# General Organic Chemistry

## for JEE Main & Advanced

Fully Solved

Includes Past
JEE & KVPY Questions

Useful for Class 11,
KVPY & Olympiads

- **Head Office :** B-32, Shivalik Main Road, Malviya Nagar, New Delhi-110017
- **Sales Office :** B-48, Shivalik Main Road, Malviya Nagar, New Delhi-110017
  **Tel. :** 011-26691021/ 26691713

**Typeset by Disha DTP Team**

*Printed at* : **Repro Knowledgecast Limited, Thane**



**For further information about the books from DISHA,**
Log on to **www.dishapublication.com** or email to **info@dishapublication.com**

# PREFACE
## REVISED EDITION

It gives us immense pleasure and satisfaction to bring out the thoroughly revised and updated edition of the book **"Disha General Organic Chemistry."** The book has been designed to give a better look & feel and to make the text more lucid. The new pattern of JEE Main & Advanced has been kept in mind throughout.

The exercises at the end of each chapter have been designed in the flavour of the new pattern of JEE Main & Advanced. The questions from the previous JEE papers have been incorporated in the different exercises. The book contains three exercises.

1. **Exercise 1 - MCQ with One correct option :** This exercise contains a collection of questions, which has been very carefully selected and it is ensured that there is no repetition. The exercise has been designed so as to cover all the concepts involved in the chapter.
2. **Exercise 2  :** This exercise contains all the four new variety of questions which have been asked in the last 3-4 JEE examinations. These variety of questions are -
    (i) **MCQ's with one or more than one correct answers :** Around 20-30 well selected problems introduced in each chapter.
    (ii) **Comprehension based questions :** More than 50 passages which tests the student's comprehension and analytical ability have been added. All these are newly framed problems.
    (iii) **Matching type questions :** Match the following type of questions with multiple matching have been introduced in each chapter. These are unique and newly framed problems which will definitely pose a big challenge to the student. I feel that this type of problem is the best way to check a student's concept.
    (iv) **Assertion & Reason type questions :** Assertion and Reason type of questions have been incorporated in each and every chapter.
3. **Exercise 3 - Subjective Problems :** This exercise contains a unique collection of subjective problems which will not only give practice to the students but will also help in revising the complete chapter.

In the end, We would like to request all readers to highlight the printing errors and come forward  with suggestions for further improvement of the book.

DR. O. P. AGARWAL

## Other Useful Books

# CONTENTS

3-methylhexane
wrong
seven-carbon chain,
but only three substituents
correct
seven-carbon chain,
four substituents

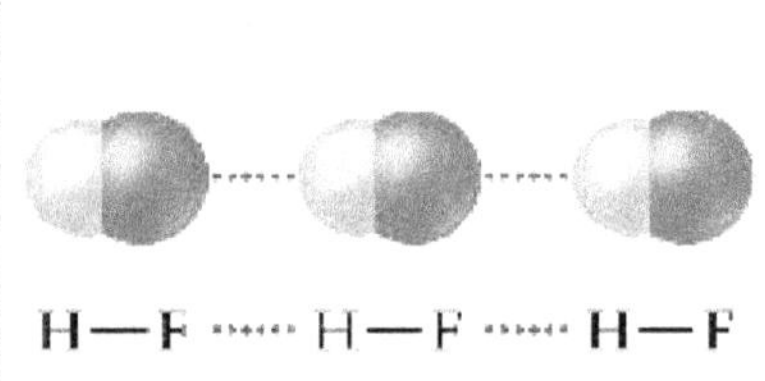

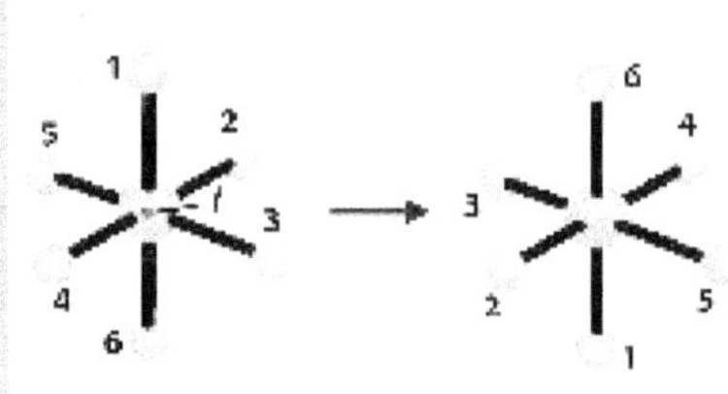

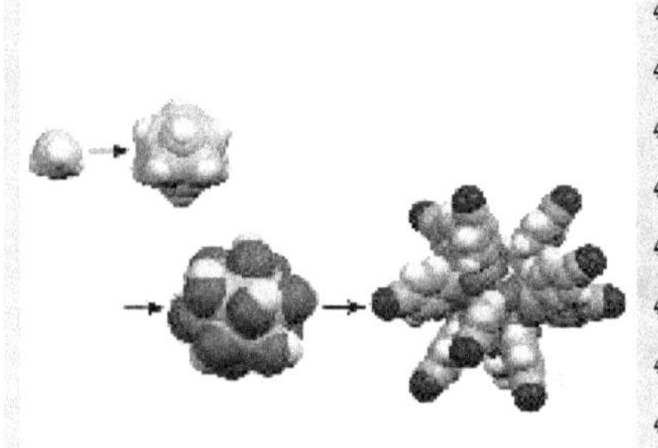

# Classification and Nomenclature of Organic Compounds

## CHAPTER HIGHLIGHTS



## 1.1  Classification of Organic Compounds

All the known organic compounds have been divided into various classes as follows.

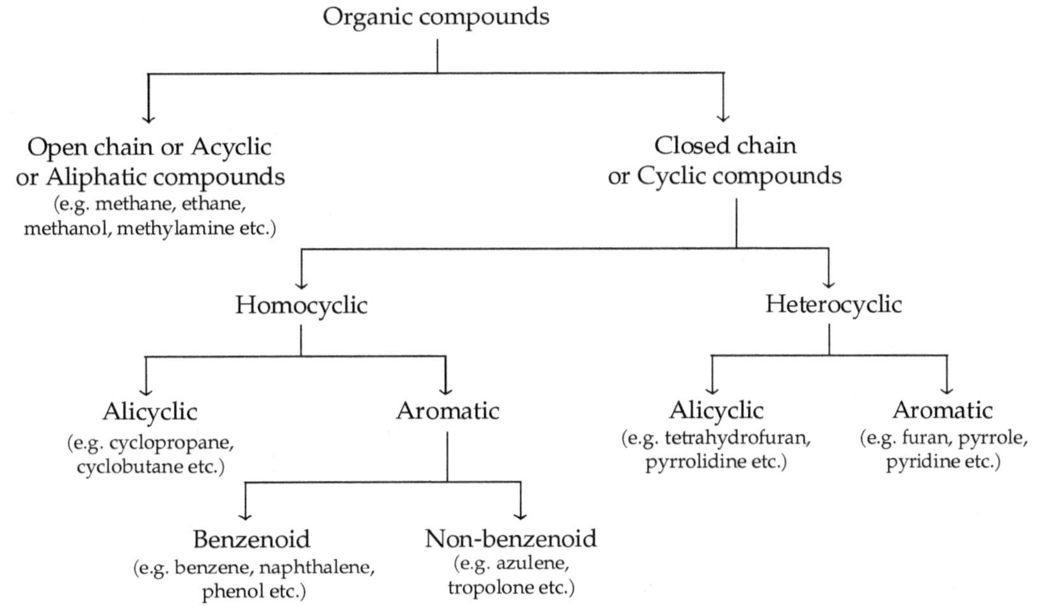

## 1.2 Nomenclature of Organic Compounds

There are two general ways for naming organic compounds, namely trivial name (common name) and IUPAC name.

**Trivial or common names.** This is unscientific system in which certain (not all) compounds are named after their source, their property or a historical aspect. These names existed long before organic chemistry became an organized branch of chemical science and structure of organic compounds was not known. Many common names became so popular that they are still widely used by chemists. Methane, ethane, propane, *n*-butane, isobutane, and neopentane are common names.

**IUPAC names.** A system built on common names is not adequate to communicate structural information of a compound, chemists developed a set of rules for naming organic compounds based on their structures, which we now call the **IUPAC rules**, where IUPAC stands for the "International Union of Pure and Applied Chemistry". Although IUPAC rules were first laid down in 1892, these have been revised at regular intervals to keep them upto-date. The system of nomenclature, based upon IUPAC rules is known as IUPAC system of nomenclature or systematic nomenclature.

The IUPAC name of an organic compound consists of three parts

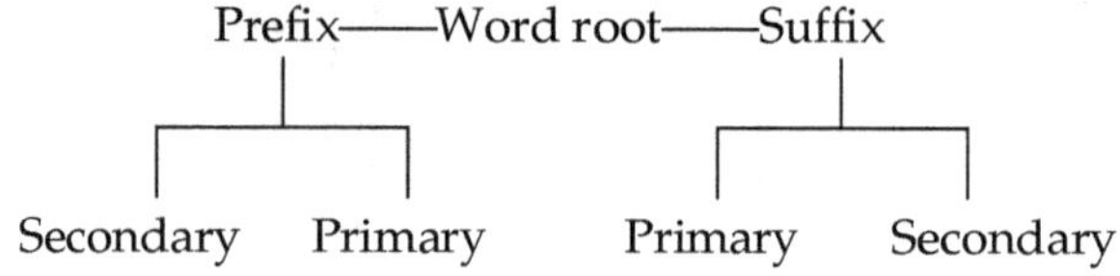

### 1.2.1 Word root

A word root indicates the nature of the basic carbon skeleton. Chains containing one to four carbon atoms are known by special word roots, while chains from $C_5$ onwards are known by Greek numerals.

| Chain length | Word root | Chain length | Word root |
|---|---|---|---|
| $C_1$ | Meth– | $C_{19}$ | Nonadec– |
| $C_2$ | Eth– | $C_{20}$ | Icos– |
| $C_3$ | Prop– | $C_{21}$ | Henicos– |
| $C_4$ | But– | $C_{22}$ | Docos– |
| $C_5$ | Pent– | $C_{23}$ | Tricos– |
| $C_6$ | Hex– | $C_{29}$ | Nonacos– |
| $C_7$ | Hept– | $C_{30}$ | Triacont– |
| $C_8$ | Oct– | $C_{31}$ | Hentriacont– |
| $C_9$ | Non– or Ennea | $C_{32}$ | Dotriacont– |
| $C_{10}$ | Dec– | $C_{40}$ | Tetracont– |
| $C_{11}$ | Undec– or Hendec– | $C_{50}$ | Pentacont– |
| $C_{12}$ | Dodec– | $C_{100}$ | Hect– |
| $C_{13}$ | Tridec– | | |

In general, the word root for any carbon chain is **alk.**

### 1.2.2 Suffix

There are two types of suffixes *viz.* primary and secondary.

*(i)* **Primary suffixes :** The degree of unsturation or saturation in the carbon chain is indicated by primary suffixes. The primary suffixes for the various saturated and unsaturated carbon chains are mentioned below.

| Nature of C chain | C—C | C = C | –C ≡ C– |
|---|---|---|---|
| **Primary suffix** | -ane | -ene | -yne |

It is added after the word root, viz. *ethane, ethene, ethyne* etc.

In case the parent carbon chain contains two, three, four or more double or triple bonds, numerical prefixes such as *di* (for two), *tri* (for three), *tetra* (for four) etc are added to the primary suffix. For example, *–diene* (for two double bonds), *–triyne* (for three triple bonds).

*(ii)* **Secondary suffixes :** Suffixes, added after the primary suffix to indicate the particular functional group (groups) present in the carbon chain, are known as **secondary suffixes.** Secondary suffixes for some important functional groups are given below.

| Class | Functional group | Secondary suffix | Class | Functional group | Secondary suffix |
|---|---|---|---|---|---|
| Alcohols | –OH | –ol | Acid amides | $-CONH_2$ | –amide |
| Aldehydes | –CHO | –al | Esters | –COOR | alkyl... –oate |
| Ketones | $>C=O$ | –one | Nitriles | –CN | –nitrile |
| Carboxylic acids | –COOH | –oic acid | Thiols | –SH | –thiol |
| Acid chlorides | –COCl | –oyl chloride | Amines | $-NH_2$ | –amine |

The significance of the word root, primary suffix and secondary suffix can be illustrated by the following examples.

| Formulae of compound | Word root | Primary suffix | Secondary suffix | IUPAC name |
|---|---|---|---|---|
| $CH_3CH_2OH$ | Eth | ane | ol | Ethanol |
| $CH_3CH_2COOH$ | Prop | ane | oic acid | Propanoic acid |
| $CH_3NH_2$ | Meth | ane | amine | Methanamine |
| $CH_2=CHCHO$ | Prop | ene | al | Propenal |
| $CH\equiv CCOOH$ | Prop | yne | oic acid | Propynoic acid |
| $CH_3CH_2CN$ | Prop | ane | nitrile | Propaneitrile |

Note that while adding the secondary suffix to the primary suffix, the terminal 'e' of the primary suffix is removed if the secondary suffix begins with a vowel (*a, e, i, o, u* or *y*) but it is retained if the secondary suffix begins with a consonant.

In all above examples except the last the terminal 'e' of the primary suffix has ben removed because the secondary suffix starts with a vowel, while in the last the secondary suffix (nitrile) starts with a consonant and hence the terminal 'e' of the primary suffix has been retained.

## 1.2.3  Prefix

Prefixes are used to indicate *(i)* the cyclic nature of the compound and *(ii)* the nature of the substituent present on the parent chain. Thus like suffixes, prefixes are of two types namely primary and secondary.

*(i)* **Primary prefix.** The primary prefix *cyclo* is added before the word root to indicate the cyclic nature of the carbon skeleton, *e.g.*

|  | Primary prefix | Word root | Prim. suffix | Sec. suffix | IUPAC name |
|---|---|---|---|---|---|
| $H_2C-CH_2$<br>$\mid \quad \mid$<br>$H_2C-CH_2$ | Cyclo | but | ane | — | Cyclobutane |

In case the compound is acyclic (open chain), no primary prefix is used.

*(ii)* **Secondary prefix.** The groups which are not considered as functional groups, in IUPAC system of nomenclature, but regarded as substituents are called **secondary prefixes.** These are added before the word root in case of acyclic compounds and before the primary suffix in case of cyclic compounds. Some important secondary prefixes are alkyl (for —R), nitro (for $-NO_2$), halo (for —X), alkoxy (for —OR) etc.

Thus in short, IUPAC name of an organic compound consists of following arrangement.

*pri-***Prefix -***sec-***prefix-word root-***pri-***suffix-***sec-***suffix**

According to the latest rules, the name of an organic compound is derived from the name of the parent hydrocarbon by using suitable suffixes, infixes and prefixes.

## 1.3   Alkyl, Alkenyl and Alkynyl Groups

These are derived by replacing one hydrogen atom from the corresponding parent compound.

| Nature of group | Primary suffix | Generic name |
| --- | --- | --- |
| Alkane minus one H atom | –yl | Alkyl |
| Alkene minus one H atom | –enyl | Alkenyl |
| Alkyne minus one H atom | –ynyl | Alkynyl |

The alkyl groups derived from alkanes having three or more carbon atoms exist in various isomeric structures, *viz.* propyl (or *n*-propyl) and isopropyl; *n*-butyl, isobutyl, *sec*-butyl and *tert*-butyl.

$$CH_3CH_2CH_2CH_2-$$ $$CH_3\overset{\overset{\textstyle CH_3}{|}}{C}HCH_2-$$ $$CH_3\overset{\overset{\textstyle CH_2CH_3}{|}}{C}H-$$ $$CH_3\overset{\overset{\textstyle CH_3}{|}}{\underset{\underset{\textstyle CH_3}{|}}{C}}-$$

*n*-Butyl          iso-Butyl          sec-Butyl          tert-Butyl

The prefix *n*-, *iso*-, *sec*-, *tert*-, and *neo*- are although used in common names, these have been integrated into the IUPAC system and are thus acceptable to systematic nomenclature too.

A carbon atom attached to one other carbon atom is known as a **primary (1°) carbon atom**, similarly carbon atoms attached to two, three, and four other carbon atoms are known as **secondary, tertiary and quaternary carbon atom** respectively. Methyl group is although a primary alkyl group, it is always categorised separately. Some typical alkyl, alkenyl and alkynyl groups are

$$CH_3CH_2CH_2CH_2CH_2-$$ $$CH_2=CH-$$ $$CH_2=CHCH_2-$$ $$CH_3CH=CH_2-$$
*n*-Pentyl or *n*-Amyl          Vinyl          Allyl          Propenyl

$$CH_3-\overset{\overset{\textstyle |}{}}{C}=CH_2$$ $$CH\equiv C-$$ $$CH_3C\equiv C-$$ $$CH\equiv C-CH_2-$$
Isopropenyl          Ethynyl          Propynyl          Propargyl

## TEST YOUR UNDERSTANDING - 1.1

1.    Give the total number of carbon atoms present in the following compounds
   (*a*)   Undecane (a principal component of aggregation pheromone, secreted by cockroaches).
   (*b*)   Hentriacontane (a principal component of bees wax).
   (*c*)   Octacosane (a compound present in certain fossil plant).

2.    Pick up the word root, suffixes (primary and secondary) and prefixes (primary and secondary) in each of the following structures.

   (*a*)   $CH_3CH_2\overset{\overset{\textstyle Cl}{|}}{C}HCH_2OH$        (*b*)   $CH_2=CH\overset{\overset{\textstyle CH_3}{|}}{C}HCHO$        (*c*)   $CH\equiv C\overset{\overset{\textstyle COOH}{|}}{C}HCH_2NH_2$

   (*d*)   $CH_3OCH_2CH_3$        (*e*)   $C_6H_{11}Br$

3.    Pick up the word root, suffixes and prefixes in each of the following IUPAC names.
   (*a*)   2-Methyl-4-oxobutanoic acid        (*b*)   3-(Carbamoylmethyl) pentanediamide
   (*c*)   3-(Formylmethyl)hexanedial        (*d*)   Pentanediel
   (*e*)   3-Carbamolymethyl) pentanediamide        (*f*)   3-(Formylmethyl)hexanedial

4.    (*a*)   Give structrues of all the $C_5H_{11}$ alkyl groups and identify them as primary, secondary or tertiary alkyl groups.
   (*b*)   Give the structure of the simplest hydrocarbon having all the four types of carbon atoms. Write down its IUPAC name too.

## 1.4   Bond-Line Formulas

Now-a-days, a very simplified formula called a bond-line formula, is used to represent structural formulas. The bond-line representation is the quickest of all to write because it shows only the carbon skeleton. The necessary number of hydrogen atoms required by each carbon are assumed to be present, and not written ; other atoms (e.g., O, Cl, N) are written inside the skeleton. Each intersection (joint) of two or more lines and the end of a line represent a carbon atom unless some other atom is written in.

| | | | |
|---|---|---|---|
| $CH_3CHClCH_2CH_3$ | 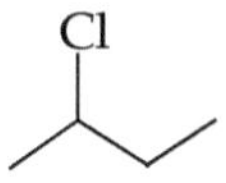 | $CH_3CH(CH_3)CH_2CH_3$ | 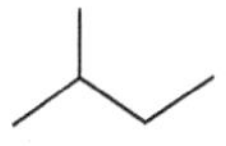 |
| $(CH_3)_2NCH_2CH_3$ | 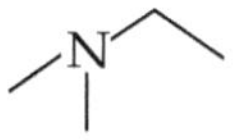 | $(CH_3)_2C = CHCH_2CH_3$ | 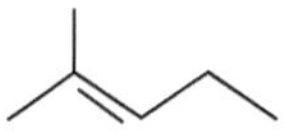 |
| $CH_2 = CHCH_2OH$ |  | 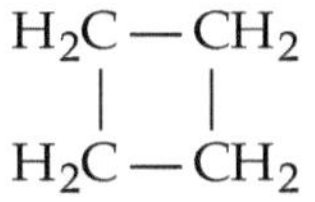 |  |



## TEST YOUR UNDERSTANDING - 1.2

1. Write the bond-line formula for

(a) $(CH_3)_2CHCH_2\overset{CH_3}{\overset{|}{C}}HCH_2OH$ (b) $CH_3COCH_2CH_2\overset{CH_3}{\overset{|}{C}}HCH_3$ (c) $(CH_3)_3CH$

(d) $CH_3C$ ° $CCH_2OH$ (e) $CH_3(CH_2)_4\overset{CH_2CH_3}{\overset{|}{C}}HCH_2Cl$ (f) $CH_3CH = CH(CH_2)_3\overset{CH_2OH}{\overset{|}{C}}HCHO$

## 1.5 Nomenclature of Branched Chain Alkanes

There are certain rules for naming a complex organic molecule according to IUPAC system. All organic compounds are regarded as substituted hydrocarbons and, therefore, these names are also known as **substitutive names.** These rules are illustrated below.

### 1.5.1 Longest chain rule

*The first step for naming an organic compound is to select the longest continuous chain of carbon atoms which may or may not be horizontal (straight).* This is called the **parent chain or main chain**, and other carbon chains attached to it are known as **side chain.** On the basis of the number of carbon atoms present in the parent chain, the parent hydrocarbon is determined. For example, if the parent chain contains six carbon atoms, the compound is considered to be a derivative of hexane.

***Example*** - The structure I has the longest chain of six carbon atoms present in a straight line; therefore it is said to be a derivative of hexane. On the other hand, in structure II the straight chain has only four or three carbon atoms while the longest possible chain may have as many as six carbon atoms (zig-zag chain).

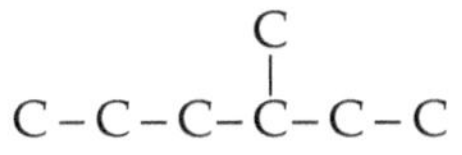

I
(Longest chain, straight)

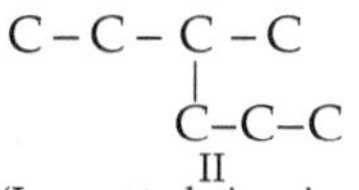

II
(Longest chain, zig-zag)

Therefore, both the structures are derivatives of hexane.

In case a molecule contains two equally long carbon chains, the one carrying larger number of side chains is selected. For example, structure III may have two parent carbon chain of equal length ($C_7$), but the one carrying there substituents is selected.

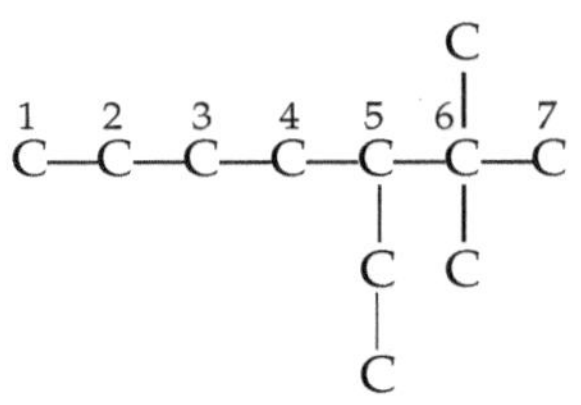

Straight parent chain of $C_7$ with three side chains **(Right)**

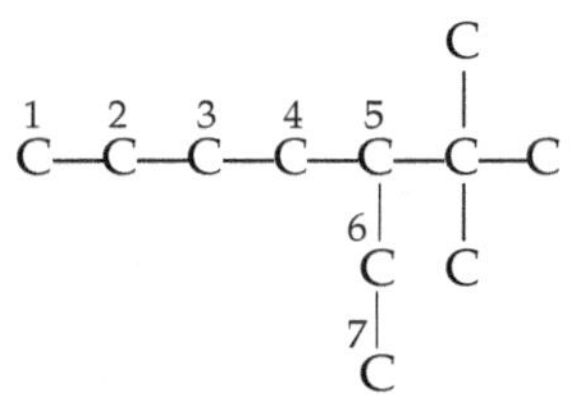

Zig-zag parent chain of $C_7$ with only one side chain **(Wrong)**

III

### 1.5.2  Lowest number *or* lowest sum rule

*The longest carbon chain is numbered as 1, 2, 3, 4, ...... etc. starting from the end that gives the smallest possible number(s) to the substituent(s).* For example, in structure IV numbering may be done in two ways ;

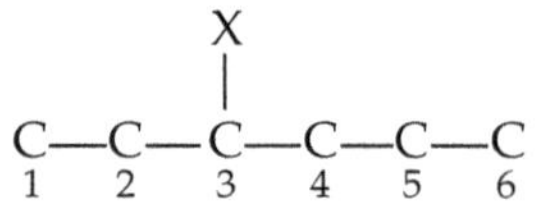

$$
\begin{array}{cccccc}
 & & X & & & \\
 & & | & & & \\
C - C - C - C - C - C \\
1 \quad 2 \quad 3 \quad 4 \quad 5 \quad 6
\end{array}
\qquad
\begin{array}{cccccc}
 & & X & & & \\
 & & | & & & \\
C - C - C - C - C - C \\
6 \quad 5 \quad 4 \quad 3 \quad 2 \quad 1
\end{array}
$$

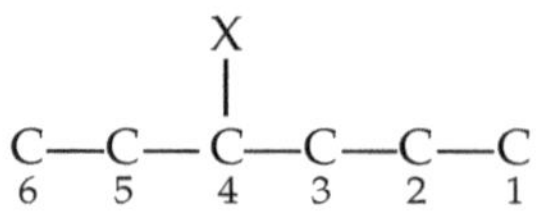

Substituent at C$_3$              Substituent at C$_4$
**(correct)**                        **(incorrect)**
IV

In one case the substituent is assigned position 3, while in other case it is assigned position 4. Hence the former, being smaller, is correct. The number that locates the position of a substituent is known as **locant**. Thus the locant for X in the above correct structure is 3.

*In case, the parent* chain *has two or more substituents, numbering must be done in such a way that the sum of the locants on the parent chain is the lowest possible.* Thus in structure V numbering may be done in two ways : in one, the sum of locants is 9 while in other it is 12, hence the former is correct while the latter is wrong.

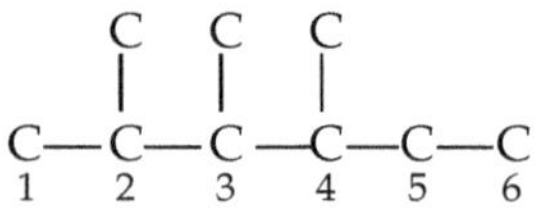

$$
\begin{array}{cccccc}
C & C & C & & & \\
| & | & | & & & \\
C - C - C - C - C - C \\
1 \quad 2 \quad 3 \quad 4 \quad 5 \quad 6
\end{array}
\qquad
\begin{array}{cccccc}
C & C & C & & & \\
| & | & | & & & \\
C - C - C - C - C - C \\
6 \quad 5 \quad 4 \quad 3 \quad 2 \quad 1
\end{array}
$$

Sum of locants : 2 + 3 + 4 = 9          Sum of locants : 3 + 4 + 5 = 12
**(correct)**                       **(incorrect)**
V

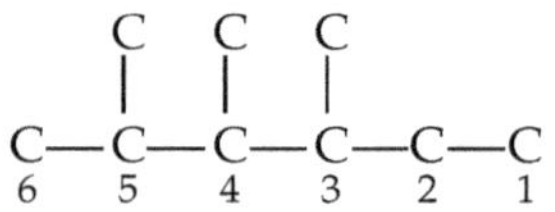

Further, if different side chains (alkyl groups) are present on the identical positions in relation to the ends of the chain, numbering must be done in a way that the first cited group (i.e. the group which comes first in alphabetic order) receives the minimum number, *e.g.* the correct name of the following compound is 3-ethyl-5-methylheptane and not 5-ethyl-3-methylheptane.

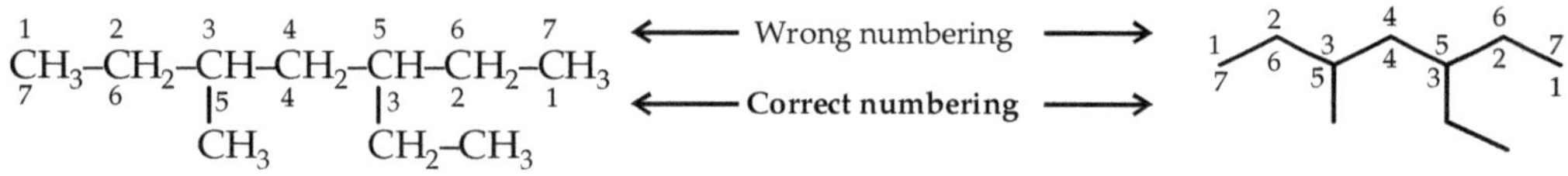

$$
\underset{\underset{\text{CH}_3}{|}}{\overset{1}{\text{CH}_3}} - \overset{2}{\text{CH}_2} - \overset{3}{\underset{5}{\text{CH}}} - \overset{4}{\text{CH}_2} - \overset{5}{\underset{3}{\text{CH}}} - \overset{6}{\text{CH}_2} - \overset{7}{\text{CH}_3}
$$

⟵ Wrong numbering ⟶

⟵ Correct numbering ⟶

3-Ethyl-5-methylheptane

Similarly, the correct name for the following compound is 2-bromo-3-chlorobutane and not 3-bromo-2-chlorobutane.

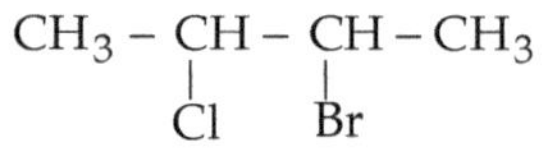

$$
\text{CH}_3 - \underset{\underset{\text{Cl}}{|}}{\text{CH}} - \underset{\underset{\text{Br}}{|}}{\text{CH}} - \text{CH}_3
$$

When two chains of equal length compete for selection as the parent chain, choose the chain with the greater number of substituents.

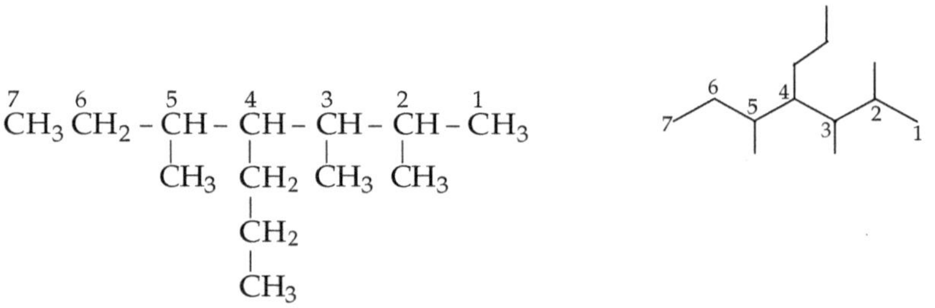

$$
\overset{7}{\text{CH}_3} \overset{6}{\text{CH}_2} - \overset{5}{\text{CH}} - \overset{4}{\text{CH}} - \overset{3}{\text{CH}} - \overset{2}{\text{CH}} - \overset{1}{\text{CH}_3}
$$

2,3,5-Trimethyl-4-propylhelptane (four substituents)

### 1.5.3

The name of the substituent is prefixed to the name of the parent hydrocarbon and its position on the main chain is indicated by writing the locant before the prefix. A hyphen (–) is inserted between the locant and the substituent name. Thus the compound VI is written as 2-methylpentane.

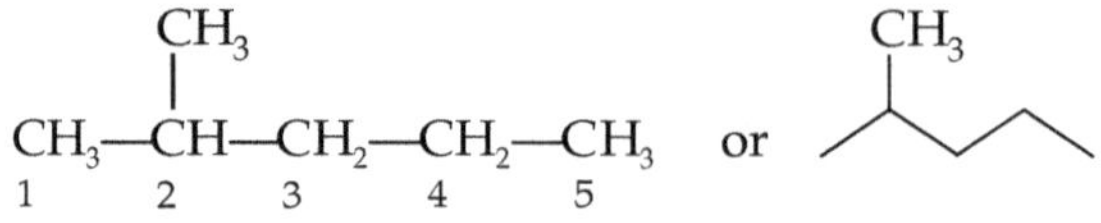

$$
\underset{\underset{\phantom{x}}{\overset{1 \quad 2 \quad 3 \quad 4 \quad 5}{}}}{\text{CH}_3 - \underset{\underset{\text{CH}_3}{|}}{\text{CH}} - \text{CH}_2 - \text{CH}_2 - \text{CH}_3} \quad \text{or}
$$

2-Methylpentane, VI

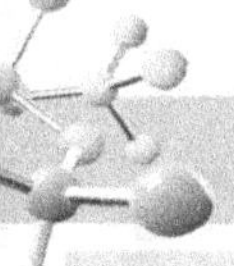



### 1.5.4  Alphabetical order of side chains

In case two or more alkyl groups (side-chains) are attached to the parent chain, these are prefixed in alphabetic order, *e.g.*

3-Ethyl-2-methylpentane and not as 2-Methyl-3-ethylpentane

### 1.5.5

*If a substituent is present two or more times, this is indicated by the prefix di–, tri–, tetra–, etc. added to the substituent.* The different locants of the substituents are separated by commas. For example,

2, 3-Dimethylpentane

### 1.5.6

If the same substituent numbers are obtained in both directions, the first cited group receives the lowest number.

**3-Ethyl-5-methylheptane** *not* **5-Ethyl-3-methylheptane**          **2-Bromo-3-chlorobutane** *not* **3-Bromo-2-chlorobutane**

4-Ethyl-3, 3-dimethylheptane

The spelling of the prefixes *di-, tri-,* and *tetra-* should not be considered while arranging the substituents alphabetically, as in the above example.

### 1.5.7

*In case the substituent on the parent chain has itself branched chain then it is named as a substituted alkyl group and its carbon chain is numbered from the carbon atom attached to the main chain.* The name of this complex substituent is written in bracket to avoid confusion with the numbers of the main chain, *e.g.*

5-(1', 2'-dimethylpropyl)nonane

The multiplicity of a substituted substituent, *i.e.* when the substituent is itself substituted and there are two or more such substituents, these are indicated by numerical prefixes like *'bis'*, *'tris'*, *'tetrakis'* etc.

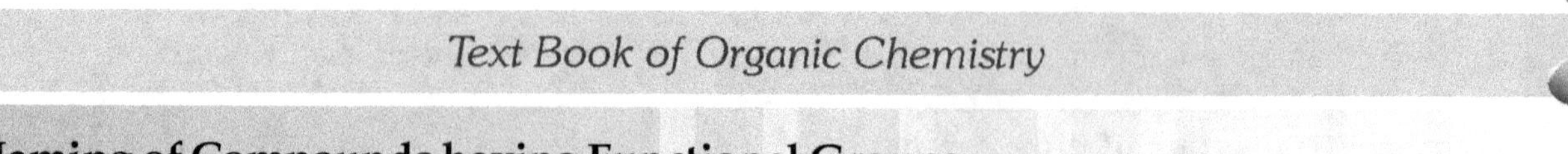

## 1.6   Naming of Compounds having Functional Groups

After studying the IUPAC nomenclature of saturated hydrocarbons, let us study the rules for naming compounds with functional groups (double and triple bonds are also considered as the functional groups).

*(i)*   *The longest carbon chain is selected in such a way as to include the maximum number of functional groups.* Thus in the example given below numbering is done in such a way that the selected carbon chain contains the alcoholic (functional) group, although the longest possible chain (but without functional group) is having five carbon atoms.

Selected chain has 4 C atoms with functional group (**Right**)    Selected chain has 5 C atoms without functional group (**Wrong**)

Similarly, if the compound contains more than one functional group ; the selected longest chain must have all the functional groups. Thus the following compound is considered as a derivative of pentane and not of hexane.

$$\overset{5}{CH_3}-\overset{4}{CH}=\overset{3}{C}-CH_2-CH_2-CH_3 \quad or$$

$$\underset{2 \quad 1}{\overset{|}{CH}=CH_2}$$

3-Propyl-1, 3-pentadiene

*(ii)*   *The numbering of carbon chain is done in such a way that the functional group(s) is (are) given minimum possible number even if it violates the lowest sum rule.* Thus, the following compound is named as

2-Methylpentanol-1 (**Right name**)    4-Methylpentanol-5 (**Wrong name**)
(functional group at $C_1$)    (functional group at $C_5$)

Similarly,

4, 4-Dimethylpentanol-2 (**Right name**)    2, 2-Dimethylpentanol-4 (**Wrong name**)
(although sum of locants ; 4 + 4 + 2 = 10)    (although sum of locants ; 2 + 2 + 4 = 8)

*(iii)*   *The name of the substituents are prefixed to the parent hydrocarbon according to IUPAC rules described earlier.*

*(iv)*   *The terminal 'e' of the hydrocarbon (alkane) is replaced by the suffix of the corresponding functional group.*

*(v)*   *Although the positional number of the functional group may be represented in either of the three ways,* **in 1993, the IUPAC recommended that the number indicating the position of the functional group should be placed immediately before the suffix, e.g. but-2-ene, butan-2-ol, etc. Although this is the latest convention used by IUPAC system, the older conventions like butene-2 or 2-butene are so widely used, that their replacement will take some time.** *So readers should take a note of it throughout the book.*

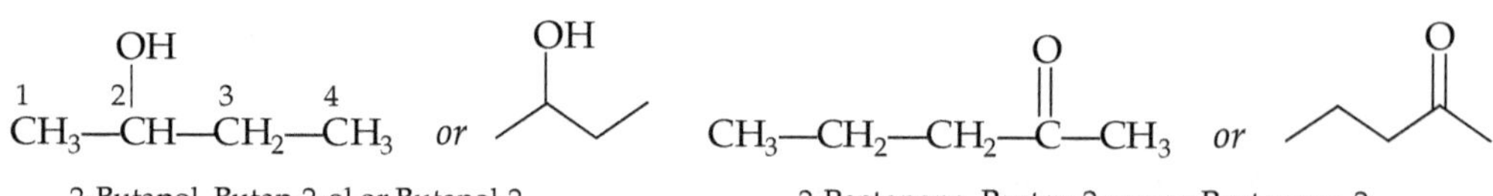

2-Butanol, Butan-2-ol or Butanol-2    2-Pentanone, Pentan-2-one or Pentanone-2

*(vi)*   *Halo, nitro and sometime amino groups are not regarded as functional groups. They are considered as substituents.*

(*vii*)　*In case the compound contains two or more different functional groups (including $C = C$ and $C \equiv C$), the principal group forms the suffix of the name while the other functional groups are considered as substituents and indicated as prefixes. The order of seniority among the principal groups is given in the following table along with their prefix and suffix names.*

Seniority table for principal groups

| Group | Prefix name | Suffix name |
|---|---|---|
| $-SO_3H$ | Sulpho– | sulphonic acid |
| –COOH | Carboxy– | –oic acid |
| –COOR | Alkyl-oxycarbonyl | –alkyl---oates |
| –COX | Haloformyl– | –oyl halide |
| $-CONH_2$ | Carbamoyl– | amide |
| –CHO | Formyl– | –al |
| –CN | Cyano– | –nitrile |
| –CO | Keto- or Oxo | –one |
| –OH | Hydroxy– | –ol |
| –SH | Mercapto– | –thiol |
| $-NH_2$ | Amino– | –amine |
| $> C = C <$ ; $-C \equiv C-$ | – | –ene, –yne |
| –X (halogen) | Halo– | – |
| $-NO_2$ | Nitro– | – |
| –NO | Nitroso– | – |
| –O– | Epoxy– | – |
| R— | Alkyl– | – |

Let us examplify the above rule by some examples.

While using prefixes such as formyl (for —CHO), cyano (for —CN), carboxy (—COOH), carbamoyl ($-CONH_2$) etc. the carbon of the substituent group is not counted in the principal chain. However, when prefix —*oxo* (for $>C = O$) is used, its carbon is counted in the principal chain. This is due to its non-terminal nature.

$$\overset{4}{O}HC\overset{3}{C}H_2\overset{2}{C}H_2\overset{1}{C}H_2\overset{}{C}OOH$$
4-Formylbutanoic acid

$$\overset{4}{C}H_3\overset{3}{C}O\overset{2}{C}H_2\overset{1}{C}OOH$$
3-Oxobutanoic acid

2, 2-Dimethylhept-3-ene-6-yne (Double bond is senior to triple, hence given lower number).

4-Amino-2-hexanone (here ketonic group is senior to amino group)

5-Vinyl-1, 3, 7-octatriene

3-Cyanopentamide (here amide group is senior to cyano).

*(viii)*   *In case two groups of the same seniority occupy indentical positions in relation to end of the chain, the lowest number should be given to the group in the alphabetical order of their prefixes.* Thus the following compound should be named as 1-bromo-4-chlorobutane.

$$\overset{4}{Cl}CH_2.\overset{3}{C}H_2.\overset{2}{C}H_2.\overset{1}{C}H_2Br \qquad\qquad \overset{1}{Cl}CH_2.\overset{2}{C}H_2.\overset{3}{C}H_2.\overset{4}{C}H_2Br$$

1-Bromo-4-chlorobutane          4-Bromo-1-chlorobutane

**(Right name)**             **(Wrong name)**

*(ix)*   Substituents, side chains and functional groups are named in alphabetical order. In short, first of all mention all substituents in alphabetical manner, then side chains in alphabetical manner, and finally functional group in alphabetical order. For example,

$$\overset{4}{CH_2}—\overset{3}{C}=\overset{2}{CH}—\overset{1}{CH_2}OH \qquad \text{or}$$

with Cl on C-4 and CH₃ on C-3.

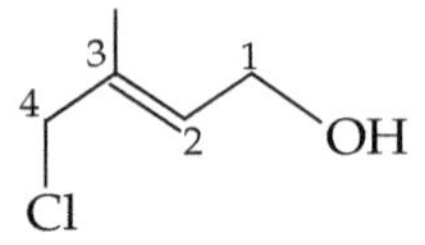

4-Chloro-3-methylbutene-2-ol-1

Thus in the compound given above two functional groups (-ene and -ol) are arranged in the alphabetical order.

*(x)*   *Prefixes like n-, iso-, sec-, tert-, neo-, etc. must be avoided in IUPAC system.*

## 1.7   IUPAC Names of Some Organic Compounds

1.   $\overset{5}{CH_3}—\overset{4}{C}(=O)—\overset{3}{CH_2}—\overset{2}{CH_2}—\overset{1}{CHO}$   or

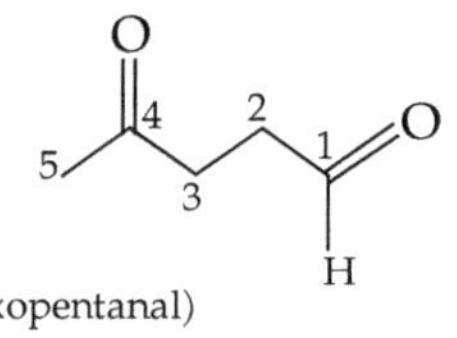

4-Ketopentanal (4-Oxopentanal)

     —CHO and >C = O are the principal and secondary functional groups respectively

2.   $NC\overset{4}{CH_2}\overset{3}{CH}(OCH_3)\overset{2}{CH_2}\overset{1}{COOCH_3}$   or

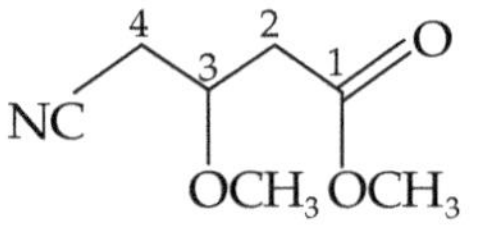

Methyl-4-cyano-3-methoxy butanoate

     Note that —COOCH₃ is the principal functional group

3.   $Cl\overset{2'}{CH_2}\overset{1'}{CH_2}\overset{2}{CH_2}\overset{4}{C}(=O)\overset{5}{CH}=CH_2$   or

with CONHCH₃ on position 1.

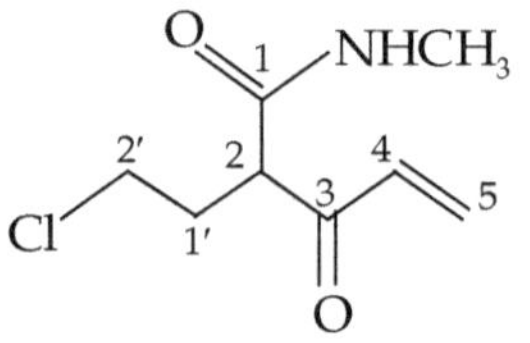

N-Methyl-2-(2′-chloroethyl)-3-keto-4-pentenamide

     Note that here —CONHCH₃ is the principal functional group

4.   $\overset{5}{CH_3}\overset{4}{CH}=\overset{3}{C}\overset{2}{CH_2}\overset{1}{COOH}$   or

with CONH₂ on position 3.

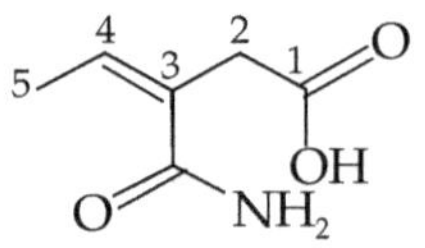

3-Carboxamido-3-pentenoic acid

     Note that —COOH is the principal functional group while —CONH₂ is considered as a substituent

## TEST YOUR UNDERSTANDING - 1.3

**1.** Try to justify the selection of the parent carbon chain and elaborate the IUPAC name for each of the following structures :

(a)

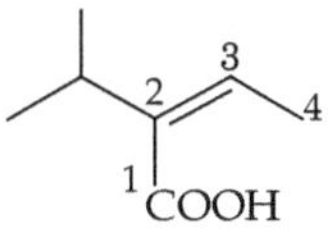

(b)

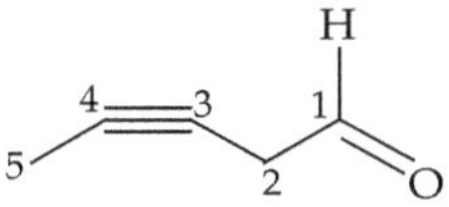

(c)

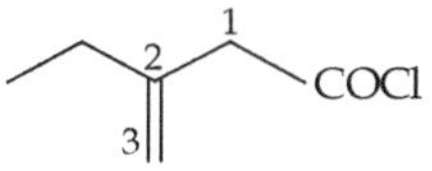

(d)

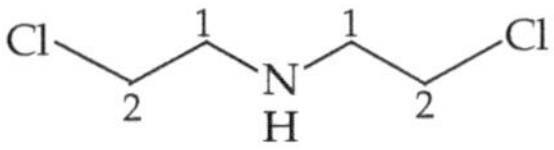

(e)

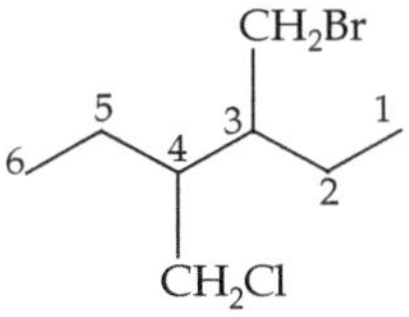

(f)

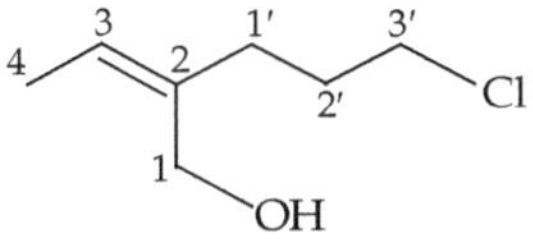

(g)

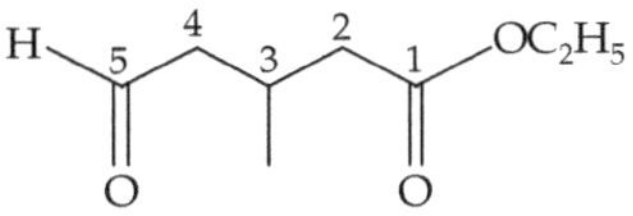

(h)

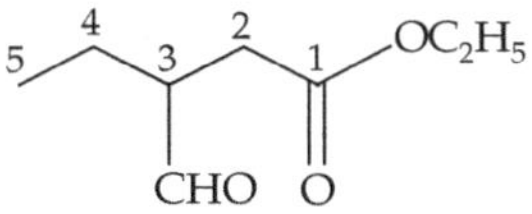

(i)

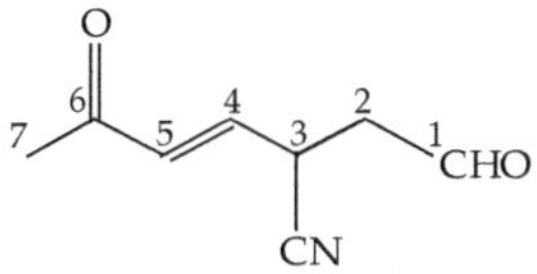

(j)

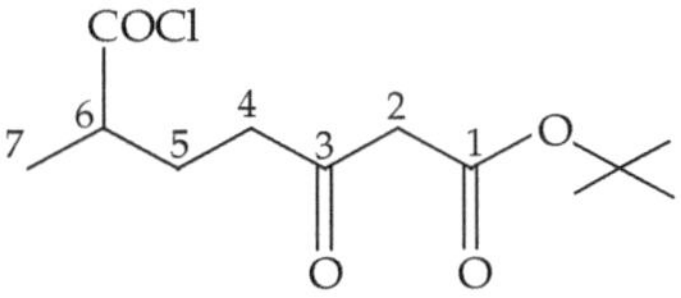

(k)

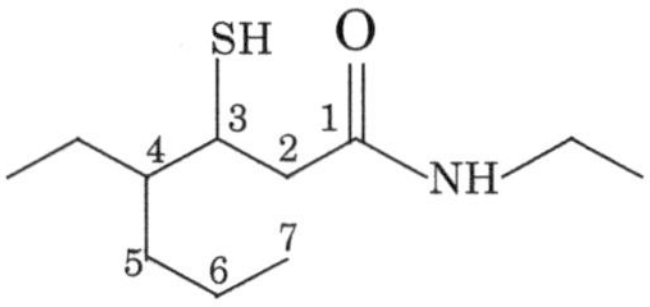

(l)

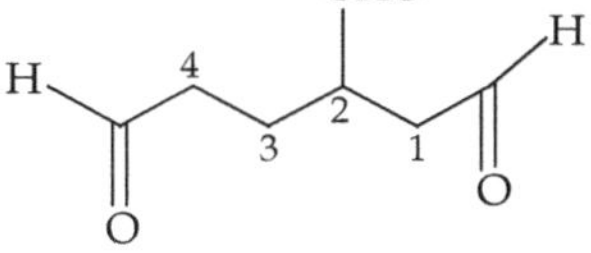

**2.** Give IUPAC names for the following compounds.

(a)

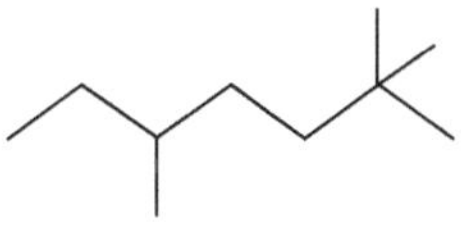

(b)

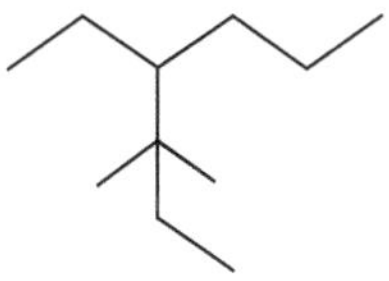

(c)

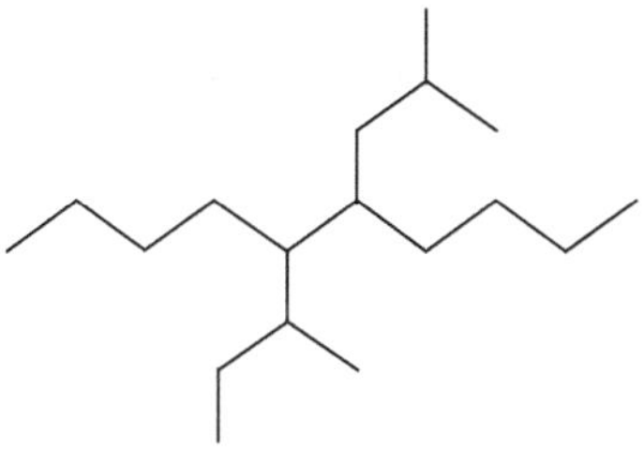

(d)

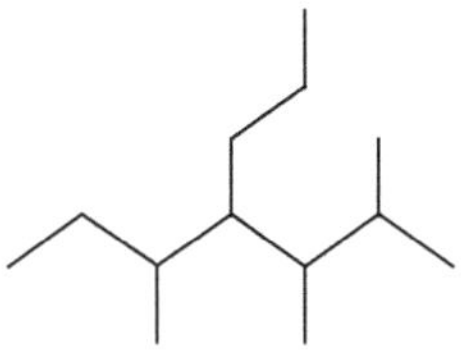

(e)

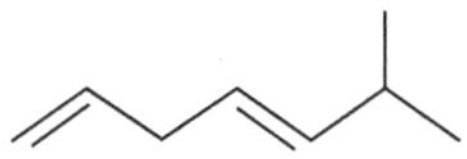

(f)

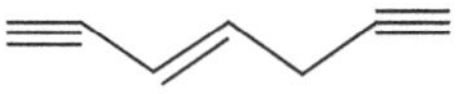

(g)

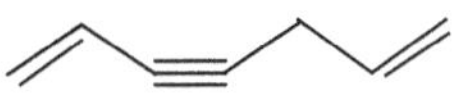

(h)

(i)

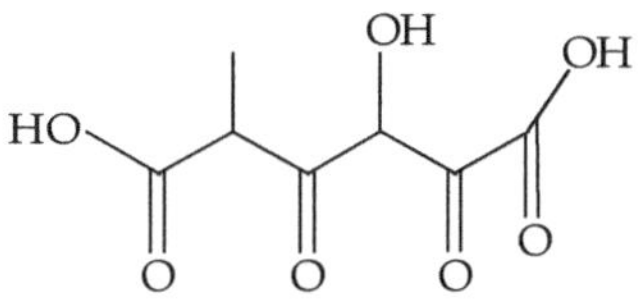

(j)

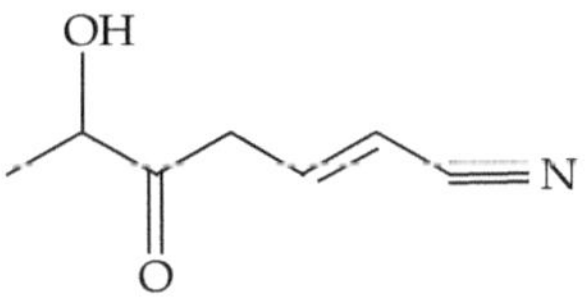

(k)

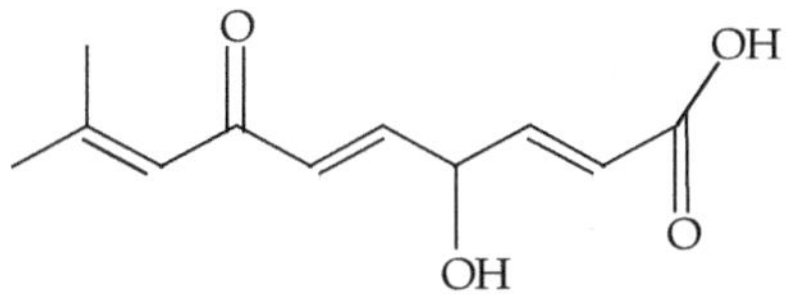

(l)

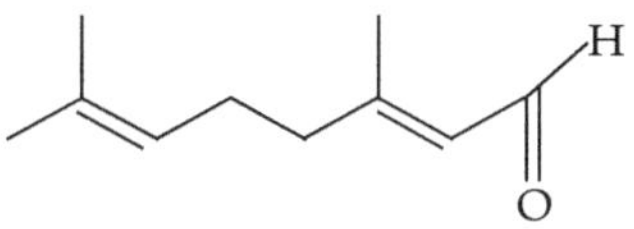

(m)

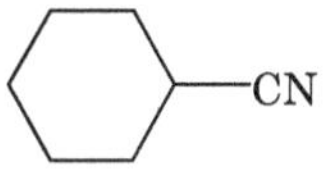

(n)

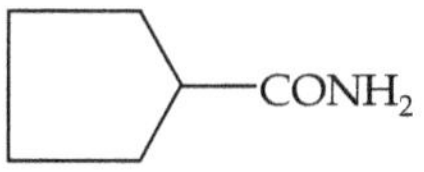

## 1.8   Naming of Polyfunctional Compounds Containing Two or More Similar Carbon-Containing Terminal Groups

Carbon-containing terminal groups are monovalent groups like —COOH, —COOR, —COCl, —CONH₂, —CHO, and —CN. When the compound contains two or more such groups, following special rules must be observed.

### 1.8.1

*When the compound contains two similar carbon-containing terminal groups*, then both of these groups must be counted in the principal chain and it is not necessary to indicate their positions (these are assumed to be present on the terminal carbon atom). For example,

$$\overset{1\,2\quad 3\quad 4}{HOOCCH_2CH_2COOH}$$

Butanedioic acid

$$\overset{1\quad 2\quad 3\quad 4}{H_2NCOCH_2CH_2CONH_2}$$

Butanediamide

$$\overset{4\quad 3\quad 2|\quad 1}{H_2NCOCH_2CHCONH_2}\quad (CH_3)$$

2-Methylbutanediamide

$$\overset{1\,2\quad 3\,4\quad 5}{NCCH_2CHCH_2CN}\quad (OH)$$

3-Hydroxypentanedinitrile

$$\overset{1\,2\quad 3\quad 4}{OHCCH_2CH_2CHO}$$

Butanedial

$$\overset{4\,3\quad 2\quad 1}{ClOCCH_2CH_2COCl}$$

Butanedioyl chloride

$$\overset{1\,2\quad 3\quad 4\quad 5}{C_2H_5OOCCH_2CH_2CH_2COOC_2H_5}$$

Diethyl pentanedioate

### 1.8.2

When the compound contains more than two similar terminal groups, all of which are not directly linked to the principal chain, then that longest principal chain should be selected which contains two such similar terminal groups at its two ends. Here the terminal groups are counted in the chain, while the third, present on side chain, is considered as a substituent.

$$\overset{1\,2\quad 3|\quad 4\quad 5}{HOOCCH_2CHCH_2COOH}\quad (CH_2COOH) \quad \text{or}$$

3-(Carboxymethyl)pentanedioic acid

$$\overset{6\,5\quad 4\quad 3|\quad 2\quad 1}{NCCH_2CH_2CHCH_2CN}\quad (CH_2CN) \quad \text{or}$$

3-(Cyanomethyl)hexanedinitrile

$$\overset{6\,5\quad 4\quad 3|2\quad 1}{OHCCH_2CH_2CCH_2CHO}\quad (CH_2CHO)(CH_2CHO) \quad \text{or}$$

3,3-Bis(formylmethyl)hexanedial

$$\overset{1\,2\quad 3|\quad 4\quad 5}{C_2H_5OOCCH_2CHCH_2COOC_2H_5}\quad (CH_2COOC_2H_5) \quad \text{or}$$

Diethyl 3-(ethyloxycarbonylmethyl)pentanedioate

**1.8.3**

*When the compound contains more than two similar groups all of which are present on the principal chain*, then none of these groups are counted in the principal chain ; and special suffixes are used to indicate  the functional group, *viz.*

| *Functional group* | *Special suffix* | *Functional group* | *Special suffix* |
|---|---|---|---|
| –COOH | –carboxylic acid | –COX | –carbonyl halide |
| –CONH$_2$ | –carboxamide | –CHO | –carbaldehyde |
| –COOR | R----carboxylate | –CN | –carbonitrile |

$$\overset{\text{CHO}}{\underset{}{}} \quad CHOCH_2CH_2CHCH_2CHO$$

CHO
$\overset{4}{} \quad \overset{3}{} \quad \overset{2}{|} \quad \overset{1}{}$
CHOCH$_2$CH$_2$CHCH$_2$CHO
Butane-1, 2, 4-tricarbaldehyde

COOH
$\overset{1}{} \quad \overset{2}{|} \quad \overset{3}{} \quad \overset{4}{}$
HOOCCH$_2$CHCH$_2$CH$_2$COOH
Butane-1, 2, 4-tricarboxylic acid

CN
$\overset{5}{} \quad \overset{4}{} \quad \overset{3}{} \quad \overset{2}{|} \quad \overset{1}{}$
NCCH$_2$CH$_2$CH$_2$CHCH$_2$CN
Pentane-1, 2, 5-tricarbonitrile

**Few examples are given below for illustration.**

**1.**　　CN
$\overset{1}{} \quad \overset{2}{|} \quad \overset{3}{}$
NCCH$_2$CHCH$_2$CN　or　

Propane-1, 2, 3-tricarbonitrile

Note that more than two —CN groups are present on the main chain, hence not counted in the main chain

**2.**　3-(Formylmethyl)hexane-1,6-dial

(Only two —CHO groups are present on the main chain, hence counted in the main chain)

**3.**　Butane-1, 3, 4-tricarbaldehyde

(More than two —CHO gps. are present on the main chain, hence their C's are not counted in the main chain)

**4.**　Butane-1, 2, 4-tricarboxamide

(Three —CONH$_2$ are present on the main chain, hence their C's are not counted)

**5.**　3-(Carbamoylmethyl)hexanediamide

(Only two —CONH$_2$ gps. are on the main chain, the third is on the side chain, hence former two are counted in main chain)

---

*Example 1 :*

**Number the different carbon atoms present in the main and side chain  of the following structures and give IUPAC name of the following compounds.**

(i)　　—CH$_2$CH$_2$CH$_2$COCH$_3$

(ii)　　OH , COOCHMe$_2$

(iii)　CH$_3$–C(CH$_2$CH$_3$)–COOC$_2$H$_5$ ; COOH

(iv)　HOCH$_2$—O, HOCH$_2$CH$_2$—O CHCOOH

(v)　　CH$_2$CH$_3$

(vi)

(vii) 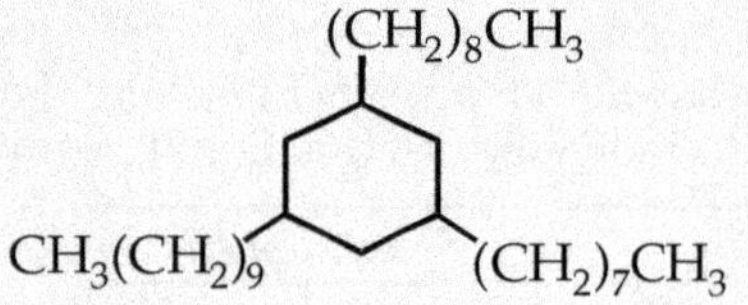 $CH_3(CH_2)_9$ — ... — $(CH_2)_7CH_3$, $(CH_2)_8CH_3$

(viii)

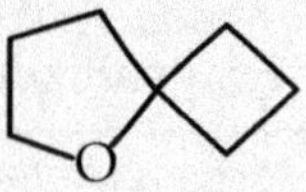

(ix) 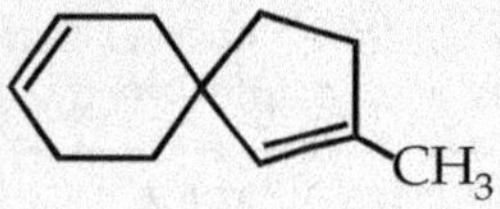 $CH_3$

(x)

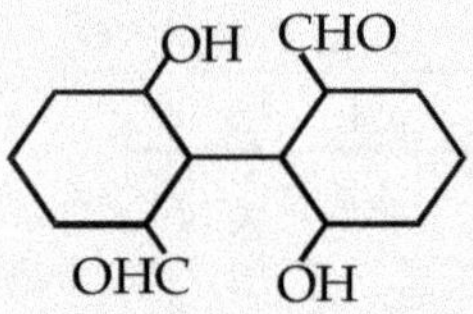

(xi) 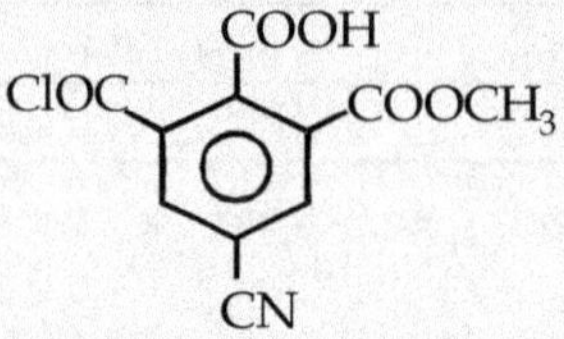 $ClOC$, $COOH$, $COOCH_3$, $CN$

(xii) 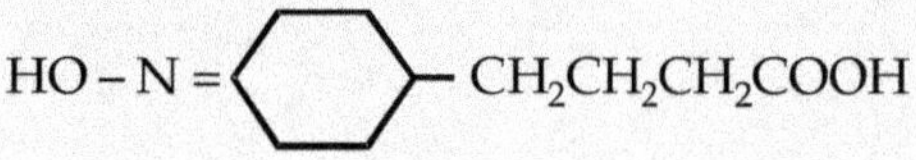 $HO-N=$ cyclohexane $-CH_2CH_2CH_2COOH$

(xiii)

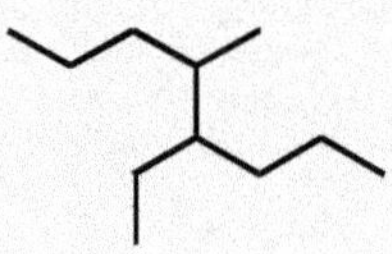

(xiv)

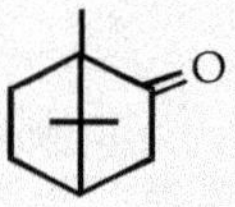

(xv) 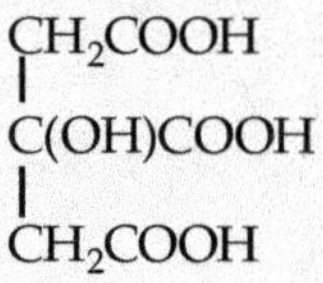 $CH_2COOH$
$C(OH)COOH$
$CH_2COOH$

**Solution :**

(i)

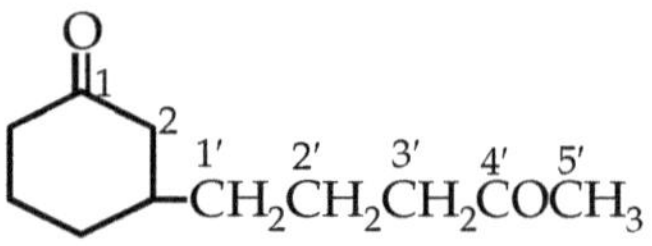

3 – (4'- Oxopentyl)cyclohexanone

(ii)

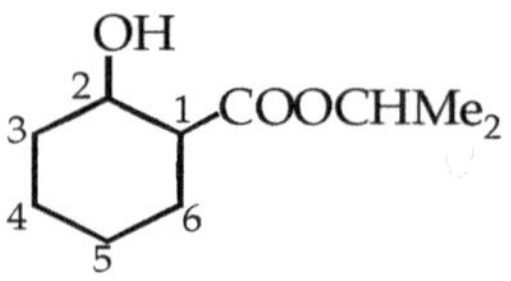

isopropyl-2-Hydroxycyclohexane carboxylate

(iii)

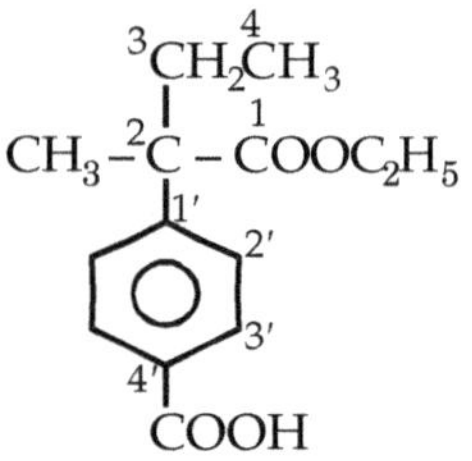

Ethyl, 2-methyl-2-(4'-carboxyphenyl) butanoate

(iv)

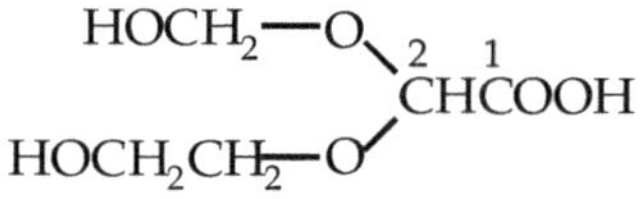

2-Hydroxyethoxy-2-hydroxymethoxyethanoic acid

(v)

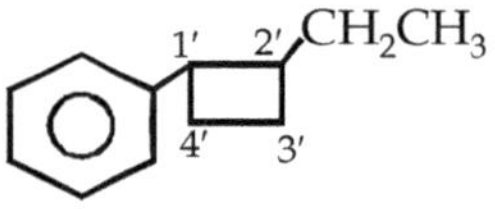

1-(2'-Ethylcyclobutyl)benzene

(vi)

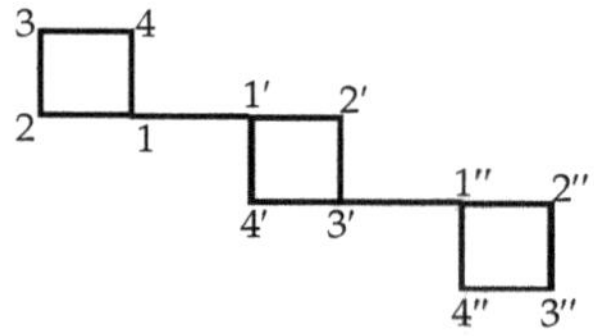

1, 1', 3', 1"-Tercyclobutane

(vii)

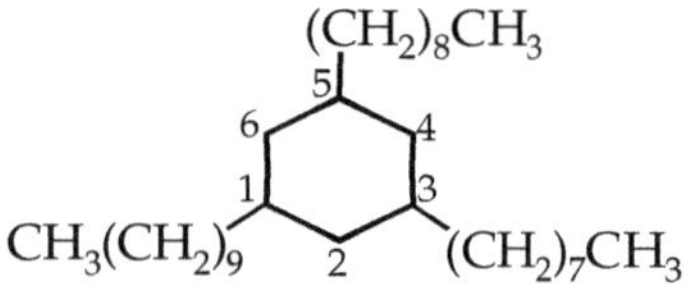

1-Decyl-5-nonyl-3-octylcyclohexane

(viii)

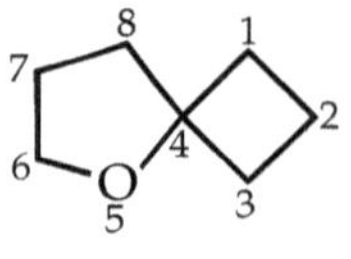

5-Oxaspiro[3, 4] octane

(ix)

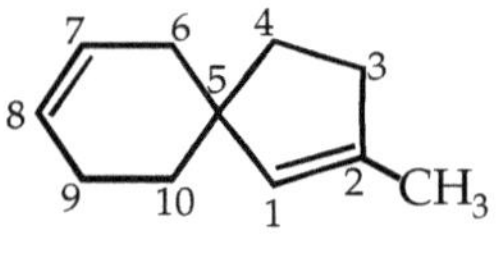

2-Methylspiro [4, 5] deca-1, 7-diene

(x)

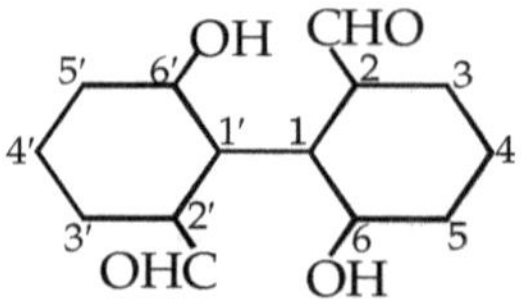

6,6-Dihydroxydiphenyl-2, 2'-dicarbaldehyde

(xi) 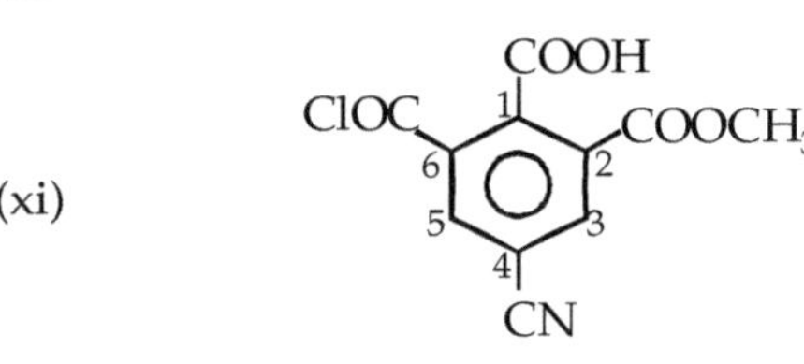

2-Methoxycarbonyl-6-chloroformyl-4-cyanobenzoic acid

(xii) 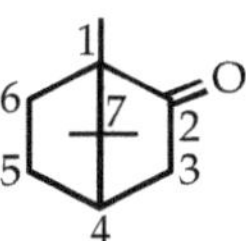

4-(4'- Hydroxyiminocyclohexyl)butanoic acid

(xiii)

5–Ethyl-4-methyloctane

(xiv)

1, 7, 7 –Trimethylbicyclo [2. 2. 1] heptan -2- one

(xv)

$$CH_2COOH$$
$$|$$
$$C(OH)COOH$$
$$|$$
$$CH_2COOH$$

2-Hydroxypropane -1, 2, 3- tricarboxylic acid
(common namecitric acid)

## 1.9 Structural Formula from the IUPAC Name

Following points should be taken into consideration

1. Identify the word root in the given IUPAC name and draw the corresponding carbon chain and number the chain from either side.
2. Identify the primary suffix (-ane, -ene, or -yne) from the name of the compound and insert the double or triple bond at the carbon atom indicated by the suffix.
3. Identify the secondary suffix *i.e.* the principal functional group and insert the proper functional group on the carbon atom indicated by the locant in the given IUPAC name. In case the secondary suffix, *i.e.* the principal functional group, does not bear any numerical prefix, it is assumed to be present at $C_1$.
4. Identify the secondary prefixes, *i.e.* secondary functional group(s) and other substituent(s) indicated by the various prefixes and insert them on the given carbon atom(s) specified by locants.
5. Add suitable number of hydrogen atom(s) so that each carbon atom in the chain becomes tetravalent. This step is not necessary in bond line formulae.

Let us illustrate it by taking the example of **3-Hydroxy-7-oxo-8-methyl-2, 5-decadienoic acid.**

(*i*) Here the word root is *deca* which indicates that the compound is a derivative of decane, hence a carbon chain having 10 carbon atoms must be drawn.

(*i*) Chain of 10 C          (*ii*) A $C_{10}$ chain having double bonds at $C_2$ and $C_5$

(*ii*) Here primary suffix is *diene* whose positions are indicated by numbers 2 and 5.
(*iii*) Here the secondary suffix, *i.e.* primary functional group is carboxylic acid, indicated by –oic acid which is a secondary suffix for –COOH. Since –oic acid does not bear any number it should be given number 1.
(*iv*) Here the secondary prefixes *i.e.* secondary functional groups and substituents are hydroxy (at $C_3$), –oxo (at $C_7$), and methyl (at $C_8$). Insert these groups at respective carbons. In line-bond formula, each carbon atom is assumed to have required number of H atoms, so there is no necessity for writing hydrogen atoms on C atoms.

(*iii*) A $C_{10}$ chain having double bonds at
$C_2$ and $C_5$, and a terminal —COOH group

(*iv*) Secondary functional groups at $C_3$ and $C_7$; methyl at $C_8$.
3-Hydroxy-7-oxo-8-methyl-2, 5-decadienoic acid

## TEST YOUR UNDERSTANDING - 1.4

**1.** Draw structure for the compounds corresponding to following IUPAC names.

    (*a*)   3-Ethyl-2-methylheptane           (*b*)   3-Ethyloctene

    (*c*)   1, 6-Hexanedioic acid              (*d*)   Methyl 2-ethyl-3-hydroxybutanoate

    (*e*)   *tert*-Butyl-3-hydroxyoct-5-enoate     (*f*)   N, N, 2-Trimethyl-3-oxohexanamide

    (*g*)   2-Cyclopropyl-1-hexene           (*h*)   *tert*-Butylcyclohexane

## 1.10   Rules for Nomenclature of Alicylic Compounds

In addition to rules mentioned earlier, following points should be taken in consideration.

**1.** If the ring contains fewer carbon atoms than the alkyl group attached to it or when more than one ring system is attached to a single chain, the compound is named as a derivative of alkane and the ring(s) is(are) treated as cycloalkyl substituent(s), otherwise it is named as a derivative of cycloalkane.

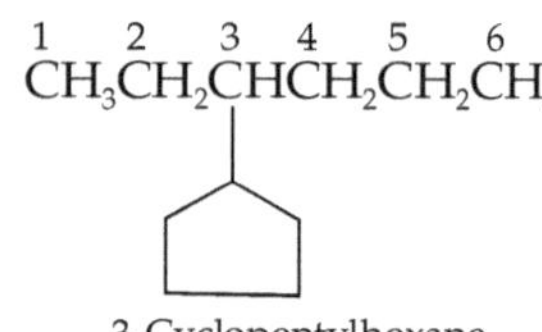

3-Cyclopentylhexane
(Ring has 5 C's, while the alkyl
group has 6)

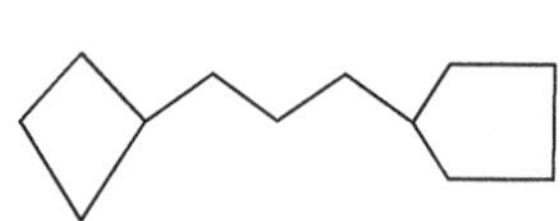

1-Cyclobutyl-
3-cyclopentylpropane

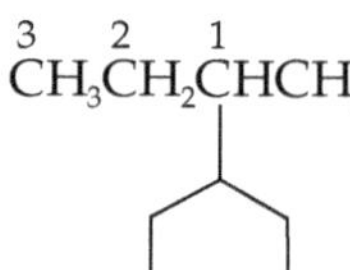

1-Methylpropylcyclopentane
(Ring has 5 C's, while alkyl group has 4)

**2.** In case, the side chain contains multiple bond or a functional group, the alicyclic ring is treated as substituent irrespective of its size.

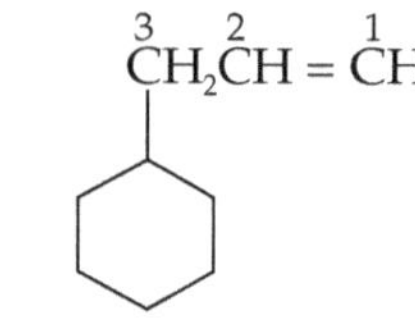

3-Cyclohexylprop-1-ene

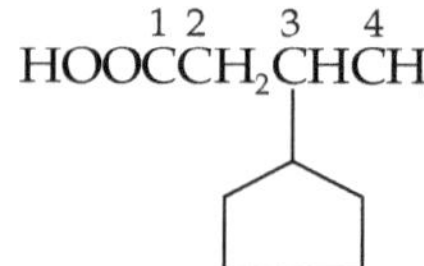

3-Cyclopentylbutanoic acid

**3.** If the functional group, directly attached to the ring contains carbon atom, it is not counted in the word root ; and special suffixes, mentioned earlier, are used to indicate the presence of such groups.

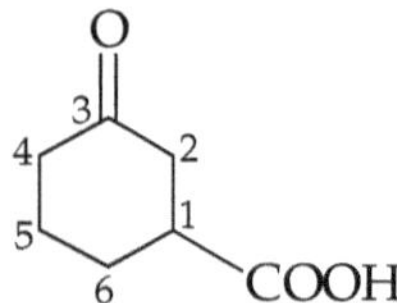

3-Oxocyclohexane-1-carboxylic acid
(Note that here the suffix for —COOH group
is –carboxylic acid rather than -oic acid,
because its carbon is not counted in word root)

3-Methylcyclopentane-1-carboxamide

In cycloalkenes, the double bond is always given number 1. In case the ring contains other substituent, the numbering should be done in a direction that gives the lower number for the substituent attached on the double bond, no matter it may violate the lowest sum rule. For example,

1,6-Dichlorocyclohexene
**not**
2,3-Dichlorocyclohexene
because 1 < 2

5-Ethyl-1-methylcyclohexene
**not**
4-Ethyl-2-methylcyclohexene
because 1 < 2

4.  Nomenclature of the alicyclic compounds containing double bond or functional in the ring as well as in the side chain. In such cases the compound is considered as a derivative of that part in which principal functional group is present.

2-(Cycloprop-3'-enyl)propanol

4-(4'-Hydroxycyclohex-2'-enyl)-3-methylbutanoic acid
(Here the principal group, —COOH is present in side chain, so ring is considered as a substituent)

4-(2'-Methyl-3'-hydroxypropyl)cyclohex-2-en-1-carboxylic acid
(Here the principal group —COOH is present in ring, so the side chain is considered as a substituent)

5.  When both ring as well as side chain contains the same functional group, then the parent hydrocarbon is decided on the basis of the number of carbon atoms (point 1).

2-(2'-Hydroxybutyl)cyclohexanol
(Here ring has 6 C's, while side chain has 4)

6-(3'-Formylcyclopentyl)hexanol
(Here ring has 5 C's, while side chain has 6)

6.  If a compound contains an acyclic ring as well as a benzene ring, it is named as a derivative of benzene.

## TEST YOUR UNDERSTANDING - 1.5

1.  Give IUPAC names for the following compounds.

(a)

(b)

(c)

(d)

(e)

(f)

## 1.11  Nomenclature for Polycyclic Compounds

1.  Compounds containing two or more fused alicyclic rings are known as polycyclic compounds. The carbon atoms common to both the rings are called **bridge head atoms**. A bond or a chain of carbon atoms connecting the two bridge heads is called a **bridge**; thus a bridge may contain 0, 1, 2 ... etc. carbon atoms.

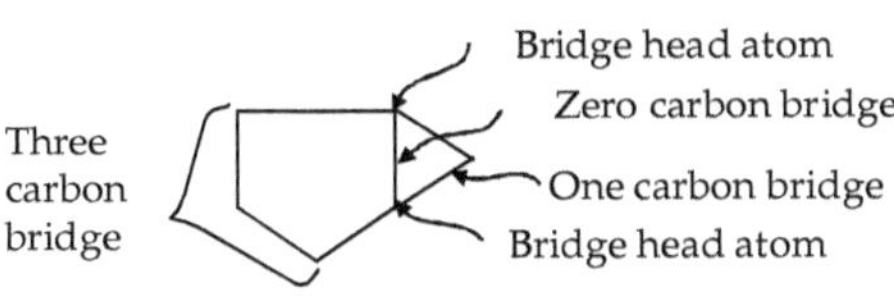


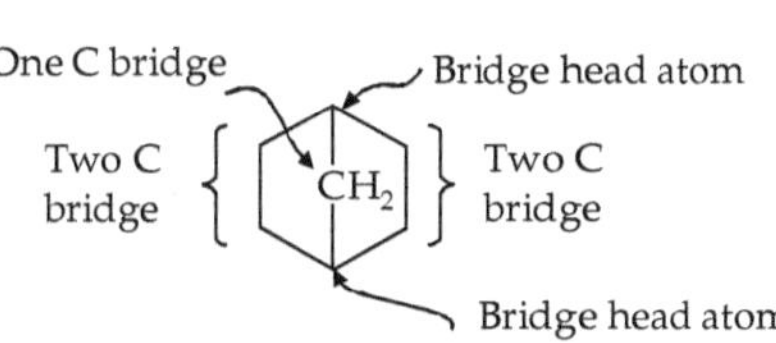

2.   A bicyclic compound is named by attaching the prefix *bicyclo* to the name of the hydrocarbon corresponding to the total number of carbon atoms in the two rings. The number of carbon atoms in each of these three bridges connecting the two bridge head carbon atoms is indicated by arabic numerals, *i.e.* 0, 1, 2, 3, ... etc. These arabic numerals are arranged in descending order, separated from one another by full stops (.) and then enclosed in square brackets. These brackets are placed between the prefix bicyclo and the name of the alkane. For example, the above two compounds are named as

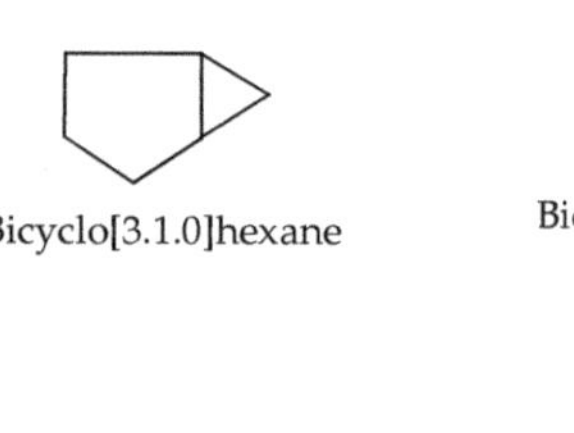

Bicyclo[3.1.0]hexane     Bicyclo[2.2.1]heptane     Bicyclo[4.4.0]decane     Bicyclo[3.1.1]heptane

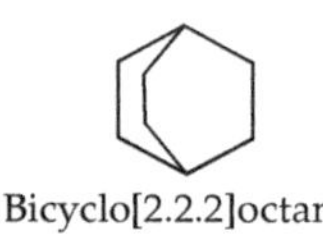

Bicyclo[2.2.2]octane     Bicyclo[1.1.1]pentane     Bicyclo[2.1.1]hexane     Bicyclo[2.2.1]heptane
(Norborane)

3.   If a substituent is present, numbering is done from one of the bridge head atoms, passes first through the longest bridge to the second bridge head atom, then to the next longest bridge and finally to the shortest bridge.

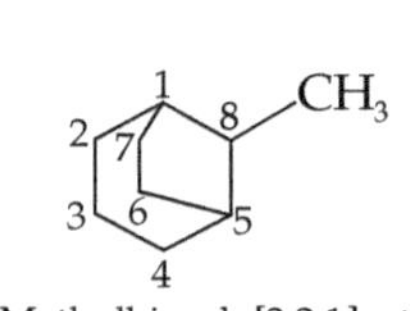

8-Methylbicyclo[3.2.1]octane     2, 6, 6-Trimethylbicyclo[3.1.1]hept-2-ene     Bicyclo[2.2.1]hept-2-ene     1, 7, 7-Trimethylbicyclo[2.2.1]heptan-2-one

Compounds in which one carbon atom is common to two different rings are called **spiro compounds,** and the common carbon atom is called the **spiro atom**. Their IUPAC name begins with the word spiro followed by brackets containing the number of carbon atoms in *ascending order*, in each ring attached to the common carbon atom and ending with the name of the hydrocarbon corresponding to the total number of carbon atoms in the two rings.

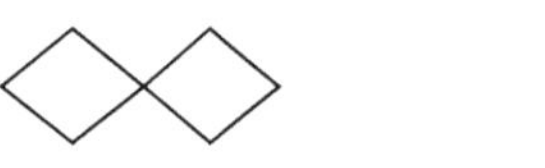

Spiro[3.3]heptane     Spiro[2.4]heptane     Spiro[3.5]nonane

## TEST YOUR UNDERSTANDING - 1.6

1.   Give IUPAC names for the following compounds.

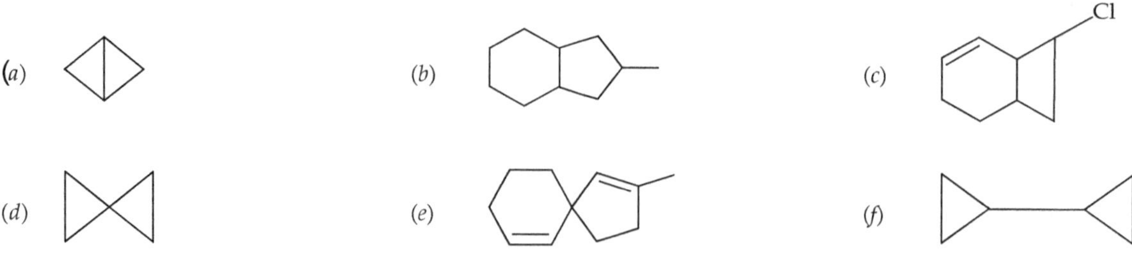

(a)          (b)          (c)

(d)          (e)          (f)

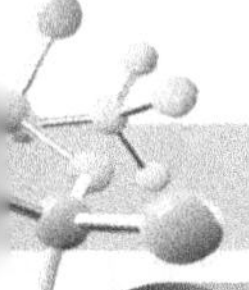

## 1.12   Nomenclature of Aromatic Compounds

Aromatic compounds are generally named as substituted benzene, however when large and complex groups are attached to the benzene ring, these are named as alkanes, alkenes, etc. and benzene ring is considered as substituent, *i.e.* aryl group. The common aryl groups are

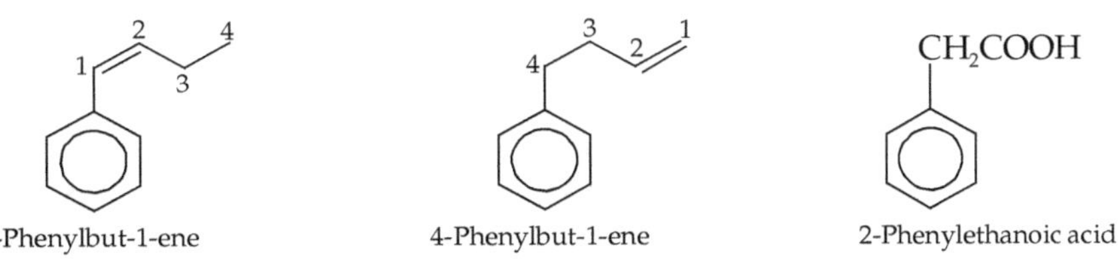

Phenyl written as $C_6H_5$—, φ—, or Ph—      Benzyl      Benzal      Benzo

*o*-Tolyl (2-Tolyl)      *m*-Tolyl (3-Tolyl)      *p*-Tolyl (4-Tolyl)

In case benzene ring has a substituted side chain, $C_6H_5$— is named as a phenyl and the compound is named as an acyclic compound.

1-Phenylbut-1-ene      4-Phenylbut-1-ene      2-Phenylethanoic acid

## TEST YOUR UNDERSTANDING - 1.7

1.    Give IUPAC name for each of the following compounds.

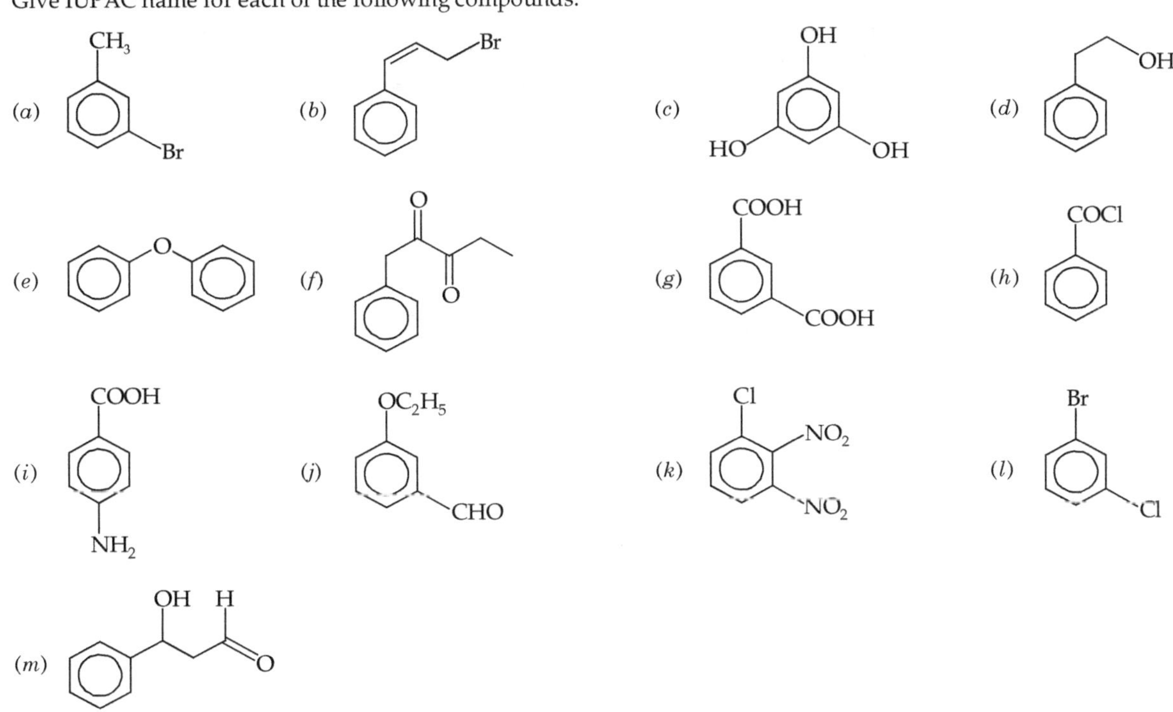

●●●●●    **IMPORTANT POINTS**    ●●●●●

1. In the common system of nomenclature, prefixes iso and neo are used for the groups $Me_2CH-$ (isopropyl) and $Me_3C-$ (*tert*-butyl) groups respectively.

2. Isocyanides or isonitriles or carbylamines have no IUPAC name.

3. The aldehyde group (a terminal group) can be represented by two types of prefixes, i.e., *oxo* (when –CHO is at the end of the carbon chain, here its carbon is counted in the chain) and formyl when –CHO is present as a substituent, its carbon is not counted in the chain). For example,

$$O = \overset{3}{C}H - \overset{2}{C}H_2 - \overset{1}{C}OOH$$
3–Oxo propanoic acid

$$HOO\overset{1}{C} - \overset{2}{C}H - \overset{3}{C}OOH$$
$$|$$
$$CHO$$
2 – Formylpropane -1, 3 – dioic acid

4. In IUPAC system, while using prefixes like carboxy, formyl and oxo, the carbon of the substituent group is not counted in the principal chain.

5. Due to different systems of nomenclature, a given organic compound can have two or more IUPAC names but one IUPAC name can't represent two compounds.

    1-(4′–Chlorophenyl)–2–(2′-chlorophenyl)ethane

    1-(2′–Chlorophenyl)–2–(4′-chlorophenyl)ethane

6. When two or more prefixes consist of identical words, (e.g. chlorophenyl in the given example) the priority for citation is given to that group which contains the lowest locant at the first point of difference.

7. Hydrocarbons containing double as well as triple bond is always named as **alkenyne** and not alkynene. However, in such cases numbering should be done in a way that it follows the lowest locant rule (sum of locants should be minimum). However, if there is a choice, the double bond should be given preference over the triple bond. For example,

← correct numbering

$$\overset{5}{C}H \equiv \overset{4}{C} - \overset{3}{C}H_2 - \overset{2}{C}H = \overset{1}{C}H_2$$

wrong numbering →
Pent–1–en–4–yne

$$\overset{1}{C}H_2 = \overset{2}{C}H - \overset{3}{C}H = \overset{4}{C}H - \overset{5}{C} \equiv \overset{6}{C}H$$

Hexa – 1, 3 – dien – 5 – yne   (correct)
Hexa – 3, 5 – dien – 1 – yne X(wrong)

8. In IUPAC system of nomenclature of **bicyclic compounds**, the numerical prefixes indicating the number of carbon atoms in the two rings and the bridge are written in **descending order**, while in the nomenculature of **spiro** compounds, the numerical prefixes indicating the number of carbon atoms in each ring are written in **ascending order**.

# EXERCISE 1.1 (MCQ - ONE option correct)

1. The correct IUPAC name for $CH_3CH_2CH_2CH_3$ is
   - (a) *n*-Butane
   - (b) Butane
   - (c) Both (a) and (b)
   - (d) None

2. Isobutyl group is a ...... alkyl group.
   - (a) primary
   - (b) secondary
   - (c) tertiary
   - (d) both (a) and (b)

3. Systematic name for the species, $—CH_2CH_2CH(CH_3)_2$ is
   - (a) Isopentyl
   - (b) *sec*-Pentyl
   - (c) 2-Methylbutyl
   - (d) 3-Methylbutyl

4. Which of the following compound has all the four types (1°, 2°, 3° and 4°) of carbon atoms?
   - (a) 2, 3, 4-Trimethylpentane
   - (b) *neo*-Pentane
   - (c) 2, 2, 4-Trimethylpentane
   - (d) None of the three

5. IUPAC name of ☰☰☰ is
   - (a) 1-Butyne-3-ene
   - (b) 1-Butene-3-yne
   - (c) both (a) and (b)
   - (d) Vinylacetylene

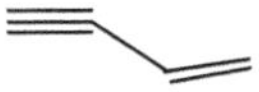

6. Choose the correct IUPAC name for ... is
   - (a) 2-Methylhept-6-yn-2-ene
   - (b) 2-Methylhept-2-en-6-yne
   - (c) 6-Methyl-5-hepten-1-yne
   - (d) 6-Methylhept-1-yn-5-ene

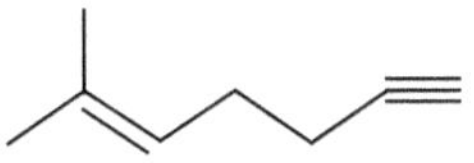

7. The correct IUPAC name for ... is
   - (a) 2-Chloro-4-ethyl-3-methyl-6-heptyn-2-ene
   - (b) 6-Chloro-4-ethyl-5-methyl-5-hepten-1-yne
   - (c) 1-Chloro-1, 2-dimethyl-3-ethylhex-1-en-5-yne
   - (d) 1-Chloro-3-ethyl-1, 2-dimethylhex-1-en-5-yne

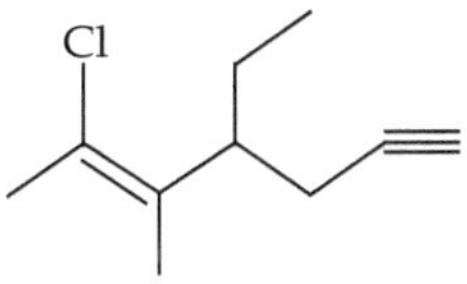

8. The most appropriate IUPAC name for $CH_3CH_2OCH_2CH_2Cl$ is
   - (a) ethyl chloroethyl ether
   - (b) 1-Chloro-2-ethoxyethane
   - (c) 2-Ethoxyethyl chloride
   - (d) 2-Chloro-1-ethoxyethane

9. IUPAC name for H—C—C—OH is
   - (a) Formylmethanoic acid
   - (b) 2-Oxoethanoic acid
   - (c) Glyoxalic acid
   - (d) 2-Oxomethanoic acid

10. The IUPAC name for ... is
    - (a) 2-Formylpentanol
    - (b) 2-Methylpentanedial
    - (c) 2-Methyl-4-oxopentanal
    - (d) 2, 4-Diformylbutane

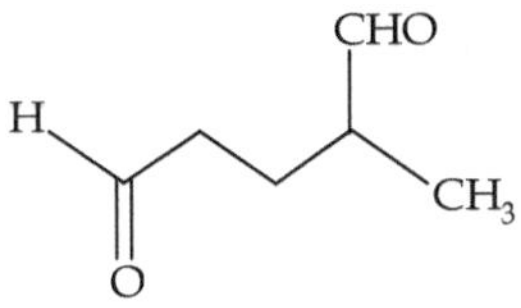

11. The IUPAC name for ... is
    - (a) 2-Ethyl-2-carboxypentanoic acid
    - (b) 2-Carboxy-2-ethylpentanoic acid
    - (c) 2-Propyl-2-ethylpropanedioic acid
    - (d) 2-Ethyl-2-propylpropanedioic acid

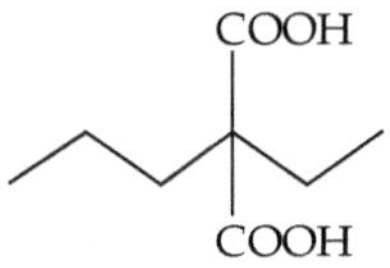

12. IUPAC name for the compound ... is
    - (a) 2-Ethyl-1-butanol-2
    - (b) Diethylmethylmethanol
    - (c) 1-Methyl-1-ethylpropanol
    - (d) 2-Ethylbutanol

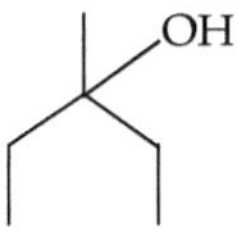

13. IUPAC name for the given structure is 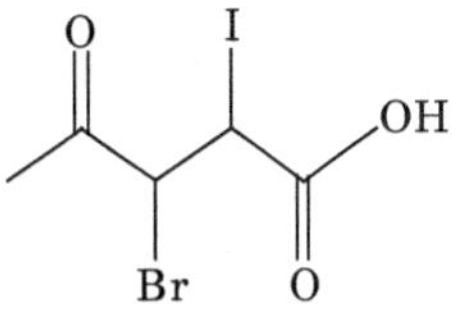
    - (a) 4-Carboxy-3-bromo-4-iodopentanoic acid
    - (b) 3-Bromo-2-iodo-4-ketopentanoic acid
    - (c) 4-Keto-3-bromo-2-iodopentanoic acid
    - (d) 2-Iodo-3-bromo-4-ketopentanoic acid

14. IUPAC name for the compound ... should be
    - (a) 5-Bromo-3-carbamoyl-2-chloroformyl-4-formylhexanoic acid
    - (b) 2-Bromo-4-carbamoyl-5-chloroformyl-3-formylhexanoic acid
    - (c) 2-Chloroformyl-3-carbamoyl-4-formyl-5-bromohexanoic acid
    - (d) 4-Formyl-2-chloroformyl-3-carbamoyl-5-bromohexanoic acid

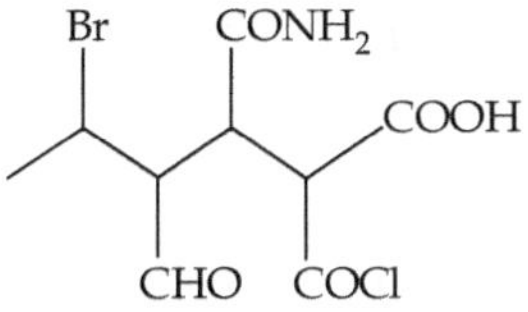

15. IUPAC name for $CH_3CON(Br)Cl$ is
    - (a) N-Bromo-N-chloroethanamide
    - (b) N-Chloro-N-bromoethanamide
    - (c) 1-Bromo-1-chloroethanamide
    - (d) N-Bromo-N-chloroacetamide

16. Which of the following statement is incorrect ?
    - (a) –COCl may be represented as carbonyl halide
    - (b) –COCl may be represented as chloroformyl
    - (c) –CN may be represented as nitrile, cyano and carbonitrile
    - (d) None of these

**17.** Pick up the correct IUPAC name in the following :

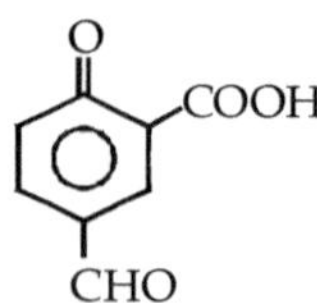

(a)  3-formyl-5-oxocyclohexane carboxylic acid
(b)  5-formyl-2-oxocyclohexane carboxylic acid
(c)  2-carboxy-4-formylcyclohexanone
(d)  3-carboxy-4-oxocyclohexane carbaldehyde

**18.** Pick up the correct IUPAC name in the following :

(a)  2-methyl-3-(2′, 4′-dimethylbutyl)cyclohexene
(b)  1-methyl-6 (2′, 4′-dimethylbutyl)cyclohexane
(c)  1-methyl-2 (2′, 4′ - dimethylbutyl)cyclohexene
(d)  (1′-methylcyclohexenyl)2, 4-dimethylbutane

**19.** Pick up the correct IUPAC name in the following :

(a)  1-vinyl–5, 8, 9, 10 – tetrahydronaphthalene
(b)  2-ethenylbicyclo [4.4.0] deca–1, 5, 8 – triene
(c)  2-vinyl – 3, 4, 7, 10 – tetrahydronaphthalene
(d)  3-ethenylbicyclo [4.4.0] deca -3, 5, 8-triene

**20.** ⬡—COOH. The correct IUPAC name for the structure is

(a)  cyclohexanoic acid
(b)  cyclohexane carboxylic acid
(c)  both
(d)  none

**21.** The  correct IUPAC name for     is

(a)  3, 5-dihydroxy-6-mercaptocyclohexene
(b)  4, 6-dihydroxy-3-mercaptocyclohexene
(c)  3-hydroxy-4-mercaptocyclohex-5-enol
(d)  3-hydroxy-6-mercaptocyclohex-4-enol

**22.** The IUPAC name for        is
(a)  5-thiohexanoic acid
(b)  5-thiohexanoic acid
(c)  5-sulphohexanoic acid
(d)  None is correct

**23.** The secondary functional group in

$$CH_3CH-C-CH-CH_2CONH_2 \text{ is}$$

with CONH₂, CONH₂ substituents and NH

(a)  carbanoyl          (b)  imino
(c)  both               (d)  none

**24.** The correct IUPAC name for

(a)  1, 4-dicyclobutylcyclobutane
(b)  1, 1′, 3′, 1″-tercyclobutane
(c)  *p*-dicyclobutylcyclobutane
(d)  1, 3′, 1″-tricyclobutane

**25.** The IUPAC name of the compound :

(a)  1-methyl-2-N-methylcyclohexanecarboxamide
(b)  1-(N-methylcarbamoyl)-2-methylcyclohexane
(c)  2-(N-,ethylcarbamoyl)-1-methylcyclohexane
(d)  N, 2-dimethylcyclohexanecarboxamide

**26.** The correct IUPAC name for         is :

(a)  2-bromo-1-chloro-3-fluoro-5-iodocyclohexane
(b)  2-bromo-3-chloro-1-fluoro-5-iodocyclohexane
(c)  1-bromo-6-chloro-2-fluoro-4-iodocyclohexane
(d)  1-bromo-2-chloro-6-fluoro-4-iodocyclohexane

**27.** The correct IUPAC name for

is

(a)  4-benzamido-2-nitrobenzoic acid
(b)  4-benzoylamino-2-nitrobenzoic acid
(c)  4-benzoylamino-6-nitrobenzoic acid
(d)  N-(3-carboxy-4-nitrophenyl) Benzamide

**28.** $CH_3NH$—⬡—⬡—$NHCH_3$        has IUPAC name

(a)  3, 4′-bis (N-methylamino) biphenyl
(b)  3, 4′-bis (methylamino) biphenyl
(c)  *p*-methylamino-*m*-methylaminobiphenyl
(d)  3, 4′-bis (aminomethyl) biphenyl

**29.** The IUPAC name of $C_6H_5COCl$ is
(a)  benzene chloro ketone
(b)  benzoyl chloride
(c)  chloro phenyl ketone
(d)  benzene carbonyl chloride

# EXERCISE 1.2   (MCQ 1 or >1 option correct, Passage based, Matching, A/R)

**DIRECTIONS for Q. 1 to Q. 7 : Multiple choice questions with one or more than one correct option(s).**

**1.** Which of the following statements are true about a homologous series?
   (a) Adjacent members of a group differ by a mass of 14
   (b) Adjacent members of a group differ by one $-CH_2$ group
   (c) members of a homologous series can be prepared by the same general methods
   (d) members of a homologous series have the same physical and chemical properties

**2.** Which of the following compounds will have only primary and tertiary carbon?
   (a) Pentane                     (b) 2-Methylbutane
   (c) 2, 3-Dimethylbutane         (d) 2-Bromo-2-methylpropane

**3.** Which of the following compounds will have only primary and secondary carbon?
   (a) Propane                     (b) 2,2,3-Trimethylpentane
   (c) 2-Methylpropane             (d) n-Propylbromide

**4.** Which of the following statements are true?
   (a) Primary carbon atom is bonded to one or no other carbon atom
   (b) Secondary carbon atom is bonded to two other carbon atoms
   (c) Tertiary carbon atom is bonded to three other carbon atoms
   (d) None of above

**5.** The IUPAC name of the compound $CH_3CHOH.CH_2CH_3$ is
   (a) 1-Methylpropanol-1          (b) 2-Butanol
   (c) Butan-2-ol                  (d) Butanol-2

**6.** The IUPAC name of the compound

$$\text{CH}_3\text{CH}_2 - \bigcirc - \text{CH}_2\text{CH}_2\text{CH}_3, \ \text{H}_3\text{C}$$

   (a) 1-Ethyl-2–methyl-4-propylcyclohexane
   (b) 2-Ethyl-1-methyl-5-propylcyclohexane
   (c) 4-Ethyl-3-methyl-1-propylcyclohexane
   (d) All the three

**7.** The IUPAC name of the compound  Cl—◇—◇—Br
   (a) 3-Bromo-3'-chloro-1, 1'-bicyclobutane
   (b) 1-Bromo-1'-chloro-4, 4'-bicyclobutane
   (c) 1-Bromo-3 (3'-chlorocyclobutyl) cyclobutane
   (d) 4-(4'-Chlorocyclobutyl)-1-bromocyclobutane

**DIRECTIONS for Q. 8 to Q. 19 : Read the following passages and answer the questions that follows :**

### PASSAGE 1
When the compound contains more than two similar groups all of which are present on the principal chain, then none of these groups are counted in the principal chain ; and special suffixes are used to indicate the functional group, *viz.*

| *Functional group* | *Special suffix* | *Functional group* | *Special suffix* |
|---|---|---|---|
| –COOH | –carboxylic acid | –COX | –carbonyl halide |
| –CONH$_2$ | –carboxamide | –CHO | –carbaldehyde |
| –COOR | R----carboxylate | –CN | –carbonitrile |

When the compound contains more than two similar terminal groups, all of which are not directly linked to the principal chain, then that longest principal chain should be selected which contains two such similar terminal groups at its two ends. Here the terminal groups are counted in the chain, while the third, present on side chain, is considered as a substituent.

**8.** This rule can't be applied on the compound containing
   (a) aldehydic group
   (b) nitrile group
   (c) ketonic group
   (d) it can be applied to all the three

**9.**  The IUPAC name of this compound is
   (a) 2, 3-Dicyanobutanecarbonitrile-4
   (b) 1-Methylpropane-1, 2, 3-tricarbonitrile
   (c) Butane-1, 2, 3-tricarbonitrile
   (d) 2, 3-Dicyanocarbonitrile

**10.**  The IUPAC name of this compound is
   (a) 2-methylhexane-1, 5, 6-tricarbonitrile
   (b) 5-methylhexane-1, 2, 6-tricarbonitrile
   (c) 3-methyl-6-cyanoctan-1, 8-dinitrile
   (d) 6-methyl-3-cyanoctan-1, 8-dinitrile

**11.**  The IUPAC name of this compound is
   (a) 3-Carboxy-4-cyanobutanoic acid
   (b) 2-Cyanomethylbutane-1, 4-dioic acid
   (c) 3-Cyanomethylbutane-1, 4-dioic acid
   (d) 3, 5-Dicarboxypentanenitrile

**12.**  The IUPAC name of this compound is
   (a) pentane-1, 4, 5-tricarbaldehyde
   (b) 3-(formylmethyl) hexane-1, 6-dial
   (c) 4-(formylmethyl) hexane-1, 6-dial
   (d) 4, 4(diformylmethyl) butanal

**13.** Which of the following is considered as a derivative of hexane?

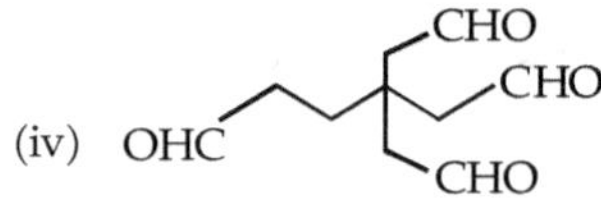

(iv)

(a)  (i) and (iii)  (b)  (ii) and (iii)
(c)  (ii), (iii) and (iv)  (d)  all the four

## PASSAGE 2

Although most of the IUPAC rules of open chain compounds are applied to alicyclic compounds, certain points deserve special attention.

(i)  In cycloalkenes, the numbering should be done in a direction that gives the lower number for the substituent attached on the double bond.

(ii)  In case the alicyclic compound has functional group in the ring as well as in the side chain, the compound is considered as a derivative of that part in which principal functional group lies.

On the basis of the following seniority table for some of the principal groups, answer the questions given below.

### Seniority table for principal groups

| Group | Prefix name | Suffix name |
|---|---|---|
| –COOH | Carboxy– | –oic acid |
| –COOR | Alkyl-oxycarbonyl | –alkyl---oates |
| –COX | Haloformyl– | –oyl halide |
| –CONH$_2$ | Carbamoyl– | amide |
| –CHO | Formyl– | –al |
| –OH | Hydroxy– | –ol |
| –X (halogen) | Halo– | – |
| R— | Alkyl– | – |

14.  $HO-$⬡$-\overset{\overset{O}{\|}}{C}-NH\,CH_3$ its correct IUPAC name should be

(a)  4-acetamidocyclohexanol
(b)  4-(N-methylamido)cyclohexanol
(c)  4-hydroxy-N-methylcyclohexanecarboxamide
(d)  4-hydroxycyclohexaneacetamide

15.  $HOOC-$⬡$-CONH_2$. The correct IUPAC name for the structure is :
(a)  4-Carbomylbenzoic acid  (b)  4-Amidobenzoic acid
(c)  4-Carboxybenzamide  (d)  4-Acetamidobenzoic acid

16.  ⬡$-Cl$. The correct IUPAC name for the structure is :

(a)  1, 2-Dichlorocyclohexene  (b)  1, 6-Dichlorocyclohexene
(c)  2, 3-Dichlorocyclohexene  (d)  any of the three

17.  Accoding to IUPAC system,

$HO-$⬡$-CH_2\overset{\overset{CH_3}{\|}}{C}HCH_2COOH$ is named as :

(a)  4-(3-Carboxy-2-methylpropyl)cyclohex-2-enol-1
(b)  4-(4'-Hydroxycyclohex-2-enyl)-3-methylbutanoic acid
(c)  4-Hydroxycyclohexenyl-3-methylbutanoic acid
(d)  4-(4'-Hydroxycyclohex-2'-enyl)-3-methylbutanoic acid

18.  $Cl\,CH_2\,CH_2\,CH_2-\overset{\overset{O}{\|}}{C}-O-CH_2\overset{\underset{Br}{\|}}{C}H-CH_3$ has its IUPAC name as

(a)  4-Chlorobutyl-2-bromopropanoate
(b)  2-Bromopropyl-1-chlorobutanoate
(c)  2-Bromopropyl-3-chlorobutanoate
(d)  2-Bromopropyl-4-chlorobutanoate

19.  Name the prefix in the following compound :

$$C_2H_5O_2C-CH_2-\overset{\overset{CH_2COOC_2H_5}{\|}}{C}H-CH_2-COOC_2H_5$$

(a)  Ethylacetato  (b)  Ethylacetoxy
(c)  Ethyloxycarbonylmethyl  (d)  Ethoxycarbonylmethyl

**DIRECTIONS for Q. 20 to Q. 21 : The following questions are matching type questions. Match Column I with Column II**

20.
| Column I | Column II |
|---|---|
| (A)  Prefix | (a)  carbonyl chloride |
| (B)  Suffix | (b)  carbamoyl |
| (C)  –CN | (c)  carbonitrile |
| (D)  –CHO | (d)  carbaldehyde |
| (E)  –COCl | (e)  chloroformyl |

21.

| Column I | Column II |
|---|---|
| (A) | (a)  carbamoyl-methyl is present |
| (B) | (b)  derivative of hexane |
| (C) | (c)  name as amide |

# EXERCISE 1.3  (Subjective Problems)

1.  Give the structural formula for a three-carbon compound containing each of the following functional groups.

(i)  $\overset{}{C}=\overset{}{C}$     (ii)  $-C\equiv C-$

(iii)  $-C\equiv N$     (iv)  $-COOH$

2.  Provide a structural formula for the compound with the smallest number of carbons that is
(a)  a cyclic alcohol  (b)  an amide,
(c)  a cyclic ether, and  (d)  an alkenylcarboxylic acid

3.  Give the bond line structure for the following compounds.
(a)  $CH_2OH(CH_2)_3COCH_3$

(b)  $CH_3CH_2NHCOCH_2CH(CH_3)_2$

(c)  $H_2NCH_2-$⬡$-C(CH_3)_3$

(d)  $CH_2=CMe_2$

4.  Give IUPAC names for the compounds with following structure.

(i)  $CH_3CH_2\overset{\overset{CH_3}{\|}}{C}H\overset{\overset{CH_3}{\|}}{C}H-\overset{\overset{CH_3}{\|}}{\underset{\underset{CH_2CH_2CH_3}{\|}}{C}}HCH_3$

(ii)  $CH_3CH_2OCH_2CH_2Cl$     (iii)  $CH_3CH_2C \equiv CCH_2CHO$

(iv)

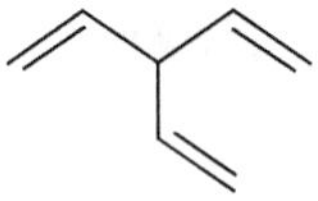

(v)

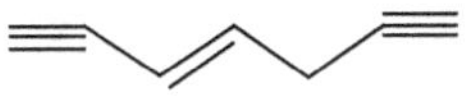

(vi)

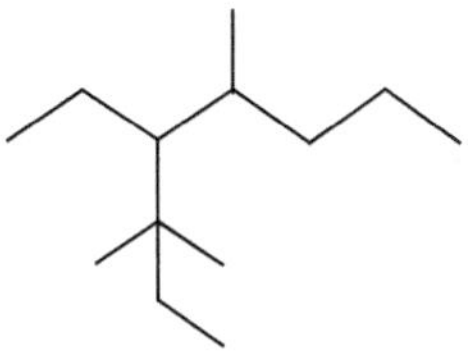

(vii)

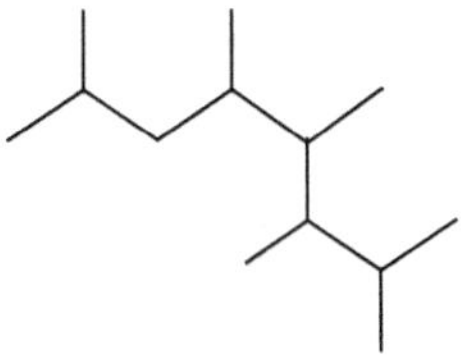

(viii)

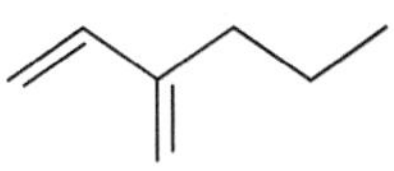

(ix)

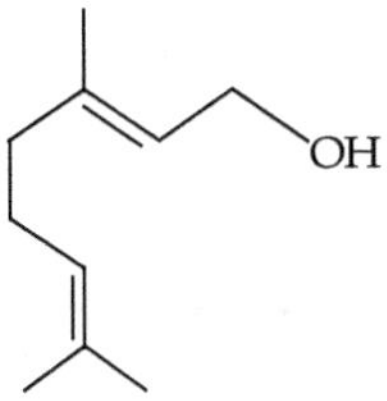

(x)

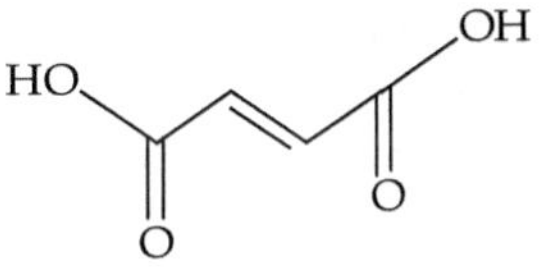

(xi)

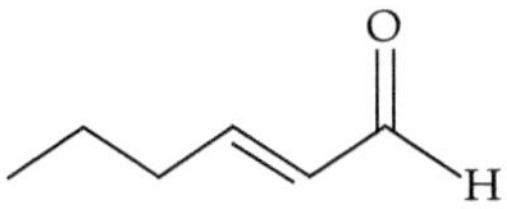

(xii)

(xiii)

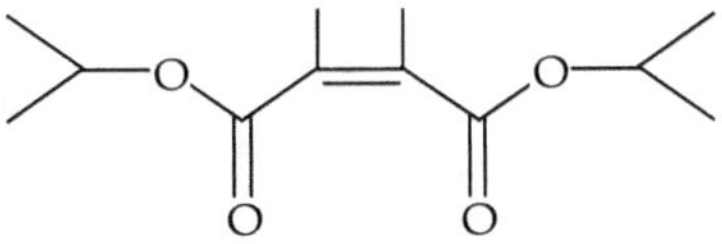

(xiv)

(xv)

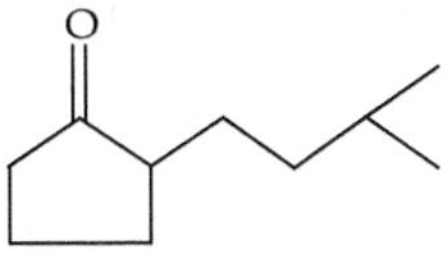

(xvi) 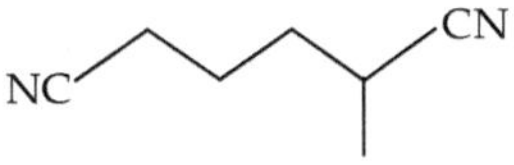  $NC$ ... $CN$

(xvii)  $NC$ ... $CN$ ... $CN$

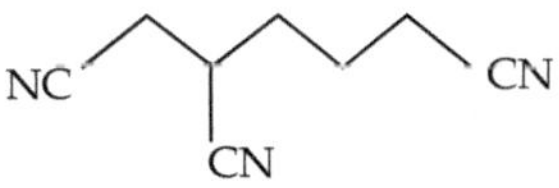

(xviii)

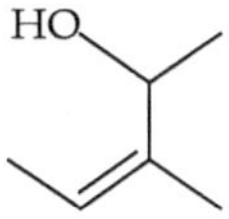

(xix)

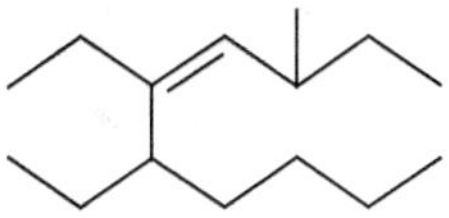

(xx)

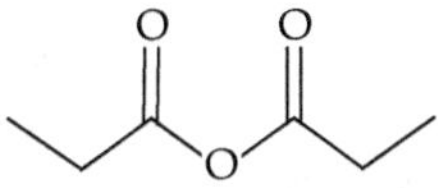

(xxi)

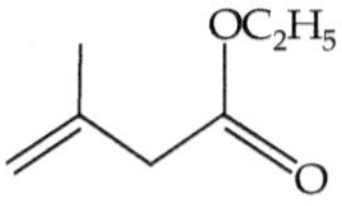

(xxii)

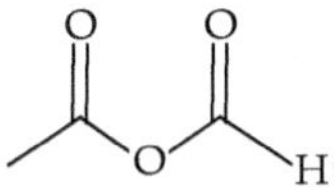

(xxiii)

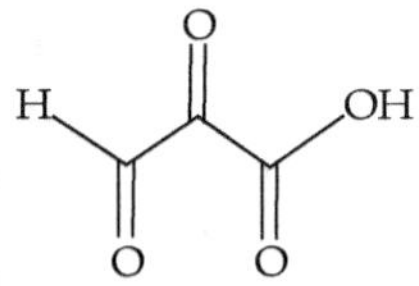

(xxiv)

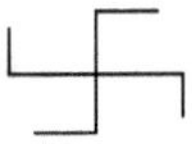

(xxv)

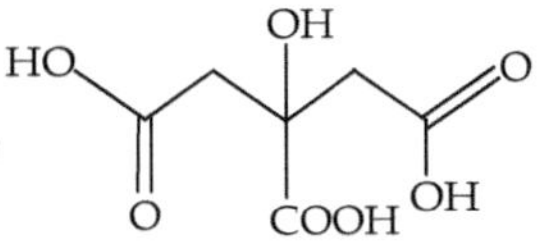

(xxvi)

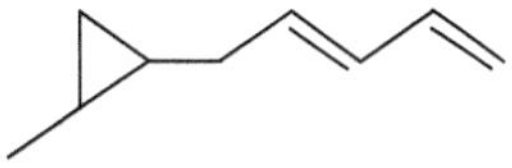

(xxvii)

(xxviii)

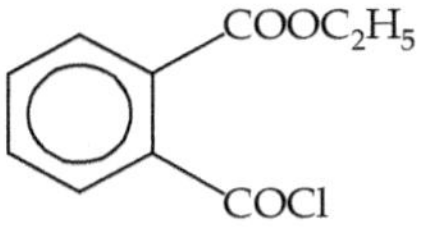

(xxix)

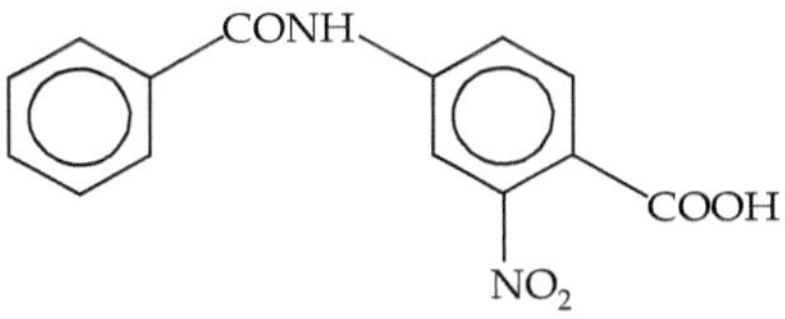

(xxx)

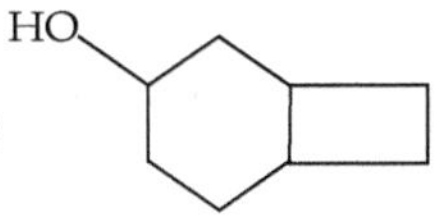

(xxxi)

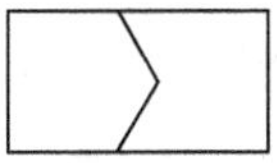

(xxxii)

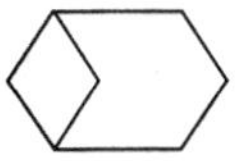

5.  Draw acceptable structure to each of the following compounds.

   (*a*)   3-Ethyloctene               (*b*)   5-Isobutyl-1-heptene

   (*c*)   2-Cyclopropyl-1-heptene   (*d*)   3-Ethyl-2-methylhexane

   (*e*)   5-*tert*-Butylnonane

   (*f*)   2-(1-Cyclobutenyl)-1-hexene

   (*g*)   Ethyl 2-chloropropanoate

   (*h*)   Octa-1-ene-4yne          (*i*)   Bicyclo[4.2.0]octane

   (*j*)   Spiro[4.5]decane

# SOLUTIONS

## TEST YOUR UNDERSTANDING - 1.1

**1.** (a) $C_{11}$   (b) $C_{31}$   (c) $C_{28}$

**2.**

| | *pri*-Prefix | *sec.*-Prefix | Word root | *pri*-Suffix | *sec.*Suffix |
|---|---|---|---|---|---|
| (a) | — | Chloro | but | ane | ol |
| (b) | — | Methyl | but | ene | al |
| (c) | — | Amino | but | yne | oic acid |
| (d) | — | Methoxy | eth | ane | — |
| (e) | Cyclo | bromo | hex | ane | — |

**3.**

| | *pri*-Prefix | *sec.*-Prefix | Word root | *pri*-Suffix | *sec.*Suffix |
|---|---|---|---|---|---|
| (a) | — | — | but | ene | ol |
| (b) | — | Oxo | but | ane | oic acid |
| (c) | — | Methyl, Oxo | but | ane | oic acid |
| (d) | — | — | pent | ane | al |
| (e) | — | Carbamoyl-methyl —CH$_2$CONH$_2$ | pent | ane | amide |
| (f) | — | Formylmethyl —CH$_2$CHO | hex | ane | al |

**4.** (a)

(i)  $CH_3CH_2CH_2CH_2CH_2-$  1°

(ii)  $CH_3CH_2\overset{|}{C}HCH_2-$  1°

(iii)  $CH_3\overset{CH_3}{\underset{|}{C}}HCH_2CH_2-$  1°

(iv)  $CH_3\overset{CH_3}{\underset{\underset{CH_3}{|}}{\overset{|}{C}}}CH_2-$  1°

(v)  $CH_3CH_2CH_2\overset{|}{C}HCH_3$  2°

(vi)  $(CH_3)_2CH_2\overset{|}{C}HCH_3$  2°

(vii)  $CH_3CH_2\overset{|}{C}HCH_2CH_3$  2°

(iv)  $CH_3\overset{|}{\underset{\underset{CH_3}{|}}{C}}CH_2CH_3$  3°

(b)  $\overset{1°}{CH_3}-\overset{2°}{CH_2}-\overset{3°}{\overset{|}{C}H}-\overset{4°}{\underset{\underset{CH_3}{|}}{\overset{CH_3\quad CH_3}{\overset{|}{C}}}}CH_3$  or

(2, 2, 3-Trimethylpentane)

## TEST YOUR UNDERSTANDING - 1.2

**1.** (a)     (b)

(c)     (d)

**(e)**

**(f)**

## TEST YOUR UNDERSTANDING - 1.3

**1.**
- (a) 2-Isopropylbut-2-enoic acid
- (b) Pent-3-ynal
- (c) 2-Ethylprop-2-enoyl chloride
- (d) Bis (2-chloroethyl)amine
- (e) 3-Bromomethyl-4-chloromethylhexane (bromomethyl should get lower locant than chloromethyl because former comes first in alphabet order).
- (f) 2-(3'-Chloropropyl)but-2-enol (Main chain must contain principal functional group, —OH as well as C = C).
- (g) Ethyl 3-methyl-5-oxopentanoate (– COOC$_2$H$_5$ is the principal functional group, CHO group is present at the end of the chain, so it is counted in the main chain and given the prefix —*oxo*, had it been in the middle of the chain its prefix would have been *formyl*, see example below).
- (h) Ethyl 3-formylpentanoate.
- (i) 3-Cyano-6-ketoheptanal (—CHO has priority over >C = O as well as —CN)
- (j) *tert*-Butyl 3-oxo-6-chloroformylheptanoate (—COOCMe$_3$ is the principal functional group).
- (k) 4-Ethyl-3-mercapto-N-ethylheptanamide (—CONHR is the principal functional group and the longest chain has 7 carbon atoms).
- (l) Butane-1, 2, 4-tricarbaldehyde (when more than two —CHO groups are present on the main chain, these are not counted in the principal chain).

**2.**
- (a) 2,2,5-Trimethylheptane
- (b) 4-Ethyl-3,3-dimethylheptane.
- (c) 5-(1'-Methylpropyl)-6-(2'-methylpropyl)decane
- (d) 2,3,5-Trimethyl-4-propylheptane (in case two or more chains are of equal length, then the chain with greater number of side chains is selected as the principal chain).
- (e) 6-Methylhepta-1,4-diene
- (f) Hept-3-ene-1,6-diyne (-*ene* is written first because it comes first in alphabetic order).
- (g) Hepta-1,6-dien-3-yne
- (h) Cyclododecane (it is having 12 C's)
- (i) 3-Hydroxy-2,4-diketo-5-methylhexanedioic acid
- (j) 6-Hydroxy-5-oxo-2-heptenenitrile (—CN has priority over >C = O as well as —OH)

(k)   4-Hydroxy-7-oxo-9-methyl-2,5,8-decatrienoic acid

(l)   3, 7-Dimethyl-2,6-octadienal

(m)   Cyclohexylmethanenitrile (Cyclohexanecarbonitrile is its chemical abstract name)

(n)   Cyclopentanecarboxamide

## TEST YOUR UNDERSTANDING - 1.4

1.   (a)   (b)   (c)   (d)   (e)   (f)   (g)   (h)

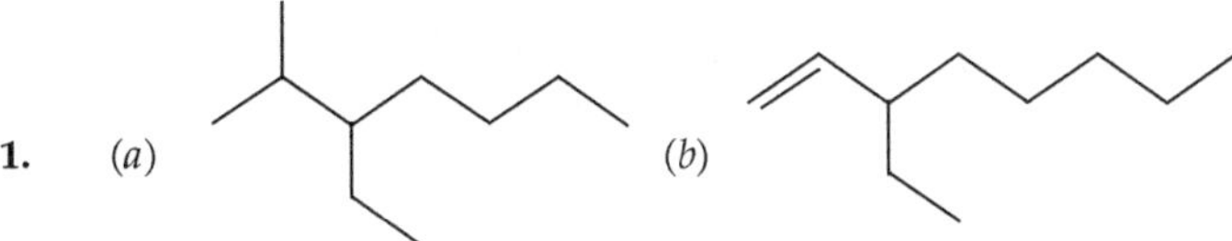

## TEST YOUR UNDERSTANDING - 1.5

1.   (a)   4-Chloro-2-ethyl-1-methylcyclohexane

(b)   1-Cyclobutylpentane

(c)   1,3-Dicyclohexylpropane

(d)   4-Ethyl-1-methylcyclohexene

(e)   4-(1-Chloro-1-methylpropyl)cyclohexene

(f)   Ethyl 3-oxocyclohexane-1-carboxylate

## TEST YOUR UNDERSTANDING - 1.6

1.   (a)   Bicyclo[1.1.0]butane

(b)   8-Methylbicyclo [4.3.0] nonane

(c)   8-Chlorobicyclo [4.2.0]oct-2-ene

(d)   Spiro [2.2]pentane

(e)   2-Methylspiro [4.5]deca-1,6-diene

(f)   1,1'-Bicyclopropane.

## TEST YOUR UNDERSTANDING - 1.7

1.   (a)   3-Bromotoluene

(b)   1-Phenyl-3-bromopropene

(c)   Benzene-1,3,5-triol

(d)   2-Phenylethanol

(e)   Phenoxybenzene

(f)   1-Phenylpentan-2, 3-dione

(g)   Benzene-1,3-dicarboxylic acid

(h)   Benzoyl chloride

(i)   4-Aminobenzoic acid

(j)   3-Ethoxybenzaldehyde

(k)   1-Chloro-2,3-dinitrobenzene (chloro is given lower locant as it comes before nitro in alphabetic order)

(l)   1-Bromo-3-chlorobenzene (Br given lower locant)

(m)   3-Hydroxy-3-phenylpropanal.

# EXERCISE 1.1

| 1 | (b) | 6 | (c) | 11 | (d) | 16 | (d) | 21 | (d) | 26 | (a) |
|---|-----|---|-----|----|-----|----|-----|----|-----|----|-----|
| 2 | (a) | 7 | (b) | 12 | (a) | 17 | (b) | 22 | (b) | 27 | (b) |
| 3 | (d) | 8 | (b) | 13 | (b) | 18 | (b) | 23 | (b) | 28 | (a) |
| 4 | (c) | 9 | (b) | 14 | (a) | 19 | (b) | 24 | (b) | 29 | (b) |
| 5 | (b) | 10 | (b) | 15 | (a) | 20 | (b) | 25 | (d) |  |  |

1.   The prefix *n-* is not part of the IUPAC system, hence the correct name for $CH_3(CH_2)_2CH_3$ is *butane*, *n*-butane is its common name, although now-a-days, it too is also acceptable to IUPAC system.

2.   Isobutyl ($Me_2CHCH_2$—) is a primary alkyl group because its potential point of attachment is a primary carbon.

3.   Numbering should be done with the end having free valency; no matter locant gets higher number.

4.   
$$\overset{1}{H_3C}-\overset{2}{\underset{\underset{CH_3}{|}}{C}}-\overset{3}{CH_2}-\overset{4}{\underset{\underset{CH_3}{|}}{CH}}-\overset{5}{CH_3}$$

with a $CH_3$ group on C-2.

$C_1$ and $C_5$ are 1°, $C_3$ is 2°, $C_4$ is 3°, and $C_2$ is 4°.

5.   A compound containing both a double bond and a triple bond is named as an *enyne*. Numbering is done in a manner which gives the lower locant to the one nearer the end of the chain. In case, both double and triple bonds are located at similar positions with respect to the two ends of the chain, double bond is assigned lower locant because *ene* comes first than *yne*.

7.   Numbering should be done from that end of the chain in which double or triple bond gets lower locant, no matter sum of locants may be higher.

8.   Among two substituents, lower locant is assigned to that substituent which comes first in alphabetical order.

9. When —CHO is present at the end of a carbon chain, it should be counted in the main chain. Further, here —CHO is not the principal functional group, hence its presence is indicated by the prefix *-oxo*.

10. When two similar carbon-bearing monovalent groups are present in the main chain, both should be counted in the main chain.

11. Since both of the —COOH groups are present on the main carbon chain, these should be counted. Further, *ethyl* should be written first because it comes first in alphabetic order than propyl.

12. Here —OH is the functional group.

13. Here —COOH is the primary functional group, all others are substituents.

14. Here —COOH is the primary functional group, all other groups are substituents, hence indicated by their corresponding prefixes.

15. When any group is present on an atom other than C, it is indicated by placing such atom like N-methyl, O-methyl, S-methyl, N-bromo etc.

24. Here ter-- is used to indicate Here the numbering is shown

25. The position of two $CH_3$ (methyl) groups is indicate by N, 2, one - $CH_3$ is attached to N-atom of $-\overset{\overset{O}{\|}}{C}-\underset{\|}{N}H$ group and other at positive number 2 in the ring.

27. The compound formula be

28. The numbering is shown below

Since $–CH_3$ is attached to N– so it is (Methylamine)

29. Carboxylic acids are named as acid chlorides.

---

# EXERCISE 1.2

| >1 | 1 | (a, b, c) | 2 | (c, d) | 3 | (a, d) | 4 | (a, b, c) | 5 | (b, c, d) | 6 | (c) |
|---|---|---|---|---|---|---|---|---|---|---|---|---|
| CORRECT OPTION | 7 | (a,c) | | | | | | | | | | |
| PASSAGE 1 | 8 | (c) | 9 | (c) | 10 | (b) | 11 | (b) | 12 | (b) | 13 | (c) |
| PASSAGE 2 | 14 | (c) | 15 | (a) | 16 | (b) | 17 | (d) | 18 | (d) | 19 | (c) |
| MATCHING TYPE | 20 | (A)-(b); (B)-(c, d); (C)-(c); (D)-(d); (E);(a, e) | | | | | | | | | | |
| QUESTIONS | 21 | (A)-(b); (B)-(c); (C)-(a,b,c) | | | | | | | | | | |

---

# EXERCISE 1.3

1. (a)   $CH_3CH = CH_2$     (b)   $CH_3C \equiv CH$

   (c)   $CH_3CH_2C \equiv N$     (d)   $CH_3CH_2COOH$

2. (a)           (b)   $H\overset{\overset{O}{\|}}{C}NH_2$

   (c)           (d)   $H_2C = CHCOOH$

3. (a) 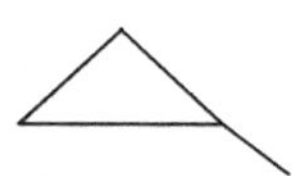

   (b) 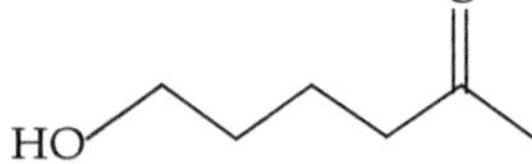

(c)

(d)

4. (i)

$$\underset{\underset{\underset{}{CH_2CH_2CH_3}}{|}}{\overset{7}{CH_3}\overset{6}{CH_2}\overset{5}{\underset{|}{\overset{CH_3}{C}}}H\overset{4}{CH}\overset{3}{\underset{|}{\overset{CH_3}{C}}}H\overset{2}{CH}\overset{1}{CH(CH_3)_2}}$$

2, 3, 5-Trimethyl-4-propylheptane

Not as

$$CH_3CH_2\overset{4}{\underset{|}{\overset{CH_3}{C}}}H\overset{3}{C}H\overset{2}{CH}\overset{1}{CH(CH_3)_2}$$

(This numbering is wrong because here number of substituents is less)

(ii)    $CH_3CH_2O\overset{2}{C}H_2\overset{1}{C}H_2Cl$

1-Chloro-2-ethoxyethane

(iii)    $\overset{6}{C}H_3\overset{5}{C}H_2\overset{4}{C} \equiv \overset{3}{C}\overset{2}{C}H_2\overset{1}{C}HO$

Hex-3-ynal

(iv) 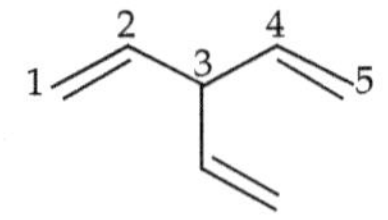    3-Vinylpenta-1, 4-diene

(v) 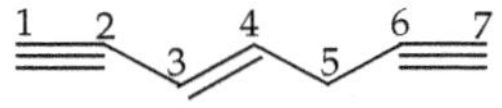    Hept-3-ene-1, 6-diyne

(vi) 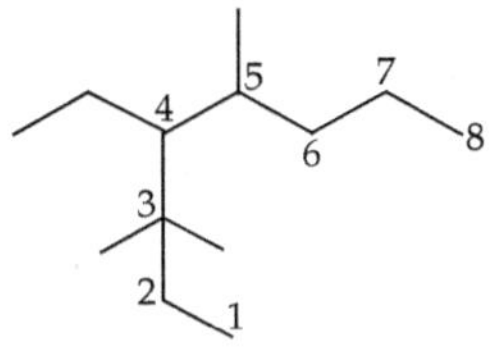    4-Ethyl-3, 3, 5-trimethyloctane

(vii) 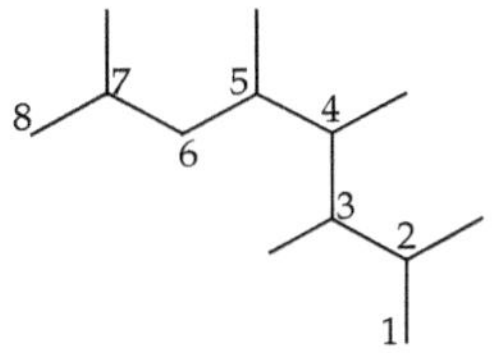    2, 3, 4, 5, 7-Pentamethyloctane

(viii) 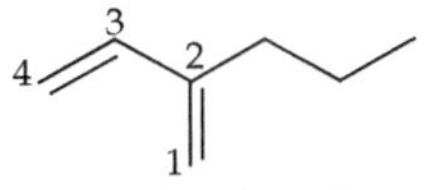    2-Propyl-1, 3-butadiene

(ix) 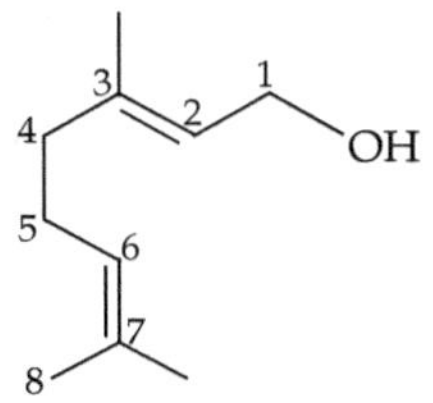    3, 7-Dimethyl-2, 6-octadienol

(x) 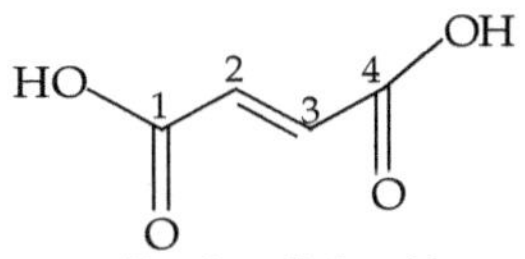    But-2-endioic acid

(xi) 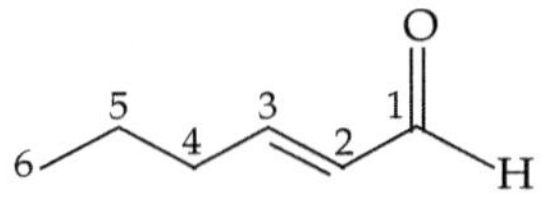    2-Hexenal

(xii)    2, 4-Hexdiyne

(xiii) 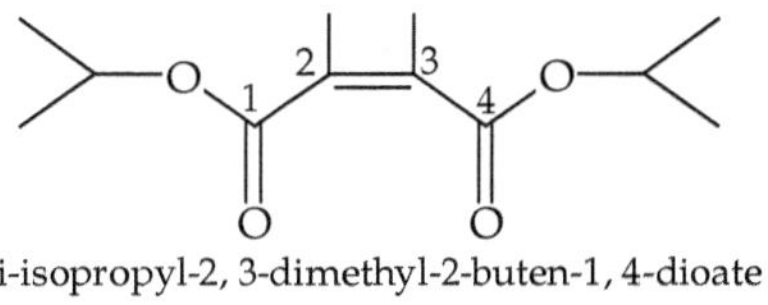    Di-isopropyl-2, 3-dimethyl-2-buten-1, 4-dioate

(xiv) 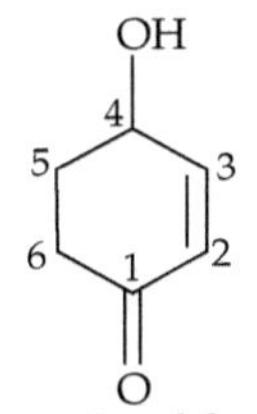    4-Hydroxy-2-cyclohexenone

(xv) 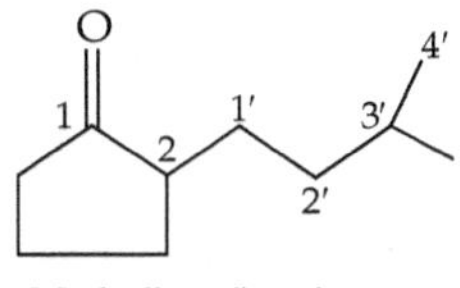    2-(3'-Methylbutyl)cyclopentanone

(xvi) 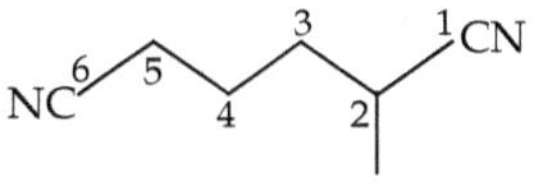    2-Methylhexanedinitrile

(xvii) 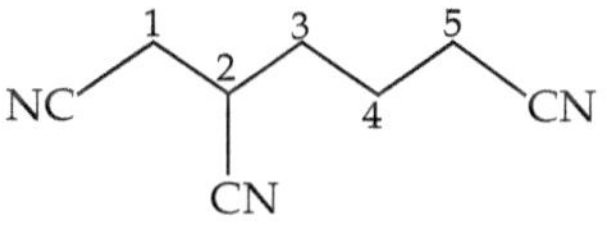    Pentane-1, 2, 5-tricarbonitrile

(xviii) 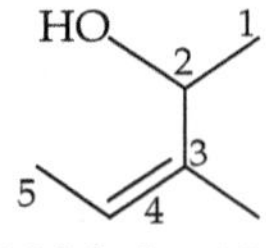    3-Methylpent-3-enol-2

(xix) 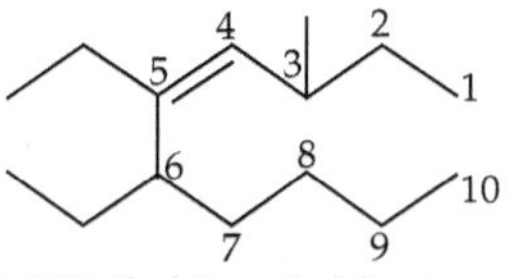    5, 6-Diethyl-3-methyldec-4-ene

(xx) 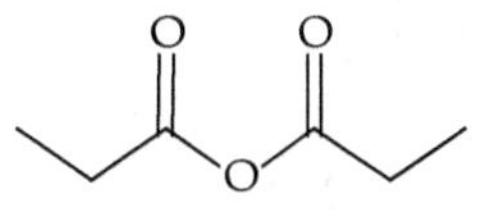    Propanoic anhydride

(xxi) 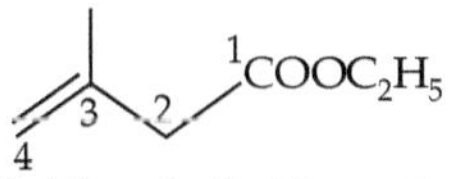    Ethyl-3-methylbut-3-enoate

(xxii)    $CH_3 - \overset{O}{\overset{||}{C}} - O - \overset{O}{\overset{||}{C}} - H$    *or*

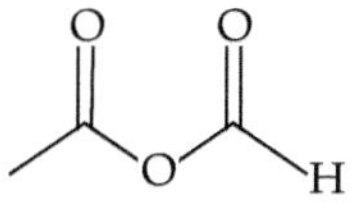

Ethanoicmethanoic anhydride

(xxiii)

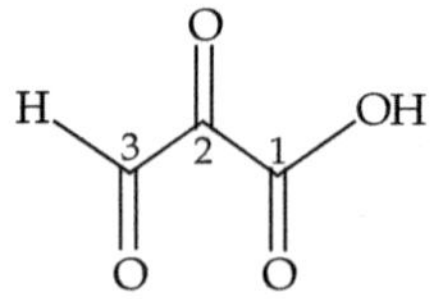

2, 3-Dioxopropanoic acid

(xxiv)

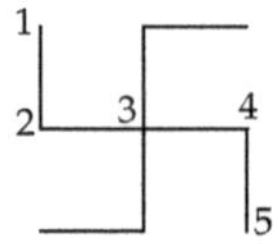

3, 3-Diethylpentane

(xxv)

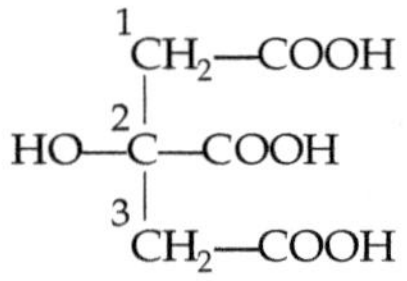

$$\overset{1}{C}H_2—COOH$$
$$HO—\overset{2}{C}—COOH$$
$$\overset{3}{C}H_2—COOH$$

2-Hydroxypropane-1, 2, 3-tricarboxylic acid

(xxvi)

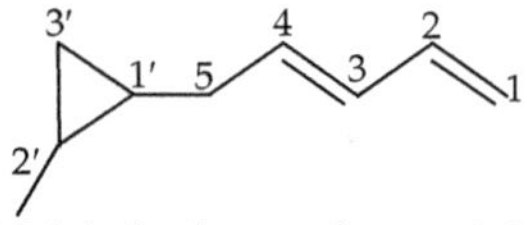

5-(2′-Methylcyclopropyl)penta-1, 3-diene

(xxvii)

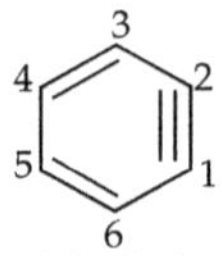

1, 2-Didehydrobenzene

(xxviii)

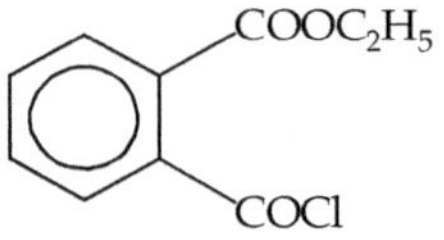

$COOC_2H_5$

$COCl$

Ethyl 2-(chloroformyl)benzoate

(xxix)

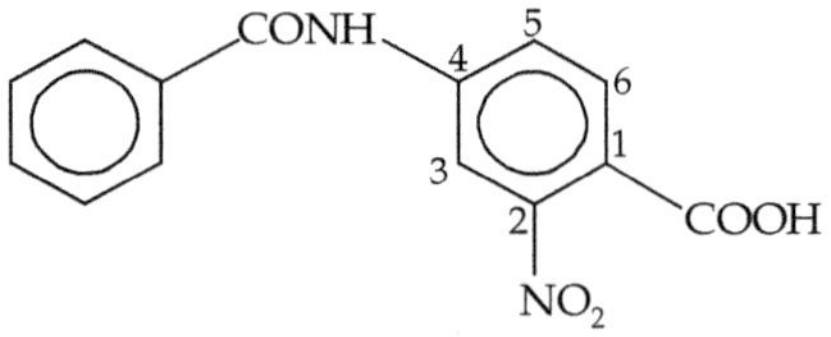

$CONH$

$COOH$

$NO_2$

4-(1-Benzoylamino) 2-nitrobenzoic acid

(xxx)

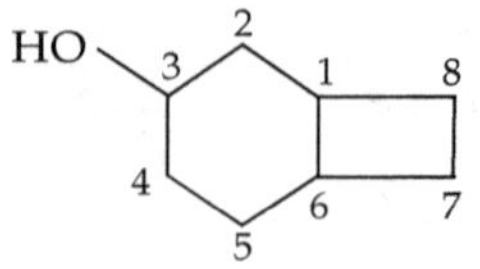

Bicyclo [4.2.0] octan-3-ol

(xxxi) Bicyclo [2.2.1]heptane

(xxxii) Bicyclo [3.1.1]heptane.

**5.**    (a)

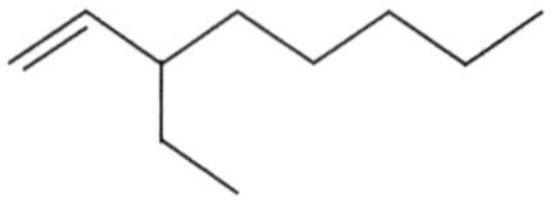

(b)

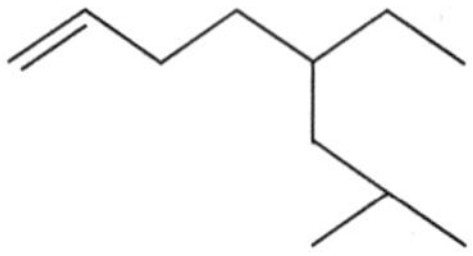

(c)

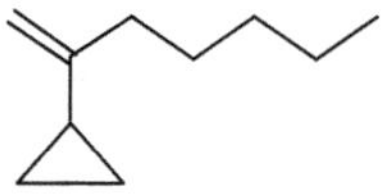

(d)

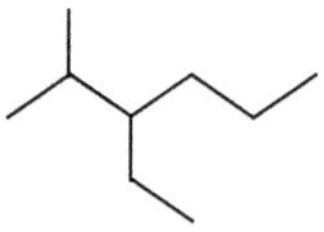

(e)

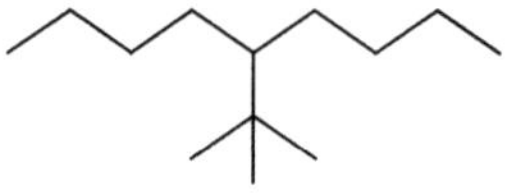

(f)

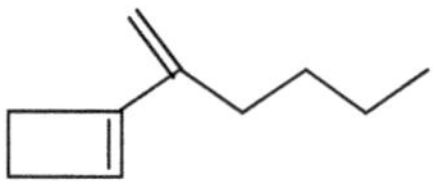

(g)

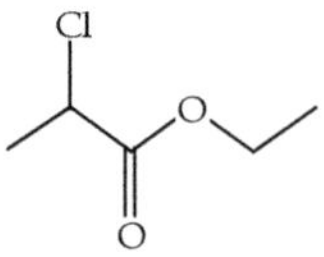

(h)

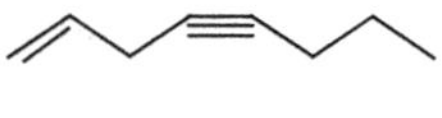

(i)

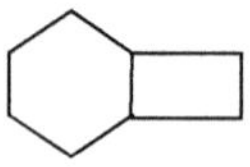

(j)

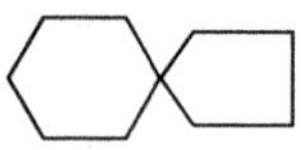

$$H\!-\!F \cdots\cdots H\!-\!F \cdots\cdots H\!-\!F$$

# 2

# Basic concepts in Organic Chemistry

CHAPTER HIGHLIGHTS



## 2.1 The Covalent Bond

We know that organic compounds are carbon compounds. Electronic configuration of carbon in the ground state ($Z = 6$ ; $1s^2$, $2s^2p^2$) indicates it to be divalent. However, the tetravalency of carbon atom was explained by the fact that carbon atom forms bonds only in excited state ($1s^2$, $2s^1p^3$). Further this electronic configuration suggests that the tetravalent carbon should have two types of bonds ; one bond is formed by electron present in non-directional orbital ($2s$) and other three identical bonds are formed by electrons present in directional orbital ($2p$). However, all the four bonds formed by carbon in a molecule like methane are equivalent. Finally, it was observed that the carbon atom does not take part in bond formation as such but its outermost orbitals, *i.e.* one $2s$ and three $2p$ orbitals mix or merge together to form new orbitals known as **hybrid orbitals** and the phenomenon in turn is known as **hybridization.** Three types of hybridization are found in organic compounds, namely $sp^3$, $sp^2$ and $sp$. It is assumed that students are familiar with the three types of hybridization ($sp^3$, $sp^2$ and $sp$) found in alkanes, alkenes, and alkynes respectively, and also with the sigma ($\sigma$) and pi ($\pi$) bonds.

| Type | Bond angle | Geometry | Number of unused p orbital(s) | % of s orbital |
|------|-----------|----------|-------------------------------|----------------|
| $sp^3$ | 109.28' | Tetrahedral | 0 | 25 |
| $sp^2$ | 120° | Trigonal planar | 1 | 33.3 |
| $sp$ | 180° | Linear | 2 | 50 |

*(i)* Hybrid orbitals *(a)* can overlap better because its head is larger than either lobe of the *p* AO and *(b)* provide greater bond angles, thereby minimize the repulsion between pairs of electrons ; and hence bond formed by a hybrid orbital is more stable than that formed by an atomic orbital.

*(ii)* Since *s* orbitals are closer to nucleus than *p* orbitals, it is reasonable to expect that **greater the *s* character of an orbital the smaller it is.** Thus the decreasing order of the size of the three hybrid orbitals is opposite ($sp^3 > sp^2 > sp$) to that of the decreasing percentage of *s* character in the three hybrid orbitals (given above in the table).

*(iii)* On the basis of the size of the hybrid orbitals, *sp* **orbital should form the shortest and** $sp^3$ **orbital the longest bond with other atom.** This is evident by the C—H and C—C bond lengths in alkanes (formed by $sp^3$ hybridized carbon atoms), alkenes (formed by $sp^2$ hybridized carbon atoms) and alkynes (formed by *sp* hybridized carbon atoms).

| Bond type (C—H) | Bond length | Bond type (C—C) | Bond length |
|---|---|---|---|
| $sp^3$—*s* (alkanes) | 1.112 Å | $sp^3$—$sp^3$ (alkanes) | 1. 54 Å |
| $sp^2$—*s* (alkenes) | 1.103 Å | $sp^2$—$sp^2$ (alkenes) | 1.34 Å |
| *sp*—*s* (alkynes) | 1.08 Å | *sp*—*sp* (alkynes) | 1.20 Å |

*(iv)* For a given atom, more is the *s* character (or less *p* character) in an orbital, lower is the energy of the electrons in that orbital and the closer are its electrons to the nucleus. In terms of decreasing energy, the order is $p > sp^3 > sp^2 > sp > s$.

*(v)* Further, *the shorter the bond, the greater the compression between atomic nuclei and hence greater is the strength of that bond.* Thus the bond formed by *sp* hybridized carbon is strongest (*i.e.*, it has maximum bond energy), while that formed by $sp^3$ hybridized carbon is the weakest (*i.e.* it has minimum bond energy). This is evident by the bond energies of the various types of C—H and C—C bonds.

| Bond type (C—H) | Bond energy(kcal/mole) | Bond type (C—C) | Bond energy(kcal/mole) |
|---|---|---|---|
| $sp^3$—*s* (in alkanes) | 104 | $sp^3$—$sp^3$ (in alkanes) | 80—90 |
| $sp^2$—*s* (in alkenes) | 106 | $sp^2$—$sp^2$ (in alkenes) | 122—164 |
| *sp*—*s* (in alkynes) | 121 | *sp*—*sp* (in alkynes) | 123—199 |

*(vi)* The electronegativity of an orbital increases with increase (or decrease) of *s* (or *p*) contribution in it. Hence electronegativity of the hybrid orbitals follows the order.

$$sp > sp^2 > sp^3 \quad \textbf{(Relative electronegativity of hybrid orbitals)}$$

*(vii)* The type of hybridization of orbitals in organic molecules can be determined on the basis of **hybrid orbital number (HON) rule.** *According to HON rule, every σ bond and an unshared pair of electrons (but not an unpaired electron) on an atom uses hybrid orbital.* Thus

*(a)* $sp^3$ hybridization is possible when the atom has

(i) four σ bonds, (ii) three σ bonds and an unshared pair of electrons (carbanions)

*(b)* $sp^2$ hybridization is possible when the atom has

(i) three σ bonds and one π bond, (ii) three σ bonds and a positive charge (carbocations), (iii) three σ bonds and an unpaired electron (free radicals), (iv) two σ bonds and unshared pair of electrons (singlet carbenes)

*(c)* *sp* hybridization is possible when an atom has

(i) two σ bonds and two π bonds either as a triple bond or as two double bonds on the same carbon, (ii) two σ bonds, one π bond and a positive charge, (iii) two σ bonds and two unpaired electrons (triplet carbenes).

*Example 1 :*

**Give the type of hybrid orbitals used by each atom other than hydrogen in each of the following compounds.**

(a)  $NH_4^+$,  (b)  $CH_2 = O$,  (c)  $CH_2 = NH$,  (d)  $HC \equiv N$,

(e)  $HO - C \equiv N$,  (f)  $H_2C = C = CH_2$,  (g)  $O = C = O$,  (h)  $H_2C = C = O$,

(i)  $BF_4^-$  (j)  $OH^-$  (k)

*Solution :*

(a)
$$N : 4\,\sigma\ bonds,\ sp^3$$

(b)
$$C : 3\,\sigma\ bonds,\ sp^2$$
$$O : 1\,\sigma\ bond,\ 2lp,\ sp^2$$

(c)
$$C : 3\,\sigma\ bonds,\ sp^2$$
$$N : 2\sigma\ bond,\ 1\ lone\ pair,\ sp^2$$

(d)  $H - C \equiv N :$
$$C : 2\,\sigma\ bonds,\ sp$$
$$N : 1\,\sigma\ bond,\ 1\ lone\ pair,\ sp$$

(e)  $H\overset{..}{O} - C \equiv N :$
$$C : 2\,\sigma\ bonds,\ sp$$
$$N : 1\,\sigma\ bond,\ 1\ lp,\ sp$$
$$O : 2\,\sigma\ bonds,\ 2\ lp,\ sp^3$$

(f)  $H_2 \overset{1}{C} = \overset{2}{C} = \overset{3}{CH_2}$
$$C_1 : 3\,\sigma\ bonds,\ sp^2$$
$$C_2 : 2\,\sigma\ bonds,\ sp$$
$$C_3 : 3\,\sigma\ bonds,\ sp^2$$

(g)  $: \overset{..}{O} = C = \overset{..}{O} :$
$$C : 2\,\sigma\ bonds,\ sp$$
$$O : 1\,\sigma\ bond,\ 2\ lp,\ sp^2$$

(h)  $H_2 \overset{1}{C} = \overset{2}{C} = \overset{..}{O} :$
$$C_1 : 3\,\sigma\ bonds,\ sp^2$$
$$C_2 : 2\,\sigma\ bonds,\ sp$$
$$O : 1\,\sigma\ bond,\ 2\ lp,\ sp^2$$

(i)  $F - \overset{F}{\underset{F}{B^-}} - F$
$$B : 4\,\sigma\ bonds,\ sp^3$$

(j)  $^-: \overset{..}{O}H$
$$O : 1\,\sigma\ bond,\ 3\ lp,\ sp^3$$

(k)
$$C_1 : 3\,\sigma\ bonds,\ sp^2$$
$$C_2 - C_4 : 4\,\sigma\ bonds,\ sp^3$$
$$Ketonic\ O : 1\,\sigma\ bond,\ 2\ lp,\ sp^2$$
$$Ether\ O : 2\,\sigma\ bonds,\ 2\ lp,\ sp^3$$

## 2.2  Effect of Unshared Pair of Electrons

This can be explained by taking the example of ammonia and water.

### 2.2.1  Ammonia (NH₃)

Electronic configuration of nitrogen ($1s^2\ 2s^2\ 2p_x^1\ 2p_y^1\ 2p_z^1$) indicates that in the formation of $NH_3$, overlapping of the three pure $2p$ orbitals with $1s$ orbitals of the three hydrogen atoms can take place. If this had been the case, the H—N—H bond angle in ammonia would have been 90°. However, the experimental value for the H—N—H bond angle has been found to be 107°. Since this value (107°) is near to the normal tetrahedral angle of 109.5° in methane, it can be assumed that here also $sp^3$ hybridisation involving $2s^2$, $2p_x^1$, $2p_y^1$ and $2p_z^1$ atomic orbitals occurs forming four $sp^3$ hybrid orbitals, one having two (paired) electrons and the other three having one electron each. The latter three orbitals form $3\sigma$ bonds with three hydrogen atoms, while the remaining (fourth) $sp^3$ hybrid orbital retains a pair of electrons commonly known as **lone pair**. Remember that $sp^3$ hybridisation although normally leads to tetrahedral shape, ammonia is found to have pyramidal shape with nitrogen at the apex and three hydrogens located at the corners of a triangular base.

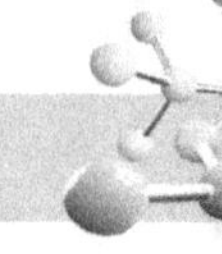

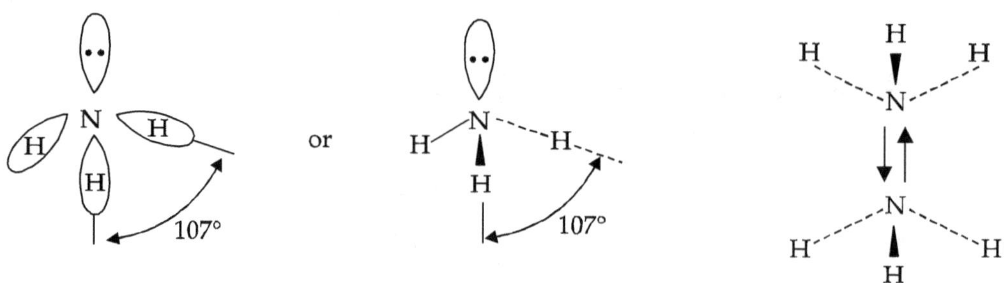

Fig. 1. Pyramidal structure of ammonia molecule.      Fig. 2. Inversion of ammonia.

Since the four pairs of electrons in ammonia are not equivalent (three $sp^3$ bonding and one $sp^3$ non-bonding), the bond angles are slightly deviated from the ideal value of 109.5°.

Note another important feature of ammonia molecule and that is its **inversion,** *i.e.* it turns inside-out. There is an energy barrier of only 6 kcal/mol between one pyramidal arrangement and the other. This energy is provided by molecular collisions, and even at room temperature the fraction of collisions can do this job. Hence at room temperature rapid transformation between pyramidal arrangements occurs and therefore no amine (even NRR′ R″ of the type) is capable of showing optical isomerism.

### 2.2.2   Water (H$_2$O)

Again the electronic configuration of oxygen ($1s^2$, $2s^2$ $2p_x^2$ $2p_y^1$ $2p_z^1$) indicates that in the formation of $H_2O$ molecule, if the two $2p$ atomic orbitals each having one electron overlaps with the $1s$ orbitals of the hydrogen atoms, the H—O—H bond angle would have been 90°.

However, experimental value for this angle is 104.5° pointing to $sp^3$ hybridisation of $2s^2$ $2p_x^2$ $2p_y^1$ and $2p_z^1$ orbitals. Out of the four $sp^3$ hybrid orbitals of oxygen, two have one electron each and they form 2σ bonds with the two hydrogen atoms; while the remaining two $sp^3$ orbitals have a pair of electrons each.

Fig. 3. Structure of water molecule.

Although the four $sp^3$ orbitals are directed towards the four corners of a tetrahedral, the H—O—H bond angle is found to be 104.5° (less than the regular tetrahedral bond angle of 109.5°). This deviation is due to non-equivalence of the four hybrid orbitals.

The deviation in bond angle in $NH_3$ and $H_2O$ from the regular (normal) tetrahedral value (109.5°) as in methane can be explained on the basis of **valence shell electron pair repulsion** (VSEPR) theory. According to this theory, for the maximum stability of a molecule, the valence electrons should be at a maximum distance from each other because of mutual repulsion. Deviation in bond angle occurs due to different type of repulsions in a molecule. However, repulsion between all electron pairs is not equal but it follows the following order.

$$lp\text{-}lp \text{ electrons } > \ lp\text{-}bp \text{ electrons } > \ bp\text{-}bp \text{ electrons}$$

where *lp* stands for lone pair, and *bp* stands for bond pair.

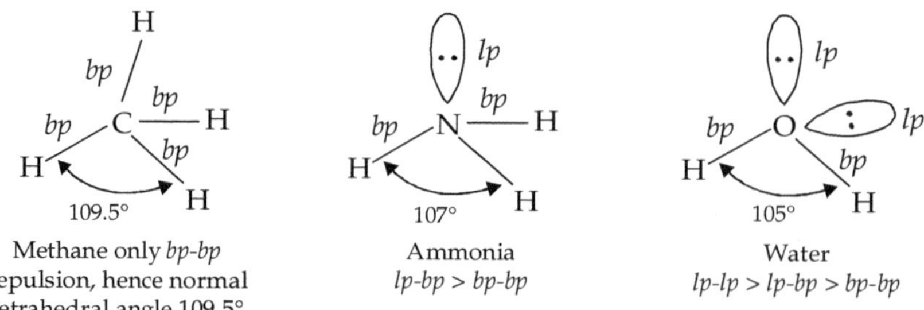


Thus if the central atom (C, N, O in the above cases) has a lone pair of electrons, the molecule will have a slightly distorted shape (as in case of $NH_3$ and $H_2O$). Since nitrogen (in $NH_3$) has *lp-bp* repulsion which is greater than *bp-bp* repulsion, it will result in the shortening of the H—N—H bond angle (107°). Further, since oxygen (in $H_2O$) exhibits *lp-lp* repulsion which is greatest, it will result shortening of the H—O—H bond angle from 109.5° to a greater extent which is found to be 104.5°.

## TEST YOUR UNDERSTANDING - 2.1

1.  Predict the shape of the following molecules

    (a)   $BF_3$,

    (b)   $BF_4^-$,

    (c)   $NH_4^+$,

    (d)   $H_3O^+$,

    (e)   $CH_3NH_2$,

    (f)   $NO_2^+$, and

    (g)   $NO_2^-$.

## 2.3  Electronegativity and Polarity of Bonds

We know that a covalent bond between two atoms is formed by equal sharing of electrons, *i.e.* their nuclei are held together by the same electron cloud. However, once a covalent bond is formed the sharing of electrons between two atoms may be equal (in case the two atoms are same as in case of Cl—Cl, H—H etc.) or different, when the two atoms are different in nature, *viz* H—Cl. Unequal sharing of common electrons by two atoms of different elements is due to their different tendency to attract electrons, a characteristic of elements known as **electronegativity**. The higher the electronegativity, the more effectively does the atom attract and hold electrons. A bond formed by atoms of dissimilar electronegativities is called **polar**, while a bond  formed between atoms having similar electronegativity or nearly zero difference in electronegativity is called **non-polar**. Relative electronegativities of a few elements are given below.

$$\begin{array}{ccccccccccc} F & > & O & > & Cl, N & > & Br & > & S, C, I & > & H \\ 4.0 & & 3.5 & & 3.0 & & 2.8 & & 2.5 & & 2.1 \end{array}$$

The *more electronegative element of a covalent bond is relatively negatively charged, while the less electronegative element is relatively positively charged.* These charges are indicated by the symbols $\delta-$ and $\delta+$ and represent only partial charges (different from complete or ionic charges). Polar bonds are indicated by $\longmapsto$, the head points towards the more electronegative atom.

## 2.4  Polarity of Molecules

A molecule having polar bonds should be polar, however, this is not true in all cases. For example, O = C = O although has two polar C—O bonds, the $CO_2$ molecule is **non-polar** ; similarly $CCl_4$ although has four C—Cl bonds, $CCl_4$ is a non-polar molecule. A **molecule is said to be polar when the center of negative charge does not coincide with the center of positive charge.** Such a molecule constitutes a *dipole*, two equal and opposite charges are separated in space. The molecule in turn possesses a *dipole moment*, $\mu$, which is equal to the multiple of magnitude of the charge ($e$) and distance ($d$), between the centers of charge.

$$\mu \quad = \quad e \quad \times \quad d$$

in debye units, $\qquad$ (D) $\qquad$ in esu $\qquad$ in cm

Since the charge on an electron is $4.80 \times 10^{-10}$ electrostatic units (esu) and the distance between charges in a polar bond is of the order of $10^{-8}$ cm, the product of charge and distance is of the order of $10^{-18}$ esu. cm. A dipole moment of $1.5 \times 10^{-18}$ esu. cm is stated on 1.5 D.

Alternatively, $\qquad$ 1 debye = $3.34 \times 10^{-30}$ coulomb meters

Charge on 1 electron = Charge on 1 proton = $1.60 \times 10^{-19}$ coulomb

If distance between an electron and a proton = 1 Å = $10^{-10}$ meter

Then $\qquad$ $\mu = (1.60 \times 10^{-19}$ coulomb$) \times (10^{-10}$ meter$) = 1.60 \times 10^{-29}$ coulomb meter

Expressing $\mu$ in debyes, $\qquad$ $\mu = \dfrac{1.60 \times 10^{-29} \text{ C.m.}}{3.34 \times 10^{-30} \text{ C.m./D}} = 4.8$ D

Thus $\qquad$ $\mu$ (in debyes) = $4.8 \times \delta$ (electron charge) $\times d$ (in Å)

Dipole moments are measured experimentally, and they can be used to calculate bond length and charge separations.

*Example 2 :*

(a)    **Determine the charge on the oxygen atom in a C = O bond, whose bond length is 1.22Å and the dipole moment is 2.30 D.**

(b)    **Use this information to evaluate the relative importance of the following two resonance contributions.**

$$\underset{\text{I}}{\underset{R}{\overset{R}{\diagdown}}C = \ddot{O}:} \quad\longleftrightarrow\quad \underset{\text{II}}{\underset{R}{\overset{R}{\diagdown}}\overset{+}{C} - \ddot{\underset{..}{O}}:^{-}}$$

*Solution :*

(a)    Dipole moment of the molecule if the bond were 100% ionic, i.e. when oxygen carries a full negative charge

$$\mu_{\text{theoretical}} = e \times d = (4.80 \times 10^{-10}\ \text{esu}) \times (1.22 \times 10^{-8}\ \text{cm}) = 5.86 \times 10^{-18}\ \text{esu.cm} = 5.86\ \text{D}$$

$$\text{Actual charge } (\delta) = \frac{\text{Experimental dipole moment}}{\text{Theoretical dipole moment}} = \frac{2.30}{5.86} = 0.39$$

**Alternatively,**

$$\mu \text{ (in debyes)} = 4.8 \times \delta \text{ (electron charge)} \times d \text{ (in Å)}$$

$$\therefore 2.30\text{D} = 4.8 \times \delta \times 1.22\text{Å} \Rightarrow \delta = \frac{2.30}{4.8 \times 1.22} = 0.39$$

Thus we can say that oxygen atom has an excess of about 0.4 electron and the carbon atom has a deficiency of about 0.4 electron. **Alternatively,** it can be said that the amount $\delta$ of charge separation is about 0.40 electronic charge, so the oxygen atom has about 40% of a negative charge and carbon has 40% of a positive charge.

(b)    When the value of charge separation is more than 0.5, it indicates that the charged structure is major contributor. Thus here resonance form I must be the major contributor. Although the form II is minor, it is quite significant, explaining in part the high polarity of the C = O.

## TEST YOUR UNDERSTANDING - 2.2

1.    Calculate the charge separation for a typical C–O single bond, with a bond length of 1.43Å and a dipole moment of 0.86 D.

Non-polar molecules always have zero dipole moment because here the value of $e$ is zero. This in turn is due to symmetrical structure of the molecule where charge developed by a part of the molecule is cancelled by the equal but opposite charge due to rest part of the molecule.

Thus we can say that polarity of the molecule and thus dipole moment also depends upon the shape of the molecule.

Ammonia ($NH_3$), water ($H_2O$) and nitrogen trifluoride ($NF_3$) have different dipole moments because the net dipole moment is a *vector sum* of the individual bond moments and bond moment due to lone pair of electron(s).

The strongly polar $C \equiv N$: triple bond has the maximum dipole moment (3.6D).

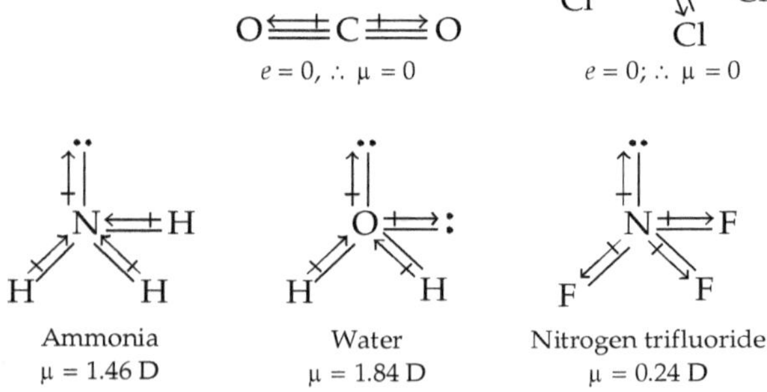



**Dipole moment and geometry of molecule :**

1.    If a molecular of the type $MX_4$ has zero dipole moment, it indicates $sp^3$ hybridisation of M (Z < 21). Examples are $CH_4$, $CCl_4$, $SiCl_4$, $SnCl_4$ etc.

2.    If a molecule of the type $MX_3$ has zero dipole moment, it indicates $sp^2$ hybridisation of M (Z < 21). Examples are $BF_3$, $AlCl_3$, etc.

3.    If a molecule of the type $MX_2$ has zero dipole moment, it indicates $sp$ hybridisation of M (Z < 21). Examples are $BeF_2$, $CO_2$, etc.

## TEST YOUR UNDERSTANDING - 2.3

1.　Although $CO_2$ and $H_2O$, both are triatomic, they have considerable difference in their dipole moments. Explain

2.　*(i)*　Ammonia has dipole moment as 1.46 D, can you predict the dipole moment of nitrogen trifluoride ?

　　*(ii)*　Dipole moment of $CH_3F$ is 1.847 D, can you predict dipole moment of $CD_3F$ ?

## 2.5　Other Factors for Polarity of Covalent Bonds

We have observed that difference in electronegativity of the two atoms forming a covalent bond produces polarity in a bond and hence in a molecule. In addition to this factor, there are other factors (or effects) which may cause displacement (partial or complete) of the bonding electrons and thus produce polarity in the bond. Some of these effects are **permanent** (*e.g., inductive, mesomeric, and hyperconjugation*) and others are **temporary** (*e.g., electromeric and inductomeric effects*). The former effects are permanently operating in the molecule and are known as **polarisation effects,** while the latter are brought into play by the attacking reagent, and as soon as the attacking reagent is removed, the electronic displacement disappears ; such effects are known as the **polarisability effects.** Here inductive, mesomeric, electromeric effects and hyperconjugation are described.

### 2.5.1　Inductive effect

It is a well known fact that a covalent bond is formed by the equal sharing of electrons between the two atoms. In case of a covalent bond between two similar atoms, the electron pair of the bond occupies central position between the nuclei of the two concerned atoms. Such a covalent bond is known as non-polar bond, *viz.*

$$H:H \qquad\qquad Cl:Cl$$

On the other hand, in case of a covalent bond between the two dissimilar atoms, the electron pair forming the bond is never shared absolutely equally between the two atoms but is attracted a little more towards the more electronegative atom. For example, in the compound C—X where X is more electronegative than C, the electron pair forming the C—X bond is somewhat more attracted towards the atom X with the result the latter attains partial negative charge (denoted by $\delta-$) while the carbon atom attains a partial positive charge (denied by $\delta+$).

$$\geq\!C\;:\;X \qquad \text{or} \qquad \overset{\delta+\;\;\;\delta-}{\geq\!C\!-\!X}$$

On the other hand, in compounds, like C—Z where Z is an electropositive element or group, *i.e.,* C is more electronegative than Z, the electron pair forming the C—Z bond is somewhat displaced towards the carbon atom and thus C and Z attain partial negative and partial positive charges respectively.

$$\geq\!C\;:\;Z \qquad \text{or} \qquad \overset{\delta-\;\;\;\delta+}{\geq\!C\!-\!Z}$$

Thus inductive effect causes a certain degree of polarity in the bond which in turn renders the bond much more liable to be attacked by other charged atoms or groups. With reference to inductive effect *it is very important to note that the electron pair, although permanently displaced, remains in the same valency shell.*

Thus, **inductive effect may now be defined as the permanent displacement of electrons forming a covalent bond towards the more electronegative element or group.**

The inductive effect is always transmitted along a chain of carbon atoms. For example, consider a carbon chain in which terminal carbon atom ($C_1$) is joined to a chlorine atom.

$$\underset{3}{C}\!\longrightarrow\!\!-\!\!-\underset{2}{C}\!\longrightarrow\!\!-\!\!-\overset{\delta+}{\underset{1}{C}}\!\longrightarrow\!\!-\!\!-\overset{\delta-}{Cl}$$

Now since chlorine has greater electronegativity than carbon, the electron pair between $C_1$ and Cl will be displaced from the middle somewhat to the chlorine atom with the result the latter will acquire a small negative charge, and the $C_1$ a small positive charge. Now further since $C_1$ is positively charged, it will attract towards itself the electron pair forming the covalent bond between $C_1$ and $C_2$ with the result $C_2$ will also acquire a small positive charge, but the charge on

$C_2$ will be smaller than on $C_1$ since the effect of chlorine atom (source) has been transmitted through $C_1$ to $C_2$. Similarly, $C_3$ will also acquire a small positive charge, but again due to the above reason the charge on $C_3$ will be smaller than on $C_2$. This effect can be relayed still further although it would decrease in intensity considerably as the distance from the source increases. In fact, it would be negligible even on $C_3$ for all practical purposes.

The inductive effect is represented by the symbol $\rightarrow$—, the arrow pointing towards the more electronegative element or group of elements. Thus in case of *n*-butyl chloride inductive effect may be represented as below.

$$\overset{\delta\delta\delta\delta+}{CH_3}\rightarrow\overset{\delta\delta\delta+}{-CH_2}\rightarrow\overset{\delta\delta+}{-CH_2}\rightarrow\overset{\delta+}{-CH_2}\rightarrow\overset{\delta-}{-Cl}$$

The decrease in the effect is denoted by using a greater number of the sign $\delta$.

The electron attraction and repulsion are compared with hydrogen as the reference in the molecule $R_3C$—H as standard. Any atom or group that attracts electrons more strongly than hydrogen is said to have a – **I effect** (electron-attracting or electron-withdrawing), *viz* $NO_2$, Cl, Br, I, F, COOH, $OCH_3$, etc. ; while the atom or group that attracts electrons less strongly than hydrogen is said to have + **I effect** (electron repelling or electron-releasing) *viz.*, $CH_3$, $C_2H_5$, $Me_2CH$ and $Me_3C$ groups. The important atoms or groups which cause negative or positive inductive effect are arranged below in the order of decreasing effect.

**– I (Electron-attracting) groups.**

$$\overset{+}{N}(CH_3)_3 > NO_2 > CN > COOH > F > Cl > Br > I > CF_3 > OR > OH > NH_2 > C_6H_5 > H$$

**+ I (Electron-repelling) groups.**

$$O^- \text{ (phenoxide)} > COO^- > (CH_3)_3C > (CH_3)_2CH > CH_3CH_2CH_2 > CH_3CH_2 > CH_3 > D > H$$

**Importance of inductive effect**

The phenomenon of inductive effect is very important in organic chemistry as it explains several facts, most important of which are given here.

(*i*)   **Reactivity of alkyl halides.** Alkyl halides, in general, are more reactive than the corresponding alkane, the reason being the presence of C—X bond in alkyl halides due to which they undergo inductive effect, *e.g.*, methyl chloride.

$$\overset{\delta+}{CH_3}—\rightarrow—\overset{\delta-}{Cl}$$

Thus due to the development of charges, the attack of a reagent on $CH_3Cl$ is facilitated as compared to that on methane. Furthermore, tertiary butyl chloride (a *tert*-halide) is more reactive than the methyl chloride because + I effect of the three methyl groups enhances the – I effect of chlorine atom by supplying electrons towards the tertiary carbon atom.

Thus *the chlorine atom in tert-butyl chloride can be very easily replaced by other atom as compared to that in methyl chloride* (a primary chloride).

*tert*-Butyl chloride

(*ii*)   **Strength of carboxylic acids.** An acid is a species that has the tendency to lose proton. Furthermore, the strength of an acid depends upon the ease with which an acid ionises to give proton. Thus any structural unit like strongly electronegative group that helps in removing the proton from the hydroxy group of the acid will have the effect of making the corresponding carboxylic acid a stronger one. For example, halogenated fatty acids are much stronger acids than the parent fatty acid and moreover the acidity among the halogenated fatty acids is increased almost proportionately with the increase in electronegativity of the halogen present. This fact can be visualised by the following table (higher the $K_a$ value, more stronger will be the acid).

| Name of the acid | Formula | $K_a$ |
|---|---|---|
| Iodoacetic acid | $I.CH_2COOH$ | $75 \times 10^{-5}$ |
| Bromoacetic acid | $Br.CH_2COOH$ | $138 \times 10^{-5}$ |
| Chloroacetic acid | $Cl.CH_2COOH$ | $155 \times 10^{-5}$ |
| Fluoroacetic acid | $F.CH_2COOH$ | $217 \times 10^{-5}$ |

Furthermore, the inductive effect in di- and tri-halogeno substituted acids is still more marked with the result these acids are progressively more stronger than the corresponding monohalogeno substituted acid which is obvious from their dissociation constants, for example, di- and tri-chloroacetic acids are more stronger than the chloroacetic acid.

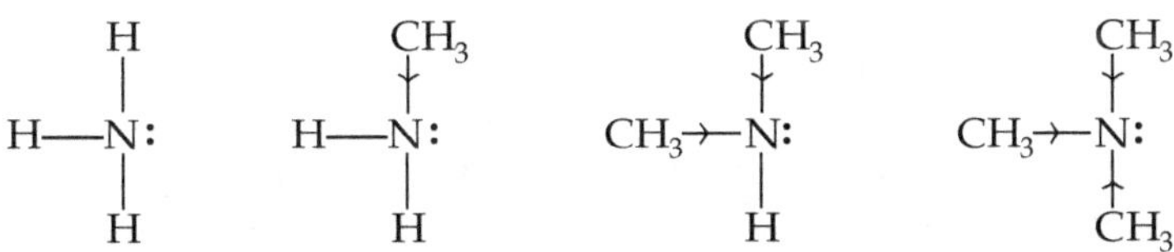

Dichloroacetic acid       Trichloroacetic acid

$(K_a = 5140 \times 10^{-5})$       $(K_a = 12100 \times 10^{-5})$

Actually, the *cumulative inductive* effect of the three chlorine atoms **in trichloroacetic acid makes this substance as strong acid as hydrochloric acid.**

However, since the inductive effect decreases rapidly as the group responsible for the effect (*e.g.* halogen atom in the present case) moves farther from the source (*e.g.* carboxyl group), the strength of the acid is proportionately decreased. Thus the chlorobutyric acids follow the following acidity order which is evident from their dissociation constants.

$$\alpha - \;>\; \beta - \;>\; \gamma - \;>\; n - \text{Butyric acids}$$

Similarly, we can explain the following order of decreasing acidic strength of a few of the fatty acids.

$$HCOOH > CH_3COOH > C_2H_5COOH > n\text{-}C_3H_7COOH$$

The decreasing acidic strength is due to increase in $+$ I effect due to alkyl groups.

$R{\rightarrow}{-}C{\rightarrow}{-}O{\rightarrow}{-}H$ (with $\overset{O}{\underset{\parallel}{}}$ above C)

**Formic acid, having no alkyl group, is the most acidic among these acids.**

(*iii*)   **Basic character of amines.** *The basic character of amines is due to the presence of unshared electron pair on nitrogen atom which accepts proton ; the ease with which the lone pair of electrons is available for co-ordination with a proton determines the relative basic strength of amines.*

Thus due to $+$ I effect of alkyl group, the nitrogen atom becomes rich in electron with the result the lone pair of electrons on nitrogen atom in amines is more easily available than in ammonia and thus amines are stronger bases than ammonia. However, it is important to note that the relative basic character of amines is not in total accordance with the inductive effect *i.e.* T > S > P, but it is in the following order

Secondary > Primary > Tertiary > $NH_3$ **(Basicity in aqueous solution)**

Tertiary > Secondary > Primary > $NH_3$ **(Basicity in gas phase)**

For explanation consult, example 3 given below.

(*iv*)   **Basic character of alcohols.** On the basis of $+$ I effect of the various alkyl groups, we can explain relative basic character of the following alcohols.

$$CH_3{\rightarrow}\ddot{O}H < CH_3CH_2 {\rightarrow} \ddot{O}H < (CH_3)_2CH {\rightarrow}\ddot{O}H < (CH_3)_3 C {\rightarrow} \ddot{O}H$$

Thus 3° alcohols are most basic and 1° alcohols least. Therefore, we can now explain the chemistry of Lucas test (Lucas reagent is a mixture of anhydrous $ZnCl_2$ and conc. HCl), where 3° alcohols react fastest and 1° slowest. Since Lucas test involves reaction between an acid (HCl) and a base (ROH), the strongest base (*i.e.* 3° alcohols) will react fastest.

$$\underset{\text{base}}{ROH} + \underset{\text{acid}}{HCl} \xrightarrow{\;ZnCl_2\;} \underset{\text{white turbidity}}{RCl\downarrow} + H_2O$$

*Example 3 :*

**Arrange $RNH_2$, $R_2NH$, $R_3N$ and $NH_3$ in decreasing order of their basic strength in (a) aqueous solution and (b) gas phase.**

*Solution :*

Two effects, induction and solvation, determine the $K_b$ of an alkyl amine. Inductive effect of alkyl groups increases basic character of alkyl amine with increase in number of alkyl groups. Further, the inductive effect of the alkyl group stabilizes the positive charge on the conjugate base. Thus, it is expected that :

$$: NH_3 \; < \; R \rightarrow \overset{R}{\underset{}{N}}H_2 \; < \; R \rightarrow NH \; < \; R \rightarrow N :  \qquad \textbf{(Relative basic character in gas phase)}$$

Least basic                     Most basic

$$NH_4^+ \; < \; R \rightarrow NH_3^+ \; < \; R \rightarrow \overset{+}{N}H_2 \; < \; R \rightarrow \overset{+}{N}H \qquad \textbf{(Stability order)}$$

Least stable                     Most stable

However, this is true in gaseous phase.

In aqueous solution, both inductive as well as solvation effect, determine the relative basic character of amines. Solvation effect plays important role in stabilising the conjugate acid as they have positive charge and hydrogen.

In terms of solvation alone, more the number of H's in the conjugate acid, the more it is stabilized by H-bonding and thus greater will be basic character of the parent base. Thus, conjugate acid of 2° amines having 2 H's will be more stable than the conjugate acid of 3° amines having only 1 H.

Inductive effect dominates in making all the three amines stronger bases than $NH_3$, and dimethylamine stronger than methylamine. However, in tertiary amines, the solvation effect has important role.

Thus the relative basic character of the three amines in aqueous solution is

$$\underset{\text{Least basic}}{NH_3} \; < \; R_3N \; < \; RNH_2 \; < \; \underset{\text{Most basic}}{R_2NH} \qquad \textbf{(Basic order in aqeuous solution)}$$

## 2.5.2    Resonance effect or Mesomeric effect

The phenomenon in which a species (molecule, ion or free radical) can be represented by two or more structures (none of which can alone explain all properties of the species) having same arrangement of atoms but different distribution of electrons is called **resonance**. The various structures are called *resonanting, contributing or canonical structures*. Consider the structure of 1, 3-butadiene and benzene.

$$CH_2 = CH - CH = CH_2 \longleftrightarrow \overset{+}{C}H_2 - CH = CH - \overset{-}{C}H_2$$

Two canonical structures of 1, 3-butadiene (Note that it is π electrons which are moving)

Two important canonical structures of benzene.

It must be understood that none of the contributing structures of a species has any existence, they exist only on paper. The real structure that can explain all properties of a species is a hybrid of all contributing structures and it is known as **resonance hybrid** of that species.

$$CH_2 \cdots CH \cdots CH \cdots CH_2$$
Resonance hybrid of 1, 3-butadiene　　　　Resonance hybrid of benzene

It should be noted that the term resonance does not mean the mixing of formal structures and, therefore, a less confusing term for this phenomenon is $\pi$–$\pi$ **electron delocalisation.**

**Rules for writing resonance structures :**

1.　Each resonating structure must conform to real Lewis structures *i.e.* there can be no structure with a penta-covalent carbon and bicovalent hydrogen.

2.　Resonance involves movement of only $\pi$ or $n$ electrons and a resonance structure can be derived from another by a series of one or more electron shifts. Thus resonance is possible only when one double is in conjugation with another double bond or an unshared pair of electrons or an electron deficient atom. For example,

(*i*)　$CH_2 = CH—CH = CH_2 \longleftrightarrow \overset{+}{C}H_2—CH = CH—\bar{C}H_2 \longleftrightarrow \bar{C}H_2—CH = CH—\overset{+}{C}H_2$

(*ii*)　$CH_2 = CH—\ddot{\underset{..}{C}l: \longleftrightarrow \overset{\ominus}{C}H_2—CH = \overset{\oplus}{C}l:}$

(*iii*)

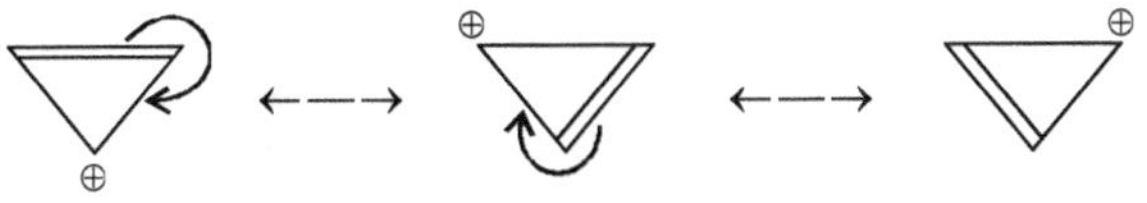

3.　In order to achieve maximum overlap of *p* orbitals, which is necessary for delocalization, it is essential that the *skeleton should be planar* in conjugated system.

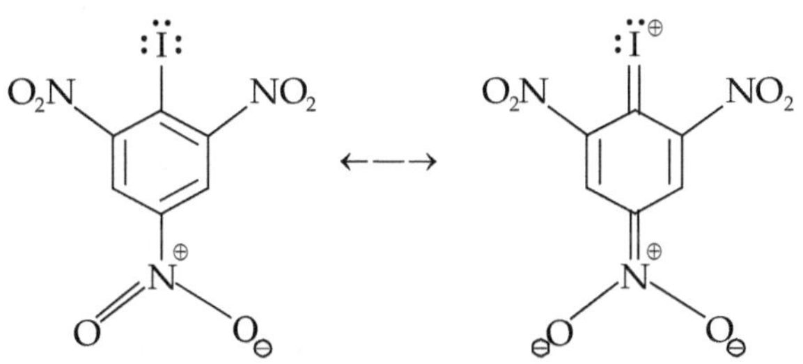

Thus any structural feature that destroys this coplanarity of the conjugated system will inhibit resonance. This inhibition is referred to as **steric inhibition of resonance.**

Picryl iodide provides a good example. A comparison of the C—N bond lengths of nitro groups in the *ortho* position (1.45 Å) with that of the nitro group in the *para* position (1.35 Å) reveals that the C—N bond of the nitro group in the *para* position has some double bond character. This is explained on the basis of involvement of the *para* nitro group in resonance because of coplanarity of benzene ring and the nitro group. On the other hand, *ortho* nitro groups do not participate in resonance as they are pushed out of the plane of the ring by bulky iodine atom. Consequently, the C—N bond length of the *ortho* nitro group is very close to that of aliphatic nitro compounds.

4.　All resonating structures must have same number of paired electrons.

5.　All resonating structures do not contribute equally to the hybrid. Lesser the energy of the structure, more will be its contribution to the hybrid. Relative energies of the contributing structures are assessed by the following rules.

(*a*)　Since each covalent bond adds about 50—100 kcal/mole to the stability of the system, it is expected that **structures with more covalent bonds are more stable** than those with fewer. For instance, the non-polar form of butadiene (having 11 covalent bonds) is more stable than the other two polar structures (having 10 double bonds).

(*b*)　Non-polar structures have less energy and hence more stable than the polar structures, *e.g.* butadiene, R—COOH etc.

$$R—\overset{\overset{\displaystyle O}{\|}}{C}—OH \longleftrightarrow R—\overset{\overset{\displaystyle \overset{\ominus}{O}}{|}}{C}=\overset{\oplus}{O}H$$
(More stable)　　　　　(Less stable)

(c) If all structures have formal charge, the more stable structure has negative charge on the more electronegative atom and positive charge on the less electronegative (more electropositive) atom. Further structure with the least number (or amount) of formal charge is more stable.

$$R_2C=\ddot{O}: \longleftrightarrow R_2\overset{+}{C}-\ddot{\underset{..}{O}}:^{-} \longleftrightarrow R_2\overset{-}{\ddot{C}}-\overset{+}{\underset{..}{O}}:$$

most important    less important    least important

(d) Structures with like charges on adjacent atoms have very high energy and hence unimportant. For example,

$$R-\overset{O}{\overset{\|}{C}}-\overset{O}{\overset{\|}{C}}-R \longleftrightarrow R-\overset{O^{\ominus}}{\underset{\oplus}{C}}-\overset{O^{\ominus}}{\underset{\oplus}{C}}-R$$

(e) Resonating structures with electron deficient, positively charged atom have high energy and hence unimportant.

(f) Equivalent contributing structures have nearly equal energies and hence contribute more to the hybrid. Thus phenomenon of resonance is of much significance when two or more **equivalent contributing structures** are possible for a species. For example,

$$\overset{\oplus}{C}H_2-CH=CH_2 \longleftrightarrow CH_2=CH-\overset{\oplus}{C}H_2$$
Allyl cation

Cyclopentadienyl anion (all contributing structures are equivalent)

(g)
$$CH_3-\overset{+}{C}H-\overset{..}{\underset{..}{O}}CH_3 \longleftrightarrow CH_3-CH=\overset{+}{\underset{..}{O}}CH_3$$
    I          II

Here, although structure II has positive charge on the electronegative atom, it helps to disperse the charge (positive) on structure I, hence resonance is possible. However, due to positive charge on the electronegative atom (oxygen), contribution of structure II to resonance hybrid is very less.

On the other hand, presence of group which intensifies charge on the atom makes the species less stable.

$$CH_3-\overset{+}{C}H \longrightarrow \overset{O}{\overset{\|}{C}}-CH_3$$

Here resonance is not possible, and the –I effect of the –COCH$_3$ group intensifies the positive charge on carbon, making it less stable.

(h) Structures in which all atoms have a complete octet of electrons are especially stable and make large contribution to the hybrid. For example,

    I           II          III          IV

In the above structures, IV is especially stable since here every atom (except hydrogen) has octet.

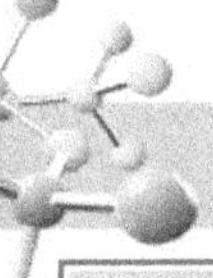



*Example 4 :*

**Write all possible contributing structures for**

**(a)　hydrazoic acid ($HN_3$),**　　　　　　　　**(b)　nitrate ion ($NO_3^-$)**

**(c)　boron trichloride ($BCl_3$)**　　　　　　　**(d)　formic acid (HCOOH)**

**(e)　diazomethane.**

**Comment on the stability of each structure.**

*Solution :*

(a)　*Hydrazoic acid, $HN_3$*

$$H\!-\!\overset{\cdot\cdot}{N}=\overset{+}{N}=\overset{\cdot\cdot}{\underset{\cdot\cdot}{N}}\!:\!^{-} \longleftrightarrow H\!-\!\overset{\cdot\cdot}{\underset{\cdot\cdot}{N}}\!-\!\overset{+}{N}\equiv N\!: \longleftrightarrow H\!-\!\overset{+}{N}=N=\overset{\cdot\cdot}{\underset{\cdot\cdot}{N}}\!:\!^{2-} \longleftrightarrow H\!-\!\overset{2+}{N}=\overset{\cdot\cdot}{N}\!-\!\overset{\cdot\cdot}{\underset{\cdot\cdot}{N}}\!:\!^{2-} \equiv H\!-\!\overset{\delta+}{N}\!\cdots\!\overset{+}{N}\!\cdots\!\overset{\delta-}{N}\!:$$

$$\text{I}\qquad\qquad \text{II}\qquad\qquad \text{III}\qquad\qquad \text{IV}\qquad\qquad \underset{\text{V}}{\text{Rsonance hybrid}}$$

Structrues I and II have least amount of formal charge (total 2), they have nearly similar energy and are the most stable. Structure III has similar charge (+) on adjacent atoms, and moreover it also has a total formal charge of 4, it has a very high energy and hence unstable. Structure IV also has a very high energy because the N bonded to H has only 6 electrons and it has a total formal charge of 4. Thus hydrazoic acid is a hybrid of only two structures, namely I and II and can be represented as V.

(b)　*Nitrate ion, $NO_3^-$*

Note that all the three structures of $NO_3^-$ ion are similar to each other and are thus equally stable. Thus resonance hybrid (IV) is composed of all the three structures.

(c)　*Boron trichloride, $BCl_3$*

(d)　*Formic acid, HCOOH*

Structure I is stable because it has no formal charge while the other structures II, III and IV have more number of covalent bonds are equivalent, and so these are equally stable and contribute more to the hybrid, V.

Structures I and II have greater number of covalent bonds, these are more stable than III or IV. Further, structure I has no formal charge it is more stable than II. Among III and IV, III is more stable because here negative charge is on O, a more electronegative element rather than on C (in IV), a lesser electronegative element than O. Structure of carboxylic acids is mainly represented by structure I, *i.e.* resonance is not of much significance in carboxylic acids.

(e)    *Diazomethane, CH$_2$N$_2$*

$$H_2C = \overset{+}{N} = \overset{\cdot\cdot}{\underset{}{N}}{}^{-} \quad \longleftrightarrow \quad H_2\overset{-}{\overset{\cdot\cdot}{C}} - \overset{+}{N} \equiv N \colon \quad \equiv \quad \overset{\delta-}{H_2C} \cdots \overset{\delta+}{N} \cdots \overset{\delta-}{N}$$

$$\text{I} \qquad\qquad\qquad \text{II} \qquad\qquad\qquad \text{III}$$

Both have same number of covalent bonds, hence these should be equally stable. However, structure II has negative charge on C, rather than N (a more electronegative element), hence I can said to be more stable than II.

---

*Example 5 :*

**Pick up the more stable ions among the following pairs with proper explanation.**

**(i)**    $(CH_3)_2 N^+ = CH - CH = CH - N(CH_3)_2$  and  $(CH_3)_2 N^+ = CH - CH = CH - OC_2H_5$
           I                                      II

**(ii)**    $CH_2 = CH - C^-(CH_3)_2$  and  $(CH_3)_2 C^- - CHO$
           III                      IV

**(iii)**    $CH_3CH_2O^-$  and  $CH_2 = CH - O^-$
           V              VI

*Solution :*

(i)    I is more stable than II because its two resonating structures are equivalent.

$$(CH_3)_2 N^+ = CH - CH = CH - \overset{\cdot\cdot}{N}(CH_3)_2 \quad \longleftrightarrow \quad (CH_3)_2 N - CH = CH - CH - N^+(CH_3)_2$$

Equivalent resonating structures

(ii)    IV is more stable than III because its one of the resonating structures has negative charge on oxygen.

$$(CH_3)_2 \overset{-}{C} - \overset{O}{\overset{\|}{C}} - H \quad \longleftrightarrow \quad (CH_3)_2 C = \overset{O^-}{\overset{|}{C}} - H$$

More stable

IV

$$\overset{-}{CH_2} = CH - \overset{-}{C}(CH_3)_2 \quad \longleftrightarrow \quad \overset{-}{CH_2} - CH = C(CH_3)_2$$

III

(iii)    VI is more stable than V because of resonance, while resonance is not possible in V.

**Resonance energy**

The most important consequence of resonance is that the resonance hybrid (*i.e.* the actual molecule) has much lower energy than the energy for any of the contributing structures. This lower energy of the resonance hybrid and hence increased stabilisation in such systems is expressed in terms of **resonance energy.** Resonance energy may be defined as the difference between energy of the actual molecule (resonance hybrid) and the energy for the most stable contributing structure. Resonance energy has been computed from the heats of hydrogenation and heats of formation.

(*i*)    **Resonance energy from heats of hydrogenation.** Resonance energy has been calculated by comparing the heat of hydrogenation of the theoretical benzene (cyclohexatriene) with the real molecule of benzene. Heat of hydrogenation of the theoretical benzene (cyclohexatriene) can be calculated as $-85.8$ kcal/mole on the basis of the fact that the heat of hydrogenation of $C = C$ is $-28.6$ kcal/mole.

$$\text{(cyclohexene)} \quad + H_2 \quad \longrightarrow \quad \bigcirc \quad ; \ \Delta H = -28.6 \text{ kcal/mole}$$

Cyclohexene

Cyclohexadiene $+ 2H_2 \longrightarrow$ (cyclohexane) ; $\Delta H = -57.2$ kcal/mole

Cyclohexatriene (hypothetical benzene) $+ 3H_2 \longrightarrow$ (cyclohexane) ; $\Delta H = -85.8$ kcal/mole

However, the heat of hydrogenation of the real benzene molecule as determined experimentally is found to be $-49.8$ kcal/mole. Thus we can say that the real structure (resonance hybrid) of benzene has 36.0 kcal/mole (85.8 $-$ 49.8 = 36.00) of energy less than the most stable canonical structure. In other words, benzene molecule is stabilized by 36.0 kcal/mole of energy which is commonly referred to as **resonance energy of benzene.**

**In short,**

Resonance energy = Theoretical heat of hydrogenation—Experimental heat of hydrogenation.

(*ii*)  **Resonance energy from heat of formation.** Resonance energy of a molecule can be computed from heats of formation in the same way as from heat of hydrogenation. For example, for benzene theoretical heat of formation of benzene can be computed from the various bond dissociation energies.

Theoretically,

$\Delta H_f = 6$ (Bond energy of C–H bond) $+ 3$ (Bond energy of C–C bond) $+ 3$ (Bond energy of C = C bond)

$\quad = 6 \times 98.8 + 3 \times 83.1 + 3 \times 145 = 1277.1$ kcal/mole.

Experimental heat of formation of benzene can be determined from heat of combustion of benzene, heat of formation of $CO_2$ and heat of formation of $O_2$ according to the following thermochemical equation.

$$C_6H_6 + 7\frac{1}{2} O_2 \longrightarrow 6CO_2 + 3H_2O + 789.1 \text{ kcal}$$

This value is found to be 1313.3 kcal/mole.

Hence resonance energy of benzene = 1313.3 $-$ 1277.1 = 36.2 kcal/mole.

**Effects of resonance :**

1.  The most important effect of resonance is to induce stability in the molecule, it is due to delocalisation of electrons which decreases reactivity and hence increases stability, of the molecule. Possibility of equivalent (two or more) resonating structrues leads to more stability. Thus we can explain greater stability of the carboxylate ion as compared to carboxylic acids.

$$R-\overset{O}{\overset{\|}{C}}-OH \longleftrightarrow R-\overset{O^-}{\overset{|}{C}} \overset{+}{=} OH$$

Non-equivalent resonating structures of carboxylic acids, resonance less important

$$R-\overset{O}{\overset{\|}{C}}-O^- \longleftrightarrow R-\overset{O^-}{\overset{|}{C}} = O$$

Equivalent resonating structures of carboxylate ion, resonance more important leads to greater stability of $RCOO^-$.

Further, more the number of equivalent resonating structures more will be stability of the species (neutral or ionic).

2.  The phenomenon of resonance gives identical bonding (concept of partial double bond in resonance hybrid) and hence identical bond lengths. Thus in benzene, carbon-carbon bond length acquires a value which lies between C—C (single bond) length (1.54 Å) and C = C (double bond) length (1.33 Å).

## 2.5.3  Mesomeric effect

Mesomeric effect is the resonance effect of certain compounds produced under the influence of certain groups attached to the conjugated system. Like inductive effect, mesomeric effect (denoted by M) may be + M and − M. It is + M when the transference of electron pair is away from the hetero atom ; and − M when transference of electron pair is towards the hetero atom. In general,

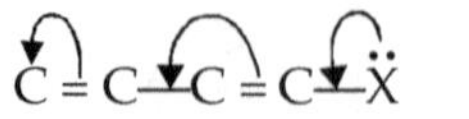

$$\overset{\frown}{C} = C \overset{\curvearrowleft}{\phantom{}} C \overset{\frown}{=} C \overset{\curvearrowleft}{\phantom{}} \overset{..}{X} \qquad\qquad C \overset{\frown}{=} C \overset{\curvearrowleft}{\phantom{}} C \overset{\frown}{=} C \overset{\curvearrowleft}{\phantom{}} C \overset{\frown}{=} \overset{..}{O}$$

+ M effect 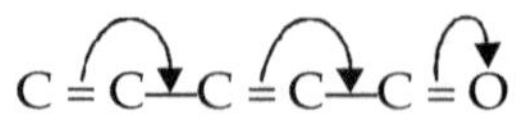　　　　　　　　　　　　　　　　－ M effect

Some common atoms or groups which cause + M and – M effect are given below.

**+ M groups.**　　　—Cl, —Br, —I, —NH$_2$, —NR$_2$, —OH, —OCH$_3$, –SH

**– M groups.**　　　—NO$_2$, —C ≡ N, > C = O, –COOH

The effect is of common occurrence in aromatic compounds and explains orientation in monosubstituted benzenes during electrophilic substitution.

Since **mesomeric effect** is a permanent effect and always operates in a non-reacting molecule, it, **like inductive effect, affects the physical properties of a molecule.** Again, like inductive effect, it may either aid or hinder a particular reaction.

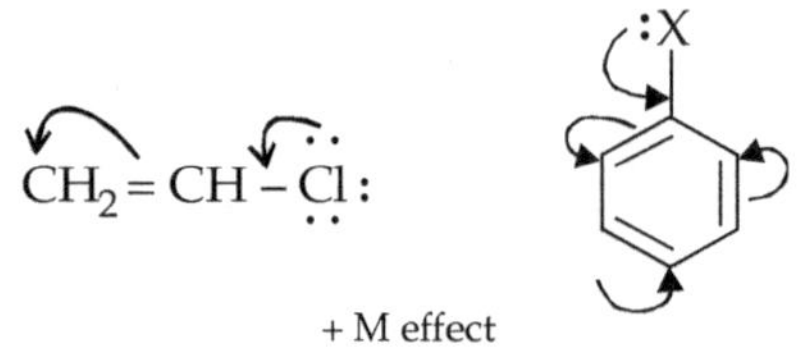

+ M effect 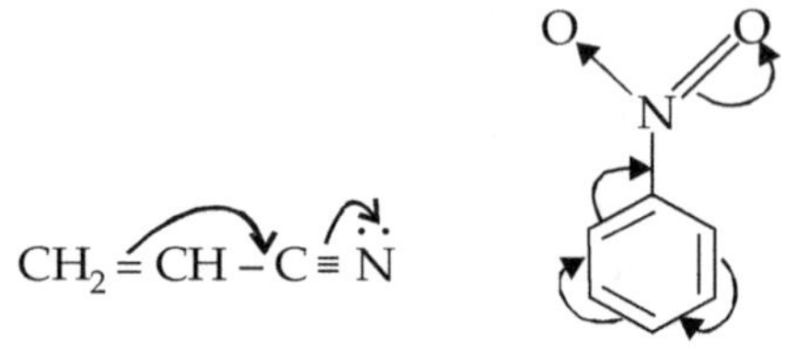　　　　　　　　　　　　　　　　　　　　　　　　　　　－ M effect

The inductive and mesomeric effects, when present together, may act in the same direction or opposite to each other. When the two effects oppose each other, the mesomeric effect is more powerful than the former. For example, in vinyl chloride, chlorine atom attains positive charge, and not negative.

$$:\overset{..}{\underset{..}{Cl}} \longleftarrow CH = CH_2 \qquad\qquad :\overset{..}{\underset{..}{Cl}} \overset{\frown}{\phantom{}} CH \overset{\frown}{=} CH_2 \longleftrightarrow \overset{\oplus}{Cl} = CH - \overset{\ominus}{CH_2}$$

– I effect of chlorine leads to　　　　　　　+ M effect due to Cl leads to positive charge on chlorine atom<br>negative charge on chlorine atom

### 2.5.4　Electromeric effect

This type of temporary displacement of electrons takes place in compounds containing multiple covalent bonds (*e.g.* C = C, C = O, C ≡ N, etc.) or an atom with a lone pair of electrons adjacent to a covalent bond. The effect involves complete transference of a pair of electrons from a multiple bond to an atom, or from a multiple bond to another bond, or from an atom with a free pair of electrons to a bond. It is the π-electrons of a multiple bond, or the *p*-electrons of an atom, which are transferred. Since the effect involves complete transference of electrons, it leads to the development of full + and – charges within the molecule. It is important to note that the electromeric effect is purely a temporary effect and is brought into play only at the requirement of attacking reagent ; it vanishes out as soon as the attacking reagent is removed from reaction mixture. For example,

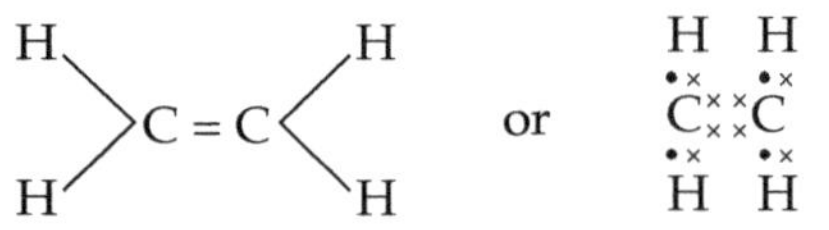

(a) Ethylene molecule before adding the reagent 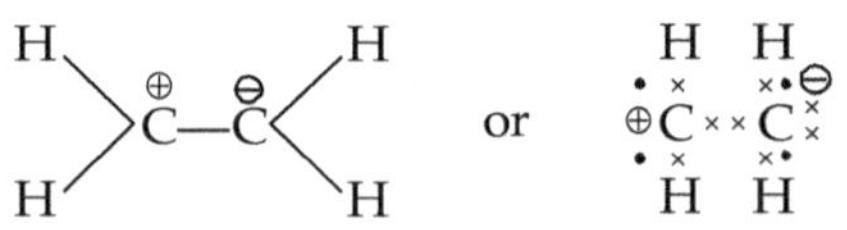　　　　　　(b) Ethylene molecule after adding the reagent.

In the above examples as soon as the attacking reagent is removed, the charged molecule (*b*) reverts to its original condition (*a*).

The electromeric effect is generally shown by curved arrow, starting at the original position of the electron pair and ending to the new position (attained by migration) of the electron pair, *e.g.*, in the carbonyl group it operates as

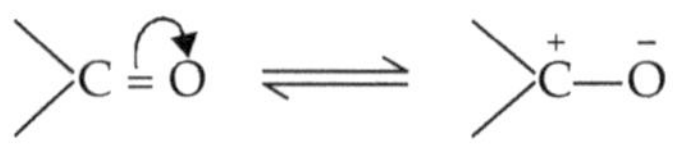

$$\underset{}{\overset{}{>}}C \overset{\frown}{=} \overset{..}{O} \;\rightleftharpoons\; \underset{}{\overset{}{>}}\overset{+}{C} - \overset{-}{\overset{..}{O}}$$

The electromeric effect is represented by the symbol E which may be + E when the displacement of electron pair is away from the hetero atom or – E when the displacement is towards the hetero atom *e.g.*,

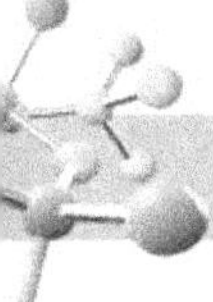



**+ E effect**    $\overset{\frown}{C} = C \overset{\frown}{-} C = C \overset{\frown}{-} \ddot{X}$    (Displacement away from atom X)

Here the attacking species adds on the atom on which electrons are transferred.

**– E effect**    $C = C \overset{\frown}{-} C = C \overset{\frown}{-} C = \overset{\frown}{O}$    (Displacement towards atom O)

Here the attacking species does not add on the atom on which electrons are transferred.

Now since the electromeric effect takes place only at the requirement of the attacking reagent it always facilitates the reaction but never inhibits it. It is important to note that **when the inductive and electromeric effects are operating in the same molecule but in the opposite directions, it is the electromeric effect** that usually **overcomes the inductive effect.**

The electromeric effect is of common occurrence during addition of polar reagents on $C = C$ and $C = O$ bonds, and in the orientation of group in monosubstituted benzene during electrophilic substitutions.

The combined mesomeric and electromeric effects of the atom or group is known as its conjugative effect. Since the conjugative effect was first recognized in connection with the phenomenon of tautomerism, it was previously known as the **tautomeric effect (± T).**

---

*Example 6 :*

**Represent the π-electron transfer due to mesomeric effect in following cases. Assign the + or – sign of effect.**

*(i)*    $CH_3O\!-\!\!-CH = CH_2$    *(ii)*   $CH_2 = CHNO_2$    *(iii)* $CH_2 = CHCH_2NO_2$

*(iv)*   $CH_2 = CHCl$    *(v)*   ⬡—$C \equiv CH$    *(vi)* ⬡—$C \equiv CH$

*(vii)* $Cl$—⬡—$C \equiv CH$    *(viii)* $O_2N$—⬡—$CH = CH_2$    *(ix)* $CH_3CH = CHCH_2CH_3$.

*Solution :*

*(i)*   $H_3C\!-\!\ddot{O}\!-\!CH = CH_2 \longleftrightarrow H_3C\!-\!\overset{\oplus}{O} = CH\!-\!\overset{\ominus}{C}H_2$    **+ M effect**

*(ii)*  $H_2C = CH\!-\!N\!\!\diagdown\!\!^O_O \longleftrightarrow H_2\overset{}{C}\!-\!CH = \overset{+}{N}\!\!\diagdown\!\!^{O^-}_O$    **+ M effect**

*(iii)* $H_2C = CH\!-\!CH_2\!-\!N\!\!\diagdown\!\!^O_O \longleftrightarrow CH_2 = CH\!-\!CH_2\!-\!\overset{+}{N}\!\!\diagdown\!\!^{O^-}_O$    **– M effect**

(Note that $C = C$ is not conjugated, hence π–electron transfer will not proceed to $- NO_2$ ; $- NO_2$ will independently undergo – M effect)

*(iv)*  $H_2\overset{\frown}{C} = CH\!-\!\ddot{C}l: \longleftrightarrow H_2\overset{\ominus}{C}\!-\!CH = \overset{\oplus}{\ddot{C}}l:$    **+ M effect**

Note that here + M effect and – I effect opposes each other. But + M > – I

*(v)*   ⬡ with $C \equiv CH$    $\longleftrightarrow$    ⬡ with $\overset{\oplus}{C} = \overset{\ominus}{C}H$

No mesomeric effect displacement
of electrons is due to + I effect

It is not given + or – sign because hetero atom (other than C) is not involved.

*(vi)*  ⬡ with $C \equiv CH$    $\longleftrightarrow$    ⬡ with $\overset{\oplus}{C} = CH$

Mesomeric effect due to - I effect

(*vii*) **(+ M effect)**

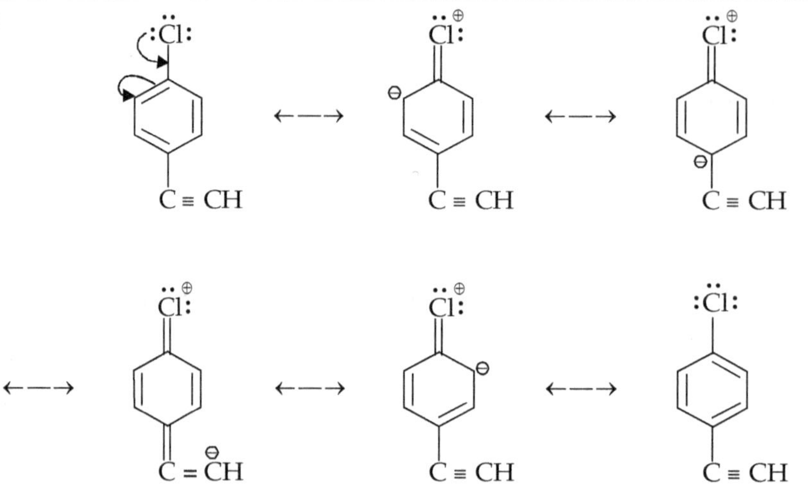

(*viii*) **(– M effect)**

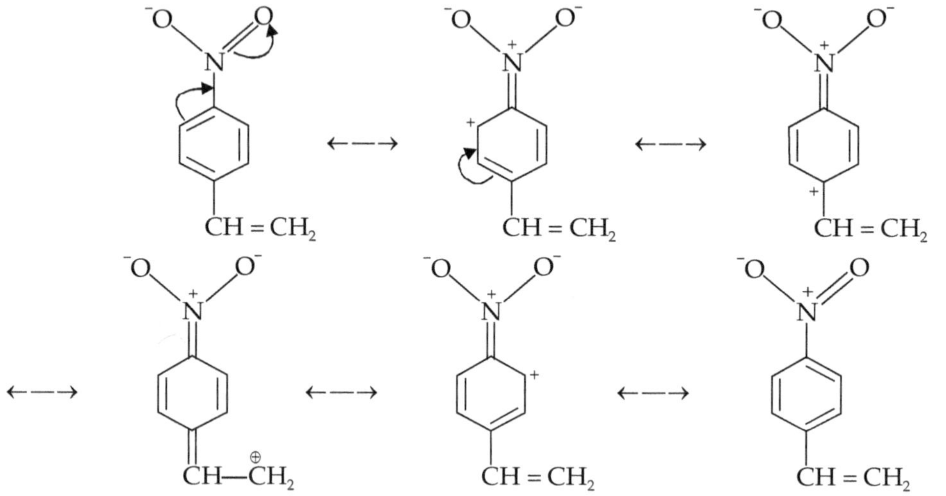

(*ix*)    $CH_3—CH = CH—CH_2CH_3 \longleftrightarrow CH_3—\overset{\ominus}{C}H—\overset{\oplus}{C}H—CH_2CH_3$

No mesomeric effect, displacement of electrons is governed by —$CH_2CH_3$ group which has more + I effect than the —$CH_3$.

# TEST YOUR UNDERSTANDING - 2.4

1.    Write down the various mesomeric structures of the following species, and also mention which one is especially stable or unstable, if any

    (*i*) 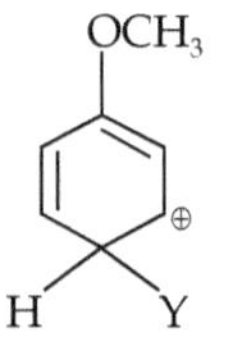             (*ii*) 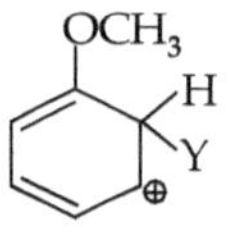             (*iii*) 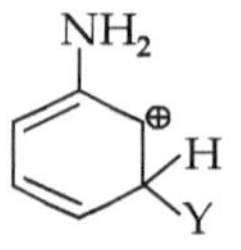             (*iv*)

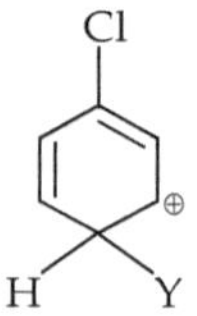

2.    Write down the resonance hybrid of the following structures.

    (*i*)    Allyl carbonium ion     (*ii*)    Acetamide       (*iii*) 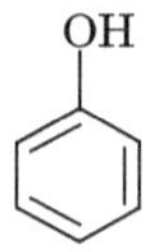                    (*iv*)

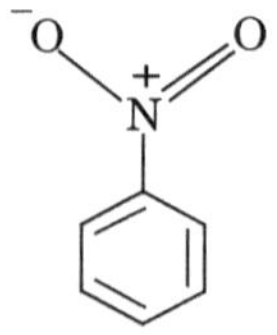

3.    Draw the resonating structure of the carbonium ion ($CH_3OCH_2^+$) and discuss the relative stability of different canonical structures.
4.    Explain why $CHCl_3$ is more acidic than $CHF_3$.

### 2.5.5 Hyperconjugation

Baker and Nathan suggested that alkyl groups with at least one hydrogen atom on the $\alpha$-carbon atom, attached to an $sp^2$ hybridised carbon atom (alkenes, carbocations or alkyl free radicals), are able to release electrons in the following way.

$$-\overset{H}{\underset{}{C}}-C=C \quad\longleftrightarrow\quad \overset{H^+}{} \quad -C=C-\overset{-}{C}$$
$$\text{I} \qquad\qquad\qquad \text{II}$$

Note that the delocalisation involves $\sigma$ and $\pi$ bond orbitals (or $p$ orbitals in case of carbocation and free radicals); thus it is also known as $\sigma - \pi$ **conjugation.** This type of *electron release due to the presence of the system* H—C—C = C is known as **hyperconjugation** or **Baker-Nathan effect.** Note that in structure II there is no definite bond between one of the carbon atoms and one of the hydrogen atoms, hence hyperconjugation is also known as **no-bond resonance.** It is a permanent effect. It is also known as **anchimeric effect.**

**Hyperconjugation in propene**

$$\underset{\text{I}}{H-\overset{H}{\underset{H}{C}}-CH=CH_2} \longleftrightarrow \underset{\text{II}}{H-\overset{H}{\underset{H}{C}}=CH-\overset{-}{C}H_2} \overset{H^+}{} \longleftrightarrow \underset{\text{III}}{H^+\overset{H}{\underset{H}{C}}=CH-\overset{-}{C}H_2} \longleftrightarrow \underset{\text{IV}}{H-\overset{H}{\underset{H^+}{C}}=CH-\overset{-}{C}H_2}$$

**Hyperconjugation in toluene**

$$\text{I} \longleftrightarrow \text{II} \longleftrightarrow \text{III} \longleftrightarrow \text{IV}$$

More the number of H—C bonds attached to the unsaturated system more will be the probability of electron release by this mechanism. Thus the electron release by this mechanism will be greater in methyl (possessing three hyperconjugated H—C bonds), less in ethyl (having two such bonds) and *iso*-propyl (one) and essentially zero in *tert*-butyl (no hyperconjugated H—C bond) group.

$$H-\overset{H}{\underset{H}{C}}-C=C \qquad H_3C-\overset{H}{\underset{H}{C}}-C=C \qquad H_3C-\overset{H}{\underset{CH_3}{C}}-C=C \qquad H_3C-\overset{CH_3}{\underset{CH_3}{C}}-C=C$$

| Methyl compound | Ethyl compound | *iso*-Propyl compound | *tert*-Butyl compound |
|---|---|---|---|
| (containing 3 H – C hyperconjugated bonds) | (containing 2 H – C hyperconjugated bonds) | (containing 1 H – C hyperconjugated bond) | (containing no H – C hyperconjugated bond) |

It is important to note that although hyperconjugation like inductive effect causes the release of electrons and thus the two effects reinforce each other in this respect, the magnitude of the two effects changes in opposite directions in passing along a series of alkyl groups.

$$CH_3—, \quad CH_3CH_2—, \quad (CH_3)_2CH—, \quad (CH_3)_3C—$$

**Increasing inductive effect, Decreasing hyperconjugation** $\longrightarrow$

The phenomenon of hyperconjugation can also be applied to group, Cl—C—C = C (*cf.* H—C—C = C) where the effect operates in the reverse direction.

$$Cl—C—C=C \quad\longleftrightarrow\quad Cl^- \quad C=C—C^+$$

**Effects of hyperconjugation*.**

(i) **Stability of alkenes.** Hyperconjugation explains the stability of certain olefins over other alkenes. For example, propene is more stable than ethene because in propene there are three H—C hyperconjugated bonds and thus the σ-electron of C—H bond can delocalise over three different structures (structures drawn above).

Further greater the number of alkyl groups attached to the doubly-bonded carbons, the more stable the alkene is. Thus 2-methylpropene and butene-2 are more stable than propene.

$$CH_3—\underset{\underset{CH_3}{|}}{C}=CH_2 \qquad\qquad CH_3—CH = CH—CH_3$$

2-Methylpropene                           Butene-2

(6 H—C hyperconjugated bonds)              (6 H—C hyperconjugated bonds)

In general, alkenes follow the following order of stability.

$$R_2C = CR_2 > R_2C = CHR > RCH = CHR > R\,CH = CH_2 > CH_2 = CH_2$$

(ii) **Stability of carbocations and alkyl free-radicals.** The concept of hyperconjugation can also be extended to explain the following relative stabilities of alkyl radicals and carbocations.

$$\text{\textit{tert}-Alkyl} > \text{\textit{sec}-Alkyl} > \text{\textit{pri}-Alkyl} > \text{Methyl radical}$$

e.g.,        $(CH_3)_3\dot{C} > (CH_3)_2\dot{C}H > CH_3\dot{C}H_2 > \dot{C}H_3$

Similarly,   $(CH_3)_3C^+ > (CH_3)_2\overset{+}{C}H > CH_3\overset{+}{C}H_2 > \overset{+}{C}H_3$

In general, more the number of hyperconjugative structures of a species higher is its stability. Thus ethyl radical may be regarded as a hybrid of the following hyperconjugative structures.

(iii) **Orienting influence of alkyl group in** *o, p*-**positions and of** —CCl₃ **group in** *m*-**position.** Observe the hyperconjugative structures of toluene, given earlier you will find high electron density on *o*- and *p*-positions.

Hyperconjugation in $C_6H_5CCl_3$ causes electron deficiency in *o*-, *p*-positions and thus *m*-positions become relatively electron rich.

The role of hyperconjugation in directive influence can be realised by knowing the fact during nitration of *p*-isopropyltoluene and *p*-*tert*-butyltoluene, —NO₂ group is introduced mainly in the *o*-position with respect to the —CH₃ group and not to isopropyl or *tert*-butyl group.

*    Hyperconjugative effect is a much weaker effect as compared to resonance effect.

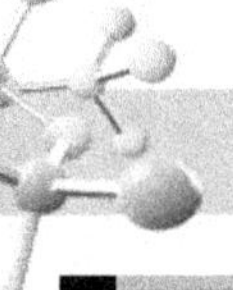

# TEST YOUR UNDERSTANDING - 2.5

1. Represent the movement of electrons in allyl bromide on additions of HBr.

## 2.6 Types of Bonding Among Covalent Molecules (Intermolecular Forces)

In an ionic compound, the structural units are ions. For example, solid sodium chloride is made up $Na^+$ and $Cl^-$ ions. Each $Na^+$ ion is attached to six $Cl^-$ ions around it and each $Cl^-$ ion is attached to six $Na^+$ ions around it. The *interionic forces are very powerful electrostatic forces and hold each ion in position.* However, in non-ionic (covalent) compounds, the structural units are molecules which *are hold together through very weak forces* of the following three types.

### 2.6.1 Dipole-dipole interaction

In polar molecules, positive end of one polar molecule is attracted by the negative end of another polar molecule and vice versa. As a result of this, dipole-dipole interaction, polar molecules are generally held to each other more strongly than the nonpolar molecules of comparable molecular mass.

### 2.6.2 Hydrogen bond

Hydrogen bond is formed between hydrogen atom linked to highly elecronegative element, X (F, O or N), and another highly electronegative element, Y (F, O or N), X—H ------ Y. Hydrogen bond may be intermolecular or intramolecular. Intermolecular hydrogen bonding causes association of the molecules and thus increases its m.p. or b.p.

### 2.6.3 London (van der Waals) forces

In non-polar compounds there is a weak intermolecular attraction due to electrostatic attraction between the nuclei of one molecule and electrons of the other. The electrostatic attraction is largely compensated by electrostatic repulsion between electrons of the two neighbouring molecules, as well as by repulsion between nuclei of the two neighbouring molecules. Thus the van der Waals forces are very weak and are significant only when the molecules are very close together. They act only between portions of different molecules which are in close contact, *i.e.,* between the surface molecules. Thus van der Waal forces are proportional to

(*a*) *surface area of a molecule.* Greater is the surface area of a molecule, greater is the number of interactions and hence stronger will be van der Waal forces. This explains why boiling point decreases on the increase in branching of a compound.

(*b*) *molecular weight of compound.* The greater the molecular weight of the molecule, the greater is the number of electrons and the greater these forces.

The relative order of attraction of the three intermolecular forces is :

**hydrogen bond > dipole-dipole > van der Waals**

The physical properties especially m.p., b.p. and solubility depend largely upon the nature of the bond present in the molecule, nature of the intermolecular forces and molecular weight of the compound.

(*a*) **Melting and boiling points.** A solid melts when the thermal energy of its particles is large enough to overcome the interparticle forces which hold them in position. Similarly, a liquid boils when the thermal energy of its particles is enough to overcome the cohesive forces which hold them in position. Since ionic compounds have very strong interionic forces which are overcome only at very high temperatures, they melt (or boil) at high temperatures. On the other hand, non-ionic (covalent) compounds have weak intermolecular forces (H-bond, dipole-dipole interaction or van der Waals forces) which are overcome at relatively low temperatures, these compounds melt (or boil) at low temperatures.

$$\overset{\delta_+}{H} - \overset{\delta_-}{F}$$

Melting points depend not only on molecular weight but also on molecular shape. Following important general relationship exists between melting point and structure of aromatic compounds.

(*i*) **Among isomeric disubstituted benzenes the para isomer generally melts considerably higher than the corresponding ortho and para.**

The higher melting point (and lower solubility) of a *para* isomer is due to molecular symmetry. The more symmetrical a compound, the better it fits into a crystal lattice and hence higher will be the melting point (and lower is the solubility). Among disubstituted benzenes, *para* isomers are the most symmetrical and hence possess highest melting point among the three isomers.

(*ii*) *trans*-Isomers have higher m.p. than the corresponding *cis*-isomer, *e.g.*

$$\begin{array}{ll} \text{H—C—COOH} & \text{H—C—COOH} \\ \quad\|\| & \quad\|\| \\ \text{H—C—COOH} & \text{HOOC—C—H} \\ \text{Maleic acid (m.p. 150° C)} & \text{Fumaric acid (m.p. 250° C)} \end{array}$$

(*iii*) In carboxylic acids, even numbered member has higher melting point than the higher molecule having odd number of carbon atoms.

(*b*) **Solubility.**

(*i*) Ionic compounds are generally soluble in water due to following reason.

In the strongly polar solvent $H_2O$, each positive ion is surrounded by water molecules due to ion-dipole attraction, and each negative ion is H-bonded to water.

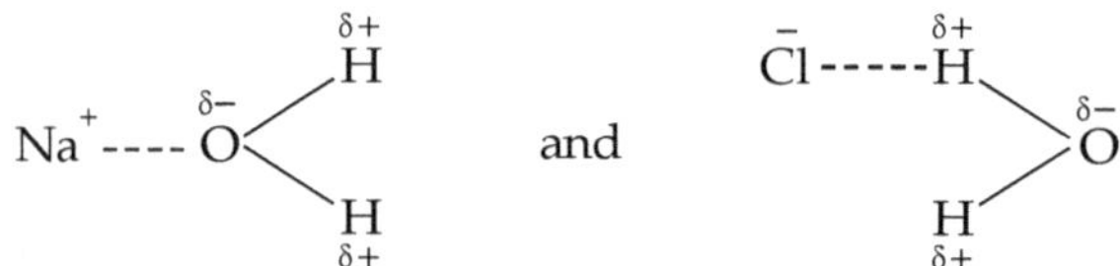

These interactions, called **solvation** (more specifically, **hydration**, since the solvent is water), causes the ions to separate and disperse in the solvent. Once the ions are hydrated, water lowers the attraction between oppositely charged ions due to its high dielectric constant.

(*ii*) Non-ionic compounds are governed by solubility rule "*like dissolves like*". Thus non-polar, weakly polar and highly polar substances are generally soluble in non-polar, weakly polar and highly polar solvents respectively. Solubility of organic compounds in water can be predicted on the basis of H-bonding.

(*a*) Compounds containing —OH, —COOH, —NH₂ and ethers are soluble in water because these functional groups are capable of forming hydrogen bonding with water.

(*b*) Hydrocarbons are almost insoluble in water ; in general larger the hydrocarbon part of an organic molecule, lower is its solubility in water. However, lower alkanes (*e.g.* $CH_4$) are sparingly soluble in water due to their similar (smaller) size with that of water molecules.

## 2.7 Hydrogen Bonding

A hydrogen atom, with only $1s$ orbital at first sight is expected to form only one valency bond but it has been found to possess the special property of forming weak bonds with certain electronegative atoms to which it is not directly attached by formal chemical bonds. There is a lot of evidence to show that in some cases hydrogen atom can, in fact, bind two atoms together, apparently forming two bonds.

Consider the hydrogen–fluorine bond in hydrogen fluoride, HF. This is a polar covalent bond in which hydrogen is attached to a strongly electronegative element. As a result, the fluorine acquires partial negative charge hydrogen acquires a partial positive charge.

The positive charge on hydrogen in a molecule of hydrogen fluoride will be attracted electrostatically by the negative charge on the fluorine atom in another molecule of hydrogen fluoride. This electrostatic attraction (dipole-dipole attraction) between different molecules of hydrogen fluoride continues resulting in the formation of a large aggregate.

$$\overset{\delta+}{\text{—H}}\overset{\delta-}{\text{—F}}\text{---}\overset{\delta+}{\text{H}}\overset{\delta-}{\text{—F}}\text{---}\overset{\delta+}{\text{H}}\overset{\delta-}{\text{—F}}\text{——}$$

Covalent bond ⟋          ⟍ Hydrogen bond

Thus we see that hydrogen in hydrogen fluoride is bonded to two highly electronegative flourine atoms; the linkage between hydrogen and one of the fluorine atoms is a usual covalent bond while the linkage between hydrogen and the other fluorine is simply due to electrostatic forces of attraction which results a weak bond, commonly known as **hydrogen bond** (protonic bridge). The new type of linkage is represented by dotted line (------).

Thus **hydrogen bond** *is an electrostatic attractive force between covalently bonded hydrogen atom of one molecule and an electronegative atom (such as F, O, N) of another molecule.* Hydrogen bond is merely a strong electrostatic attractive force and not a normal chemical bond. It is very weak (strength about 2—10 kcal mol$^{-1}$ or 8.4—42 kJ mol$^{-1}$) as compared to a covalent bond (strength 50—100 kcal mol$^{-1}$ or 209—418.4 kJ mol$^{-1}$).

**Conditions for hydrogen bonding**

(*i*)    *The molecule must possess a higher electronegative atoms such as F, O or N, directly linked to hydrogen atom.*

(*ii*)    *The size of the electronegative atom should be small.*

These conditions are met only by F, O and N* atoms and only these atoms form effective hydrogen bonding. Thus hydrogen bonds are usually encountered in hydrogen fluoride (HF), water (H$_2$O), ammonia (NH$_3$), alcohols (ROH), carboxylic acids (RCOOH), and amines (RNH$_2$). Further, greater the electronegativity and smaller the size of the atom (F, O, N), the stronger is the hydrogen bond which is evident from the relative order of energies of hydrogen bonds in the three elements.

$$H—F - - - H > H—O - - - H > H—N - - - H$$
10 kcal/mole        7 kcal/mole        2 kcal/mole

*Comparison of hydrogen bonding formed by halogens.* Among halogens, only fluorine forms hydrogen bonding because other halogens are not too electronegative to form hydrogen bonding. The non-existence of hydrogen bonding in HCl, HBr and HI explains the non-existence of molecules like KCl– – –HCl (KHCl$_2$), KBr – – –HBr (KHBr$_2$) and KI– – –HI (KHI$_2$), although KF– – –HF (KHF$_2$) has been isolated. Actually, the HF$_2^-$ anion has the strongest known hydrogen bond (bond energy = 27 kcal/mole).

$$[F------H—F]^-$$

Experimentally, it has been found that hydrogen atom is in midway between the two fluorine atoms. The HF$_2^-$ ion consists of two F$^-$ ions shielded from each other by a proton (H$^+$).

**Types of hydrogen bonding.** Generally, the hydrogen bonds are classified into two groups, *viz.* intermolecular and intramolecular.

## 2.7.1   Intermolecular hydrogen bonding

In such type of linkage the two or more than two molecules of the same compound combine together to give a polymeric aggregate. For example,

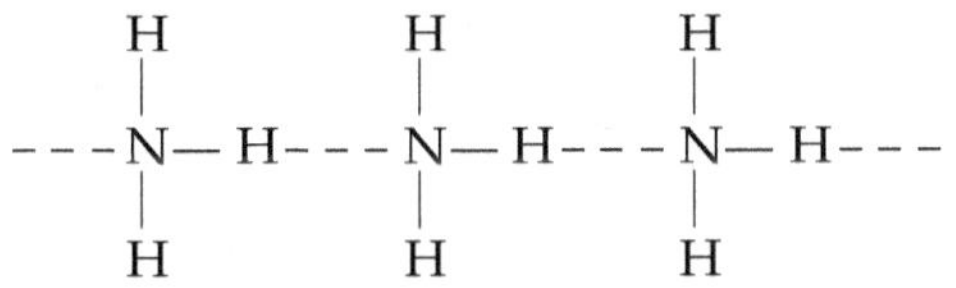

Hydrogen bonding in ammonia 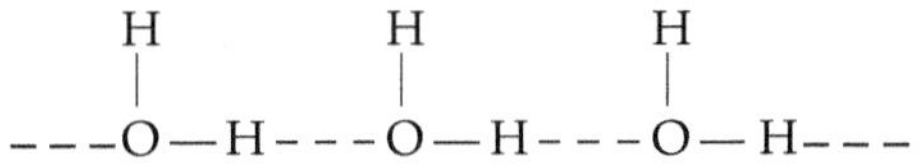          Hydrogen bonding in water

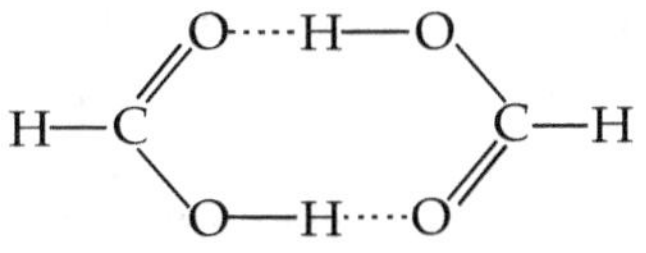

Hydrogen bonding in formic acid (dimerisation) 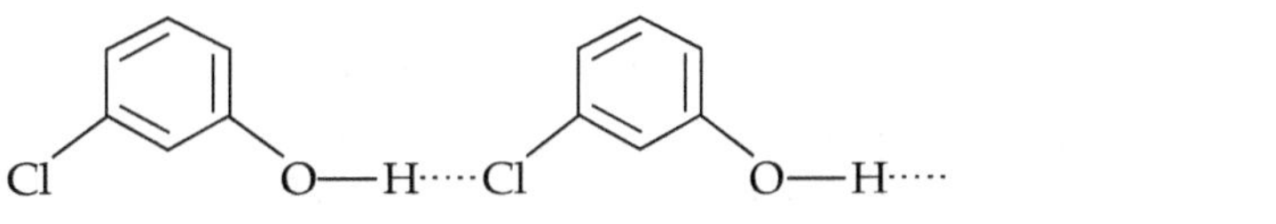          Hydrogen bonding in m-chlorophenol

*Intermolecular hydrogen bonding* between molecules of the same type (*association*) *increases the boiling point of the compound.* The increase in boiling point is because of association of several molecules of the compound with the result the effective molecular weight of the compound increases and hence more energy (large amount of heat) is required to dissociate the molecules for vaporization.

Intermolecular hydrogen bonding between molecule of a compound and water molecule, increases solubility of that compound in water (remember *a compound is said to be soluble in water if it is capable forming hydrogen bonding with water*).

## 2.7.2   Intramolecular hydrogen bonding

In this type, hydrogen bonding occurs within two atoms of the same molecule. This type of hydrogen bonding is commonly known as **chelation** and frequently occurs in organic compounds. Intramolecular hydrogen bonding is possible when a six or five-membered ring can be formed. Some examples are given below.

---

*    Although Cl has same electronegativity as nitrogen, it does not form effective hydrogen bonds. This is because of its larger size than that of N with the result its electrostatic attractions are weak. Similarly, sulphur forms a very weak hydrogen bond due to its low electronegativity, although oxygen present in the same group forms a strong hydrogen bond.

Intramolecular hydrogen bonding in *o*-chlorophenol, *o*-nitrophenol and 2, 6-dihydroxybenzoic acid.

*Intramolecular hydrogen bonding (chelation) decreases the boiling point of the compound and also its solubility in water.* This is because of fact that the chelation between the *ortho* substituted groups restricts the possibility of intermolecular hydrogen bonding and thus prevents association of the molecules which would have raised the melting and boiling points. Chelation is not possible in the corresponding *m*- and *p*-isomers because the two groups (atoms) are far away from each other. Hence in such cases, intermolecular hydrogen bonding takes place which in turn increases the boiling point. Thus we can explain *the low m.p. and b.p. of the ortho isomers of hydroxy and nitro-carbonyl compounds than the corresponding m-and p-isomers.* Decrease of solubility in water is again due to chelation which prevents hydrogen bonding between compound and water.

Intramolecular hydrogen bonding in
*o*-hydroxybenzoic acid (Note that —CO group not
available to form hydrogen bond with water)

Intermolecular H-bonding between
*p*-hydroxybenzoic acid and water (—CO group is
available to form hydrogen bond with water)

## EFFECTS OF HYDROGEN BONDING

1. **Boiling point.** The boiling point of a liquid is the temperature at which kinetic energy of the molecule is sufficient to overcome the intermolecular attractive forces. Thus it seems to be reasonable that heavier the molecule and stronger the intermolecular forces higher will be the boiling point of the compound. Thus, if the intermolecular forces are equal, the melting and boiling points of similar compounds should increase with the increase in molecular weight of the compound. This explains why the melting and boiling points generally increase with increase in number of carbon atoms in most of the homologous series.

   On the other hand, if the two similar compounds under study are having different intermolecular forces, their melting and boiling points differ very much. It is due to the fact that molecules of the compound having greater attractive intermolecular force have a greater tendency of association with the result the effective molecular weight and subsequently melting and boiling* points of the compound increase. Best familiar examples of this type of compounds are water, alcohols, hydrogen fluoride, amines and amides.

   (*a*) **Water.** Although water has minimum molecular weight amongst hydrides of the 16th group of the periodic table, it has the highest melting and boiling points and is liquid (while others are gases) under ordinary conditions.

   This is explained on the basis that water molecules associate through hydrogen bonding and thus require more energy to get separated for vaporization.

   As far as sulphur is concerned, its lesser electronegative nature than oxygen gives S—H bond a smaller ionic character than the O—H bond and thus $H_2S$ forms very weak hydrogen bond.

---

*    Alternatively, since extra energy is required to break the hydrogen bond, intermolecular hydrogen bonding increases the melting and boiling points of substances.

The two unusual properties of water, namely (*a*) low density in the solid state than that in the liquid state, and (*b*) contraction when heated between 0°C and 4°C, can be explained on the basis of hydrogen bonding in water.

Note the following features of the above structure.

(*i*)　The $H_2O$ molecules are tetrahedrally oriented with respect to one another.

(*ii*)　Each oxygen atom is surrounded tetrahedrally by four H atoms.

(*iii*)　One water molecule is capable of forming four hydrogen bonds.

(*iv*)　Hydrogen bonds are weaker and, therefore, longer than the covalent bonds.

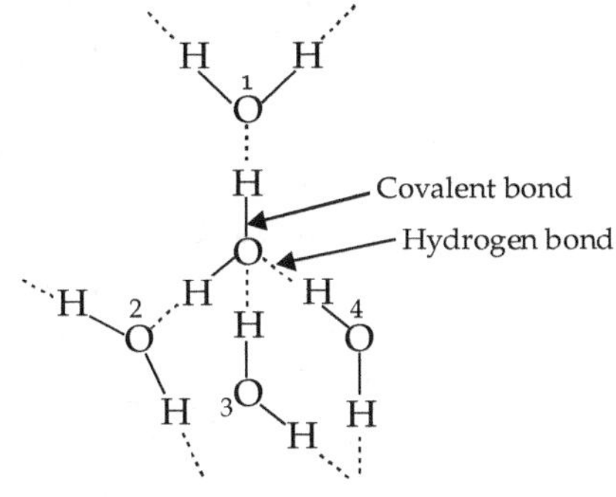


The tetrahedral open cage-like structure of ice.

(*b*)　***Alcohols.*** The boiling points of alcohols are higher than those of the corresponding thiols (mercaptans) and ethers. Higher boiling point of an alcohol than that of the corresponding thiol is due to the association of alcohol molecules in the same way as in water.

$$------O-H------\ O-H------\ O-H------\ O-H------$$
$$\quad\ \ |\qquad\qquad |\qquad\qquad |\qquad\qquad |$$
$$\quad\ \ R\qquad\qquad R\qquad\qquad R\qquad\qquad R$$

Similarly, we can explain the higher boiling points of polyhydric alcohols than their ethers. The successive replacement of hydrogen atom of the OH group of alcohol by alkyl group to form ether blocks the probability of hydrogen bonding, and thus the boiling points of the products (*i.e.* ethers) progressively decrease in spite of increase in molecular weights.

| | | |
|---|---|---|
| $CH_2OH$ | $CH_2OCH_3$ | $CH_2OCH_3$ |
| \| | \| | \| |
| $CH_2OH$ | $CH_2OH$ | $CH_2OH_3$ |
| **b.p.**　197°C | 125°C | 84°C |

Now let us compare the hydrogen bonding in water and alcohols (*e.g.*, ethyl alcohol). Although both the compounds are having the hydroxyl group responsible for forming hydrogen bonds, water having low molecular weight boils at a high temperature than ethyl alcohol having higher molecular weight.

| | $H_2O$ | $C_2H_5OH$ |
|---|---|---|
| **Mol. wt.** | 18 | 46 |
| **b.p.** | 100°C | 78°C |

The higher boiling point of water than ethyl alcohol is because of greater degree of hydrogen bonding in water than in alcohol with the result greater number of water molecules are associated than the ethyl alcohol.

The high degree of hydrogen bonding in water is due to more contribution of —OH group in water (H — OH) molecule than that in alcohol (R—OH) molecule where a larger alkyl group is present in place of smaller hydrogen atom. The alcohols, due to alkyl group, behave somewhat like hydrocarbons as far as hydrogen bonding is concerned. This is further evidenced by the fact that larger the alkyl group or more the number of alkyl groups in an alcohol, lesser will be its tendency of forming hydrogen bonding. Thus primary alcohols have the highest boiling point while the tertiary alcohols have the lowest boiling point in the isomeric alcohols.

| | OH | OH |
|---|---|---|
| | \| | \| |
| $CH_3CH_2CH_2CH_2OH$ | $CH_3CHCH_2CH_3$ | $CH_3-C-CH_3$ |
| | | \| |
| | | $CH_3$ |
| 1-Butanol (1° alcohol) | 2-Butanol (2° alcohol) | Methyl-2-propanol |
| b.p. 118°C | b.p. 99°C | (3° alcohol) b.p. 83°C |

Glycerol, $CH_2OHCHOHCH_2OH$, having three — OH groups per molecule can form more hydrogen bonds per molecule than that of water. This increases attraction between all the molecules and hence increases the resistance of flow, *i.e.* viscosity.

(c)    ***Hydrogen fluoride.*** Like the hydride of oxygen (water) among the hydrides of group 16 elements, hydrogen fluoride among the hydrides of group 17 elements, although has the lowest molecular weight, yet it is liquid and has the highest boiling point while others are gaseous in nature with low b.p.The abnormally high boiling point of HF is explained on the basis of the fact that due to greater electronegativity and smaller size, fluorine forms much stronger intermolecular hydrogen bonds than other halogens.

(d)    ***Amines.*** Like water and alcohols, primary and secondary amines, but not tertiary, are capable of forming intermolecular hydrogen bonding (— N—H ------N) and thus primary and secondary amines boil at higher temperatures than the isomeric tertiary amine.

**By now we have discussed the examples where the boiling points is increased due to hydrogen bonding** (*intermolecular*) **but there are certain cases where the boiling point is decreased due to hydogen bonding** (*intramolecular*). For example, *the ortho-hydroxy- nitro,-carbonyl,-carboxylic or -chloro compounds have lower melting and boiling points than the respective meta or para isomer.* The reason being that intramolecular hydrogen bonding takes place between the two ortho substituted groups and thus prevents association of the molecules which would have raised the melting and boiling points.

On the other hand, intramolecular hydrogen bonding is not possible in case of *m*- and *p*-isomers because of the size of the ring which would have been formed. Thus here the intermolecular hydrogen bonding takes place which causes some degree of association with the result the *m*- and *p*-isomers melt and boil at higher temperatures.

Hydrogen bonding in enolic form of acetoacetic ester.

Chelation also explains low boiling point of the enolic form of acetoacetic ester than that of the ketonic form (although usually alcohols possess higher boiling points than that of the corresponding ketones, *e.g.* isopropyl alcohol boils at 82°C while acetone at about 56°C).

2.    **Water solubility.** *A substance is said to be soluble in water if it is capable of forming hydrogen bonding with water molecules.* On the other hand, compounds in which hydrogen bonding with water is not possible (or restricted due to intramolecular hydrogen bonding) would be insoluble or less soluble in water.

Thus organic compounds like alkenes, alkanes and ethers which lack the formation of hydrogen bonds with water are insoluble in water while alcohols and acids which are capable of forming hydrogen bonds with water are readily soluble in water.

Hydrogen bonding between alcohol and water

However, it is important to note that when the alkyl group (R —) in alcohols has four or more carbon atoms, the alkyl group predominates and hydrogen bond formation is restricted with the result the solubility of such alcohols in water decreases. Alcohols containing more than seven carbon atoms are insoluble in water, while methyl, ethyl and propyl alcohols are fairly soluble in water.

When a compound has a large ratio of — OH groups to hydrocarbon group, it will be very much soluble in water. Thus sugars, certain starches and polyvinyl alcohol are quite soluble in water.

Thus we can explain the solubility of alcohols, phenols, primary and secondary amines in water since these compounds easily form hydrogen bonds with water molecules. The success of non-ionic detergents[1] is due to the powerful solubilizing effect of hydroxyl groups. Since the water soluble portion of these detergents has neutral hydorxy, ether or amino groups, they are easily dissolved in water as a result of hydrogen bonding.

The insolubility of tertiary amines[2] in water is probably due to a steric effect rather than lack of N - - - - -H—O bonding because tertiary amines with the alkyl groups tied back by ring formation, such as pyridine, are soluble in water.

It is important is note that while *the intermolecular hydrogen bonding increases solubility of the compound in water, the intramolecular hydrogen bonding decreases.* This is due to the fact that the formation of internal hydrogen bond prevents hydrogen bonding between the compound and water which thus reduces solubility of the compound in water.

One practical application of the contrasting effects of chelation and association upon boiling point and water solubility is made in the separation of a mixture of *ortho*- and *para*-hydroxy-carbonyl or-nitro compounds by steam distillation. In case of *ortho* isomers, association of the hydroxyl group with water molecules is prevented due to chelation and thus these isomers are only sparingly soluble in water and possess lower boiling point and

---

1.    Non-ionic detergents are the derivatives of di- and tri-ethanolamines or the condensation products of ethylene oxide with alcohols or phenols.
2.    However, the first member of the series, trimethylamine is about 41% soluble in water.

are thus much volatile that the *para* isomers with the result the *ortho* isomers can be steam distilled so much rapidly than the *para* isomers that a practical separation of the two isomers can be achieved.

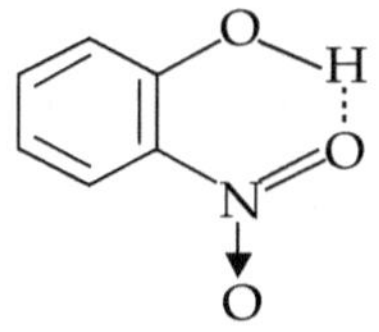

*o*-Nitrophenol

Due to chelation, —OH group is not available to form hydrogen bond with water hence it is sparingly soluble in water. Further, association of the molecules due to intermolecular hydrogen bonding is also not possible hence it has lower boiling point.

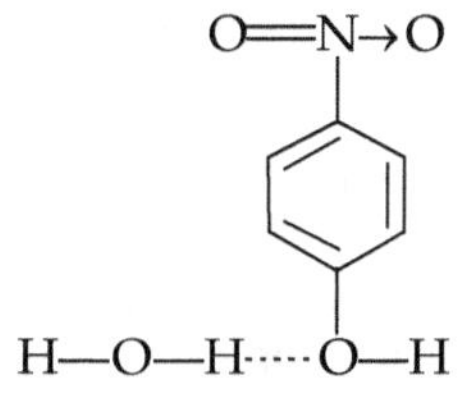

*p*-Nitrophenol

—OH group available to form hydrogen bond with water, hence it is completely soluble in water. Chelation is not possible, hence association of the molecules is possible due to intermolecular hydrogen bonding. Hence it has high boiling point.

3. **Strength of acids.** The dissociation of an acid and hence its acidity is sufficiently increased, if its anion is stabilized by chelation. This can be proved by the ionization constants of the three isomeric hydroxy-and methoxy-benzoic acids in water.

| | *ortho* | *meta* | *para* |
|---|---|---|---|
| $OH \cdot C_6H_4 \cdot COOH$ | $105 \times 10^{-5}$ | $8.3 \times 10^{-5}$ | $2.9 \times 10^{-5}$ |
| $OCH_3 \cdot C_6H_4 \cdot COOH$ | $8.1 \times 10^{-5}$ | $8.2 \times 10^{-5}$ | $3.4 \times 10^{-5}$ |

The abnormally high dissociation constant of the *o*-hydroxybenzoic acid in the above table is due to the fact its anion is stabilized by chelation. Its dissociation is 17 *times more than that of benzoic acid. The fact that hydrogen bonding increases the acidity of the o-isomer is proved by the very low dissociation constant of the o-methoxybenzoic acid where hydrogen is not available for hydrogen bonding. Furthermore, the dissociation of 2, 6-dihydroxybenzoic acid is 800 times as large as that of benzoic acid which is again due to greater stabilization of its anion by hydrogen bonding.*

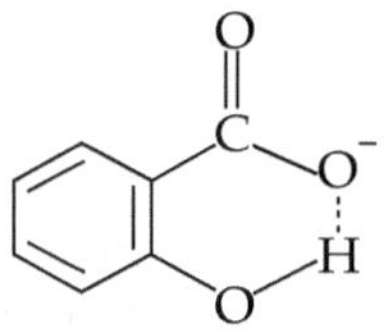

Salicylate ion 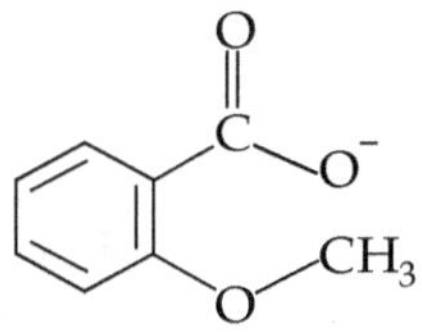     *o*-Methoxybenzoate anion<br>(Hydrogen bonding is not possible)     2, 6-Dihydroxybenzoate anion

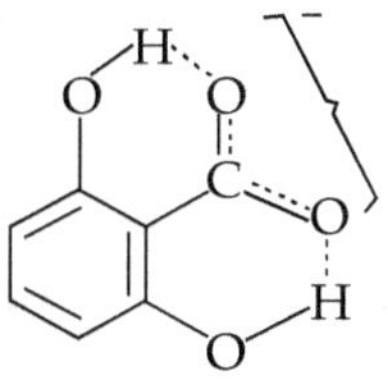

Similarly, we can explain very strong acidic character of maleic acid than fumaric acid. If one proton is removed from each of the acids, the corresponding ions are formed. But the maleate ion can be stabilized by chelation because hydrogen and oxygen responsible for forming hydrogen bond are very near to each other. On the other hand, fumarate ion can not stabilise by chelation because hydrogen and oxygen are on the opposite sides to each other, hence the formation of fumarate ion does not take place. This explains why maleic acid is a stronger acid than its isomer, fumaric acid.

In case, the dissociating hydrogen atom is involved in hydrogen bond, enough energy will be required for its removal and thus the dissociation constant will be abnormally low. This explains why the *o*-halogenophenols are weaker acids than the *m*- or *p*-isomers. It also explains why the second dissociation constant of maleic acid is very low as compared to that of $K_{a_1}$.

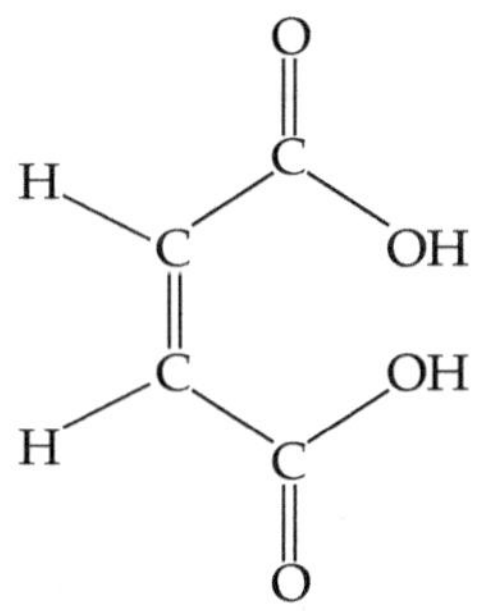

Maleic acid 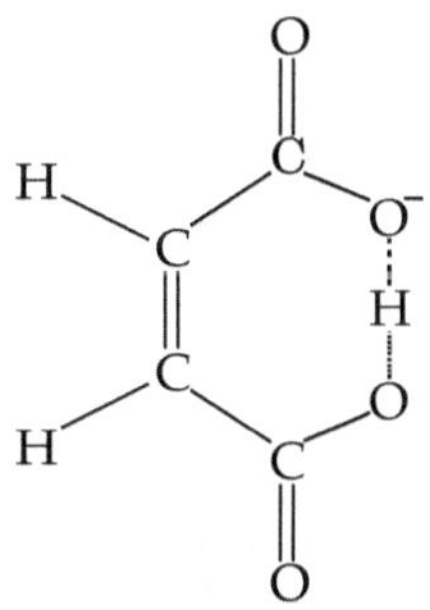     Maleate ion<br>(chelation possible)     Fumaric acid 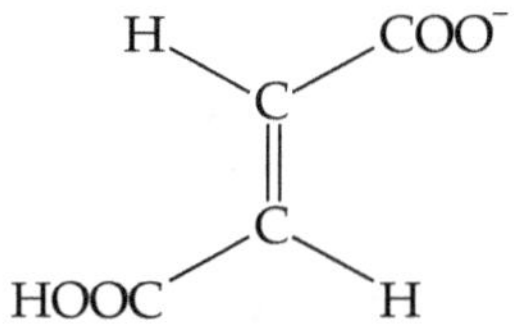     Fumarate ion<br>(chelation not possible)

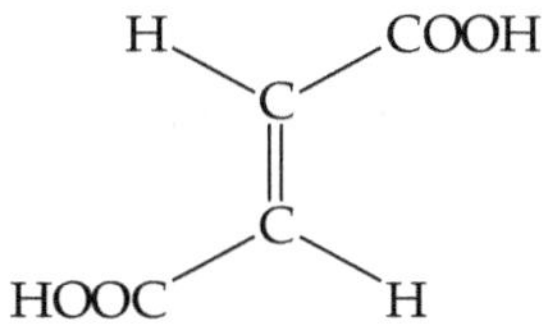

Similarly, we can explain why HF is a less stronger acid than any other halogen acid. Since HF is capable of forming strong hydrogen bonds, its proton is dissociated with a great difficulty as compared to other halogen acids. Thus acidity among halogeno acids follows the following order :

$$HF < HCl < HBr < HI$$

4.     **Basic strength of amines.** Compounds like $NH_3$, $MeNH_2$, $Me_2NH$ and $Me_3N$ are weak bases, while the quaternary compound $Me_4N^+OH^-$ is a very strong base can be explained in the following way. When dissolved in water, the first four bases combine with water to yield species I which owing to the formation of hydrogen bond can not be regarded as fully ionic.

$$CH_3-\underset{\underset{H}{|}}{\overset{\overset{H}{|}}{N}}---H-OH \qquad\qquad \left[H_3C-\underset{\underset{CH_3}{|}}{\overset{\overset{CH_3}{|}}{N}}-CH_3\right]^+ + OH^-$$

I                    II

On the other hand, the tetramethylammonium hydroxide, lacking a hydrogen atom on the nitrogen, cannot exist in a form analogous to I. It exists only in the completely ionized form II with the result the compound is a strong base, quite comparable in strength to potassium hydroxide.

5.     **Chemical properties :** Hydrogen bonding also affects chemical properties of certain compounds. For example, dibenzoylmethane $C_6H_5COCH_2COC_6H_5$ neither gives certain typical reactions of the ketonic group, viz. it does not add HCN and $NaHSO_3$, nor some typical reactions of the enolic group, viz. acetylation and reaction with Grignard reagent. It is due to enolisation and hydrogen bonding.

(keto form)             (enol form)

Dibenzoylmethane

6.     **Hydrogen bonding in biological systems.** Hydrogen bonding also plays a very important role in biological systems. Most of water (which generally constitutes over 50% of the weight of the plant or animal) present in plants and animal is attached to proteins by hydrogen bond. The significance of hydrogen bonding in biological system can best be illustrated by its role in the structure of proteins and nucleic acids. Hydrogen bonding stabilises the usual structure of proteins and nucleic acids.

## TEST YOUR UNDERSTANDING - 2.6

1.     Account for the following :

      (*i*)     Although $CH_3Cl$ molecule is more polar than $CH_3Br$ and $CH_3I$, it has lowest boiling point among the three.

      (*ii*)     Although *n*-pentane and neopentane have same molecular weight and similar polarity, they differ in their boiling points.

      (*iii*)     Ethyl alcohol boils at 78.3°C, while its isomer dimethyl ether boils at a very low temperature (− 24°C).

      (*iv*)     Mineral oil, a mixture of high-molar mass hydrocarbons, dissolves in *n*-hexane but not in ethanol.

## 2.8    Acids and Bases

The terms acids and bases have been defined in a number of ways, however, here we shall take up only two ways.

### 2.8.1    Lowry-Bronsted definition

*An acid is a substance that donates a proton, and a base is a substance that accepts a proton.* The strength of acids or bases is measured by the extent to which they lose or gain protons, respectively. In acid-base reactions, acids and bases are converted to their conjugate bases and conjugate acids respectively. Remember that a strong acid (base) has always a weak conjugate base (acid), and a weak acid (base) always has a strong conjugate base (acid).

| | Stronger acid | | Stronger base(conjugate base) | | | Weaker acid (conjugate acid) | | Weaker base |
|---|---|---|---|---|---|---|---|---|
| (i) | $H_2SO_4$ | + | $H_2O$ | ⇌ | | $H_3O^+$ | + | $HSO_4^-$ |
| (ii) | $HCl$ | + | $NH_3$ | ⇌ | | $NH_4^+$ | + | $Cl^-$ |
| (iii) | $H_3O^+$ | + | $OH^-$ | ⇌ | | $H_2O$ | + | $H_2O$ |
| (iv) | $NH_4^+$ | + | $OH^-$ | ⇌ | | $H_2O$ | + | $NH_3$ |

Following important conclusions are drawn from the above examples.

(a) *A substance acts as an acid only when another substance capable of accepting a proton (i.e., a base) is present.* For example, hydrogen chloride or acetic acid solution in benzene is not acidic (but neutral) because benzene is not in a position to take up protons. On the other hand, HCl or $CH_3COOH$ solution in water is definitely acidic because HCl or $CH_3COOH$ can ionise in water.

(b) *In aqueous solution, $H^+$ ion exists as hydrated ion $H^+H_2O$ or $H_3O^+$* (**hydronium ion**) and not as free $H^+$ ion.

(c) *Not only molecules but even ions may act as acids or bases.*

Table 3.1. Bronsted-Lowry Acids and Bases

| Type | Acid | Base |
|---|---|---|
| Molecular | $HCl$, $HBr$, $HClO_4$, $H_2SO_4$, $H_3PO_4$, $H_2O$ | $NH_3$, $NH_2NH_2$, amines, $H_2O$ |
| Cationic | $NH_4^+$, $[Fe(H_2O)_6]^{3+}$, $[Al(H_2O)_6]^{3+}$ | $[Fe(H_2O)_5(OH)]^{2+}$, $[Al(H_2O)_5(OH)]^{2+}$ |
| Anionic | $HS^-$, $HCO_3^-$, $HSO_4^-$, $H_2PO_4^-$ | $Cl^-$, $Br^-$, $OH^-$, $HSO_4^-$, $CO_3^{2-}$, $SO_4^{2-}$ |

(d) *Water, the most common solvent, can act both as an acid as well as a base* because it can give off a proton [example (iv)] as well as can receive it [example (i)]. Its dual behaviour may be represented by the following equation.

$$\underset{\text{Acid}_1}{H_2O} + \underset{\text{Base}_2}{H_2O} \rightleftharpoons \underset{\text{Acid}_2}{H_3O^+} + \underset{\text{Base}_1}{OH^-}$$

(e) The strength of an acid (or a base) depends upon the tendency of the base (or the acid) which accept (or donate) proton, *i.e.,* on medium which acts as base (or acid), *e.g.*

(i)　$HCl + H_2O \longrightarrow H_3O^+ + Cl^-$　　　　(ii)　$HCl + NH_3 \longrightarrow NH_4^+ + Cl^-$

(iii)　$HCl + C_6H_6 \longrightarrow$ No Reaction　　　(iv)　$HCl + CH_3COOH \longrightarrow CH_3COOH_2^+ + Cl^-$

(v)　$HCl + HF \longrightarrow H_2Cl^+ + F^-$

Thus it is obvious that HCl acts as

an acid in water as in the above equation No. (i)

a stronger acid in $NH_3$ as in the above equation No. (ii)

a neutral in $C_6H_6$ as in the above equation No. (iii)

a weak acid in $CH_3COOH$ as in the above equation No. (iv)

a weak base in HF as in the above equation No. (v)

(f) In acid-base reactions, equilibrium favours the formation of the weaker acid and weaker base.

**Classification of solvents on the basis of proton**

(i)　*Protophilic.* Solvents which have a greater tendency to accept proton *e.g.*, $H_2O$, alcohol, liquor ammonia etc.

(ii)　*Protogenic.* Solvents which have a greater tendency to donate proton, *e.g.*, $H_2O$, $HCl(l)$, glacial acetic acid etc.

(iii)　*Amphiprotic.* Solvents which can both accept and donate a proton, *e.g.*, $H_2O$, liquor ammonia, alcohol etc.

(iv)　*Aprotic.* Solvents which can neither accept nor can donate a proton, *e.g.*, benzene, $CS_2$, $CCl_4$, etc.

## TEST YOUR UNDERSTANDING - 2.7

1.　Write down the conjugate acids and bases in the reaction of $H_2O$ with gaseous (a) HCl and (b) $NH_3$.

　　Also mention the direction in which the reaction will mainly occur in each case.

2.　Rewrite the following equations to show the Lowry-Bronsted acids and bases actually involved. Represent in which direction the reaction will mainly proceed.

　　(a)　$NH_3(aq) + HNO_3(aq) \longrightarrow NH_4NO_3(aq)$　　　(b)　$NaCN(aq) \longrightarrow HCN(aq) + NaOH(aq)$

　　(c)　$NaH + H_2O \longrightarrow H_2 + NaOH$　　　　　　　(d)　$CaC_2 + H_2O \longrightarrow Ca(OH)_2 + C_2H_2$.

**Strength of acids and bases.** The ease with which an acid loses a proton is known as its strength and similarly the ease with which a base takes up a proton is known as the strength of a base. The strength of an acid or a base is usually measured in terms of their ionisation constants ($K_a$ and $K_b$). Furthermore, since the $K_a$ values are very small and are expressed in negative powers of 10, they are converted into $pK_a$ ($pK_a = -\log_{10} K_a$), e.g. $K_a$ and $pK_a$ values of $CH_3COOH$ in water are $1.79 \times 10^{-5}$ and 4.76 respectively. In general, the stronger an acid (base), the larger is its $K_a(K_b)$ and smaller is its $pK_a(pK_b)$ *value.* The ionisation constant of acid and base are related as below.

$$pK_a + pK_b = pK_w = 14.00 \text{ (at } 25°C).$$

If $pK_a$ or $pK_b$ value is negative, it indicates that the acid (or base) is completely ionised (strong acid or base).

### 2.8.2 Lewis definition

*According to Lewis, an acid is a substance that can take up an electron pair, while a base is a substance that can furnish an electron pair to form a covalent bond. Thus a Lewis acid is an electron-pair acceptor (electrophile or electron deficient) and a Lewis base is an electron-pair donor (nucelophile or electron rich).* This is the most fundamental and most general concept for acids and bases.

Remember that **all the Bronsted-Lowry bases are also Lewis bases but all Bronsted-Lowry acids are not Lewis acids.** Thus according to Lewis, an acid may also be a species without any proton **(aprotic).** Actually, **Lewis acids** may be of several types.

(i)    *Compounds whose central atom has an incomplete octet.* In other words, acids of this type are electron deficient molecules such as $BF_3$, $AlCl_3$, $GaCl_3$, etc.

$$F{-}B(F)(F) \ + \ :NH_3 \ \longrightarrow \ F{-}B(F)(F):NH_3$$

Acid           Base<br>(electron acceptor)    (electron donor)

Strength of such Lewis acids increases with

(*a*)    an increase in nuclear charge (*i.e.* positive charge) on the central atom, e.g. $H_3O^+ > H_2O > OH^- > O^{2-}$

(*b*)    an increase in the number and relative electronegativity of atom attached on the central atom, e.g. $SO_2 < SO_3$.

However, note the anomaly in case of relative acidic character of $BX_3$.

$$BF_3 < BCl_3 < BBr_3 < BI_3$$

(*c*)    a decrease in atomic radius of the central atom.

(ii)    *Compounds in which the central atom has available d-orbitals and may acquire more than an octet of valence electrons ;* $SiF_4$, $SnCl_2$ and $SnCl_4$ are typical examples.

$$SiF_4 \quad + \quad 2\overset{..}{\underset{..}{F}}:^- \quad \longrightarrow \quad SiF_6{}^{2-}$$

Lewis acid       Lewis base       Complex

Some other examples of this type are $PF_3$, $PF_5$, $SF_4$, $SeF_4$, $TeCl_4$, $TiX_4$ and $GeX_4$.

(iii)    *All simple cations, e.g.* $Na^+$, $Ag^+$, $Cu^{2+}$, $Al^{3+}$, $Fe^{3+}$ etc. They can combine with electron pair, e.g.

$$Ag^+ + 2:NH_3 \longrightarrow (H_3N:Ag:NH_3)^+$$

Acid strength of simple cations increases with

(*a*)    an increase in positive charge on the ion, e.g. $Fe^{2+} < Fe^{3+}$

(*b*)    a decrease in ionic radius, e.g. $K^+ < Na^+ < Li^+$

(*c*)    an increase in nuclear charge on atoms, e.g. $Li^+ < Be^{2+} < B^{3+}$

(iv)    *Molecules with a multiple bond between atoms of dissimilar electronegativities.* Examples are $O=C=O$, $O=S=O$, etc.

Here positive end of the $\pi$ bond dipole acts as an acid, e.g. $\overset{\delta-}{O} = \overset{\delta+}{C} = \overset{\delta-}{O}$.

(v)    *Elements with an electron sextet.* Oxygen and sulphur atoms contain six electrons in their valency shells and, therefore, act as Lewis acids.

**Lewis bases** may be of following types.

(i)    *All the simple negative ions, such as* $:\overset{..}{\underset{..}{C}}l:^-$, $:\overset{..}{\underset{..}{F}}:^-$

(ii)    Molecules with one or two unshared pair of electrons, e.g. $H_2O$, $NH_3$, $PH_3$, $ROH$, $R_2O$, $R_2S$, pyridine, $NX_3$ etc.

$$H-\overset{..}{\underset{..}{O}}-H \qquad\qquad :NH_3$$

The Lewis base nature of nitrogen trihalides follows the order : $NF_3 < NCl_3 < NBr_3 < NI_3$

This can be explained in terms of electronegativity of halogens. More is the electronegativity difference in the N—X bond, more is partial positive charge on N atom and thus lesser is the tendency of the electron pair to be donated by N.

(*iii*) Molecules with a multiple bond between atoms of dissimilar electronegativity, *e.g.* $O = C = O$, $O = S = O$, etc.

Here negative end of a π bond dipole acts as a base, *e.g.* $\overset{\delta-}{O} = \overset{\delta+}{C} = \overset{\delta-}{O}$.

(*iv*) Unsaturated hydrocarbons like $CH_2 = CH_2$, $HC \equiv CH$ etc. Here π electrons are available to Lewis acids.

## 2.9 Relative Strength of Acids and Bases

To be acidic in the *Lowry-Bronsted sense*, a molecule must of course contain hydrogen. Thus degree of acidity of these acids is determined largely by the ability of the atom holding hydrogen to accommodate the electron pair left behind after removing proton. The better this atom accommodates these electrons, the greater the extent to which the conjugate base is formed, and hence stronger will be the original acid. Two factors that mainly determine the ability of an atom to accommodate electrons are

(*a*) *Electronegativity.* By definition, a more electronegative atom has a greater avidity for electrons. Since among atoms of the row of the periodic table, electronegativity increases from left to right, we can explain following acidic order.

    (*i*)   $H—CH_3 < H—NH_2 < H—OH < H—F$      (*ii*)   $H—SiH_3 < H—PH_2 < H—SH < H—Cl$

(*b*) *Size of the atom.* Since a bigger atom permits greater dispersal of the charge of the electrons, it tends to stabilize a charged species. Further since among atoms of the same family, size increases on moving down the group, acidity also increases on moving down the group.

    (*i*)   $H—F < H—Cl < H—Br < H—I$      (*ii*)   $H—OH < H—SH < H—SeH < H—TeH$

Among **organic acids**, appreciable Lowry-Bronsted acidity can be expected from compounds containing O—H, N—H and S—H groups. Factors responsible for relative acidic character of organic acids are hybridisation, inductive effect, resonance, hydrogen bonding etc.

To be acidic in the **Lewis sense,** a molecule must be electron deficient, *i.e.* it should have an atom having only a sextet of electrons.

(*i*) *Electronegativity.* More is the electronegativity of the atom holding the electron pair less will be its basicity.

(*ii*) *Size of the atom.* The bigger the atom, weaker will be base.

(*iii*) *Charge on atom.* For a given atom, availability of electrons is greatest in an electron-rich, negatively charged molecule, and least in an electron-poor, positively charged molecule as in the following example.

$$OH^- > H_2O > H_3O^+; \qquad S^{2-} > HS^- > H_2S ; \qquad NH_2^- > NH_3$$

## TEST YOUR UNDERSTANDING - 2.8

1. Predict the relative acidity of

    (*a*)  $CH_3OH$ and $CH_3SH$    (*b*)  $NH_4^+$ and $H_3O^+$    (*c*)  $NH_4^+$ and $NH_3$    (*d*)  $H_2O$ and $OH^-$.

2. Arrange the following in the order of increasing acidity.

    (*a*)  $H_2O$, $NH_3$, HF and $CH_4$      (*b*)  HCl, HBr, HF and HI

3. Arrange the following in order of decreasing basic character.

    (*i*)  $CH_3OH$, $CH_3NH_2$ and $CH_3F$    (*ii*)  $OH^-$, $NH_2^-$, $CH_3^-$ and $F^-$    (*iii*)  $OH^-$, $SH^-$ and $SeH^-$

    (*iv*)  $F^-$, $Cl^-$, $Br^-$ and $I^-$.    (*v*)

4. Explain the fact that neither pure $H_2SO_4$ nor pure $HClO_4$ conducts electric current, but a mixture of the two does.

5. Account for the fact that nearly every oxygen containing organic compound dissolves in cold conc. $H_2SO_4$ to give a solution from which the compound can be recovered by dilution with water.

To be basic in either the **Lowry-Bronsted** *or* **the Lewis sense,** a molecule must have an electron pair available for sharing. The better an atom accommodates the electron pair, less will be the availability of this pair for sharing and hence weaker will be the base. The availability of these unshared electrons is determined largely by the following characteristics of the atom holding this pair.

## ISOMERISM

The existence of two or more compounds with the same molecular formula but different properties (physical, chemical or both) is known as isomerism ; and the compounds themselves are called *isomers*. The term was given by Berzelius. The difference in properties of the two isomers is due to the difference in the arrangement of atoms within their molecules. Isomerism may be of two types : structural isomerism and stereoisomerism. Here only structural isomerism is discussed, stereoisomerism is discussed in a separate chapter.

## 2.10 Structural Isomerism

When the isomers differ only in the arrangement of atoms or groups within the molecule, without any reference to space, these are known as **structural isomers** and the phenomenon as **structural isomerism.** Thus the structural isomers have the same molecular formula, but possess different structural formulae. Structural isomerism may again be of several types.

### 2.10.1 Chain, nuclear or skeleton isomerism

This type of isomerism is *due to the difference in the nature of the carbon chain (i.e. straight or branched)* which forms the nucleus of the molecule, *e.g.,*

(a)  $CH_3CH_2CH_2CH_3$   and  $CH_3\overset{\overset{\displaystyle CH_3}{|}}{C}HCH_3$    (b)  $CH_3CH_2CH=CH_2$   and  $CH_3\overset{}{C}=CH_2$

                                                     1-Butene                          Isobutene       $CH_3$

(c)  $CH_3CH_2CH_2CH_2OH$  and  $CH_3\overset{\overset{\displaystyle CH_3}{|}}{C}HCH_2OH$   (d)   [benzene ring with $CH_2CH_2CH_3$]   and   [benzene ring with $CH(CH_3)_2$]

         *n*-Butanol             Isobutanol                       *n*-Propylbenzene        Isopropylbenzene

### 2.10.2 Position isomerism

*It is due to the difference in the position of the substituent atom, group or an unsaturated linkage in the same carbon chain.* Such isomers are also called **regiomers.** Examples are

**$C_3H_7OH$ :**        $CH_3—CH_2—CH_2—OH$              $CH_3—\overset{\overset{\displaystyle OH}{|}}{C}H—CH_3$

                       *n*-Propanol (Propanol-1)         iso-Propanol (Propanol-2)

**$C_4H_8$ :**        $CH_2=CH—CH_2—CH_3$            $CH_3—CH=CH—CH_3$

                         Butene–1                        Butene -2

**$C_6H_{14}$ :**      $CH_3CH_2CH_2\overset{}{C}HCH_3$           $CH_3CH_2\overset{}{C}HCH_2CH_3$

                           $CH_3$                       $CH_3$

                       2-Methylpentane               3-Methylpentane

**$C_8H_{10}$**         [benzene ring with $CH_3$, $CH_3$]    [benzene ring with $CH_3$, $CH_3$]    [benzene ring with $CH_3$, $CH_3$]    [benzene ring with $CH_2CH_3$]

                       *o*-Xylene       *m*-Xylene       *p*-Xylene       Ethylbenzene

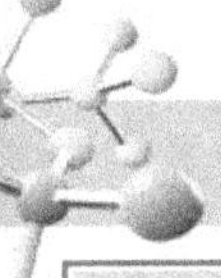

*Example 7 :*

**Write the total number of isomeric alkenes corresponding to molecular formula $C_5H_{10}$.**

*Solution :*

For knowing the possible number of isomers of a compound, follow the following points.

(*i*)  First write down the possible number of isomeric parent alkanes.

(*ii*)  Take one isomeric alkane, introduce the given functional group (*e.g.* double bond) at different positions so as to get different isomeric compounds.

(*iii*)  Repeat the procedure for other isomeric alkanes.

(*iv*)  Observe the possibility of geometrical and optical isomerism in all the isomeric compounds, so obtained.

Take the example of $C_5H_{10}$.

(*i*)  The parent hydrocarbon, pentane, has three isomers.

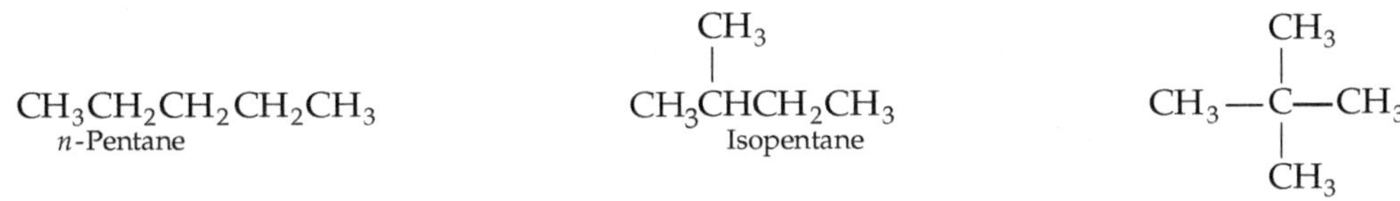

(*ii*)  Now introduce one double bond, first in *n*-pentane for which there are two possibilities.

$$CH_3CH_2CH_2CH=CH_2 \qquad CH_3CH_2CH=CHCH_3$$
Pentene-1 · · · · · Pentene-2 (*cis* and *trans*)

From the formula of pentene-2, it is obvious that it can exist in *cis* and *trans* forms.

(*iii*)  Now introduce one double bond in various possible positions in isopentane.

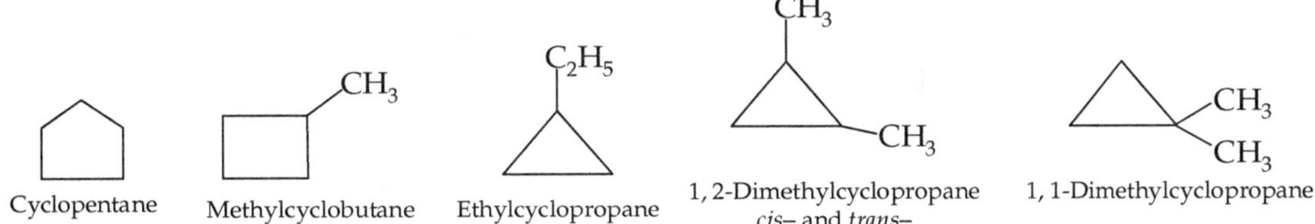

Observe that none of them can exhibit geometrical and optical isomerism.

(*iv*)  From the formula of neopentane it is evident that a double bond can't be introduced at any position.

So total number of isomeric alkenes corresponding to $C_5H_{10}$ is **six**.

Remember that $C_5H_{10}$ can also exist as cycloalkanes of following structures :

Cyclopentane    Methylcyclobutane    Ethylcyclopropane    1, 2-Dimethylcyclopropane *cis*– and *trans*–    1, 1-Dimethylcyclopropane

## 2.10.3  Ring-chain isomerism

This type of isomerism is *due to difference in mode of linkage of carbon atoms and the isomers may have either open chain or closed structure, e.g.,*

$C_3H_6$ :  $CH_3$—$CH=CH_2$

Propene

Cyclopropane

$C_4H_6$ :  $CH_3CH_2C \equiv CH$    $CH_2=CH$—$CH=CH_2$

1-Butyne    1, 3-Butadiene    Cyclobutene

### 2.10.4 Functional isomerism

This type of isomerism is *due to difference in the nature of functional group present in the isomers.* The following pairs of compounds always form functional isomers with each other.

(*i*)   Dienes, allenes and alkynes

(*ii*)  Alchols and ethers

(*iii*) Aldehydes, ketones and unsaturated alchols

(*iv*)  Carboxylic acids and esters

(*v*)   1°, 2° and 3° amines

(*vi*)  Nitroalkanes and alkyl nitrites

(*vii*) Cyanides and isocyanides

(*viii*) Aromatic alcohols, phenols and ethers

Few examples of each pair are given below.

(*a*)   $C_4H_6$:

$CH_2 = CH—CH = CH_2$ , $CH_2 = C = CHCH_3$ , $CH_3—CH \equiv C—CH_3$

Buta-1, 3-diene  ·  1,2–Butadiene (allene)  ·  Butyne-2

(note the presence of two C = C linkage)  ·  (note the C $\equiv$ C linkage)

(*b*)   $C_2H_6O$:

$CH_3—CH_2OH$         $CH_3—O—CH_3$

Ethyl alcohol           Dimethyl ether

(note the alcoholic group)  (note the ether group)

(*c*)   $C_3H_6O$:

$CH_3CH_2CHO$         $CH_3COCH_3$         $CH_2 = CH—CH_2OH$

Propanal                 Acetone                Allyl alcohol

(note the different functional groups in 3 isomers)

(*d*)   $C_3H_6O_2$:

$CH_3CH_2COOH$         $CH_3COOCH_3$

Propanoic acid          Methyl acetate

(note the acidic group)   (note the ester group)

(*e*)   $C_3H_9N$:

$CH_3CH_2CH_2NH_2$       $CH_3NHC_2H_5$         $(CH_3)_3N$

n-Propylamine            Methylethylamine       Trimethylamine

(a primary amine)        (a sec. amine)         (a *tert*-amine)

(*f*)   $RNO_2$:

$RNO_2$                  $RONO$

Nitroalkanes            Alkyl nitrites

(Note the nitro group)   (Note the nitrite group)

(*g*)   $RCN$:

$RC \equiv N$            $RN \overset{+}{\equiv} C$

Alkyl cyanides          Alkyl isocyanides

(Note the cyanide group)  (Note the isocyanide group)

(*h*)   $C_7H_8O$:

Benzyl alcohol  ·  o-, m-, p- Cresols

(Note the **alcoholic group**)  (Note the **phenolic group**)

(*i*)   $C_8H_8O$:

Acetophenone   Phenylacetaldehyde  ·  o-, m-, p-Methylbenzaldehydes

### 2.10.5 Metamerism

*It is due to difference in nature of alkyl groups attached to the same functional group.* This type of isomerism is shown by compounds of the same homologous series. For example,

$CH_3—O—C_3H_7$-n          $CH_3—O—CH(CH_3)_2$          $C_2H_5—O—C_2H_5$

Methylpropyl ether          Methylisopropyl ether          Diethyl ether

## 2.10.6 Tautomerism

*Tautomerism[1] may be defined as a phenomenon in which a single compound exists in two readily interconvertible structures that differ markedly in the relative position of at least one atomic nucleus, generally hydrogen.* The two different structures are known as tautomers of each other. Sometimes the term tautomerism is also called as **desmotropism** (Greek *desmos-bond* ; *tropos-turn*), since the interconversion of the two forms involves a change of bonds, or **dynamic isomerism** as the two forms are in dynamic equilibrium with each other. Other uncommon names for the tautomerism are *kryptomerism, allelotropism* or *merotropy* ; however, tautomerism is the most widely accepted term.

Alternatively, tautomerism may be of two types.

(a)  **Dyad system.** When the hydrogen atom migrates from atom number one to atom number two, e.g.

$$H-C \equiv N \rightleftharpoons C \overset{-}{\equiv} N - H \qquad\qquad H - N \overset{O}{\underset{O}{\diagdown}} \rightleftharpoons H - O - N = O$$

$$\text{nitrile} \qquad \text{isonitrile} \qquad\qquad \text{nitro} \qquad\qquad \text{nitrite}$$

(b)  **Triad system.** When the hydrogen atom migrates from atom one to atom three in a chain. It may again be of several types, viz.

(i)  Keto-enol system :
$$-\overset{H}{\underset{|}{\overset{|}{C}}}{}^1-\overset{|}{\overset{2}{C}}=\overset{3}{O} \rightleftharpoons -C=\overset{|}{C}-OH$$
$$\text{keto} \qquad\qquad \text{enol}$$

(ii)  Lactam-lactim or amido-imido system :
$$-\overset{H}{\underset{|}{\overset{|}{N}}}{}^1-\overset{2}{C}=\overset{3}{O} \rightleftharpoons -N=\overset{|}{C}-OH$$

(iii)  Nitro-acinitro system :
$$-\overset{H}{\underset{|}{\overset{|}{C}}}-N\overset{O}{\underset{O}{\diagdown}} \rightleftharpoons -\overset{|}{C}=N\overset{OH}{\underset{O}{\diagdown}}$$

Among the several types of tautomerism *keto-enol tautomerism* is the most important. In this type, one form (tautomer) exists as a *ketone* while the other exists as an enol[2]. The two simplest examples are of acetone and phenol.

$$CH_3-\overset{O}{\overset{||}{C}}-CH_3 \rightleftharpoons CH_3-\overset{OH}{\overset{|}{C}}=CH_2$$

*keto* form         *enol* form
                    (negligible amount)
        Acetone

*keto* form         *enol* form
(negligible amount)  Phenol

However, the most widely studied example of keto-enol tautomerism is that of acetoacetic ester (ethyl acetoacetate).

$$H_3C-\overset{O}{\overset{||}{C}}-CH_2COOC_2H_5 \rightleftharpoons CH_3-\overset{OH}{\overset{|}{C}}=CHCOOC_2H_5$$
$$\text{\textit{keto} form (92.3\%)} \qquad\qquad \text{\textit{enolic} form (7.7\%)}$$

Acetoacetic ester

The two forms are readily interconvertible by acid or base catalyst, and under ordinary conditions surface of the glass is sufficient to catalyse the interconversion. The exact composition of the equilibrium depends upon the nature of the compound, solvent, temperature, etc. *The conversion of a keto form into enol form is known as* **enolisation.** The two forms of the acetoacetic ester have been isolated under suitable conditions.

---

1.  The term was introduced by Laar.
2.  When the hydroxyl group is attached to a carbon atom which in turn is attached to another carbon atom by means of a double bond, its nature becomes acidic (difference from alcoholic hydroxyl group which is neutral). This type of hydroxyl group is known as enolic. In short,

$$-\overset{OH}{\underset{}{\overset{|}{C}}}=C \qquad\qquad -\overset{OH}{\underset{|}{\overset{|}{C}}}-C$$

enolic group (acidic)         hydroxyl group (neutral)

**Mechanism of acid catalysed enolisation :**

$$CH_3-\overset{O}{\overset{||}{C}}-CH_2R \underset{}{\overset{H^+}{\rightleftharpoons}} CH_3-\overset{OH}{\underset{+}{\overset{|}{C}}}-\overset{\underset{|}{CHR}}{\underset{H}{}} \xrightarrow[-H^+]{H_2O} CH_3-\overset{OH}{\overset{|}{C}}=CHR$$

**Mechanism of base catalysed enolisation :**

$$CH_3-\overset{O}{\overset{||}{C}}-CH_2R \overset{OH^-}{\rightleftharpoons} CH_3-\overset{O}{\overset{||}{C}}-\bar{C}HR \longrightarrow CH_3-\overset{O^-}{\overset{|}{C}}=CHR \xrightarrow[\text{by } H_2O]{\text{protonation}} CH_3-\overset{OH}{\overset{|}{C}}=CHR$$

The decreasing ease of enolisation of the various ketones is

$$\underset{\text{Nearly 100\% enolic form}}{\underbrace{\overset{OH}{\underset{}{\bigcirc}} \quad \approx \quad \overset{O}{\underset{}{\bigcirc}}\text{-CHO} \quad \approx \quad C_6H_5-\overset{O}{\overset{||}{C}}-CH_2-\overset{O}{\overset{||}{C}}-C_6H_5}} > C_6H_5-\overset{O}{\overset{||}{C}}-CH_2-\overset{O}{\overset{||}{C}}-CH_3$$

$$> CH_3-\overset{O}{\overset{||}{C}}-CH_2-\overset{O}{\overset{||}{C}}-CH_3 > CH_3-\overset{O}{\overset{||}{C}}-\underset{\underset{CH_3}{|}}{CH}-\overset{O}{\overset{||}{C}}-CH_3 > CH_3-\overset{O}{\overset{||}{C}}-CH_2-\overset{O}{\overset{||}{C}}-OC_2H_5$$

Steric hindrance decreases stability

$$\underset{\text{Negligible enolic form}}{\underbrace{> H_5C_2O-\overset{O}{\overset{||}{C}}-CH_2-\overset{O}{\overset{||}{C}}-OC_2H_5 > R-CH_2-\overset{O}{\overset{||}{C}}-CH_2-R > R-CH_2-\overset{O}{\overset{||}{C}}-H}}$$

Keto-enol tautomerism in acetoacetic ester is proved by the fact that under ordinary conditions, the compound gives the properties of the ketonic group (reaction with hydroxylamine to form oxime, reaction with phenylhydrazine to form phenylhydrazone, reduction to form secondary alcohol etc.) as well as that of the enolic group (reaction with PCl$_5$, NH$_3$, bromine water, FeCl$_3$, acidic character etc.)

$$\underset{\substack{\textit{ketonic} \text{ form} \\ \text{(note the presence of a ketonic group)}}}{H_3C-\overset{O}{\overset{||}{C}}-CH_2COOC_2H_5} \rightleftharpoons \underset{\substack{\textit{enolic} \text{ form} \\ \text{(note the presence of a double bond and} \\ \text{acidic —OH group)}}}{H_3C-\overset{OH}{\overset{|}{C}}=CHCOOC_2H_5}$$

Note that in *all the examples of keto-enol tautomerism the two isomeric forms are interconvertible by the migration of a proton from one atom (carbon) to other with the simultaneous shifting of bonds.* Remember that *keto-enol tautomerism is possible only in those* **aldehydes and ketones which have at least one α-hydrogen atom** which can convert the ketonic group to the enolic group. Examine the following compounds.

(*i*)
$$\underset{\text{ketonic form}}{CH_3-\overset{O}{\overset{||}{C}}-CH_2-\overset{O}{\overset{||}{C}}-CH_3} \rightleftharpoons \underset{\substack{\text{enolic form} \\ \text{Acetylacetone}}}{CH_3-\overset{OH}{\overset{|}{C}}=CH-\overset{O}{\overset{||}{C}}-CH_3}$$

(*ii*)
$$\underset{\substack{\text{ketonic form} \\ \text{Acetophenone}}}{C_6H_5-\overset{O}{\overset{||}{C}}-CH_3} \rightleftharpoons \underset{\text{enolic form}}{C_6H_5-\overset{OH}{\overset{|}{C}}=CH_2}$$

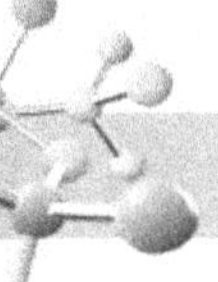

(*iii*)
$$CH_3-CH_2-\overset{\overset{O}{\|}}{C}-H \rightleftharpoons CH_3-CH=\overset{\overset{OH}{|}}{C}-H$$
ketonic form    enolic form
Propionaldehyde

(*iv*) ketonic form ⇌ enolic form
Cyclohexanone

(*v*) ⇌ (Tautomerism possible)

(*vi*) ⇌ (Tautomerism possible)

(*vii*) ⇌ (Tautomerism possible)

(*viii*)
$$C_6H_5-\overset{\overset{O}{\|}}{C}-H$$
Benzaldehyde
**(tautomerism not possible)**

(*ix*)
$$C_6H_5-\overset{\overset{O}{\|}}{C}-C_6H_5$$
Benzophenone
**(tautomerism not possible)**

(*x*)
**(Tautomerism not possible)**

(*xi*)
**(Tautomerism not possible)**

**Distinction from resonance***. The tautomeric forms are quite chemically distinct entites and can be separated (in suitable cases *e.g.* acetoacetic ester) and characterised. On the other hand, resonating forms differ only in the distribution of electrons and can never be separated from one another since neither of them has any real existence. Moreover, the position of an ion (cation, generally $H^+$ or anion) in tautomers differs by several Angstrom units whereas the position of the nuclei in resonating structures never differ by more than 0.3 Angstrom units *e.g.* in the two resonating structures of benzene the two extremes for the carbon-carbon bond differ only by 0.20 Å (C—C, 1.54 Å ; C = C, 1.34 Å). The important differences between resonance and tautomerism can be summarised below.

1. Tautomerism involves a change in the position of atom (generally hydrogen), while resonance involves a change in the position of the unshared or π electron only.

2. Tautomers are definite compounds and may be separated and isolated. Resonating structures are only imaginary and can't be isolated.

3. The two tautomeric forms have different structures (*i.e.* functional groups). The various resonating structures have the same functional group.

4. Tautomers are in dynamic equilibrium with each other, resonating structures are not in dynamic equilibrium.

5. Tautomerism has no effect on bond lengths, while resonance affect the bond lengths (single bond is shortened while the double bond becomes lengthier).

6. Tautomerism does not lower the energy of the molecule and hence does not play any role in stabilising the molecule, while resonance decreases the energy and hence increases the stability of the molecule.

7. Tautomerism is indicated by '⇌' while resonance by '⟷'.

8. Tautomerism may occur in planar or non-planar molecules, while resonance occurs only in planar molecules.

---

*    When two or more structures have practically the same position of all the atomic nuclei but differ only in the average distribution of electrons, the structures are known as resonating structures and the phenomenon as resonance.

**Distinction from isomerism.** In fact there is no sharp line of distinction between isomers and tautomers since some substances which are isomers under normal conditions can be converted into tautomeric forms under more drastic conditions. For example, propyl and iso-propyl bromides are isomeric compounds under normal conditions but form an equilibrium mixture on heating at 250°C in a sealed tube.

$$CH_3CH_2CH_2Br \xrightleftharpoons{250°C} \underset{\text{Isopropyl bromide}}{CH_3\overset{\displaystyle Br}{\underset{\displaystyle |}{C}}HCH_3}$$

$$\underset{\text{Propyl bromide}}{\phantom{CH_3CH_2CH_2Br}}$$

And hence the *dynamic isomerism* represents the better term for this phenomenon than *tautomerism*.

**Distinction from molecular rearrangement.** Although there is no sharp difference between tautomerism and molecular rearrangement, yet the two can be distinguished by the fact that the former is a rapid and reversible phenomenon whereas the latter needs neither be reversible nor rapid.

**Percentage composition of tautomeric mixture.** The percentage composition of keto-enol tautomeric mixture depends upon the relative stabilities of the two forms.

(i) Ketonic form predominates in simple monocarbonyl compounds like acetaldehyde, acetone and cyclohexanone. This is due to greater strength (about 364 kJ mol$^{-1}$) of the carbon oxygen double bond present in the ketonic form than the carbon-carbon double bond (250 kJ mol$^{-1}$) present in enolic form.

(ii) Enolic form predominates in compounds containing two carbonyl groups separated by a —$CH_2$— group ; *i.e.* 1, 3-dicarbonyl compounds, *viz.* acetoacetic ester, acetylacetone, benzoylacetophenone. This is due to greater stabilization of the enolic form due to following two factors.

    (a) Presence of conjugation which increases stability of molecule due to resonance.

    (b) Formation of intramolecular hydrogen bonds between enolic hydroxyl group and second carbonyl group which leads to stabilisation of the molecule.

Intramolecular hydrogen bonding in
the enolic form of acetylacetone

Intramolecular hydrogen bonding
in acetoacetic ester

Thus polar protic solvent (like water, methanol, acetic acid etc.) which tends to stabilise the keto form relative to the enol form will reduce the enol content. On the other hand, non-polar solvents (like benzene, hexane etc.) which do not form hydrogen bonds, tend to increase the enol content. Thus the enol content of acetylacetone in ethanol is only 76%, while in hexane it is as much as 92%.

*Example 8 :*

**Write down structures of the isomeric nitroalkanes of the formula $C_4H_9NO_2$. Which of them will show phenomenon of tautomerism?**

*Solution :*

$C_4H_9NO_2$ (Nitrobutane) can have following isomeric structures

The last one, 3° nitroalkane, can't exhibit tautomerism.

**Example 9 :**

Give mechanism of the following reactions : $C_6H_5 - \overset{\overset{O}{\|}}{C} - CD_2CH_3 \xrightarrow{H^+}$

**Solution :**

$$C_6H_5 - \overset{\overset{O}{\|}}{C} - CD_2CH_3 \underset{}{\overset{H^+}{\rightleftharpoons}} C_6H_5 - \overset{\overset{OH}{|}}{\overset{+}{C}} - CDCH_3 \longrightarrow C_6H_5 - \overset{\overset{OH}{|}}{C} - \overset{+}{C}DCH_3 \longrightarrow C_6H_5 - \overset{\overset{OH}{|}}{C} = CDCH_3 + D^+$$

(with D shown on the α-carbon and β-positions)

**Example 10 :**

**Which of the following compound can exhibit tautomerism?**

(a) 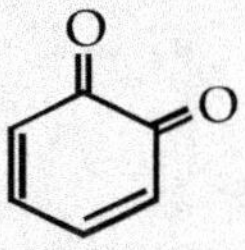 cyclohexadienone (2,4-dien-1-one with additional ketone)

(b) 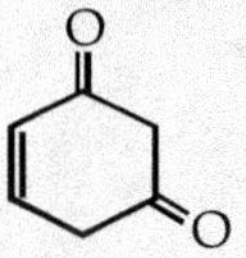 cyclohex-2-ene-1,4-dione type structure

(c) 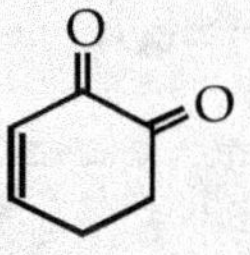 cyclohex-2-enone with additional ketone

(d) 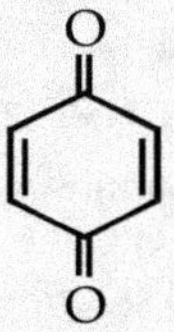 benzoquinone (1,4-dione)

(e) $H_2N - \overset{\overset{O}{\|}}{C} - NH_2$

(f) 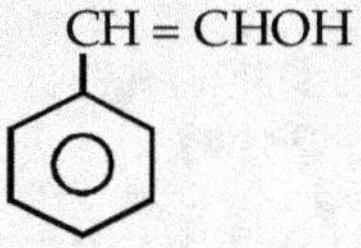 benzene ring with $CH = CHOH$

(g) 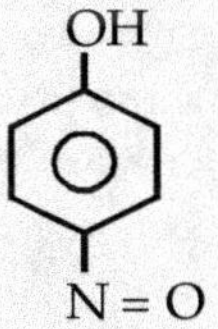 phenol ring with $OH$ at top and $N = O$ at bottom

(h) $H_2N - \overset{\overset{S}{\|}}{C} - NH_2$

**Solution :**

All except (a) and (d) show tautomerism, (a) and (d) do not have any α-H.

# EXERCISE 2.1 (MCQ - ONE option correct)

1. In ammonia, nitrogen is $sp^3$ hybridised. Which statement is true about the hybrid orbitals of nitrogen in ammonia?
   (a) All the four $sp^3$ hybrid orbitals are equivalent
   (b) One $sp^3$ hybrid orbital is different from the remaining three
   (c) Two $sp^3$ hybrid orbitals are different from the remaining two
   (d) All the four $sp^3$ orbitals are non-equivalent.

2. In which of the following you would expect, the normal tetrahedral bond angle (109.5°) ?
   (a) $NH_3$      (b) $H_2O$
   (c) $BF_4^-$      (d) None of the three.

3. Which of the following statements is true ?
   (a) Toluene has zero dipole moment
   (b) Toluene has a definite dipole moment due to + I character of the —$CH_3$ group
   (c) Toluene has a definite dipole moment due to difference in electronegativity of the carbon atom of the nucleus and that of the side chain.
   (d) Toluene has a definite dipole moment due to resonance.

4. Which of the following is true regarding the direction of the dipole ?
   (a) C $\rightleftharpoons$ H and C $\rightleftharpoons$ D
   (b) C $\leftrightharpoons$ H and C $\leftrightharpoons$ D
   (c) C $\rightleftharpoons$ H and C $\leftrightharpoons$ D
   (d) C $\leftrightharpoons$ H and C $\rightleftharpoons$ D.

5. Isocyanic acid, HNCO can be represented by the following three contributing structures

$$H—\overset{..}{N} = C = \overset{..}{\underset{..}{O}} \longleftrightarrow H—\overset{..}{\underset{..}{N}}—C \equiv \overset{+}{O}: \longleftrightarrow H—\overset{+}{N} \equiv C—\overset{..}{\underset{..}{O}}:{}^{-}$$
$$\quad\quad I \quad\quad\quad\quad\quad\quad\quad II \quad\quad\quad\quad\quad\quad\quad III$$

   Order of stability of the three contributing structures is
   (a) I > II > III      (b) I > III > II
   (c) I > II = III      (d) I = II = III.

6. Which of the following resonating structure is not possible for 2, 4, 6-trinitroiodobenzene

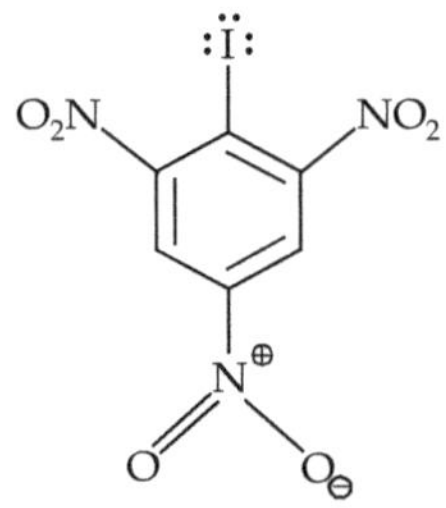

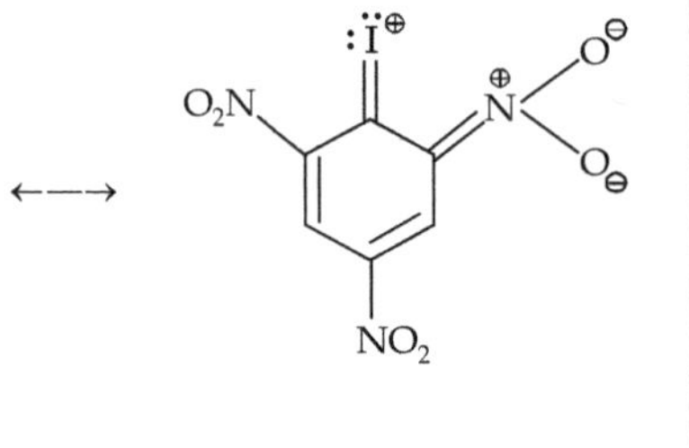

(a) I      (b) II
(c) III      (d) None of them.

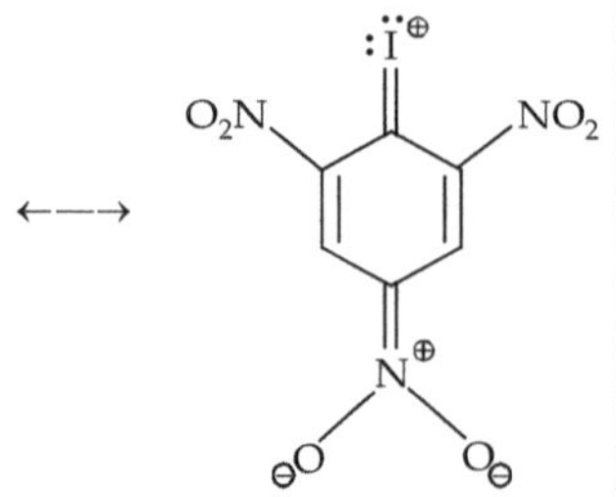

7. Which of the following statement is true regarding the stability of $NH_4^+$ and $CH_3^+$ ?
   (a) Both are equally stable
   (b) $NH_4^+$ ion is less stable than $CH_3^+$ ion because is the former +ve charge is present on the more elecronegative element
   (c) $NH_4^+$ ion is more stable than $CH_3^+$ because the former is an inorganic ion, while the latter is an organic ion
   (d) $NH_4^+$ ion is more stable because here N has complete octet of electrons, while H has duet.

8. The carbon-oxygen bond length in sod. formate and $CaCO_3$ is respectively
   (a) 1.27 Å and 1.31 Å    (b) 1.31 Å and 1.27 Å
   (c) 1.27 Å and 1.27 Å    (d) 1.31 Å and 1.31 Å.

9. Which is the correct order of stability of the following three carbonium ions ?

$$CH_2 = CH\overset{+}{C}HCH_3 \quad CH_2 = \overset{\overset{\displaystyle CH_3}{|}}{C}—\overset{+}{C}H_2 \quad CH_3CH = CH\overset{+}{C}H_2$$
$$\quad\quad I \quad\quad\quad\quad\quad\quad II \quad\quad\quad\quad\quad\quad III$$

   (a) I > II > III      (b) II > I > III
   (c) I ≈ III > II      (d) All are equally stable.

10. Hyperconjugation is not possible in
    (a) $CH_3 C \equiv CH$      (b) $CH_3CH_2CHO$
    (c) $CH_3CN$      (d) $(CH_3)_3CCH = CH_2$.

11. Which of the forces is responsible for the solubility of NaCl in water?
    (a) Ion-dipole attraction   (b) Hydrogen bond
    (c) Both (a) and (b)      (d) None of the two.

12. Stain produced by butter on a cloth is removed by
    (a) rubbing with water because of formation of hydrogen bond
    (b) benzene because of dipole-dipole interaction
    (c) carbon tetrachloride because of presence of very weak forces between butter and carbon tetrachloride
    (d) none of the above.

13. Which of the following statement is true?
    (a) Lithium acetylacetonate and beryllium acetylacetonate are soluble in chloroform and have very high melting points
    (b) Both are insoluble in chloroform and have low melting points
    (c) The two differs in their melting points and resemble in solubility
    (d) None of the above is true.

14. Which of the following statement is true for *n*-butanol and diethyl ether ?
    (a) Both have same solubility in water & also boil at high temperature than expected from their molecular weight
    (b) *n*-Butanol is more soluble in water and boils at a higher temperature than diethyl ether
    (c) Both have same solubility in water, but *n*-butanol boils at a higher temperature than diethyl ether
    (d) None of the above is true.

15. Which of the following structures are expected to have a net dipole moment ? Assuming that electronegativities of atoms A, X and Y are 5, 3 and 1 respectively.

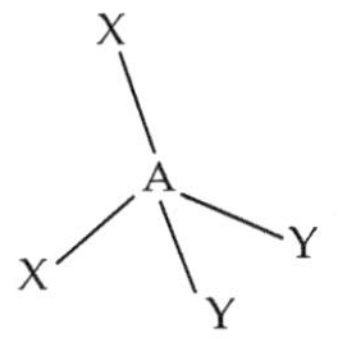

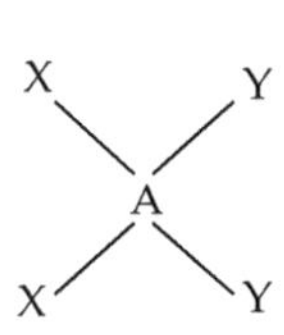

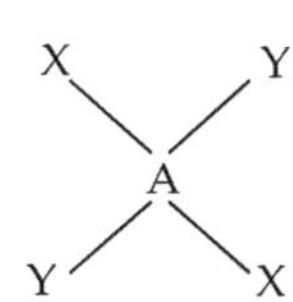

Tetrahedral, (*i*)  Square, (*ii*)  Square, (*iii*)

(*a*)  (*i*) and (*ii*)

(*b*)  (*ii*) and (*iii*)

(*c*)  (*i*) and (*iii*)

(*d*)  All the three.

**16.** Among closely related molecules where the same atom loses proton, which of the following statement is true ?

(*a*)  Increase in positive charge decreases acidity

(*b*)  Increase in negative charge decreases acidity

(*c*)  Increase in negative charge increases acidity

(*d*)  Nothing can be said.

**17.** Which of the following is true regarding basic character of the two species ?

$$H_3C \bar{\colon} \qquad \colon \bar{\ddot{F}} \colon$$
$$\text{I} \qquad\qquad \text{II}$$

(*a*)  I and II have nearly equal basic character

(*b*)  I is much more stronger base than II

(*c*)  II is much more stronger base than I

(*d*)  II is slightly more basic than I.

**18.** Which of the following is true ?

(*a*)  Acetic acid is a stronger acid in water than in methanol

(*b*)  Acetic acid is a stronger acid in methanol than in water

(*c*)  Acetic acid is as acidic in water as in methanol

(*d*)  None of the above in true.

**19.** The total number of chain isomers for the compound shown in side is

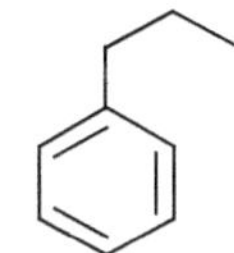

(*a*)  2

(*b*)  4

(*c*)  5

(*d*)  8.

**20.** The possible number of metamers of the compound shown in side is

—OCH$_2$CH$_3$

(*a*)  2

(*b*)  3

(*c*)  4

(*d*)  5.

**21.** Predict the product P

$$CH_3CO\ CH_2COOC_2H_5 \xrightarrow{D^+} P$$

(*a*)  $CH_3C(OH) = CHCOOC_2H_5$

(*b*)  $CH_3C(OD) = CHCOOC_2H_5$

(*c*)  $CH_3C(OH) = CDCOOC_2H_5$

(*d*)  $CH_3C(OD) = CDCOOC_2H_5$.

**22.** In which of the following property *cis*-3-hexene differs from *trans*-3-hexene ?

(*a*)  melting point

(*b*)  dipole moment

(*c*)  solubility in ethanol

(*d*)  All of the three.

**23.** The number of isomers possible for $C_4H_8$ is

(*a*)  2

(*b*)  3

(*c*)  4

(*d*)  5

**24.** The possible number of isomers for $C_4H_4O_4$ is

(*a*)  2

(*b*)  3

(*c*)  4

(*d*)  5

**25.** Keto enol tautomerism is observed in

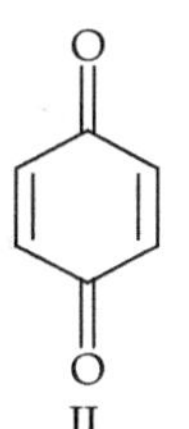

I    II    III    IV

(*a*)  IV

(*b*)  I, III, IV

(*c*)  I, IV

(*d*)  II, III, IV.

**26.** Which one of the following has most acidic α-hydrogen atom?

(*a*)  $CH_3CHO$

(*b*)  $CH_3COCH_3$

(*c*)  $CH_3COCH_2COOC_2H_5$

(*d*)  $CH_3COCH_2CHO$.

**27.** Urea can show which type of isomerism ?

(*a*)  Position

(*b*)  Functional

(*c*)  Keto-enol tautomerism

(*d*)  both (*b*) and (*c*).

**28.** Which of the following has a bond formed by overlap of $sp^3$–$sp$ hybrid orbitals ?

(*a*)  $CH_3—C \equiv C—H$

(*b*)  $CH_3—CH = CH—CH_3$

(*c*)  $CH_2=CH—CH=CH_2$

(*d*)  $HC \equiv CH$.

**29.** The hybridisation of carbon atoms in C—C single bond of $HC \equiv C—CH = CH_2$ is

(*a*)  $sp^3$–$sp^3$

(*b*)  $sp^2 - sp^3$

(*c*)  $sp - sp^2$

(*d*)  $sp^3 - sp$.

**30.** In the compound $CH_2 = CH—CH_2—CH_2—C \equiv CH$, the $C_2$—$C_3$ bond is of the type

(*a*)  $sp - sp^2$

(*b*)  $sp^3 - sp^3$

(*c*)  $sp - sp^3$

(*d*)  $sp^2 - sp^3$.

**31.** Formic acid is considered as a resonance hybrid of the four structures.

I    II    III    IV

Which of the followings order is correct for the stability of the four contributing structures ?

(*a*)  I > II > III > V

(*b*)  I > II > IV > III

(*c*)  I > III > II > IV

(*d*)  I > IV > III > II.

**32.** Examine the following two structures for the anilinium ion and choose the correct statement from the ones, given below.

I    II

(*a*)  II is not an acceptable canonical structure because carbonium ions are less stable than ammonium ion

(*b*)  II is not an acceptable canonical structure because it is non-aromatic

(*c*)  II is not an acceptable canonical structure because the nitrogen has 10 valence electrons

(*d*)  II is an acceptable canonical structure.

**33.** The most unlikely representation of resonance structures of *p*-nitrophenoxide ion is

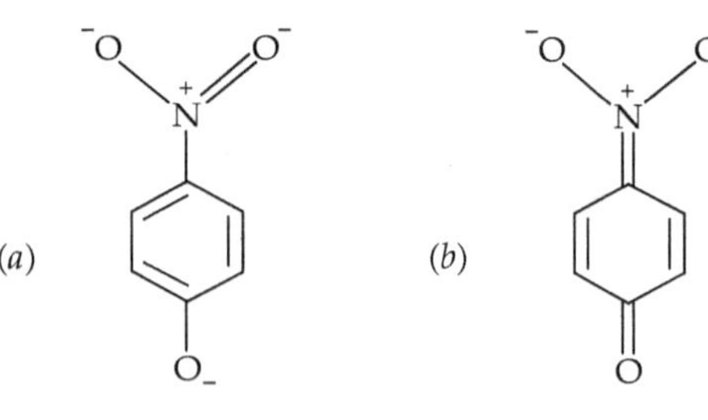

(*a*)             (*b*)

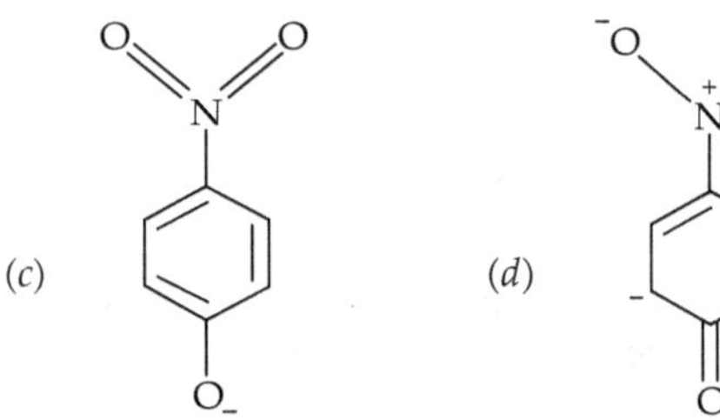

(*c*)             (*d*)

**34.** The total number of isomers for the compound of the formula $C_7H_8O$ is

(*a*)   3            (*b*)   4

(*c*)   5            (*d*)   6.

**35.** The enolic form of acetone contains

(*a*)   9 σ bonds, 1 π bond and 2 lone pairs

(*b*)   8 σ bonds, 2 π bonds and 2 lone pairs

(*c*)   10 σ bonds, 1 π bond and 1 lone pair

(*d*)   9 σ bonds, 2 π bonds and 1 lone pair.

**36.** Tautomerism is not shown by

(*a*) 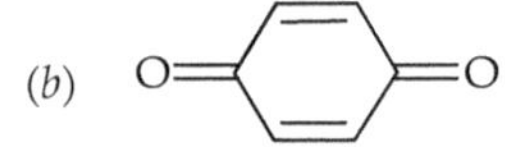 $—CH = CH—OH$

(*b*) 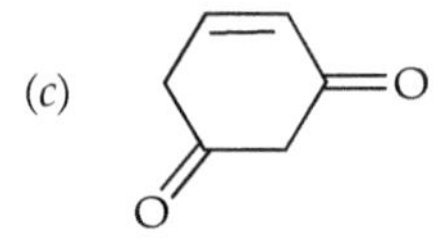

(*c*) 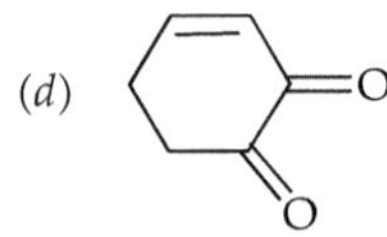

(*d*) 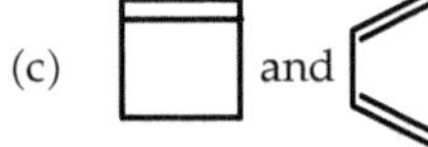

**37.** Which of the following statement is true regarding acidity of $CH_3COCH_2CH_3$(I) and $CH_2(CN)_2$(II).

(*a*)   I > II          (*b*)   I < II

(*c*)   I = II          (*d*)   Not definite

**38.** Which of the following pairs represent the phenomenon of resonance?

(*a*)   $CH_3CH_2 - \overset{\overset{O}{\|}}{C} - H$ aend $CH_3CH = \overset{\overset{OH}{|}}{C} - H$

(*b*)   $CH_3 \overset{+}{C}HOH$ and $CH_3CH = \overset{+}{O}H$

(*c*) 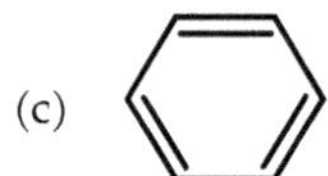 and

(*d*)   None

**39.** Cyanate ion, $CNO^-$ has three important resonating structures

$$O = C = N^- \longleftrightarrow \;^-O - C \equiv N \longleftrightarrow \;^+O \equiv C - N^{2-}$$
$$\quad\quad\text{I} \quad\quad\quad\quad\quad\quad \text{II} \quad\quad\quad\quad\quad\quad \text{III}$$

Which of the above structures contributes more to the resonance hybrid?

(*a*)   I           (*b*)   II

(*c*)   I and II equal      (*d*)   All equal

**40.** The oxidation states of O, C and N in the above II structure respectively are

(*a*)   –2, +4, 3        (*b*)   –2, +4 and –3

(*c*)   –1, +4 and zero   (*d*)   –2, +4 and +5

**41.** Arrange the following structures in decreasing order of σ to π bond ratio

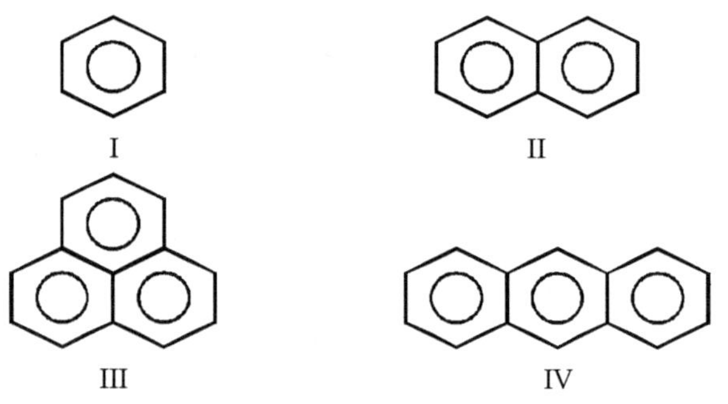

(*a*)   IV > III > I > II     (*b*)   III > I > II > IV

(*c*)   III = IV > II > I     (*d*)   III = IV > I > II

**42.** The carbon-chlorine bond length is shortest in

(*a*)   $CH_3Cl$        (*b*)   $CH_2Cl_2$

(*c*)   $CHCl_3$        (*d*)   $CCl_4$

**43.** The number of *p*-orbitals in $\overset{+}{C}H_3$ is

(*a*)   2           (*b*)   3

(*c*)   4           (*d*)   zero

**44.** In which of the following C – C bond distance is maximum?

(*a*)   $H_2C = CH_2$      (*b*)   $BrHC = CHBr$

(*c*)                (*d*)   $H_2C = CBr_2$

**45.** The bond between Li and F is ionic, while that between Li and Cl it is covalent, what should be the nature of bond between Li and Br?

(*a*)   ionic         (*b*)   covalent

(*c*)   coordinate     (*d*)   nothing certain

**46.** Which of the following involves cleavage of covalent bond?

(*a*)   melting of KCN    (*b*)   melting of silica

(*c*)   boiling of $H_2O$    (*d*)   boiling of $CF_4$

**47.** A diatomic molecule has a dipole moment of 1.2 D, if the bond distance between the atoms is 1Å, the percentage of electronic charge on each atom would be

(*a*)   29%        (*b*)   25%

(*c*)   20%        (*d*)   15%

**48.** Let the heat of hydrogenation of benzene is 61 kcal/mol. and its resonance energy is 36 kcal/mol., then the heat of hydrogenation of cyclohexene and cyclohexadiene per mole respectively are

(*a*)   20.3, 40.6     (*b*)   40.6, 20.3

(*c*)   32.3, 64.6     (*d*)   25, 50

**49.** The average bond energy of the C–H bond in methane is the mean of the four bond dissociation energies, viz. $CH_3$–H to $CH_3$; $CH_2$–H to $CH_2$; CH–H to CH and CH to C; which bond cleavage has minimum bond dissociation energy?

(a)  $H_3C \!\mid\! H$

(b)  $H_2C \!\mid\! H$

(c)  $HC \!\mid\! H$

(d)  $C \!\mid\! H$

**50.** Which of the following has minimum dipole moment?

(a)  $CH_3CH_2Cl$

(b)  $CH_2=CHCl$

(c)  $CH_2=CHCH_2Cl$

(d)  $CH_3Cl$

**51.**

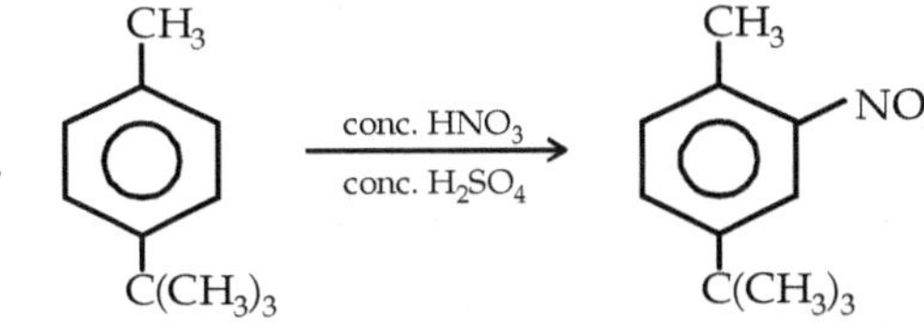

Introduction of $-NO_2$ group at the given position in the above reaction can be explained on the basis of

(a)  inductive effect

(b)  hyperconjugation

(c)  both

(d)  resonance

**52.** The $C_2 - C_3$ bond length in 1,3-butadiene is

(a)  1.54Å

(b)  1.35Å

(c)  1.46Å

(d)  1.20Å

**53.** Arrange the following carbocations in decreasing order of stability

$$CH_3 \overset{+}{C}HOCH_3 \qquad \text{I}$$

$$CH_3 \overset{+}{C}HCOCH_3 \qquad \text{II}$$

$$CH_3 \overset{+}{C}HCH_3 \qquad \text{III}$$

(a)  III > I > II

(b)  I > III > II

(c)  I > II > III

(d)  III > I = II

**54.** Resonance has impact on the stability or unstability of which carbocation?

(a)  $CH_3 \overset{+}{C}HCH_3$

(b)  $CH_3 \overset{+}{C}HOCH_3$

(c)  $CH_3 \overset{+}{C}HCOCH_3$

(d)  All the three

**55.** How many cyclic isomers are possible for $C_5H_{10}$?

(a)  3

(b)  4

(c)  5

(d)  6

**56.** Which of the following compounds cannot show tautomerism?

(a)  $CH_2=CHOH$

(b)  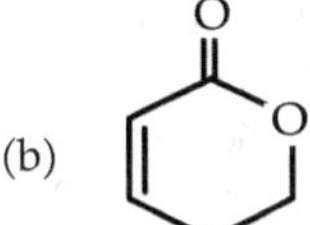

(c)  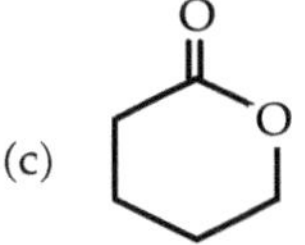

(d)  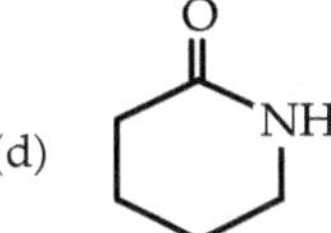

**57.**  $C_6H_5 - \overset{\overset{O}{\|}}{C} - CH_2CD_3 + D_3O^+ \longrightarrow$ Product is

(a)  $C_6H_5 - \overset{\overset{OD}{|}}{C} = CDCD_3$

(b)  $C_6H_5 - \overset{\overset{OD}{|}}{C} = CHCD_3$

(c)  $C_6H_5 - \overset{\overset{OH}{|}}{C} = CDCD_3$

(d)  $C_6H_5 - \overset{\overset{OD}{|}}{C} = CDCH_2D$

**58.** Maximum enol content is in

(a)  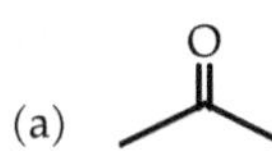

(b)  

(c)  

(d)  

**59.** Which of the following has a bond formed by overlap of $sp^3$–sp hybrid orbitals?

(a)  $CH_3 - C \equiv C - H$

(b)  $CH_3 - CH = CH - CH_3$

(c)  $CH_2 = CH - CH = CH_2$

(d)  $HC \equiv CH$

**60.** Carbon tetrachloride has no net dipole moment because of

(a)  its planar structure

(b)  its regular tetrahedral structure

(c)  similar size of carbon and chlorine atoms

(d)  similar electron affinities of carbon and chlorine

**61.** What is the decreasing order of strength of the bases $OH^-, NH_2^-, H - C \equiv C^-$ and $CH_3 - CH_2^-$?

(a)  $CH_3 - CH_2^- > NH_2^- > H - C \equiv C^- > OH^-$

(b)  $H - C \equiv C^- > CH_3 - CH_2^- > NH_2^- > OH^-$

(c)  $OH^- > NH_2^- > H - C \equiv C^- > CH_3 - CH_2^-$

(d)  $NH_2^- > H - C \equiv C^- > OH^- > CH_3 - CH_2^-$

**62.** Among the following compounds, the strongest acid is

(a)  $HC \equiv CH$

(b)  $C_6H_6$

(c)  $C_2H_6$

(d)  $CH_3OH$

**63.** How many types of H's are present in the structure of the compound drawn below?

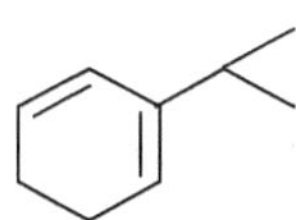

(a)  3

(b)  4

(c)  5

(d)  6

**64.** The increasing order of boiling points of the below mentioned alcohols is

(I)  1,2-dihydroxy benzene

(II)  1,3-dihydroxy benzene

(III)  1,4-dihydroxy benzene

(IV)  Hydroxy benzene

(a)  I < II < IV < III

(b)  I < II < III < IV

(c)  IV < II < I < III

(d)  IV < I < II < III

**65.** The number of structural isomers for $C_6H_{14}$ is

(a)  3

(b)  4

(c)  5

(d)  6

**66.** Hyperconjugation involves overlap of the following orbitals

(A)  σ-σ

(B)  σ - p

(C)  p- p

(D)  π-π

# EXERCISE 2.2 (MCQ 1 or >1 option correct, Passage based, Matching, A/R)

**DIRECTIONS for Q. 1 to Q. 18 :** Multiple choice questions with one or more than one correct option(s).

**1.** Resonance can explain the stability of

(a) $(CH_3)_2 \overset{+}{C}OH$

(b) *(structure: phenolate with para-NO₂)*

(c) *(structure: phenolate with meta-NO₂)*

(d) *(structure: benzyl alkoxide $CH_2O^-$ with para-NO₂)*

**2.** Pick up the correct statement
   (a) The $k_1$ of maleic acid is high than that of fumaric acid, while the $k_2$ of maleic acid is very low than that of fumaric acid
   (b) Fluorine forms stronger H-bond than oxygen, hence HF should boil at a higher temperature than $H_2O$
   (c) Delocalisation of $\pi$ electrons does not always lead to stabilisation
   (d) Delocalisation of $\pi$ electrons always leads to stabilisation

**3.** In which of the following pairs of carbocations, the second carbocation is less stable than the first?
   (a) $CH_2 = CH\overset{+}{C}H_2$ and $CH_2 = CHCH_2\overset{+}{C}H_2$
   (b) $CH_3NH\overset{+}{C}H_2$ and $\overset{+}{C}H_2OH$
   (c) $CH_3\overset{+}{C}HCH_2CH_2CH_3$ and $CH_3CH_2\overset{+}{C}HCH_2CH_3$
   (d) $CH_3OCH_2\overset{+}{C}H_2$ and $CH_3O\overset{+}{C}H_2$

**4.** Which of the following compounds show tautomerism?

(a) *(structure: phenol with N=O, nitrosophenol)*

(b) $H_2N-\overset{O}{\overset{\|}{C}}-NH_2$

(c) $H_2N-\overset{S}{\overset{\|}{C}}-NH_2$

(d) 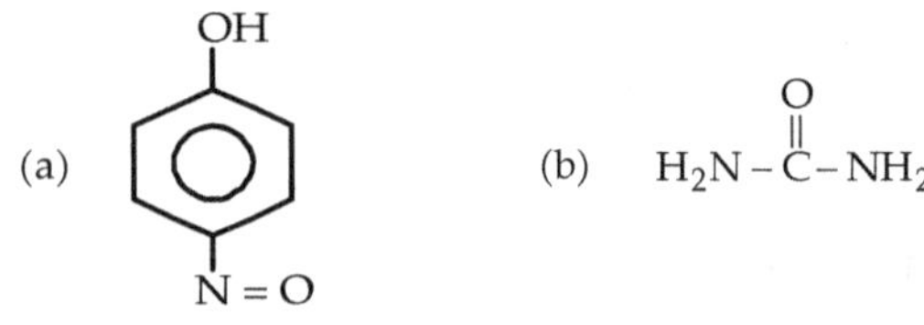

**5.** Enolic form of methyl 3-oxobutanoate is more stable than its keto form, this is due to
   (a) resonance stabilization of the enol form
   (b) intermolecular hydrogen bonding
   (c) intramolecular hydrogen bonding
   (d) carbonyl group on each side of $-CH_2-$ group

**6.** Tautomerism is exhibited by

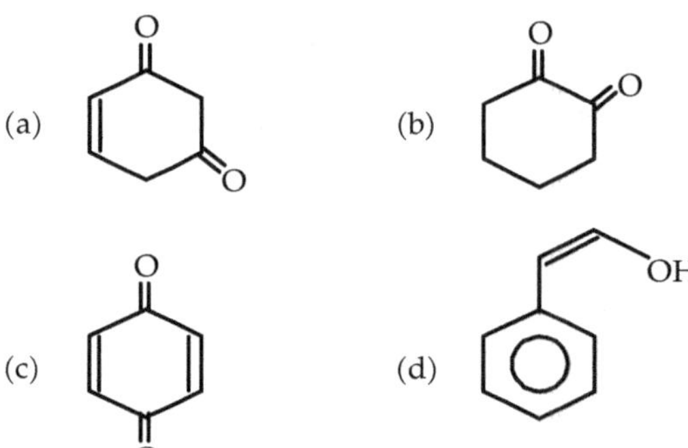

**7.** All of the given structures show ring-chain tautomerism, in which of the following cyclic form is more stable than the open chain form?
   (a) $CHOCH_2CH_2OH$
   (b) $CH_3COCH_2CH_2OH$
   (c) $CHOCHOHCHOHCH_2OH$
   (d) $CH_2OHCOCHOHCHOHCH_2OH$

**8.** Which of the following compounds have only one type of hybrid carbon?
   (a) $CH_2=CH-CH=CH_2$     (b) $HC\equiv C-C\equiv CH$
   (c) $CH_3-CH_2-CH_2-CH_3$ (d) $CH_3-C\equiv C-CH_3$

**9.** In which of the following compounds are all the carbon atoms in the $sp^3$ state of hybridization
   (a) $CH_4$ (b) $C_2H_6$
   (c) $C_3H_8$ (d) $C_4H_{10}$

**10.** Resonance structure of a molecule should have
   (a) identical arrangement of atoms
   (b) nearly the same energy content
   (c) the same number of paired electrons
   (d) identical bonding

**11.** Hydrogen bonding is possible in
   (a) Ethers (b) Hydrocarbons
   (c) Water (d) Alcohols

**12.** Dipole moment is shown by :
   (a) $1,4$-dichlorobenzene
   (b) *cis* $1,2$-dichloroethane
   (c) *trans* $1,2$-dichloroethene
   (d) *trans* $1,2$-dichloro-2-pentene

**13.** Which of the following will show hyperconjugation :
   (a) $CH_3 - CH = \overset{|}{C} -$
   (b) $CH_3 - CH_2 - CH = \overset{|}{C} -$
   (c) $CH_3 - \overset{|}{\underset{CH_3}{C}}H - CH = C -$
   (d) $CH_3 - \overset{CH_3}{\underset{CH_3}{\overset{|}{C}}} - CH = \overset{|}{C} -$

**14.** $C - C$ and $C = C$ bond lengths are equal in :
   (a) benzene (b) $1,3$-butadiene
   (c) $1,3$ cyclohexadiene (d) none

15. Resonance stabilised compounds are :

(a) 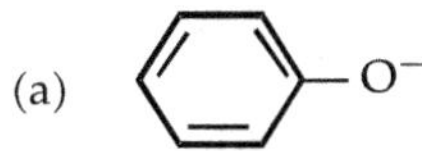

(b) $CH_2 = CH - Cl$

(c) 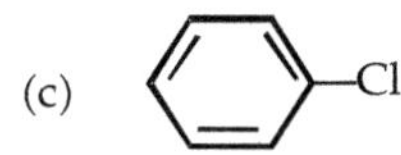

(d)

16. The compounds which is(are) isomeric with diethyl ether is (are)
    (a) n-propyl methyl ether
    (b) butan-1-ol
    (c) 2-methylpropan-2-ol
    (d) butanone
17. Out of the following compounds, which will not have a zero dipole moment?
    (a) 1, 1-dichloroethylene
    (b) *cis*-1, 2-dichloroethylene
    (c) *trans*-1, 2-dichloroethylene
    (d) All have zero dipole moments
18. The type of hydrogen present in the above structure is
    (a) 2° allylic
    (b) vinylic
    (c) 3° allylic
    (d) benzylic

INSTRUCTION for Q. 19 to 56 : Read the passages given below and answer the questions that follow.

PASSAGE 1

The statement that molecule having polar bonds should be polar, is not always true; e.g. $O = C = O$ has two polar $C - O$ bonds, yet $CO_2$ is non-polar. A molecule is said to be polar when the centre of negative charge does not coincide with the centre of positive charge. The polarity of every bond results in dipole moment which can be calculated as below.

$$\mu \text{ (in debye)} = charge \text{ (in esu unit)} \times d \text{ (in Å)}$$

Alternatively, $\mu$ (in debyes) = 4.8 × electron charge × $d$ (in Å)

Dipole moment is a vector quantity, and thus the net dipole moment of a polyatomic molecule is the vector sum of the dipole moments of various bonds. The magnitude of the resultant dipole moment is dependent upon the spatial orientation of various bonds present in the molecule. If the molecule is symmetrical, the resultant dipole moment of the molecule is zero.

19. Dipole moment can be used for calculating
    (a) bond length between two atoms
    (b) charge on the more electronegative atom
    (c) charge on both of the atoms
    (d) polar nature of the molecule
20. The central atom in each of the three molecules $CCl_4$, $H_2O$, and $NH_3$ is $sp^3$ hybridised; carbon tetrachloride has zero dipole moment, what do you expect about the dipole moment of $H_2O$ and $NH_3$?
    (a) Water has zero dipole moment, while $NH_3$ has a definite dipole moment
    (b) $NH_3$ has zero dipole moment, while $H_2O$ has definite dipole moment
    (c) $H_2O$ and $NH_3$, both have zero dipole moments
    (d) $H_2O$ and $NH_3$, both have definite dipole moments
21. The dipole moment of $NH_3$ is 1.46D, what should be the dipole moment of $NF_3$?
    (a) 1.70D
    (b) 0.24D
    (c) zero
    (d) 1.46D

22. Different values of dipole moment of $NH_3$ (1.46 D) and $H_2O$ (1.84D) is due to
    (a) difference in electronegativities of N and O
    (b) difference in lone pair on electrons on N and O
    (c) different direction of dipole in the N – H and O – H bonds
    (d) difference in hybridisation of the central atom
23. Which has least dipole moment?
    (a) H – Cl
    (b) H – F
    (c) H – Br
    (d) H – I
    (size of the four halogen is I > Br > Cl > F)
24. A diatomic molecule has a dipole moment of 1.98D and bond length of 0.92Å; the bond between two atoms should have ........ ionic character.
    (a) 52.5%
    (b) 50%
    (c) 44.8%
    (d) 26.6%

PASSAGE 2

Hydrogen bond is an electrostatic attractive force between covalently bonded hydrogen atom of one molecule and electronegative atom of small size of another molecule. The three atoms satisfying these conditions are F, O and N. Hydrogen bonding may be intermolecular as well as intramolecular. Intramolecular hydrogen bonding, also known as chelation, is possible when a 6- or 5-membered ring can be formed. Intermolecular hydrogen bonding increases the boiling point of the compound and also solubility of the compound in water. Intramolecular hydrogen bonding decreases boiling point and also its solubility in water.

25. Strongest hydrogen bond is possible in case of
    (a) higher electronegativity and greater size of the atom
    (b) lesser electronegativity and lesser size of the atom
    (c) higher electronegativity and smaller size of the atom
    (d) higher electronegativity irrespective of size of the atom
26. Which of the following compound is soluble in water?

(a) 

(b) 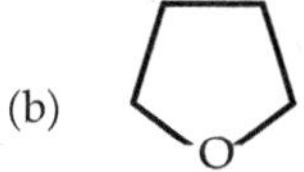

(c) 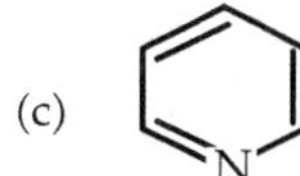

(d) none

27. Among the following pairs, pick up the incorrect order with reference to boiling points.

(a) $CH_3 \overset{OH}{\underset{|}{C}}HCH_3 \; > \; CH_3 \overset{O}{\overset{||}{C}}CH_3$

(b) $H_2O > H_2S$

(c) $CH_3 \overset{OH}{\underset{|}{C}} = CHCOOC_2H_5 \; > \; CH_3 \overset{O}{\overset{||}{C}}CH_2COOC_2H_5$

(d) None of the three

28. The relative acidic character of halogen acids (HX) can be explained on the basis of
    (a) inductive effect
    (b) hydrogen bonding
    (c) hybridization
    (d) all the three
29. HCl does not form H-bonding, while HF does so because
    (a) HCl is less polar than HF
    (b) of weak electrostatic attraction between Cl and H
    (c) larger size of Cl
    (d) any other reason

**30.** Tetramethylammonium hydroxide is as basic as potassium hydroxide because
   (a)   it exists only in ionized form
   (b)   it can't form hydrogen bonding
   (c)   both of the factors
   (d)   none of the two

**31.** Intramolecular hydrogen bonding is possible in

   (a)   $Cl_3C - \overset{\overset{H}{|}}{\underset{\underset{OH}{|}}{C}} - OH$

   (b)   $CH_3COOH$

   (c)   $CH_3 - \overset{\overset{OH}{|}}{C} = CH - \overset{\overset{O}{||}}{C} - CH_3$

   (d) 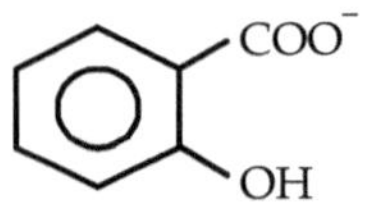   [structure: benzene ring with COO⁻ and OH ortho groups]

**32.** Which hydrogen atom of 2,6-dihydroxybenzoate can form intramolecular hydrogen bond?

   [structure: benzene ring with $OH^\alpha$, $COO^-$, $OH^\beta$ groups]

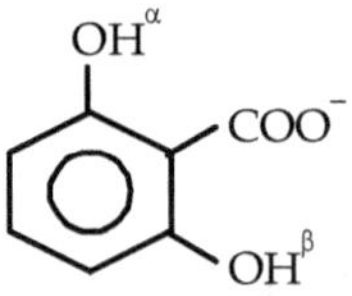

   (a)   $\alpha$                      (b)   $\beta$
   (c)   both                      (d)   none

**33.** Which of the following molecules dimerises in non-polar solvents?
   (a)   HCOOH               (b)   ArCOOH
   (c)   $CH_3COOH$          (d)   ArOH

PASSAGE 3

Tautomerism may be defined as a phenomenon in which a single compound exists in two readily interconvertible structures that differ in the relative position of hydrogen. It is broadly of two types :- dyad system in which hydrogen migrates from atom one to atom two, and similarly defined *triad system*. Keto-enol tautomerism is the most important and its most usual example is ethyl acetoacetate.

$$CH_3 - \overset{\overset{O}{||}}{C} - CH_2 - \overset{\overset{O}{||}}{C} - OC_2H_5 \rightleftharpoons CH_3 - \overset{\overset{OH}{|}}{C} = CH - \overset{\overset{O}{||}}{C} - OC_2H_5$$

The two forms are readily interconvertible under ordinary conditions by acid or base catalyst.

Stability of the enolic form depends upon several factors, viz. its stabilization (through resonance) and nature of solvent. Non-polar solvents generally stabilise the enolic form, while polar protonic solvent stabilises the ketonic form.

**34.** Which of the following is not an example of triad system of tautomerism?

   (a)   $CH_3 - \overset{\overset{O}{||}}{C} - CH_3 \rightleftharpoons CH_2 = \overset{\overset{OH}{|}}{C} - CH_3$

   (b)   $C_6H_5 - \overset{\overset{O}{||}}{C} - NH_2 \rightleftharpoons C_6H_5 - \overset{\overset{OH}{|}}{C} = NH$

   (c)   $CH_3 - N\overset{O}{\underset{O}{\diagup}} \rightleftharpoons CH_2 = N\overset{OH}{\underset{O}{\diagup}}$

   (d)   $H - N\overset{O}{\underset{O}{\diagup}} \rightleftharpoons H - O - N = O$

**35.** In which of the following enol content is maximum?
   (a)   $CH_3COCH_2COOC_2H_5$   (b)   $CH_3COCH_2COCH_3$
   (c)   $C_6H_5COCH_2COCH_3$   (d)   $C_6H_5COCH_2COC_6H_5$

**36.** Which of the following statement is/are incorrect about ethyl acetoacetate?
   (a)   It reacts with $NaHCO_3$ to form addition product
   (b)   It does not discharge bromine solution
   (c)   It has an ester linkage
   (d)   It has two ketonic groups

**37.** Tautomerism is not possible in

   (a) 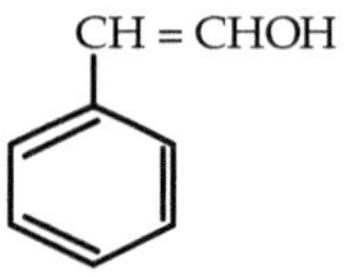   [structure: benzene ring with CH = CHOH group]

   (b) 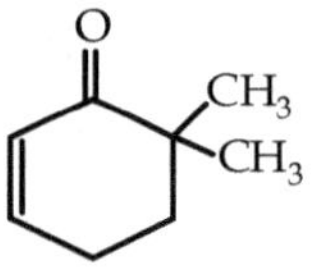   [structure: cyclohexenone with two $CH_3$ groups]

   (c) 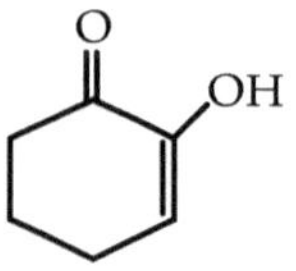   [structure: cyclohexenone with OH group]

   (d)   $CH_3 - \overset{\overset{O}{||}}{C} - \overset{\overset{\overset{CH_3}{|}}{}}{\underset{\underset{CH_3}{|}}{C}} - \overset{\overset{O}{||}}{C} - OC_2H_5$

**38.** Which of the following constitutes enolic form of dimethyl acetoacetic ester?

   (a)   $CH_3 - \overset{\overset{OH}{|}}{C} = \overset{\overset{\overset{CH_3}{|}}{}}{\underset{\underset{CH_3}{|}}{C}} - \overset{\overset{O}{||}}{C} - OC_2H_5$

   (b)   $CH_2 = \overset{\overset{OH}{|}}{C} - \overset{\overset{\overset{CH_3}{|}}{}}{\underset{\underset{CH_3}{|}}{C}} - \overset{\overset{O}{||}}{C} - OC_2H_5$

   (c)   $CH_3 - \overset{\overset{O}{||}}{C} - \overset{\overset{\overset{CH_3}{|}}{}}{\underset{\underset{CH_3}{|}}{C}} = \overset{\overset{OH}{|}}{C} - OC_2H_5$

   (d)   None of the three

**39.** You are given two samples of acetylacetone, $CH_3 - \overset{\overset{O}{||}}{C} - CH_2 - \overset{\overset{O}{||}}{C} - CH_3$ in different solvents, namely ethyl alcohol and *n*-hexane. Which of the following statement is true?
   (a)   Both samples have equal percentage of the keto form
   (b)   Sample in ethanol has higher percentage of the keto form than that in the *n*-hexane sample
   (c)   Sample in *n*-hexane has higher percentage of the keto form than that in ethanol sample
   (d)   Sample in ethanol does not have keto form at all

**40.** Phenols and amines undergo methylation when treated with $CH_3I$. How many methylated products can be formed when isatin is methylated?

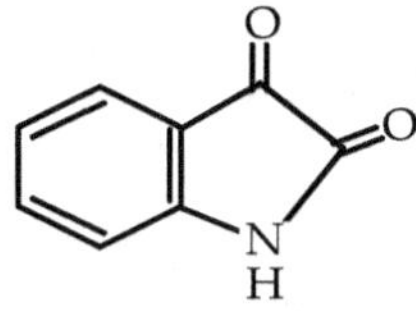

   (a)   One            (b)   Two
   (c)   Three         (d)   Four

**41.** The species formed during enolisation of ethyl acetoacetate in presence of acids is

(a)    $CH_3 - \overset{\overset{\displaystyle +OH}{\|}}{C} - CH_2 - \overset{\overset{\displaystyle O}{\|}}{C} - OC_2H_5$

(b)    $CH_3 - \overset{\overset{\displaystyle O}{\|}}{C} - CH_2 - \overset{\overset{\displaystyle +OH}{\|}}{C} - OC_2H_5$

(c)    $CH_3 - \overset{\overset{\displaystyle O}{\|}}{C} - CH_2 - \overset{\overset{\displaystyle O}{\|}}{C} - \overset{+}{O}C_2H_5$

(d)    All the three

### PASSAGE - 4

**Conditions for hydrogen bonding**

*(i)*  *The molecule must possess a higher electronegative atoms such as F, O or N, directly linked to hydrogen atom.*

*(ii)*  *The size of the electronegative atom should be small.*

**Types of hydrogen bonding.** Generally, the hydrogen bonds are classified into two groups, *viz.* intermolecular and intramolecular.

**1.**  **Intermolecular hydrogen bonding.** In such type of linkage the two or more than two molecules of the same compound combine together to give a polymeric aggregate.

**2.**  **Intramolecular hydrogen bonding.** In this type, hydrogen bonding occurs within two atoms of the same molecule. Intramolecular hydrogen bonding is possible when a six or five-membered ring can be formed.

**42.** Hydrogen bonding is possible in
   (a)  *o*-chlorobenzoic acid   (b)  HCl
   (c)  HF                (d)  KF

**43.** Which of the following explains the high boiling point of *m*-chlorophenol than the *o*-chlorophenol?
   (a)  Intermolecular H-bond
   (b)  Intramolecular H-bonding
   (c)  Both
   (d)  None

**44.** Which of the following factor explains insolubility of salicyclic acid in water?
   (a)  Its bulky aryl group
   (b)  Chemical reaction between –OH and –COOH groups
   (c)  Chelation
   (d)  Association

### PASSAGE 5

A molecule having polar bonds should be polar, however this is not true in all cases. A molecule is said to be polar when the center of negative charge does not coincide with the center of positive charge. A polar molecule has a dipole moment, $\mu$, which is equal to the multiple of magnitude of the charge ($e$) and distance ($d$) between the centers of charge.

$$\mu = e \times d$$

**45.** The correct order of the dipole moments of the four alkyl halides should be

$$\underset{\text{I}}{CH_3F} \qquad \underset{\text{II}}{CH_3Cl} \qquad \underset{\text{III}}{CH_3Br} \qquad \underset{\text{IV}}{CH_3I}$$

   (a)  I > II > III > IV     (b)  IV > III > II > I
   (c)  II > I > III > IV     (d)  II > III > I > IV

**46.** Which of the following statement is false about $BCl_3$?
   (a)  It has three polar bonds
   (b)  It is a polar molecule
   (c)  It is a non-polar molecule
   (d)  Its central atom has no lone pair of electrons

**47.** Dipole moment can be used for
   (a)  calculating bond length between two concerned polar atoms
   (b)  calculating the percentage ionic character of the concerned bond
   (c)  differentiating between ionic and covalent bond
   (d)  all the above three purposes

### PASSAGE – 6

Following criteria should be taken in consideration for resonance.

The major contributor is the one with the lowest energy. Good contributors generally have all octets satisfied, as many bonds as possible and as little charge separation as possible. Negative charges are more stable on the more electronegative atoms.

Resonance stabilization is most important when it serves to delocalize a charge over two or more atoms.

**48.** The two important resonating structures of nitromethane are:

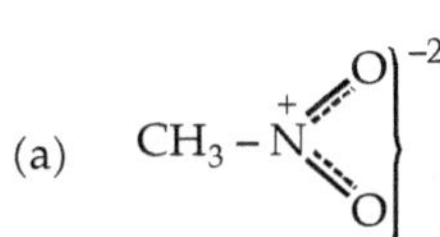

the resonance hybrid of nitromethane can be written as

(a)  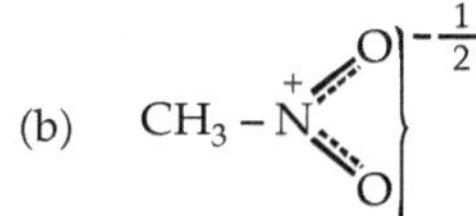

(b)   structure

(c)  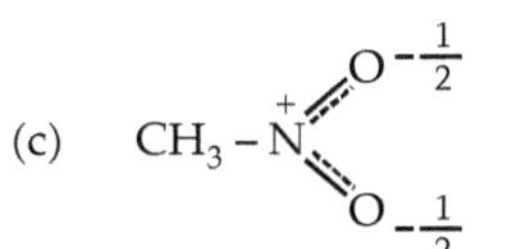

(d)   structure

**49.** Observe the following structures :

$$\underset{\text{I}}{H_2C = \overset{+}{N}H_2} \longleftrightarrow \underset{\text{II}}{\overset{+}{C}H_2 - NH_2}$$

   (a)  Structure I is major contributor in the two resonating structures
   (b)  Structure II is major contributor in the two resonating structures
   (c)  Both are equal stable
   (d)  Resonance is not possible

**50.** How many resonating structures can be drawn for 2, 4-pentadienyl radical?
   (a)  1             (b)  2
   (c)  3             (d)  4

## PASSAGE 7

Resonance involves movement of only π or *n* electrons and a resonance structure can be derived from another by a series of one or more electron shifts. Thus resonance is possible only when one double bond is in conjugation with another double bond or an unshared pair of electrons or an electron deficient atom.

Further for resonance, it is essential that the *skeleton should be planar* in conjugated system. Thus any structural feature that destroys this coplanarity of the conjugated system will inhibit resonance. This inhibition is referred to as **steric inhibition of resonance.**

Structures in which all atoms have a complete octet of electrons are especially stable and make large contribution to the hybrid.

**51.** In picryl chloride which of the –$NO_2$ group (as indicated by a, b, c) is involved in resonance.

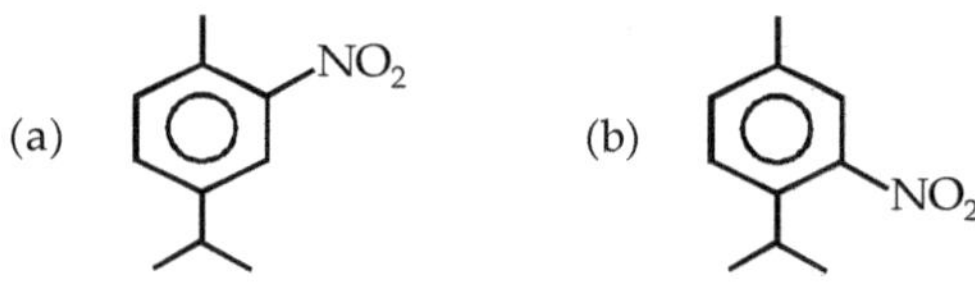

(a) a     (b) b
(c) c     (d) all

**52.** The C–Cl bond length in $CH_2 = CHCl$ and $CH_2=CHCH_2Cl$ respectively is most likely to be
(a) shorter, longer  (b) longer, shorter
(c) equal     (d) shorter, shorter

**53.** Which of the following is more stable than others

(a) I     (b) II
(c) IV    (d) all equal

## PASSAGE 8

Alkyl groups with at least one hydrogen atom on the α-carbon atom, attached to an unsaturated carbon atom, are able to release electrons in the following way.

Note that the delocalisation involves σ and π bond orbitals (or *p* orbitals in case of free radicals) ; thus it is also known as σ – π **conjugation.** This type of *electron release due to the presence of the system* H—C—C = C is known as **hyperconjugation.**

The phenomenon of hyperconjugation can also be applied to group, Cl—C—C = C, where the effect operates in the reverse direction.

More the number of H—C bonds attached to the unsaturated system more will be the probability of electron release by this mechanism. Thus the electron release by this mechanism will be greater in methyl (possessing three hyperconjugated H—C bonds), less in ethyl (having two such bonds) and *iso*-propyl (one) and essentially zero in *tert*-butyl (no hyperconjugated H—C bond) group.

It is important to note that although hyperconjugation like inductive effect causes the release of electrons and thus the two effects reinforce each other in this respect, the magnitude of the two effects changes in opposite directions in passing along a series of alkyl groups.

More is the number of hyperconjugative structures, more will be the stability of the species.

**54.** On the basis of hyperconjugation which of the following alkene is more stable ?
(a) 2-Methylpropene  (b) Butene - 2
(c) Both equal
(d) Hyperconjugation has nothing to do with the relative stability of the two alkenes.

**55.** [benzene] $\xrightarrow{\text{Nitration}}$ P. P is most likely to be

(c) Both in equal amounts (d)

**56.** Which of the following statements is regarding the electron substitution in toluene and benzotrichloride, $C_6H_5CCl_3$. Substitution takes place in o-position in toluene and m-position in $C_6H_5CCl_3$.
(a) This can be explained by both inductive as well as hyperconjugation.
(b) This can be explained only by inductive effect.
(c) This can be explained only by hyperconjugation.
(d) This can be explained by inductive effect and mesomeric effect.

**Instructions for Q. 57 to 63 : Following questions are Multiple Matching type Questions :**

**57.**

| | Column I | | Column II |
|---|---|---|---|
| (A) | Enol form of $CH_3COCH_2COOC_2H_5$ | (a) | resonance stabilization |
| (B) | Higher acidity of maleic acid than fumaric acid | (b) | Hydration |
| (C) | Higher acidity of potassium fumarate than sodium maleate | (c) | Intramolecular hydrogen bonding |
| (D) | Solubility of NaCl in water | (d) | Intermolecular hydrogen-bonding |

**58.**

| | Column I | | Column II |
|---|---|---|---|
| (A) | $O = C = O$ | (a) | C is sp hybridised |
| (B) | $OH^-$ | (b) | O has two lone pair of electrons |
| (C) | HCHO | (c) | C is $sp^2$ hybridised |
| (D) | $CH_2 = C = CH_2$ | (d) | O is $sp^3$ bybridised |

**59.**

| | Column I | | Column II |
|---|---|---|---|
| (A) | Inductive effect | (a) | Temporary effect |
| (B) | Hyperconjugation | (b) | Lucas's test for the three types of alcohols |
| (C) | Mesomeric effect | (c) | Involves σ electrons |
| (D) | Electronic effect | (d) | Involves π electrons |

**60.**

| | Column I | | Column II |
|---|---|---|---|
| (A) | $H_2O$ | (a) | Protophilic solvent |
| (B) | Liquid ammonia | (b) | Amphiprotic solvent |
| (C) | Benzene | (c) | Aprotic solvent |
| (D) | $C_2H_5OH$ | (d) | Protogenic solvent |

**61.**

| | Column I | | Column II |
|---|---|---|---|
| (A) | sp hybridization | (a) | square planar |
| (B) | $sp^2$ hybridization | (b) | tetrahedral |
| (C) | $sp^3$ hybridization | (c) | octahedron |
| (D) | $dsp^2$ hybridization | (d) | trigonal bipyramidal |
| (E) | $d^2sp^3$ hybridization | (e) | linear |
| (F) | $dsp^3$ hybridization | (f) | triangluar planar |

**62.**

| | Column I | | Column II |
|---|---|---|---|
| (A) | o - Hydroxybenzoic acid | (a) | Tautomerism |
| (B) | p- hydroxybenzoic acid | (b) | Intramolecular H- bonding |
| (C) | Acetylacetone | (c) | Intermolecular H- bonding |
| (D) | Acetoacetic ester | (d) | Soluble in water |

**63.**

| | Column I | | Column II |
|---|---|---|---|
| (A) | $CH \equiv CH$ | (a) | Markownikoff addition |
| (B) | (cyclohexene) | (b) | Acidic hydrogen |
| (C) | $CH_3COCH_2COOC_2H_5$ | (c) | Wohl-Ziegler reaction |
| (D) | $CH_3NO_2$ | (d) | Tautomerism |

**Instructions for Q. 64 to 70 : Following questions are Assertion and Reasoning Type Questions :**

**Note : Each question contains STATEMENT-1 (Assertion) and STATEMENT-2 (Reason). Each question has 5 choices (a), (b), (c), (d) and (e) out of which ONLY ONE is correct.**

(a) Statement-1 is True, Statement-2 is True; Statement-2 is a correct explanation for Statement-1.

(b) Statement-1 is True, Statement-2 is True; Statement-2 is NOT a correct explanation for Statement-1.

(c) Statement -1 is True, Statement-2 is False.

(d) Statement -1 is False, Statement-2 is True.

(e) Statement -1 is False, Statement-2 is False.

**Q.64 Statement - 1 :** Dipole moment of Azulene 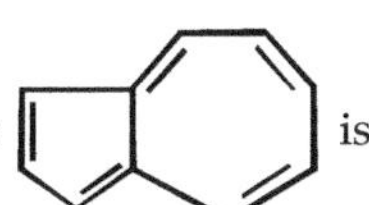 is more than naphthalene.

**Statement- 2 :** Azulene exists as dipolarion due to the aromatic nature obtained in both rings.

**65. Statement I :** 3-Phenylbutan-2-one racemises in presence of dilute acid or dilute base.

**Statement II :** Its keto form is thermodynamically more stable form then the enol form.

**66. Statement - 1 :** $CH_3OH$ boiling point is more than $CH_3SH$ while $CH_3–O–CH_3$ boiling point is less than $CH_3–S–CH_3$.

**Statement - 2 :** Hydrogen bonding is stronger in $CH_3OH$ than $CH_3SH$ while no hydrogen bonding exist in $CH_3–O–CH_3$ and $CH_3–S–CH_3$.

**67. Statement I :** 2,4,6 trinitro N, N-diemethylaniline is 40,000 times more basic than 2,4,6-trinitroaniline.

**Statement II :** In the former steric inhibition or resonance causes the availability of $\ell$p on N whereas in the later due to H-bonding of $NH_2$ with $NO_2$ groups make $NH_2$ planar with benzene ring, so easy delocalisation of electron pair of N in benzene ring.

**68. Statement 1 :** p-Hydroxybenzoic acid has a lower boiling point than o-hydroxybenzoic acid.

because

**Statement 2 :** o-Hydroxybenzoic acid has intramolecular hydrogen bonding.

**69. Statement 1 :** Trichloroacetic acid is stronger than acetic acid.

**Statement 2 :** Electron withdrawing substituents decrease the activity.

**70. Statement 1:** Neopentane forms one mono substituted compound.

**Statement 2 :** Neopentane is isomer of pentane.

**Instructions for Q. 71 to 82 : The following questions are True/False Type Questions :**

**71.** Vinyl chloride has higher dipole moment than allyl chloride.

**72.** The relative values of dipole moment of vinyl chloride and allyl chloride is due to resonance which here decreases dipole moment.

**73.** The *meta*-directing influence of $–CCl_3$ group in benzotrichloride is due to inductive as well as hyperconjugation.

**74.** Both $CH_3 \overset{+}{C}HCH_2CH_3$ and $CH_3 \overset{+}{C}HCH_3$ are 2° carbocations, hence equally stable.

**75.** Maleic and fumaric acids have similar acidic character, while fumarate ion is a stronger acid than maleate ion.

**76.** $CH_3O\overset{+}{C}H_2$ is more stable than $CH_3OCH_2\overset{+}{C}H_2$.

**77.** Resonance effect involves delocalisation of π or p electrons, while inductive effect involves delocalisation of σ electrons.

**78.** In $CH_2 = CH\overset{+}{N}H_3$, the π electrons are delocalised in the following way.

$$CH_2 = CH - \overset{+}{N}H_3 \quad \longleftrightarrow \quad \overset{+}{C}H_2 - CH = NH_3$$
$$I \qquad\qquad\qquad\qquad II$$

**79.** 1,3-Butadiene is stabilised by resonance, while cyclobutadiene is destabilised by resonance.

**80.** Boiling points of hydrogen halides follow the order HF > HCl > HBr > HI.

**81.** Chelation may explain increasing acidic character as well as decreasing acidic character of certain compounds.

**82.** Stability of enolic form of acetylacetone is due to resonance as well as hydrogen bonding.

# EXERCISE 2.3 (Subjective Problems)

1. Predict the shape of the following species.

   (*i*)   $(CH_3)_3B$     (*ii*)   $CH_3^-$     (*iii*)   $CH_3^+$

   (*iv*)   $NH_2^-$     (*v*)   $BF_4^-$     (*vi*)   $(CH_3)_2O$.

2. Write the conjugate acid and conjugate base of the following :

   (*a*)   $HNO_3$     (*b*)   $H{:}^-$     (*c*)   $:CH_3^-$

   (*d*)   $Cl^-$     (*e*)   $H_2C = CH_2$     (*f*)   $CH_3O^-$.

   Which of the following species is amphoteric in nature ?

3. Which is the stronger base in each of the following pairs ?

   (*a*)   $NH_3$ and $PH_3$

   (*b*)   $NH_2^-$ and $OH^-$

   (*c*)   $HS^-$ and $F^-$.

4. Ethanol and water both form hydrogen bond and ethanol has high molecular weight than water, even then water boils at a much higher temperature than ethanol. Explain

5. Arrange the following alkenes in increasing order of stability. Explain you answer with proper reason.

   $CH_3CH = CH_2$, $CH_2{=}CH_2$, $(CH_3)_2 C = CH_2$, $(CH_3)_2C = CHCH_3$, $(CH_3)_2 C = C (CH_3)_2$

6. Explain the following :

   (*i*)   Guanidine behaves as a strong base.

   (*ii*)   Vinyl alcohol is acidic in nature

   (*iii*)   Acidic nature of $\alpha$-hydrogen of aldehydes and ketones

   (*iv*)   The $F^-$ of dissolved NaF is more reactive in dimethyl sulphoxide, $(CH_3)_2SO$ or acetonitrile than in methanol.

   (*v*)   Melting point of NaCl is much higher than that of $AlCl_3$.

   (*vi*)   In acylium ion, the structure $R{-}C \equiv O^+{:}$ is more stable than $R{-}C^+ = O$.

7. Give the enolic forms of acetylacetone, ethyl acetoacetate and diethyl malonate and explain their stability involving intramolecular H—bonding.

8. Indicate the type of hybridisation of each carbon atom in the following compounds.

   (*i*)   $CH_3CN$     (*ii*)   $CH_3CH = CH_2$

   (*iii*)   $CH_3{-}C \equiv C {-} CH_3$     (*iv*)   $HC \equiv C{-}CH = CH_2$.

9. (*a*)   Write the structural formulae of all the possible isomers of $C_2H_2Cl_2$ and indicate which of them is non-polar.

   (*b*)   What effect should the following resonance of vinyl chloride have on its dipole moment ?

   $$CH_2 = CH{-}Cl \longleftrightarrow \overset{\ominus}{C}H_2{-}CH = \overset{\oplus}{C}l$$

   (*c*)   Write the tautomeric forms for phenol.

10. (*a*) Write the two resonance structures of ozone which satisfy the octet rule.

    (*b*)   Write all possible resonance structures of the following that satisfy the octet rule.

    $$NO_3^- \quad \text{and} \quad N_3^-.$$

11. Arrange 2, 2-dimethylbutane, 3-methylpentane and *n*-hexane in order of decreasing boiling point. Explain your answer with proper reasoning.

12. Arrange the following in order of increasing boiling point

    (*i*)   *n*-butane, *n*-butanol, *n*-butyl chloride and isobutane

    (*ii*)   *n*-butane, ethanol, water and propane.

13. Arrange the following in increasing order of expected enol content in $CH_3CH_2CHO$, $CH_3COCH_3$, $CH_3CHO$, $CH_3COCH_2COCH_3$.

14. Is there any relationship between following three structures?

I           II           III

# SOLUTIONS



**1.** For predicting the shape of each molecule, one must know the number of orbitals required by the central atom for holding the atoms attached to it and also unshared pairs of electrons, if any. For example, if the molecule requires 4 orbitals, $sp^3$ hybridisation is indicated.

(a) **$BF_3$.**

$_5B = 1s^2\ 2s^2\ p_x^1\ p_y^0\ p_z^0$     (ground state)

$_5B = 1s^2\ 2s^1\ p_x^1\ p_y^1\ p_z^0$     (excited state)

Thus $BF_3$ molecule will be trigonal planar, each F—B—F bond angle is $120°$ and the empty $p_z$ orbital is at right angles to the plane of the molecule.

(b) **$BF_4^-$.**

$$_5B = 1s^2\ \underbrace{2s^1\ 2p_x^1\ 2p_y^1\ 2p_z}_{sp^3\ \text{Hybridisation}}$$

The empty $sp^3$ hybrid orbital overlaps with a filled orbital of $F^-$ holding two electrons. The shape is regular tetrahedral with a bond angle of $109.5°$.

(c) **$NH_4^+$.** Four hydrogen atoms of N indicate $sp^3$ hybridisation, $NH_4^+$ species has no lone pair of electrons, giving regular tetrahedral shape with the normal tetrahedral bond angle of $109.5°$.

(d) **$H_3O^+$.** In $H_3O^+$, oxygen is $sp^3$ hybridised and the shape of the molecule is a distorted tetrahedral (pyramidal) due to the presence of lone pair of electrons.

(e) **$CH_3\ NH_2$.** The central atom (N) is $sp^3$ hybridised ; three $sp^3$ orbitals form the usual N—H, N—H and N—C sigma bonds, the fourth $sp^3$ orbital has a lone pair of electrons. Thus here again shape of $CH_3NH_2$ will be distorted tetrahedral.

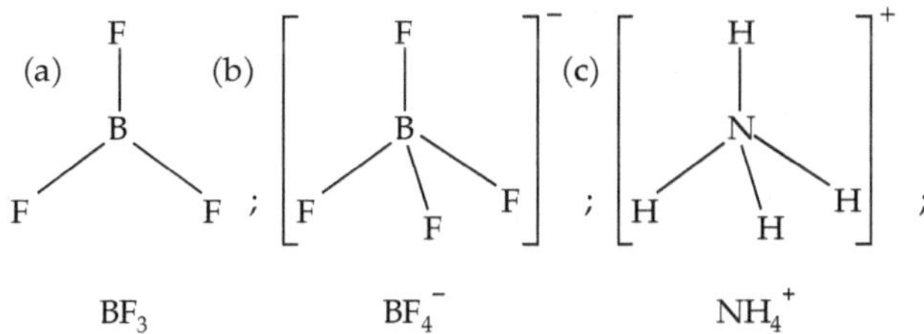



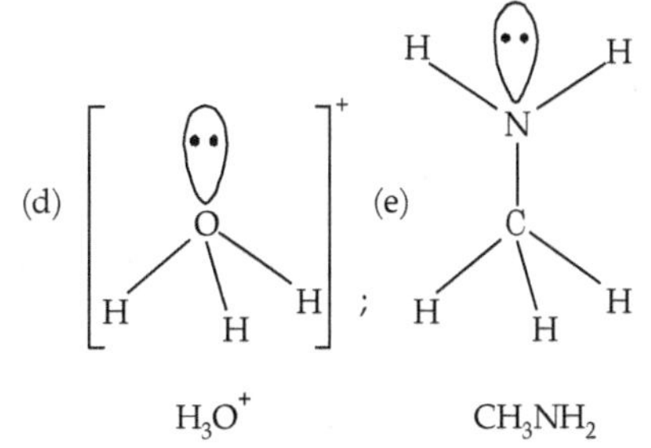



(f) **$NO_2^+$ ($:\overset{+}{\ddot{O}} = N = \ddot{O}:$).** Here the central atom (N) has two σ bonds and no lone pair of electrons ; thus it needs two hybrid orbitals which indicates $sp$ hybridised state of N. Thus $NO_2^+$ will be linear in shape.

(g) **$NO_2^-$ ($:\ddot{O} = \ddot{N}—\ddot{O}:^-$).** Here N has two σ bonds and one unshared pair of electrons and, thus it requires three hybrid orbitals indicating $sp^2$ hybridisation of N. Thus $NO_2^-$ will have a trigonal planar shape.



**1.** $0.86\ D = 4.8 × δ × 1.43\ \text{Å};$      $δ = 0.125\ e$

Thus the amount of charge separation is about $0.125$ electronic charge, so the carbon atom has about an eighth of a positive charge, and the oxygen atom has about an eighth of a negative charge.



**1.** Carbon dioxide ($CO_2$) has zero dipole moment while water ($H_2O$) has a considerably large value of dipole moment ($1.84$ D). This is due to difference in their shape, $CO_2$ is a linear molecule (dipole moment of one C—O bond cancels that of the other C—O bond), while water has

$$O = C = O$$
$$μ = 0.0\ D$$

$m = 1.84\ D$

a bent shape distorted tetrahedral, hence the dipole moment of the one O—H bond does not completely cancel that of other.

**2.** (i) In ammonia, dipole moment due to N—H bonds and due to lone pair of electrons reinforce each other

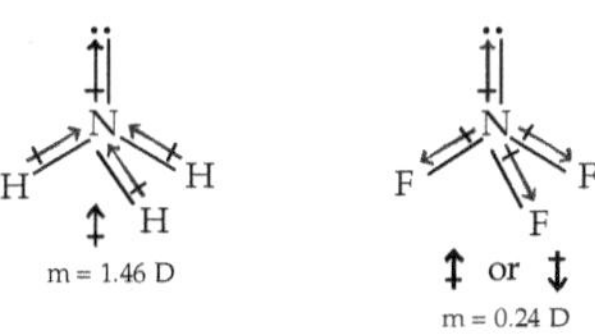

$m = 1.46\ D$      $m = 0.24\ D$

On the other hand, in $NF_3$, dipole moment due to N—F bonds is opposed by the dipole moment due to unshared pair of electrons. These opposing moments are *nearly* of the same size which produces a small moment, in any direction. However, remember in $NH_3$ the observed moment is mainly due the unshared pair, augumented by the sum of the bond moments.

(ii) Dipole moment of $CD_3F$ will be higher ($1.858$ D) than that of $CH_3F$ ($1.847$ D). The higher $μ$ for $CD_3F$ is due to higher value of charge ($e$) because $d$ is same for the two molecules. Higher value of $e$ in turn is due to the fact that F pulls electrons from D more easily than from H, *i.e.* D is more electron-releasing than H.



**1.** (i)

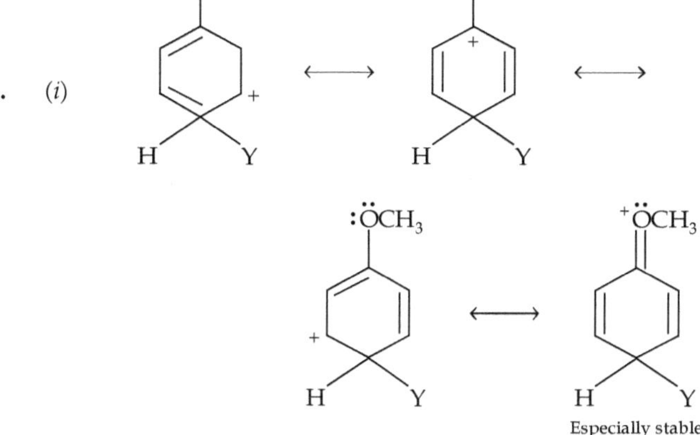

Especially stable
every atom has octet

For writing resonating structures of an ion or a free radical, put the charge or odd electron in the various alternate positions. Remember that whenever in a structure every atom has a complete octet of electrons, it is considered to be more stable ignoring the fact that the charge is present on the more or less electronegative atom.

(*ii*)

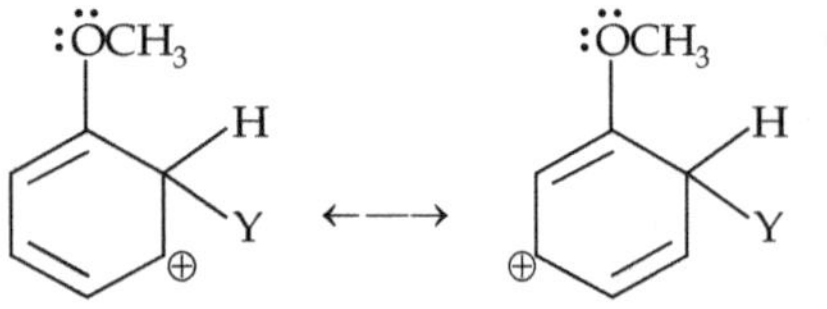

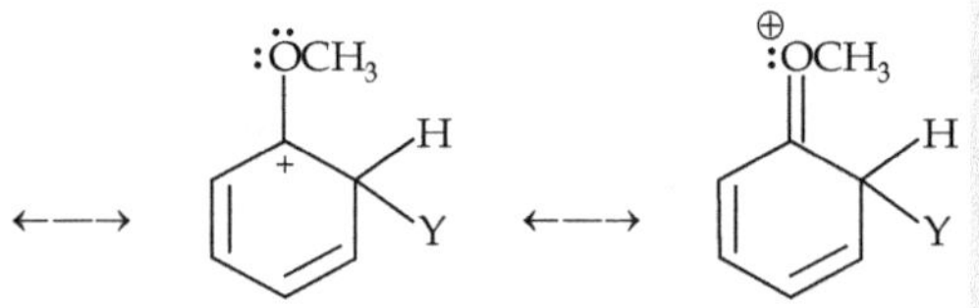

Especially stable every atom has octet

(*iii*)

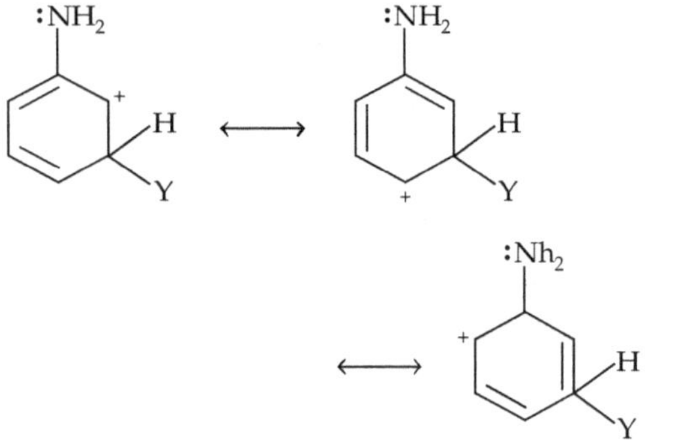

(*iv*)

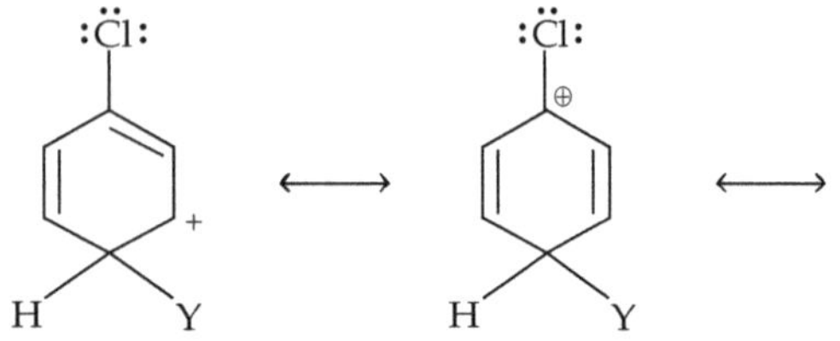

Especially unstable + charge on C bearing – I group

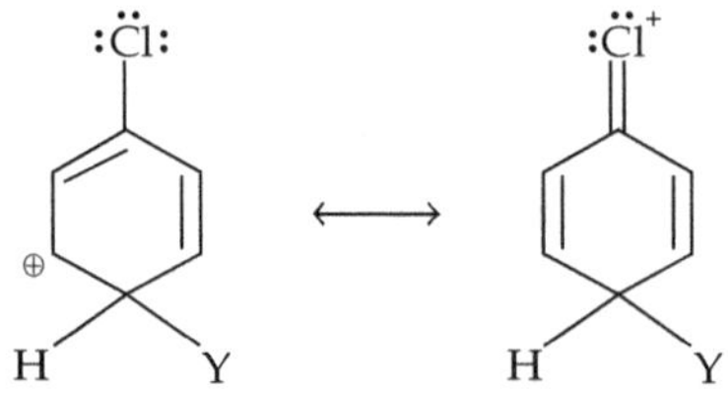

Comparatively stable every atom has octet

**2.** (*i*) $\overset{\delta+}{CH_2}$ ⋯ CH ⋯ $\overset{\delta+}{CH_2}$  (*ii*)

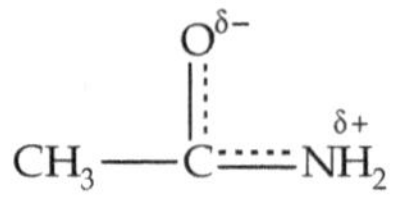

(*iii*)

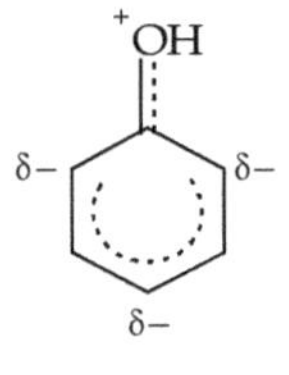

(*iv*)

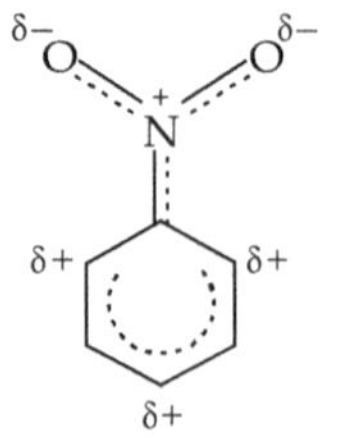

(*v*)

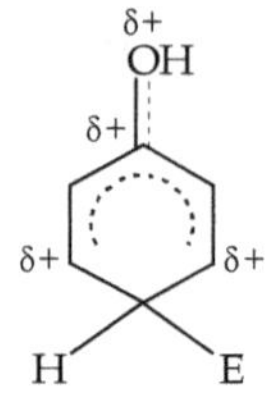

**3.** $CH_3-\ddot{O}-\overset{+}{C}H_2 \longleftrightarrow CH_3-\overset{+}{O}=CH_2$

Carbonium ion — Oxonium ion, Especially stable every atom has complete octet

This situation is comparable with the $CH_3^+$ and $H_3O^+$ where again latter is more stable due to complete octet of electrons of oxygen.

**4.** $Cl_3C:^-$ is less basic than $F_3C:^-$. This can be explained in terms of delocalization ; F can disperse charge only by an inductive effect, while Cl can disperse charge by an inductive as well as by *p-d* π bonding (F has no *d* orbital hence delocalization by *p-d* π bonding is not possible).

## TEST YOUR UNDERSTANDING - 2.5

**1.**

Electromeric effect due to – I effect

Electromeric effect due to hyperconjugation

Here hyperconjugative effect is strong than the inductive effect of Br, so mainly electromeric effect takes place in the second way.

## TEST YOUR UNDERSTANDING - 2.6

**1.** For determining the relative boiling points, try to know the type of intermolecular force present among molecules of the same type. Higher is the attraction, greater is the force and more will be the boiling point. Relative order of attraction for the three important intermolecular forces is H-bond >> dipole-dipole > London forces. In case, two or more compounds have similar type of intermolecular force, then consider the molecular weight of such compounds, higher is the molecular weight more will be the boiling point.

(*i*) Order of polarity of the three alkyl halides is

$$CH_3Cl > CH_3Br > CH_3I$$

while the order of molar mass is

$$CH_3I > CH_3Br > CH_3Cl$$

However, here order of molar mass predominates, thus the boiling points of the three halides will be governed by their molar masses rather than the weak dipole-dipole attraction.

(*ii*) *n*-Pentane and neopentane are structural isomers, hence they have similar molar mass and polarity (both are non-polar). Thus here, shape of the molecule should be considered. The shape of *n*-pentane is rod-like, while that of neopentane is sphere-like. Now we know that rods can touch along their entire length, and thus provide larger surface area while spheres touch only at a point and thus have lower surface area. More is the surface area, greater will be the London forces and hence higher will be the boiling point.

(*iii*) Both, ethyl alcohol ($C_2H_5OH$) and dimethyl ether ($CH_3OCH_3$) are polar molecules and hence exhibit dipole-dipole attraction. However, hydrogen bonding (a strong intermolecular force) is possible only in ethyl alcohol, hence it boils at a higher temperature. In $CH_3OCH_3$, no hydrogen is present on O, hence hydrogen bonding is not possible.

(*iv*) Attractive forces between nonpolar molecules such as mineral oil and *n*-hexane are very weak ; hence *such molecules can mutually mix and hence formation of solution is easy.* Actually, the nonpolar molecules cannot overcome the strong H-bonds present between polar solvent (*e.g.* ethanol) molecules and therefore nonpolar molecules do not dissolve in polar protic solvents like $C_2H_5OH$ and water.

### TEST YOUR UNDERSTANDING - 2.7

**1.** (*a*)

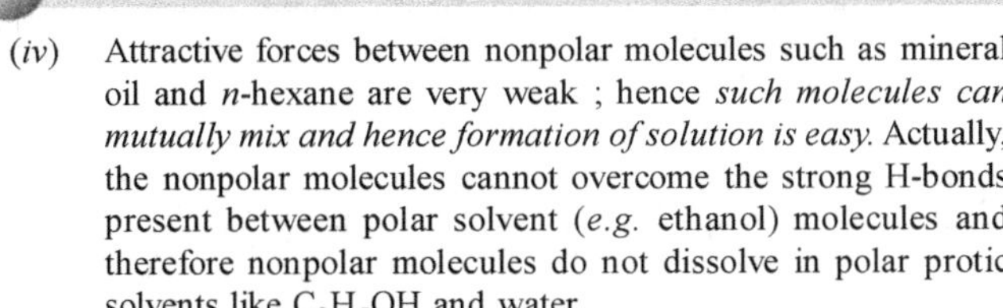

The reaction goes in the right direction because HCl is a good proton donor and hence a strong acid. Remember that an acid-base reaction goes in the direction of weak acid-weak base.

(*b*)

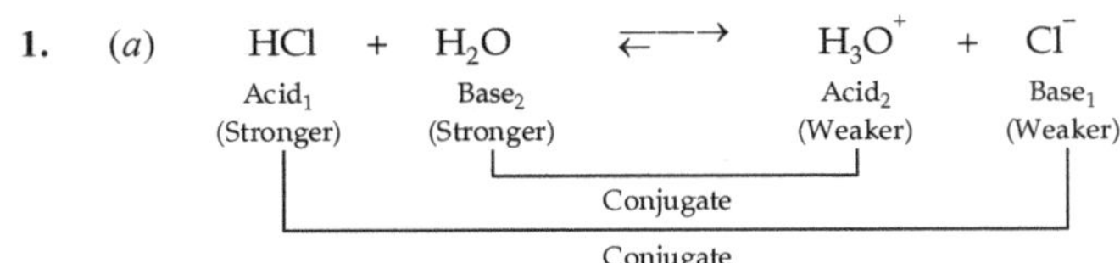

The reaction goes in the left direction because $NH_3$ is a poor proton acceptor (a weak base). Note the amphoteric (acidic as well as basic) character of $H_2O$.

**2.** (*a*)

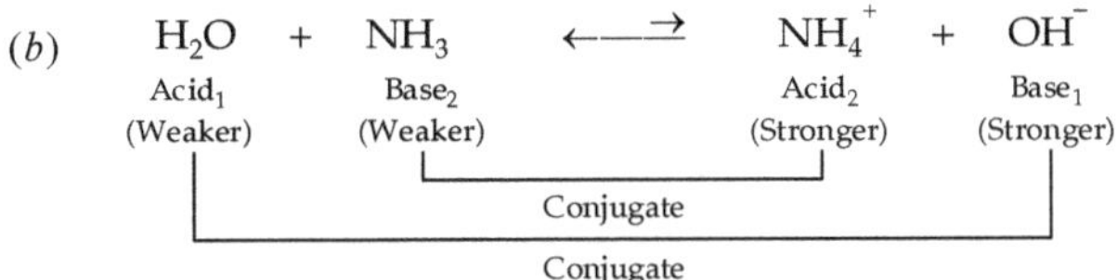

$$\underset{\text{Stronger base}}{NH_3} + \underset{\text{Stronger acid}}{H_3O^+} \xleftarrow{\hspace{1cm}} \underset{\text{Weaker acid}}{NH_4^+} + \underset{\text{Weaker base}}{H_2O}$$

(*b*)
$$\underset{\text{Weaker base}}{CN^-} + \underset{\text{Weaker acid}}{H_2O} \xrightarrow{\hspace{1cm}} \underset{\text{Stronger acid}}{HCN} + \underset{\text{Stronger base}}{OH^-}$$

(*c*)
$$\underset{\text{Stronger base}}{H^-} + \underset{\text{Stronger acid}}{H_2O} \longrightarrow \underset{\text{Weaker acid}}{H_2} + \underset{\text{Weaker base}}{OH^-}$$

(*d*)
$$\underset{\text{Stronger base}}{C_2^{2-}} + \underset{\text{Stronger acid}}{H_2O} \longrightarrow \underset{\text{Weaker base}}{2OH^-} + \underset{\text{Weaker acid}}{C_2H_2}$$

### TEST YOUR UNDERSTANDING - 2.8

**1.** Consider the conjugate base of the various species

(*a*) $CH_3O^-$ and $CH_3S^-$ are conjugate bases of $CH_3OH$ and $CH_3SH$ respectively. Here oxygen and sulphur are in the same family of the periodic table, and sulphur is bigger than oxygen causing greater dispersal of the charge. Thus formation of $CH_3S^-$ will be easier *i.e.* it is more stable. Hence *Acidity* $CH_3OH < CH_3SH$.

(*b*) Conjugate bases of $NH_4^+$ and $H_3O^+$ are $NH_3$ and $H_2O$ respectively. Here N and O are in the same row (period) of the period table, and oxygen is more electronegative than nitrogen, thus $H_2O$ will be more stable than $NH_2$. Hence *Acidity* $NH_4^+ < H_3O^+$.

(*c*) Conjugate bases of $NH_4^+$ and $NH_3$ are $NH_3$ and $NH_2^-$ respectively. Here lone pair of electrons formed by loss of proton is better accommodated in : $NH_3$ (a neutral species) than in : $NH_2^-$ (a negatively charged species). Hence

Stability $\qquad NH_2^- < NH_3$ ; Acidity $\qquad NH_3 < NH_4^+$

(*d*) Conjugate bases of $H_2O$ and $OH^-$ are $OH^-$ and $O^{2-}$ respectively. Here lone pair of electrons due to loss of proton is better accommodated in $OH^-$ (single negative charge) than in $O^{2-}$ (a doubly negatively charged). Hence

Stability $\qquad O^{2-} < OH^-$ ; Acidity $\qquad OH^- < H_2O$

**2.** First write down the conjugate base.

(*a*) The four species are $H_2O$, $NH_3$, HF and $CH_4$. Their conjugate bases are $OH^-$, $NH_2^-$, $F^-$ and $CH_3^-$. The central atoms of these species (O, N, F and C) are present in the same row *i.e.* in the same periodic table. Hence their electronegativity will determine their stability.

Electronegativity order $\qquad C < N < O < F$

Hence stability order $\qquad CH_3^- < NH_2^- < OH^- < F^-$

Hence acidity order $\qquad CH_4 < NH_3 < H_2O < HF$

(*b*) The four species are HCl, HBr, HF and HI. Their conjugate bases are $Cl^-$, $Br^-$, $F^-$ and $I^-$.

Atoms of these ions belong to the same group of the periodic table, hence their size increases on going down the group. Thus

*Size order* $\qquad F < Cl < Br < I$

*Stability order* $\qquad F^- < Cl^- < Br^- < I^-$

Remember that bigger the size of the ion, more will be its stability.

Hence *acidity* $\qquad HF < HCl < HBr < HI$.

**3.** For determining the relative basic character, follow the following points.

(*a*) In case the atoms bearing electron pair are in the same row of the periodic table, observe their *electronegativity* (more is the electronegativity of the atom less will be the basic character of the species bearing it).

(*b*) In case the atoms bearing electron pair are in the same family (group) of the periodic table, observe their *size* (the bigger the atom, more its ability to accommodate the electron pair and hence lesser will be the basic character of the species bearing it).

(*i*) *Basic character* $\qquad CH_3NH_2 > CH_3OH > CH_3F$

(*ii*) *Basicity* $\qquad CH_3^- > NH_2^- > OH^- > F^-$

(*iii*) *Basicity* $\qquad OH^- > SH^- > SeH^-$

(*iv*) *Basicity* $\qquad F^- > Cl^- > Br^- > I^-$

(*v*) Decreasing basic character.

We know that more the availability of lone pair of electrons, more is the basic character. Structures I and II do not exhibit resonance, and thus lone pair of electrons is localised and easily available for protonation, compound II is less basic than I because of presence of electronegative oxygen atom.

In compound III also, although lone pair of electrons on N is not involved in resonance but it is present on N attached to C by a double bond, hence it is less available than the N of I and II. In IV, lone pair of electrons on N is involved in resonance and hence least available for protonation.

**4.** Neither pure acid is ionized. However, in the mixture of $HClO_4$ and $H_2SO_4$, the stronger one ($HClO_4$) acts as an acid and thus donates a proton to $H_2SO_4$ (here a weaker acid) to form a mixture of ions.

$$\underset{\text{Acid}_1}{HClO_4} + \underset{\text{Base}_2}{H_2SO_4} \xleftarrow{\hspace{1cm}} \underset{\text{Acid}_2}{H_3SO_4^+} + \underset{\text{Base}_1}{ClO_4^-}$$

$HClO_4$ is a stronger acid than $H_2SO_4$ because of the two conjugate bases ($ClO_4^-$ and $HSO_4^-$), $ClO_4^-$ is a weaker base than $HSO_4^-$ because of more electronegativity of Cl than that of S. Hence here $H_2SO_4$ is acting as a base.

**5.** Reversible protonation of an unshared electron pair on an oxygen atom converts the organic compound into an ionic compound, a salt, which is soluble in the highly polar solvent, conc. $H_2SO_4$.

$$-\ddot{O}- + H_2SO_4 \xleftarrow{\hspace{1cm}} \underset{\text{Ionic compound}}{-\overset{\overset{\displaystyle H^+}{|}}{\underset{\ \ }{O}}} + HSO_4^-$$

# EXERCISE 2.1

| 1 | (b) | 6 | (b) | 11 | (c) | 16 | (b) | 21 | (b) | 26 | (d) | 31 | (b) | 36 | (b) | 41 | (b) | 46 | (b) | 51 | (b) | 56 | (b) | 61 | (a) |
|---|-----|---|-----|----|-----|----|-----|----|-----|----|-----|----|-----|----|-----|----|-----|----|-----|----|-----|----|-----|----|-----|
| 2 | (c) | 7 | (d) | 12 | (c) | 17 | (b) | 22 | (d) | 27 | (b) | 32 | (c) | 37 | (b) | 42 | (d) | 47 | (b) | 52 | (c) | 57 | (b) | 62 | (d) |
| 3 | (c) | 8 | (a) | 13 | (d) | 18 | (a) | 23 | (d) | 28 | (a) | 33 | (c) | 38 | (b) | 43 | (d) | 48 | (c) | 53 | (b) | 58 | (c) | 63 | (b) |
| 4 | (c) | 9 | (c) | 14 | (c) | 19 | (d) | 24 | (c) | 29 | (c) | 34 | (d) | 39 | (b) | 44 | (c) | 49 | (d) | 54 | (b) | 59 | (a) | 64 | (d) |
| 5 | (b) | 10 | (d) | 15 | (a) | 20 | (d) | 25 | (c) | 30 | (d) | 35 | (a) | 40 | (b) | 45 | (b) | 50 | (b) | 55 | (d) | 60 | (b) | 65 | (c) |
|   |     |   |     |    |     |    |     |    |     |    |     |    |     |    |     |    |     |    |     |    |     |    |     | 66 | (b) |

**1.** In ammonia, $2s^2\, 2p_x^{\,1}$, $2p_y^{\,1}$ and $2p_z^{\,1}$ orbitals of nitrogen undergo hybridisation to form four $sp^3$ orbitals, one having 2 electrons and the remaining three have 1 electron each.

**2.** In $BF_4^-$, the central atom (B) has only bonding electrons, *i.e.* no lone pair of electrons is present on the $sp^3$ hybridised B.

**3.** Dipole moment is due to difference in electronegativity of the two atoms. In toluene carbon atom of nucleus is $sp^2$ hybridised and hence more electronegative than that of side chain which is $sp^3$ hybridised.

**4.** D is more electron-releasing than H ; hence relative to the C—H bond, the C—D bond has a dipole from D to C.

**5.** Structure I is most stable as it has no formal charge, while structure II is least stable because the negative charge is present on N rather than the more electronegative O as in III.

**6.** Structure II is not possible because the bulky iodine atom will push the *ortho* —$NO_2$ groups out of the plane of the ring, hence the two —$NO_2$ groups can't participate in resonance (*steric inhibition of resonance*).

**7.** An ion in which all atoms have complete octet of electrons and hydrogen has duet is more stable than the other.

**8.** The carbonate ion is a hybrid of three equivalent structures ; each carbon-oxygen bond is double (C = O) in one structure and single (C—O) in the other two. Thus each carbon-oxygen bond has less double bond character and hence is longer, than the bonds in formate ion which is hybrid of two equivalent structures.

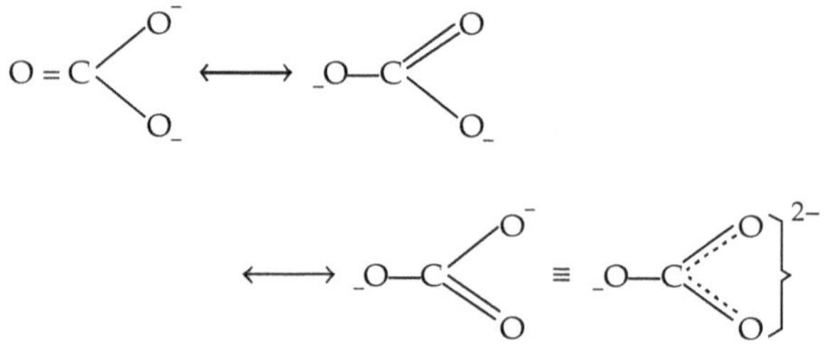

Resonating structures of $CO_3^{2-}$

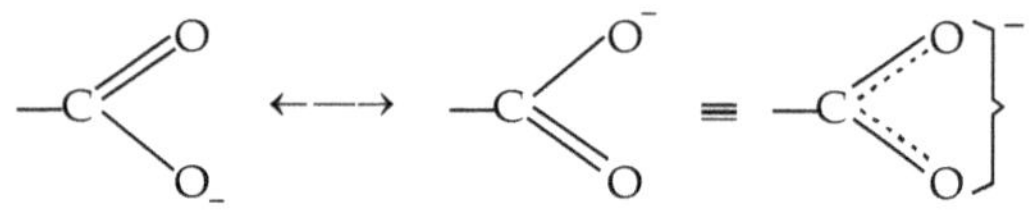

Resonating structures of —$COO^-$ ion

**9.** Let us first write the resonance hybrid of the three allyl carbonium ions.

$$\overset{1}{C}H_2 \cdots \overset{2}{C}H \cdots \overset{3}{C}H \leftarrow CH_3 \qquad\qquad CH_2 \cdots \overset{\underset{\displaystyle CH_3}{\big|}}{C} \cdots CH_2$$

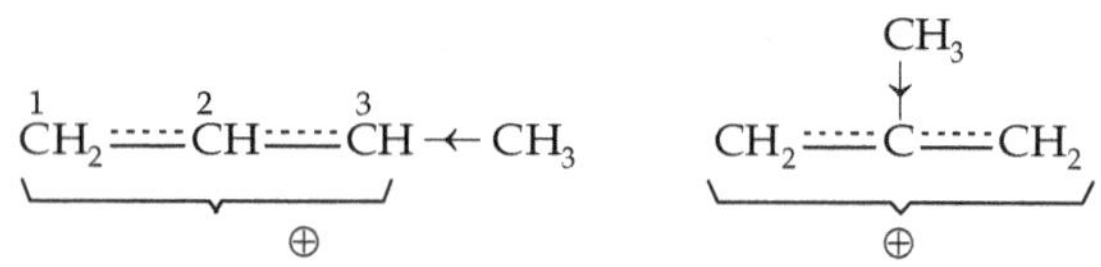

I $\oplus$      II $\oplus$

$$CH_3 \rightarrow \overset{3}{C}H \cdots \overset{2}{C}H \cdots \overset{1}{C}H_2$$

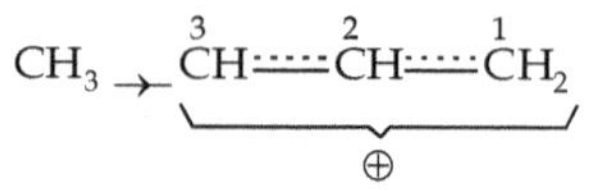

III $\oplus$

We know that better the dispersal of + charge, more will be the stability of the carbonium ion. Further, we know that $C_1$ and $C_3$ carry most of the positive charge which is

$$\overset{1}{C}H_2 = \overset{2}{C}H - \underset{\oplus}{\overset{3}{C}H} \leftarrow CH_3 \quad\longleftrightarrow\quad \underset{\oplus}{\overset{1}{C}H_2} - \overset{2}{C}H = \overset{3}{C}H - CH_3$$

dispersed by the methyl group (+ I group) present on I and III, thus these two are more and equally stable than the II in which methyl group is present on $C_2$ which carry little of the positive charge.

**10.** In all structures except (*d*), $\pi$ bond is in conjugation with the hyperconjugated H—C bonds represented by bold H.

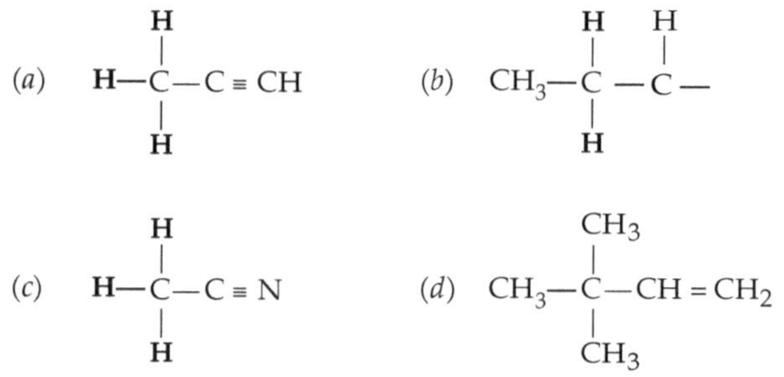

(*a*)    H—C—C $\equiv$ CH      (*b*)    $CH_3$—C —C—

(*c*)    H—C—C $\equiv$ N      (*d*)    $CH_3$—C—CH = $CH_2$

**11.** Solution of a salt, such as NaCl, necessitates separation of the attracting ions (*i.e.* $Na^+$ and $Cl^-$ ions). In presence of strong polar solvents like $H_2O$, both ions ($Na^+$ as well as $Cl^-$) are surrounded by water molecules in the following ways :

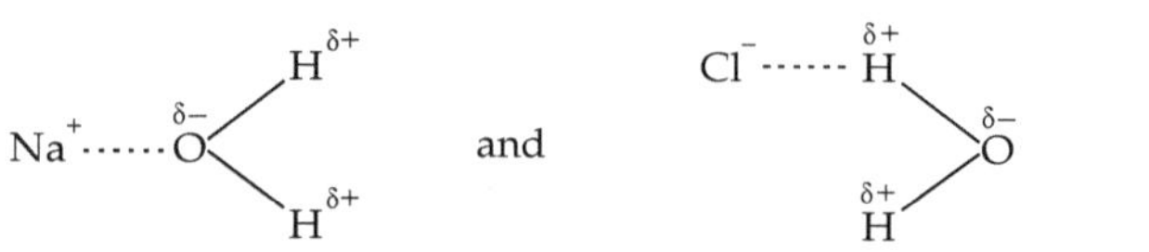

Ion-dipole attraction     and     Hydrogen bond between $Cl^-$ and $H_2O$

**12.** Butter and $CCl_4$, both have very weak forces between them, hence they mix with each other.

**13.** Lithium compounds are ionic, hence are insoluble in organic solvents and have high melting points ; while beryllium salts are covalent, hence soluble in organic solvents and will melt at low temperatures.

**14.** *n*-Butanol molecules can form hydrogen bonding between themselves (association) raising its boiling point, it can also form hydrogen bonding between water molecules (intermolecular hydrogen bonding) leading to its solubility in water. Diethyl ether, on the other hand, can't associate because of absence of H atom on O, hence its b.p. will be low than the isomeric *n*-butanol ;

however it can form H-bonding with water through its O with the H of water.

$$C_2H_5\text{—}O\cdots H\text{—}O\text{—}H \quad (C_2H_5)$$

(*a*) Diethyl ether

(*b*) *n*-Butanol

**15.**

Tetrahedral, (*i*)　　Square, (*ii*)　　Square, (*iii*)
Net moment　　　Net moment　　　Net moment = 0

In (*i*) and (*ii*) bond moments in opposite directions are not cancelled, while in (*iii*) individual bond moments are cancelled.

**16.** Increase in positive charge in closely related species increases acidity while increase in negative charge decreases acidity because the conjugate base (formed by loss of proton) will become less stable with the increase in negative charge.

$$O^{2-} \; < \; OH^- \; < \; H_2O$$

Stability of the three conjugated bases.

This is because the electron pair left behind upon the loss of proton is easily accommodated in a neutral conjugate base, followed by univalent ion, then bivalent ion, and so on.

Hence $\quad OH^- \; < \; H_2O \; < \; H_3O^+$

Stability of the three conjugate acids

**17.** $H_3C:^-$ is much stronger base than $:\ddot{F}:^-$ due to following two factors.

(*a*) F is much more electronegative than C.

(*b*) Electron density of $F^-$ is dispersed over its entire surface (100%), while that of $H_3C^-$ is dispersed over only one-fourth of its surface (25%), the remaining three-fourth surface is occupied by three hydrogens. Thus electrons of $F^-$ are more dispersed (and hence less available for protonation) than that of $CH_3^-$.

**18.** The difference of $CH_3COOH$ as an acid in water and methanol is due to difference in solvation of the ions. Water solvates ions better than does methanol, hence

(*i*) $CH_3COOH + H_2O \; \rightleftharpoons \; CH_3COO^- + H_3O^+$

(*ii*) $CH_3COOH + CH_3OH \; \rightleftharpoons \; CH_3COO^- + CH_3OH_2^+$

reaction (*i*) is shifted more toward the right than the reaction (*ii*)

**19.** 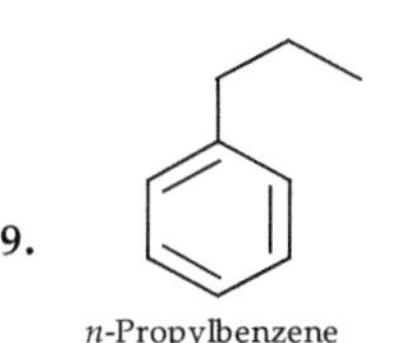

*n*-Propylbenzene　　*iso*propylbenzene　　*o*-, *m*- and *p*-Ethyltoluenes

**20.**

1, 2, 3-, 1, 2, 4- and 1, 3, 5-Trimethylbenzenes

**21.** For this we must know the mechanism of enolisation. Note that α–H atom in II is more labile than in the ketone I

$$CH_3\text{—}\overset{O}{\overset{\|}{C}}\text{—}CH_2COOC_2H_5 \; \underset{D^+}{\rightleftharpoons} \; CH_3\text{—}\overset{+OD}{\overset{\|}{C}}\text{—}\overset{}{\underset{H}{CH}}COOC_2H_5$$

Ketone, I　　　　　　　Conjugate acid, II

$$\overset{slow}{\rightleftharpoons} \; CH_3\text{—}\overset{OD}{\overset{|}{C}} = CHCOOC_2H_5 + H^+$$

**22.** Geometrical isomers differ in all physical properties.

**23.** $\quad CH_3CH_2CH = CH_2 \qquad CH_3CH = CHCH_3$

1-Butene　　　　　　*cis*-2-Butene
　　　　　　　　　　*trans*-2-Butene

Cyclobutane　　　Methylcyclopropane

**24.** 

Maleic acid　　　　　Fumaric acid

Unsaturated dicarboxylic acid　　Cyclic ester

**25.** Only I and IV have α-hydrogen atoms.

**26.** Carbanion of all the four compounds are stabilised by resonance, hence α-hydrogen atom of all will be acidic. However, resonance stabilisation of the carbanion formed by (*c*) and (*d*) is more than that from (*a*) and (*b*). Further among (*c*) and (*d*), parent compound

(c) also shows resonance due to $—\overset{..}{\text{O}}\text{C}_2\text{H}_5$ group, hence its carbanion will be relatively less stable than that of the (d).

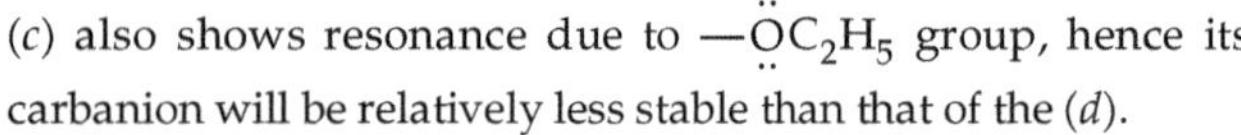

$$CH_3—\overset{O}{\overset{||}{C}}—CH_2—\overset{O}{\overset{||}{C}}—\overset{..}{\underset{..}{O}}C_2H_5 \longleftrightarrow CH_3—\overset{O}{\overset{||}{C}}—CH_2—\overset{:\overset{..}{\underset{..}{O}}:^{\ominus}}{C}=\overset{+}{\underset{..}{O}}C_2H_5$$
(c)
Resonance due to —OC$_2$H$_5$ grouping

$$CH_3—\overset{O}{\overset{||}{C}}—CH_2—\boxed{\overset{O}{\overset{||}{C}}—H}$$
(d)   no resonance is possible in this group.

Hence compound (d) will have more tendency to be converted to carbanion.

**27.** Urea, $H_2NCONH_2$ can show lactam-lactim tautomerism, or functional isomerism with $NH_4CNO$ (ammonium cyanate).

$$H_2N—\overset{O}{\overset{||}{C}}—NH_2 \rightleftharpoons HN=\overset{OH}{\overset{|}{C}}—NH_2$$

**30.** Since olefinic bond has upper position in the seniority table, it should be given lower number in numbering than the acetylenic linkage. $C^2$ is having double bond one side *i.e.* it is $sp^2$ hybridised while $C^3$ has single bonds on both sides, it is $sp^3$ hybridised.

**31.** I and II have greater number of covalent bonds and thus more stable than either III or IV. Further I has no formal charge, thus it is more stable than II having formal charges. Further IV is less stable because here negative charge is present on carbon (a lesser electronegative atom than oxygen) and positive charge on oxygen (a more electronegative element) ; while it is reverse in III which is in accordance with the nature of the two atoms (oxygen and carbon).

**32.** A resonating structure in which every atom has 8 valence electrons (octet) is said to be the most stable, on the contrary a structure having more than 8 valence electrons in any of its atoms is said to be most unstable.

**33.** Structure (c) has 10 valence electrons in N.

**34.** $C_4H_8O$ corresponds to general formula, $C_nH_{2n}O$ for aldehydes and ketones. Thus different isomeric aldehydes, ketones and unsaturated alcohols are

(i)   $CH_3CH_2CH_2CHO$      (ii)   $CH_3\overset{CHO}{\overset{|}{CH}}CH_3$
    1° aldehyde              2° aldehyde

(iii)   $CH_3COCH_2CH_3$      (vi)   $CH_2=CHCH_2CH_2OH$
    ketone                  1° alcohol

(v)   $CH_3CH=CHCH_2OH$   (vi)   $CH_2=CH\overset{OH}{\overset{|}{CH}}CH_3$
    1° alcohol              2° alcohol

**35.**
$$H—\overset{H}{\underset{H}{\overset{|}{\underset{|}{C}}}}—\overset{:\overset{..}{O}—H}{\overset{|}{C}}=\overset{H}{\overset{|}{C}}—H$$
Acetone (enolic form)

No. of σ bonds = 9
No. of π bond = 1
No. of lone pairs = 2

**36.** Enolisation is possible only in those structures which have at least one α-hydrogen atom to the ketonic group ; in structure (b) α-hydrogen atom to ketonic group is not present.

# EXERCISE 2.2

| >1 | 1 | (a,b,c) | 2 | (a,c) | 3 | (a,b,c) | 4 | (a,b,c,d) | 5 | (a,c) | 6 | (a,b,d) |
|---|---|---|---|---|---|---|---|---|---|---|---|---|
| **CORRECT** | 7 | (c,d) | 8 | (a, b, c) | 9 | (a,b,c,d) | 10 | (a, b, c) | 11 | (c, d) | 12 | (b, d) |
| **OPTION** | 13 | (a, b, c) | 14 | (a, b) | 15 | (a,b,c,d) | 16 | (a,b,c) | 17 | (a,b) | 18 | (a,b,c) |
| **PASSAGE 1** | 19 | (a,b,c,d) | 20 | (d) | 21 | (b) | 22 | (a,b) | 23 | (d) | 24 | (c) |
| **PASSAGE 2** | 25 | (c) | 26 | (b) | 27 | (d) | 28 | (b) | 29 | (b, c) | 30 | (a,b,c) |
| | 31 | (a,b,c) | 32 | (a,b,c) | 33 | (a,b,c) | | | | | | |
| **PASSAGE 3** | 34 | (d) | 35 | (d) | 36 | (b,d) | 37 | (b) | 38 | (b) | 39 | (b) |
| | 40 | (b) | 41 | (a) | | | | | | | | |
| **PASSAGE 4** | 42 | (a, c) | 43 | (a) | 44 | (c) | | | | | | |
| **PASSAGE 5** | 45 | (c) | 46 | (b) | 47 | (d) | | | | | | |
| **PASSAGE 6** | 48 | (c) | 49 | (a) | 50 | (c) | | | | | | |
| **PASSAGE 7** | 51 | (c) | 52 | (a) | 53 | (c) | | | | | | |
| **PASSAGE 8** | 54 | (b) | 55 | (a) | 56 | (a) | | | | | | |
| **MATCHING TYPE QUESTIONS** | 57 | (A) - a, c; (B) - c; (C) - c; (D) - b, d | | | | | 58 | (A) - a, b ; (B) -d ; (C) - b, c ; (D) - a | | | | |
| | 59 | (A) - b, c ; (B) - c, d ; (C) -d (D) - a,d | | | | | 60 | (A) – a,b,d; (B) – a,b; (C) – c; (D) – a,b | | | | |
| | 61 | (A)-e; (B)-f; (C)-b; (D)-a; (E)-c; (F)-d | | | | | 62 | (A) - b ; (B) - c, d ; (C) -a, b (D) -a, b | | | | |
| | 63 | (A)-a, b ; (B)-a, c ; (C)-b, d ; (D)-b, d | | | | | | | | | | |
| **A/R** | 64 | (a) | 65 | (b) | 66 | (a) | 67 | (a) | 68 | (d) | 69 | (c) |
| | 70 | (b) | | | | | | | | | | |
| **TRUE/FALSE** | 71 | FALSE | 72 | **TRUE** | 73 | TRUE | 74 | **FALSE** | 75 | FALSE | 76 | **TRUE** |
| | 77 | FALSE | 78 | **FALSE** | 79 | TRUE | 80 | **FALSE** | 81 | TRUE | 82 | **TRUE** |

**65.**

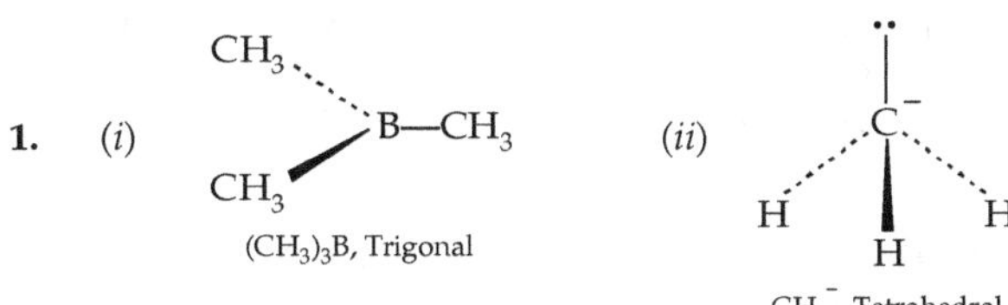

Statement-1 is True, Statement-2 is True but reason is not the correct explanation of assertion.

**68.** p-Hydroxybenzoic acid has higher boiling point than o-hydroxybenzoic acid due to intermolecular hydrogen bonding. Thus, statement-1 is false. o-Hydroxybezoic acid shows intramolecular H-bonding thus, statement-2 is true.

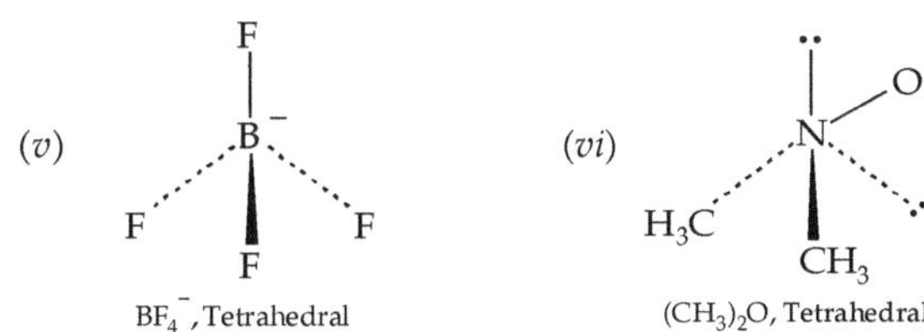

**69.** Trichloro acedic acid is stronger acid as three chloro substituents are electron withdrawing.

**70.** Neopentane forms one mono substituted compound as shown below :

$$CH_3-\underset{\underset{CH_3}{|}}{\overset{\overset{CH_3}{|}}{C}}-CH_3 \xrightarrow{CH_2} H_3C-\underset{\underset{CH_3}{|}}{\overset{\overset{CH_3}{|}}{C}}-CH_2Cl$$

It is 1-chloro 2, 2-dimethyl propane.
It forms only one mono substituted compound not because it is isomer of pentane but because its structure is symmetrical (all the form carbons are symmetrically situated around central carbon).

# EXERCISE 2.3

**1.** *(i)* (CH₃)₃B, Trigonal    *(ii)* CH₃⁻, Tetrahedral

*(iii)* CH₃⁺, Trigonal    *(iv)* NH₂⁻, Tetrahedral

*(v)* BF₄⁻, Tetrahedral    *(vi)* (CH₃)₂O, Tetrahedral

**2.**

| Species | Conjugate acid | Conugate base |
| --- | --- | --- |
| (a) $HNO_3$ | $H_2NO_3^+$ | $NO_3^-$ |
| (b) $H{:}^-$ | $H_2$ | None |
| (c) $:CH_3^-$ | $CH_4$ | $:CH_2^{2-}$ |
| (d) $Cl^-$ | $HCl$ | None |
| (e) $CH_2 = CH_2$ | $CH_3-CH_2^+$ | $CH_2 = \ddot{C}H^-$ |
| (f) $CH_3O^-$ | $CH_3OH$ | $:CH_2O^{2-}$ |

However, practically conjugate bases in (c) and (f) are difficult to form, hence it can be said that $CH_3O^-$ and $:CH_3^-$ have no conjugate bases.

Thus $HNO_3$ and $CH_2 = CH_2$ are amphoteric.

**3.** *(a)* $NH_3$ is stronger base than $PH_3$ because of smaller size of N.

*(b)* $NH_2^-$ is stronger base than $OH^-$ because of less electronegativity of N than that of O. Moreover in $:NH_2^-$, electron density is dispersed over one-third (33%) of the surface while in $OH^-$ electron density is dispersed over half (50%) of the surface.

*(c)* Basic character of $HS^-$ and $F^-$ cannot be compared because F and S are in different groups and different periods of the periodic table.

**4.** Degree of association is very high in water as compared to that in ethanol because presence of bulky alkyl groups hinders the formation of intermolecular hydrogen bonding.

**5.** Relative stability of alkenes can be explained on the basis of hyperconjugation, more the number of hyperconjugative structures (*i.e.* α—H atoms, written, below the each member), more will be the stability of the alkene.

$$\overset{\alpha}{C}H_3 —CH = CH_2 \qquad H_2C = CH_2 \qquad \underset{\underset{6}{\overset{\alpha}{C}H_3}}{\overset{\overset{\alpha}{C}H_3}{}}C = CH_2$$

3-Hyperconjugative structures    No    6-Hyperconjugative structures

9 Hyperconjugate structures    12 Hyperconjugative structures

Hence order of stability is
$$(CH_3)_2C = C(CH_3)_2 > (CH_3)_2C = CHCH_3 > (CH_3)_2C = CH_2 > CH_3CH = CH_2 > CH_2 = CH_2.$$

**6.** *(i)* Guanidine is a strong base because it can accept proton very easily and the protonated guanidine is quite stable as it is a resonance hybrid of three equivalent structures.

Three equivalent resonating structures

Note that protonation occurs only at $sp^2$ hybridised nitrogen atom because this leads to a species very much stabilised by three *equivalent* resonating structures. Protonation on $sp^3$ hybridised N atom gives species which is not stabilised by resonance to any significant extent.

*(ii)* Vinyl alcohol behaves as a weak acid because the ion formed by deprotonation is more stable than the parent compound.

$$CH_2 = CH—\overset{..}{\underset{..}{O}}H \longleftrightarrow \overset{\ominus}{\overset{..}{C}H_2}—CH = \overset{+}{O}H$$

Less stable due to charge separation

$\downarrow -H^+$

$$CH_2 = CH—\overset{..}{\underset{..}{O}}\overset{\ominus}{:} \longleftrightarrow \overset{..}{\underset{..}{C}H_2}—CH = O$$

More stable due to absence of charge separation

*(iii)* α-Hydrogen atom of aldehydes and ketones is acidic in nature because the carbanion formed by its loss is stablised by resonance.

$$H_3C—\overset{\overset{O}{\|}}{C}—R \xrightarrow{-H^+} H_2\overset{\ominus}{C}—\overset{\overset{O}{\|}}{C}—R \longleftrightarrow H_2C = \overset{\overset{O^-}{|}}{C}—R$$

Aldehydes/ketones (No resonance)     Resonance stabilization of carbanion of aldehydes/ketones

*(iv)* In methanol, fluoride ion is linked to $CH_3OH$ via H—bond ($CH_3OH - - - F^-$) with the result reactivity of $F^-$ is decreased. The other two solvents are incapable of forming H—bond.

*(v)* NaCl is electrovalent, while $AlCl_3$ is covalent.

*(vi)* In acylium ion, $R—C \equiv \overset{+}{O}$ : is more stable than $R—\overset{+}{C} = O$, the ordinary carbonium ion, because in the former the octet of every atom is complete while in the later, the carbon atom has only 6 electrons.

**7.** If a structure is capable of forming 5- or 6-memberd ring structure it is said to be stable. In the enolic form of the given compounds 6-membered ring is formed due to hydrogen bonding, thus the enolic forms of these compounds are said to be stable.

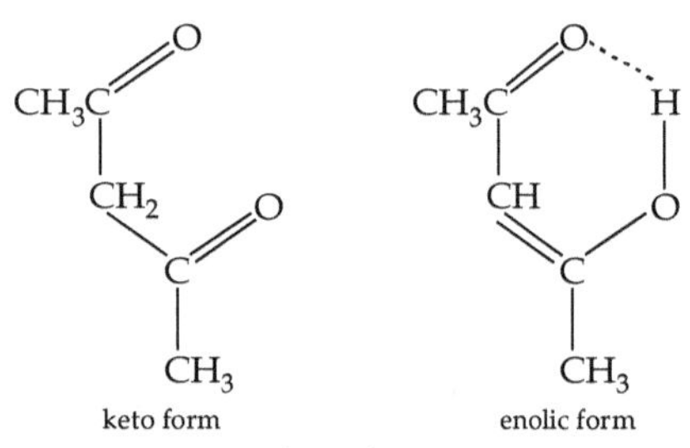

keto form     enolic form

**Acetylacetone**

keto form     enolic form

**Ethyl acetoacetate**

keto form     enolic form

**Diethyl malonate**

**8.** *(i)* $sp^3, sp$     *(ii)* $sp^3, sp^2, sp^2$
   *(iii)* $sp^3, sp, sp, sp^3$     *(iv)* $sp, sp, sp^2, sp^2$.

**9.** *(a)*

$$\begin{matrix} H—C—Cl \\ \| \\ H—C—Cl \end{matrix} \qquad \begin{matrix} H—C—Cl \\ \| \\ Cl—C—H \end{matrix}$$

*cis*-1,2-Dichloroethylene (Polar)    *trans*-1,2-Dichloroethylene (Non-polar)

*(b)* Resonance decreases the dipole moment of vinyl chloride. The positive charge on Cl and a negative charge on C (developed by resonance) oppose each other and hence diminish the electronegativity of Cl and thus polarity (and dipole moment) of the bond. The dipole moments of vinyl chloride and chlorobenzene are 1.4 D and 1.7D respectively, while the dipole moment of alkyl halides is 2– 2.2 D.

*(c)*

end     keto

**10.** *(a)* $:\overset{..}{O} = \overset{+}{O}—\overset{..}{\underset{..}{O}}: \longleftrightarrow :\overset{..}{\underset{..}{O}}—\overset{+}{O} = \overset{..}{O}:$

*(b)* $:\overset{-}{\underset{..}{O}}—\overset{+}{N}\overset{\overset{..}{O}:}{\underset{\overset{..}{\underset{..}{O}}:}{}} \longleftrightarrow :\overset{..}{O} = \overset{+}{N}\overset{\overset{..}{O}:}{\underset{\overset{..}{\underset{..}{O}}:}{}}$

$$\longleftrightarrow :\overset{-}{\underset{..}{O}}—\overset{+}{N}\overset{\overset{..}{\underset{..}{O}}:^-}{\underset{\overset{..}{O}:}{}}$$

and

$:\overset{..}{N} = \overset{+}{N} = \overset{..}{\underset{..}{N}}:^- \longleftrightarrow {}^{2-}:\overset{..}{\underset{..}{N}} - \overset{+}{N} \equiv N:$

$\longleftrightarrow :N \equiv \overset{+}{N}—\overset{..}{\underset{..}{N}}:^{2-} \longleftrightarrow :\overset{+}{N} = \overset{..}{N}—\overset{..}{\underset{..}{N}}:^{2-}$

**11.** Branching decreases the surface area of the molecule with the result vander Waal forces becomes less and hence the molecule boils at lower b.p. Thus the boiling point order is

    *n*-Hexane > 3-Methylpentane > 2, 2-Dimethylbutane

**12.** *(i)*

| | *iso*-Butane < | *n*-Butane < | *n*-Butyl chloride < | *n*-Butanol |
|---|---|---|---|---|
| Intermolecular forces | Weaker vander Waal | Stronger vander Waal | Dipole-dipole | H-bond |

*(ii)*

| | Propane < | *n*-Butane < | Ethanol < | Water |
|---|---|---|---|---|
| Intermolecular forces | Weaker vander Waal | Stronger vander Waal | Weaker H-bond | Stronger H-bond |

**13.** $CH_3CHO < CH_3COCH_3 < CH_3COCH_2CHO$
             $< CH_3COCH_2COCH_3$

**14.** I and II are tautomers (lactam-lactim type) ; II and III are resonating structures.

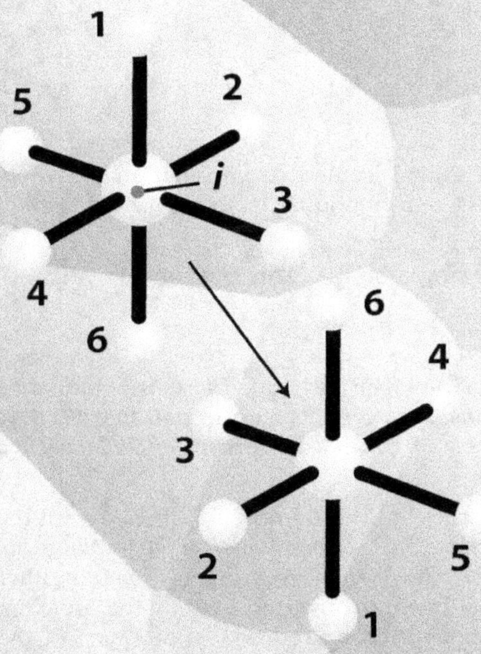

# Stereochemistry



Stereochemistry is the study of the three-dimensional structure of molecules. The foundation of organic stereochemistry was laid by Van't Hoff and Le Bel in 1874. They, independently, proposed that the four bonds to carbon were directed towards the corners of a tetrahedron. Stereochemistry explains the existence of *stereochemical isomers* or *stereoisomers*, namely *conformational* (those that can be interconverted by rotation about a sigma bond) and *configurational* (those that can be interconverted only by breaking and reforming of bonds). Two important sub-classes of configurational isomers are *geometrical isomers* (those in which restricted rotation in a ring or at a multiple bond determines the relative spatial arrangement of atoms) and *optical isomers* (those that differ in the three-dimensional relationship of substituents about one or more atoms).

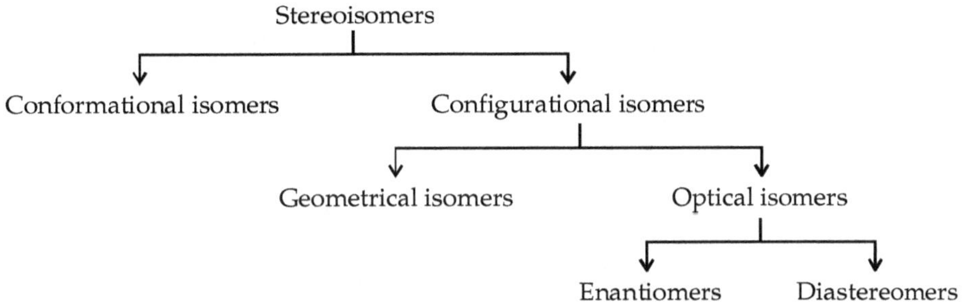


**Diastereomers (steroisomers that are not enantiomers) may not necessarily be optical isomers, geometrical isomers are also examples of diastereomers.**

## 3.1 Conformational Isomers

The isomers which differ in the conformation are known as conformational isomers. Conformational isomers are rapidly interconverted at room temperature, so **they cannot be sparated**. Conformational isomers are also called **conformers**. There are two kinds of conformational isomers.

(a)   Conformational isomers due to free rotation about carbon-carbon single bonds. This is found in alkanes, cycloalkanes and their substituted derivatives.

(b)   Conformers due to amine inversion, discussed in enantiomers.

**Conformations of alkanes.** There is restricted (but not free) rotation about a single bond. *The restricted rotation leads to the existence of a single compound of one configuration into more than one spatial arrangements* **(conformations).** So now **conformation** *may be defined as the term used to denote any one of the infinite number of spatial arrangements of the atoms of a molecule that can arise from rotation about a single bond.*

**Difference between conformation and configuration.** The term conformation should not be confused with the **configuration** *which relates to those spatial arrangements of the atoms of a molecule that can be changed only by the breaking and making of bonds* whereas the *spatial arrangements in* **conformation** *are changed simply by rotation about a single bond.* In other words we can say that the various stereoisomers that differ in configuration can be interconverted only by the breaking and making of bonds whereas the conformational arrangement may be interconverted by rotation of one part of the molecule with respect to the rest of the molecule about a single bond joining these two parts. The various conformations of some of the important compounds are dealt in the book to clarify the point.

**Representation of conformation.** Conformation of alkanes can best be represented with the help of Newmann projection formulae since eclipsing (overlapping or crowding) of hydrogen atoms can best be represented by this formula. In the Newmann projection formula, the carbon atoms nearer to the eye (*i.e.*, the front carbon) and the groups attached to it are represented by equally spaced radii and the distant carbon atom (*i.e.* the carbon atom farther from the eye or the rear carbon) and the groups attached to it are represented by a circle with three equally spaced radial extensions.

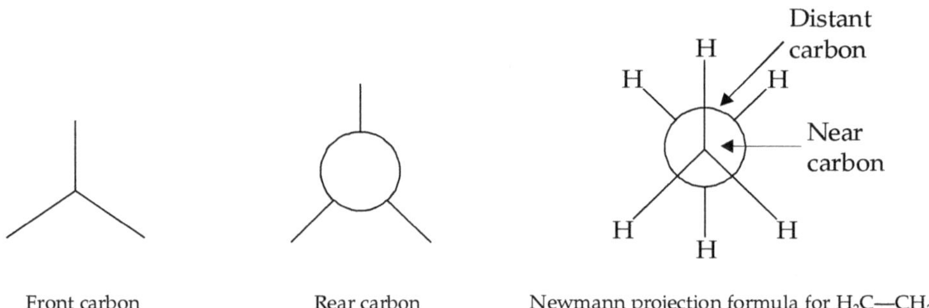

Front carbon          Rear carbon          Newmann projection formula for $H_3C$—$CH_3$

(a)   **Conformations of ethane.** The conformation of ethane, $H_3C$—$CH_3$ affords the simplest possible introduction of the subject. Imagine that one of the methyl groups is rotated along the C—C axis keeping the rest of molecule undisturbed. An infinite number of possible arrangements of the rotated methyl group with respect to the undisturbed methyl group are possible, each of these possible arrangement represents a **conformation.**

Any conformation can be specified by its **torsion angle or dihedral angle** ($\theta$), the angle between the C–H bonds on the front carbon atom and the C–H bonds on the back carbon in the Newmann projection.

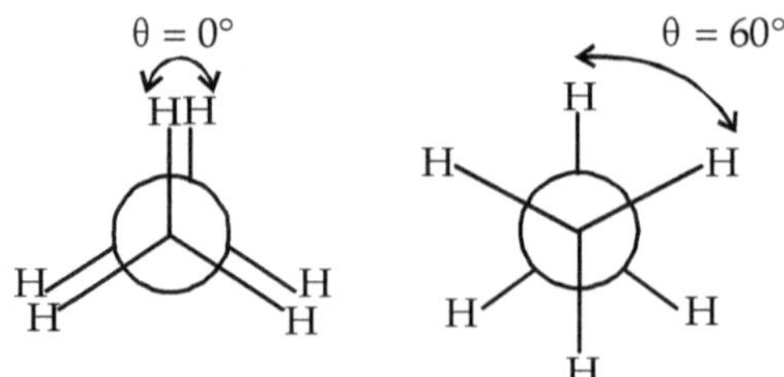

$\theta = 0°$          $\theta = 60°$

---

*   It is important to note that the bonds of the rear carbon in the eclipsed form in the Newmann projection formula are shown slightly displaced simply to make them visible otherwise in practice they eclipse (overlap) completely. However, this can beautifully be realised in the ball-and-stick model of the eclipsed form of ethane.

In ethane, the conformation with θ = 0° is called the **eclipsed conformation**, while the conformation with θ = 60° is called the **staggered conformation**.

However, for the sake of convenience each rotation is done in the instalment of 60°. Thus in such case we will obtain six different conformations of ethane. Of these six conformations, the two extreme ones are worth studying because these are very much different from each other, while the intermediate four conformations are almost similar to each other but of course different from the two extreme forms. Thus in short there will be three conformations of ethane, the two extremes and the third which will be the intermediate of the two extremes.

1. One extreme conformation will be such in which the rear methyl group is completely eclipsed by the front methyl group and thus only the front methyl group, *i.e.*, three hydrogen atoms of the methyl group nearer to the eye are visible. Such conformation is known as **eclipsed conformation.** In the Newmann projection formula of the eclipsed form, the hydrogen atoms are crowded, *i.e.* the two hydrogen atoms come close to each other.

2. Another extreme conformation will be such in which the rear methyl group has been rotated upside down and thus both the methyl groups, *i.e.*, all the six hydrogen atoms are visible and are as far apart from each other as possible. Such conformation is known as **staggered.**

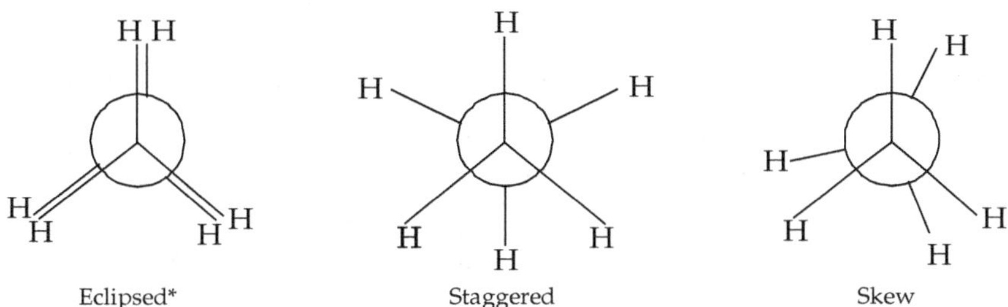

| Eclipsed* | Staggered | Skew |

3. The infinite number of possible intermediate conformations between the two extreme conformations are referred to as **skew conformations.** In these conformations, hydrogen atoms are closer than in staggered but away than in eclipsed conformation.

It is important to note that all the above conformations of ethane are not equally stable. Among the infinite number of conformations the *staggered conformation* in which hydrogen atoms are as far apart as possible *is the most stable* while the *eclipsed conformation* in which hydrogen atoms are perfectly eclipsed *is the least stable ;* stabilities of the skew conformations lie in between these two extreme limits. Hence the relative stabilities of the various conformations of ethane are in the following order.

Staggered > Skew > Eclipsed

This stability order can be explained in terms of repulsive interactions (non-bonded) between bonding pairs of electrons, *i.e.* electrons pair which form six C—H bonds in ethane. In the staggered conformation, the electron clouds of six carbon-hydrogen bonds are as far apart as possible with the result there is minimum repulsive interactions between these electron clouds. Hence this conformation is quite stable. On the other hand, in the skew and eclipsed conformations, the electron clouds start coming closer. This causes repulsive interactions which is maximum in the eclipsed conformation where there is minimum separation of the electrons of the six C—H bonds. Hence the potential energies of the skew and eclipsed conformations increase and thus their stabilities decrease which is minimum in case of eclipsed conformation.

*The repulsive interaction between the electron clouds which affects the stability of a conformation is known as* **torsional strain.** Of all the conformations of ethane, staggered conformation has the least torsional strain and hence most stable while eclipsed conformation has the maximum torsional strain and hence least stable. Due to torsional strain, certain energy called **torsional energy**, is required to allow rotation around the C—C single bond. In other words, an ethane molecule having staggered conformation will have to cross an energy barrier equivalent to the torsional energy for being converted into eclipsed conformation.

The energy difference between the staggered and eclipsed conformations of ethane is found to be 2.8 kcal/mole which constitutes the energy barrier to rotation about the C—C bond, *i.e.*, for the conversion of staggered to eclipsed conformation. However, this energy barrier of 2.8 kcal/mole is too small for either form to remain stable, *i.e.*, the two forms are interconvertible because even at ordinary temperature, ethane molecules have an average energy of 15—20 kcal/mole which can easily overcome the small barrier of 2.8 kcal/mole. This implies that *rotation about the carbon-carbon single bond in ethane is almost free for all practical purposes,* and it is not possible to separate the different conformations of ethane. Remember that ordinarily, ethane is mostly in staggered form.

**(b)**    **Conformations of butane :** Butane has three carbon-carbon single bonds, and the molecule can rotate about each of them. One of the staggered and one of the eclipsed conformations of butane due to rotation about the $C_1$–$C_2$ bond are drawn below.

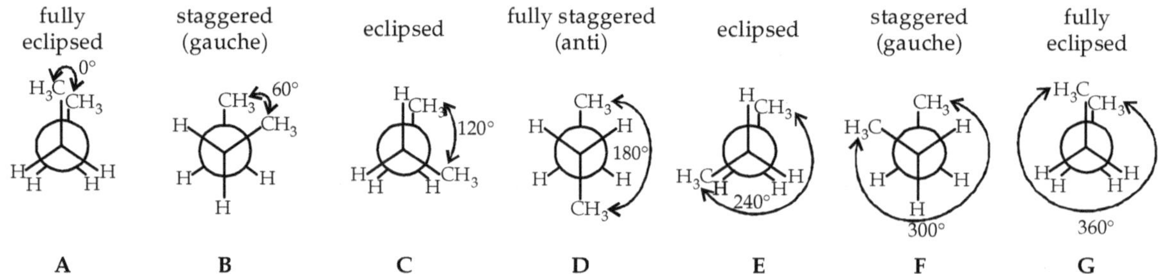

$$\overset{1}{C}H_3 - \overset{2}{C}H_2 - \overset{3}{C}H_2 - \overset{4}{C}H_3$$

A staggered conformation       An eclipsed conformation
due to rotation about the $C_1$–$C_2$    due to rotation about the $C_1$–$C_2$
bond in butane            bond in butane

It is important to note that all the staggered conformers due to rotation about the $C_1$–$C_2$ bond in butane have same energy (difference from the staggerred conformers due to rotation about the $C_2$–$C_3$ bond). The six important conformations of butane obtained due to rotation about the $C_2$–$C_3$ bond are drawn below.

| fully eclipsed | staggered (gauche) | eclipsed | fully staggered (anti) | eclipsed | staggered (gauche) | fully eclipsed |
|---|---|---|---|---|---|---|
| A | B | C | D | E | F | G |

Note that six different configurations are broadly of two types.

**(i)**    **Staggered :** Structures B, D and F in which the substitutents on the $C_2$ and $C_3$ are as far apart as possible. Hence they have less **steric strain** (**steric hindrance**) and thus more stable than the other three (A, C and E).

Further among the three staggered conformers, the conformer D is different from the other two staggered conformers B and F because in D the two methyl (bulky) groups are maximum possible away from each other, hence this conformation exerts less steric strain than the D and F, and thus it has less energy and more stable. The two types of staggered conformers are known as **anti** (D) and **gauche** (B and F) **conformers.**

**(ii)**    **Eclipsed :** Like the three staggered conformers (B, D and F), there are three eclipsed conformers (A, C and E) in which the substituents on $C_2$ and $C_3$ are closest to each other. Thus they have more steric strain, more energy and less stability. Further among the three eclipsed conformers, the eclipsed conformer A has two large ($CH_3$) groups closest to each other, while the other two (C and E) has two $CH_3$ groups away from each other. Hence A (called totally eclipsed) is less stable than the C and E (called eclipsed), although all the three A, C and E are less stable than B, D and F.

The order of stability of these conformations is

Anti  >  Gauche  >  Eclipsed  >  Fully eclipsed
D       B=F       C=E       A

In an alkane, most molecules are in staggered conformations, and further more molecules are in an anti conformation than in a gauche conformation (the two types of staggered conformers). The preference for a staggered conformation causes carbon chains to orient themselves in a zigzag fashion.

## TEST YOUR UNDERSTANDING - 3.1

**1.**    **(a)**    What structural features are necessary for a compound to exhibit conformational isomerism? Which of the following compounds have conformations?

            (i)   $CH_3Cl$         (ii)   $H_2O_2$         (iii)   $H_2NOH$         (iv)   $CH_2 = CH_2$

     **(b)**    Draw the two important conformational isomers of methanol.

**2.**    Draw the six conformations of propane.

**3.**    Using Newmann projections, draw the most stable conformer for the following.

     **(a)**    3-Methylbutane, considering rotation about the $C_2$ – $C_3$ bond.

     **(b)**    3,3-Dimethylhexane, considering rotation about the $C_3$ – $C_4$ bond.

**4.** Three conformations of 1, 1, 2, 2-tetrabromoethane are given below.

$$\text{I} \qquad\qquad \text{II} \qquad\qquad \text{III}$$

Answer the following regarding these.

(*i*)  Can any of the above conformation exhibit optical isomerism ?

(*ii*)  Is there any known relation between the three, if so mention it ?

**5.** Complete the following reactions

(*i*)  $CH_2OH.CHOH.CH = CH_2 \xrightarrow[\text{alk. KMnO}_4]{\text{Cold}} \underset{\text{Optically active}}{A} + \underset{\text{Optically inactive}}{B}$

(*ii*)  $CH_2OH.CHOH.CHOH.CH_2OH \xrightarrow{\text{1 mole HBr}} \underset{\text{(Optically active)}}{C}$

(*iii*)  2-Ethyl-3-methyl-1-pentene $\xrightarrow{H_2} \underset{\text{(Optically active)}}{D} + \underset{\text{(Optically inactive)}}{E}$

**6.** 1, 2-Dibromoethane has a zero dipole moment, while ethylene glycol has a measurable dipole moment. Explain.

## 3.2  Configurational Isomers

These isomers differ in the configuration (arrangement of substituents around a central atom). Since these isomers are not readily interconverted at room temperature, they can be separated. There are two kinds of configurational isomers : (a) *cis-trans isomers,* and (b) *isomers due to chirality centre (optical isomers).* Before going into details of the two types of configurational isomers, we must be familiar with the concept of configuration.

**Configuration :** In the study of the optical isomerism among organic compounds three different conventions are frequently used : D and L- ; *d*- and *l*- and (+) and (–)- ; the latter two have the same significance and are used to indicate the sign of rotation of the two enantiomers. The first convention, *i.e.,* D- and L-, is used to show the *configuration* of the compound. *By the term configuration we mean the arrangement of atoms or groups around the chiral centre* which is most commonly a carbon or nitrogen atom. It must be very clear to the reader that there is no significant relation between the sign of rotation and the configuration of an enantiomer because a compound and its derivatives having the same configuration may have different sign of rotation, *e.g.,* lactic acid and its esters, although having same configuration, possess opposite sign of rotation, *viz.* + 3.82° and – 8.25°, respectively. Two systems have been developed for studying the configuration of organic compounds.

### 3.2.1  Relative configuration (D, L-Nomenclature)

Before 1951, there was no method for determining the **absolute configuration** (actual arrangement of atoms in space) of a compound and hence the configuration of all the compounds were studied with respect to glyceraldehyde[1] **(relative configuration),** the configuration of which was taken as an arbitrary standard. (+) – Glyceraldehyde, having the —OH group on the right and the hydrogen atom on the left, the —CHO and —CH$_2$OH groups being at the top and bottom, respectively, was arbitrarily given the configurational symbol D. The mirror image compound (–)- gylceraldehyde, in which the –OH group is on the left and hydrogen on right was given the configuration, L.

$$\begin{array}{ccc}
& CHO & \\
H & —\overset{|}{\underset{|}{C}}— & OH \\
& CH_2OH &
\end{array}
\qquad\qquad
\begin{array}{ccc}
& CHO & \\
HO & —\overset{|}{\underset{|}{C}}— & H \\
& CH_2OH &
\end{array}$$

D-(+)-Glyceraldehyde[2]            L-(–)-Glyceraldehyde[2]
(having —OH to the right)        (having —OH to the left)

---

1.  Rosanoff chose glyceraldehyde as arbitrary standard for studying relative configuration because of its relationship to carbohydrates.

2.  (+)- and (–)-signs indicate that the two forms are dextro- and laevorotatory, respectively, but it must also be taken in mind that it is not necessary that all the compounds belonging to D- and L-series will be dextro- and laevorotatory, respectively.

Any compound that can be prepared from, or converted into D- (+)-glyceraldehyde will belong to the D-series, and similarly any compound that can be prepared from, or converted into, L–(–)-glyceraldehyde will belong to the L-series (**relative configuration**). For example, D-glyceraldehyde can be converted to glyceric acid by simple oxidation and thus the configuration of glyceric acid obtained must be D.

$$
\begin{array}{ccc}
\text{CHO} & & \text{COOH} \\
| & & | \\
\text{H—C—OH} & \xrightarrow{[O]} & \text{H—C—OH} \\
| & & | \\
\text{CH}_2\text{OH} & & \text{CH}_2\text{OH}
\end{array}
$$

D–(+)-Glyceraldehyde       D–(–)-Glyceric acid

Similarly, lactic acid obtained from D- (+)-glyceraldehyde in the following way is also assigned D-configuration.

$$
\begin{array}{c}
\text{CHO} \\
| \\
\text{H–C–OH} \\
| \\
\text{CH}_2\text{OH}
\end{array}
\xrightarrow{\text{oxidation}}
\begin{array}{c}
\text{COOH} \\
\text{H}\!\!-\!\!|\!\!-\!\!\text{OH} \\
\text{CH}_2\text{OH}
\end{array}
\xrightarrow{\text{PBr}_3}
\begin{array}{c}
\text{COOH} \\
| \\
\text{H–C–OH} \\
| \\
\text{CH}_2\text{Br}
\end{array}
\xrightarrow{\text{reduction}}
\begin{array}{c}
\text{COOH} \\
| \\
\text{H–C–OH} \\
| \\
\text{CH}_3
\end{array}
$$

D–(+)–Glyceraldehyde    D–(–)-Glyceric acid    D–(–)–3–Bromo–    D–(–)–Lactic acid<br>2–hydroxypropanoic acid

Although D,L-nomenclature also known as Fischer-Rosanoff convention is ambiguous, it is still widely used in the chemistry of amino acids and sugars. The D,L-configuration of all α-amino acids can be represented below.

$$
\begin{array}{cccc}
\text{COOH} & \text{COOH} & \text{COOH} & \text{COOH} \\
\text{H}\!\!-\!\!|\!\!-\!\!\text{NH}_2 & \text{H}_2\text{N}\!\!-\!\!|\!\!-\!\!\text{H} & \text{H}\!\!-\!\!|\!\!-\!\!\text{NH}_2 & \text{H}_2\text{N}\!\!-\!\!|\!\!-\!\!\text{H} \\
\text{CH}_2\text{OH} & \text{CH}_2\text{OH} & \text{CH}_2\text{CH}_2\text{COOH} & \text{CH}_2\text{CH}_2\text{COOH}
\end{array}
$$

D-(+)-Serine     L-(–)-Serine     D-(–)-Glutamic acid     L-(+)-Glutamic acid

Most naturally occuring amino acids have the L configuration but it never means that all L-amino acids will be (–)-enantiomer. Actually there is no relation between configuration (D, L) and sign of rotation [(+) and (–)]; as is evident from the example of glutamic acid.

In case of sugars, when the bottom asymmetric carbon atom has H on left and OH on right, it is said to belong to D series, if the configuration at the bottom asymmetric carbon atom is opposite (H on right and OH on left), it is said to belong to L series. Most naturally occurring sugars belong to D series.

$$
\begin{array}{ccc}
 & & \text{CHO} \\
 & & \text{H}\!\!-\!\!|\!\!-\!\!\text{OH} \\
 & & \text{HO}\!\!-\!\!|\!\!-\!\!\text{H} \\
\text{CHO} & & \text{H}\!\!-\!\!|\!\!-\!\!\text{OH} \qquad \text{CHO} \\
\text{H}\!\!-\!\!|\!\!-\!\!\text{OH} & & \text{H}\!\!-\!\!|\!\!-\!\!\text{OH} \qquad \text{HO}\!\!-\!\!|\!\!-\!\!\text{H} \\
\text{CH}_2\text{OH} & & \text{CH}_2\text{OH} \qquad\quad \text{H}\!\!-\!\!|\!\!-\!\!\text{OH} \\
 & & \qquad\qquad\qquad \text{CH}_2\text{OH}
\end{array}
$$

D-(+)-Glyceraldehyde     D-(+)-Glucose     D-(–)-Threose

## 3.2.2   Absolute configuration (R and S System of Nomenclature)

The D, L system of relating the configuration has a basic defect that sometimes the configuration of the same molecule may not be related to both D and L series. Moreover, it is cumbersome to apply it to molecules having complicated structure and to compounds having more than one chiral carbon atoms. These difficulties are, however, removed by an unambiguous system devised by Cahn, Ingold and Prelog ; which is based *on the actual three-dimensional formula*. The system of assigning configuration involves the following steps.

**Step I**

The four atoms or groups attached to the chiral carbon atom are assigned a sequence of priorities in accordance with a set of rules, known as **sequence rules** (described below).

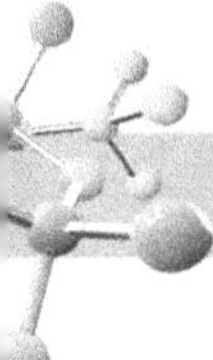

**Sequence rule 1.**

*In case all the four atoms directly attached to the chiral carbon atom are different from one another, sequence of priorities is determined by their atomic numbers.* The atom of highest atomic number gets the highest priority while the atom having the lowest atomic number is given the least order of priority. Thus the sequence of priority of the four atoms in bromochloroiodomethane (BrCHCII) is I (Z = 53), Br (Z = 35), Cl (Z = 17) and H (Z = 1).

In case the chiral centre has two isotopic atoms, such as deuterium (D) and hydrogen (H), the isotopes of higher mass number gets higher priority.

**Sequence rule 2.**

*If two or more atoms directly attached to the chiral carbon atom have the same atomic number, the priority may be determined by comparing the next atom in the group.* If even this does not solve the problem, the comparison is extended to the next atom and so on.

$$CH_3CH_2-\overset{\overset{\displaystyle H}{|}}{\underset{\underset{\displaystyle OH}{|}}{C}}-CH_3$$

Let us consider the case of *sec*-butyl alcohol in which the four atoms or groups attached to the chiral centre are $CH_3CH_2—$, H, $—CH_3$ and $—OH$.

The relative priorities of the $—CH_3$ and $—C_2H_5$ groups can't be decided by the first atom linked to the chiral carbon which is carbon in both cases. The next atoms in $—CH_3$ group are H, H and H while in $CH_3—CH_2—$ group the next atoms are C, H and H. Now since C has a higher atomic number than H, $CH_3CH_2$ — (having C, H and H atoms) gets higher priority to $CH_3$ (having H, H and H atoms).

**Sequence rule 3.**

*Treat double and triple bonds as if each were a singly bonded to two (or three) of those atoms.* For this method, imagine that each π bond is broken and the atoms at both ends duplicates. Note that when you break a bond, you always add two imaginary atoms.

By the application of these rules, some common substituents are arranged in the following priority sequence.

I, Br, Cl, $SO_3H$, F, OCOR, OR, OH, $NO_2$, $NR_2$, NHCOR, NHR, $NH_2$, $CCl_3$, COCl, COOR, COOH, $CONH_2$, COR, CHO, $CH_2OH$, CN, $C_6H_5$, $CR_3$, $CHR_2$, $CH_2R$, $CH_3$, D and H.

**Step II.**

After assigning priorites to the four groups or atoms attached to the chiral carbon, proceed as below.

**For structures drawn as a perspective formule :**

If the group (or atom) with the lowest priority (4) is bonded to a hatched wedge, draw a curved arrow from the group (or atom) with the highest priority (1) to the group/atom with the second highest priority (2). If the arrow points in a clockwise direction, the compound has the *R* (*R* is for *rectus*, which is Latin for "right") of configuration, in case it points to anticlockwise direction, the compound has the *S* (*S* is for *sinister*, which is Latin for "left") configuration.

(*R*)–2-Bromobutane      (*S*)–2-Bromobutane

However, if the group/atom with the lowest priority (4) is not bonded by a hatched wedge, interchange a pair of groups so that group (4) is bonded by a hatched wedge and then proceed as mentioned above. The configuration now you get will be the *configuration of the enantiomer of the original molecule*, hence the configuration of the original molecule will be other than that of enantiomer.

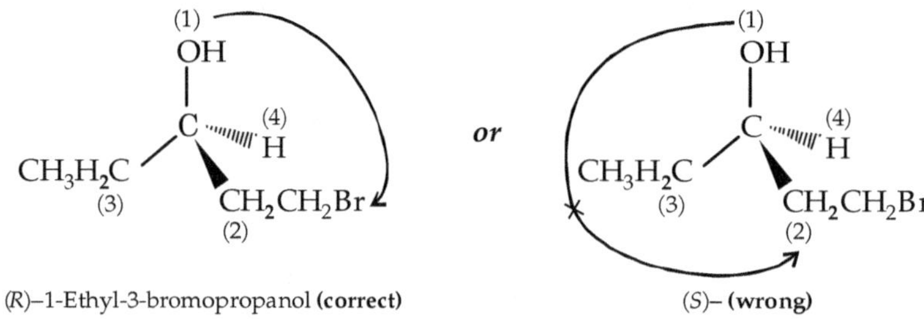

($R$)–2-Propanol which means the configuration before interchanging had the ($S$)-configuration

Sometimes there are two options for drawing the arrow from group (1) to group (2).

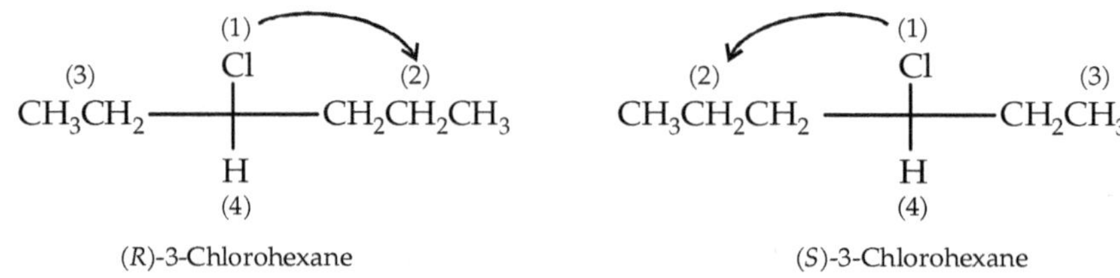

($R$)–1-Ethyl-3-bromopropanol **(correct)**　　　　　　　　　　　($S$)– **(wrong)**

In such case, remember that while drawing an arrow you can pass over (*ignore*) the lowest priority group (4) but never the next lowest priority group (3). Thus in the above example, the correct configuration is $R$ but not $S$.

**For structures drawn as a Fischer projection :**

If we assume that a clockwise arrow specifies an $R$ configuration and a counterclockwise arrow specifies an $S$ configuration, the configuration of Fischer projection formulas can be remembered by a mnemonic "Very true when the lowest priority group (4) is present on a **V**ertical bond and **H**orribly wrong if the lowest priority group is present on a **H**orizontal bond. Thus remember that when the lowest priority group is present on a horizontal bond clockwise direction of the arrow signifies $S$ configuration, not the $R$ configuration.

($R$)-3-Chlorohexane　　　　　　　　　　　($S$)-3-Chlorohexane

**Note that here lowest priority group is on a vertical bond.**

($S$)-2-Butanol　　　　　　　　　　　($R$)-2-Butanol

**Note that here lowest priority group is on a horizontal bond.**

As in perespective projection, while drawing an arrow you can pass over the group with the lowest priority (4), but never the group (3).

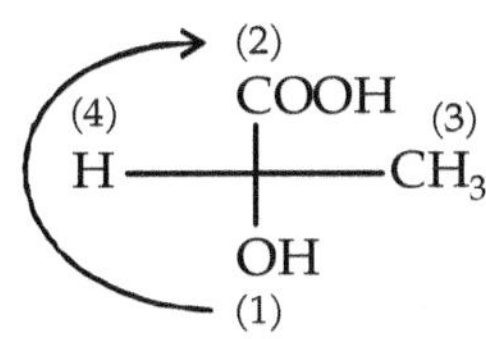

**Correct** drawing of arrow
(*S*)-Lactic acid　　　　**Wrong** drawing of arrow

Here since the lowest priority group is on a horizontal bond, so clockwise direction of arrow signifies *S*-configuration, the enantiomer of this will be having *R*-configuration.

Thus the easiest way to determine whether two molecules (drawn on a two-dimensional piece of paper) with one chirality center and with the same set of substituents are enantiomers or identical molecules is to know their configuration. If one has the *R* configuration and the other has the *S* configuration, we can say that they are enantiomers but which one is dextro-and which one is laevo can be ascertained only by polarimeter. If the two molecules have the same (*R* or *S*) configuration, they are identical.

---

*Example 1 :*

**(a)　Draw the staggered conformations of 2,3-dimethylbutane in order of increasing energy.**

**(b)　Draw the eclipsed conformations of 2,3-dimethylbutane in order of increasing energy.**

*Solution :*

(a)

(b)

---

*Example 2 :*

**Arrange the following groups (ligands) in decreasing order of priority.**

**(a)　(CH₃)₂CH– and cyclohexyl　　(b)　Cyclohexyl and phenyl　　(c)　Phenyl and tert-butyl**

*Solution :*

(a)　Cyclohexyl > –HC(CH₃)₂

First point of difference lies at $C_2$; in cyclohexyl $C_2$ has only two H and one C, while $C_2$ of (CH₃)₂CH– has three H.

(b)　Phenyl – > Cyclohexyl–. Here first point of difference lies at $C_1$ because the $C_1$ of phenyl is doubly bonded and hence counted as attached to three C's.

(c)　Phenyl – > (CH₃)₃C– . Here first point of difference lies at $C_2$.

**Example 3 :**

**Convert the following structures to the Fischer projection formulas.**

H ⫼⫼C—CH₃   *or*    (Newman: Br, CH₃)   *and*    H₃C—C⫼⫼H   *or*    (Newman: H₃C, Br)    with Cl (top) and Br (bottom) — *R* and *S*

**Solution :**

In the Fischer formula, the chiral carbon is assumed to be present at the crossing of a horizontal and a vertical line. The horizontal bonds project out of the plane of the paper, toward the viewer, while the vertical bonds project behind the plane of the paper, away from the viewer. Now put the Cl back so the H and Cl are behind the plane with the Cl on the top and the H below. The Me and Br project in front of the paper on the horizontal bond, the Me to the right and Br to the left of the viewer.

Fischer projections:

Br —|— CH₃ with Cl (top) and H (bottom) — *R*      H₃C —|— Br with Cl (top) and H (bottom) — *S*

**Example 4 :**

**Draw the Fischer projection formula for (S)-2-butanol. What happens when**

(a)      ligands across the horizontal bond are exchanged

(b)      ligands across the vertical bond are switched

(c)      both of the above switches are performed

(d)      a ligand attached to a horizontal bond is switched with the ligand attached to a vertical bond.

**Solution :**

H —|— OH with CH₃ (top) and C₂H₅ (bottom)

(S)-2-Butanol

(a)    HO —|— H with CH₃ (top) and C₂H₅ (bottom)    (R)-2-Butanol

(b)    H —|— OH with C₂H₅ (top) and CH₃ (bottom)    (R)-2-Butanol

(c)    HO —|— H with C₂H₅ (top) and CH₃ (bottom)    (S)-2-Butanol

(d)    H —|— C₂H₅ with CH₃ (top) and OH (bottom),    H₃C —|— OH with H (top) and C₂H₅ (bottom),    H —|— CH₃ with OH (top) and C₂H₅ (bottom)  *or*  C₂H₅ —|— OH with CH₃ (top) and H (bottom)

**All are (R)-2-Butanol**

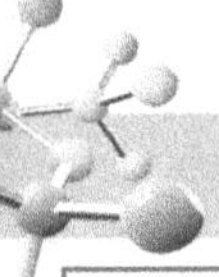

*Example 5 :*

**(a)** Designate the compound A as R or S and then give its relation with the three other structures B, C and D for the same compound.

$$
\begin{array}{cccc}
CH_3 & OH & CH=CH_2 & H \\
H-\!\!-OH & H-\!\!-CH_3 & H_3C-\!\!-OH & HO-\!\!-CH=CH_2 \\
CH=CH_2 & CH=CH_2 & H & CH_3 \\
A & B & C & D
\end{array}
$$

**(b)** How many interchange(s) are required for the conversion of A to other structures, namely B, C and D?

*Solution :*

**(a)** The priority order for the four groups is $OH > CH=CH_2 > CH_3 > H$. In the given structure, the direction of arrangement of groups i.e. from highest priority (1) to the second highest priority (2) is clockwise.

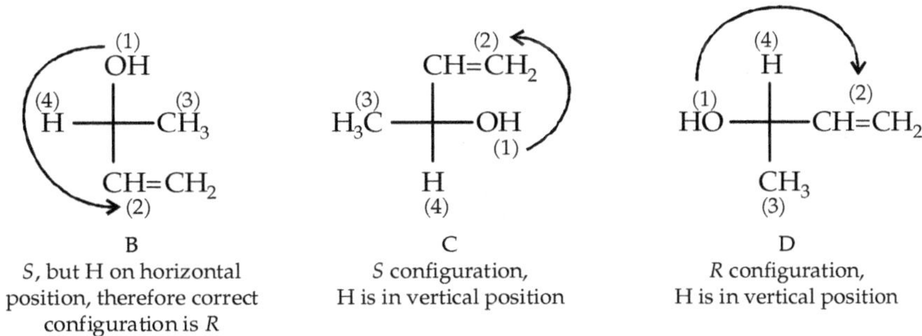

However, here the lowest priority substituent (H) is on the horizontal side, so correct configuration of A should be *S*. **Alternatively** bring lowest priority substituent (H) on the vertical bond by making **two** switches; now the arrangement of groups (1) to (2) is counterclockwise giving it *S* configuration.

**(b)**

$$
\begin{array}{ccc}
CH_3 & & CH_3 \\
H-\!\!-OH & \xrightarrow[\text{of } CH_3 \text{ and } OH]{\text{interchange}} & H-\!\!-CH_3 \\
CH=CH_2 & & CH=CH_2 \\
A & & B
\end{array}
$$

Therefore number of interchange is **one**.

$$
\begin{array}{ccccc}
CH_3 & & CH=CH_2 & & CH=CH_2 \\
H-\!\!-OH & \xrightarrow[\text{of } CH_3 \text{ and } CH=CH_2]{\text{interchange}} & H-\!\!-OH & \xrightarrow[\text{of H and } CH_3]{\text{interchange}} & H_3C-\!\!-OH \\
CH=CH_2 & & CH_3 & & H \\
A & & & & C
\end{array}
$$

Therefore number of interchanges is **two**.

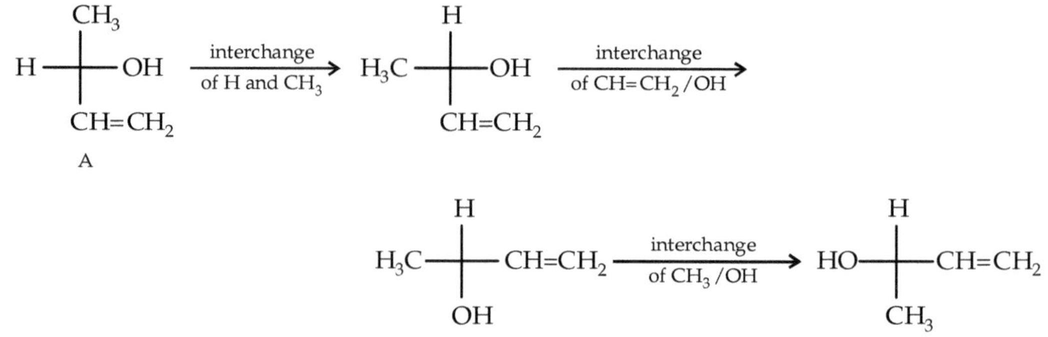

Therefore number of interchanges is **three**.

**The R, S system of nomenclature for isomers with more than one chirality center :**

If a compound has more than one chirality center, we analyze each center separately and decide whether it is $(R)$ or $(S)$. As an example, let us name the following stereoisomer of 3-bromo-2-butanol.

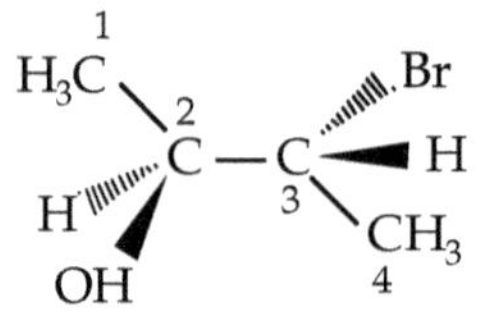

3-Bromo-2-butanol

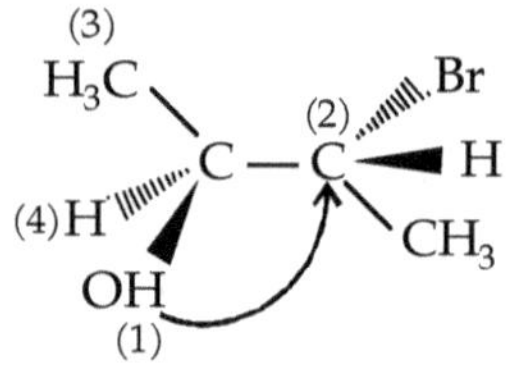

Priority orders of the four substituents at C-2

*Configuration at the chiral carbon-2 :* The priority order of the four groups at C-2 is shown above. Here the lowest priority substituent (4) is bonded by a hatched wedge, so draw an arrow from the group (1) to group (2) and note that the direction of arrow is counterclockwise indicating the configuration at C-2 as $S$.

*Configuration at the chiral carbon-3 :* Analyse the priority order of the four substituents at C-3, and observe that the lowest priority substituent (4) is not bonded by a hatched wedge so bring it temporarily on a hatched bond by interchanging H and Br.

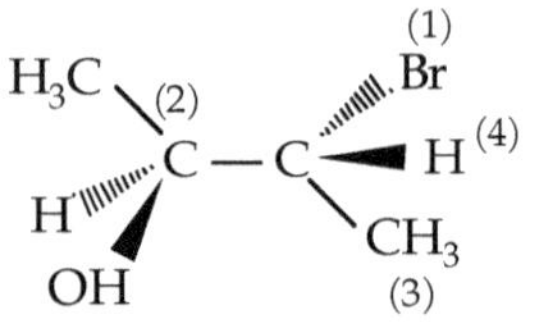

Priority orders of the four substituents at C-3

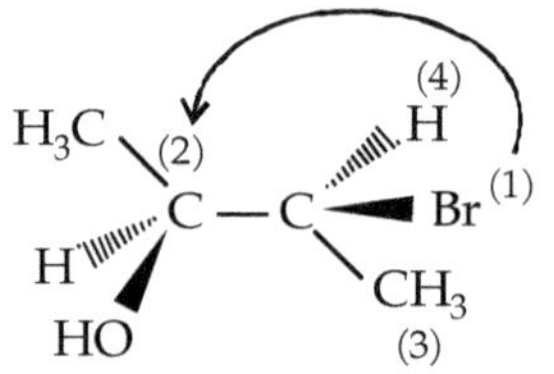

$S$-configuration on the imaginary structure, so the configuration at C-3 on the original (left) structure should be $R$

Counterclockwise indicating $S$-configuration

Thus the stereoisomer in question is $(2S, 3R)$-3-bromo-2-butanol.

Let us study the configurations at the two chiral carbons of 3-bromo-2-butanol, when drawn according to Fischer projection.

**Configuration at C-2**

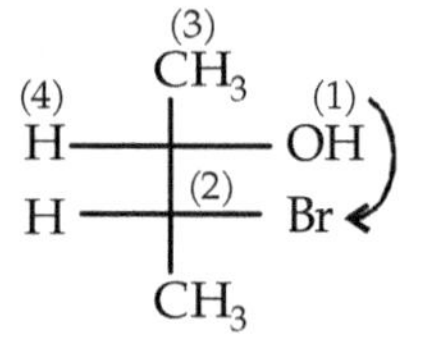

**Configuration at C-3**

Clockwise direction indicates $(R)$ configuration. However, note that group(4) is present on horizontal bond, so the correct configuration at C-2 will be $(S)$.

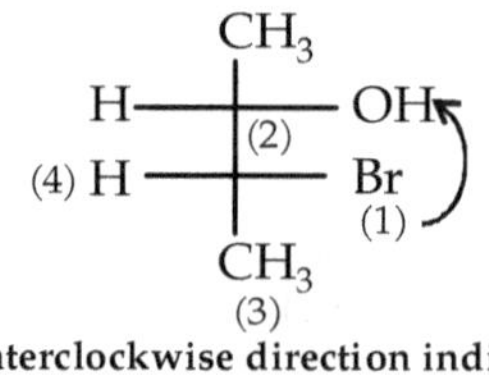

Counterclockwise direction indicates $(S)$ configuration which is obtained when substituent (4) is present on horiztonal bond (Horribly wrong) so correct configuration at C-3 is opposite to $(S)$, i.e. $(R)$

*Example 6 :*

**Draw perspective formulas for the following compounds -**

**(a)    (S)-2-Butanol and (R)-2-Butanol**                          **(b)    (2R, 3S)-3-Chloro-2-pentanol.**

*Solution :*

(a)    (i)    Write down the structural formula for the given compound to know what groups are bonded to the chirality center  $CH_3 \overset{*}{C} H(OH)CH_2CH_3$

(ii)    Assign the priority order to the four substituents; –OH (1),–CH$_2$CH$_3$ (2), –CH$_3$ (3), and –H (4).

(iii)    Draw the tetrahedral carbon atom;

(iv)    Put the lowest priority substituent on the hatched wedge; and the highest priority group (1) on any of the remaining three bonds.

(v)    Now take into consideration the configuration, you want, if you want *R* enantiomer, draw an arrow clockwise from the highest priority group (1) to the next available bond and put the group with the next priority (2) on that bond. In case you want *S* configuration, draw an arrow anticlockwise from the highest priority group (1) to the next available bond and put the group (2) on that bond.

(vi)    Put the remaining substituent on the bond available.

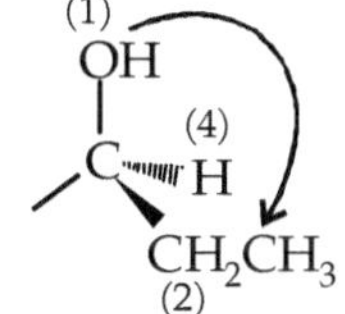

Clockwise arrow for *R*

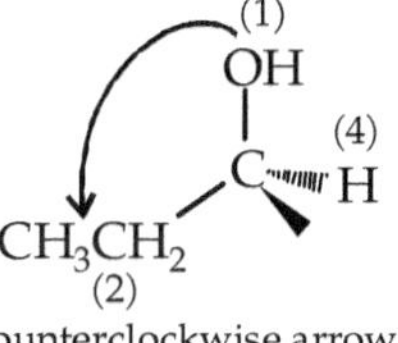

Counterclockwise arrow for *S*

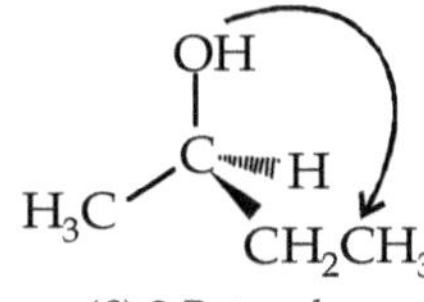

(*S*)-2-Butanol          (*R*)-2-Butanol

(b)    (i)    $CH_3 \overset{*}{C} H \overset{*}{C} HCH_2CH_3$ , with Cl and OH substituents

3-Chloro-2-pentanol

(ii)    The priority order of the four groups on the two carbon atoms are –OH(1), –CHClCH$_2$CH$_3$ (2), –CH$_3$ (3) and –H (4) on one carbon; and –Cl (1), –CHOHCH$_3$ (2), –CH$_2$CH$_3$ (3) and –H (4).

(iii)    The perspective respresentation of the two chiral carbon atoms.

(iv)    Putting the lowest priority group (4) on the hatched wedge of each chirality center.

(v)    For each chirality center, put the highest priority group (1) on that bond from which when arrow is drawn to the nexty priority group (2) gives clockwise direction (for *R* configuration) or counterclockwise direction (for *S* configuration).

(vi)    Place the remaining group on each chiral carbon.

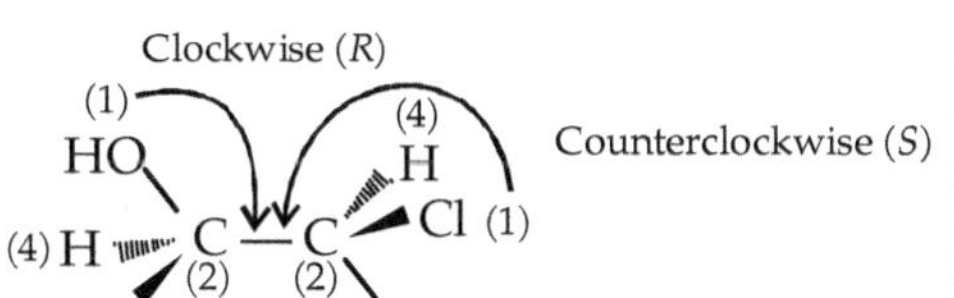


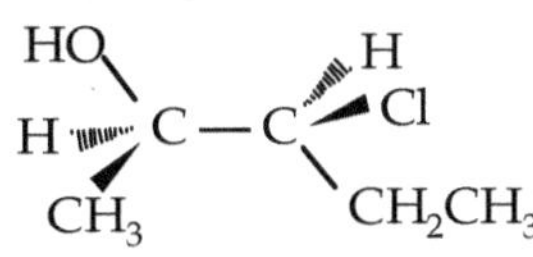

## TEST YOUR UNDERSTANDING - 3.2

1. Ephedrine is the principal constituent of the herb Ephedra and used for treating asthma. It has two chiral carbon atoms and thus has four stereoisomers. However, the isomer having following configuration is pharmacologically active. Assign the configuration at each of the carbon atoms.

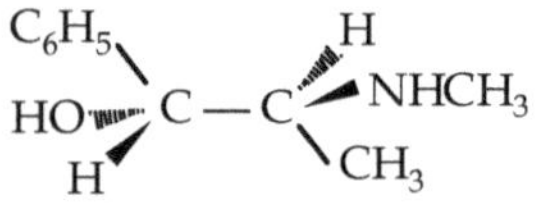

2. Star (*) the asymmetric carbon atom(s) in each of the following structures, and determine whether it has the (R) or the (S) configuration.

    (a) 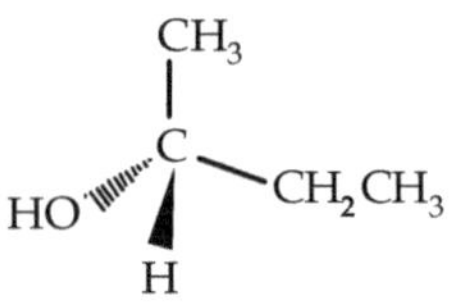    (b) 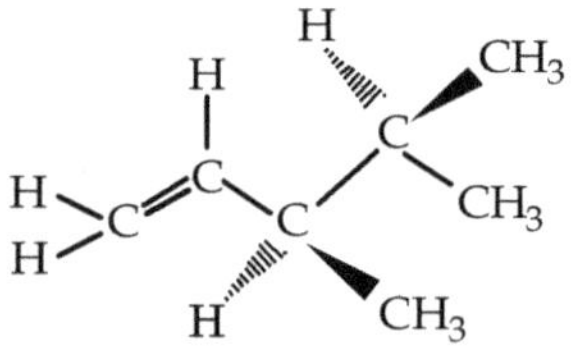    (c)

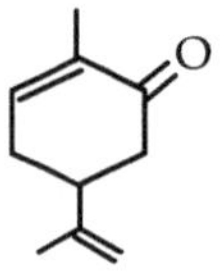

    (d) 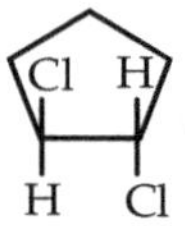    (e) 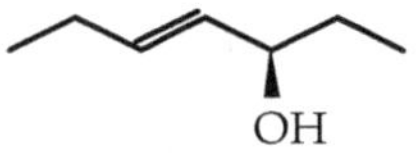    (f)

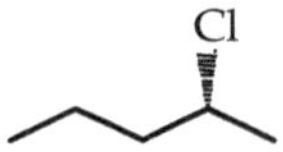

3. Do the following structures represent identical molecules or a pair of enantiomers?

    (a) 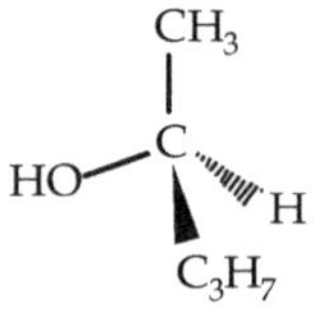    (b)

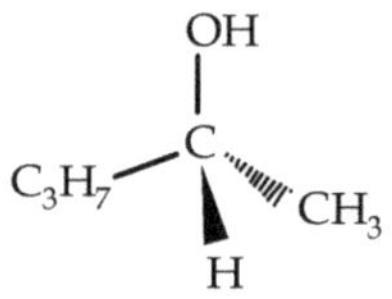

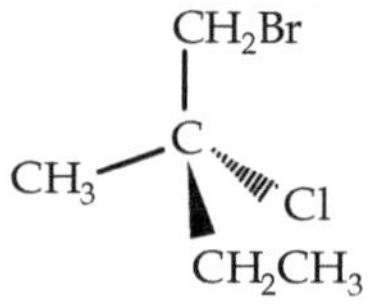

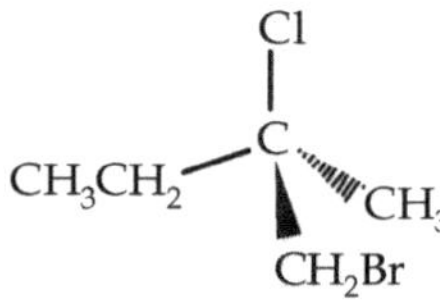

    (c) 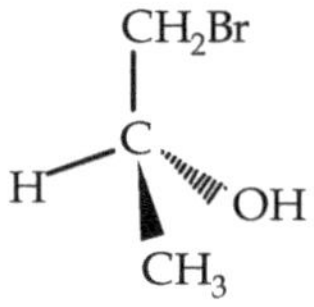    (d)

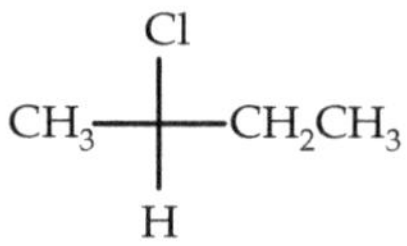

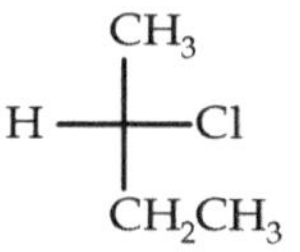

4. Account for the fact that chlorination of *n*-butane to 2-chlorobutane (*sec*-butyl chloride) gives racemic mixture, while chlorination of any one enantiomer 2-chlorobutane (*sec*-butyl chloride) gives optically active product.

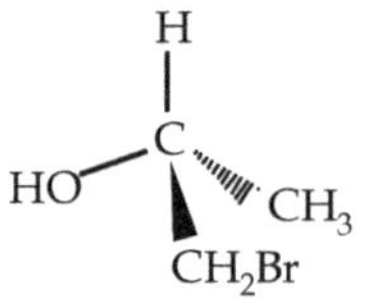

5. Detrmine the percentage composition of a mixture of enantiomers of 2-bromo-octane having specific rotation of + 18° ; given the specific rotation of the (R)-(–)-2-bromo-octane is – 36°.

6. (*a*)   Give priority order of the 1°, 2°, 3° alkyl and $CH_3$ groups according to sequence rule.

    (*b*)   Draw cross formula (Fischer projection formula) for the following compounds and assign configuration R/S to the fromula drawn.

    (*i*)  α-Deuterioethyl brimide     (*ii*)  3-Chloro-1-pentene     (*iii*)  Malic acid

    (*iv*)  Alanine     (*v*)  Methylethyl-*n*-propylisopropylmethane     (*vi*)  1- Amino-1-phenylethane.

7. Give the number of isomers formed during free radical mono-chlorination of isopentane. Predict which isomer(s) will be obtained in racemic form ? Draw their R/S formulae.

    Geometrical isomerism is due to hindered rotation either due to two doubly bonded atoms (e.g. C = C, C = N and N = N) or due to cyclic structure.

### 3.2.3   Geometrical isomerism in alkenes

Due to absence of rotation about a carbon-carbon double bond, an alkene in which each of the two doubly bonded carbon atoms is differently substituted can exist in two different configurations. Thus following types of compounds cannot exist as geometrical isomers.

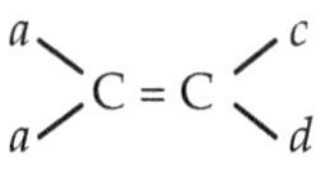

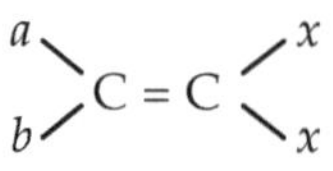

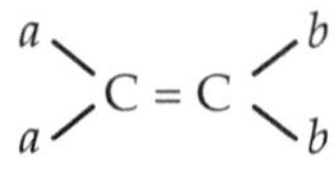

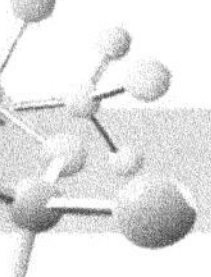

On the other hand, following types of compounds can exist as geometrical isomers.

$$\begin{array}{c} a \\ b \end{array}\!\!\!>\!\!C=C\!\!<\!\!\begin{array}{c} a \\ b \end{array} \qquad \begin{array}{c} a \\ b \end{array}\!\!\!>\!\!C=C\!\!<\!\!\begin{array}{c} c \\ d \end{array}$$

When the similar substituents are on the same side, the isomer is called *cis-*, while when the similar substituents are on the opposite sides, the isomer is called *trans*. Hence geometrical isomerism is also known as *cis-trans* isomerism. Few examples are given below.

cis-2-Butene

trans-2-Butene

Maleic acid (*cis*)

Fumaric acid (*trans*)

Cinnamic acid (*cis*)

(*trans*)

Isocrotonic acid (*cis*)

crotonic acid

When a compound contains $n$ number of dissimilarly substituted double bonds, the number of geometrical isomers is $2^n$, e.g.

*tanns-trans*

*tanns-cis*

*cis-trans*

*cis-cis*

However, the number of geometrical isomers is less than $2^n$ when the two double bonds are substituted by similar groups, viz. 2,4-hexadiene, $CH_3CH = CHCH = CHCH_3$, having two double bounds have only three geometrical isomers instead of four.

*cis-cis*, I

*trans-trans*, II

*cis-trans*, III

*trans-cis*, IV

Structures III and IV are identical.

# TEST YOUR UNDERSTANDING - 3.3

1. Draw the *cis-* and *trans-* isomers for the following compounds :

   (a)  3,4-Dimethyl-3-heptene

   (b)  2-Methylbut-2-en-1,4-dioic acid

2. Some of the following examples can show geometric isomerism, and some cannot. Draw the line bond structures for all and name as *cis* and *trans* isomers for those that show geometric isomerism.

   (a)  3-Hexene

   (b)  2,4-Dimethyl-2-pentene

   (c)  1,3-Butadiene

   (d)  1-Chloro-2-butene

   (e)  4,5-Dibromo-1-pentene

   (f)  1,4-Dichloro-2-pentene

3. Draw the structures for the *cis-trans* isomers of the following compounds

   (a)  1-Ethyl-3-methylcyclobutane

   (b)  1-Bromo-3-chlorocyclohexane

**Distinction between *cis*- and *trans*-isomers.**

(i) **By cyclization method.** Generally, the *cis*-isomers are comparatively less stable because of mutual repulsion between the groups. Hence, the *cis*-isomer (*e.g.* maleic acid) cyclises on heating to form the corresponding anhydride while the *trans*-isomer does not form its anhydride at all.

$$
\begin{array}{ccc}
\text{H—C—COOH} & & \text{H—C—CO} \\
\| & \xrightarrow{\text{heat}} & \| \quad\quad\rangle O \\
\text{H—C—COOH} & & \text{H—C—CO} \\
\text{Maleic acid (\textit{cis})} & & \text{Maleic anhydride}
\end{array}
$$

Note that the two reacting groups (—COOH) are near to each other.

$$
\begin{array}{cc}
\text{H—C—COOH} & \\
\| & \xrightarrow{\text{heat}} \text{ No anhydride} \\
\text{HOOC—C—H} & \\
\text{Fumaric acid (\textit{trans})} &
\end{array}
$$

Note that the two reacting groups (—COOH) are quite apart form each other, hence cyclisation is not possible.

(ii) **By hydroxylation** (*Oxidation by mean of* $KMnO_4$, $OsO_4$ *or* $H_2O_2$ *in presence of* $OsO_4$). Oxidation (hydroxylation) of alkenes by means of these reagents proceeds in the *syn*-manner. Thus the two geometrical isomers of an alkene lead to different products by these reagents.

However, addition of $Br_2$ and halogen acid (HX) on alkenes gives *anti*-addition product. Thus here also, the two geometrical isomers of an alkene lead to different products.

The term *syn* addition means the two atoms or groups are added on available sites, i.e. on the same side on *cis* and on different sides on *trans* isomer. On the other hand, the term *anti* addition means the two atoms or groups are added on different sides on *cis* isomer, and on same side on *trans* isomer.

$$
\underset{\substack{\textit{rac}\ \text{-2, 3-Dibromobutan-}\\ \text{1, 4-dioic acid}}}{
\begin{array}{c}
\text{COOH} \\ | \\ \text{H – C – Br} \\ | \\ \text{Br – C – H} \\ | \\ \text{COOH}
\end{array}}
\xleftarrow[\text{(\textit{anti}–addition)}]{Br_2}
\underset{\substack{\text{Maleic acid (\textit{cis})}}}{
\begin{array}{c}
\text{COOH} \\ | \\ \text{H – C} \\ \| \\ \text{H – C} \\ | \\ \text{COOH}
\end{array}}
\xrightarrow[\text{(\textit{syn}–addition)}]{\text{alk.}KMnO_4}
\underset{\substack{\textit{meso}\ \text{-Tartaric acid}}}{
\begin{array}{c}
\text{COOH} \\ | \\ \text{H – C – OH} \\ | \\ \text{H – C – OH} \\ | \\ \text{COOH}
\end{array}}
$$

$$
\underset{\substack{\textit{meso}\ \text{-2, 3-Dibromobutan-}\\ \text{1, 4-dioic acid}}}{
\begin{array}{c}
\text{COOH} \\ | \\ \text{H – C – Br} \\ | \\ \text{H – C – Br} \\ | \\ \text{COOH}
\end{array}}
\xleftarrow[\text{(\textit{anti}–addition)}]{Br_2}
\underset{\substack{\text{Fumaric acid (\textit{trans})}}}{
\begin{array}{c}
\text{COOH} \\ | \\ \text{H – C} \\ \| \\ \text{C – H} \\ | \\ \text{COOH}
\end{array}}
\xrightarrow[\text{(\textit{syn}–addition)}]{\text{alk.}KMnO_4}
\underset{\substack{\textit{rac}\ \text{-Tartaric acid}}}{
\begin{array}{c}
\text{COOH} \\ | \\ \text{H – C – OH} \\ | \\ \text{HO – C – H} \\ | \\ \text{COOH}
\end{array}}
$$

(iii) **By studying their dipole moments.** The *cis*-isomer of a symmetrical alkene (alkenes in which both the carbon atoms have similar groups) has a definite dipole moment, while the *trans*-isomer has zero dipole moment. For example, 1, 2-dichloroethylene and butene-2.

$$
\underset{\substack{\textit{cis}\text{-1, 2-Dichloroethylene}\\ (\mu = 1.9\ D)}}{
\begin{array}{c}
\text{H—C} \rightleftharpoons \text{Cl} \\ \| \\ \text{H—C} \rightleftharpoons \text{Cl}
\end{array}}
\qquad
\underset{\substack{\textit{trans}\text{-1, 2-Dichloroethylene}\\ (\mu = 0.0\ D)}}{
\begin{array}{c}
\text{H—C} \rightleftharpoons \text{Cl} \\ \| \\ \text{H} \rightleftharpoons \text{C—H}
\end{array}}
\qquad
\underset{\substack{\textit{cis}\text{-Butene-2}}}{
\begin{array}{c}
\text{H—C} \rightleftharpoons \text{CH}_3 \\ \| \\ \text{H—C} \rightleftharpoons \text{CH}_3
\end{array}}
\qquad
\underset{\substack{\textit{trans}\text{-Butene-2}}}{
\begin{array}{c}
\text{H—C} \rightleftharpoons \text{CH}_3 \\ \| \\ \text{H} \rightleftharpoons \text{C—H}
\end{array}}
$$

In *trans*-isomer of the symmetrical alkenes, the effect produced in one half of the molecule is cancelled by that in the other half of the molecule.

In case of unsymmetrical alkenes, the *trans*-isomer has lower dipole moment than the corresponding *cis*-isomer. For example,

$$
\underset{\substack{\textit{cis}\text{-2, 3-Dichloropentene-2 (high dipole moment)}}}{
\begin{array}{c}
\text{H}_3\text{C—C—Cl} \\ \| \\ \text{CH}_3\text{CH}_2\text{—C—Cl}
\end{array}}
\qquad\qquad\qquad
\underset{\substack{\textit{trans}\text{-2, 3-dichloropentene-2 (less dipole moment)}}}{
\begin{array}{c}
\text{CH}_3\text{—C—Cl} \\ \| \\ \text{Cl—C—CH}_2\text{CH}_3
\end{array}}
$$

Similar is the case with pentene-2.

H—C⇌CH₂CH₃       H—C⇌CH₂CH₃

H—C⇄CH₃       H₃C⇄C—H

*cis*-pentene-2 (more polar)     *trans*-pentene-2 (more ploar)

Note that the —$CH_2CH_3$ has more + I effect than the —$CH_3$ group, hence dipole moment of the two polar bonds do not cancel each other in the *trans* isomer. Thus *trans*-isomer is also polar, but less than he corresponding *cis*-isomer.

*(iv)* **By studying other physical properties.**

   *(a)* The *cis*-isomer of a compound has higher boiling point and higher solubility in water due to higher polarity, higher density, higher heat of hydrogenation, higher heat of combustion and higher refractive index than the corresponding *trans*-isomer **(Auswers-skita rule)**.

| | $CH_3$—C—H<br>$CH_3$—C—H | $CH_3$—C—H<br>H—C—$CH_3$ | H—C—Cl<br>H—C—Cl | H—C—Cl<br>Cl—C—H |
|---|---|---|---|---|
| | *cis*-2-Butene | *trans*-2-Butene | *cis*-1, 2-Dichloroethene | *trans*-1, 2-Dichloroethene |
| **b.p.** | 4°C | 1°C | 60°C | 48°C |
| **m.p.** | – 139°C | – 106°C | – 80°C | – 50°C |

   *(b)* The *trans*-isomer has higher melting point than the *cis*-isomer due to symmetrical nature and more close packing of the *trans*-isomer.

## 3.2.4   Geometrical Isomerism in Oximes (compounds containing C = N group)

Oximes are the condensation products of aldehydes/ketones with hydroxylamine.

Aromatic aldoximes and aromatic ketoximes also show geometrical isomerism. In aldoximes, when H and OH groups are on the same side, the isomer is known as *syn* (analogous to *cis*) and when these groups are on the opposite sides, the isomer is known as *anti* (analogous to *trans*).

$C_6H_5$—C—H       $C_6H_5$—C—H

N—OH       HO—N

*syn*-Benzaldoxime       *anti*-Benzaldoxime

In ketoximes the prefixes *syn* and *anti* indicate which group of ketoxime is *syn* (on the same side) or *anti* (on the opposite side) to the OH group.

$p$-$CH_3.C_6H_4$—C—$C_6H_5$       $p$-$CH_3.C_6H_4$—C—$C_6H_5$

N—OH       HO—N

*syn*-Phenyl-*p* tolylketoxime     *syn*-*p*-Tolylphenylketoxime

(*anti*-*p*-Tolylphenylketoxime)     (*anti*-phenyl-*p*-tolylketoxime)

However, remember that all aromatic ketoximes do not show geometrical isomerism *e.g.*, $(C_6H_5)_2C = NOH$, benzophenone oxime having two similar aryl groups does not show geometrical isomerism.

**Determination of configuration of aldoximes**

The two forms (*syn* and *anti*) of aromatic aldoximes resemble each other in many ways, but differ in the behaviour of their acetyl derivatives towards sodium carbonate solution. The acetyl derivative of the *anti*-isomer gives cyanide, whereas that of *syn*-isomer is reconverted into aldoxime back on treatment with aqueous sodium carbonate.

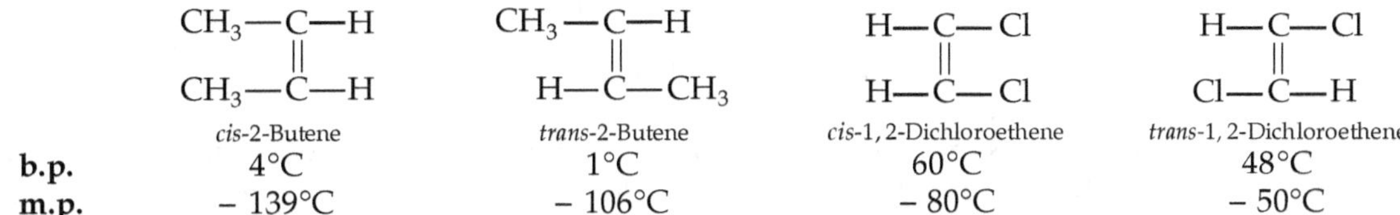

Acetate of *anti*-aldoxime     Cyanide     Acetate of *syn*-aldoxime     Aldoxime

Behaviour of aldoxime acetate towards aqeous $Na_2CO_3$

**Determination of configuration of ketoximes.**

Like aliphatic and aromatic aldoximes, aliphatic and aromatic ketoximes also occur in one and two forms, respectively. But it must be noted that unlike aromatic aldoximes, the aromatic ketoximes can exist in two isomeric forms only when one aryl and another alkyl or two different aryl groups are present. The aromatic ketoxime having two same aryl groups do not show the phenomenon of geometrical isomerism, *e.g.* benzophenone oxime, $Ph_2C = NOH$, does not show the phenomenon of geometrical isomerism. The configuration of geometrical isomerism is determined with the help of Beckmann rearrangement.

**Beckmann rearrangement.**

The Beckmann rearrangement consists in the conversion of ketoximes to N-substituted amides by heating with some acidic reagent, *viz.* conc. $H_2SO_4$, $BF_3$, polyphosphoric acid (PPA), $P_2O_5$, $PCl_5$, $SO_3$, $SOCl_2$, $C_6H_6SO_2Cl$, etc.

$$\underset{\text{Ketoxime}}{R-\overset{\overset{\displaystyle NOH}{\|}}{C}-R'} \xrightarrow{H_2SO_4} R'CONHR \quad \text{or} \quad RCONHR'$$

The two different amides, thus formed, can be identified by their hydrolysis to different acids and amines. In this rearrangement the shift or migration of groups is always *trans-(anti)* to the leaving group [*e.g.* —OH].

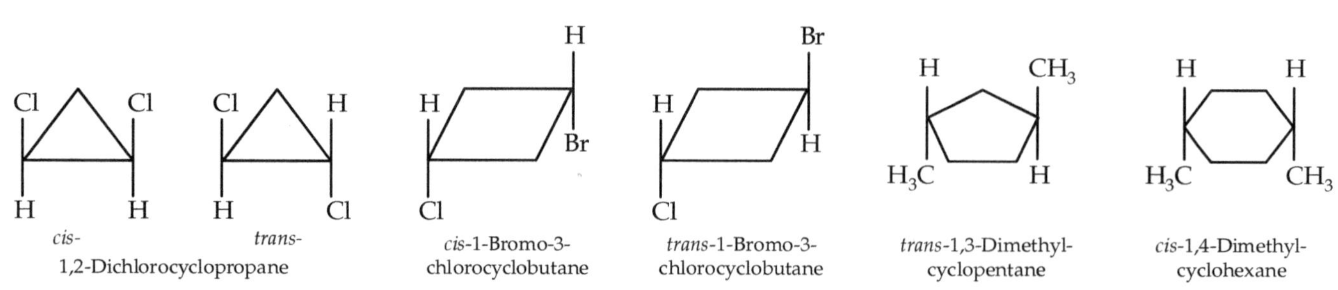

Ketoxime → Amide → RCOOH + R'NH₂

Ketoxime → Amide → R'COOH + RNH₂

**Geometrical isomerism due to N = N bond.**

$$\underset{syn\text{-Azobenzene}}{\overset{\displaystyle C_6H_5-N}{\underset{\displaystyle C_6H_5-N}{\|}}} \qquad \underset{anti\text{-Azobenzene}}{\overset{\displaystyle C_6H_5-N}{\underset{\displaystyle N-C_6H_5}{\|}}}$$

## 3.2.5   Geometrical isomerism in cyclic compounds

Like double bonds, cyclic system prevents free rotation about the single bond. In the cyclic system, the group attached to the top of the vertical line is said to be above the plane of the ring and the group attached to the bottom of the vertical line is said to be below the plane of the ring. Thus properly substituted cycloalkanes show geometrical isomerism; the *cis* isomer has substituents on the same side **of the ring**, whereas the *trans* isomer has substituents on opposite sides of the ring.

Disubstituted cyclobutanes and cyclopentanes show two position isomers (1, 2- and 1, 3-) each of which can exhibit geometrical isomerism. Disubstituted cyclohexanes show three position isomers (1, 2-, 1, 3- and 1, 4-) each of which can exihibit geometrical isomerism.

*cis-*
1,2-Dichlorocyclopropane

*trans-*
1,2-Dichlorocyclopropane

*cis*-1-Bromo-3-chlorocyclobutane

*trans*-1-Bromo-3-chlorocyclobutane

*trans*-1,3-Dimethyl-cyclopentane

*cis*-1,4-Dimethyl-cyclohexane

In cycloalkenes, *cis-trans* isomerism is possible only in large rings (at least 8 carbon atoms) because *trans* cycloalkenes with less than 8 carbon atoms are unstable at room temperature. *trans*-Cyclo-octene is stable at room temperature, although the *cis* isomer is still more stable. For cyclodecene and larger cycloalkenes, the *trans* isomer is nearly as stable as the *cis* isomer.

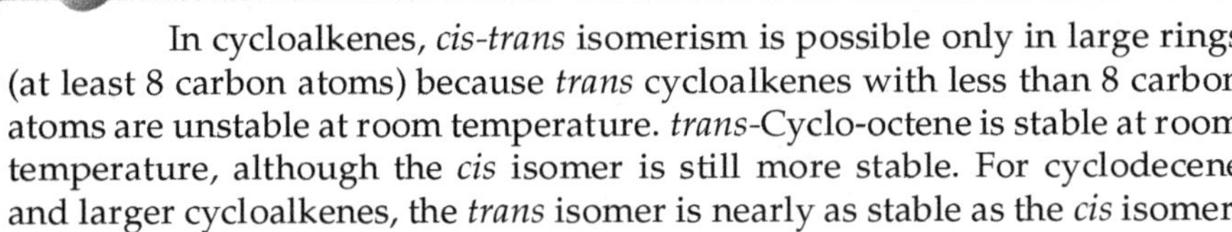

*cis*-Cyclodecene       *trans*-Cyclodecene

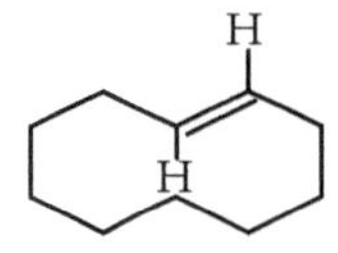

## 3.2.6 The *E* and *Z* Nomenclature of Geometrical Isomers

As discussed earlier, the geometrical isomerism is possible in structures of the following three types.

**Type 1.**

$$\underset{b}{\overset{a}{>}}C=C\underset{b}{\overset{a}{<}} \quad \text{and} \quad \underset{b}{\overset{a}{>}}C=C\underset{a}{\overset{b}{<}}$$

     *cis*              *trans*

**Type 2.**

$$\underset{b}{\overset{a}{>}}C=C\underset{x}{\overset{a}{<}} \quad \text{and} \quad \underset{b}{\overset{a}{>}}C=C\underset{a}{\overset{x}{<}}$$

     *cis*              *trans*

**Type 3.**

$$\underset{b}{\overset{a}{>}}C=C\underset{y}{\overset{x}{<}} \quad \text{and} \quad \underset{b}{\overset{a}{>}}C=C\underset{x}{\overset{y}{<}}$$

     *cis*              *trans*

In the first two types, the geometrical isomers are labelled as *cis* and *trans* on the basis of the fact that the common groups are on the same or opposite sides of the double bond. But in type 3 where all the four substituents are different, *cis-trans* type of isomerism cannot be applied. Moreover, the *cis-trans* system (also *syn-anti* system in oximes) is often ambiguous because the configurational descriptions have not been defined according to any general and clear set of rules. So an unambiguous system of configurational assignments for all types of structures showing geometrical isomerism was developed in 1968. This system is known as E-Z system of nomenclature and is based upon the sequence rules of Cahn, Ingold and Prelog originally developed for naming optical isomers on the R-S system. The following procedure is followed in specifying the configuration of such compounds.

(*i*)     Assign the priority order to the two groups attached to each of the doubly bonded carbon in accordance with the sequence rules, discussed earlier.

(*ii*)     Select the atom/group with higher priority on each doubly bonded carbon. If the atoms/groups of higher priority (denoted by H) on each carbon are on the same side of the double bond, the isomer is assigned the configuration Z (from the German word, *zusammen* meaning together). On the other hand, if the atoms/groups of higher priority on each carbon are on the opposite sides of the double bond, the isomer is assigned the configuration E (from the German word *entgegen* meaning against).

$$\underset{L}{\overset{H}{>}}C=C\underset{L}{\overset{H}{<}} \quad \text{and} \quad \underset{L}{\overset{H}{>}}C=C\underset{H}{\overset{L}{<}}$$

      *Z*-isomer                *E*-isomer

Where H and L represent the atoms (groups) of higher and lower priority respectively.

Now let us consider example of an alkene in which one of the doubly bonded carbon atom has Br and I and the other has F and Cl. Now since I has a higher atomic number than Br, it is assigned higher priority ; similarly Cl is of higher priority than F on the second olefinic carbon atom. Thus the E and Z configurations of the two isomers of 1-bromo-2-chloro-2-fluoro-1-iodoethene are assigned.

$$\underset{I}{\overset{Br}{>}}C=C\underset{Cl}{\overset{F}{<}} \quad \text{and} \quad \underset{I}{\overset{Br}{>}}C=C\underset{F}{\overset{Cl}{<}}$$

        *Z*                  *E*

Thus the *cis-* and *trans*-isomers of 2-butene become Z- and E-2-butenes respectively.

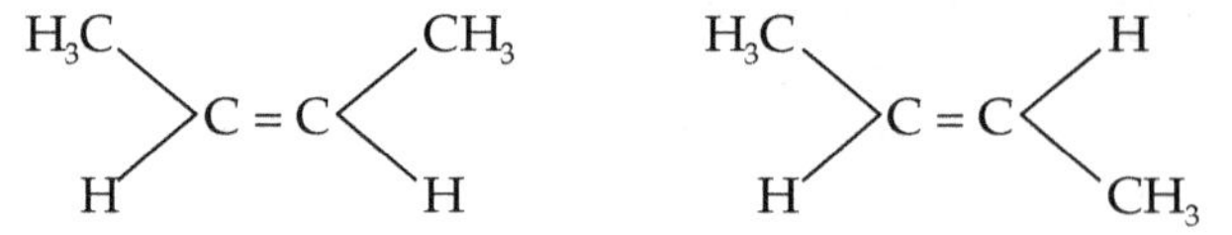

Z-2-Butene                    E-2-Butene

Remember that there is no relation between *cis-trans* isomers and *E, Z* isomers.

(Z)-3-Methylpent-2-ene        (E)-3-Methylpent-2-ene

**Note that** here, the similar groups ($CH_3$) is on the same side in the (*E*)-isomer, so it should be *cis-* on the basis of *cis-trans* isomerism. However, in 2-butene the *cis*-2-butene is Z-2-butene.

Similarly, following structures are assigned to the configuration mentioned below them.

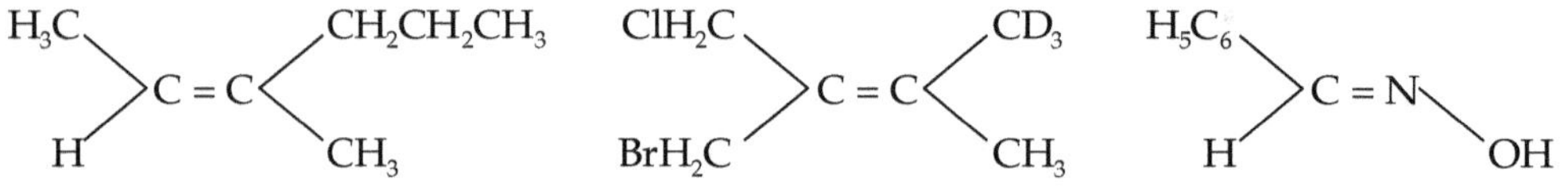

Z-isomer                    E-isomer              E-isomer

---

*Example 7 :*

**Write down the structure of the product, mentioning stereochemistry in each case.**

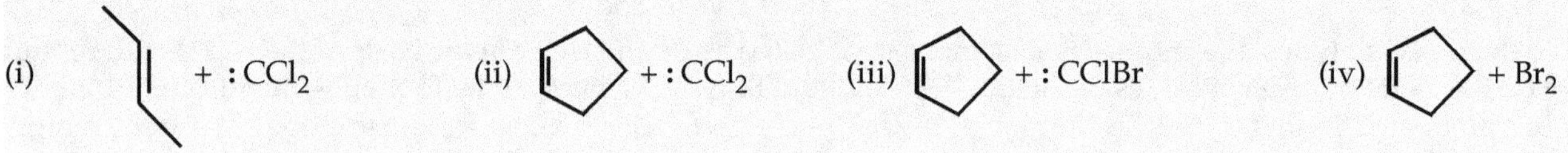

(i)  [structure] $+ : CCl_2$    (ii) [structure] $+ : CCl_2$    (iii) [structure] $+ : CClBr$    (iv) [structure] $+ Br_2$

*Solution :*

(i) [structure] $+ : CCl_2$ $\xrightarrow{syn-addition}$ [structure] Cl, Cl

*trans*-Butadiene

*trans*-1, 1-dichloro-2, 3-dimethylcyclopropane

(ii) [structure] $+ : CCl_2$ $\xrightarrow{syn-addition}$ [structure] Cl, Cl

*meso*

(iii) [structure] $+ : CClBr$ $\xrightarrow{syn\ addition}$ [structure] Cl, Br

*race-*

(iv) [structure] $+ Br_2$ $\xrightarrow{anti-addition}$ [structure] Br, Br

*rac*

---

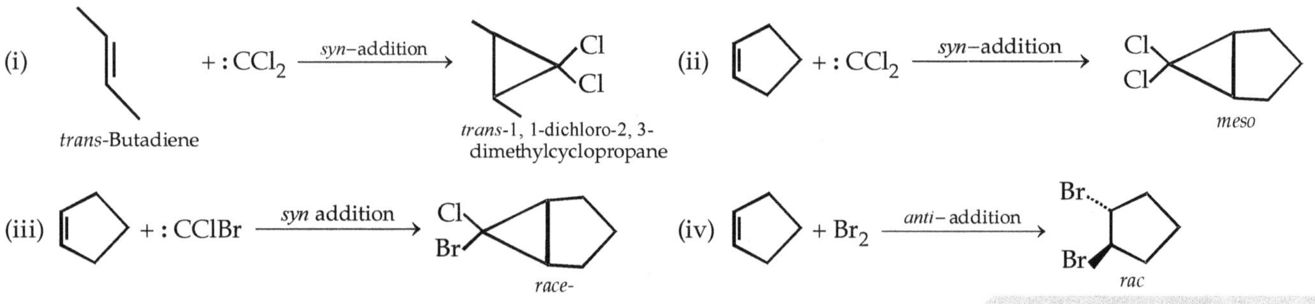

*Example 8 :*

**Three isomeric hydrocarbons of the formula $C_4H_8$ decolorise bromine water. Write down the structure in each case, mentioning stereochemistry. Also give structure of the other isomer (if possible) for the compound.**

*Solution :*

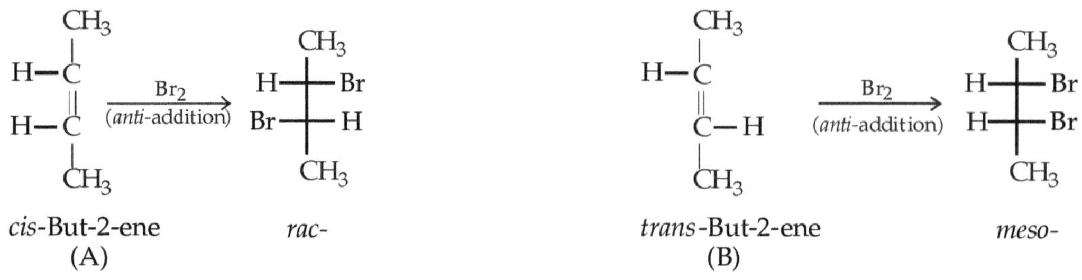

[structure]   $\xrightarrow[\text{(anti-addition)}]{Br_2}$   [structure]

*cis*-But-2-ene          *rac-*
(A)

[structure]   $\xrightarrow[\text{(anti-addition)}]{Br_2}$   [structure]

*trans*-But-2-ene         *meso-*
(B)

$$\underset{CH_3}{\overset{CH_3}{>}}C = CH_2 \xrightarrow{Br_2} \underset{CH_3}{\overset{CH_3}{>}}C(Br)CH_2Br$$

But-1-ene (C)                          (achiral)

Two other isomers of $C_4H_8$ are ☐ and △

cyclobutane            methylcyclo-
                       propane

## TEST YOUR UNDERSTANDING - 3.4

1. (a) How many isomeric nitroalkanes are possible for the molecular formula $C_4H_9NO_2$ ? Also draw the structure of tautomer of each isomer.

   (b) Draw structure of the tautomer of

2. Draw structures of the possible geometrical isomers of 2, 4-hexadiene.

3. Assign E or Z configuration to the following structures.

   (i)            (ii)            (iii)

   (iv)            (v)            (vi)

## 3.3  Enantiomers and Chiral Molecules

The word chiral comes from the Greek word Cheir, meaning "hand"; thus chiral objects and chiral molecules are said to possess "handedness".

Handedness means analogy of the two isomers of a molecule, of course chiral, with the left and right hand. Just as the left hand is a non-superimposable mirror image of the right hand, the structure of an isomer of a chiral molecule is the non-superimposable mirror image of the other isomer. Thus **a chiral molecule** *is defined as one that is not identical with a mirror image; a non-identical (non-superimposable) mirror image is called an* **enantiomer** *of the original molecule; and a pair of non-identical mirror images is called* **a pair of enantiomers**. Objects (and molecules) that are superimposable on their images are **achiral**. Note that gents socks are achiral while ladies socks with fingers and thumb and gloves are chiral.

*How to know the possibility of enantiomers with one chirality centre?* A pair of enantiomers is always possible for molecules that contain one tetrahedral atom, with four different groups attached to it. A tetrahedral atom with four different groups is known as a **chirality centre** (the latest IUPAC name approved for the earlier names like *stereogenic centre, stereocentre, a chiral centre, and an asymmetric atom*). Actually, the term chirality centre belongs to a broader term called stereocentre. **A stereocentre (or stereogenic atom) is any atom at which the interchange of any two groups gives a stereoisomer.** Asymmetric carbon and the doubly-bonded carbon atoms in *cis-trans* isomers are the most common types of stereocentre.

* Carbon is a stereocentre         * Carbons are stereocentres
as well as chirality centre          but not chirality centre

---

* It must be noted that aliphatic oximes exist only in one form and that is the *anti* form.

In a cyclic compound, a carbon atom can be stereogenic if it has two different substituents, and the path traced around the ring from that carbon in clockwise direction is different from that traced in anticlockwise direction.

However, remember that this is the one way but not the only way for assessing the possibility of enantiomerism because as we will see that some of the molecules containing more than one tetrahedral chiral carbon show enantiomerism while some do not exhibit enantiomerism, even though they contain chiral center.

Interchanging of any two groups present on a chirality centre converts one enantiomer into other. However, an interchange of groups requires the breaking and reforming of $\sigma$ bonds at the centre of chirality, which in turn require a large input of energy, hence enantiomers do not interconvert spontaneously (difference from **conformational isomers** which are interconverted spontaneously by rotations about $\sigma$ bonds).

## 3.3.1   Drawing of enantiomers

### (i)   Perspective formulas

Show two of the bonds to the chirality center in the plane of the paper, one bond as a solid wedge coming out of the paper, and the fourth bond as a hatched wedge projecting back from the paper. The four groups may be attached to the chirality center in any order. If any two of the groups (or atoms) bonded to the chirality center are interchanged, the molecule obtained will be the enantiomer of the parent molecule



Perspective (three-dimensional) formulas of the enantiomers of 2-bromobutane
(Here H and $CH_3$ are interchanged)

### (ii)   Fischer projection formulas : 
Use the point of intersection of two perpendicular lines to represent the chirality centre; horizontal lines represent the bonds that project out of the plane of the paper toward the viewer, and vertical lines represent the bonds that project back from the plane of the paper away from the viewer. The carbon chain is drawn vertically with C – 1 at the top of the chain :



Fischer projections for the enantiomers of 2-bromobutane

Here also interchange of the two groups (or atoms) of an enantiomer gives the second enantiomer, however many organic chemists prefer to interchange the two horizontal groups because the enantiomers then look like mirror images on paper. Note that **interchanging one pair of groups gives enantiomer,** while interchanging two pairs of groups (or atoms) gives an identical (original) molecule.

In short, **if two structural formulas of a compound differ by an odd number of interchanges, they are enantiomers; if by an even number, they are identical.**

*Example 9 :*

**Seven Fischer projection formulas are drawn below for CHBrFCl. Give the relation of structures (ii) to (vii) with respect to (i).**

*Solution :*

It two structural formulas differ by odd number of interchanges, they are enantiomers; if by an even number, they are identical.

| Structure | Sequence of group interchange | Number of interchanges | Relationship to (i) |
|---|---|---|---|
| (ii) | H, Br | 1 (odd) | enantiomer |
| (iii) | H, F | 1 (odd) | enantiomer |
| (iv) | H, F ; Br, Cl | 2 (even) | identical |
| (v) | H, Br ; Cl, F | 2 (even) | identical |
| (vi) | F, Br ; Br, Cl | 2 (even) | identical |
| (vii) | F, Br; Br, Cl ; H, Cl | 3 (odd) | enantiomer |

## 3.3.2 Tests for chirality

The ultimate test for molecular chirality of a molecule is non-superimposability over its mirror image. If two structures are mirror image of each other, and these are not superimposable over each other, these are said to be chiral. However, certain structural features related to molecular symmetry can **sometimes** help us in knowing whether a molecule is chiral or achiral. For example, a molecule having either a plane of symmetry or a center of symmetry is superimposable on its mirror image, and thus it will be **achiral**.

**A plane of symmetry,** also called internal mirror plane of symmetry is defined as an imaginary plane that bisects a molecule in such a way that the two halves of the molecule are mirror images of each other. The plane may pass through atoms, between atoms, or both. For example, difluorochloromethane has a plane of symmetry (defined by the atoms H–C–Cl) and thus the molecule is **achiral**.

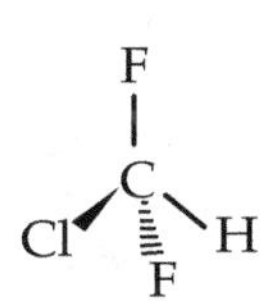

Difluorochloromethane
(it has a plane of symmetry
along the atoms Cl–C–H)

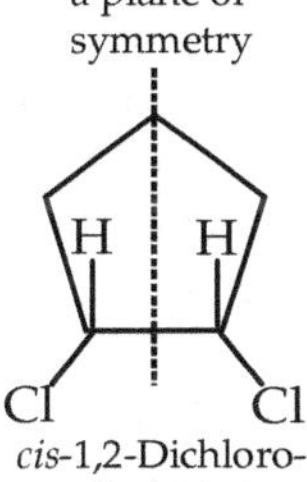


*cis*-1,2-Dichloro-
cyclopentane

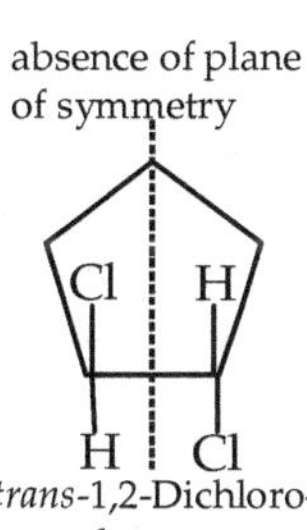


*trans*-1,2-Dichloro-
cyclopentane

Similarly, *cis*-1,2-dichloropentane has a plane of symmetry while the corresponding *trans*-isomer does not have any plane of symmetry so the former is achiral whereas the latter is chiral.

**A center of symmetry** is an imaginary point in the center of a molecule from which if lines are drawn, on any group, on both the sides to an equal distance, it divides the molecule into two equal halves which are the mirror images of each other. For example, 2,4-dimethylcyclobutane-1,3-dicarboxylic acid has a center of symmetry which is the center of the ring.

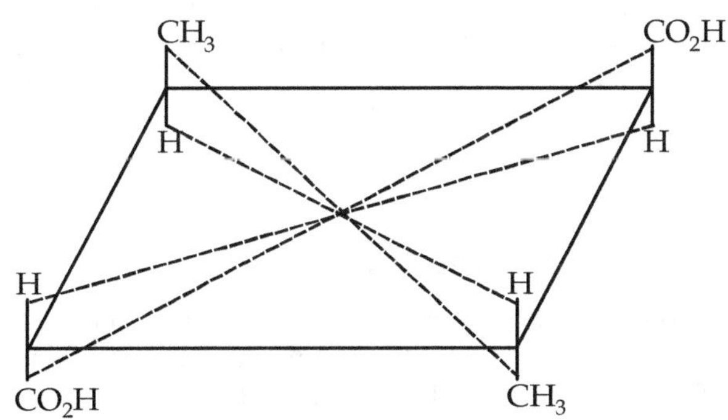

Thus from the above discussion, we can generalize the principle that *any molecule with a plane of symmetry or a center of symmetry is achiral, even though it may contain asymmetric carbon atoms.* However, the converse is not always true i.e. the absence of these symmetry elements does not necessarily mean that the molecule is chiral. Thus remember that a molecule lacking a plane of symmetry or a center of symmetry is likely (**not necessarily**) to be chiral.

## TEST YOUR UNDERSTANDING - 3.5

1.    Locate any plane of symmetry or center of symmetry in each of the following compounds. Which of the following compounds are chiral/achiral?

    (a)    (*E*)-1,2-Dichloroethene                 (b)    (*Z*)-1,2-Dichloroethene

    (c)    *cis*-1,2-Dichlorocyclopropane         (d)    *trans*-1,2-Dichlorocyclopropane

2.    Which of the following compounds are chiral? Star all asymmetric carbon atoms in the molecule. Point out plane of symmetry or center of symmetry in the structure of the molecule, also predict whether the molecule is optically active or inactive.

    (a)    *meso*-2,3-Dibromo-2,3-dichlorobutane       (b)    (2*R*, 3*S*) $\overset{4}{C}H_2OH\,\overset{3}{C}HBr\,\overset{2}{C}HOH\,\overset{1}{C}H_2OH$

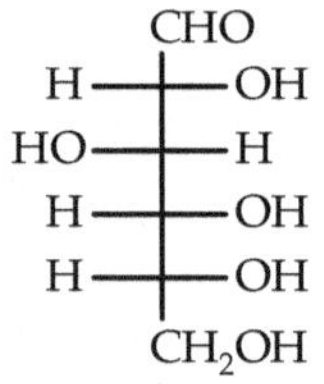

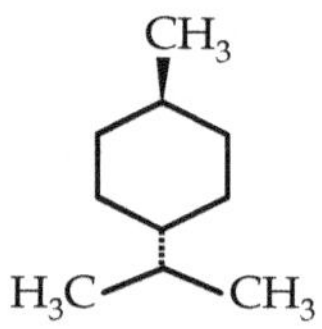

### 3.3.3 Optical activity

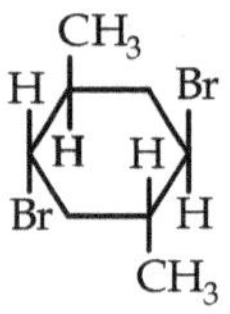

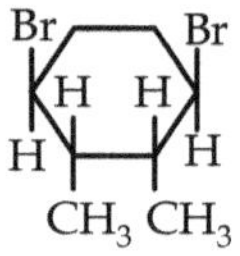

Since the molecules of enantiomers are not superimposable one over the other, these are considered to be different compounds. However, the two enantiomers have most of their physical properties (e.g. melting points, boiling points, solubilities, etc.) similar because these properties depend on the magnitude of the intermolecular forces operating between the molecules which is identical in the enantiomers. Enantiomers show different rates of reaction when they interact with other chiral substances. They also differ in solubilities in solvents that consist of a single enantiomer or an excess of a single enantiomer. The easily observable way in which enantiomers differ is their behaviour toward plane-polarized light.

**What is plane-polarized light?** Ordinary light consists of electromagnetic waves vibrating randomly in all directions. Plane-polarized light is composed of waves that vibrate in only one plane. Plane-polarized light is produced by passing normal light through a polarizer such as a polarized lens or a Nicol prism. When plane-polarized light passes through a solution of an achiral compound, the light emerges from the solution with its plane of polarization unchanged because there is no asymmetry in the molecules. Thus in short *an achiral compound does not rotate the plane of polarization and hence called* **optically inactive**.

However, when plane-polarized light passes through a solution of a chiral compound, the light emerges with its plane of polarization changed (rotated) because of *asymmetric* nature of the molecules. Thus, a chiral compound rotates the plane of polarization either in clockwise or in counterclockwise direction. If one enantiomer rotates the plane of polarization in clockwise direction, its mirror image will rotate the plane of polarization exactly to the same extent but in counterclockwise direction. *A compound that rotates the plane of polarized light is said to be* **optically active**. Before the relationship between chirality and optical activity was known, enantiomers were called **optical isomers** *because they rotate the plane of polarized light through some angle.* However, now this ambiguous term (*optical isomers*) has been replaced by the well defined term **enantiomers**.

### 3.3.4 Stereochemistry of molecules with one chiral centre

If an optically active compound rotates the plane of polarization in a clockwise direction, it is called **dextrorotatory**, indicated by (+). If an optically active compound rotates the plane of polarization in a counterclockwise direction, it is called **levorotatory**, indicated by (–). *Dextro* and *levo* are latin prefixes for "to the right" and "to the left", respectively; these are sometimes abbreviated by a lowercase *d* or *l* respectively.

Do not confuse (+) and (–) with $R$ and $S$. The (+) and (–) symbols indicate the direction in which an optically active compound rotates the plane-polarized light, whereas $R$ and $S$ indicate the arrangement of the groups about a chirality center. There is no relation between these two conventions. Some compounds with the $S$ configuration are (+) and some are(–). For example, (S)-lactic acid is dextrorotatory whereas (S)-sodium lactate is levorotatory.

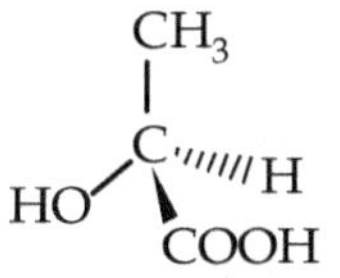

$(S)$-(+)-Lactic acid 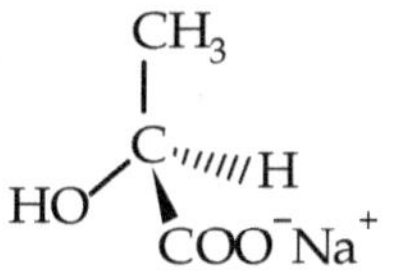          $(S)$-(–)-Sodium lactate

By looking at the structure of a compound we can tell whether it has the $R$ configuration or the $S$ configuration, but whether a compound is detxtrorotatory, (+) or levorotatory, (–) can be known only with the help of a polarimeter.

The angular rotation of polarized light by a chiral compound is a characteristic property of that compound. The rotation ($\alpha$) observed in a polarimeter depends on the concentration of the sample solution, the length of the cell, optical activity of the compound, temperature and the wavelength of the light source. To use the rotation of polarized light as a characteristic property of a compound, the rotation is measured under the specific condition and called **specific rotation**, $[\alpha]$.

$$[\alpha]_D^{25} = \frac{\alpha \text{ (observed)}}{c.\ell}$$

where, $\alpha$ (observed) = Rotation observed          $c$ = Concentration in g/mL

$\ell$ = Length of sample cell (path length) in decimeters          D = Represents the D line of the sodium spectrum

25 = Represents that the measurement is made at 25°C.

## TEST YOUR UNDERSTANDING - 3.6

1.   If (S)-lactic acid is dextrorotatory and the corresponding sodium salt is levorotatory, then can you predit the nature of (R)-lactic acid and its sodium salt?

2..   A chiral sample gives a rotation that is close to 180°. How will you tell whether this rotation is +180° or −180°?

### 3.3.5   Stereochemistry of molecules with more than one chirality centre

When a molecule contains two stereocentres, as in 2,3-dihydroxybutanoic acid, it can exist in four stereoisomeric forms. These four isomers are simply all the permutations of $(R)$ and $(S)$ configurations at the two chiral carbon atoms, C2 and C3.

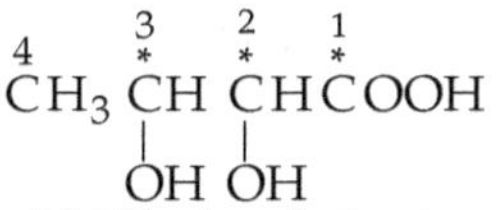

$$\underset{\text{2,3-Dihydroxybutanoic acid}}{\overset{4\quad\overset{3}{*}\;\overset{2}{*}\;1}{CH_3\,CH\,CHCOOH}} \quad \begin{array}{cccc} (2R,\,3R) & (2S,\,3S) & (2R,\,3S) & (2S,\,3R) \\ I & II & III & IV \\ & \text{Enantiomers} & & \text{Enantiomers} \end{array}$$

In order to convert a molecule with two stereogenic centres to its enantiomer, the configurations at both centres must be changed. Reversing the configuration at only one stereogenic centre converts it to a disastereomeric structure (diastereomers are stereoisomers that are not enantiomers). Thus here I and III, I and IV, II and III, and II and IV are diastereomers.

A compound with $n$ dissimilar chiral carbon atoms can have a maximum of $2^n$ stereoisomers. Thus 2,3-dihyroxybutanoic acid having 2 chiral carbon atoms can have as many as four ($2^2 = 4$) stereoisomers.

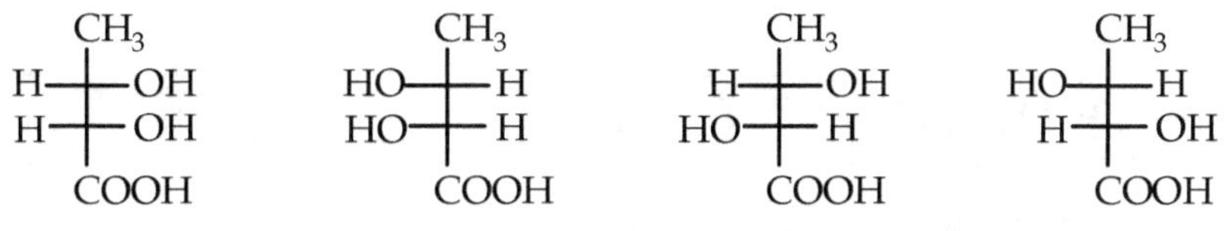

|         I        |        II        |        III       |        IV        |
|:----------------:|:----------------:|:----------------:|:----------------:|
| Enantiomers, or erythro enantiomers | | Enantiomers, or threo enantiomers | |

Here I and III, I and IV, II and III, and II and IV all are diastereomers. Remember that *cis-trans* isomers of a compound are also considered as diastereomers because they are stereomers but not enantiomers.

However, remember that when two of the chiral carbon atoms have identical substituents and opposite configuration, the number of stereoisomers will be less than $2^n$.

### 3.3.6   Meso compounds (Achiral molecules with two stereogenic centres)

A structure with two stereocenters does not *always* have four possible stereoisomers. The formula $2^n$ gives correct number of stereoisomers only when all the chiral carbon atoms are differently substituted. In case when a molecule has two chiral centers that are equivalently substituted as in 2,3-butanediol, the number of stereoisomers will be *three instead of four*. Of the four theoretically possible structures, two (A and B) are enantiomers of each other, while the *remaining two (C and D) are not enantiomers* because the mirror image of one superimposes over its original form, i.e. the two structures are superimposable. Thus in short, structures C and D are same and represent only one molecule, hence the compound has only three stereoisomers.

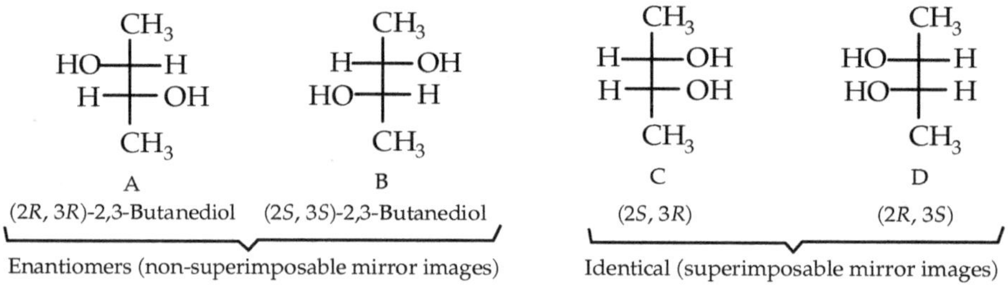

| A | B | C | D |
|---|---|---|---|
| (2R, 3R)-2,3-Butanediol | (2S, 3S)-2,3-Butanediol | (2S, 3R) | (2R, 3S) |

Enantiomers (non-superimposable mirror images)     Identical (superimposable mirror images)

To know whether the two structures are identical or not, rotate one of the structures by 180° in the plane of the paper, if now it superimposes over the other then two structures are identical. It is found to be so in case of structures C and D.

The molecules represented by structure C or D is not chiral even though it contains two chiral carbons. Such molecules are called **meso compounds** (*achiral compounds that have chirality centers*). The ultimate test for molecular chirality is to construct a model (or write the structure) of the molecule and then test whether the model (or structure) is superimposable on its mirror image. If it is superimposable, the molecule is achiral, if not superimposable, the molecule is chiral.

The achiral nature of the *meso* isomer is due to the presence of a **plane of symmetry**. Because of the plane of symmetry, a meso compound does not rotate the plane of polarized light, and hence it is optically inactive. Few examples of *meso* compounds are given below.

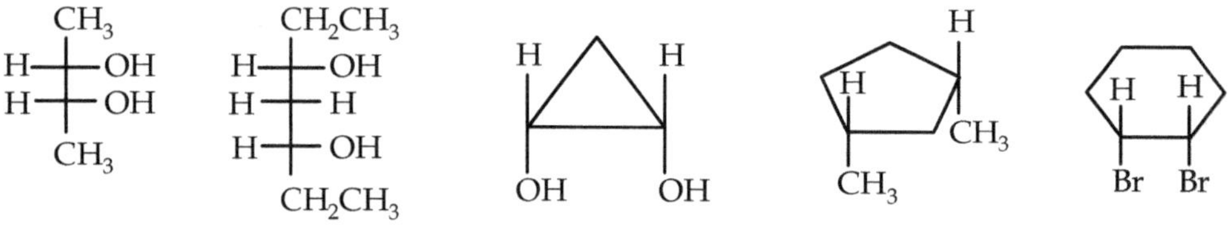

### 3.3.7   Erythro and threo nomenclature

When Fischer projections are drawn for stereomers with two adjacent chirality centres, the pair of enantiomers with similar groups on the same side of the carbon chain is called the **erythro enantiomers**. The pair of enantiomers with similar groups on opposite sides is called **threo enantiomers**. Thus, the above drawn I and II stereoisomers in (e) are the *erythro* enantiomers, while the III and IV are the *threo* enantiomers.

## TEST YOUR UNDERSTANDING - 3.7

1.     Cholesterol, an important compound, has I as its structure

    (a)    How many chirality centers does it have?

    (b)    Also predict the maximum number of stereoisomers of cholesterol?

I, Cholesterol

II, Tetracycline

2.    Tetracycline is a broad-spectrum antibiotic. It is assigned structure II. How many chirality centers does tetracycline have?

3.    Cholic acid, an important constituent of bile acids, has eleven chiral carbon atoms. Can you predict the possible number of diastereomers of cholic acid?

## 3.3.8   Properties of enantiomers and diastereomers

Enantiomers have identical physical properties (except for the direction in which they rotate plane-polarized light) and identical chemical properties - they react at the same rate with a given *achiral* reagent.

Since diastereomers are not mirror images of each other, they have different physical properties (like m.p., b.p., solubilities, specific rotations, and so on) and different chemical properties - they react with the same reagent at different rates. In this respect, these diastereomers resemble diasteromeric alkenes like *cis-* and *trans-*2-butene. Because diastereomers have different physical properties, they can be separated by ordinary methods like distillation and recrystallization (note that enantiomers can't be separated by either of the two methods).

## TEST YOUR UNDERSTANDING - 3.8

1.    Predict the nature of the two stereoisomers in each of the following case of a compound having two chirality centers.

   (a)    The configuration of both chirality centers in the two isomers is same.

   (b)    When the configuration of both chirality centers in one isomer is opposite to that of the configuration of the chirality centers in the other isomer.

   (c)    When the configuration of one of the chirality centers has the same configuration in the both isomers but the other chirality center has opposite configuration in the two isomers.

2.    (a)    Draw Fischer projections of the four stereoisomeric 3-amino-2-butanols and label each as erythro or threo.

   (b)    The (2R, 3R)-3-amino-2-butanol is liquid while the (2R, 3S)-isomer is a crystalline solid. Name the remaining two stereomers with their physical state.

3.    Using *R* and *S* descriptors, write all the possible combinations for a molecule with three stereogenic centers.

## 3.3.9   Prediction of number of optical isomers in compounds having chiral centre

1.    **When the molecule is chiral.**

   Number of *d* and *l* isomers $(a) = 2^n$ , Number of meso forms $(m) = 0$

   $\therefore$   Total number of optical isomers $= (a + m) = 2^n$

   Where $n$ is the number of differently substituted chiral carbon atom(s).

   Common example is $CH_3.CHBr.CHBr.COOH$

2.    **When the molecule is symmetrical and has even number of chiral carbon atoms.**

   Number of *d* and *l* isomers $(a) = 2^{(n-1)}$ , Number of meso forms $(m) = 2^{(n/2)-1}$

   $\therefore$   Total number of optical isomers $= (a + m)$

   Common example is tartaric acid, $HOOC.CHOH.CHOH.COOH$

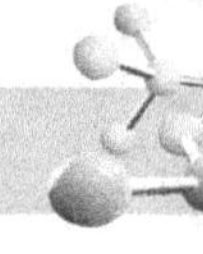

3.  **When the molecule is symmetrical and has an odd number of chiral carbon atoms.**

Number of $d$ and $l$ forms $(a) = 2^{(n-1)} - 2^{(n/2) - 0.5}$   Number of meso forms $(m) = 2^{(n/2) - 0.5}$

$\therefore$   Total number of opital isomers $= (a + m) = 2^{(n-1)}$

Common example is

$$HOOC - \overset{*}{C}HOH - \overset{*}{C}HOH - \overset{*}{C}HOH - COOH$$

A carbon atom which is attached to two different atoms or groups as well as two identical carbon atoms is called **pseudo chiral carbon atom**. For example, in trihydroxyglutaric acid, the central carbon atom is *pseudo chiral* while the terminal carbon atoms are chiral.

---

*Example 10 :*

**How many monohydric primary alcohols can be derived from the hydrocarbon $C_5H_{12}$. Draw their structures.**

*Solution :*

$n$-Pentane $\longrightarrow$ ($-$OH on $C_1$) $1°$ ; ($-$OH on $C_2$) $2°$   ($-$OH on $C_3$) $2°$

$iso$-Pentane $\longrightarrow$ ($-$OH on $C_1$) $1°$ ; ($-$OH on $C_2$) $3°$   ($-$OH on $C_3$) $2°$   ($-$OH on $C_4$) $1°$

$neo$Pentane $\xrightarrow{\text{All CH}_3 \text{ groups are identical}}$ ($-$OH on $C_1$ or $C_3$) $1°$

Hence total number of monohydric $1°$ alcohols $= 1 + 2 + 1 = 4$.

---

*Example 11 :*

**Draw structures of the following compounds in line bond notations.**

(*i*)   **Z-1, 3-Pentadiene**                    (*ii*)  **E-1, 3-Pentadiene**

(*iii*) **2E, 4E-3-Ethyl-2,4-hexadiene**          (*iv*) **2Z, 4E-3-Ethyl-2,4-hexadiene**

(*v*)   **2Z, 4Z-3-Ethyl-2,4-hexadiene.**

*Solution :*

For drawing line bond formulae for geometrical isomers, proceed according to following points.

(*a*)   Write down the structure of the compound. Pick up the doubly bonded carbon atoms responsible for geometrical isomerism. In case the compound has two or more such centres, take one by one.

(*b*)   Observe the atom or group attached on each carbon atom and determine their priority according to sequence rule.

(*c*)   Draw the line representing other group in the same direction for $Z$ or *cis* isomer, or in opposite direction for the $E$ or *trans* isomer.

(*d*)   In case compound has more than one double bond causing geometrical isomers, repeat steps (*b*) and (*c*) for each such double bond.

Let us illustrate the above points on $Z$-1-, 3-pentadiene and $E$-1, 3-pentadiene.

(*a*)   $\overset{1}{C}H_2 = \overset{2}{C}H - \overset{3}{C}H = \overset{4}{C}H - \overset{5}{C}H_3$. Here only double bond between $C_3$ and $C_4$ can produce geometrical isomers.

(*b*)   $C_3$ has H and $-CH = CH_2$ group where $-CH = CH_2$ has priority over H ; while $C_4$ has H and $CH_3$ group where $-CH_3$ has priority over H.

(c)    For *Z* isomer draw lines in such manner that lines representing —CH = CH$_2$ and —CH$_3$ lie on the same side ; similarly for *E*, draw lines on opposite directions.

(*i*) 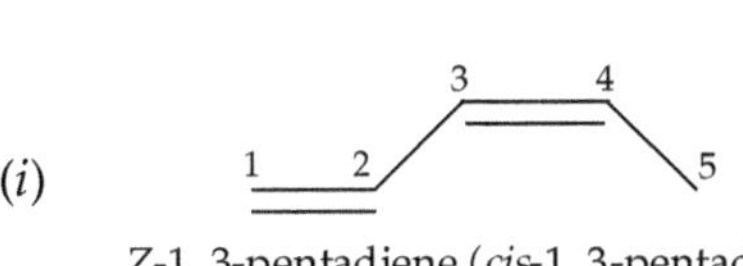

Z-1, 3-pentadiene (*cis*-1, 3-pentadiene)
CH$_2$ = CH— and —CH$_3$
are on same side

(*ii*) 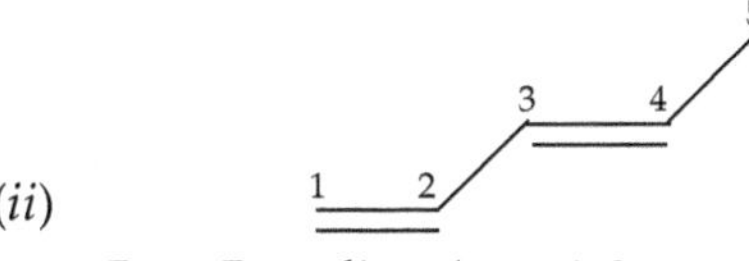

E-1, 3-Pentadiene (*trans*-1, 3-pentadiene)
CH$_2$ = CH— and —CH$_3$
are on opposite sides

(*iii*) 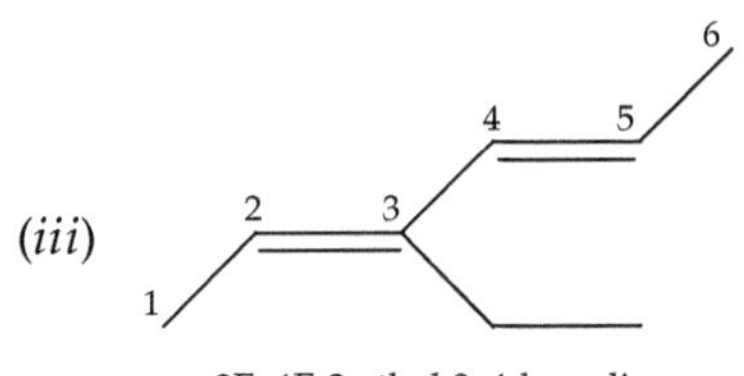

2E, 4E-3-ethyl-2, 4-hexadiene

(*iv*) 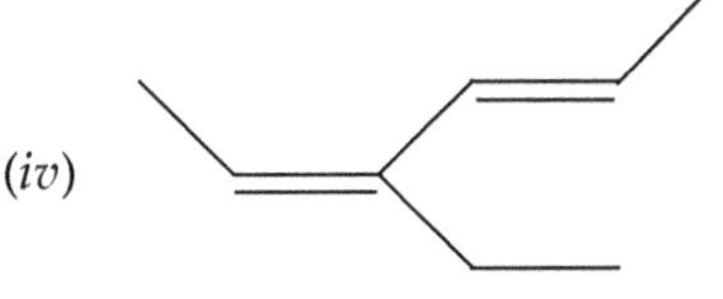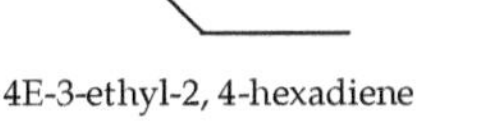

2Z, 4E-3-ethyl-2, 4-hexadiene

(*v*) 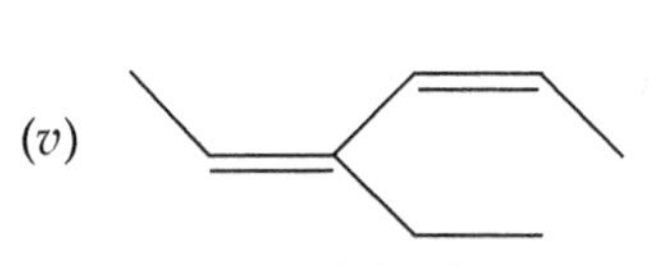

2Z, 4Z-3-ethyl-2, 4-hexadiene

---

*Example 12 :*

**Which of the following compounds has a meso stereoisomer?**

(a)    **2,4-Dibromopentane**     (b)  **3,4-Dimethylhexane**      (c)  **2-Bromo-3-methylpentane**
(d)    **1,3-Dichlorocyclohexane**     (e)  **1,4-Dichlorocyclohexane**      (f)  **1,2-Dichlorocyclohexane**
(g)    **3,4-Dimethylhexane**      (h)  **1-Chloro-2-methylcyclohexane**

*Solution :*

First of all draw structure for each of the compound

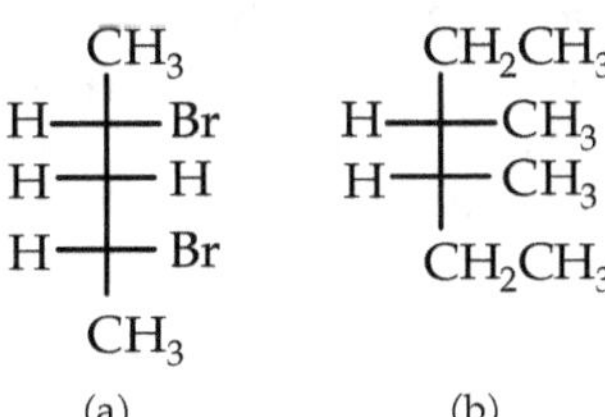

The essential condition for a compound to exist in meso stereomeric form is the presence of two equivalently substituted chiral centers. Thus here

(i)    Compounds (e) and (g) do not have any chiral carbon so they do not show even stereoisomerism, what to speak of meso compound.

(ii)   Compounds (c) and (h) have two chiral centers, but the two chiral carbons of each compound are different, so they do not have any meso isomer.

(iii)  Each of the compounds (a), (b), (d) and (f) have two equivalently substituted two chiral centers. Further, the meso isomer has a plane of symmetry which can be easily observed in acyclic compound when drawn as a Fischer projection, and in cyclic compounds when drawn with a flat ring.

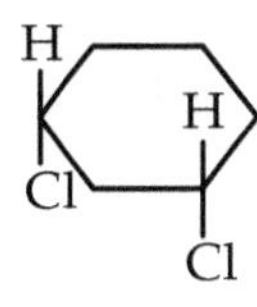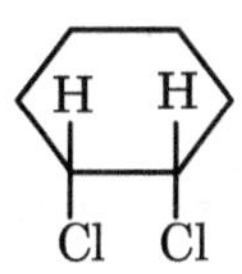

## TEST YOUR UNDERSTANDING - 3.9

1. Classify each of the following pair as enantiomers, diastereomers or identical.

   (a) ($2R$, $3S$)-2,3-dibromohexane and ($2S$, $3R$)-2,3-dibromohexane

   (b) ($2S$, $3R$)-2,3-dichlorohexane and ($2R$, $3R$)-2,3-dichlorohexane

   (c)

   (d)     and     (e)     and

   (f)     and     (g)     and

   (h)     and its mirror image     (i)     and

2. Draw all the distinct stereoisomers for each structure and show their relationship as enantiomers, diastereomers, etc. Label any meso isomer, if any and draw in any mirror plane of symmetry.

   (a) $CH_3CHClCHOHCOOH$

   (b) $COOH.CHOH.CHOH.COOH$

   (c) $HOOC.CHBr.CHOH.CHOH.COOH$

   (d)

3. Which of the following compounds has meso as one of the stereoisomers in each case?

   (a) 2,3-Dimethylbutane    (b) 3,4-Dimethylhexane    (c) 2-Bromo-3-methylpentane

   (d) 1,3-Dimethylcyclohexane    (e) 1,4-Dimethylcyclohexane    (f) 1,2-Dimethylcyclohexane

   (g) 3,4-Dimethylhexane    (h) 1-Bromo-2-methylcyclohexane

### 3.3.10 Enantiomerism in Compounds having no chiral centre

We have learnt that the essential condition for a molecule to be chiral is that it is not superimposable on its mirror image. The most important and common examples of chiral compounds contain a tetrahedral atom with four different substituents. However, several chiral molecules are known which although do not contain any chiral (asymmetric) atom, yet they are chiral. In these types of compounds, chirality to the molecule is associated with the molecular shape. Here the chirality is better known as **disymmetry**.

**Allenes :** Dienes containing double bonds between successive carbon atoms are called allenes or cumulenes.

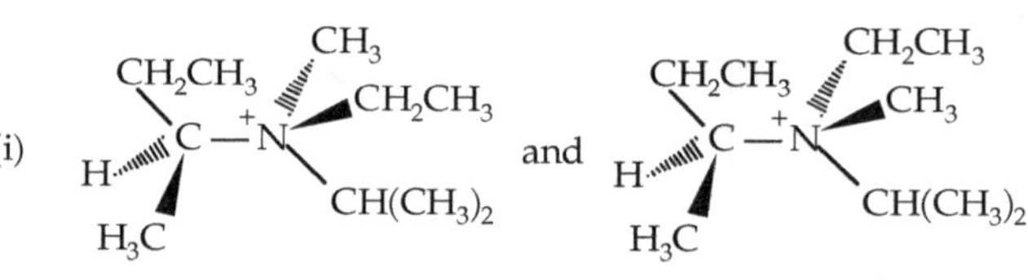

The central carbon atom is in *sp* hybrid state and thus the two π bonds lie in mutually perpendicular planes. This geometry of the π bonds causes the groups attached to the end carbon atoms to lie in perpendicular planes. Thus allenes with different substituents on the end carbon atoms are chiral and hence show enantiomerism (allenes do not show *cis-trans*-isomerism).

Enantiomers of 2,3-pentadiene

**Conformational enantiomerism in biphenyls :**

Although the two benzene nuclei of the biphenyl are different, they can't be distinguished because of very fast rotation around the C–C single bond.

However, this rotation can be avoided by placing bulky groups on the *ortho* positions of the two benzene rings, and thus such biphenyls can exist in two structures.

However, these two structures are superimposable mirror images over each other, hence they do not show enantiomerism. In case, the *ortho*-positions of each of the benzene rings are differently substituted by bulky groups, the biphenyls show enantiomerism.

Thus it is concluded that *the essential condition for enantiomerism is the molecular disymmetry or molecular chirality and not the mere presence of chiral centre.*

## 3.3.11 Racemic Mixture

A mixture of equal amounts of the two enantiomers is called a **racemic mixture, a racemic modification, or a racemate**. A racemic mixture does not rotate plane-polarized light. They are optically inactive because for every molecule in a racemic mixture that rotates the plane of polarized light in one direction, there is a mirror-image molecule that rotates the plane in the opposite direction; hence these are often designated as being (±) or *d, l*. For example, a racemic form of (R)-(−)-2-butanol and (S)-(+)-2-butanol is designated as (±)-2-butanol or (*d,l*)-2-butanol.

Many reactions lead to racemic products, especially when an achiral molecule is converted to a chiral molecule in absence of any chiral reagent or solvent. For example, addition of hydrogen across the C=O double bond of a ketone produces a racemic mixture of the alcohol.

2-Butanone

(achiral molecule)

(±)–2–Butanol

[chiral molecules but 50:50 mixture of (R) and (S)]

The formation of racemic mixture can be explained by the fact that if the addition of hydrogen to one face of the double bond of a carbonyl group (a flat molecule) produces the *R*-enantiomer, addition of hydrogen to the other face forms the *S*-enantiomer.

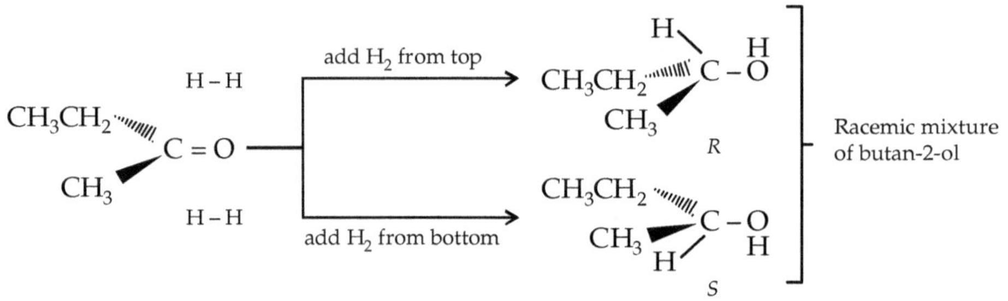


## 3.3.12 Enantioselective synthesis

If a reaction that leads to the formation of enantiomers produces a preponderance of one enantiomer over its mirror image, it is called **enantioselective**. For a reaction to be enantioselective, a chiral reagent, solvent, or catalyst must assert an influence on the course of the reaction. The enantioselective syntheses taking place in nature is due to the chiral influence of proteins, present in enzymes. The active site of proteins (enzymes) is chiral, and hence ***only one enantiomer of a chiral reactant fits it properly*** causing the reaction to occur. For example,

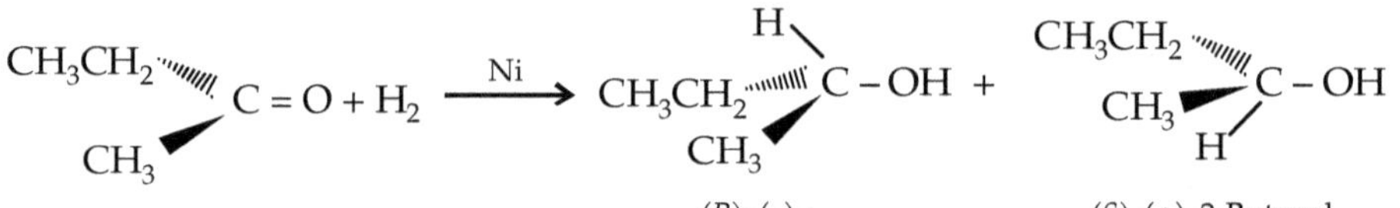


(*R*)-(–)- (*S*)-(+)-2-Butanol

(Racemate)

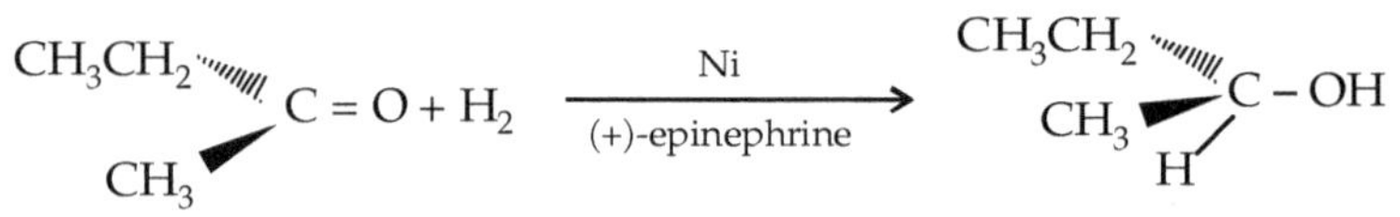


(*S*)-(+)-2-Butanol
(Major)

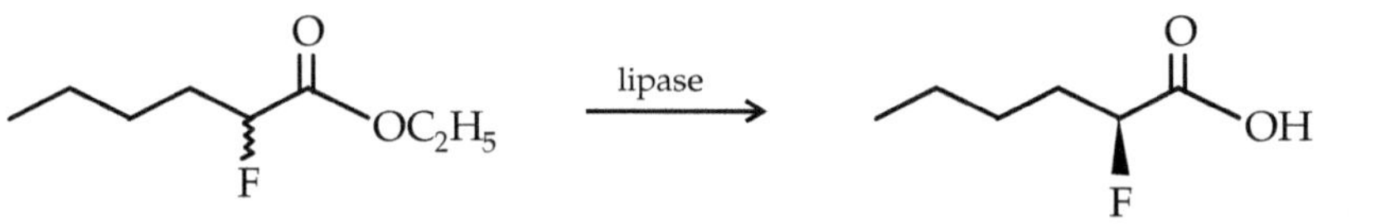


Ethyl (±)-2-fluorohexanoate (*S*)-(–)-2-Fluorohexanoic acid (About 84%)

On similar ground, the therapeutic use of only the (*S*)-enantiomer of the following drugs can be explained.

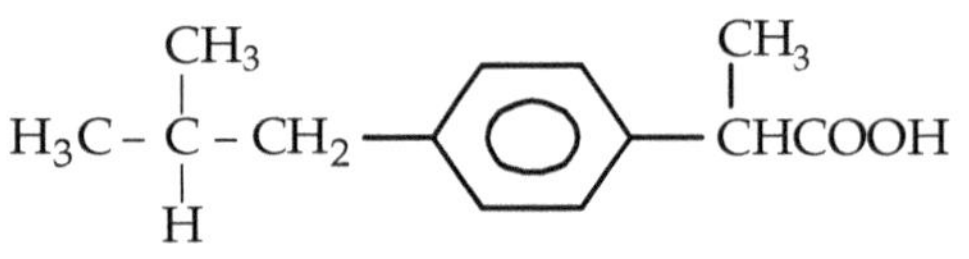

Ibuprofen

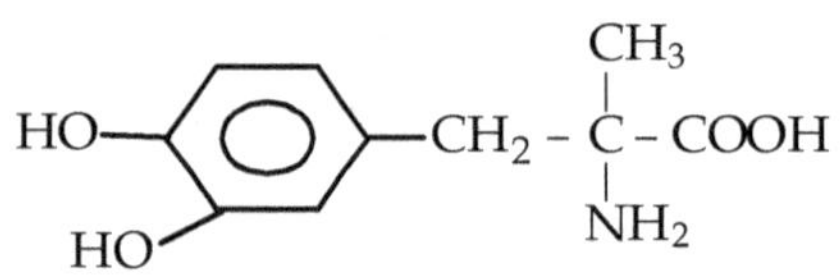

Methyldopa

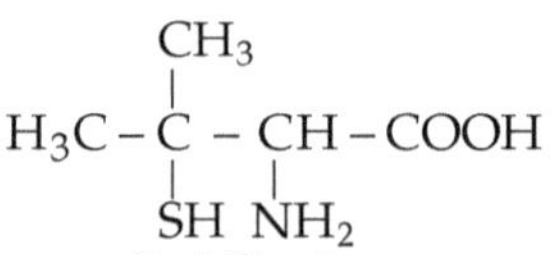

Penicillamine

## TEST YOUR UNDERSTANDING - 3.10

1. Draw three dimensional representations of the following compounds. Which one has asymmetric carbon atom and which has no asymmetric carbon atom but still chiral?

   (a)   1-Chloro-3-methyl-1,2-butadiene          (b)   1-Chloro-1,3-butadiene

   (c)   2,2'-Dibromo-6-iodo-6'-methylbiphenyl     (d)   2,2'-Dideuteriobiphenyl

2. Write three-dimensional formula for the (*S*)-enantiomers of

   (a) ibuprofen, (b) methyldopa, and (c) penicillamine

### 3.3.13 Enantiomeric excess and optical purity

Sometimes we deal with mixtures that are neither optically pure (all molecules are of one enantiomer) nor racemic (equal amounts of two enantiomers). In these cases, we specify optical purity (**o.p.**) of the mixture. The optical purity of a mixture is defined as the ratio of its rotation to the rotation of a pure enantiomer.

$$\text{Optical purity} = \frac{\text{Observed specific rotation}}{\text{Specific rotation of pure enantiomer}}$$

For example, if a sample of 2-bromobutane whose (*S*)-enantiomer has specific rotation of +23.1° has an observed specific rotation of +9.2°, its optical purity will be 0.40, i.e. it will be 40% optically pure.

$$\text{Optical purity} = \frac{+9.2°}{+23.1°} = 0.40 \text{ or } 0.40 \times 100 = 40\%$$

The positive specific rotation (+9.2°) of the sample indicates that the sample has excess amount of (*S*)-(+)-2-bromobutane. Thus the optical purity (40%) of the mixture indicates the following composition of the mixture.

$$40\% \ (+) \text{ enantiomer} + 60\% \ (\pm)\text{-mixture}$$

$$\text{or } 40\% \ (+) + 30\% \ (+) + 30\% \ (-) \text{ enantiomer}$$

$$\text{or } 70\% \ (+) \text{ enantiomer} + 30\% \ (-) \text{ enantiomer}$$

In other words, the mixture has 40% excess of one enantiomer, hence this amount (40%) which is equal to optical purity is also known as **enantiomeric excess (e.e.)**.

Algebraically, we use the following formula

$$\text{O.p} = \text{e.e.} = \frac{[d-l]}{(d+l)} \times 100\% = \frac{\text{Excess of one over the other}}{\text{Entire mixture}} \times 100\%$$

Since in the above calculation, units cancel out, the formula can be used whether the amounts of the enantiomers are expressed in concentrations, grams or percentages.

## TEST YOUR UNDERSTANDING - 3.11

1. (+)-Mandelic acid has a specific rotation of +158°. What would be the observed specific rotation of a mixture having 25% (+)-mandelic acid and 75% (–)-mandelic acid?

2. If the observed specific rotation of a mixture of (*R*)-glyceraldehyde and (*S*)-glyceraldehyde is +1.4°, determine the percentage composition of (*R*,*S*)-glyceraldehyde; the $[\alpha]_D^{25}$ for (*S*)-(–)-glyceraldehyde is –8.7°C.

3. Calculate the enantiomeric excess and the specific rotation of a mixture containing 6 g of (+)-2-butanol and 4 g of (–)-2-butanol. The specific rotation of the pure (–)-2-butanol is –13.5°.

4. A solution having 10 mL of 0.10 M solution of the *R* enantiomer and 30 mL of a 0.10 M solution of the *S* enantiomer has a specific rotation of +4.8°. Determine the specific rotation of each of the enantiomer.

5. Catalytic reduction of 2-butanone in presence of (–)-epinephrine gives a product with a specific rotation of –0.45°. Calculate the percentage composition of the product, (+)-2-butanol and (–)-2-butanol, obtained. The specific rotation of (+)-2-butanol is +13.5°.

### 3.3.14 Separation of Enantiomers

The separation of a mixture of enantiomers into pure enantiomers is called **resolution**. Since enantiomers have identical boiling points and solubilities, they can't be separated by the conventional separation techniques, such as crystallization and distillation.

Pasteur separated racemic mixture of the crystalline sodium ammonium tartrate by using a microscope and a pair of tweezers. The separation was based on the fact that the crystals of the two enantiomers were not identical, crystals of one enantiomer were "right-handed" while that of other enantiomer were "left-handed".

However, separation of enantiomers by hand is not universally useful method of resolving a racemic mixture because only a few compounds form asymmetric crystals. A more commonly used method is to convert the enantiomers into diastereomers. Diastereomers can be separated by the usual conventional methods like distillation and fractional crystallization because they have different physical properties. After separation, the individual diastereomers are converted back into the original enantiomers. For example, a racemic mixture of a carboxylic acid can be separated (resolved) into two enantiomers by using a naturally occurring 100% optically pure base (a resolving agent); morphine, strychnine, and brucine are naturally occurring chiral bases commonly used for this purpose.

$$(R)\text{–R–COOH} \quad \xrightarrow{(S)\text{–base}} \quad (R)\text{–RCOO}^{-} (S)\text{-base H}^{+}$$
$$+ \qquad\qquad\qquad\qquad +$$
$$(S)\text{–R–COOH} \qquad\qquad\qquad (S)\text{–RCOO}^{-} (S)\text{-base H}^{+}$$

A pair of enantiomers       A pair of diastereomers

Separate

$$(R)\text{–RCOO}^{-} (S)\text{-base H}^{+} \qquad\qquad (S)\text{–RCOO}^{-} (S)\text{-base H}^{+}$$

$$\downarrow \text{HCl} \qquad\qquad\qquad\qquad \downarrow \text{HCl}$$

$$(S)\text{-base H}^{+} + (R)\text{–RCOOH} \qquad (S)\text{–RCOOH} + (S)\text{-base H}^{+}$$

Enantiomers can also be separated by **chromatography**. The racemic mixture to be separated is dissolved in a solvent and the solution is then passed through a column packed with a *chiral* adsorbent. The two enantiomers move through the column at different rates because of their different affinities (adsorption) for the chiral adsorbent (a right hand prefers a right-hand glove), so one enantiomer will emerge from the column before the other.

## TEST YOUR UNDERSTANDING - 3.12

1.  $(R, S)$-2-Butanol is treated with $(R, R)$-tartaric acid to form salts.

    (a)  How many different salts can be formed?      (b)  Predit the total number of chirality centers in each salt.

    (c)  How many chirality centers are identical to that in the other salt and how many are different?

2.  Which of the following pairs of compounds can be separated by recrystallisation or distillation?
    (a)  $(\pm)$-Tartaric acid and *meso*-tartaric acid.

    (b)    (c)

    (d)

3.  Draw the structures of $(R)$-2-butyl-$(R,R)$-tartrate, $(S)$-2-butyl-$(R,R)$-tartrate, and their mirror images. Give the relationship of the four compounds as enantiomers, diastereomers, or identical.

### 3.3.15 Compounds capable of Showing Enantiomerism as well as Geometric Isomerism

A molecule having both stereogenic centers and double bonds will show enantiomerism as well as geometric isomerism, provided each of the doubly bonded atom is differently substituted. For example, 3-penten-2-ol may be either *R* or *S*, and *R* may be *R, E* or *R, Z*; similarly *S* may be *S, E* or *S, R*. Thus there are four stereoisomers of 3-penten-2-ol, although it has only one stereogenic center.

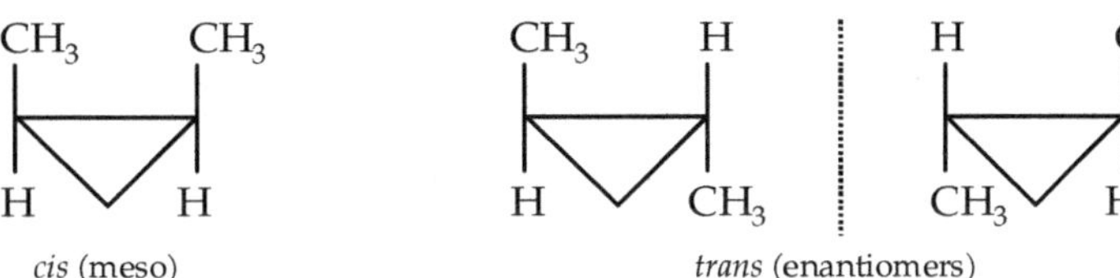

(2*R*, 3*E*)-3-penten-2-ol     (2*S*, 3*E*)-3-penten-2-ol     (2*R*, 3*Z*)-3-penten-2-ol     (2*S*, 3*Z*)-3-penten-2-ol

### 3.3.16 Stereoisomerism in Carbocyclic Compounds

(i)     Monosubstituted carbocyclic compounds do not have stereoisomers.

(ii)     1,2-Dimethylcyclopropane have three stereoisomers

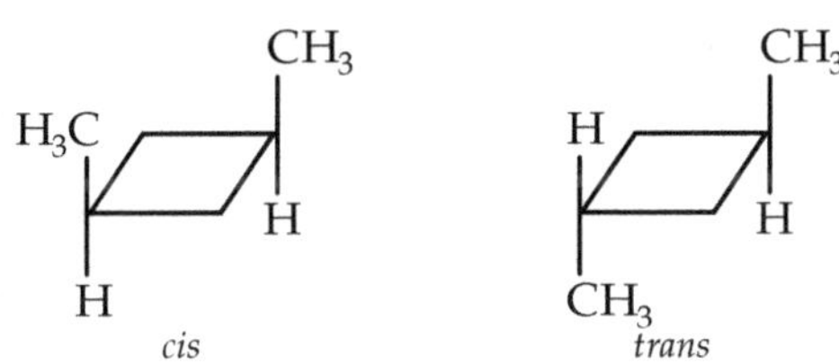

*cis* (meso)        *trans* (enantiomers)

(iii)     1,2-Dimethylcyclobutane has also three stereoisomers : *cis* (meso) and *trans* (enantiomers).

(iv)     1,3-Dimethylcyclobutane has two stereoisomers.

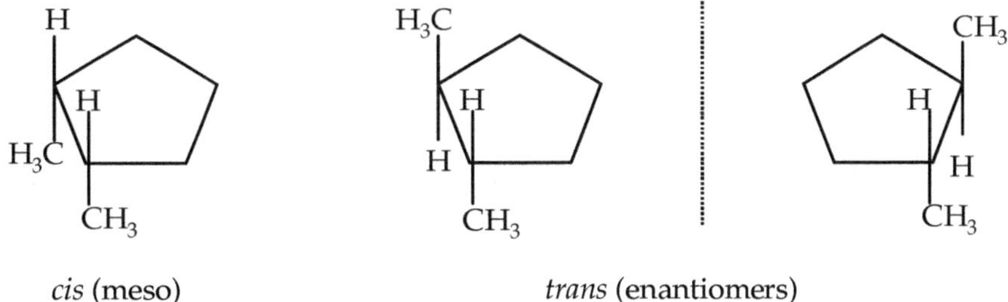

*cis*        *trans*

(v)     All *cis*-isomers of 1,2- and 1,3-dimethylcyclopentanes are *meso*, while all *trans*-isomers exist as a pair of enantiomers.

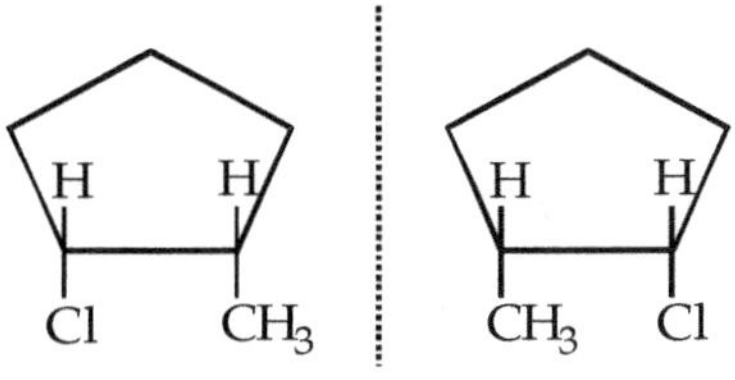

*cis* (meso)        *trans* (enantiomers)

However, when the two carbons are differently substituted, both *cis*- and *trans*- isomers exist as pair of enantiomers.

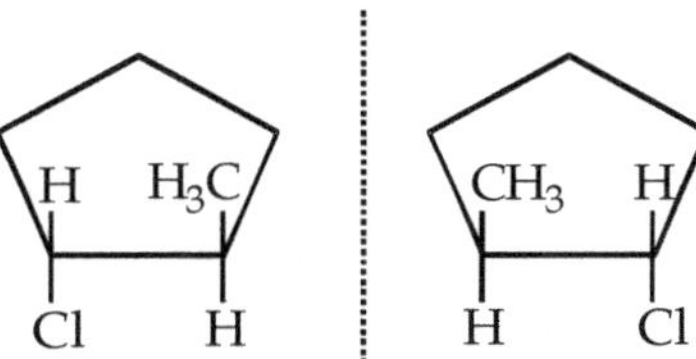

*cis*-1-Chloro-2-methylcyclopentane        *trans*-1-Chloro-2-methylcyclopentane

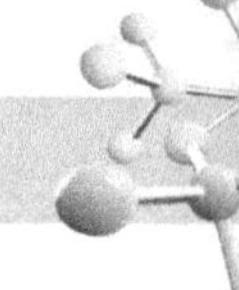

(vi)    Stereoisomers in the various substituted disubstituted cyclohexanes.

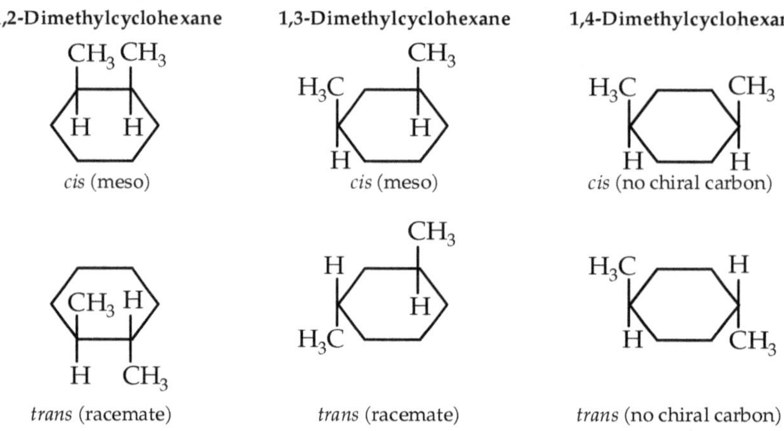

## TEST YOUR UNDERSTANDING - 3.13

**1.**    How many stereoisomers are possible for the following compound. Draw their structures.

$$CH_3CH_2CH(Br)CH_2CH = CHCH_3$$

**2.**    Draw the enantiomers of

(a)    3-bromocyclohexene, and (b) 4-bromocyclohexene

### 3.3.17 Reactions of compounds bearing chirality center (Relative and absolute configuration)

When a compound that contains a chirality center undergoes a reaction, two situations may arise.

(a)    The reaction takes place without cleavage of any of the four bonds to the chirality center. In such cases, the relative positions of the groups bonded to the chirality center will not change. For example,

$CH_3 \overset{\displaystyle CH_2CH_2CH_3}{\underset{\displaystyle H}{\vert}} CH_2CH_2Cl \quad \xrightarrow{\text{OH}^-} \quad CH_3 \overset{\displaystyle CH_2CH_2CH_3}{\underset{\displaystyle H}{\vert}} CH_2CH_2OH$

(*S*)-1-Chloro-3-methylhexane        (*S*)-3-Methyl-1-hexanol

Relative configuration of reactant and product is same.
Absolute configuration of reactant and product is same.

However, it is very important to note that although the relative positions of the four groups same in the reactant as well as product, it does not **always** mean that an *S*-reactant will always yield an *S* product. For example,

(*S*)-1-Chloro-3-methylhexane     $\xrightarrow{\text{LiAlH}_4}$     (*R*)-3-Methylhexane

Relative configuration of reactant and product is same.
Absolute configuration of reactant and product is different.

In this example, although the four groups bonded to chirality center maintained their relative positions (**relative configuration**) during the reaction, the absolute configurations of the two are opposite; one is *S* and the other is *R*. This is due to change in the relative priorities of the four groups as indicated by the encircled numbers.

(b) If a bond to the chirality center is broken, the product may have the same or opposite relative configuration to the reactant. The nature of the product actually depends upon the mechanism of the reaction.

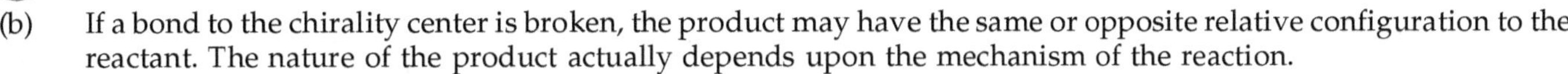

Relative configuration of reactant and product may be same or different.

## Rate of reaction of a chiral compound :

Enantiomers have the same chemical properties, so they react with **achiral** reagents (e.g. OH⁻) at the same rate. However, if the reagent is *chiral*, the enantiomers react at different rates. The common example of chiral reagent is an enzyme. The enzyme, being chiral, reacts only with one enantiomer, leaving another unchanged. If we imagine an enzyme to be a right-handed glove, then it will fit **only** into the right-handed hand (enantiomer), not at all into the left-handed hand (enantiomer).

---

*Example 13 :*

**How many stereoisomers are formed when (R)-2-chlorobutane is monochlorinated? Give the stereochemistry of each stereoisomer.**

*Solution :*

A  
(R)-2-Chlorobutane

B (S)  C  D (2R, 3R and 2R, 3S)  E (R)

(i) Compound B is chiral having the same relative configuration at $C_2$ as A, but it is S since priority order is changed ($CH_2Cl > CH_2CH_3$), in A the priority order was $CH_2CH_3 > CH_3$.

(ii) Compound C is achiral.

(iii) In D, a new chiral carbon is introduced hence it can exist in two diastereomeric forms: 2R, 3R (optically active), and 2R, 3S (meso).

(iv) E has same relative configuration at $C_2$ as in A, further like A it is also $R$ because the priority order is not changed. It was $CH_2CH_3 > CH_3$ in A; it is $CH_2CH_2Cl > CH_3$ in E.

## 3.3.18 Compounds with stereocentres other than Carbon

A tetrahedral atom with four different groups attached to it is a stereocenter (**chirality center**). Thus when an atom like silicon, germanium, nitrogen or phosphorus has four different substituents bonded it, it becomes chiral and the molecule bearing such atom will show enantiomerism and the enantiomers can be separated.

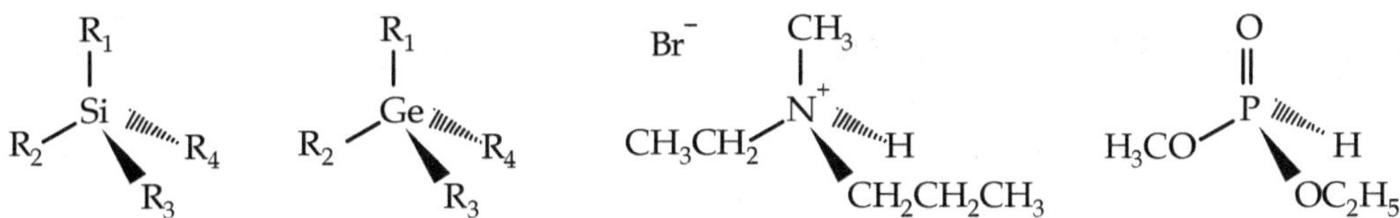

Enantiomerism in tetrahedral molecules other than carbon.

Trigonal pyramidal molecules (molecules in which one of the four positions is occupied by a pair of non-bonding electrons) are also chiral provided the central atom bears three different groups. Hence, such molecules should also show enantiomerism, however the two enantiomers can't be separated at the same ease in all cases because of different rate of pyramidal inversion that interconverts enantiomers.

(a)    In case of amines, pyramidal inversion at nitrogen is very rapid ($E_{act} = 24 - 40$ kJ mol$^{-1}$ or 6 to 10 kcal mol$^{-1}$) and thus an enantiomer of amines (having no stereogenic center other than nitrogen) is rapidly converted to other enantiomer causing immediate racemization.

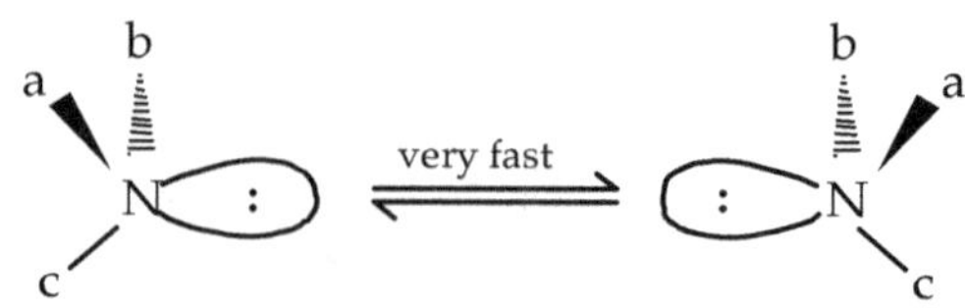

(b)    Tricoordinate phosphorus compounds (phosphines), however, undergo pyramidal inversion much more slowly than amines ($E_{act} = 120 - 140$ kj mol$^{-1}$ or 30-35 kcal mol$^{-1}$), and thus a number of optically active phsophines have been prepared.

(c)    Tricoordinate sulphur compounds bearing three different substituents around sulphur have also been resolved because the rate of pyramidal inversion at sulphur is rather slow. Optically active sulphoxides are examples of this type.

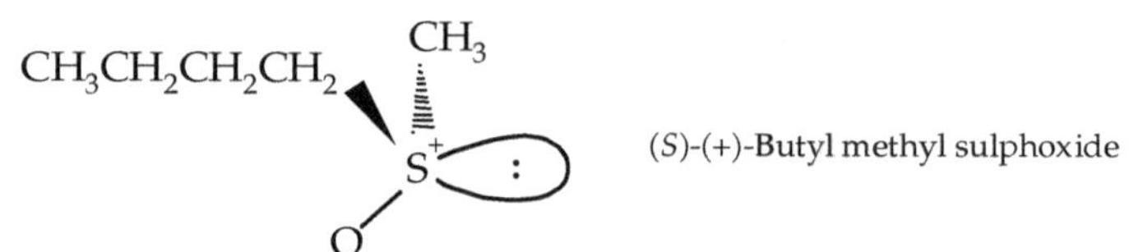


## 3.4   Diastereomers

All stereomers that are not mirror images are called diastereomers. Diastereomers include (a) all geometric isomers, and (b) compounds containing two or more chiral centers (usually asymmetric carbons). These have been discussed earlier in detail.

### Stereochemistry of Reactions

When we study the stereochemistry of a reaction, we are concerned with the following questions.

(a)    If a chiral center or a double bond is generated during a reaction, there are possibilities that a single stereoisomer or all possible stereoisomers are formed. In case the reaction leads to the preferential formation of one stereoisomer over another, it is called a **stereoselective reaction**. Depending on the degree of preference for a particular stereoisomer, a reaction can be described as *moderately stereoselective, highly stereoselective, or completely stereoselective.*

     **A stereoselective reaction :**   A $\longrightarrow$ B + C , where B and C are stereoisomers.

(b)    If the reactant can exist as stereoisomers, it is just possible that one stereoisomer reacts while the other does not react, or the two isomers form different products, the reaction is said to be **stereospecific**.

     **A stereospecific reaction :**   A $\longrightarrow$ B, C $\longrightarrow$ D where A and C are stereoisomers and B and D are stereoisomers.

In the above reaction, we observe that stereoisomer A forms only the stereoisomer B but not the D, so, in addition to stereospecific, the reaction is also stereoselective. Many reactions (like addition of bromine on the carbon-carbon double bond) *are both stereoselective and stereospecific.* But this is not always true; some reactions are stereoselective but not stereospecific, one particular stereoisomer is the predominant product regardless of the stereochemistry of the reactant, or regardless of whether the reactant even exists as stereoisomers.

*Some reactions are stereospecific but not stereoselective* because (i) although the stereoisomers may react at different rates, but form the same stereoisomers as the product, or (ii) form products that differ in ways other than in their stereochemistry. Sometimes one stereoisomer reacts readily, while the other does not react at all, as in the biological reactions.

Further stereospecificity toward enentiomers is called **enantiospecificity**, and stereospecificity toward diastereomers is called **diastereospecificity**.

Whenever a reaction can lead to the formation of two structural (constitutional) isomers, one of which predominates the other, the reaction is called **regioselective reaction**.

## TEST YOUR UNDERSTANDING - 3.14

1.    Draw the structure of the reactant and products formed in the following reaction. Give the R/S designations to each

$$(R) - C_2H_5CH(CH_3)CH = CH_2 + D_2 \xrightarrow{\text{Pd}}$$

# EXERCISE 3.1 (MCQ - ONE option correct)

**1.** Which of the following statements is true?
   (a) All stereocenters are chiral
   (b) All chiral centers are stereocenters
   (c) Both of the above
   (d) None of the two

**2.** Which of the following is false?
   (a) A compound with a stereocenter is always optically active
   (b) A compound with a stereocenter may or may not be optically active
   (c) A compound with a stereocenter is never optically active
   (d) Both (a) and (c)

**3.** Which of the following has stereogenic center?

(a) 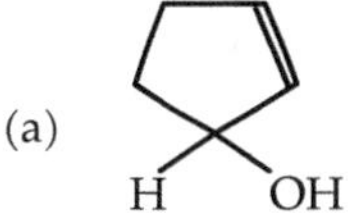   (b) 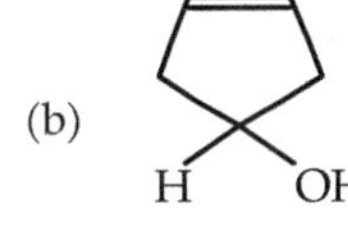

   (c) Both          (d) None

**4.** Theoretically, which type of intermediate can serve as a chiral center?
   (a) $R^1R^2R^3C^+$       (b) $R^1R^2R^3C^-$
   (c) $R^1R^2R^3C^{\bullet}$       (d) None of these

**5.** Which of the following type of compound can be resolved?

(a) $\overset{1\ 2\ 3\ \overset{..}{+}}{R\,R\,R\,S}X^-$       (b) $\overset{1\ 2\ 3\ ..}{R\,R\,R\,P}$

(c) $\overset{1\ 2}{R\,R}\,\underset{..}{S}=O$       (d) All of these

**6.** Which of the following can show optical activity?
   (a) 3-Methylpentene-1   (b) 3-Methylpent-1-yne
   (c) 2,3-Dimethylpentane   (d) All the three

**7.** The observed rotation of a solution of coniine (0.75 g/10 mL) in a 1 decimeter tube at 25°C (D line) is found to be +1.2°. The specific rotation of the coniine present will be
   (a) +1.2°       (b) −1.2°
   (c) +16°        (d) −16°

**8.** Find the observed rotation of a solution of coniine containing 0.35 mg/mL as measured in a 5.0 cm tube (D line), assuming the specific rotation of the sample coniine as −16°
   (a) +16°       (b) −1.2°
   (c) +2.8°      (d) −2.8°

**9.** Which of the following statement is true?
   (a) Doubling the concentration of the solution doubles the observed and specific rotation
   (b) Doubling the concentration of the solution halves the observed and specific rotation
   (c) Doubling the concentration of the solution doubles the observed rotation without affecting the specific rotation
   (d) Doubling the concentration of the solution and doubling the length of the tube increases the observed rotation by four times

**10.** Preparation of a compound X leads to a mixture with 20% racemization and 80% retention. What should be the observed rotation of the mixture, if $[\alpha]_D = -12°$ ?
   (a) +9.6°       (b) −9.6°
   (c) +2.4°       (d) −2.4°

**11.** The fact that two enantiomers of carvone have different smells suggests that
   (a) the two enantiomers are associated with different impurity.
   (b) the two have different volatility
   (c) the receptor sites in the nose are achiral
   (d) the receptor sites in the nose are chiral

**12.** If the structure of (+)-carvone is 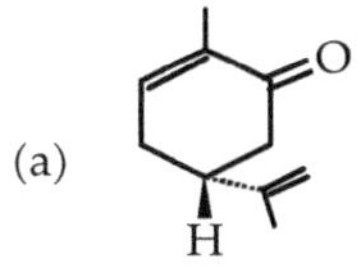 , the structure for (−)-carvone will be

(a) 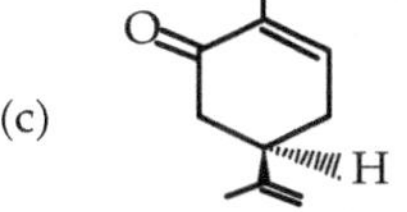   (b) 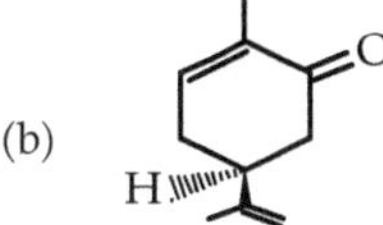

(c) 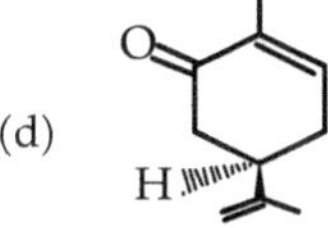   (d)

**13.** Which of the following is most reliable test for assessing the enantiomerism in a compound?
   (a) Absence of plane of symmetry or center of symmetry
   (b) Nonsuperimposability of the mirror image
   (c) Both of these
   (d) None of these

**14.** Which of the following has two stereoisomers?

$$CH_3-\overset{\overset{\displaystyle CH=CH_2}{|}}{\underset{\underset{\displaystyle CH_2CH_3}{|}}{N^+}}-H \quad (I)$$

$$CH_3-\overset{\overset{\displaystyle CH=CH_2}{|}}{\underset{\underset{\displaystyle CH_3}{|}}{N^+}}-H \quad (II)$$

$$H_3C-\overset{\overset{\displaystyle CH=CH_2}{|}}{\underset{\displaystyle \cdot\cdot}{N}}-H \quad (III)$$

   (a) None of these       (b) Only I
   (c) Only III            (d) I and III

**15.** Which of the following reaction produces optically inactive product?

(a) $\underset{\text{Fumaric acid}}{\overset{\displaystyle CHCOOH}{\underset{\displaystyle CHCOOH}{\|}}} + H_2O \underset{\xleftarrow{\hspace{1cm}}}{\overset{\text{fumarase}}{\xrightarrow{\hspace{1cm}}}} \overset{\displaystyle CH(OH)COOH}{\underset{\displaystyle CH_2COOH}{|}}$

(b) $(\pm)-CH_3CHOHC_2H_5 + (R)-\text{tartaric acid} \longrightarrow$ Tartrate

(c) $CH_3CH=CH_2 \xrightarrow{CH_3CO_3H} CH_3CH-CH_2 \backslash O /$

(d) All the above three

**16.** Meso stereoisomer is possible in which of the following compounds?
   (I) 2,4-Dibromopentane   (II) 2,3-Dibromopentane
   (III) 3-Bromo-2-pentanol   (IV) *cis*-1,3-Dimethylcyclohexane
   (V) *trans*-1,3-Dimethyl cyclohexane
   (a) I       (b) I and III
   (c) I and IV   (d) None of these

17. In the resolution of 1-phenylethylamine using (–)-malic acid, if the compound obtained by recrystallization of the mixture of diastereomeric salts is (R)-1-phenylethylammonium (S)-malate, the configuration of the more soluble salt will be
    (a) (R)-1-phenylethylammonium (R)-malate
    (b) (S)-1-phenylethylammonium (R)-malate
    (c) (S)-1-phenylethylammonium (S)-malate
    (d) (S)-1-phenylethylammonium (R)-malate

18. From the structures of the three stereoisomers of tartaric acid, which statement should be true?

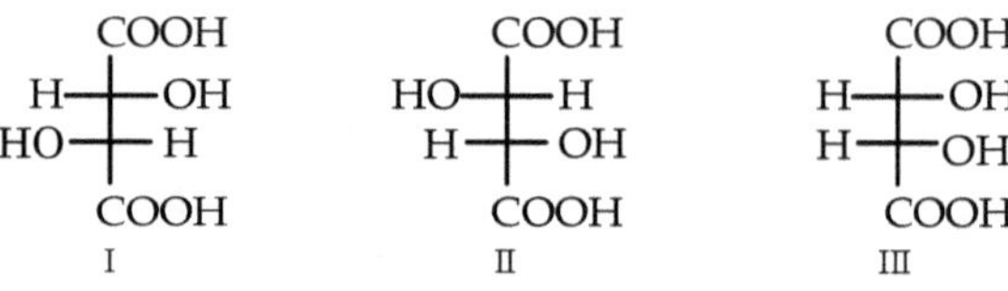

    (a) I is (+)–, II is (–)–, and III is optically inactive
    (b) I is (–)–, II is (+)–, and III is optically inactive
    (c) I is (+)–, II is (–)–, and III is meso
    (d) III is optically inactive, but nothing can be said about I and II

19. Compounds A and B are related as

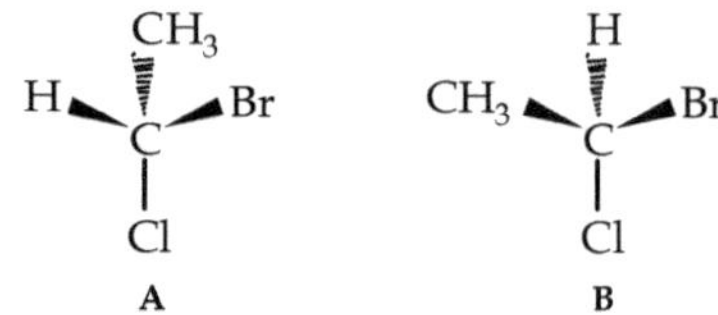

    (a) diastereomers　　　(b) conformational isomers
    (c) enantiomers　　　(d) same compound

20. The priority sequence of the alkyl groups is
    (a) $1° > 2° > 3° > CH_3$　　(b) $CH_3 > 1° > 2° > 3°$
    (c) $3° > 2° > 1° > CH_3$　　(d) $3° > 2° > CH_3 > 1°$

21. The first point of difference in determining the priority order among $C_6H_5$– and $(CH_3)_3C$– is at
    (a) $C_1$　　　　　(b) $C_2$
    (c) $C_3$　　　　　(d) $C_4$

22. The configurations of the compounds A and B respectively are

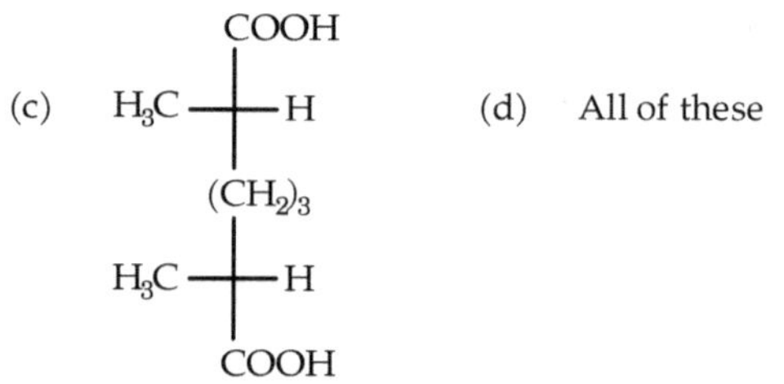

    (a) R and R　　　(b) S and S
    (c) R and S　　　(d) S and R

23. (R)-2-Butanol has the structure as

then the structure for (S)-2-butanol should be

    (a) ...　　　(b) ...
    (c) ...　　　(d) None of these

24. Reaction of (–)-lactic acid with methyl alcohol gives (+)-methyl lactate

$$CH_3CH(OH)COOH + CH_3OH \xrightarrow{HCl} CH_3CH(OH)COOCH_3$$
$$\text{(–)–Lactic acid} \qquad\qquad \text{(+)–Methyl lactate}$$

    This reaction involves
    (a) change in observed rotation
    (b) change in configuration
    (c) both (a) and (b)
    (d) racemization

25. Which of the R / S designation for meso-2,3-butanediol is incorrect?
    (a) 2R, 3S　　　　(b) 2S, 3R
    (c) R, S　　　　　(d) None of these

26. Which of the following stereoisomers is meso?

    (a) ...　　　(b) ...

    (c) ...　　　(d) All of these

27. The number of stereoisomers formed during monochlorination of butane is
    (a) 1　　　　　(b) 2
    (c) 3　　　　　(d) 4

28. $(S) - C_3H_7CH(OH)CH = CH_2 + H_2$

$$\xrightarrow{\text{Pt catalyst}} C_3H_7CH(OH)CH_2CH_3$$

    From the above reaction, we can definitely say that
    (a) the product and reactant are S
    (b) the product and reactant have same specific rotation
    (c) the product and reactant have same sign of specific rotation
    (d) (a) and (c) are correct

29. What would happen when (+)-2-iodobutane is kept in a solution of NaI?
    (a) (–)-2-iodobutane will be formed
    (b) (±)-2-iodobutane will be formed
    (c) (+)-2-iodobutane will be major product
    (d) Nothing will happen

30. The two enantiomers of 3,4-hexanediol can form as much as
    (a) two diastereomers　　(b) three diastereomers
    (c) four diastereomers　　(d) only one diastereomer

31. Select the compound which shows cis-trans isomerism but can't be named as cis and trans?
    (a) 3-Octene　　　(b) 3-Chloropent-2-ene
    (c) 1,3-Butadiene　　(d) 4,5-Dibromo-1-pentene

**32.** Which of the following compound does not show *cis-trans-* isomerism?
(a) 1,4-Dimethylcyclohexane
(b) 1,3-Dimethylcyclohexane
(c) 1-Vinyl-3-methylcyclopentane
(d) Vinylcyclopentane

**33.** Which of the following does not show geometric isomerism?
(a) 1,2-Dimethylcyclohexane
(b) 1,4-Dimethylcyclohexane
(c) 1-Bromo-3-chlorocyclohexane
(d) None of the three

**34.** Which of the following statement is true regarding *cis-* and *trans-* 2-butenes?
(a) Both have similar vander Waals attractions
(b) Both have similar dipole-dipole attractions
(c) Both are true
(d) Both isomers have similar van der Waals attractions, but only the *cis* isomer has dipole-dipole attractions

**35.** A hydrocarbon with the minimum number of carbon atoms, capable of showing geometric isomerism as well as optical isomerism is
(a) 3-Methylpentene    (b) 3-methylpentene-2
(c) 4-Methylhexene-2   (d) 4-Methylheptene-3

**36.** Following isomeric pair constitutes an example of

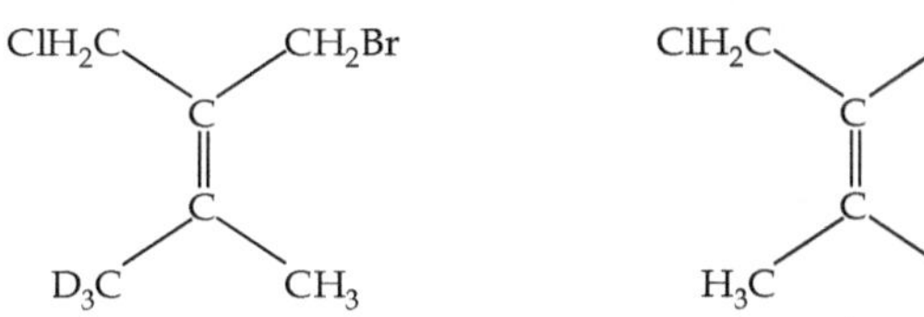

(a) Structural isomers    (b) Enantiomers
(c) Functional isomers    (d) Diastereomers.

**37.** How many stereoisomers are possible for monochloroisopentane?
(*a*) 2        (*b*) 4
(*c*) 6        (*d*) zero.

**38.** Which of the following statement is true regarding following structures ?

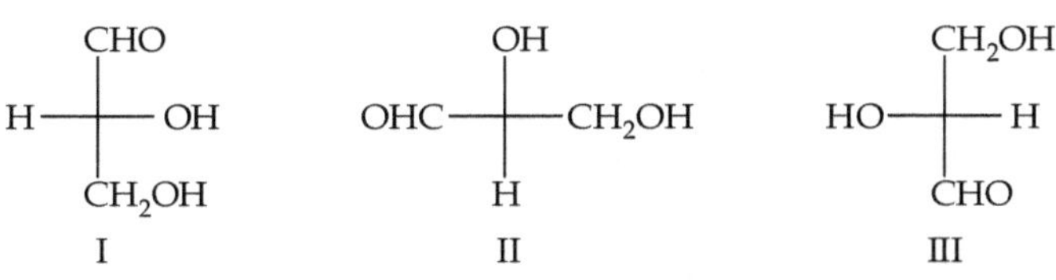

(*a*) I, II and III are identical
(*b*) I and II are identical, while I and III are enantiomers
(*c*) I and III are identical, while I and II are enantiomers
(*d*) II and III are identical, while I and II are enantiomers.

**39.** Which of the following statement is true ?
(*a*) The two enantiomers of 2-methyl-1-butanol react with acetic acid at the same rate
(*b*) The two enantiomers of 2-methyl-1-butanol react with (+)-lactic acid at the same rate
(*c*) A molecule containing chiral carbon atom is always chiral
(*d*) A chiral molecule always has at least one chiral atom.

**40.** In which of the following compounds meso form is possible ?
(*i*) 3, 4-Dibromo-3, 4-dimethylhexane
(*ii*) 2, 3-Dihydroxybutan-1, 4-dioic acid
(*iii*) 2, 4-Dibromopentane
(*iv*) 1, 2, 3, Tribromobutane
(*a*) (*i*) and (*ii*)        (*b*) only (*ii*)
(*c*) (*i*), (*ii*) and (*iii*)    (*d*) All the four.

**41.** Structure written below, has which of the following R, S configuration ?

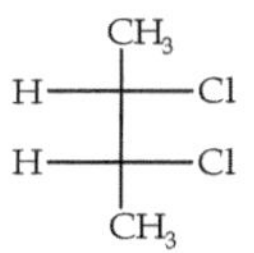

(*a*) 2(R)– 3(R)–        (*b*) 2(S) – 3(S)–
(*c*) 2(R) –3(S)–        (*d*) 2(S) – 3(R)–.

**42.** When (+)-2-butanol is allowed to stand in an aqueous acidic solution for some time, the product will be
(*a*) dextro-rotatory    (*b*) laevo-rotatory
(*c*) optically inactive  (*d*) either of the these.

**43.**

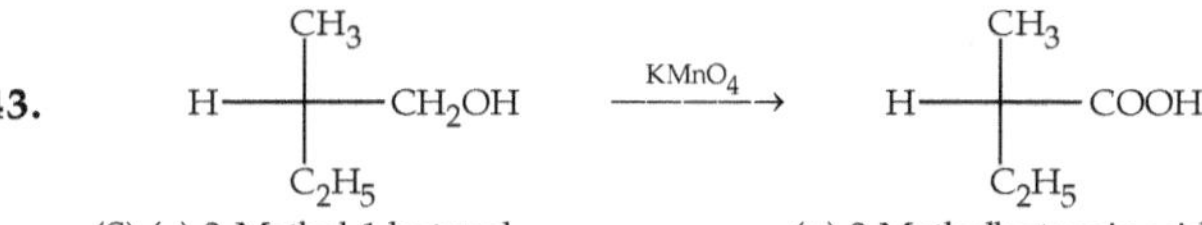

(S)-(–)-2-Methyl-1-butanol    (+)-2-Methylbutanoic acid

The above reaction indicates that the configuration of the product is
(*a*) R            (*b*) S
(*c*) RS           (*d*) can't be predicted.

**44.** Which of the following reaction can be used to establish relative configuration ?
(*a*) (R)–CH$_3$CH$_2$C(CH$_3$)(OH)CH$_2$Cl
$$\xrightarrow{PCl_5} CH_3CH_2C(CH_3)(Cl)CH_2Cl$$
(*b*) (S)–CH$_3$CHClCH$_2$CH$_3$
$$\xrightarrow{CH_3ONa} CH_3CH(OCH_3)CH_2CH_3$$
(*c*) (R)–CH$_3$CH$_2$CHOHCH$_3$
$$\xrightarrow{Na} CH_3CH_2CH(O^-Na^+)CH_3$$
(*d*) (S)–(CH$_3$)$_2$C(OH)CHBrCH$_3$
$$\xrightarrow{CN^-} (CH_3)_2C(OH)CHCNCH_3.$$

**45.** Which of the following compounds will exhibit geometrical isomerism ?
(*a*) 1-Phenyl-2-butene    (*b*) 3-Phenyl-1-butene
(*c*) 2-Phenyl-1-butene    (*d*) 1, 1-Diphenyl-1-propene.

**46.** Number of stereoisomeric forms of the compound CH$_3$.CH = CH. CHBr.CH$_3$ is
(*a*) 3        (*b*) 6
(*c*) 2        (*d*) 4.

**47.** The optically active tartaric acid is named as D –(+) – trataric acid because it has a positive
(*a*) optical rotation and is derived from D-glucose
(*b*) pH in organic solvent
(*c*) optical rotation and is derived from D – (+) – glyceraldehyde
(*d*) optical rotation only when substituted by deuterium.

**48.** A solution of (+) – 2-chloro-2-phenylethane in toluene racemises slowly in the presence of small amount of SbCl$_5$ due to formation of
(*a*) carbanion     (*b*) carbene
(*c*) free radical   (*d*) carbocation.

**49.** The following pair of structures are examples of :

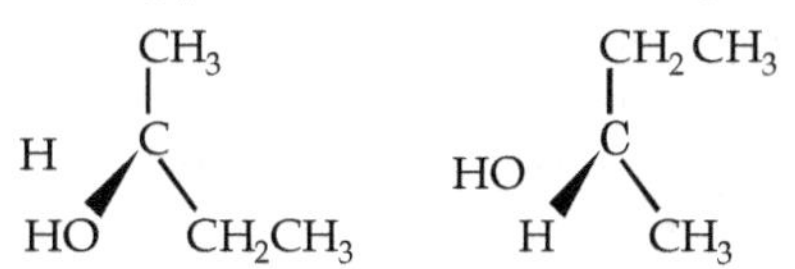

(a) same molecule     (b) enantiomers
(c) diastereomers     (d) regiomers

**50.** The following compounds are :

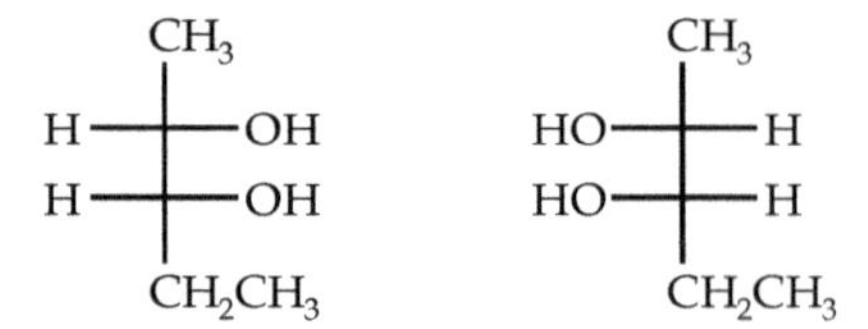

(a) enantiomers (b) diastereomers
(c) identical (d) epimers

**51.** Which of the following has a stereogenic centre?

(a) 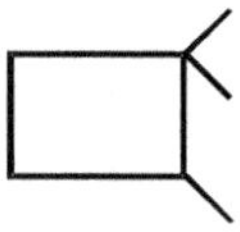 (b) 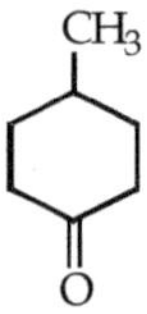

(c) 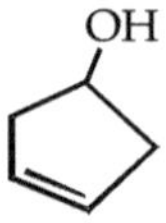 (d) 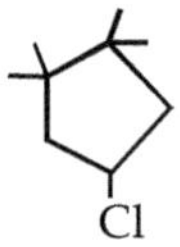

**52.** Which of the following represents enantiomeric pair?

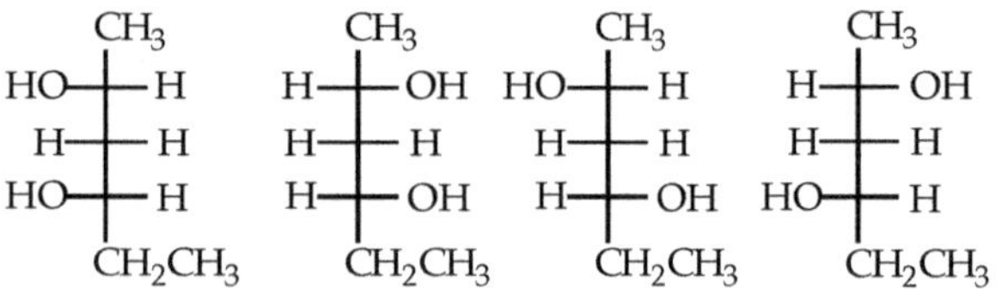

I II III IV

(a) I and II (b) I and III
(c) I and IV (d) II and III

**53.** Which of the following structures can show geometrical as well as optical isomerism?

(a) 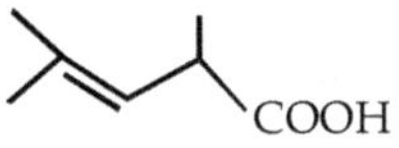 (b) HO – N =N – OH

(c) 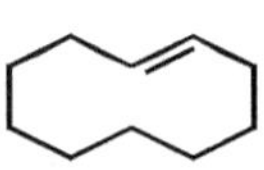 (d) 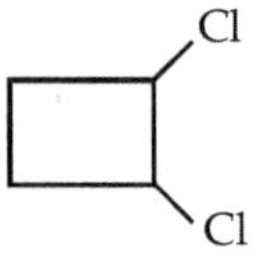

**54.** An enantiomerically pure acid is treated with racemic mixture of an alcohol having one chiral carbon. The ester formed will be
(a) optically active mixture
(b) pure enantiomer
(c) meso compound
(d) racemic mixture

**55.** 2-Methylpenta-2, 3-diene is achiral because it has
(a) a plane of symmetry
(b) a centre of symmetry
(c) a $C_2$ axis of symmetry
(d) both a plane and a centre of symmetry

**56.** *n*-Heptane can be made chiral by introducing a substituent on
(a) $C_1$ (b) $C_3$
(c) $C_4$ (d) any of the carbon

**57.** Pick up the correct statement regarding following two pairs.

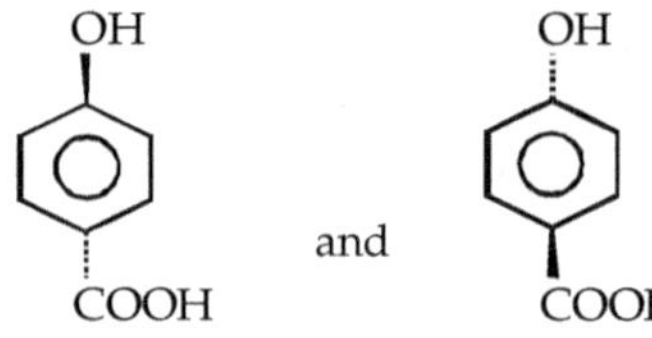

I and II

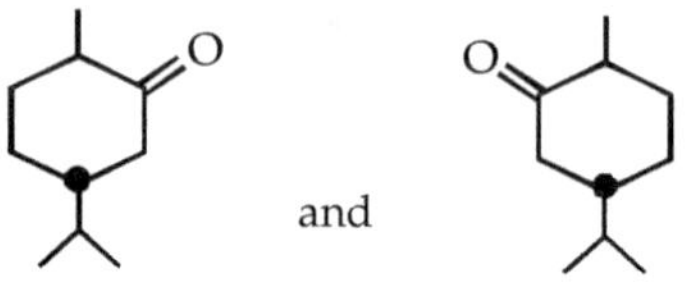

III and VI

(a) I and II as well as III and IV are enantiomers,
(b) I and II are enantiomers, while III and IV are identical.
(c) I and II as well as III and IV are identical.
(d) I an II are identical, while III and IV are diastereomers.

**58.** The compounds I and II are

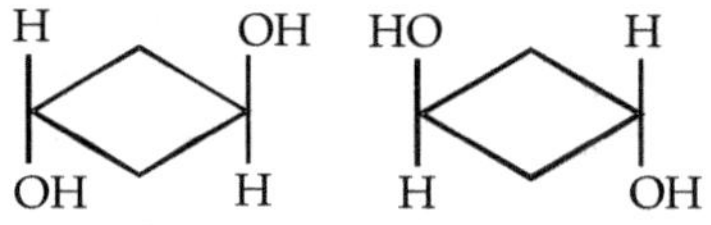

I II

(a) same
(b) enantiomers
(c) achiral identical mirror images
(d) geometrical isomers

**59.** The number of chiral carbon atoms in 1, 2-dimethyl-cyclohexane (A), 3-methylcyclohexene (B) and 4-methylcyclopentene (C) respectively are
(a) 1, 1, 1 (b) 2, 1, 0
(c) 2, 0, 1 (d) 2, 1, 1

**60.** Optical isomerism is shown by
(a) butanol-1 (b) butanol-2
(c) 3-pentanol (d) 4-heptanol

**61.** meso-Tartaric acid is optically inactive due to the presence of
(a) two chrial carbon atoms
(b) molecular unsymmetry
(c) molecular symmetry
(d) external compensation

**62.** Which of the following compounds will exhibit cis-trans (geometrical) isomerism?
(a) 2-butene (b) 2-butyne
(c) 2-butanol (d) butanal

**63.** The structure 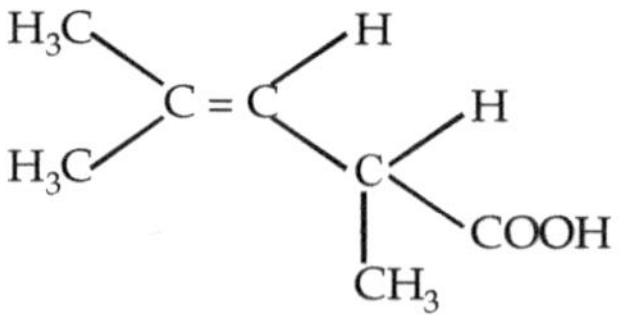 shows

(a) geometrical isomersism
(b) optical isomerism
(c) geometrical & optical isomerism
(d) tautomerism.

**64.** Which of the following compounds exhibits stereoisomerism?
(a) 2-methylbutene-1 (b) 3-methylbutyne-1
(c) 3-methylbutanoic acid (d) 2-methylbutanoic acid

# EXERCISE 3.2   (MCQ 1 or >1 option correct, Passage based, Matching, A/R)

**DIRECTIONS for Q. 1 to Q. 22 :** Multiple choice questions with one or more than one correct option(s).

1. Observe the following structures and pick up the correct option(s) mentioned below :

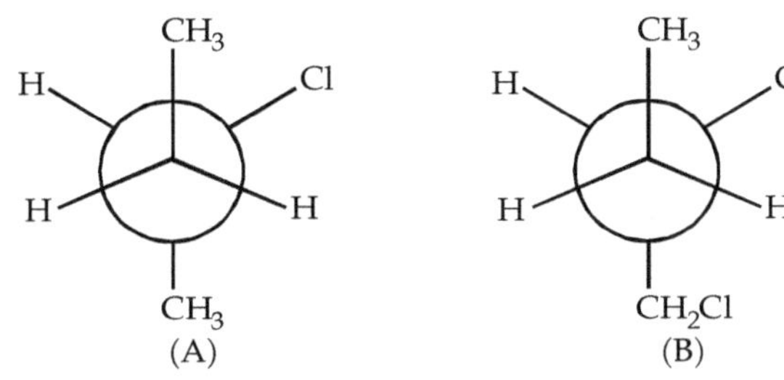

(a)  The two are position isomers
(b)  None of the two shows optical isomerism
(c)  Only A shows optical isomerism
(d)  The two are not related to each other regarding isomerism

2. 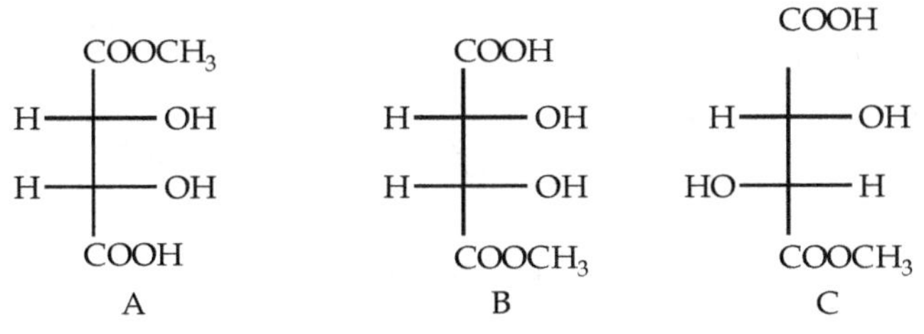

(a)  I and II are enantiomers
(b)  I is 2S, 3S; while II is 2S, 3R
(c)  I is 2R, 3R; while II is 2R, 3S
(d)  I and II are diastereomers

3. Which of the following statements are true regarding following structures?

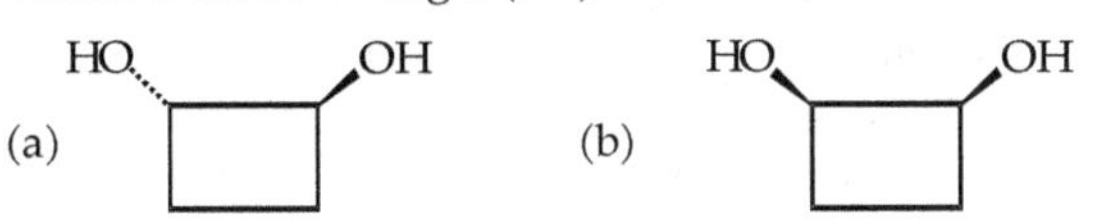

(a)  A and B are diastereomers
(b)  A and C are diastereomers
(c)  B and C are diastereomers
(d)  A and B are enantiomers

4. The R and S enantiomers of an optically active compound differ in
(a)  their reactivity with chiral reagents
(b)  their melting points
(c)  their optical rotation of plane polarized light
(d)  their solubility in achiral reagents

5. Which of the following is (are) chiral?

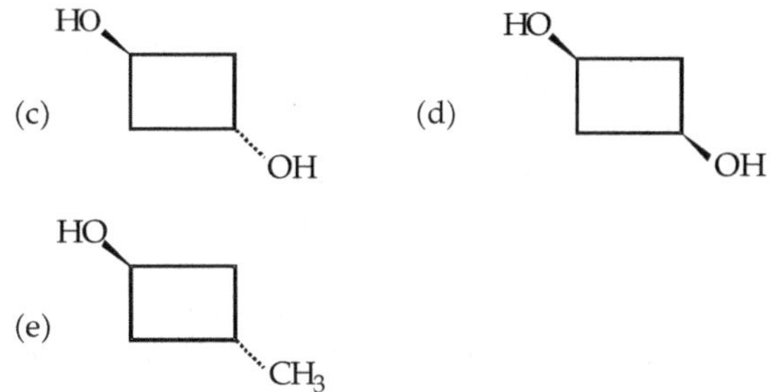

(a)     (b)

(c)     (d)

(e)

6. Which of the following can show diastereoisomerism?

(a)     (b)  $HO-N=N-OH$

(c)     (d)

7. Pick up the correct statements.
(a)  Sodium potassium tartarate will show enantio-merism.
(b)  $CH_3 - \overset{Cl}{\underset{H}{C}} - CH_2CH_3$ and $Cl - \overset{CH_3}{\underset{CH_2CH_3}{C}} - H$ are enantiomers.
(c)  $CH_3COCH_3$ on reaction with HCN followed by acidic hydrolysis gives racemic mixture.
(d)  $CH_3CH_2NO_2$ will show functional isomerism and tautomerism.

8. 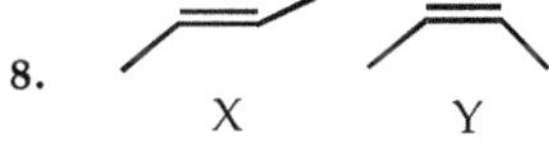

X     Y

Which of the following statments(s) is (are) incorrect?
(a)  X is *cis-* and Y is *trans*
(b)  X is Z and Y is E
(c)  X is *trans* and Y is *cis*
(d)  X and Y are diastereomers

9. Which of the following has S configuration?

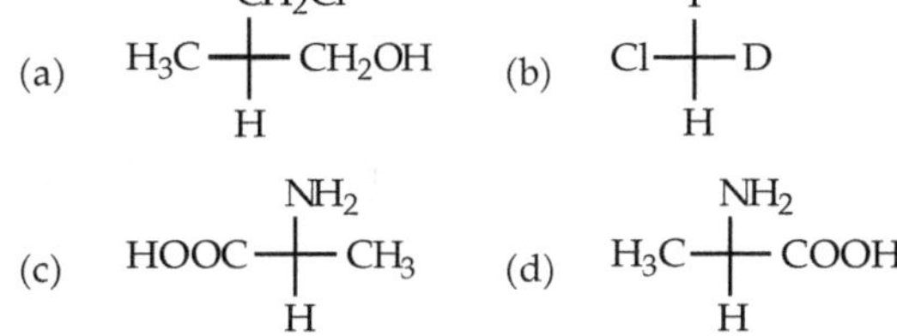

10. Which of the following shows *cis-trans* isomerism?

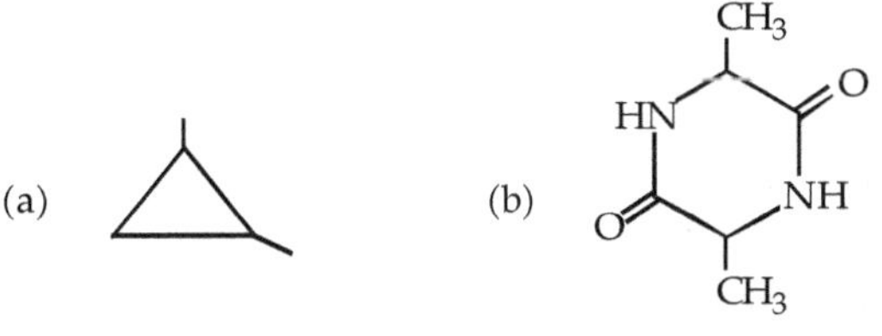

(d)  1, 2-Dimethylcyclobutane

**11.** Which of the following statement(s) is (are) incorrect?
- (a) Malic acid is less soluble in water than fumaric acid.
- (b) The presence of chiral carbon is an essential condition for enantiomerism.
- (c) Reduction of butanone with a chiral reagent gives (R)- and (S)-2-butanols in equal amounts.
- (d) Diastereoisomers are always optically active.

**12.** Which of the following have different rates of reaction?
- (a) Reaction of (+) and (−)- enantiomers with a chiral reagent.
- (b) Reaction of diastereomers with a chiral reagent.
- (c) Reaction of distereomers with an achiral reagent
- (d) Reaction of (+) and (−) enantiomers with an achiral reagent.

**13.** Which of the following is (are) threo isomers (s)?

- (a) 
- (b) 
- (c) 
- (d) 

**14.** Which of the following Newmann projections represent *meso* isomer?

- (a) 
- (b) 
- (c) 
- (d) 

**15.** Select the correct statement(s) about the following compound

- (a) It is an achiral molecule
- (b) It is erythro isomer
- (c) It has three stereoisomers
- (d) It has no plane of symmetry

**16.** Which of the following compounds will show geometrical isomerism?
- (a) 2–butene
- (b) propene
- (c) 1–phenylpropene
- (d) 2–methyl–2–butene

**17.** Tautomerism is exhibited by

- (a) 
- (b) 
- (c) 
- (d) 

**18.**   ... and ... are ............. isomer :
- (a) position
- (b) optical
- (c) geometrical
- (d) diastereomer

**19.** Which can show tautomerism?
- (a) $CH_3CH_2NO_2$
- (b) 
- (c) 
- (d) HCN

**20.** In which case chiral carbon is generated?
- (a) $CH_3COCH_3 + HCN \xrightarrow{H_3O^+}$
- (b) $CH_3CHO + HCN \xrightarrow{H_3O^+}$
- (c) $CH_3COCOOH + HCN \xrightarrow{H_3O^+}$
- (d) $C_6H_5-CHO + HCN \xrightarrow{H_3O^+}$

**21.** The correct statements(s) concerning the structures E, F and G is (are) –

(E)    (F)    (G)

- (a) E, F, and G are resonance structures
- (b) E, F and E, G are tautomers
- (c) F and G are geometrical isomers
- (d) F and G are diastereomers

**22.** The correct statement(s) about the compound given below is (are)

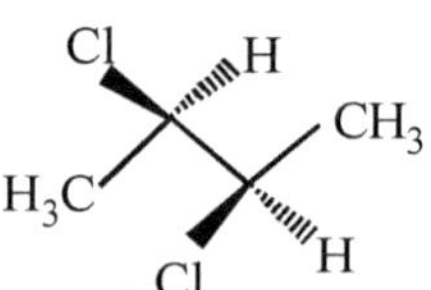

- (a) The compound is optically active
- (b) The compound possesses centre of symmetry
- (c) The compound possesses plane of symmetry
- (d) The compound possesses axis of symmetry

**INSTRUCTION for Q. 23 to 32 : Read the passages given below and answer the questions that follow.**

## PASSAGE 1

A compound with $n$ dissimilar chiral carbon atoms can have maximum of $2^n$ stereomers.

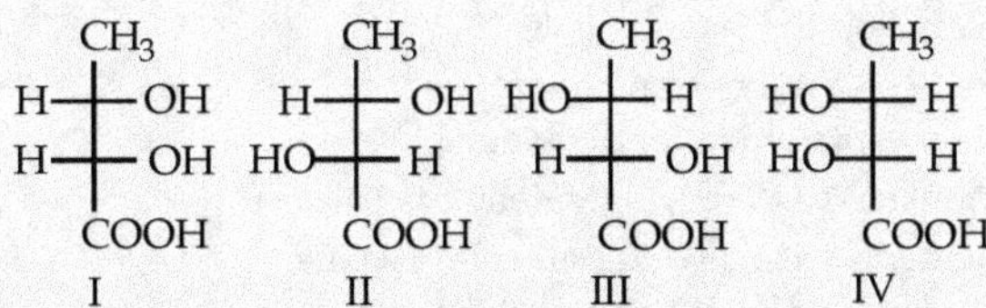

    I       II      III     IV

Since all of the above structures are devoid of plane of symmetry, they are chiral and hence optically active. Reversing of configuration at one of the stereogenic centres results in a diastereoisomer, while reversing of configuration at both stereogenic centres results in enantiomer. Diastereomers are stereoisomers that are not enantiomers. Since enantiomers are mirror image of each other they have identical physical and chemical properties; thus they have same b.p., solubilities and identical reactivity with achiral reagents.

**23.** Which of the following pairs are not diastereomers?
- (a) I and II
- (b) II and IV
- (c) I and IV
- (d) II and III

**24.** If COOH group is replaced by $CH_3$, which pair structure will be achiral?
- (a) I
- (b) IV
- (c) II
- (d) None

**25.** All of the above compounds are treated (separately) with an optically active base, which of them will react at different rates?
- (a) I and II
- (b) II and IV
- (c) I and IV
- (d) All the three

**26.** All of the above compounds are treated (separately) with an achiral acid, which of them will react at different rate?
- (a) I and II
- (b) II and IV
- (c) I and IV
- (d) All the three

## PASSAGE 2

Isomers are compounds that have the same chemical formula but different structures. There are two fundamental types of isomerism: constitutional isomerism and stereoisomerism. Constitutional isomers are compounds whose atoms are connected differently. Stereoisomers are compounds whose atoms are connected in the same order but with a different geometry. Sub-types of stereoisomers include enantiomers (mirror-image stereoisomers) and diastereomers (non-mirror-image stereoisomers). Further, diastereomers can be classified as either cis-trans diastereomers or configurational diastereomers

**27.** What kind of isomers are the two compounds below?

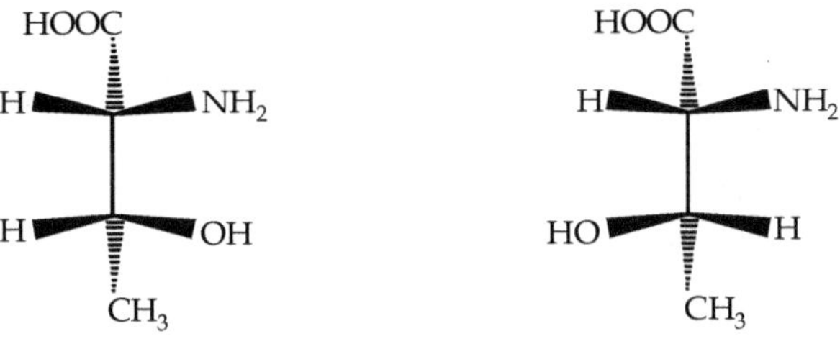

- (a) Configurational diastereomers
- (b) Enantiomers
- (c) Constitutional isomers
- (d) cis-trans diastereomers

**28.** What kind of isomers are the two compounds below?

- (a) Configurational diastereomers
- (b) Enantiomers
- (c) Constitutional isomers
- (d) They are exactly the same compound

**29.** What kind of isomers are the two compounds below?

- (a) Configurational diastereomers
- (b) Enantiomers
- (c) cis-trans diastereomers
- (d) They are exactly the same compound

## PASSAGE 3

Alkenes are characterized by C=C bonds. As such, they are subject to electrophilic addition reactions. Most electrophilic additions obey Markovnikov's rule; however, there are some exceptions. Examples of alkenes are shown below

**30.** When HBr adds to compound 2 above, the main product is

**31.** What is the order of reactivity of the compounds above to electrophilic addition of HBr?
- (a) $1 > 2 > 3 > 4$
- (b) $3 > 1 > 4 > 2$
- (c) $4 > 1 > 2 > 3$
- (d) $2 > 4 > 1 > 3$

**32.** What is the major product of the following reaction?

(a)   $H_3C$—$CH$($CH_3$)($CH_3$)—$CH$($CH_3$)($Br$)

(b)   $H_3C$—$CH$($CH_3$)($CH_3$)—$CH$($Br$)($CH_3$)

(c)   $H_3C$—$CH$($CH_3$)($CH_3$)—$CH_2$($CH_2Br$)

(d)   $(H_3C)(H_3C)C = CH(CH_3)$

---

**Instructions for Q. 33 to 35 : Following questions are Multiple Matching type Questions :**

**33.**

| Column I | Column II |
|---|---|
| (A) Dimethylcyclo-hexane | (a) Position isomerism |
| (B) | (b) Plane of symmetry |
| (C) | (c) Enantiomerism |
| (D) | (d) Geometrical isomerism |

**34.**

| Column I | Column II |
|---|---|
| (A) $CH_3NHC_2H_5$ | (a) Enantiomerism |
| (B) $CH_3CH(Cl)C_2H_5$ | (b) Resolvable |
| (C) $CH_3CH = C = CHCH_3$ | (c) Non-resolvable |
| (D) $\begin{array}{c} COOH \\ H\,C\,OH \\ H\,C\,OH \\ COOH \end{array}$ | (d) Enantiomerism not possible |

**35.**

| Column I | Column II |
|---|---|
| (A) Geometrical isomers | (a) Diastereomers |
| (B) Enantiomers | (b) Same properties |
| (C) Meso compounds | (c) Different properties |
| (D) Tautomers | (d) |

---

**Instructions for Q. 36 to 40 : Following questions are Assertion and Reasoning Type Questions :**

**Note : Each question contains STATEMENT-1 (Assertion) and STATEMENT-2 (Reason). Each question has 5 choices (A), (B), (C), (D) and (E) out of which ONLY ONE is correct.**

(a)   Statement-1 is True, Statement-2 is True; Statement-2 is a correct explanation for Statement-1.

(b)   Statement-1 is True, Statement-2 is True; Statement-2 is NOT a correct explanation for Statement-1.

(c)   Statement -1 is True, Statement-2 is False.

(d)   Statement -1 is False, Statement-2 is True.

(e)   Statement -1 is False, Statement-2 is False.

**36.**   **Statement I :** 3-Phenyl-butan-2-one racemises in presence of dilute acid or dilute base.

    **Statement II :** Its keto form is thermodynamically more stable form then the enol form.

**37.**   **Statement I :** Restricted rotation about a bond is the necessary condition for geometrical isomerism.

    **Statement II :** Two different orientations are possible due to restricted rotation about a bond if the end groups are different.

**38.**   **Statement I :** Compounds having only one chiral centre can have both enantiomer and diastereomer.

    **Statement II :** Diastereomer may or may not have chirality.

**39.**   **Statement I :** Cis-1, 3-dihydroxy cyclohexane exists in boat conformaton.

    **Statement II :** In the chair form, there will not be hydrogen bonding between the two hydroxyl groups.

**40.**   **Statement I :** Diastereoisomers have different physical properties.

    **Statement II :** They are non-superimposable mirror images.

---

**Instructions for Q. 41 to 46 : The following questions are True/False Type Questions :**

**41.**   Dichlorocyclopentane does not exhibit structural isomerism but only stereoisomerism.

**42.**   Maleic acid and fumaric acid are diastereomers.

**43.**

The above two structures are equally stable.

**44.**   Dimethylcyclohexanes do not have any plane of symmetry, hence show enantiomerism.

**45.**   $\begin{array}{c} CH_3 \\ H-OH \\ Cl-H \\ C_2H_5 \end{array}$ and $\begin{array}{c} CH_3 \\ HO-CH_3 \\ H-C_2H_5 \\ Cl \end{array}$ are identical.

**46.**   $CH_3\overset{..}{C}HCH_2CH_3$ and $CH_3\overset{..}{C}HCOCH_3$ are optically inactive.

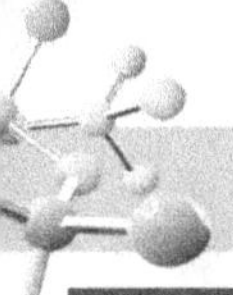

# EXERCISE 3.3 (Subjective Problems)

1. Draw structures of the various possible geometrical isomers of 2, 4-heptadiene.
2. An optically active dichloro derivative of propane (A), on further chlorination gives trichloro derivative. Suggest the structure of A, write down structures of the various possible trichloro derivatives and predict which isomer, if any, is optically active.
3. Assign R/S configuration to the chiral carbon atoms in the following compounds.

(*i*) 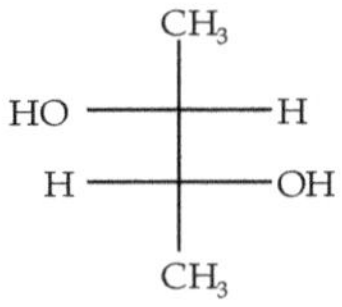
CH3
HO
H
H
OH
CH3

(*ii*) 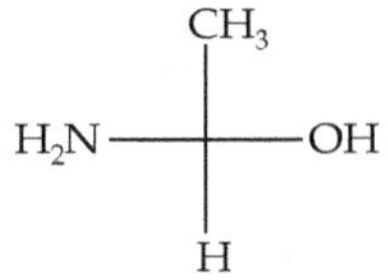
CH3
H2N
OH
H

(*iii*) 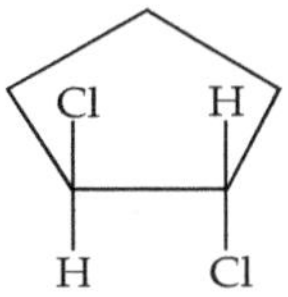
Cl
H
H
Cl

(*iv*) 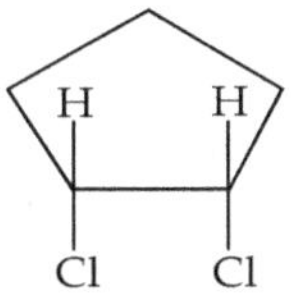
H
H
Cl
Cl

(*v*) 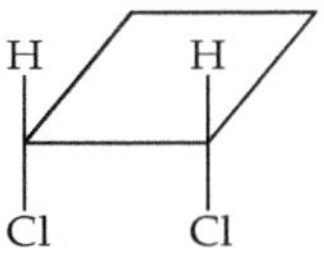
H
H
Cl
Cl

4. (*a*) Write down structures of stereoisomers of the following compounds.
   (*i*) 2, 3-Dihydroxybutane
   (*ii*) 3-Phenyl-2-propenoic acid.
   (*b*) Identify the pairs of enantiomers and diasteromers from the following compounds, I, II and III.

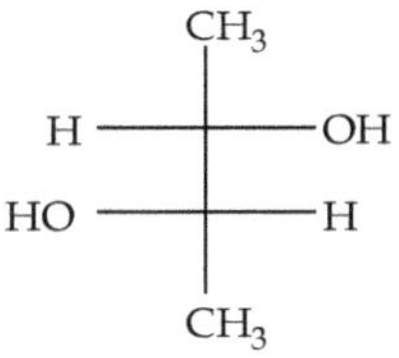
CH3
H
OH
HO
H
CH3
I

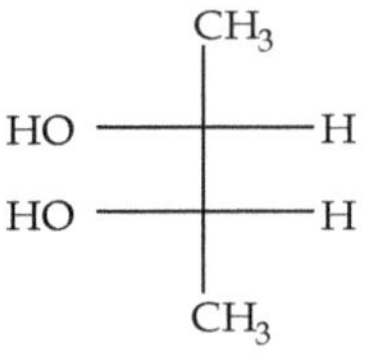
CH3
HO
H
HO
H
CH3
II

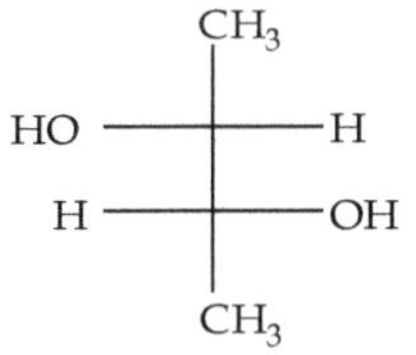
CH3
HO
H
H
OH
CH3
III

5. Acetophenone on reaction with hydroxylamine hydrochloride can produce two isomeric oximes. Write structures of the oximes.
6. Write down the name of the following compounds.

(*a*) 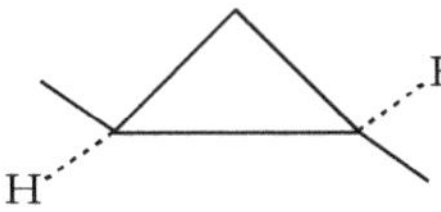
H
H

(*b*) 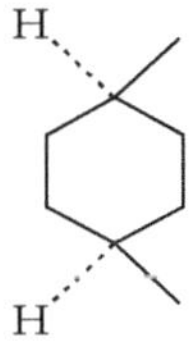
H
H

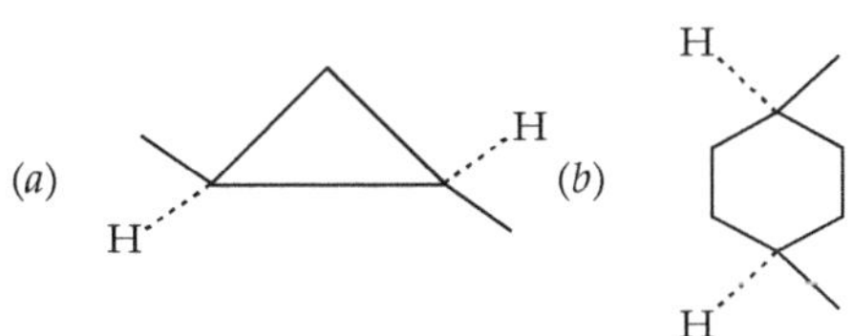

7. How many enantiomeric pairs are possible in the simplest possible alkene?
8. Give the stereochemical relationships between each pair of isomers.
   (*i*) $CH_3CN$ (*ii*) $CH_3CH = CH_2$
   (*iii*) $CH_3—C \equiv C — CH_3$ (*iv*) $HC \equiv C—CH = CH_2$.

(*a*) 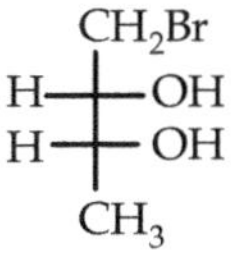 and 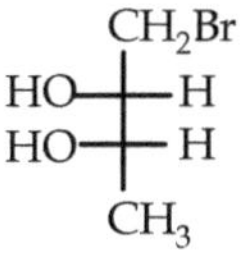
CH2Br
H
OH
H
OH
CH3

(*b*) 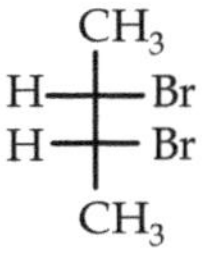 and 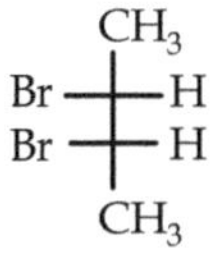
CH3
H
Br
H
Br
CH3

(*c*) 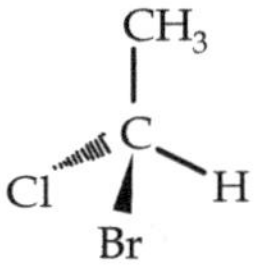 and 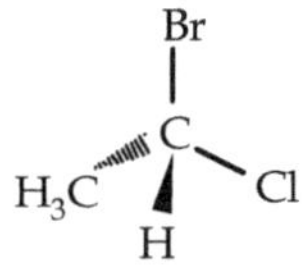
CH3
C
Cl
H
Br

(*d*) 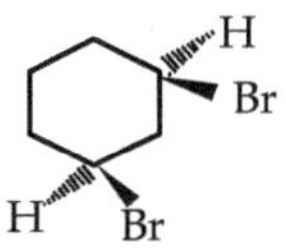 and 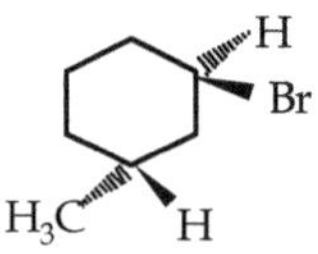
H
Br
H
Br

(*e*) 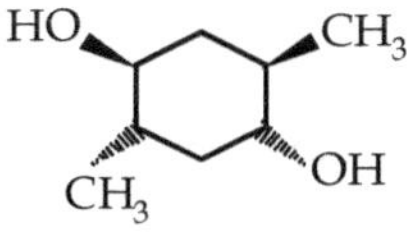 and 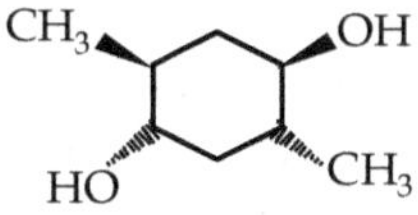
HO
CH3
OH
CH3

9. In each of the following structure, star (*) any asymmetric carbon atom. Draw any internal mirror planes of symmetry, if any.

(a) 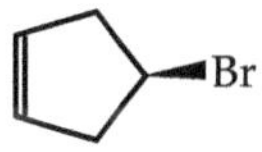
Br

(b) 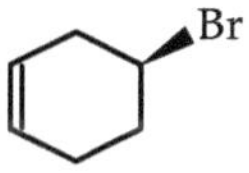
Br

(c) 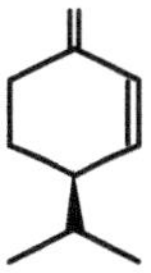

(d) 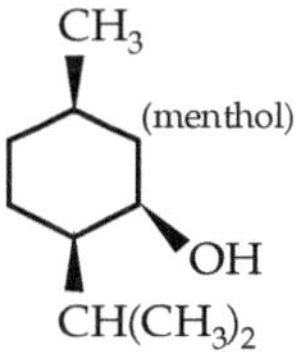
CH3
(menthol)
OH
CH(CH3)2

(e) 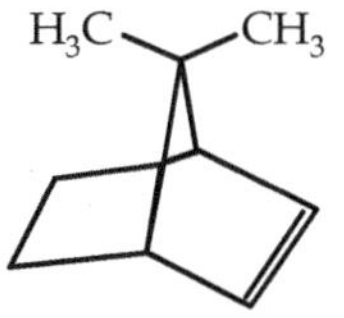
H3C
CH3

(f) 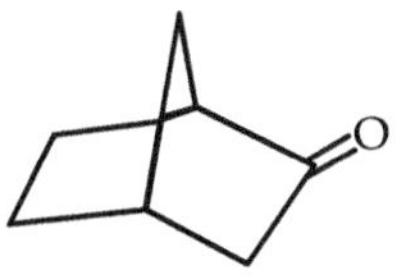
O

(g) 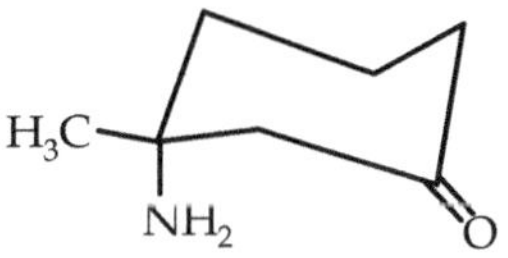
H3C
NH2
O

10. Draw the structure of each of the following compounds and its enantiomer. Also draw the structure of the diastereomer(s), where possible
    (a) (2*R*, 3*S*)-2,3-Dibromohexane
    (b) *meso*-3,4-Dibromohexane
    (c) (*R*)-1,1,2-Trimethylcyclohexene
    (d) (1*R*, 2*R*)-1,2-Dibromocyclohexane

**11.** (a) Draw all stereoisomers of 2,3,4-tribromopentane and give the relationship between them. Star (*) the asymmetric carbon atom(s) in each.

    (b) Give the stereogenic and chirality character of $C_3$ in the various isomers.

**12.** Draw all stereoisomers for the following structures.

(a)

(b)

**13.** Each of the two optically active alkenyl chlorides, A and B, of the same molecular formula, $C_5H_9Cl$ takes up one mole of hydrogen to form compound C (optically inactive) and D (optically active) respectively. Assign structures to the two alkenes.

**14.** How many stereoisomers are possible for 2,3,4,5-tetrahydroxyhexane-1,6-dioic acid? Give their $R$ / $S$ designations. How many of these are optically active and how many are optically inactive?

**15.** Does tri-*sec*-butylmethane show stereoisomerism?

**16.** How many *meso* diastereomers are possible for the compound with the formula $C_6H_{12}Cl_2$ ?

**17.** How many stereoisomers can be obtained by catalytic hydrogenation of both double bonds in the following compound

**18.** The following cyclohexanone was enzymatically reduced to form a cyclohexanol derivative.

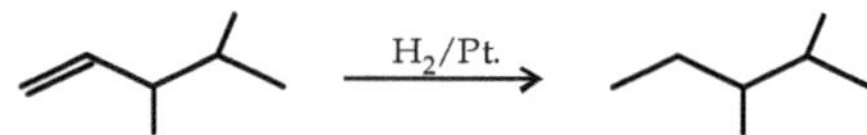

    (a) How many stereocenter(s) is(are) present in the product?

    (b) Does the product possess any asymmetric carbon atom?

    (c) What is the fate of the product regarding its optical activity?

**19.** Observe the following reaction and answer the questions given below :

    (a) Mark the star (*) on the chiral carbon(s).

    (b) Predict the $R,S$ designation of the two compounds.

    (c) On the basis of structure of the molecules, can we ascertain whether the molecules are *d-* or *l- rotatory?*

**20.** (a) An aqueous solution of pure stereoisomer A of concentration 0.10 g/mL had observed rotation –30° in a 10 dm tube at 589.6 mm (the sodium D line) and 25°C. How do you calculate its specific rotation at 25°C?

    (b) Under identical conditions but with concentration 0.050 g/mL, a solution of A had observed rotation +165°. Rationalize how this could be and recalculate the specific rotation for the stereoisomer *A*.

    (c) If the optical rotation of a substance studied at only concentration is 0°, can it definitely be concluded to be achiral or racemic?

**21.** An organic compound X ($C_3H_6O_2$) is found containing one –OH group, but no carbonyl group, can exist in two stereoisomeric forms. Assign structure to the two stereoisomers.

# SOLUTIONS



**1.** (a) There must be four atoms bonded sequentially only by *sigma bonds*, i.e. A-B-C-D.

CH$_3$Cl has only three atoms bonded sequentially, and CH$_2$ = CH$_2$ has a π bond in addition to a sigma bond between the two carbons. Thus only H$_2$O$_2$ and H$_2$NOH have conformations.

(b) (i)  *or*

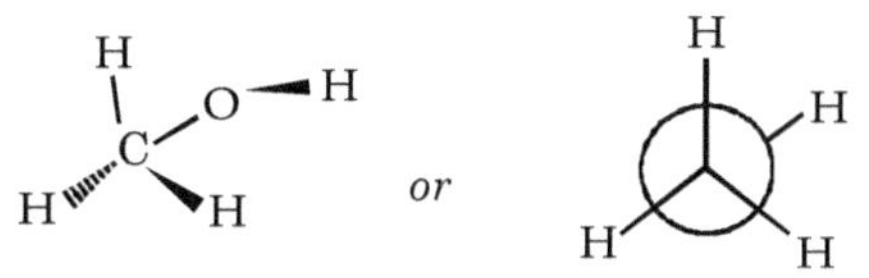

O is behind C, hence not visible

(ii)  *or*

**2.** 

**3.** (a) 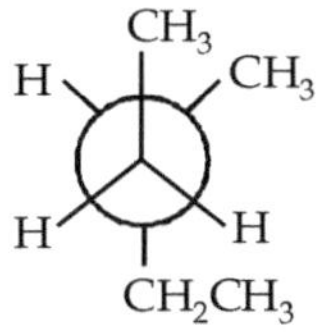 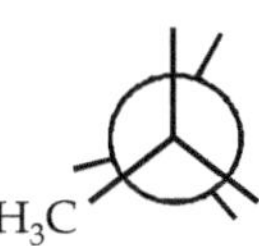 (b)

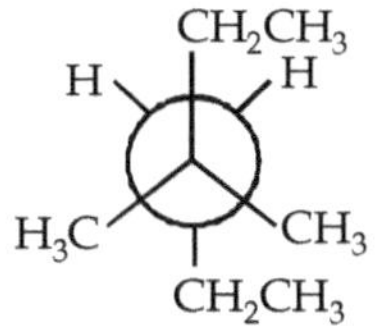

**1.** C$_1$ has $R$, while C$_2$ has $S$ configuration.

**2.** (a) (S)– (b) R

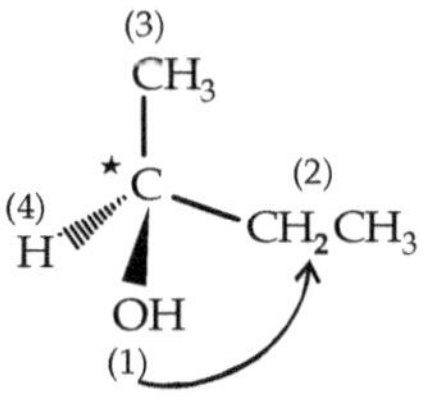

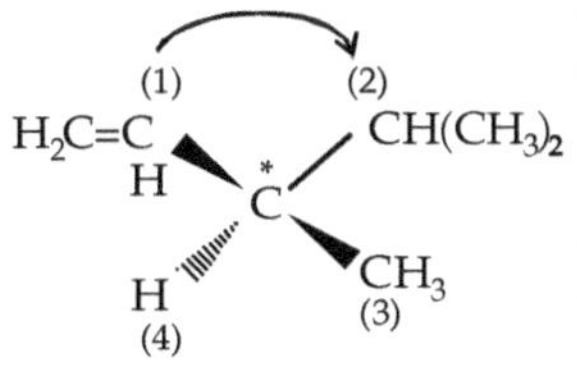

(c) 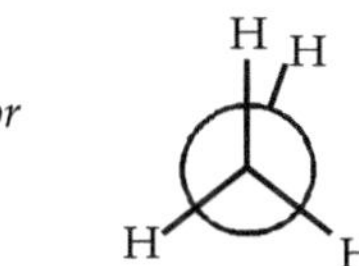 (S)-

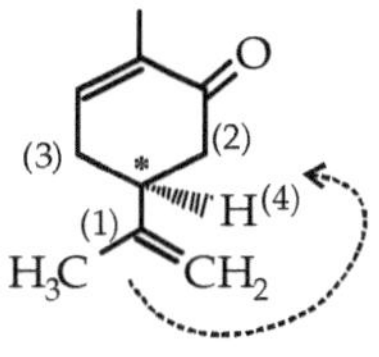

(d) 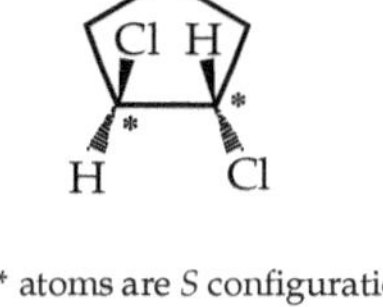

Both * atoms are $S$ configuration

(e) R (f) R

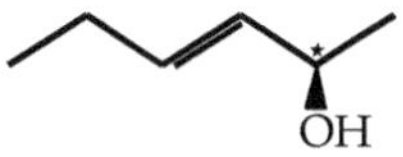

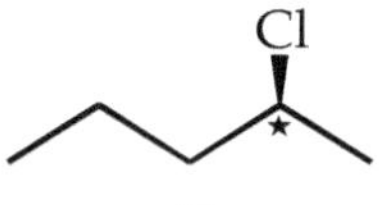

**3.** (a) The first structure has the $S$ and the second has the $R$ configuration, hence the two structures represent a pair of enantiomers.

(b) Enantiomers

(c) Enantiomers

(d) Enantiomers



**1.** (a) *cis*

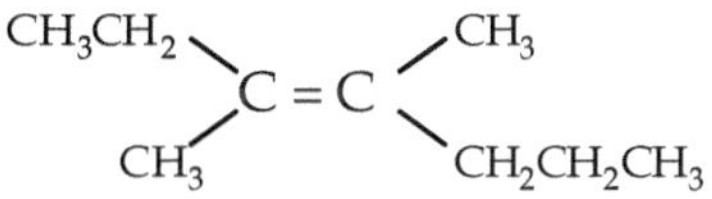

*trans*

(b) *cis*

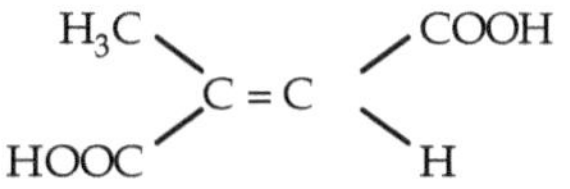

*trans*

**2.** (a) *cis* *trans*

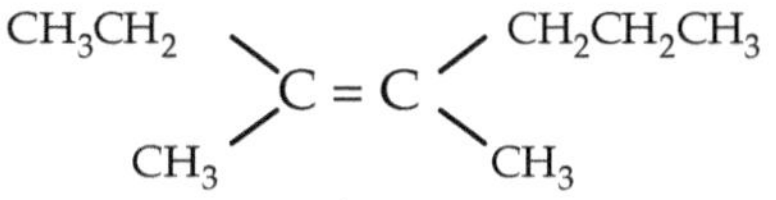

*or*

*cis* *trans*

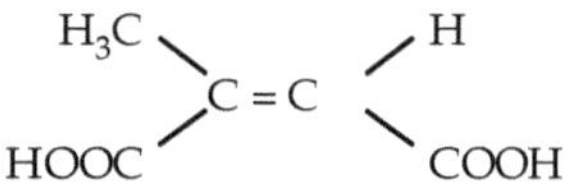

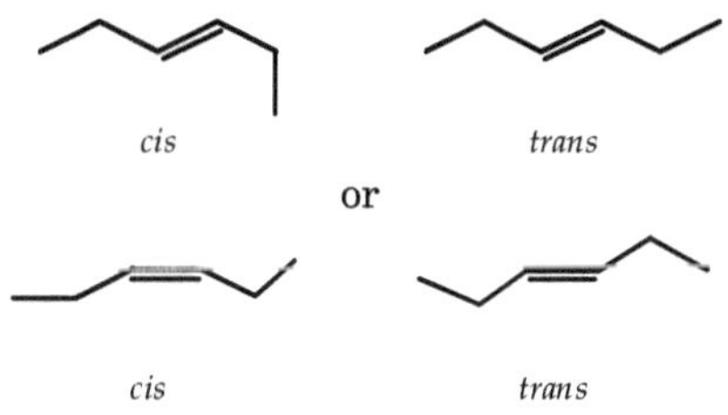

(b)

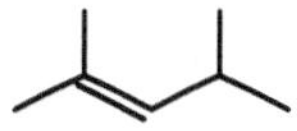

(c)

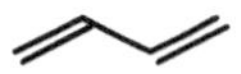

Geometric isomerism not possible in (b) and (c).

**(d)**

    *cis*        *trans*

**(e)**

Geometric isomerism not possible

**(f)**

    *cis*        *trans*

**3.**   **(a)**

    *cis*        *trans*

**(b)**

    *cis*        *trans*

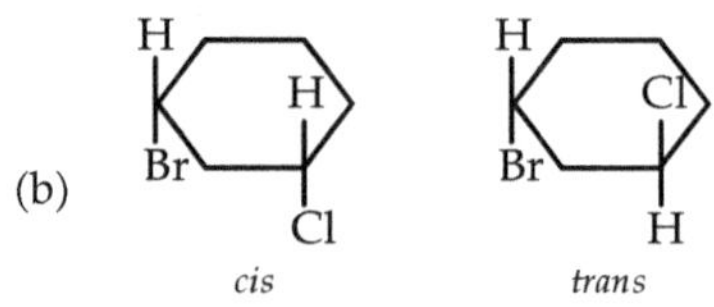



**1.**   **(a)**

$$CH_3CH_2CH_2CH_2-N \rightleftharpoons CH_3CH_2CH_2CH=N-OH$$

1° Nitroalkane

$$CH_3CHCH_2-N \rightleftharpoons CH_3CHCH=N-OH$$

1° Nitroalkane

$$CH_3CH-N \rightleftharpoons CH_3C=N-OH$$

2° Nitroalkane

$$CH_3-C-N$$

Tautomerism not possible because of absence of $\alpha-H$ atom

3° Nitroalkane

**(b)**

---

**2.**   2, 4-Hexadiene ($CH_3CH = CHCH = CHCH_3$) can exist in three geometrical isomeric forms.

   **(i)**   Take one of the double bonds at a time and draw structures of the possible geometrical isomers, by taking rest of structure as a substituent.

       *cis*          *trans*

   **(ii)**   Now draw structure(s) of the possible isomers by considering next double bond, in each of the above two isomers.

For *cis*

      *cis-cis*, I       *cis-trans*, II

For *trans*

      *trans-trans*, III       *trans-cis*, IV

   **(iii)**   In case, identical structures are obtained, take only one isomer. Thus here structure II and IV are same because both alkyl groups are similar, hence only one of them should be considered. Thus three geometrical isomers (I, II and III) are possible for 2, 4-hexadiene

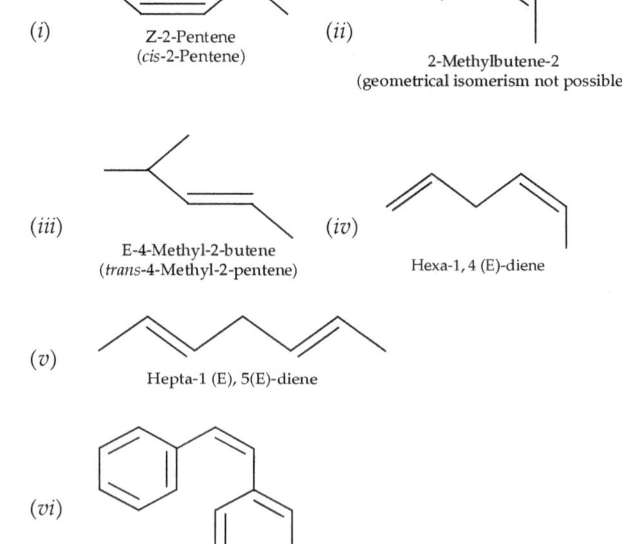



**3.**   **(i)**    **(ii)**

   **(iii)**    **(iv)**

   **(v)**

   **(vi)**

## TEST YOUR UNDERSTANDING - 3.5

1.  (a)   (*E*) - 1,2-Dichloroethene is a planar molecule. The molecular plane is a plane of symmetry. Further, the molecule also has a center of symmetry located at the center of the carbon-carbon double bond. It is an *achiral* molecule.

    (b)   (*Z*)-1,2-Dichloroethene is *achiral*. The plane of the molecule is a plane of symmetry. A second plane of symmetry is perpendicular to the plane of the molecule and bisects the carbon-carbon double bond.

    (c)   *cis*-1,2-Dichlorocyclopropane has a plane of symmetry that bisects the $C_1$-$C_2$ bond and passes through $C_3$. It is *achiral*.

    (d)   *trans*-1,2-Dichlorocyclopropane has neither a plane of symmetry nor a center of symmetry. It is a *chiral* molecule.

2.  (a) 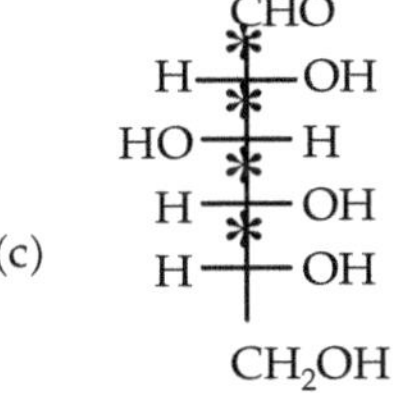

    meso structure
    (not optically active)

    (b)   HO—*—H ; Br—H
    $CH_2OH$ ... $CH_2OH$
    optically active

    (c)   (optically active)

    (d) 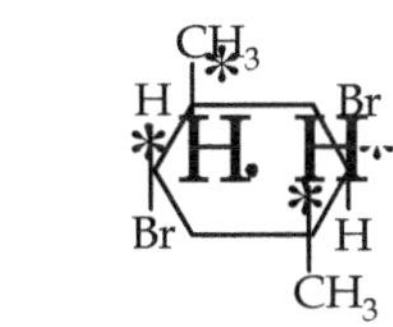

    center of symmetry present
    (not optically active)

    (e)   *meso*
    (not optically active)

    (f)   *meso*
    (not optically active)

## TEST YOUR UNDERSTANDING - 3.6

1.  Yes, when (*S*)-lactic acid is dextrorotatory, the (*R*)-isomer should be levorotatory. Similarly, when the (*S*)-sodium lactate is levorotatory the (*R*)-sodium lactate should be dextro.

2.  Dilute the solution to about one-fourth of its concentration and then measure the rotation which will give the value of either +45° or –45°.

## TEST YOUR UNDERSTANDING - 3.7

1.  (a)   Eight   (b)   $2^8 = 256$
2.  It has 5 chiral centers.
3.  Cholic acid has $2^{11} = 2048$ stereoisomers of which one is an enantiomer of cholic acid. Now since an object can have only one mirror image, so the number 2048 has (+)-cholic acid, (–)-cholic acid and 2046 other stereoisomers which are not enantiomers. Thus the number of diastereomers of cholic acid = 2046.

## TEST YOUR UNDERSTANDING - 3.8

1.  (a)   Identical              (b)   Enantiomers
    (c)   Diastereomers

2.  (a) 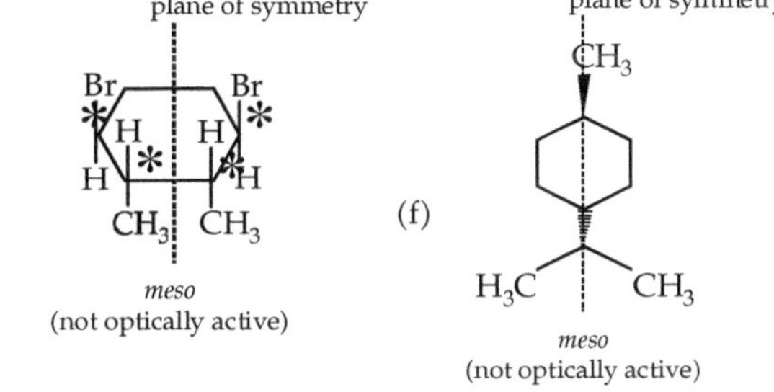

    (b)   (2*S*, 3*S*) is liquid, (2*S*, 3*R*) is solid.
3.  No. of isomers with three stereogenic centers = $2^3 = 8$.
    *RRR, RRS, RSR, SRR, SSS, SSR, SRS, RSS*

## TEST YOUR UNDERSTANDING - 3.9

1.  (a)   Configurations at both chiral carbons inverted – **enantiomers.**
    (b)   Configuration at only one chiral carbon inverted – **diastereomers.**
    (c)   Configuration at only one chiral carbon (the left one) inverted – **diastereomers.**
    (d)   The position of C=C bond shifted – **constitutional isomers.**
    (e)   Chiral, the two are mirror images – **enantiomers.**
    (f)   Configuration at only one chiral carbon (the top one) inverted – **diastereomers.**
    (g)   Configurations at all chiral carbon inverted – **enantiomers.**
    (h)   Superimposable mirror images – **same compound.**
    (i)   Configuration at only one chirality center (nitrogen) inverted - **diastereomers.**

2.  (a)   Total number of stereoisomers = $2^2 = 4$

    I and II; III and IV are **enantiomers.** I and III, I and IV, II and III, and II and IV are **diastereomers.**

    (b)   Compound has two identical chiral carbon, therefore number of stereoisomers will be **less than ($2^2$) 4.**

    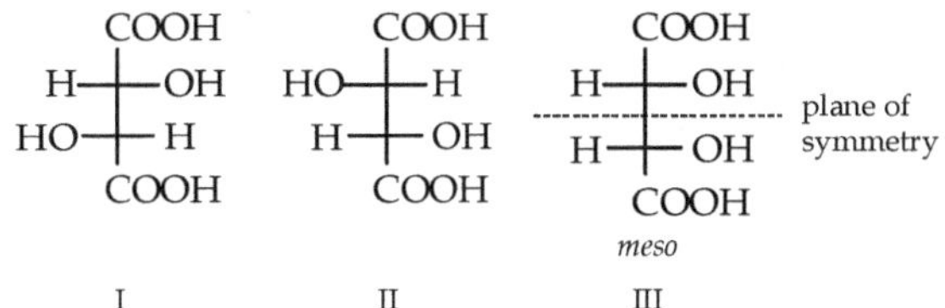

    I and II are **enantiomers,** I and III; II and III are **diastereomers.**

(c)  Here no chiral carbons are identical, therefore, number of stereoisomers = $2^3$ = 8.

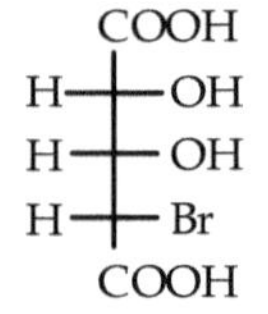

$$
\begin{array}{c}
\text{COOH} \\
\text{H——OH} \\
\text{H——OH} \\
\text{H——Br} \\
\text{COOH} \\
\text{I}
\end{array}
\qquad
\begin{array}{c}
\text{COOH} \\
\text{HO——H} \\
\text{HO——H} \\
\text{Br——H} \\
\text{COOH} \\
\text{II}
\end{array}
$$

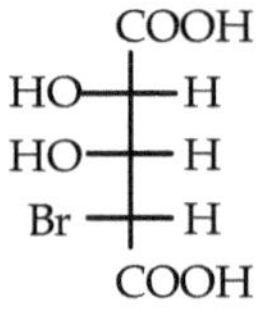

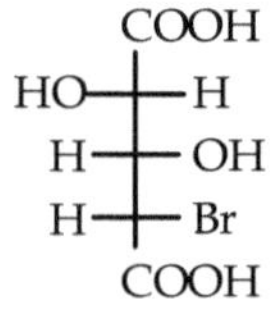

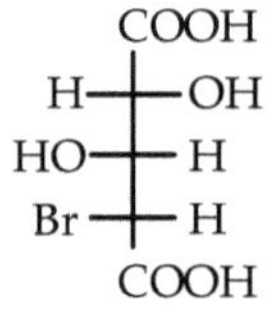

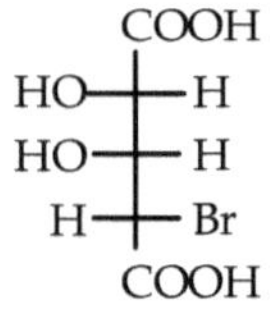

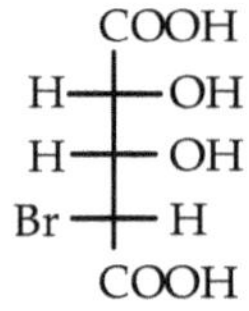

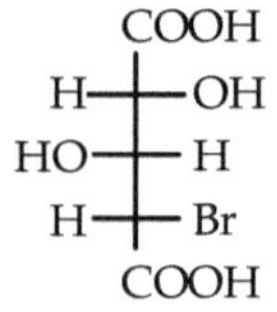

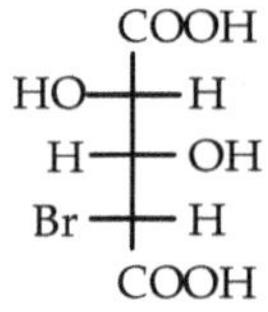

$$
\begin{array}{c}
\text{COOH} \\
\text{HO——H} \\
\text{H——OH} \\
\text{H——Br} \\
\text{COOH} \\
\text{III}
\end{array}
\qquad
\begin{array}{c}
\text{COOH} \\
\text{H——OH} \\
\text{HO——H} \\
\text{Br——H} \\
\text{COOH} \\
\text{IV}
\end{array}
$$

$$
\begin{array}{c}
\text{COOH} \\
\text{HO——H} \\
\text{HO——H} \\
\text{H——Br} \\
\text{COOH} \\
\text{V}
\end{array}
\qquad
\begin{array}{c}
\text{COOH} \\
\text{H——OH} \\
\text{H——OH} \\
\text{Br——H} \\
\text{COOH} \\
\text{VI}
\end{array}
$$

$$
\begin{array}{c}
\text{COOH} \\
\text{H——OH} \\
\text{HO——H} \\
\text{H——Br} \\
\text{COOH} \\
\text{VII}
\end{array}
\qquad
\begin{array}{c}
\text{COOH} \\
\text{HO——H} \\
\text{H——OH} \\
\text{Br——H} \\
\text{COOH} \\
\text{VIII}
\end{array}
$$

**Enantiomers :**  I and II; III and IV; V and VI; VII and VIII.

**Diastereomers :**  Any pair which is not enantiomeric, e.g. I and III, I and IV, I and V, I and VI,

I and VII, I and VIII, II and III, and so on.....

(d)

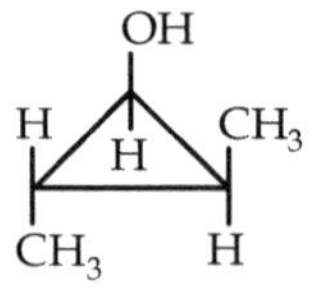

I

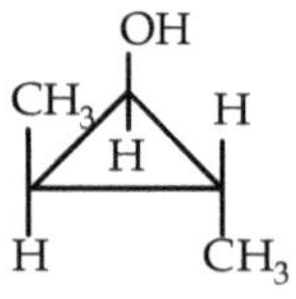

II

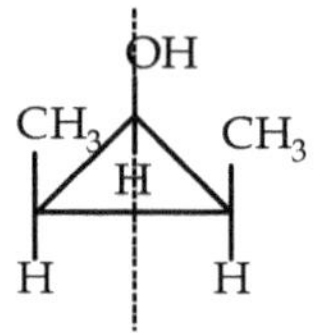

*plane of symmetry*     *plane of symmetry*

*meso* (III)         *meso* (IV)

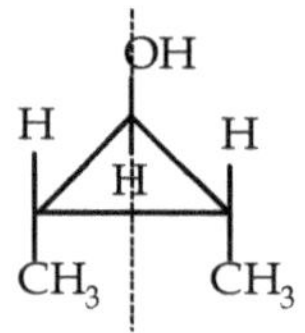

**Enantiomers :**  I and II
**Diastereomers :**  I and III, I and IV, II and III, II and IV, III and IV.

3.  (i)  Compounds *a*, *e* and *g* do not have any chiral center, so they will not show enantiomerism, hence no question of *meso* form.

(ii)  Compounds *c* and *h*, each have two different chiral centers, so they will not have *meso* stereoisomer.

(iii)  Compounds *b*, *d* and *f*, each will have *meso* stereoisomer because each contains two identical chiral carbons; and hence possess a plane of symmetry.

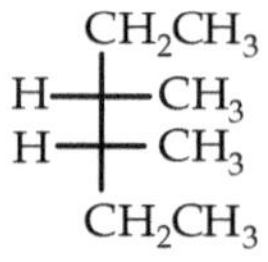

$$
\begin{array}{c}
\text{CH}_2\text{CH}_3 \\
\text{H——CH}_3 \\
\text{H——CH}_3 \\
\text{CH}_2\text{CH}_3
\end{array}
$$

(b) 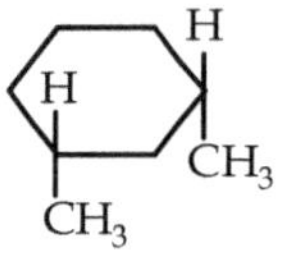          (d) 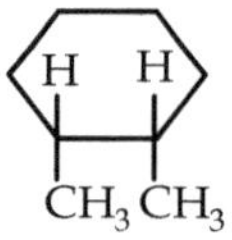          (f)



1.  (a)

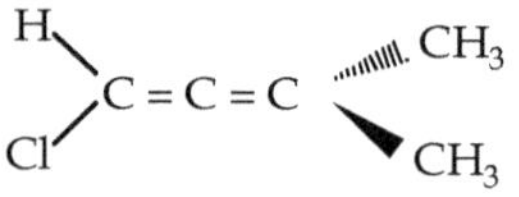

no asymmetric carbon, but the allene has a plane of symmetry between the two methyls. Hence the molecule is not chiral

(b)

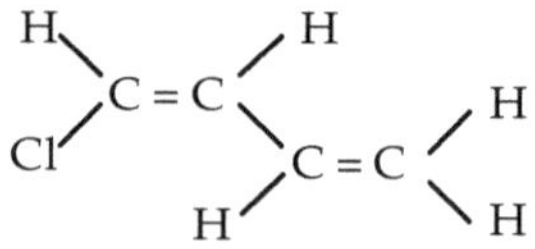

planar molecule, no asymmetric carbon, not a chiral molecule

(c)

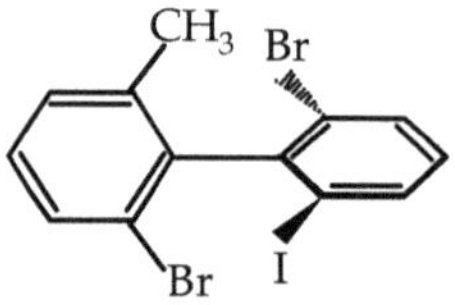

no asymmetric carbon, but the molecule is chiral due to restricted rotation

(d)

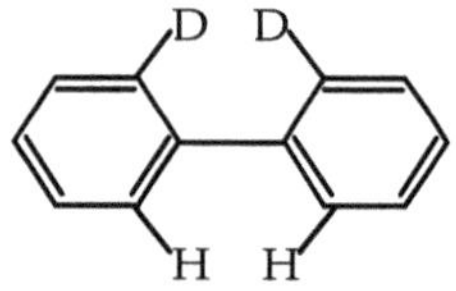

No asymmetric carbon, and the substituents at *ortho* positions are not large enough to restrict rotation, hence the molecule is not chiral

2.  (a)

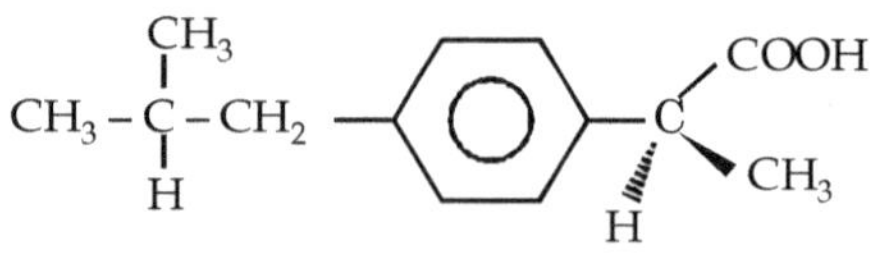

$$
\text{CH}_3 - \underset{\underset{\text{H}}{|}}{\overset{\overset{\text{CH}_3}{|}}{\text{C}}} - \text{CH}_2 -
$$

(*S*)–Ibuprofen

(b)

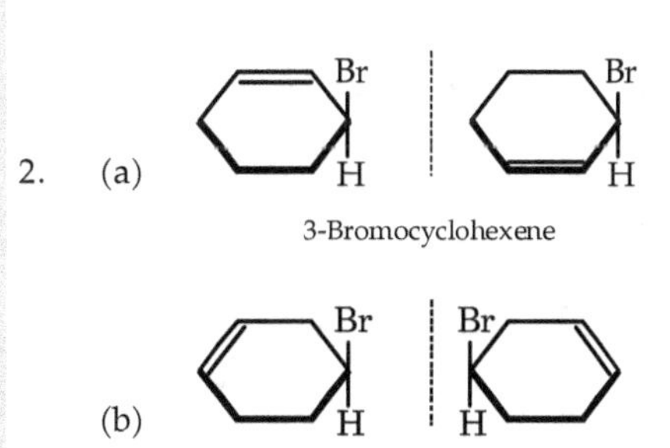

(S)–Methyldopa

(c)

(S)–Penicillamine

## TEST YOUR UNDERSTANDING - 3.11

1.  $\text{o.p.} = \dfrac{75 - 25}{100} = 0.5$

    ∴ Observed rotation of the mixture = Rotation of pure enantiomer × o. p. = $-158 \times 0.5 = -79°$.

2.  $\text{o.p.} = \dfrac{+1.4}{+8.7} = 0.16 \text{ or } 16\%$

    Optical purity of 16% means that the mixture has 16% (R) and 84% (RS)–; i.e. $16 + 42 = 58\%$ of R and 42% of S enantiomer.

3.  $\text{o.p.} = \text{e.e.} = \dfrac{(6-4)}{(6+4)} = 0.2 \text{ or } 20\%$

    Enantiomeric excess of 20% indicates that the (+)–enantiomer is 20% excess; in other words the composition of the mixture is 20% (+)–enantiomer + 80% (±)-mixture **or** 20% (+)-enantiomer + 40% (+)–enantiomer + 40% (–)–enantiomer
    Observed rotation = rotation of pure * enantiomer × o.p. = $+13.5° \times 0.2 = +2.7°$.
    *Since the mixture has excess amount of (+)–enantiomer, rotation of (+)–pure enantiomer should be taken which is +13.5°.

4.  The given solution has
    (i)    10 mL × 0.10 M = 1 mmol. of the R enantiomer,  and
    (ii)   30 mL × 0.10 M = 3 mmol. of the S enantiomer.
    Thus the solution has total of 4 mmoles of which $1 + 1 = 2$ mmol. are present as racemic mixture and 2 mmol. as pure S enantiomer.

    ∴ $\text{o.p.} = \dfrac{\text{excess of one enantiomer over the other}}{\text{entire mixture}} = \dfrac{2}{4} = 0.5$

    We know that

    $\text{o.p.} = \dfrac{\text{observed specific rotation}}{\text{specific rotation of the pure enantiomer}}$

    $0.50 = \dfrac{+4.8°}{x}; \quad x = +9.6°$

    It is important to note that here the S enantiomer is in excess, hence +9.6° is the specific rotation of the S enantiomer and –9.6° will be the specific rotation of the R enantiomer.

5.  The specific rotation of (–)–2-butanol = $-13.5°$

    $\text{o.p.} = \dfrac{-0.45°}{-13.5°} = 0.33 \text{ or } 3.3\%$

    Thus the product has 3.3% excess of one of the enantiomers of 2-butanol which is (–)–enantiomer because the product has (–)–specific rotation. Thus the product has 3.3% (–)–enantiomer + 96.7% (±)-mixture or 3.3% + 48.4% (–)–enantiomer + 48.3% (+)–enantiomer   or   51.7%(–)–enantiomer + 48.3% (+) enantiomer.

## TEST YOUR UNDERSTANDING - 3.12

1.  (a)   Two (a diastereomeric pair)
    (b)   Three
    (c)   Two chirality centers are identical due to same R,R-tartaric acid component, and one chirality center due to 2-butanol component is different.

2.  Any diastereomeric pair could be separated by a physical process like distillation or crystallization. Diastereomers are found in parts (a), (b) and (d). Since the two structures in (c) are enantiomers, they could not be separated by normal physical means.

3.

(R)-2-Butyl (R, R)-tartrate  |  (S)-2-Butyl (S, S)-tartrate

(S)-2-Butyl (R, R)-tartrate  |  (R)-2-Butyl (S, S)-tartrate

## TEST YOUR UNDERSTANDING - 3.13

1.  The compound has a carbon-carbon double bond whose each $sp^2$ hybridised carbon is differently substituted, so it will show geometrical isomerism. Further, it also has one chiral carbon, each of the geometric isomer (cis and trans) can exist in (R) and (S) form. So on the whole, there will be 4 stereomeric isomers.

cis - R
cis - S

trans - R
trans - S

2.  (a)

3-Bromocyclohexene

(b)

4-Bromocyclohexene

**TEST YOUR UNDERSTANDING - 3.14**

**1.**

$$CH_3 \overset{C_2H_5}{\underset{CH=CH_2}{|}} H \ + \ D_2 \ \xrightarrow{Pd} \ CH_3 \overset{C_2H_5}{\underset{CH_2D}{|}} H \ + \ CH_3 \overset{C_2H_5}{\underset{CH_2D}{|}} H$$

$R$       (2R, 3R)–    (2R, 3S)–
1,2-Dideutero-3-methylpentane

---

# EXERCISE 3.1

| 1 | (b) | 6 | (d) | 11 | (d) | 16 | (c) | 21 | (b) | 26 | (d) | 31 | (b) | 36 | (d) | 41 | (d) | 46 | (d) | 51 | (a) | 56 | (b) | 61 | (c) |
|---|---|---|---|---|---|---|---|---|---|---|---|---|---|---|---|---|---|---|---|---|---|---|---|---|---|
| 2 | (b) | 7 | (c) | 12 | (d) | 17 | (c) | 22 | (d) | 27 | (c) | 32 | (d) | 37 | (b) | 42 | (c) | 47 | (c) | 52 | (a) | 57 | (d) | 62 | (a) |
| 3 | (a) | 8 | (d) | 13 | (b) | 18 | (d) | 23 | (d) | 28 | (a) | 33 | (d) | 38 | (c) | 43 | (b) | 48 | (d) | 53 | (d) | 58 | (c) | 63 | (b) |
| 4 | (b) | 9 | (c) | 14 | (b) | 19 | (c) | 24 | (a) | 29 | (a) | 34 | (d) | 39 | (a) | 44 | (c) | 49 | (a) | 54 | (a) | 59 | (b) | 64 | (d) |
| 5 | (d) | 10 | (b) | 15 | (c) | 20 | (c) | 25 | (d) | 30 | (d) | 35 | (c) | 40 | (c) | 45 | (a) | 50 | (a) | 55 | (c) | 60 | (b) | | |

**1.** When switching (interchanging) of two ligands attached to an atom result in a new stereoisomer, the atom is called *stereocenter*. If the new stereocenter is an enantiomer, the stereocenter is a chiral center, otherwise not. Thus all stereocenters are not chiral but the reverse is true, i.e. all chiral centers are stereocenters.

**2.** Note the definitions from the above question. Maleic acid has a stereocenter, but not optically active, $CH_3CH(OH)COOH$ has a stereocenter and is optically active.

**3.** A tetrahedral atom bearing four different substituents is known as stereogenic center. In (b) the tetrahedral carbon bears two identical substituents.

**4.** The carbon of a carbocation and a free radical ($C^+$, $C^{\bullet}$) is $sp^2$ hybridized leading to a flat geometry. Thus such carbon has a plane of symmetry and is achiral, no matter it may have three different groups. On the other hand, carbon of carbanion is $sp^3$ hybridised and thus theoretically it can exist as a pair of enantiomers provided the three ligands attached to carbon are different. However, in practice a rapid "umbrella" type inversion converts either enantiomer to a racemic mixture.

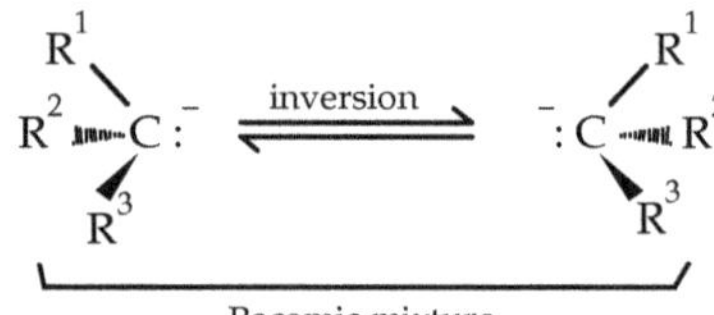

Racemic mixture

The energy required for this inversion is very low in carbon, thus leading to rapid inversion.

**5.** The energy required for inversion about S and P (third period elements) is sufficiently high so the properly substituted sulphur and phosphorus compounds can be resolved.

$$\left[ R^1 - \overset{+}{\underset{\underset{R^3}{|}}{S}} - R^2 \right] X^- \qquad R^1 - \overset{\overset{O}{||}}{\underset{}{S}} - R^2 \qquad R^1 - \overset{}{\underset{\underset{R^3}{|}}{P}} - R^2$$

A sulphonium salt     A sulphoxide     A phosphine

**6.** (a) $CH_3CH_2 \overset{*}{\underset{\underset{CH_3}{|}}{C}}HCH=CH_2$ (b) $CH_3CH_2 \overset{*}{\underset{\underset{CH_3}{|}}{C}}HC\equiv CH$

(c) $CH_3CH_2 \overset{*}{\underset{\underset{CH_3}{|}}{C}}H \ \underset{\underset{CH_3}{|}}{C}HCH_3$

**7.** $[\alpha]_D = \dfrac{[\alpha]_{obs.}}{\ell c}$, where $c$ is concentration in g/mL and $\ell$ is length of the tube in dm (decimeters).

$\therefore [\alpha]_D = +1.2°/(1)(0.075) = +16°$

**8.** $[\alpha]_{obs.} = [\alpha]_D \times \ell c = -16° \times 0.50 \times 0.35 = -2.8°$

**9.** Observed rotation depends on the concentration of the solution and the length of the tube containing the solution. Specific rotation is a constant and is independent of concentration and path length.

**10.** $\alpha_{obs.} = 0.80(-12°) = -9.6°$

**11.** The fact that the carvone enantiomers smell differently is due to the fact that the receptor sites in the nose are chiral, and only the correct enantiomer will fit its particular site ( just as a hand requires a glove of the correct chirality for a proper fit).

**12.** Structure (d) is the non superimposable mirror image of the given structure of (+)-carvone.

**13.** Nonsuperimposability of mirror image is the sole criteria for enantiomerism.

**14.** A rapid umbrella type inversion rapidly converts the structure III to its enantiomer; hence the two enantiomers are not separable.

**15.** Reaction (a) is enzyme catalysed so it will form only one enantiomer of malic acid, reaction (b), again involves a chiral reagent, so the product will give two diasteromers, reaction (c) is an example where achiral reactant is converted into chiral product without the use of any chiral reagent, so the resultant product will be a racemic mixture.

**16.** I and IV, both are symmetric molecules.

**17.** Racemic mixture to be resolved is (R,S)-1-phenylethylamine, while the resolving agent that remains common in the two diastereomers formed is (–)-malic acid.

The resolving agent (–)– malic acid is found to be (S)- as shown by the name of one of the diastereomer, so the other diastereomer will be (S)-1-phenylethylammonium (S)-malate.

18. III is *meso* so it is certain that it is optically inactive. Although I and II are enantiomers, it is not certain which one is (+)-stereoisomer and which one is (–)–. It can be determined only by polarimeter.

19. Structure A is converted into B by switching two groups.

20.

$$C-\underset{\underset{C}{|}}{\overset{\overset{C}{|}}{C}}- \qquad C-\underset{\underset{C}{|}}{\overset{\overset{H}{|}}{C}}-$$

tert–alkyl                    *sec*–alkyl

$$C-\underset{\underset{H}{|}}{\overset{\overset{H}{|}}{C}}- \qquad H-\underset{\underset{H}{|}}{\overset{\overset{H}{|}}{C}}-$$

primary alkyl

21. Each carbon of phenyl group is doubly bonded, hence it is counted to have three C's. In $(CH_3)_3C-$ group the $C_1$ has three C's while all other carbons are having only one C and three H.

22. The priority order of the four groups is different in two cases
(A) OH, $CH_2CH_3$, $CH_3$, H
(B)  OH, CHO, $CH_2OH$, H

23. Each of the three structures can be obtained from the parent compound (*S*)-2-butanol by two switches, hence all the three are (*S*)-2-butanol.

24. Sign of rotation is a molecular property unrelated to configuration.

25. For *meso* structure the 2*R*, 3*S* is identical with the 2*S*, 3*R*, it is not necessary to indicate the number and thus *R*, *S* or *S*, *R* designation is also correct.

26. The stereoisomers (a) and (c), i.e. those where $n = 1$ or an odd number, have a plane of symmetry cutting through the central carbon. The stereoisomer where $n = 2$ or an even number has the symmetry plane cutting through the central C–C bond.

27. $CH_3CH_2CH_2CH_2Cl$, $CH_3CH_2CHClCH_3$ (enantiomers)

28. Sign of rotation and R/S designation of different compounds have no relation. Here the reactant and product belong to the same designation because there is no change in the priority order of the four substituents.

29. Optically active 2-iodobutane reacts with $I^-$ with inversion at chiral carbon, leading to racemization.

$$(+)-CH_3CHICH_2CH_3 + I^- \rightleftharpoons (-)-CH_3CHICH_2CH_3$$

30. An enantiomer can be converted into diastereomer by inverting two groups on the asymmetric carbon atom.

$$\begin{array}{ccc} CH_2CH_3 & CH_2CH_3 & CH_2CH_3 \\ H-\!\!\!-OH & HO-\!\!\!-H & HO-\!\!\!-H \\ HO-\!\!\!-H & H-\!\!\!-OH & HO-\!\!\!-H \\ CH_2CH_3 & CH_2CH_3 & CH_2CH_3 \\ I & II & \text{III (From I or II)} \end{array}$$

Enantiomers                    Diastereomer

31. $CH_3CH = C(Cl)CH_2CH_3$. Here all the four groups around doubly bonded carbon are different, so *cis-trans* nomenclature is not possible.

32. Vinylcyclopentane

33. All show geometric isomerism

34. Since *trans*-2-butene is non-polar, it does not have dipole-dipole attraction.

35. Hydrocarbon with minimum carbon, and capable of showing *cis, trans* as well as optical isomerism should have following structure.

$$CH_3CH = CH\,CH\underset{\underset{CH_3}{|}}{}C_2H_5$$

36. Stereoisomers which are not enantiomers are known as diastereomers. The former is E–(*trans*)– isomer while the latter is Z–(*cis*-) isomer.

37. First of all write down all possible isomers of monochloroisopentane ; observe the chiral carbon atom(s) in all isomers

$$CH_3-\underset{\underset{CH_3}{|}}{CH}-CH_2CH_3 \longrightarrow ClCH_2\underset{\underset{CH_3}{|}}{\overset{*}{CH}}-CH_2CH_3 \; ;$$

Isopentane
I

$$CH_3-\underset{\underset{CH_3}{|}}{\overset{\overset{Cl}{|}}{C}}-CH_2CH_3 \; ; \qquad CH_3-\underset{\underset{CH_3}{|}}{CH}-\underset{\underset{Cl}{|}}{\overset{*}{C}}HCH_3 \; ;$$

II                    III

$$CH_3-\underset{\underset{CH_3}{|}}{CH}-CH_2CH_2Cl$$

IV

Thus only structures I and III can exhibit optical isomerism. Further each is having 1 chiral carbon atom, so 2 stereoisomers (*d* and *l*) are possible for each compound.

38. Structure I is changed to II by three (even number) interchange of groups, thus they should be enantiomers.

$$\begin{array}{c} CHO \\ H-\!\!\!-OH \\ CH_2OH \\ I \end{array} \xrightarrow[\text{interchange}]{\text{one}} \begin{array}{c} OH \\ H-\!\!\!-CHO \\ CH_2OH \end{array} \xrightarrow[\text{interchange}]{\text{2nd}}$$

$$\begin{array}{c} OH \\ H-\!\!\!-CH_2OH \\ CHO \end{array} \xrightarrow[\text{interchange}]{\text{3rd}} \begin{array}{c} OH \\ OHC-\!\!\!-CH_2OH \\ H \\ II \end{array}$$

On the other hand, structure III is derived from I by two interchanges, thus they should be identical.

$$\begin{array}{c} CHO \\ H-\!\!\!-OH \\ CH_2OH \\ I \end{array} \longrightarrow \begin{array}{c} OH \\ H-\!\!\!-CHO \\ CH_2OH \end{array} \longrightarrow \begin{array}{c} OH \\ HOH_2C-\!\!\!-CHO \\ H \\ III \end{array}$$

**39.** Rate of reaction between a chiral molecule and an achiral reagent is same with both of the enantiomers, while it is different with a chiral reagent in the two enantiomers. Every molecule containing chiral carbon atom is not chiral, *e.g.* mesotartaric acid has two chiral carbon atoms yet the molecule is achiral. A chiral molecule does not necessarily have chiral atom, *e.g.* properly disubstituted allenes have no chiral atom, yet they show enantiomerism.

**40.** A compound having two similar chiral atoms can form *meso* form. The first three compounds have two similar chiral atoms, while in (*iv*) the chiral atoms are different.

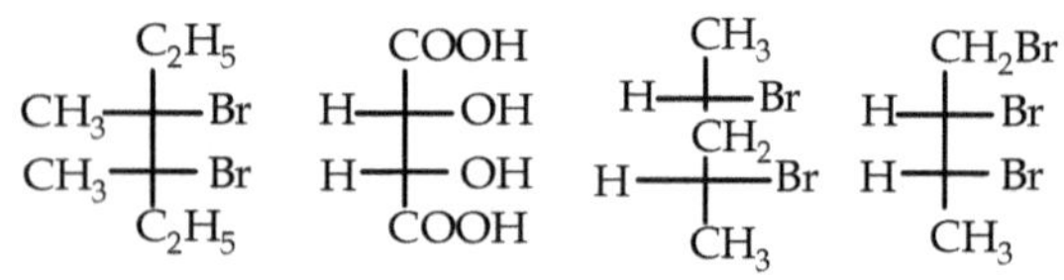

(i)        (ii)        (iii)        (iv)

**41.** $2(S) - 3(R) -$        $2(R) - 3(S) -$

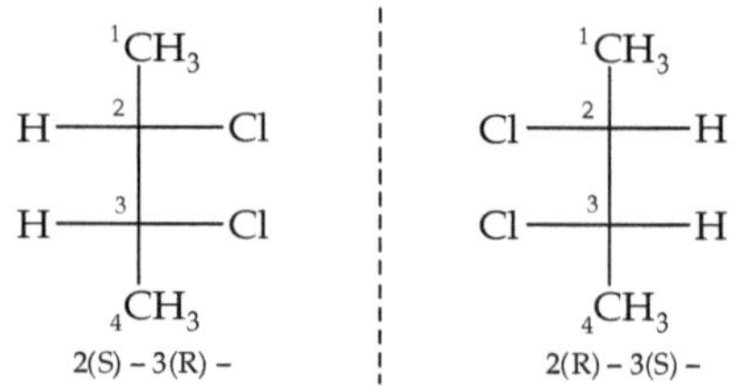

**42.**

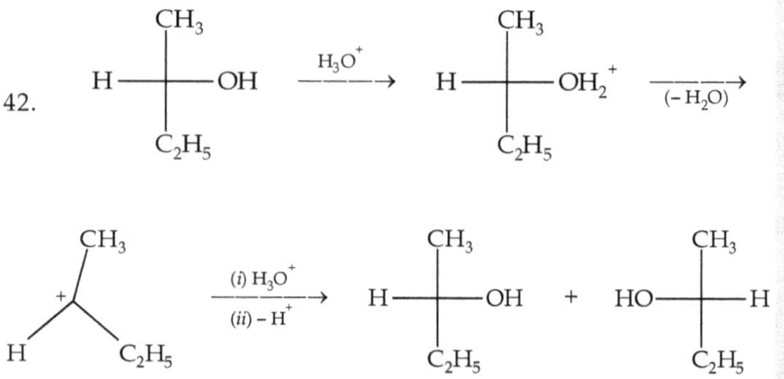

Racemic modification (optically inactive)

**43.** Configuration of the product changes (from that of reactant) only when the bond attached to the chiral atom is broken during the reaction. Since, here configuration of the reactant is S, the product should also have S configuration, no matter the sign of rotation is different.

**44.** Only reaction *c* does not involve breaking of bonds to the chiral C, other reactions involve breaking of bonds to the chiral C.

**45.** Draw structure and observe each of the doubly bonded carbon atom. Geometrical isomerism is not possible in compounds *b*, *c* and *d* due to carbon atom represented by bold letter.

$C_6H_5CH_2CH = CHCH_3$

1-Phenyl-2-butene (*a*)

$CH_2 = CH. CH.CH_3$ with $C_6H_5$ substituent

3-Phenyl-1-butene (*b*)

$CH_2 = CCH_2CH_3$ with $C_6H_5$ substituent

2-Phenyl-1-butene (*c*)

$(C_6H_5)_2C = CHCH_3$

1, 1-Diphenyl-1-propenen (*d*)

**46.**

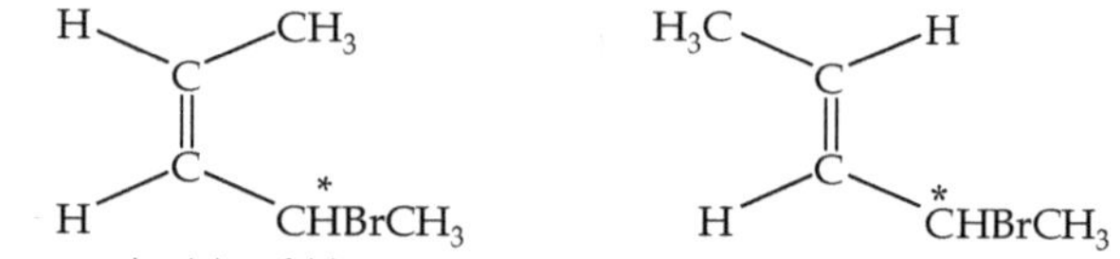

*cis-* ; (+)- and (−)-

*trans-* ; (+)- and (−)-

(+) − and (−) − isomers in each is possible because of presence of chiral carbon atom, marked by asterisk.

**47.** D − (+) − Glyceraldehyde is taken as arbitrary standard for D, L-nomenclature of configuration.

**48.** $SbCl_5$, being a Lewis acid, will take up chlorine as chloride ion forming a carbocation as an intermediate, which, being planar, can be attacked on either side of the plane forming equal amount of the two enantiomers.

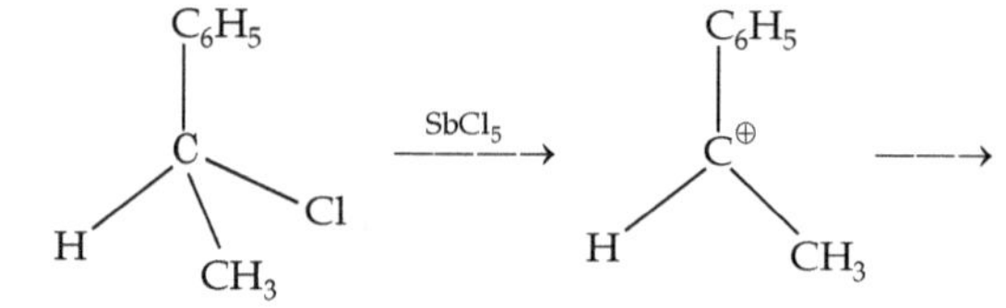

(+)-2-Phenyl-2-chloroethane     $\xrightarrow{SbCl_5}$     Carbocation (planar)    $\longrightarrow$

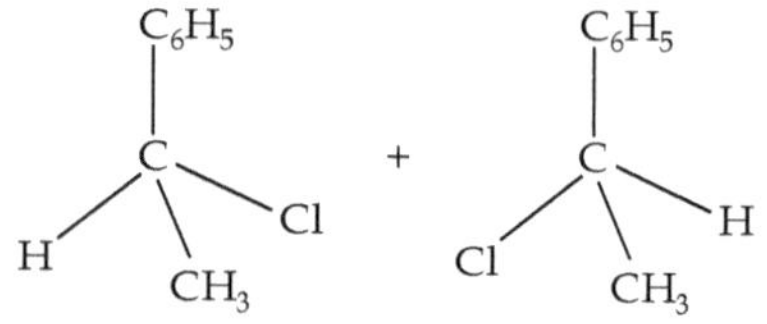

Racemic mixture

**49.**

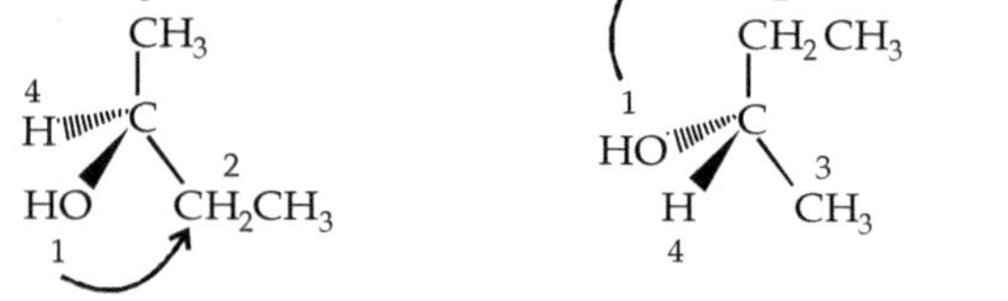

Here the lowest priority group (H) is away from the observer, hence usual R/S nomenclature is applicable. Thus it is *S*.

Here the lowest priority group is towards the observer, hence the usually assigned (R) configuration is reversed to *S*.

Thus the two structures are *S, S*, hence identical.

Regiomers are those structural isomers which differ in the position of the functional group.

# EXERCISE 3.2

| | | | | | | | | | | |
|---|---|---|---|---|---|---|---|---|---|---|
| >1 ONE CORRECT OPTION | **1** | (a,c) | **2** | (b,d) | **3** | (b,c,d) | **4** | (a,c) | **5** | (b,c,d,e) |
| | **6** | (a,b,c,d) | **7** | (a,d) | **8** | (a,b) | **9** | (a,b,d) | **10** | (a,b,d) |
| | **11** | (b,c,d) | **12** | (a,b,c) | **13** | (a,b) | **14** | (a,d) | **15** | (a,b) |
| | **16** | (a, c) | **17** | (a, c, d) | **18** | (b, c) | **19** | (a, b, c, d) | **20** | (b, c, d) |
| | **21** | (b, c, d) | **22** | (a, d) | | | | | | |
| PASSAGE 1 | **23** | (c,d) | **24** | (c) | **25** | (d) | **26** | (a,b) | | |
| PASSAGE 2 | **27** | (b) | **28** | (a) | **29** | (c) | | | | |
| PASSAGE 3 | **30** | (a) | **31** | (c) | **32** | (b) | | | | |
| MATCHING TYPE QUESTION | **33** | (A) - a, b, c, d; (B) - b, d; (C) - c, d; (D) - c, d | | | | | | | | |
| | **34** | (A) - a, c ; (B) - a, b ; (C) - a, b (D) - d, c | | | | | | | | |
| | **35** | (A) - a, c ; (B) - b ; (C) - d, c (D) - c | | | | | | | | |
| A/R | **36** | (b) | **37** | (a) | **38** | (d) | **39** | (d) | **40** | (c) |
| True / False | **41** | FALSE | **42** | TRUE | **43** | FALSE | **44** | FALSE | **45** | TRUE |
| | **46** | FALSE | | | | | | | | |

**1.** Convert these Newmann projections into open chain structures.

$$A \equiv CH_3 - \underset{\underset{H}{|}}{\overset{\overset{H}{|}}{C}} - \overset{*}{\underset{\underset{CH_3}{|}}{\overset{\overset{H}{|}}{C}}} - Cl \quad ; \quad B \equiv CH_3 - \underset{\underset{H}{|}}{\overset{\overset{H}{|}}{C}} - \underset{\underset{H}{|}}{\overset{\overset{H}{|}}{C}} - CH_2Cl$$

optically active ; optically inactive

**2.**

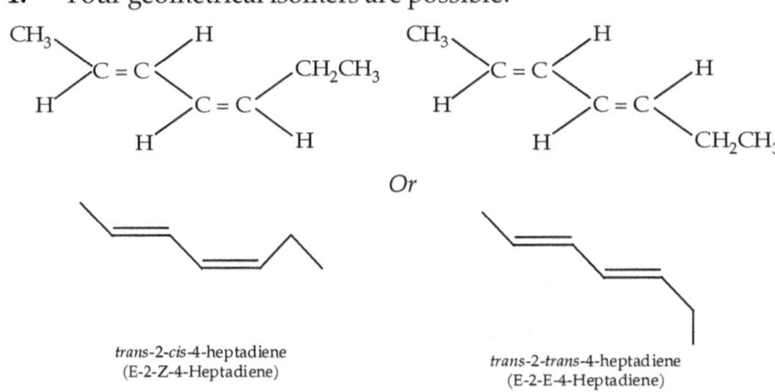

2S, 3S

2S, 3R

**3.** Rotation of A through 180° within the plane of the paper gives A′. Now since A = A′, hence A is an enantiomer of B.

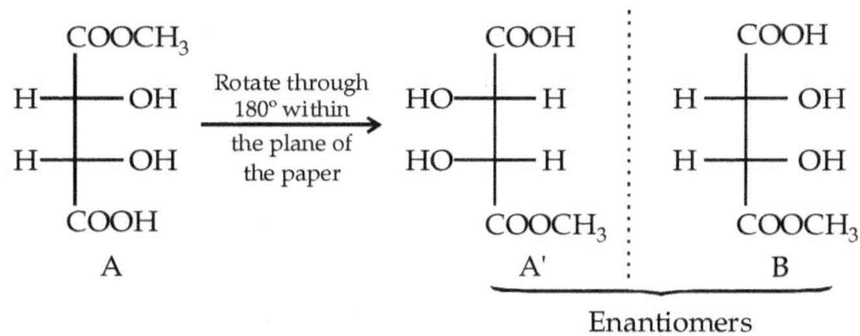

A

A'

B

Enantiomers

Further C is diastereomer of A and B.

# EXERCISE 3.3

**1.** Four geometrical isomers are possible.

*trans*-2-*cis*-4-heptadiene
(E-2-Z-4-Heptadiene)

*Or*

*trans*-2-*trans*-4-heptadiene
(E-2-E-4-Heptadiene)

*cis*-2-*cis*-4-Heptadiene
(Z-2-Z-4-Heptadiene)

*Or*

*cis*-2-*trans*-4-Heptadiene
(Z-2-E-4-Heptadiene)

**2.**

$$CH_3CH_2CH_3 \xrightarrow{Cl_2} CH_2Cl\,\overset{*}{C}HClCH_3 \xrightarrow{Cl_2}$$

Optically active (A)

$$CH_2ClCHClCH_2Cl + CHCl_2\overset{*}{C}HClCH_3 + CH_2ClCCl_2CH_3$$
Optically inactive    Optically active    Optically inactive

**3.** *(i)*

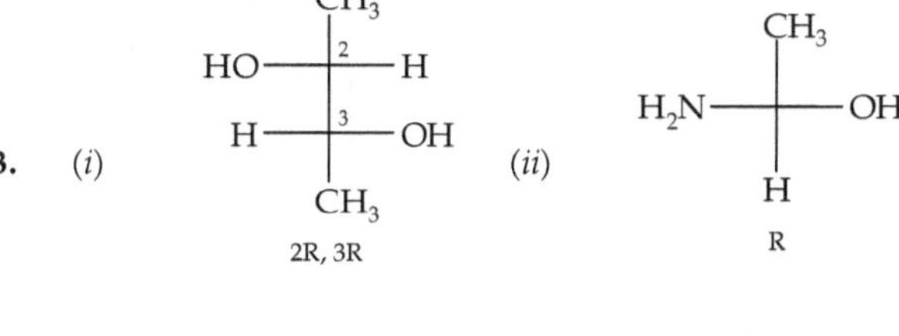

2R, 3R

*(ii)*

$$H_2N - \underset{\underset{H}{|}}{\overset{\overset{CH_3}{|}}{C}} - OH$$

R

*(iii)*

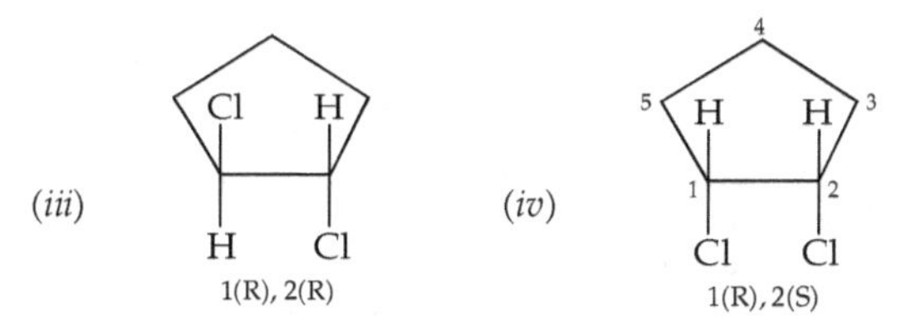

1(R), 2(R)

*(iv)*

1(R), 2(S)

(v) 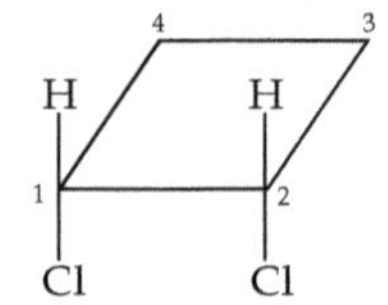 [structure: cyclohexane-type ring with H at position 4, H at position 3, Cl at position 1, Cl at position 2] **1R, 2S**

**4.** (a) (i) $CH_3.CH.CH.CH_3$ (with OH OH on carbons). Like tartaric acid, it can exist in three stereoisomeric forms (*d-, l-* and *m-*).

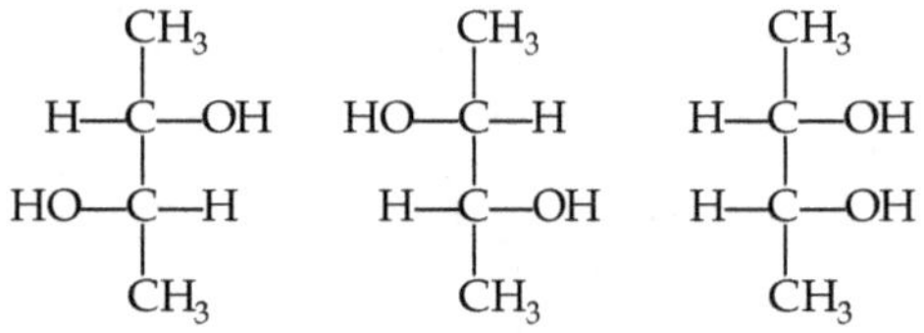

[Three Fischer projections:
I: CH₃ / H—C—OH / HO—C—H / CH₃
II: CH₃ / HO—C—H / H—C—OH / CH₃
III: CH₃ / H—C—OH / H—C—OH / CH₃]

(ii) $C_6H_5.CH = CH.COOH$. It can exist in two stereoisomeric forms (*cis-* and *trans*)

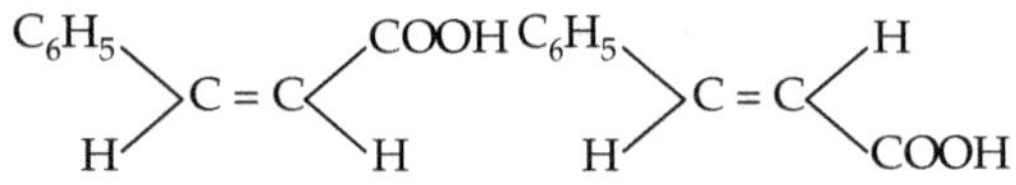

[Two structures: C₆H₅ and H on one carbon, COOH and H across double bond — *cis* and *trans*]

*cis*          *trans*

(b) I and III are enantiomers; while I and II; and II and III are diastereomeric pairs.

**5.** 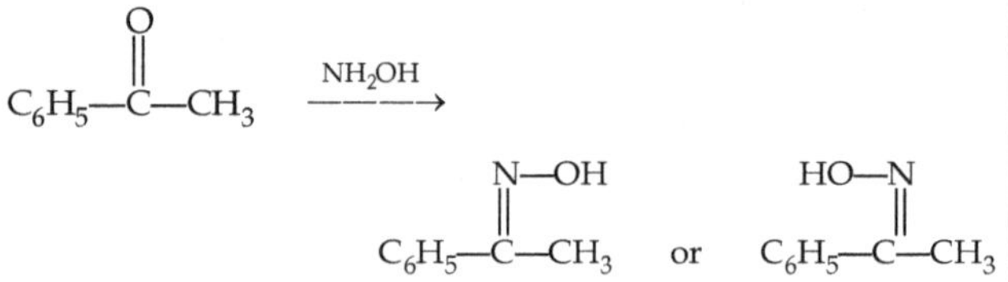 $C_6H_5-\overset{O}{\underset{\|}{C}}-CH_3 \xrightarrow{NH_2OH}$

[Products:] $C_6H_5-\overset{N-OH}{\underset{\|}{C}}-CH_3$   or   $C_6H_5-\overset{HO-N}{\underset{\|}{C}}-CH_3$

*syn-* and *anti-*Ketoximes

**6.** (a) *trans*-1, 2-Dimethylcyclopropane.
    (b) *cis*-1, 2-Dimethylcyclohexane.

**7.** The simplest possible optically active alkane has H, $CH_3$, $C_2H_5$ and $C_3H_7$ as ligands.

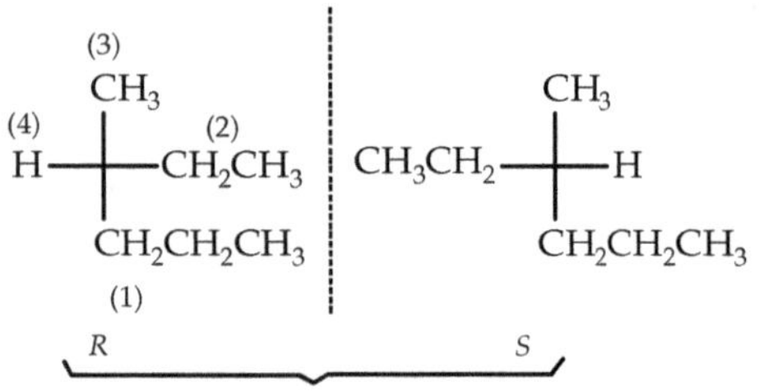

[Two Fischer projections labeled R and S]
3-Methylhexane

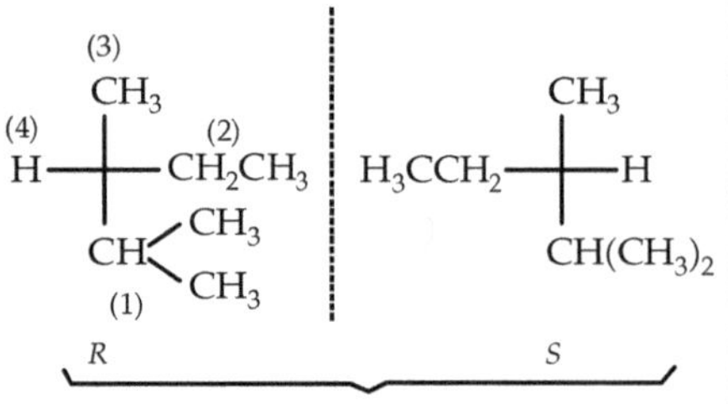

[Two Fischer projections labeled R and S]
2,3-Dimethylpentane

**8.** (a) Enantiomers     (b) Same
    (c) Enantiomers (three exchanges)
    (d) Diastereomers
    (e) Same (one can be converted to other when rotated through 180°).

**9.** (a) 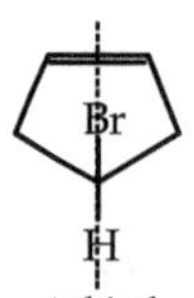 [structure] Achiral (plane of symmetry)
    (b) 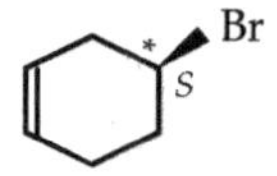 [structure with Br, S] Chiral
    (c) 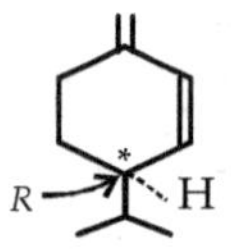 [structure] Chiral
    (d) 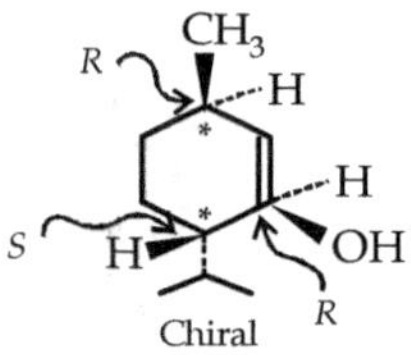 [structure] Chiral
    (e) 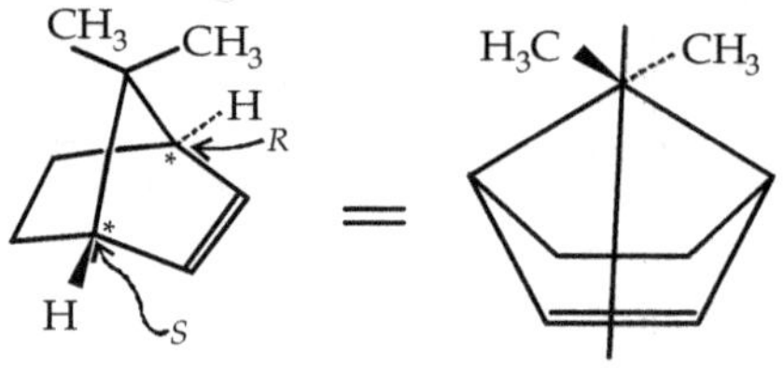 [bicyclic structures] Plane of symmetry meso, achiral
    (f) 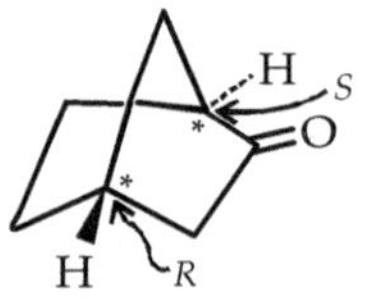 [structure] Chiral
    (g) 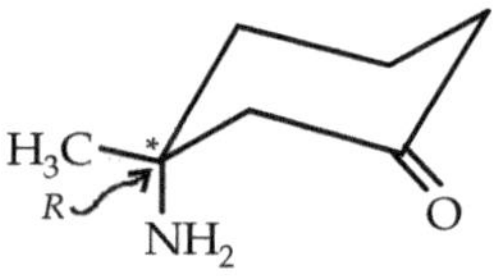 [structure with NH₂] Chiral

**10.** (a) 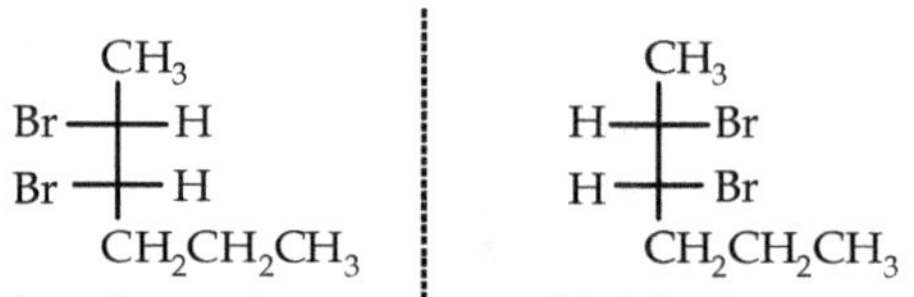 [Two Fischer projections:
Left: CH₃ / Br—H / Br—H / CH₂CH₂CH₃ — no plane of symmetry
Right: CH₃ / H—Br / H—Br / CH₂CH₂CH₃ — chiral structure]
Enantiomers

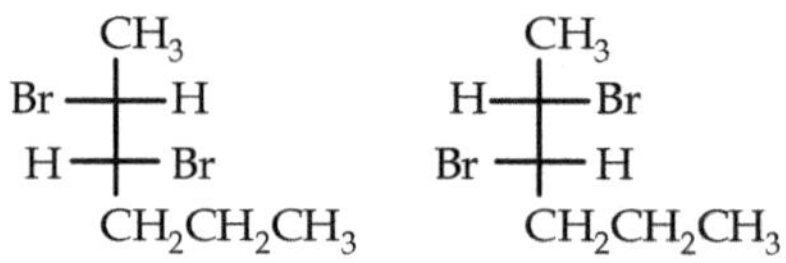

[Two Fischer projections:
Left: CH₃ / Br—H / H—Br / CH₂CH₂CH₃
Right: CH₃ / H—Br / Br—H / CH₂CH₂CH₃]
chiral structure (diastereomers)

(b) 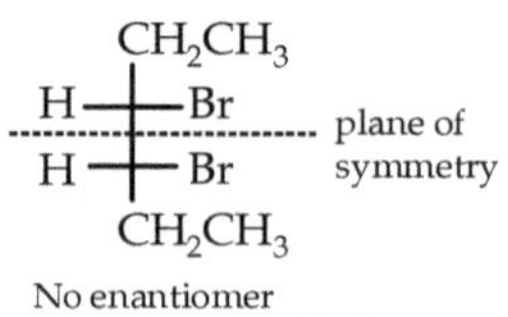 [Fischer projection: CH₂CH₃ / H—Br / H—Br / CH₂CH₃ — plane of symmetry]
No enantiomer a meso structure, not chiral

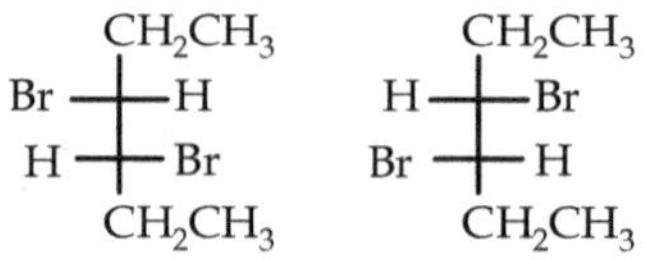

[Two Fischer projections:
Left: CH₂CH₃ / Br—H / H—Br / CH₂CH₃
Right: CH₂CH₃ / H—Br / Br—H / CH₂CH₃]
chiral structure Diastereomers

(c) 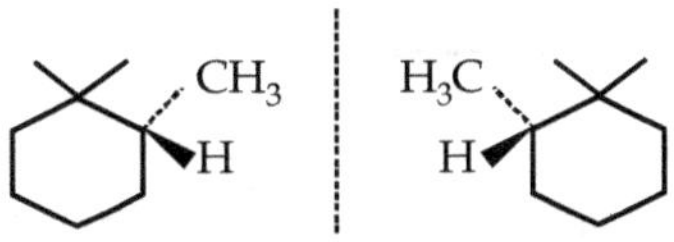 Enantiomers
Chiral structure, no plane of symmetry
no diastereomer

(d) 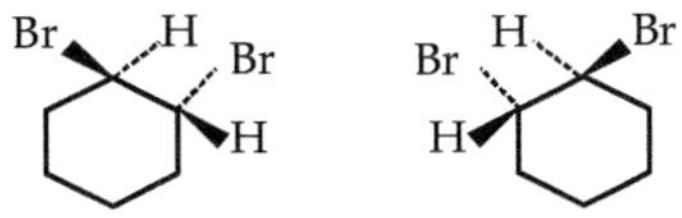 No plane of symmetry
Chiral structure

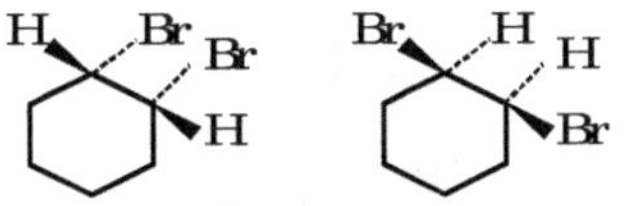

Chiral structure
Diastereomers

11. (a)

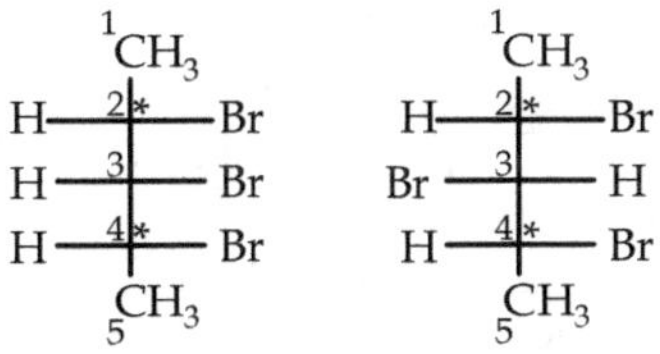

A (2S, 4R)    B (2S, 4R)

*meso*, diastereomers

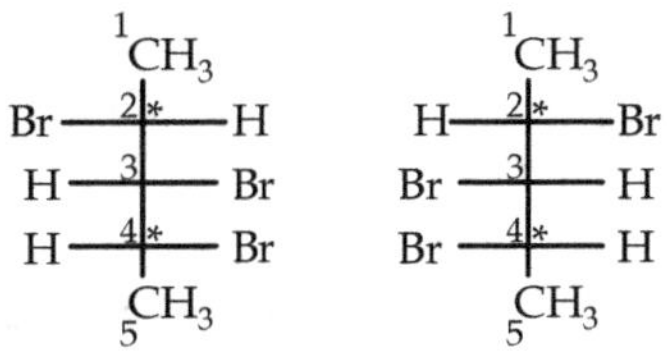

C (2R, 4R)    D (2S, 4S)

enantiomers

(b) In structures A and B, **C–3** is not chiral because it has two identical groups. However, it **is stereogenic** because interchanging the H and Br at C–3 in A gives the different meso (diastereomer) structure B.

In structures C and D, C–3 is not stereogenic because when H and Br at C–3 are interchanged and the structure is rotated through 180°, C is converted into D. Hence, **C–3 is not stereogenic**.

12. (a)

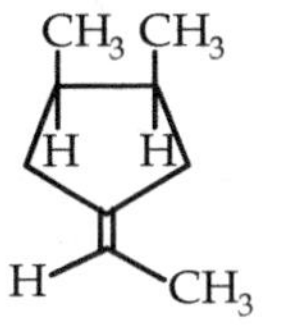

I 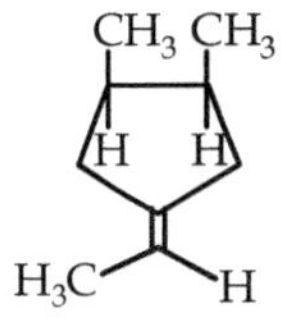    II

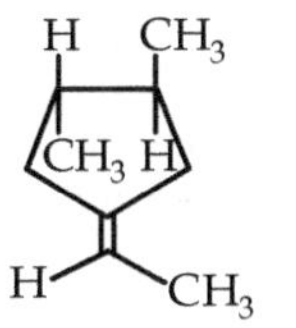

III 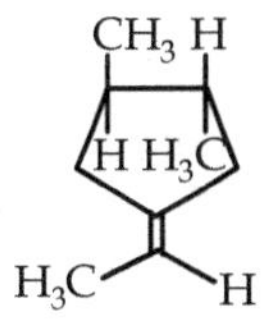    IV

I and II; III and IV are enantiomers. All other pairs are diastereomers.

12. (b)

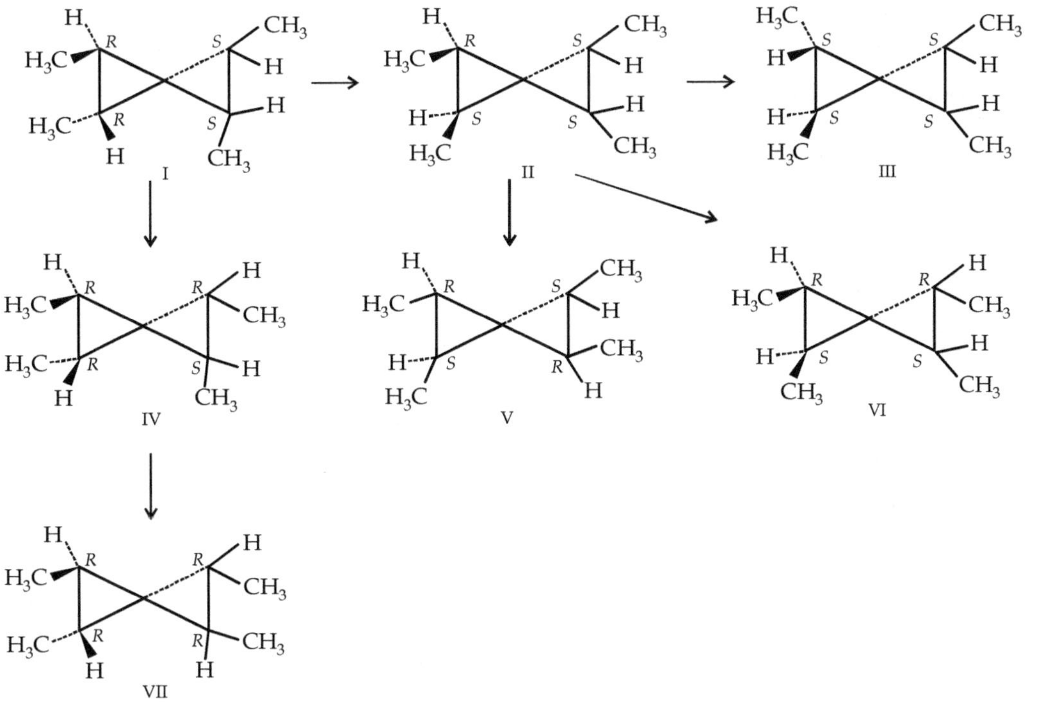

I    II    III

IV    V    VI

VII

II and IV; III and VII; V and VI are enantiomers; I is *meso*.

13.

$$\underset{A}{CH_3CH_2\overset{\overset{\displaystyle Cl}{|}}{C}HCH = CH_2}$$

$$\underset{B}{ClCH_2\overset{\overset{\displaystyle CH_3}{|}}{C}HCH = CH_2}$$

14.

$$\begin{array}{l} ^1COOH \\ ^2CHOH \\ ^3CHOH \\ ^4CHOH \\ ^5CHOH \\ _6COOH \end{array}$$

It has four chiral carbons, of which $C_2$ and $C_5$ are identical, and $C_3$ and $C_4$ are identical. The total number of stereoisomers is 10, of which 8 (four enantiomeric) are optically active and two are optically inactive (*meso*). Four enantiomeric pairs are *RRRR* and *SSSS*; *RRRS* and *SSSR*; *RRSR* and *SSRS*; *RSSR* and *SRRS*; the two *meso* isomers are *RRSS* and *RSRS*.

15. Yes;

$$\begin{array}{c} CH(CH_3)C_2H_5 \\ | \\ H - C - CH(CH_3)C_2H_5 \\ | \\ CH(CH_3)C_2H_5 \end{array}$$

Note the presence of three chiral carbons, one on each *tert*-butyl group. Since all three alkyl groups are equivalent, *RSR = SRR = RRS*, so only two enantiomeric pairs are possible; *RRR* and *SSS*; *RRS* and *SSR*.

16.

$$\begin{array}{c} CH_2Cl \\ H\!\!-\!\!\!\!-\!\!CH_3 \\ H\!\!-\!\!\!\!-\!\!CH_3 \\ CH_2Cl \end{array} \qquad \begin{array}{c} C_2H_5 \\ H\!\!-\!\!\!\!-\!\!Cl \\ H\!\!-\!\!\!\!-\!\!Cl \\ C_2H_5 \end{array} \qquad \begin{array}{c} C_2H_5 \\ Cl\!\!-\!\!\!\!-\!\!H \\ H\!\!-\!\!\!\!-\!\!Cl \\ C_2H_5 \end{array}$$

17. Three. If $H_2$ adds to both double bonds from the same face, the product will be *meso*. If $H_2$ adds to the double bond from opposite faces, the product will be racemic.

*meso*                racemate

18. (a) The product has three stereocenters; the carbon bearing H and OH, and the two carbons bearing double bond.

    (b) No, the product has no asymmetric carbon atom.

    (c) Although the product has no asymmetric carbon atom, yet the molecule is chiral and hence it is optically active. Interchange of two bonds of any of the stereocenter makes the enantiomer.

19. (a)    [structure] $\xrightarrow{H_2/Pt}$ [structure]

    (b) The four ligands on the chiral carbon are $CH_2 = CH$, H, $CH_3$, $CH(CH_3)_2$ whose priority order in decreasing sequence is $CH = CH_2$, $CH(CH_3)_2$, $CH_3$ and H. However, in the product the decreasing priority order of the groups is changed : $CH(CH_3)_2$, $CH_2CH_3$, $CH_3$ and H, so the product will be *R*.

    (c) Specific rotation is a molecular property which can be determined only by polarimeter.

20. (a) $$[\alpha]_D = \frac{-30°}{(0.10\ g/\ mL)\ (1.0\ dm)} = -300°$$

    (b) $$[\alpha]_D = \frac{+165°}{(0.05\ g/\ mL)\ (1.0\ dm)} = +3300°$$

The two rotation values can be explained by recognizing that the substance is a powerful optically active substance. The first reading (−30°) was really +330° (+360° − 30°).

$$[\alpha]_D = \frac{+330°}{(0.10\ g/\ mL)\ (1.0\ dm)} = +3300°$$

Thus the specific rotation in both cases is +3300°.

    (c) No, the apparent 0° rotation could be +360° or −360°, or an integral multiple of these values.

21. The molecular formula $C_3H_6O_2$ of X indicates that it has an index of hydrogen deficiency of 1. Thus compound X could possess a carbon-carbon double bond, or a ring. Stereoisomeric forms are not possible in a $C_3$ compound having carbon-carbon double bond. Hence, the compound X should be a cyclic compound containing oxygen in the ring (oxirane).

     [structure: $CH_2OH$]     [structure: $HOCH_2$]     An enantiomeric pair

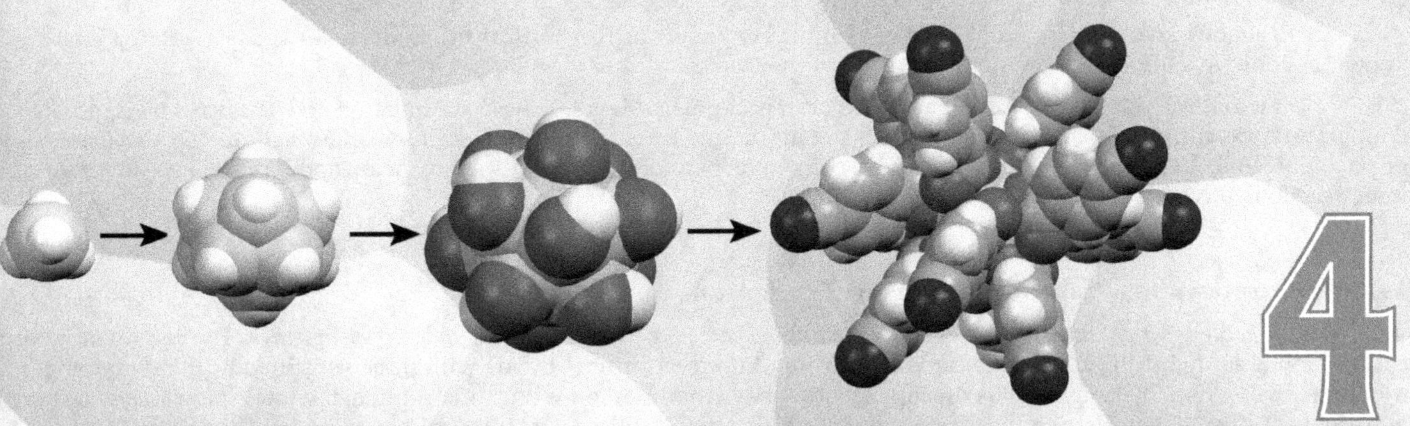

# Organic Reactions and their Mechanism

# 4



## 4.1   Types of Reaction Intermediates

Reactions involving organic compounds are known as organic reactions. Generally, organic reactions involve two steps: (*i*) breaking of the old bond and (*ii*) formation of new bond. Breaking of old bond may take place either homolytically (one electron remains with each of the two atoms) leading to the formation of **free radicals** as intermediate or heterolytically (both the bonding electrons go to the electronegative atom) leading to the formation of *ions* (**carbocations** or **carbanions**).

$$H_3C\cdot \qquad H_3C^{\oplus} \qquad H_3C:^-$$

Free radical     Carbocation        Carbanion

electron rich (nucleophiles)

electron deficient

Thus on the whole, there are three reaction intermediates, all of which are trivalent and have a tendency to become tetravalent accounting for high reactivity of these species.

When above types of reaction intermediates are formed, formation of the new bond may take place in a separate and next step by combining other reagent. However, in some cases, both steps (breaking of old bond as well as formation of new bond) occur simultaneously. Thus in such cases, well known intermediates are not formed but an imaginary **transition state** having zero life time is formed.

$$H\ddot{O}^- \ + \ CH_3\!-\!Cl \longrightarrow H\ddot{O}\cdots CH_3\cdots \overset{\delta-}{Cl} \longrightarrow HOCH_3 + Cl^-$$

Transition state

Reactions involving formation of free radicals are known as **free radical reactions,** while those involving ions are known as **ionic reactions.**

Free radical reactions occur in gas phase or in non-polar solvents. These are initiated and catalysed by light, high temperature, oxygen or peroxides and their rate is not influenced by change in temperature. Ionic reactions occur in presence of polar solvents. These are not effected by light, oxygen or peroxides but catalysed by acids and bases. Generally, rate of ionic reactions increase with increase in temperature.

## 4.1.1  Carbocations, Carbonium ions or Carbenium ions

*Carbocations are defined as species with a positively charged carbon having only three covalent bonds.* The carbon atom of carbocation is $sp^2$ hybridized. The three $sp^2$ orbitals are utilised in forming bonds with three substituents, the remaining $p$ orbital of carbon remains empty. Thus during reaction of a carbonium ion with a nucleophile, the latter may attach to it on either side of the plane leading to the formation of racemic mixture (of course, if the parent compound is chiral).

**Formation :** Carbocations are generally formed in acid catalysed reactions and in solvolysis of the C—X bond.

(a)  (i)  $CH_2 = CH_2 \overset{H^+}{\rightleftharpoons} CH_3 - \overset{+}{C}H_2$        (ii)  $R - OH \overset{H^+}{\rightleftharpoons} R - \overset{+}{O}H_2 \rightleftharpoons \overset{+}{R} + H_2O$

(b)  (i)  $(CH_3)_3C \overset{\frown}{-} Cl \longrightarrow (CH_3)C^+ + Cl^-$

(ii)  $C_6H_5 - N^+ \equiv NCl^- \longrightarrow C_6H_5 \overset{\frown}{-} N^+ \equiv N \longrightarrow C_6H_5^+ + N_2$

On the basis of relative stability*, carbocations are classified into two types, *viz.* less stable or transient (*e.g.* simple alkyl) and stable (*e.g.* aryl substituted methyl and allyl) carbocations. **Relative stability of simple alkyl carbocations is explained on the basis of inductive effect** and **hyperconjugation.**

|  |  |  |  |
|---|---|---|---|
| *tert*-Alkyl | *sec*-Alkyl | *pri*-Alkyl | Methyl carbocation |
| (+ charge dispersed by 3 alkyl groups) | (+ charge dispersed by 2 alkyl groups) | (dispersed only by 1 alkyl group) | (+ charge not dispersed) |

Similarly, due to **hyperconjugation,** positive charge on different types of carbocations is dispersed on different number of hydrogen atoms, *e.g.* on ethyl carbocation the positive charge can disperse over 4 positions.

Dispersal of positive charge over 4 positions in ethyl carbocation

In case of *sec*-carbocation, more equivalent structures can be written than for ethyl carbocation (a primary carbocation); further still greater number of such structures can be written for a tertiary carbocation. Hence the relative stability of the simple alkyl carbocations will follow the following order.

---

*  Remember that greater the probability of the positive charge (in case of carbocations), negative charge (in case of carbanions) or an odd electron (in case of free radicals) to be neutralised or dispersed in a species, more will be its stability. Conversely, greater is the probability of the charge to be concentrated over a particular atom, lesser will be the stability of that species. In other words, dispersal of the charge or the odd electron present on a species produces stability, while concentration of the charge produces unstability.

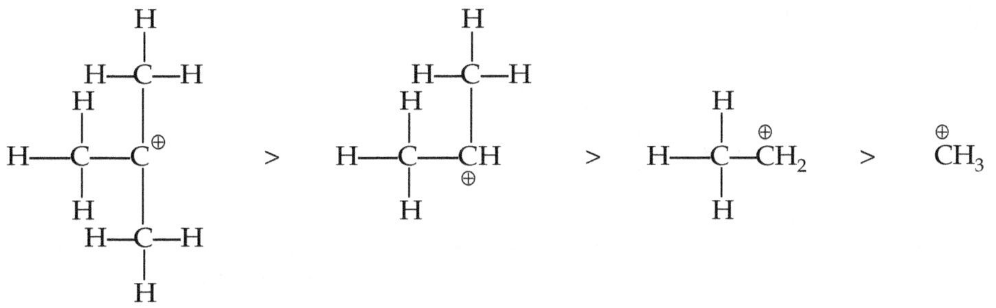

*tert*-Butyl carbocation
(+ charge can disperse
over 9 other positions)

*sec*-Isopropyl carbocation
(+ charge can disperse
over 6 other positions)

Ethyl carbocation
(+ charge can disperse
over 3 other positions)

Methyl carbocation
(No dispersal
of + charge)

A carbocation is more electron deficient (they have 6 electrons) than a free radical (with 7 electrons); hence stability of alkyl carbocations due to hyperconjugation is greater than that of radicals.

**Higher stability of allyl and aryl substituted methyl** (*e.g.* $Ph_3 \overset{+}{C} > Ph_2 \overset{+}{C} H > Ph \overset{+}{C} H_2$) carbocations is due to dispersal of positive charge due to resonance.

$$CH_2 = CH - \overset{+}{C}H_2 \longleftrightarrow \overset{+}{C}H_2 - CH = CH_2$$

Resonating structures of allyl carbocation

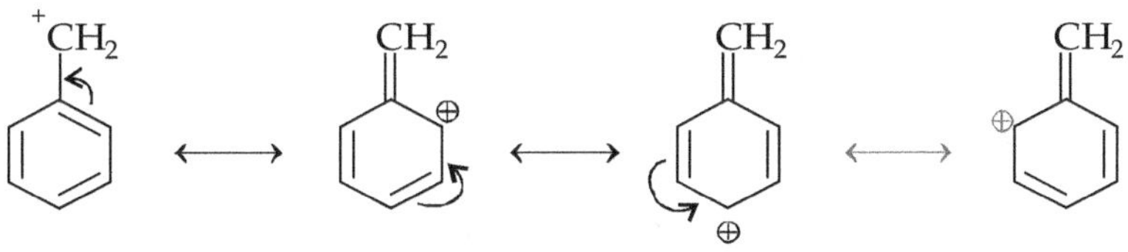

Resonating structures of benzyl carbocation

Since positive charge on $Ph_2 \overset{+}{C} H$ can disperse over 7 positions, while that on $Ph_3 \overset{+}{C}$ over 10 positions, relative stability of these carbocations follows the order.

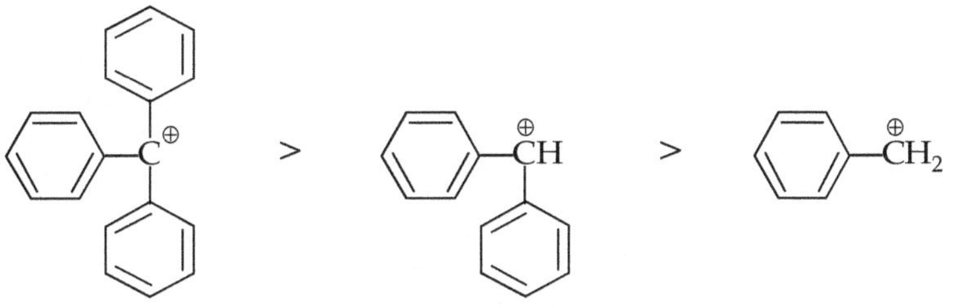

Triphenylmethyl carbocation
(dispersal of + charge
on 9 other positions)

Diphenylmethyl carbocation
(7 other positions)

Benzyl carbocation
(3 other positions)

The overall stability order of carbocations is

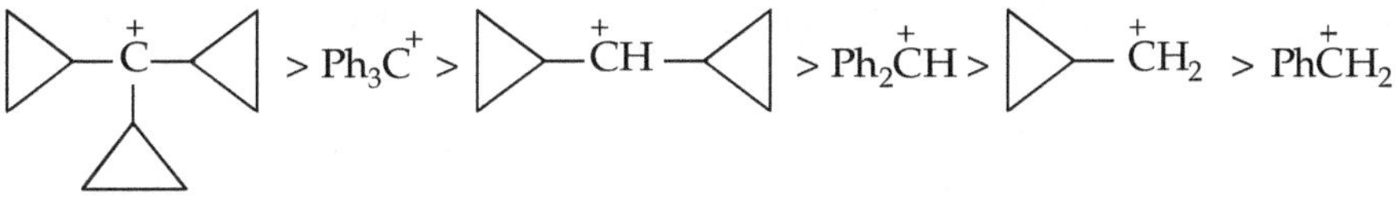

$$3° > CH_2 = CH\overset{+}{C}H_2 > 2° > 1° > \overset{+}{C}H_3$$

Stability of *tert*-carbocations as well as *tert*-radicals is largely due to *steric relief* achieved in their formation. In the parent compound (*e.g. tri*-isopropylmethyl chloride), carbon atom is tetrahedral and thus has a bond angle of 109.5° with the result the three bulky (isopropyl) groups are pushed by each other producing *steric strain*. When this compound is converted into carbocation or a free radical, the bond angle extends from 109.5° ($sp^3$) to 120° ($sp^2$) resulting in the relief of this strain due to increase in space between the bulky groups. Actually such a carbocation would resist addition of a nucleophile because it would again result in the crowding of bulky groups together.

## Important Points regarding Stability

(i)    Stability of the carbocation decreases with the increase in $s$-character of the carbon bearing positive charge. Thus

$$\% \ s\text{-character} \quad CH_3\overset{+}{C}H_2 > CH_2 = \overset{+}{C}H > CH \equiv \overset{+}{C}$$
$$\phantom{\% \ s\text{-character} \quad} 25 \qquad\quad 33.3 \qquad 50$$

(ii)    Presence of electron-donating substituents tends to stabilize the carbocation as it helps in dispersing the positive charge. Presence of electron-withdrawing groups destabilize the carbocation since it intensifies the positive charge. Thus

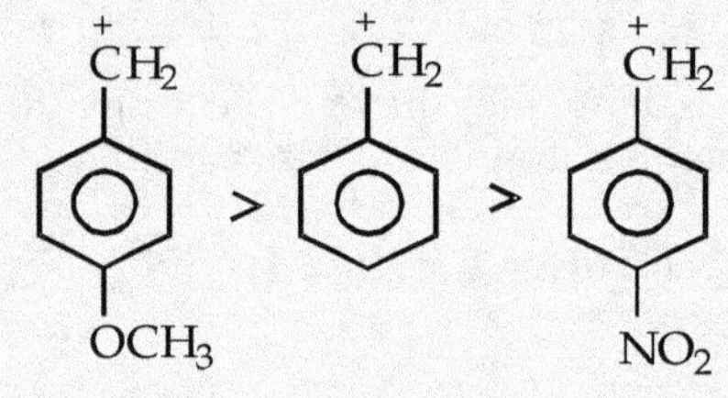

(iii)    If a hetero atom (O, N etc.) having a lone pair of electrons is present next to positively charged carbon, stability of the carbocation increases due to resonance.

$$CH_3 - \overset{+}{C}H - \overset{..}{\underset{..}{O}}CH_3 \longleftrightarrow CH_3 - CH = \overset{+}{\underset{..}{O}}CH_3$$

(iv)    Because of resonance, acylium ion is almost as stable as *tert*-butyl carbocation

$$CH_3 - \overset{+}{C} = \overset{..}{\underset{..}{O}} : \longleftrightarrow CH_3 - C \equiv \overset{+}{O} :$$

**Reactions :**

     Carbocations undergo mainly three reactions, *viz.* (*i*) combination with a nucleophile,(*ii*) elimination of a proton, if any, from the α-carbon atom, and

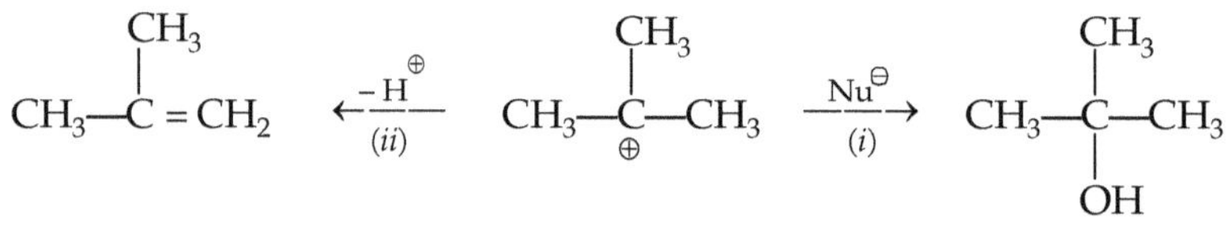

(*iii*) wherever possible, a less stable carbocation (1° or 2°) rearranges to the more stable (2° or 3°) carbocation. This is possible by 1, 2-hydride shift or by 1, 2- $:CH_3^-$ shift

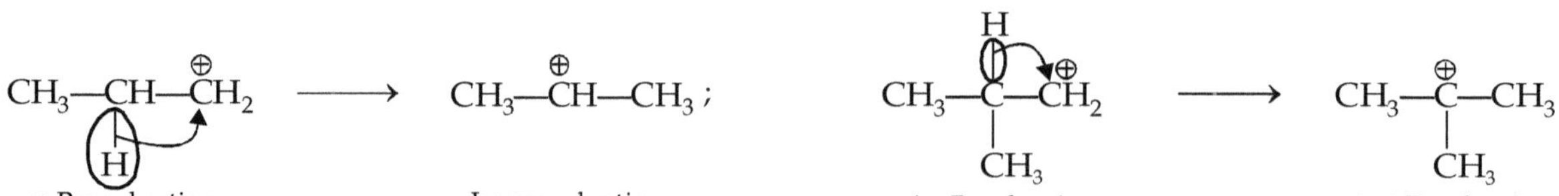

*n*-Propyl cation      Isopropyl cation      *iso*-Butyl cation      *tert*-Butyl cation
(less stable, 1°)      (more stable, 2°)      (less stable, 1°)      (more stable, 3°)

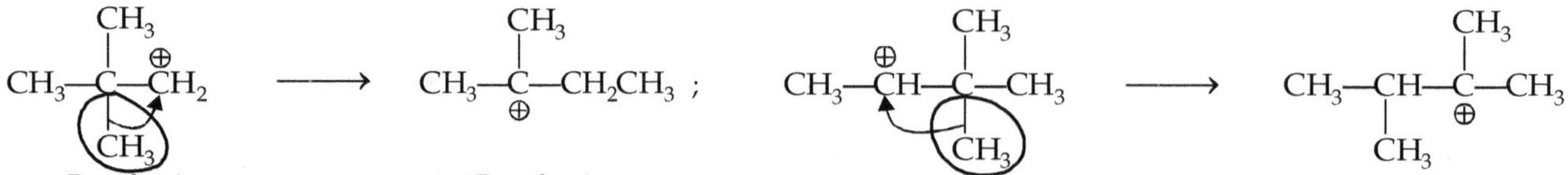

*neo*-Pentyl cation      *tert*-Pentyl cation      (less stable, 2°)      (more stable, 3°)
(less stable, 1°)      (more stable, 3°)

### 4.1.2 Carbanions

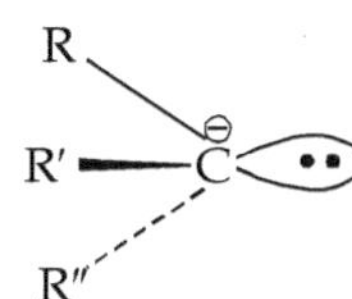

*Carbanions are anions of carbon generated by the removal of one of the group attached to a carbon without removing the bonding electrons.* The, a carbanion possesses one unshared pair of electrons and three pairs of bonding electrons around the central carbon atom which is $sp^3$ hybridised.

However, the bond angle between two bonding orbitals is slightly less than 109.5° due to two types of repulsions (*bp-bp* and *lp-bp*; and *lp-bp > bp-bp*). The methyl anion is similar to ammonia in shape (pyramidal) ; the two are also *isoelectronic*. Due to tetrahedral geometry, carbanion having three different substituents (chiral carbanion) should show enantiomerism but it is not so because the unshared pair of electrons and central carbon rapidly oscillate from one side of the plane to the other.

This rapid equilibrium between enantiomeric pyramidal structures thus explains the loss of optical activity associated with the asymmetric carbanions.

Rapid equilibrium between two enantiomers of a carbanion

Although unconjugated carbanions are $sp^3$ hybridised, conjugated carbanions are $sp^2$ hybridised because electron delocalisation results in formation of a double bond in which all involved atoms should be coplanar.

$$\overset{\ominus}{C}H_2-\overset{\overset{O}{\|}}{C}-CH_3 \longleftrightarrow CH_2=\overset{\overset{O^-}{|}}{C}-CH_3$$

Thus such carbanions will be optically inactive even when it has three different groups (chiral carbanion), because asymmetry of the negative carbon is destroyed with the formation of a carbon-carbon double bond.

**When formed** – Carbanions are formed by compound having group like –CN, –NO$_2$, etc. On a doubly bonded carbon atom.

$$C_2H_5O^- + CH_2=CH-C\equiv N \longrightarrow C_2H_5OCH_2-\overset{-}{C}H-C\equiv N$$

(a) having electrons attracting substituents such as —NO$_2$, —CN or carbonyl which render α-hydrogen atoms relatively acidic. Further once the carbanion is formed by these compounds, it is stabilised by delocalisation of the negative charge.

$$CH_3C\equiv N \xrightarrow{-H^+} \overset{\ominus}{C}H_2-C\equiv N \longleftrightarrow CH_2=C=\overset{\ominus}{N}$$

$$CH_3-\overset{\overset{O}{\|}}{C}-H \xrightarrow{-H^+} \overset{\ominus}{C}H_2-\overset{\overset{O}{\|}}{C}-H \longleftrightarrow CH_2=\overset{\overset{O^-}{|}}{C}-H$$

(b) having acetylenic hydrogen atom so that the negative charge is present on acetylenic carbon atom which can accommodate it easily because of its greater *s* character. Thus the relative stability of the following carbanions can be explained.

$$RC\equiv CH + B: \longrightarrow RC\equiv C^-: + BH$$

$$RC\equiv\overset{\ominus}{C} \quad > \quad R_2C=\overset{\ominus}{C}H \quad > \quad R_3C-\overset{\ominus}{C}H_2$$

| Acetylenic C | Alkenyl C | Alkyl C |
|---|---|---|
| (50% *s* character) | (33.3% *s* character) | (25% *s* character) |

(c) whose one hydrogen atom is removed forming anion which along with π electrons of the molecule can form *delocalised aromatic system*, characteristic stability of aromatic compounds, *e.g.* cyclopentadiene.

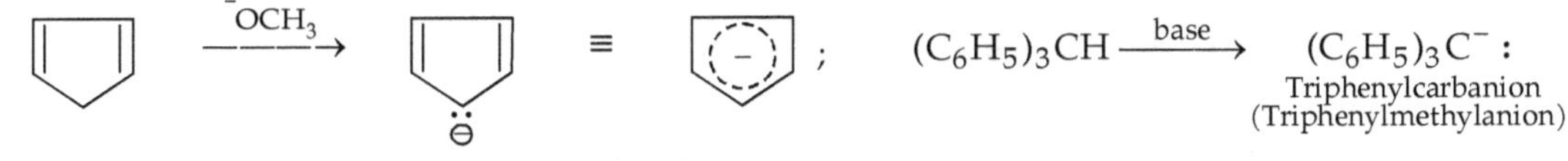

$$(C_6H_5)_3CH \xrightarrow{base} (C_6H_5)_3C^- :$$

Triphenylcarbanion
(Triphenylmethylanion)

Cyclopentadiene                    Cyclopentadienyl anion

**Stability :**

Usually, a carbanion is stabilised by resonance if a double bond is located α- to the anionic carbon. This explains the stability of allylic and benzylic carbanions.

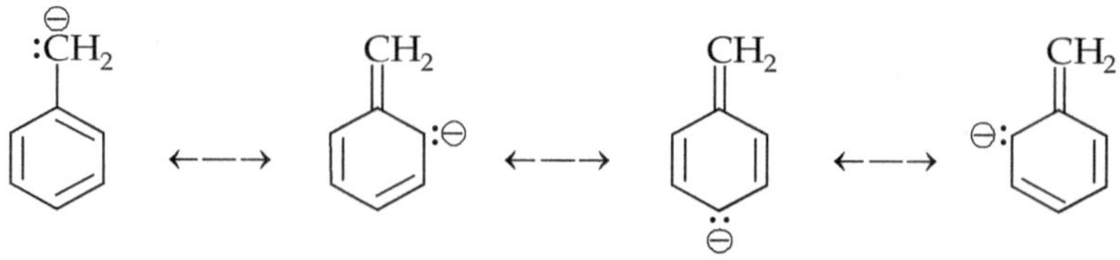

$$CH_2 = CH - CH_2 \longleftrightarrow \overset{\ominus}{C}H_2 - CH = CH_2$$

If the α-position of a carbanion has an electronegative element (like halogen) or a functional group with a multiple bond, viz. $C = C$, $C = O$, $C \equiv N$, $NO_2$ etc. such carbanions are stabilized by resonance.

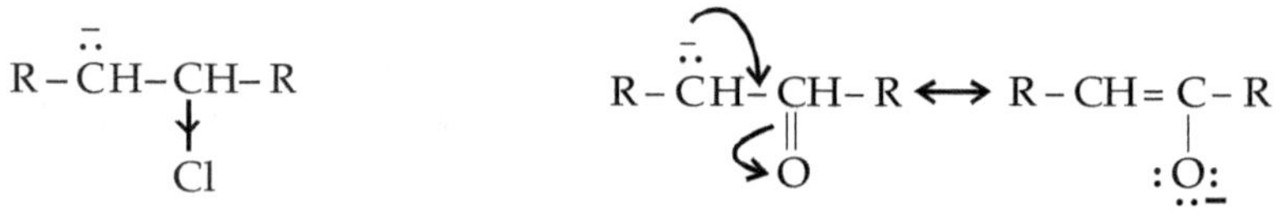

$$R - \overset{..}{C}H - CH - R \qquad\qquad R - \overset{..}{C}H - CH - R \longleftrightarrow R - CH = C - R$$
$$\qquad\qquad | \qquad\qquad\qquad\qquad\qquad \| \qquad\qquad\qquad\qquad\qquad |$$
$$\qquad\qquad Cl \qquad\qquad\qquad\qquad\qquad O \qquad\qquad\qquad\qquad :\overset{..}{O}:\underline{\phantom{.}}$$

　　　　−ve charge is dispersed due to −I effect　　　　−ve charge is dispersed due to resonance

The stability effect of the various α-substituents follows the order :

$$- NO_2 > -COR > -COOR > - CN > -X \text{ (halogen)}$$

Thus the relative stability of carbanion having different number of phenyl groups on anionic carbon can also be explained on the basis of resonance.

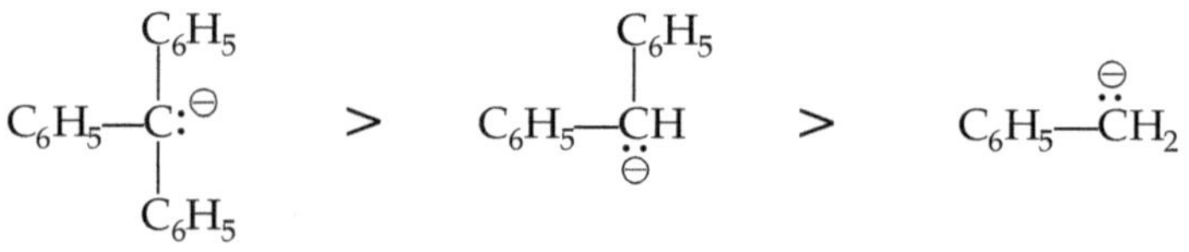

$$C_6H_5 - \underset{C_6H_5}{\overset{C_6H_5}{|}} \overset{\ominus}{C} : \quad > \quad C_6H_5 - \underset{\ominus}{\overset{C_6H_5}{|}}{C}H \quad > \quad C_6H_5 - \overset{..}{C}H_2$$

Presence of electron-donating substituents in bezene ring decreases the stability of the carbanion, while presence of electron-withdrawing substituents increases the stability (reverse to the order of corresponding carbocations). For example,

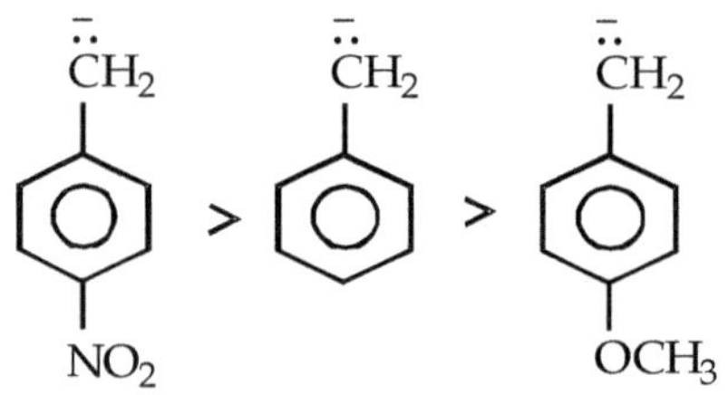

Stability of the carbanions increases with the increase in *s*-character of the carbon bearing negative charge.

$$CH_3\overset{..}{C}H_2 < CH_2 = \overset{..}{C}H < CH \equiv \overset{..}{C}$$

Since presence of electron withdrawing groups increases stability of carbanion as they help in dispersing negative charge on C, presence of electron-pushing groups (alkyl groups) will decrease the stability of carbanions as they concentrate (increase) negative charge on C. Thus the stability order of the simple carbanions is

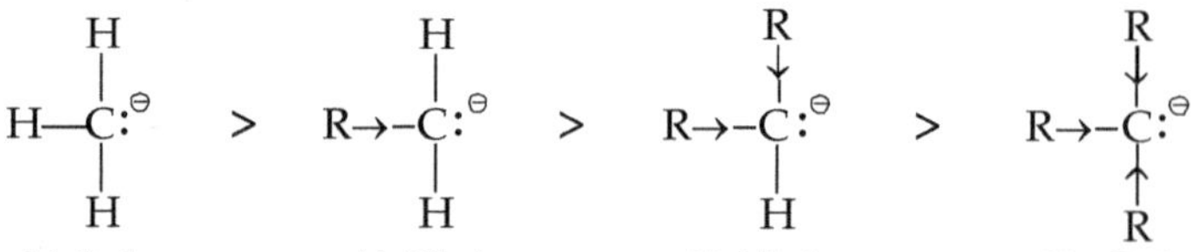

|  |  |  |  |
|---|---|---|---|
| Methyl | 1°-Alkyl | 2°-Alkyl | 3°-Alkyl |

Remember that here the stability order is exactly reverse to that of carbocations and free radicals.

(*i*)     $HC \equiv \bar{C} > Ph_3\bar{C} > Ph_2\bar{C}H > Ph\bar{C}H_2 > CH_2 = CH\bar{C}H_2 > C_6\bar{H_5} > CH_2 = \bar{C}H > \bar{C}H_3$

(*ii*)

$$\underset{NO_2}{\overset{\bar{C}H_2}{\bigcirc}} \;\; > \;\; \underset{NO_2}{\overset{\bar{C}H_2}{\bigcirc}} \;\; > \;\; \underset{NO_2}{\overset{\bar{C}H_2}{\bigcirc}}$$

## Reactions :

Among common reactions of carbanions are their nucleophilic character, viz. (*i*) nucleophilic substitution, and (*ii*) nucleophilic addition (addition to carbonyl carbon, *aldol condensation*).

(*i*)     $CH_3CH_2Br + CH \equiv C^{\ominus} \longrightarrow CH_3CH_2C \equiv CH$

(*ii*)     $\underset{}{CH_3\overset{O}{\overset{\|}{C}}{-}H} + \overset{\ominus}{\ddot{C}}H_2CHO \longrightarrow CH_3{-}\underset{CH_2CHO}{\overset{\overset{O^-}{|}}{C}}{-}H$

Usually, carbanions do not undergo rearrangement reactions.

## 4.1.3   Free Radicals

*Free radicals are neutral species having an odd or unpaired electron* which imparts it paramagnetism. A free radical is found to have a **planar** configuration in which the carbon atom bearing the odd electron is $sp^2$ hybridised (as in carbocations) and the odd electron remains in the *p* orbitals.

## Formation :

Free radicals are often produced when a molecule is supplied sufficient energy (thermal or photochemical). In addition, oxidation-reduction reactions involving the gain or loss of a single electron can also generate free radicals.

$$H_3C{-}N=N{-}CH_3 \xrightarrow{\text{heat}} 2H_3C^{\cdot} + N_2$$

$$CH_3COCH_3 \xrightarrow{h\nu} {}^{\cdot}CH_3 + {}^{\cdot}COCH_3 \longrightarrow {}^{\cdot}CH_3 + CO$$

$$RCOO^- \xrightarrow[(-e^-)]{\text{anode}} R{-}C{-}\ddot{O}: \longrightarrow R^{\cdot} + CO_2$$

## Stability :

Stability of free radicals is explained on the basis of resonance (in case of allyl and aryl substituted methyl free radicals) and hyperconjugation (in case of alkyl radicals : $3° > 2° > 1°$).

$$\underset{CH_3}{\overset{CH_3}{H_3C{-}\overset{|}{\underset{|}{C}}{}^{\cdot}}} \longleftrightarrow \underset{CH_3}{\overset{CH_2\,H^{\cdot}}{H_3C{-}\overset{\|}{\underset{|}{C}}}} \longleftrightarrow \underset{CH_2\,H^{\cdot}}{\overset{CH_3}{H_3C{-}\overset{|}{\underset{\|}{C}}}} \longleftrightarrow \underset{CH_3}{\overset{CH_3}{H^{\cdot}H_2C = \overset{|}{\underset{|}{C}}}}$$

              (2 other such structures)       (2 other such structures)       (2 other such structures)

Hyperconjugation in *tert*-butyl radical

Since allyl and benzyl radicals are stabilized by resonance, these are more stable than alkyl free radicals.

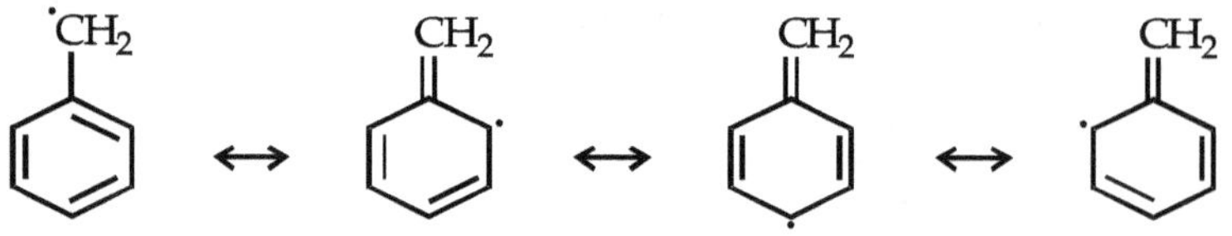

**Reactions :**

Among the important chemical reactions of free radicals are : (*i*) formation of new free radicals, (*ii*) combination with other free radical, and (*iii*) disproportionation (possible only in selected higher radicals).

(*i*)    $CH_4 + Cl\cdot \longrightarrow HCl + \cdot CH_3$        (*ii*)   $\cdot CH_3 + \cdot CH_3 \longrightarrow CH_3CH_3$

     $\cdot CH_3 + Cl_2 \longrightarrow CH_3Cl + Cl\cdot$        (*iii*)   $\cdot CH_3CH_2 \longrightarrow CH_3CH_3 + CH_2 = CH_2$ (Disporportionation)

Free radicals have lesser tendency for rearrangement because of the fact that the difference in stability between a primary and a tertiary radical is not as much as that between a primary and a tertiary carbocation.

**Radical ions :**

A free radical obtained by the addition of an electron to a $\pi$ system is called *radical anion*, while the free radical obtained by the removal of an electron from a $\pi$ bond is called *radical cation*.

*Example 1 :*

Arrange the following free radicals / carbocations in decreasing order of stability.

(a)

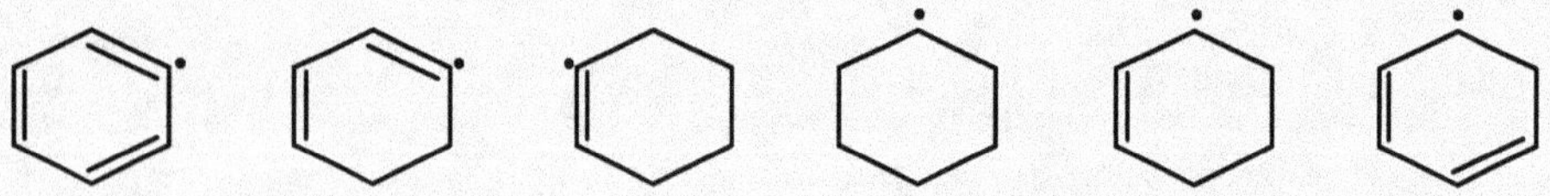

(b)

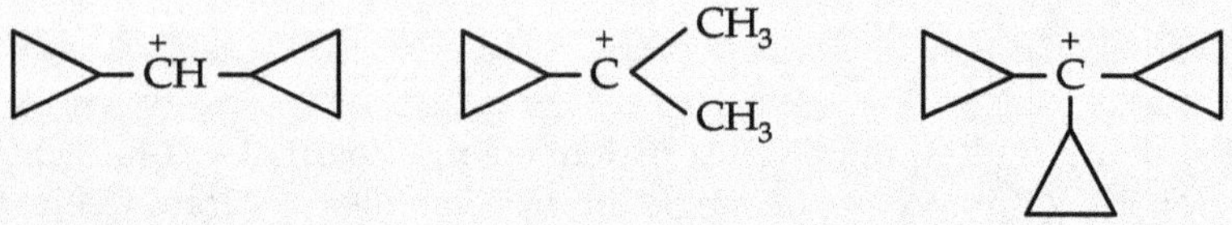

*Solution :*

(a)

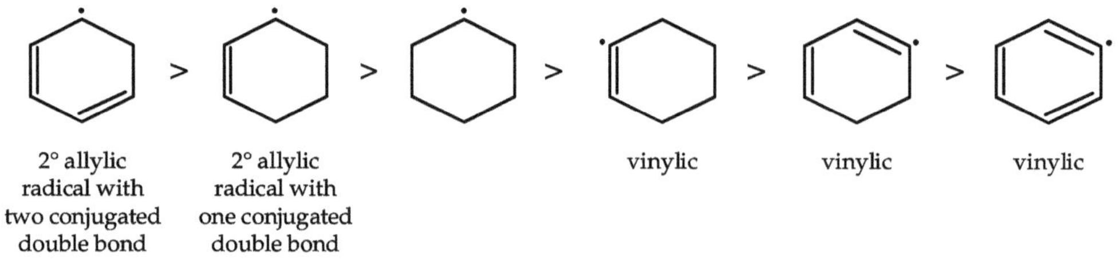

     2° allylic       2° allylic            vinylic        vinylic        vinylic
    radical with     radical with
  two conjugated   one conjugated
   double bond     double bond

(b)

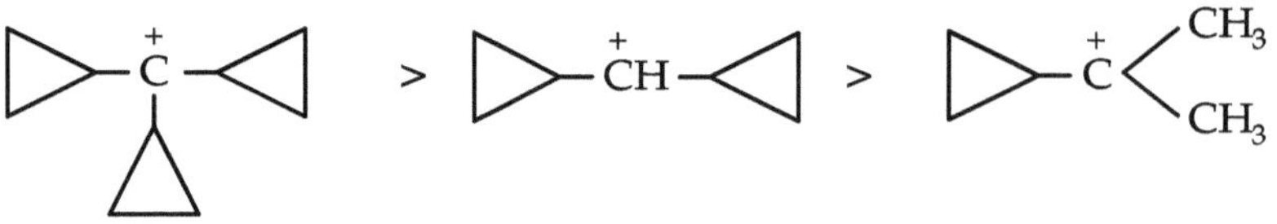

## 4.1.4 Carbenes

Carbenes are neutral, divalent carbon intermediates in which a carbon is covalently bonded to two atoms and has two non-bonding orbitals containing two electrons between them. Carbenes are of two types, singlet and triplet. Singlet carbene has $sp^2$ hybridised carbon atom, two of which are used in forming covalent bonds with the two substituents, the third one has the unshared pair of electrons ; while the *p*-orbital remains vacant. Thus a *singlet carbene is diamagnetic* and *resembles carbocation.*

Singlet carbene    Triplet carbene

Triplet carbon has *sp* hybridised carbon atom, the two hybrid orbitals form covalent bonds with two groups and two electrons are placed, one each, in the equivalent, mutually perpendicular $p_y$ and $p_z$ orbitals, i.e. here the two unshared electrons are not paired, thus a triplet carbene is paramagnetic and resembles a free radical (diradical).

In a singlet carbene, two electrons are present in the same orbital i.e. electrons are paired, interelectronic repulsion takes place and hence a singlet carbene is generally less stable than the triplet carbene.

**Formation :**

Carbenes are formed during alkaline hydrolysis of chloroform and decomposition of diazo compounds and ketenes.

(*i*) $\quad CHCl_3 \overset{OH^-}{\rightleftharpoons} \overset{\ominus}{C}Cl_3 \rightleftharpoons \underset{\text{Dichlorocarbene}}{:CCl_2} + Cl^-$    (*ii*) $\quad CH_2 = \overset{\oplus}{N} = \overset{\ominus}{\underset{..}{N}}: \overset{heat}{\longrightarrow} \underset{\text{Carbene}}{:CH_2} + N_2$

(*iii*) $\quad CH_2 = C = O \overset{heat}{\longrightarrow} :CH_2 + CO$

Carbenes have never been purified or even made in a high concentration, because when two carbenes collide, they immediately dimerize to given an alkene.

$$R_2C: + :CR_2 \overset{\text{very fast}}{\longrightarrow} R_2C = CR_2$$

Carbenes in which the carbene carbon is attached to two atoms, each having a lone pair of electrons are relatively more stable than the carbene itself due to resonance.

**Reactions :**

Carbenes undergo mainly two types of reactions ; *cycloaddition* with an alkene and *insertion* between the C—H bond.

$$H_2C = CH_2 + :CH_2 \longrightarrow \underset{\text{(due to cycloaddition)}}{H_2C-CH_2} + \underset{\text{(due to insertion)}}{CH_3CH = CH_2}$$

cis    singlet    cis

**Insertion reaction :**

$$R-\overset{\overset{\displaystyle H}{|}}{\underset{\underset{\displaystyle H}{|}}{C}}-H \;+\; R_2C: \;\longrightarrow\; R-\overset{\overset{\displaystyle H}{|}}{\underset{\underset{\displaystyle H}{|}}{C}}-\overset{\overset{\displaystyle R}{|}}{\underset{\underset{\displaystyle R}{|}}{C}}-H$$

Further it can be inserted in all the possible positions (1°, 2°, 3°).

$$CH_3CH_2CH_3 + :CH_2 \longrightarrow CH_3CH_2CH_2CH_3 + CH_3\underset{\underset{\displaystyle CH_3}{|}}{C}HCH_3$$

Carbenes are involved as intermediates in some well reactions like Riemer-Tiemann reaction, carbylamine reaction, Wittig reaction and Wolff rearrangement.

## 4.1.5   Nitrenes (*Imidogens*)

Nitrenes are neutral monovalent nitrogen species i.e. these are analogs of carbenes. These are electron deficient species and thus act as strong electrophiles. Like carbenes, nitrenes also exist in singlet and triplet states. Triplet state is the ground state and most nitrenes exist in this state. These can be generated in situ by the following methods.

(i)      By the decomposition of azides in presence of heat or light.

$$\underset{\text{Alkyl azide}}{R-\ddot{N}=N^+=\ddot{N}:^-} \xrightarrow[\text{Light}]{\text{Heat or}} \underset{\text{Alkyl nitrene}}{R-\ddot{N}:} + N\equiv N$$

(ii)      By the action of bromine in presence of base on a 1° amide (Hofmann bromamide reaction).

$$\underset{}{R-\overset{\overset{\displaystyle O}{\|}}{C}-NH_2} \xrightarrow{Br_2/NaOH} R-\overset{\overset{\displaystyle O}{\|}}{C}-N^-HBr \xrightarrow{OH^-} R-\overset{\overset{\displaystyle O}{\|}}{C}-\ddot{N}^- \overset{\curvearrowright}{Br} \xrightarrow{(-Br^-)} \underset{\text{Acylnitrene}}{R-\overset{\overset{\displaystyle O}{\|}}{C}-\ddot{N}}$$

Nitrenes, particularly acyl nitrenes are formed as intermediates in Hofmann, Curtius and Lossen rearrangements.

## 4.1.6   Arynes

*Arynes may be defined as aromatic compounds containing a formal carbon-carbon triple bond.* The best known example is benzyne which is benzene minus two ortho hydrogens and thus sometimes it is also called *dehydrobenzene.*

Remember that the benzyne bond is not like the triple bond of acetylene. In benzyne, one of the π components of the bond is part of delocalized π system of the aromatic ring. The second π component is obtained by overlapping of two $sp^2$ hybridized orbitals (not $p$-$p$ overlap). These two $sp^2$ orbitals lie in the plane of the ring and does not interact with the aromatic π system. Further the two contributing $sp^2$ orbitals are not oriented properly for effective overlap, the π bond formed is relatively weak and hence benzynes are not stable but extremely reactive.

The degree of overlap of these $sp^2$ orbitals is smaller than in the triple bond of an alkyne

Benzyne formation has been observed in following reactions.

(*i*)      Reaction of aryl halides with a strong base as during formation of (*a*) aniline from bromobenzene and (*b*) phenol from chlorobenzene.

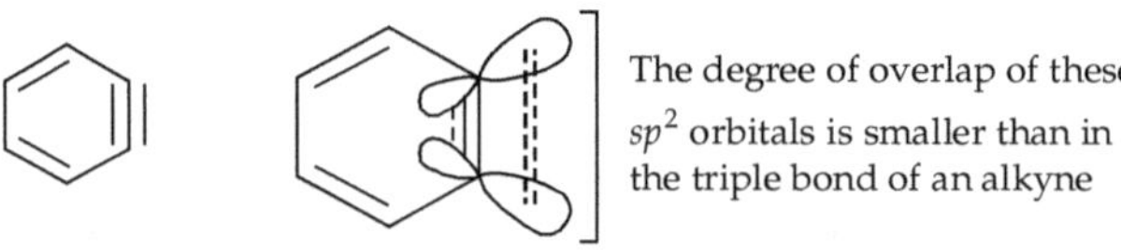

(*ii*)  By heating benzenediazonium-2-carboxylate.

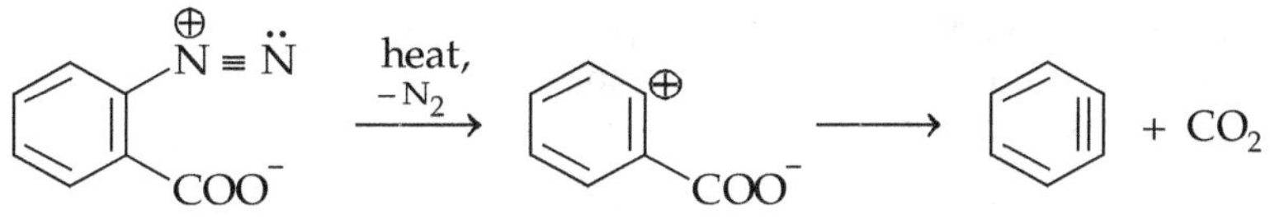

Benzene diazonium-2-carboxylate

(*iii*)  By heating *o*-fluorophenyl magnesium bromide

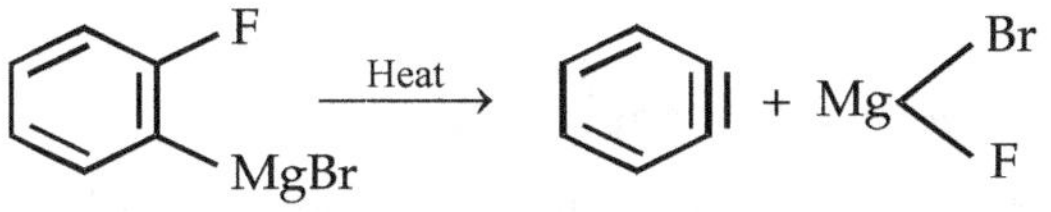

Benzynes undergo nucleophilic addition with a wide variety of nucleophiles like $H_2O$, $NH_3$, $RNH_2$, $C_6H_5Li$ etc. They also undergo dimerization reactions and react with olefins to form addition bicyclic compounds.

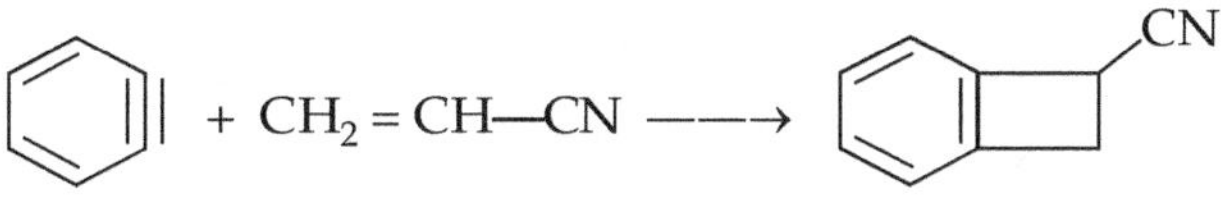

## 4.2  Types of Reagents

Heterolysis of a covalent bond is carried out by two types of reagents : electrophiles and nucleophiles.

### 4.2.1  Electrophiles

*An electrophile* (electron loving) *is a reagent that is deficient in electrons* and thus they attack at the electron rich site of the molecule. They are also called cationoid reagents and either carry a positive charge or have incomplete valence shell or have an atom which can acquire more electrons, *e.g.* $SiF_4$. Some commonly used electrophilic reagents are $H^\oplus$, $H_3O^\oplus$, $NO_2^\oplus$, $R_3C^+$, $X^\oplus$, $RC^+O$, $BF_3$, $AlCl_3$, $ZnCl_2$, $FeCl_3$, $SiF_4$, $ICl$, $R^{\bullet}$ (free radicals), $:CR$ (carbenes), $:\overset{..}{N}R$ (nitrenes), etc. Since electrophiles are capable of accepting electron pair, they are **Lewis acids.**

Positively charged electrophiles are more reactive than the neutral ones. Since presence of electron withdrawing substituents tends to concentrate positive charge on the reacting site of the electrophile, such electrophiles will be more reactive. Smaller cations are stronger electrophiles than the larger cations belonging to the same group because the positive charge is dispersed over a smaller surface.

In addition to the above list, **cation carriers** like $Br-Br$, $H-Br$, $Cl-OH$, etc. and oxidising agents like $Fe^{3+}$, $O_3$, $R-O-O-R$, etc. also act as electrophilic reagents.

### 4.2.2  Nucleophiles

*A nucleophile* (nucleus loving) *is a reagent that has at least one unshared pair of electrons on one of its atoms.* They are also called anionoid reagents. These are negatively charged species, neutral compounds of oxygen, nitrogen or sulphur which always carry at least one unshared pair of electrons on them or compounds having $\pi$ electrons. Common examples are

$OH^-$, $OR^-$, $Br^-$, $CN^-$, $NH_2^-$, $RCOO^-$, $RC \equiv C^-$, $CH_3COCH_2^-$, $(COOC_2H_5)_2CH^-$, $H_2\overset{..}{O}:$, $ROH$, $ROR$, $RSH$, $NH_3$, $H_2C = CH_2$,etc.

As expected, nucleophiles react at a positive or a partially positive site of a reactant. Fully charged ions like $OR^-$ and $OH^-$ are stronger nucleophiles than neutral substances like alcohols and water. Nucleophilic character is also enlarged by the presence of electron-donating groups (*e.g.* alkyl) which tend to concentrate negative charge on the reacting site of the nucleophile, *e.g.*, $OCH_3^-$ is a better nucleophile than $OH^-$.

Reactions instigated by nucleophiles and electrophiles are respectively known as *nucleophilic and electrophilic reactions.*

In addition, **anion carriers**, e.g. $R-MgX$, $H-H_3AlLi$, $H-C_6H_5$, $>C=C<$ etc. and reducing agents like $Fe^{2+}$, $[Fe(CN)_6]^{4-}$ etc. also act as nucleophilic reagents.

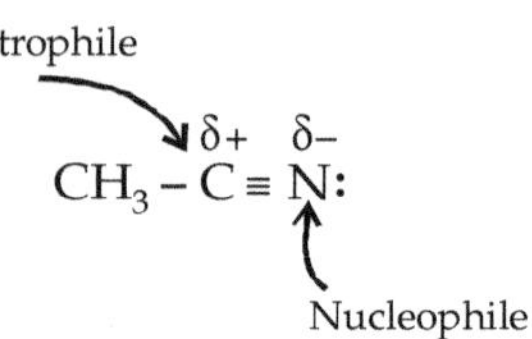

### 4.2.3 Ambiphiles or Ambidents

Reagents having both electron attracting (electrophilic) as well as electron-repelling (nucleophilic) site have dual (amphoteric) nature and known as **ambiphiles**. For example, HOH, ROH, $RPH_2$, organic compounds having $C = O$ or $C \equiv N$ linkage etc.

Electrophile

$$CH_3 - C \equiv N:$$

$\delta+ \quad \delta-$

Nucleophile

Other important examples of ambident nucleophiles are $^-O - \overset{..}{N} = O$, $-\overset{||}{\underset{O}{C}} - \overset{\ominus}{CH} - \overset{||}{\underset{O}{C}} -$ etc.

### 4.2.4 Comparison of Nucleophilicity and Basicity

Both of these two characteristics depend upon the availability of a lone pair of electrons. If this lone pair of electrons is donated to a hydrogen atom, it is called **basicity** and if it is donated to a carbon atom, it is called **nucleophilicity**. For example,

$$Nu\!:^- \; + \; \underset{}{C}\!-\!X \longrightarrow Nu\!-\!C \; + \; X\!:^- \qquad \text{[Nucleophilicity]}$$

$$Nu\!:^- \; + \; H\!-\!A \rightleftharpoons Nu\!-\!H \; + \; A\!:^- \qquad \text{[Basicity]}$$

Thus, nucleophilicity depends upon the rate constant of the reaction, while basicity depends upon the equilibrium constant ($K_b$). In other words, nucleophilicity governs the kinetics of a reaction while basicity determines its thermodynamics. Nucleophilicity and basicity may be similar or different as indicated by the following points.

(*i*)      If the nucleophilic centre of two or more species is same, nucleophilicity parallels basicity, *i.e.* more basic the species, stronger is its nucleophilicity

$$CH_3O^- \; > \; HO^- \; > \; CH_3COO^- \; > \; H_2O$$

— Basicity and nucleophilicity decrease ⟶

In all of the above species, nucleophilic atom is same, hence nucleophilicity parallels basic strength which in turn depends upon the relative strength of the conjugate acid (stronger the conjugate acid, weaker will be the base).

(*ii*)      For the same nucleophilic centre, the basicity increases but due to steric hindrance the nucleophilicity decreases as the size of the nucleophile increases. For example,

——— increasing basicity ⟶

$$CH_3O^-, (CH_3)_2CHO^-, (CH_3)_3CO^-$$

⟵—— increasing nucleophilicity ——

(*iii*)      In going from left to right across a period, the basicity and nucleophilicity are directly related. Both of the characteristics decrease as the electronegativity of the atom bearing lone pair of electrons increases. For example,

$$H_3C\!:^- \; > \; H_2N\!:^- \; > \; H\overset{..}{O}\!:^- \; > \; \overset{..}{\underset{..}{F}}\!:^-$$

——— Basicity and nucleophilicty decrease ⟶

(*iv*)      In moving down a group, the basicity and nucleophilicity are inversely related, *i.e.* nucleophilicity increases while basicity decreases. For example,

$$F^-, Cl^-, Br^-, I^- ; \quad NH_3, PH_3 ; \quad H_2O, H_2S$$

——— Basicity decreases, while nucleophilicity increases ⟶

This opposite behaviour is because of the fact that basicity and nucleophilicity depend upon different factors. Basicity is directly related to the strength of the H–Element bond, while nucleophilicity is indirectly related to the electronegativity of the atom to which proton is attached.

Bond dissociation energy of the H–Element : H—F > H—Cl > H—Br > H—I

Thus basicity follows the order : $F^- > Cl^- > Br^- > I^-$

Electronegativity of the atom : F > Cl > Br > I

Thus nucleophilicity follows the order : $I^- > Br^- > Cl^- > F^-$.

(*v*) When the atom bonded to the nucleophilic centre also has a lone pair of electrons, the nucleophilicity increases while the basicity decreases. For example, $H - \overset{..}{\underset{..}{O}} - \overset{..}{\underset{..}{O}}:^-$ (peroxide ion) is more nucleophilic than $OH^-$ ion but it is less basic than the $OH^-$ ion. Similarly, hydrazine $(H_2\overset{..}{N} - \overset{..}{N}H_2)$ is more nucleophilic but less basic than $NH_3$.

**Effect of solvent on nucleophilicity :** Anionic nucleophiles are less reactive in protic solvents (viz. ROH, HOH) than in aprotic solvents (viz. acetonitrile $CH_3CN$, DMF, $HCONH_2$, acetone). For example, fluoride ion is a poor nucleophile in protic solvents, however it is a good nucleophile in an aprotic solvent. The reason is very simple, anionic nucleophiles, especially smaller one like $F^-$, are solvated through H-bonds in protic solvents and hence their attack on the substrate will require breaking of some of the hydrogen bonds which reduce their nucleophilicity.

---

*Example 2 :*

**Are base strength and nucleophilicity, both inolving reaction of an electron pair with a positive site, identical? Explain.**

*Solution :*

No, although they are parallel quantities, they differ from each other because

(i) **Strength of a base** is based on the $K$ for the reaction of the base with a proton-donating Bronsted acid;

$$B:^- + HA \rightleftharpoons B:H + A:^-$$

(ii) **nucleophilicity** is measured by the rate of reaction with an electrophile, usually a carbon atom.

$$B:^- + \ -\overset{|}{\underset{|}{C}}- Br \longrightarrow B - \overset{|}{\underset{|}{C}} - \ + \ Br^-$$

---

*Example 3 :*

**Compare the basicities of the following pairs of bases :**

(a) $F^-$ and $I^-$       (b) $OH^-$ and $SH^-$       (c) $OH^-$ and $NH_2^-$

(d) $CH \equiv C^-$ and $CH_2 = CH^-$       (e) $NH_2OH$ and $NH_3$       (f) $Cl_3C^-$ and $F_3C^-$

*Solution :*

(a) For elements in the same group of the periodic table, the larger the basic site atom higher will be the possibility of delocalization of the charge, hence lesser will be its availability for proton. Thus

$$I^- < F^-$$

(b) Here also S and O lies in the same group, but S lies in higher period than O.

$$SH^- \quad < \quad OH^-$$
$$\text{(S lies in 3rd period)} \quad \text{(O lies in 2nd period)}$$

(c) When the basic site elements are in the same period of the periodic table and carry negative charge, more the number of electron pairs on the site atom, more will be delocalization of the negative charge and thus weaker is the base. Thus

$$:\overset{..}{N}H_2^- \ < \ :\overset{..}{\underset{..}{O}}H^-$$

(d) More is the *s*-character of the orbital having unshared (lone) pair of electrons, more it will be closer to carbon and thus lesser will be the basicity.

$$\underset{sp}{CH \equiv \overset{..}{C}{}^-} \ < \ \underset{sp^2}{CH_2 = \overset{..}{C}H^-}$$

(e) When the basic site has no negative charge, but has a group like –X, –OH, –OR which causes electron-attraction due to inductive effect decreases electron density on the basic site leading to decrease in basicity. Thus

$$H_2\overset{..}{N} \longrightarrow OH \ < \ \overset{..}{N}H_3$$

(f)     At first sight, one would conclude that $^-CF_3$ is less basic than $^-CCl_3$ due to more electron-withdrawing nature of F than Cl.

$$F \overset{F}{\underset{F}{\leftarrow}} \ddot{C}: ^- \quad < \quad Cl \overset{Cl}{\underset{Cl}{-}} \ddot{C}: ^-$$

However, this is not true because in $Cl_3C:^-$, the unshared electron pair on C in the $p$-orbital undergoes extended $p$-$d\pi$ bonding into an empty $d$-atomic orbital of each of the three chlorines ($p$-$d\pi$ bonding is not possible in $F_3C:^-$ because F has no $d$-orbital). Thus $Cl_3C:^-$ is in a weaker base than $F_3C:^-$.

$$:\ddot{C}l - C = \ddot{C}l:^- \longleftrightarrow {}^-:\ddot{C}l = C - \ddot{C}l: \longleftrightarrow \ddot{C}l: - C - \ddot{C}l:$$

Remember that resonance stabilization is more important than the inductive effect.

---

*Example 4 :*

**Explain the following :**

**(a)**     $NH_3$ **is more basic than** $PH_3$**. Explain it on the basis of their bond angle; bond angle in** $NH_3$ **and** $PH_3$ **are 107°  (app.) and 90° (app.) respectively.**

**(b)**     **Methaneselanate,** $CH_3SeO_3^-$ **is a stronger base than methanesulphonate,** $CH_3SO_3^-$**.**

*Solution :*

(a)     Both N and P are in group 5 of the periodic table, but P lies in third period while N in second period. Thus P, being larger in size than N, its hydride ($PH_3$) will be less basic than $NH_3$.

**Explanation on the basis of bond angle :** The 90° H–P–H bond angle indicates that P uses $p$ AO's for bonding and hence the unshared electron pair lies in $s$-orbital which being closer to nucleus, is less available for protonation. The 107° H–N–H bond angle indicates that N uses $sp^3$ HO's, hence electron pair lies in $sp^3$ orbital having 25% $s$-character. Thus unshared electron pair on N (in $NH_3$) is more available than the unshared electron pair on P (in $PH_3$).

(b)     Both S and Se atom are capable of forming $p$-$d\pi$ bonds, causing dispersal (delocalization) of negative charge. However, $p$-$d\pi$ bonding is more important in $CH_3SO_3^-$ which involves overlapping of $2p$ AO's of oxygen with $3d$-orbital of S, overlapping in $CH_3SeO_3^-$ involves $2p$-orbital of oxygen and $4d$-orbital of Se, hence it is less effective. Thus there is less effective overlap and delocalization of the negative charge in $CH_3SeO_3^-$, hence it is stronger base than $CH_3SO_3^-$.

---

*Example 5 :*

**(a)**     **Write chemical equations for the reaction of** $CH_3NH_2$ **with (i)** $H_2O$**; (ii) gaseous HCl and (iii)** $(CH_3)_3B$**.**

**(b)**     **Whether the amine is behaving as a base or as a nucleophile in the three cases.**

*Solution :*

(a)     (i)    $\underset{\text{base}}{CH_3NH_2} + \underset{\text{acid}}{H_2O} \rightleftharpoons \underset{\text{salt}}{CH_3NH_3^+OH^-}$       (ii)    $\underset{\text{base}}{CH_3NH_2} + \underset{\text{acid}}{HCl(g)} \longrightarrow \underset{\text{salt}}{CH_3NH_3^+Cl^-} \text{ (solid)}$

(iii)    $\underset{\substack{\text{nucleophile}}}{CH_3NH_2} + \underset{\substack{\text{electrophile} \\ \text{(B is electron deficient)}}}{B(CH_3)_3} \longrightarrow \underset{\text{complex compound}}{CH_3NH_2^+ - B^-(CH_3)_3}$

(b)     In (i) and (ii) $CH_3NH_2$ acts as a Bronsted base; while in (iii), it is acting as a nucleophile.

## 4.3   Types of Organic Reactions

The most common organic reactions can be classified into four groups namely substitution, addition, elimination and rearrangements.

### 4.3.1   Substitution Reactions

*The replacement of an atom or group from a molecule by a different atom or group is known as* **substitution** *or* **displacement reaction.** The species to be substituted may be either a nucleophile, an electrophile or a free radical.

In **nucleophilic substitution,** a nucleophile provides an electron pair to the substrate and the leaving group departs with an electron pair.

$$Nu{:} \; + \; R{-}X \longrightarrow R-Nu \; + \; X{:}^{\ominus}$$

These are usually written as $S_N$ (S stands for substitution and N for nucleophilic) and are common in aliphatic compounds especially in alkyl halides and acyl halides.

In **electrohphilic substitution,** the attacking species is an electrophile and the departing group leaves the molecule without pair of bonding electrons. These are usually written as $S_E$ (S stands for substitution and E for electrophilic) and are more common in aromatic compounds which provides electron rich site.

In **free radical substitution,** a free radical attacks the substrate to form new free radical which is converted into substituted product, the leaving atom departs the substrate with an electron. These reactions are initiated by sunlight, oxygen and other free radical producing agents. Most common examples are halogenation of alkanes.

$$CH_4 + Cl_2 \xrightarrow{\text{light}} CH_3Cl + HCl$$

### 4.3.2   Addition Reactions

In addition reactions, the reagent adds to a molecule which generally has a multiple bond. Like substitution, here also the attacking species may be a nucleophile, electrophile or a free radical.

$$CH_2 = CH_2 + HBr \longrightarrow CH_3 - CH_2Br$$

In **electrophilic addition,** an electrophile approaches a multiple bond (source of electrons) to form a carbocation which in the next step combines with a nucleophile to give addition product.

$$CH_2 = CH_2 \xrightarrow{H^{\oplus}} CH_3{-}CH_2^{\oplus} \xrightarrow{Br^{\ominus}} CH_3{-}CH_2Br$$

However, when the addition of HBr to alkenes is carried out in presence of peroxides, addition occurs through *radical mechanism.*

In **nucleophilic additions,** a nucleophile provides a pair of electrons to a carbon atom joined to oxygen by a multiple bond.

**Free radical addition reactions** are initiated by free radicals. For example,

$$CH_3CH = CH_2 + HBr \xrightarrow{\text{peroxide}} CH_3CH_2CH_2Br$$

### 4.3.3   Elimination Reactions

An elimination reaction involves removal of two atoms from the same molecule, thus it is said to be reverse of an addition reaction. For example,

$$CH_3CH_2Cl \xrightarrow{\text{alc. KOH}} CH_2 = CH_2 + HCl$$

Generally, two atoms or groups are lost from adjacent carbon atoms to form an unsaturated compound, such reactions are known as β-**elimination.** Acid-catalyzed dehydration of alcohols and base-catalysed dehydrohalogenation of alkyl halides are common examples.

(i)    $CH_2$—$CH_2$—$\overset{\cdot\cdot}{\underset{\cdot\cdot}{O}}H$ $\xrightarrow{H^\oplus}$ $CH_2$—$CH_2$—$\overset{\oplus}{O}H_2$ $\xrightarrow{-H_2O}$ $CH_2$—$\overset{\oplus}{C}H_2$ $\xrightarrow{H^\oplus}$ $CH_2 = CH_2$

(ii)    $CH_2$—$CH_2$—$Cl$ $\longrightarrow$ $H_2O + CH_2 = CH_2 + Cl^\ominus$

In few elimination reactions, two atoms or groups are lost from the same carbon atom to form highly reactive species, known as *carbenes* (α-**elimination**). For example,

$$OH^- + H - \overset{Cl}{\underset{|}{C}}Cl_2 \longrightarrow :CCl_2 + H_2O + Cl^-$$
$$\text{Dichlorocarbene}$$

### 4.3.4   Molecular Rearrangements

A rearrangement reaction involves the migration of an atom or a group (including a double bond) within the molecule.

(i)    $CH_3CH(X)CH = CH_2 \longrightarrow CH_3CH = CHCH_2X$

(ii)    $CH_3$—$\overset{CH_3}{\underset{\underset{H}{|}}{\overset{|}{C}}}$—$\overset{\oplus}{C}H_2$ $\dashrightarrow$ $CH_3$—$\overset{CH_3}{\overset{|}{\underset{\underset{\oplus}{}}{C}}}$—$CH_3$

       (1° carbocation)         (3° carbocation)

(iii)    $NH_4CNO \longrightarrow NH_2CONH_2$

# TEST YOUR UNDERSTANDING - 4.1

1.    Pick up the species which can act as (*a*) an electrophile, (*b*) a nucleophile, (*c*) both *i.e.* electrophile as well as nucleophile and (*d*) neither electrophile nor nucleophile.

   $H^+, H_2, H_2O, Cl^+, Cl^-, Cr^{3+}, CH_4, NO_2^+, BeCl_2, CH_2O, CH_3CH = CH_2, SnCl_4, CH_3CN, SiF_4$

2.    Some of the commonly used reagents are given below. Identify which part of the reagent can act as an electrophile ?

   $Cl_2, H_2O, HBr, HOCl, CH_3COOH, CH_3COCl, C_6H_5SO_2OH$

3.    In $CH_3COCl$ and $ICl$, every atom has complete octet of electrons, even then they behave as electrophiles. Explain.

4.    Classify the following reactions as addition, substitution, elimination, rearrangement or redox, note that a single reaction may belong to more than one type

   (i)    $H_2C = CH_2 + HCl \longrightarrow CH_3CH_2Cl$        (ii)    $H_2C = CH_2 + H_2 \xrightarrow{Pt} CH_3CH_3$

   (iii)    $\triangle \longrightarrow CH_3CH = CH_2$        (iv)    $CH_3CHClCHClCH_3 + Zn \longrightarrow CH_3CH = CHCH_3 + ZnCl_2$

(v)  $\triangle$ + $Br_2$ $\longrightarrow$ $BrCH_2CH_2CH_2Br$  (vi)  $NH_4CNO \longrightarrow H_2NCONH_2$

(vii)  $CHCl_3 + OH^- \longrightarrow :CCl_2 + H_2O + Cl^-$  (viii)  $CH_3CH_2Br + H^- \longrightarrow CH_3CH_3 + Br^-$

(ix)  $\searrow\!\!\!/ \xrightarrow{H_2} \searrow\!\!\!<$

5.  Think of the intermediate formed during following reactions :

(i)  $(CH_3)_3COH + H^+ \longrightarrow$ [Intermediate] $+ H_2O$  (ii)  $CH_2I_2 + Zn \longrightarrow [\ \ ] + ZnI_2$

(iii)  $(CH_3)_3CCl + AlCl_3 \longrightarrow [\ \ ] + AlCl_4^-$  (iv)  $CH_3—N=N—CH_3 \longrightarrow [\ \ ] + N_2$

(v)  $CH_2N_2 \longrightarrow [\ \ ] + N_2$  (vi)  $CH_2=CH_2 + DBr \longrightarrow [\ \ ] + Br^-$

(vii)  $(CH_3)_2Hg \longrightarrow [\ \ ] + .Hg.$  (viii)  $C_2H_2 + Na \longrightarrow [\ \ ] + Na^+ + \frac{1}{2}H_2$

6.  The rate expression for the following reaction is given by the expression $r = k\,[Me_3CBr][Ag^+]$.

$Me_3CBr + CH_3COO^- + Ag^+ \longrightarrow$ Products

Write down the product of the reaction and explain it by a plausible mechanism showing the reacting electrophiles and nucleophiles.

7.  Arrange the following free radicals in decreasing order of stability.

(i)  [structures I, II, III, IV, V]  (ii)  $CH_2=\overset{\bullet}{C}H$  $CH_2=\overset{\bullet}{C}H—CH_2$  [structures III, IV]

I  II  III  IV  V  I  II  III  IV

---

 **4.4  Energetics of Organic Reactions**

Every chemical reaction can proceed in either direction, even if it goes in one direction to a microscopic extent. Thus for every reaction, a **state of equilibrium** is reached when the concentrations of A, B, C and D no longer change even though the reverse and forward reactions are taking place. The equilibrium constant of a reaction depends upon following thermodynamic quantities.

$$e\,A + f\,B \rightleftharpoons g\,C + h\,D$$

(i)  **Enthalpy change ($\Delta H$).** It is the quantity of heat released or absorbed when a mole of reactant is converted into a mole of product. Alternatively, $\Delta H$ of a chemical reaction is the difference in the enthalpies of the products, $H_P$ and the reactants, $H_R$, *i.e.* $\Delta H = H_P - H_R$.

If the bonds in the products are more stable than the bonds in the reactants, *i.e.* when the sum of bond energies of the products are more than that of the reactants, $\Delta H$ is negative and the reaction is **exothermic.**

$$H_3C—H + Cl—Cl \longrightarrow H_3C—Cl + H—Cl$$

Bond energy  435  243  339  431  ;  $\Delta H = -92$ kJ mol$^{-1}$

678 kJ mol$^{-1}$  770 kJ mol$^{-1}$

(ii)  **Entropy change ($\Delta S$).** Since entropy is a measure of randomness, change in entropy is the measure of the energy consumed (or released) in the reaction to create more order (or randomness) in products relative to reactants. For a reaction,

$$\Delta S = S_P - S_R$$

(iii)  **Free energy change ($\Delta G$).** When entropy change is taken with the absolute temperature (T), it gives the free energy change ($\Delta G$) according to the following relation.

$$\Delta G = \Delta H - T\Delta S$$

A reaction proceeds in the forward direction only when $\Delta G$ is negative that is there is overall release of energy. A positive $\Delta G$, on the other hand, indicates that the reaction has a tendency to go backward.

## Rates of reactions

Although a negative value of $\Delta G$ tell us that the reaction is thermodynamically feasible in the forward direction, it does not necessarily tell us that the reaction will proceed at a measurable rate. The **rate of reaction** and its dependence on the concentration of the various reacting species is predicted by kinetic studies. Consider the following reaction.

$$e\,A + f\,B \longrightarrow g\,C + h\,D$$

The rate of the above reaction is given by

$$\text{rate} = k\,[A]^x\,[B]^y$$

where $k$ is the rate constant at temperature T. The numerical values of the exponents $x$ and $y$ are determined experimentally, they need not be the same as $e$ and $f$, the coefficients of the chemical reaction. The sum of the values of the exponents is defined as the order of the reaction.

Under a given set of conditions (concentration, temperature, nature of solvent, presence of catalyst etc.), following factors determine the rate of a given reaction.

(*i*)    **Number of collisions per unit time.** The greater the chances for molecular collision, the faster the reaction. Probability of collision is proportional to the molar concentrations.

(*ii*)    **Enthalpy of activation** (activation energy, $E_{act}$, $\Delta H^{\neq}$). Reaction may take place only when colliding molecules have some enthalpy content in excess of average ($E_{act}$). The smaller the value of $E_{act}$, the more successful will be the collisions and the faster the reaction.

(*iii*)    **Entropy of activation** ($\Delta S^{\neq}$). All collisions between molecules possessing requisite $E_{act}$ does not result the reaction. Collisions between molecules must also occur in certain orientation, reflected by the value of entropy of activation. The more organized or less random is the required orientation of the colliding molecules, lower is the entropy of activation and thus slower is the reaction.

## Transition state and enthalpy diagrams

When reactants having sufficient enthalpy of activation and proper orientation collide, they pass through a hypothetical transition state in which some bonds are breaking while others are being formed. The relationship of the transition state to the reactants and products is shown by energy (enthalpy) diagrams.

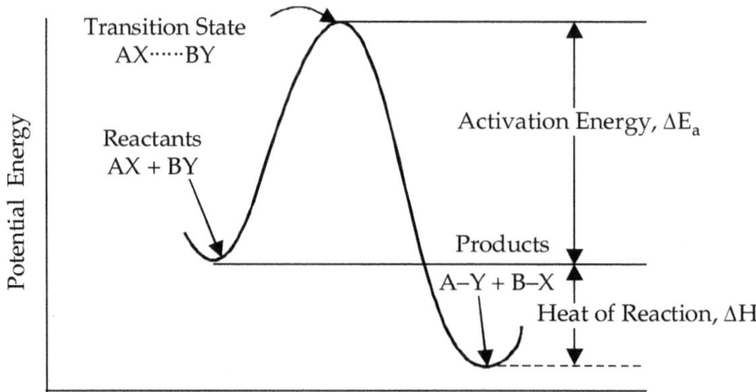


Enthalpy diagram for exothermic reactions.

From the above plot it is obvious that for the reaction to proceed, energy must be supplied to the reactants in order to carry them over the hump. This energy is required, essentially, to stretch and ultimately to break any bond as may be necessary in the reactants. This amount of work necessary to get the reactants upto the top of the hump is called the **free energy of activation, activation energy or energy of activation.** Therefore, reactions with high activation energies occur more slowly than those with low activation energies, since at ordinary temperature the kinetic energy of only a small fraction of the reactant molecules will be great enough to provide sufficient energy on collision to reach the transition state. Thus we see that it is the activation energy and not the heat of reaction which determines the reaction. The top of the energy hump corresponds to the least stable configuration through which the reactants pass on their way to products and this is generally known as the **transition state or activated complex.** The activated complex is not a true molecule. It contains partial bonds, and the energy content of the system is maximum. Its life is extremely short, and hence it cannot be isolated; it always decomposes into reactants or products.

An endothermic reaction similarly has a specific activation energy required to reach its transition state. But here the activation energy must be greater or least equal to the heat of reaction.

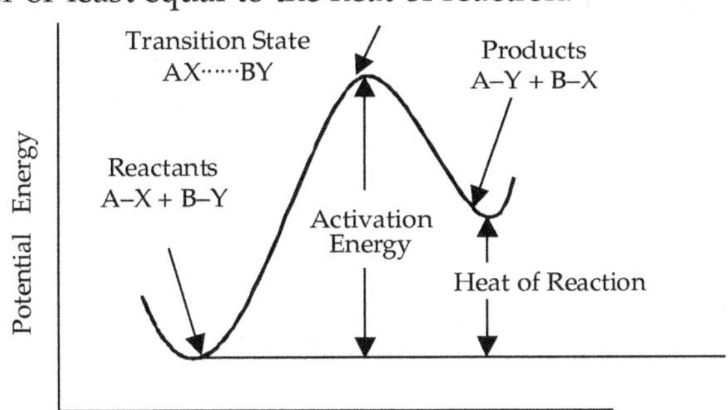



Enthalpy diagram for endothermic reaction

However, many common reactions are not so simple and do not proceed through a single transition state as the above two examples, but involve the formation of one or more actual intermediates. The overall such reactions consist of two or more separate reactions, *viz.* (*i*) reactants → intermediate, and (*ii*) intermediate → products, and thus two or more activation energies will be involved–one leading to a transition state for formation of the intermediate, and a second leading to a transition state between the intermediate and the final products. The step with the highest activation energy will usually be the slower and therefore the **rate determining step** of the over-all reaction.

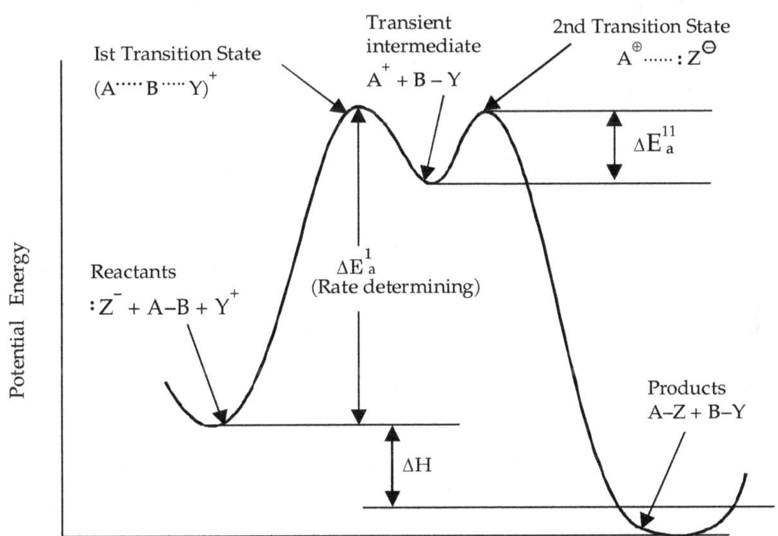



Enthalpy diagram for an exothermic reaction with a transient intermediate

If a reaction proceeds through a true intermediate, there will be a minima in the energy diagram. The greater the dip, the more stable will be the intermediate, and *vice versa i.e.,* the shallower the dip, the less stable will be the intermediate. In the extreme case, the dip may be so shallow that the intermediate is indistinguishable from the transition state. It should be noted here that each intermediate has its own transition state.

## TEST YOUR UNDERSTANDING - 4.2

1.　Predict the sign of $\Delta S$ (positive or negative) in the following reactions :

(*i*)　$CH_2 = CH_2 + H_2 \longrightarrow CH_3CH_3$

(*ii*)　$H_2C \underset{\diagdown}{\overset{\diagup}{\phantom{ }}} \overset{CH_2}{\phantom{ }} CH_2 \xrightarrow{heat} CH_3CH = CH_2$

(*iii*)　$CH_3COO^- (aq) + H_3O^+ (aq) \longrightarrow CH_3COOH + H_2O$

2.　Predict the effect on the rate of a reaction if a change in the solvent causes (*i*) a decrease in $\Delta H^{\ddagger}$ and an increase in $\Delta S^{\ddagger}$, (*ii*) an increase in $\Delta H^{\ddagger}$ and a decrease in $\Delta S^{\ddagger}$, (*iii*) an increase in $\Delta H^{\ddagger}$ and $\Delta S^{\ddagger}$, and (*iv*) a decrease in $\Delta H^{\ddagger}$ and $\Delta S^{\ddagger}$.

3.　Catalyst generally speeds up reactions by lowering $\Delta H^{\ddagger}$. Explain how this occurs in terms of reactant and transition state enthalpies.

4. The rate of the reaction (A + B → C + D) can be expressed in three ways.

 (*i*) rate = $k$[A][B], (*ii*) rate = $k$[A], or (*iii*) rate = $k$[B]. Give plausible mechanisms consistent with the above expressions.

5. Give mechanism for the reaction, 2A + 2B $\longrightarrow$ C + D, whose rate = $k$[A]$^2$[B], assuming that no step is termolecular.

6. The rate of the reaction A + 2B $\longrightarrow$ C + D is expressed as rate = $k$[A][B]$^2$. If the rate determining step of the reaction is unimolecular, give the possible mechanism of the reaction.

## 4.5   Competitive Reactions (Thermodynamic and Kinetic Control)

Many reactions produce a mixture of products formed from a common intermediate. For example, hydrogen halides add to 1, 3-butadiene to give a mixture of two regioisomeric allylic halides.

$$CH_2 = CHCH = CH_2 \xrightarrow[(-80°C)]{HBr} CH_3\overset{\displaystyle Br}{\overset{|}{CH}}CH = CH_2 \;+\; CH_3CH = CHCH_2Br$$

$$\text{1, 3-Butadiene} \qquad \text{3-Bromo-1-butene (81\%)} \quad \text{1-Bromo-2-butene (19\%)}$$
$$\text{(1, 2-Addition)} \qquad \text{(1, 4-Addition)}$$

Both of the above products are derived from the same allylic carbocation.

$$[CH_3\overset{+}{C}HCH = CH_2 \longleftrightarrow CH_3CH = CH\overset{+}{C}H_2] \xrightarrow{Br^-} CH_3\overset{\displaystyle Br}{\overset{|}{CH}}CH = CH_2 \;+\; CH_3CH = CHCH_2Br$$

$$\quad\text{2° (More stable)} \qquad\qquad \text{(1° Less stable)} \qquad\qquad \text{3-Bromo-1-butene (81\%)} \quad \text{1-Bromo-2-butene (19\%)}$$
$$\textbf{(Major)} \qquad\qquad \textbf{(Minor)}$$

The secondary carbocation is more stable than the primary *i.e.* it bears more of the positive charge than does the primary carbon, hence attack by the nucleophile (Br$^-$) is faster at 2° carbocation forming 1, 2-addition product as the major product.

*When the major product of a reaction is that which is formed at the fastest rate, it is known as* **kinetically controlled** or **rate-controlled product,** *and the reaction is known as kinetically controlled reaction.* Such reactions take place at low temperature. Most organic reactions fall into this category, and the addition of HBr to 1, 3-butadiene at low temperature is a kinetically controlled reaction.

However, addition of HBr to 1, 3-butadiene at room temperature gives 1-bromo-2-butene (1, 4-addition product) as the major product.

$$CH_2 = CHCH = CH_2 \xrightarrow[\text{room temp.}]{HBr} CH_3\overset{\displaystyle Br}{\overset{|}{CH}}CH = CH_2 \;+\; CH_3CH = CHCH_2Br$$

$$\qquad\qquad\qquad \text{3-Bromo-1-butene (44\%)} \quad \text{1-Bromo-2-butene (56\%)}$$
$$\text{(1, 2-addition)} \qquad\qquad \text{(1, 4-addition)}$$

*When the major product of the reaction is that which is relatively more stable, it is known as* **thermodynamically-controlled** or **equilibrium controlled product,** *and the reaction is known as thermodynamically-controlled reaction.* Such products are formed at room temperature (high temperature).

Thus, it can be concluded that the temperature of the reaction exerts a major influence on the product composition. This can be explained on the basis of the fact that at elevated temperature, the 1, 2 and 1, 4-addition products *interconvert rapidly* by allylic rearrangement. Heating the product mixture to 45°C in the presence of hydrogen bromide leads to a mixture in which the ratio of 3-bromo-1-butene to 1-bromo-2-butene is 15 : 85.

$$CH_3\overset{\displaystyle Br}{\overset{|}{CH}}CH = CH_2 \;\rightleftharpoons\; \underset{\underset{Br^-}{}}{\overset{H}{\underset{CH_3CH \cdots\; \cdots CH_2}{\overset{|}{\overset{+}{C}}}}} \;\rightleftharpoons\; CH_3CH = CHCH_2Br$$

$$\text{3-Bromo-1-butene} \qquad\qquad\qquad\qquad\qquad \text{1-Bromo-2-butene}$$
$$\text{(Less stable)} \qquad\qquad\qquad\qquad\qquad\qquad \text{(More stable)}$$

The predominance of the 1, 4-addition product (1-bromo-2-butene) is due to its high stability owing to the presence of *internal double bond* than the 1, 2-addition product (3-bromo-1-butene) which has a terminal double bond.

When addition occurs under such conditions where the products can equilibrate, the composition of the product is not in accordance to the relative rates of formation of the products (or the relative stability of the intermediate carbocation) but tends to reflect their relative stabilities.

However, it must be remembered that if the conditions of the reaction do not permit interconversion (like low temperature), *i.e.* when the reaction is irreversible the kinetically controlled product will invariably predominate. The irreversible nature of the reaction at low temperature is because of slow isomerization which in turn in due to insufficient thermal energy to permit the products to surmount the energy barrier for ionization. At higher temperatures, isomerization is possible and the more stable product predominates.

## 4.6   Mechanism of Substitution Reactions

As described earlier substitution reactions may follow of free-radical or ionic path. Further, ionic mechanism may be nucleophilic (when the reagent is nucleophile) or electrophilic. Thus, on the whole there are three types of substitution reactions namely free radical, nucleophilic and electrophilic depending upon the nature of the reactant, reagent and reaction conditions.

### 4.6.1   Free-Radical Mechanism

This mechanism occurs when the reaction conditions or reagent are free-radical producing, *viz.* UV light, high temperature or presence of certain free radical initiators (*e.g.* peroxides, tetraethyl lead, etc.). This mechanism is observed in halogenation of alkanes. For details of halogenation, readers are referred to Ch. on 'Alkanes'. However, here three necessary steps encountered in halogenation of alkanes are summarised below.

(*i*)   *Initiation step (Formation of free-radical).* A reactive particle, typically an atom or free-radical, is needed to start the reaction. It is the generation of this reactive particle that requires the vigorous conditions, *viz.* presence of UV light, high temperature etc.

$$X - X \xrightarrow[\text{or } 250\text{-}400°C]{\text{UV light}} 2X\cdot$$

(*ii*)   *Propagation steps.*   $X\cdot + H{-}CH_3 \longrightarrow HX + \cdot CH_3$

$$\cdot CH_3 + X_2 \longrightarrow CH_3X + X\cdot$$

These two steps are repeated until finally a chain is terminated.

(*iii*)   *Termination step.* The above propagation steps, *i.e.* chain reaction stops by coupling of any two radicals.

$$X\cdot + X\cdot \longrightarrow X - X$$

$$\cdot CH_3 + X\cdot \longrightarrow CH_3{-}X$$

$$\cdot CH_3 + \cdot CH_3 \longrightarrow CH_3{-}CH_3$$

When the ratio of $CH_4$ to $X_2$ is high, $CH_3X$ is formed predominantly and when $X_2$ is in excess, $CCl_4$ is the final product.

**Relative reactivity of hydrogens toward free radical halogenation :** It is in accordance with the relative stability of the free radicals.

$$\text{Benzyl} > \text{allyl} > 3° > 2° > 1° > \text{vinyl} > \text{methyl}$$

Halogenation at allylic or benzylic carbon takes place by means of $Cl_2$ or $Br_2$ at high temperatures (500-800°C). However, allylic bromination is carried out more easily with NBS (N-bromosuccinimide). The weak N-Br bond in NBS can be cleaved homolytically into radical upon warming or exposure to visible light. For more details of allylic bromination consult (6.4.15).

**Stereochemistry :**

(i)     If the reaction creates a chirality centre in the product both the R and S enantiomers are formed.

CH$_3$ · H—|—H · CH$_2$CH$_3$  $\xrightarrow[hv]{Br_2}$  CH$_3$ · H—|—Br · CH$_2$CH$_3$  +  Br—|—H · CH$_3$ · CH$_2$CH$_3$

enantiomers

(ii)     In case, the parent compound already has a chiral centre, and another chirality centre is developed, a pair of diastereomers is formed.

CH$_3$ · H—|—Cl · H—|—H · CH$_3$  $\xrightarrow[hv]{Br_2}$  CH$_3$ · H—|—Cl · H—|—Br · CH$_3$  +  CH$_3$ · H—|—Cl · Br—|—H · CH$_3$

diastereomers

## 4.6.2   Nucleophilic Substitution (S$_N$) Reactions

These reactions occur when the attacking agent is a nucleophile. Such reactions are mainly encountered in alkyl halides and acyl halides.

**Nucleophilic substitution in alkyl halides :** The carbon-halogen bond in an alkyl halide is polar ($\overset{\delta+}{R} - \overset{\delta-}{X}$) and cleaved heterolytically on attack by a nucleophile.

$$R—\ddot{\underset{\cdot\cdot}{X}}: \; + \; Y:^- \; \xrightarrow{\text{Solvent}} \; R—Y \; + \; \ddot{\underset{\cdot\cdot}{X}}:^-$$

**Nucleophiles** may be anions or neutral molecules having lone pair of electrons. Relative reactivity of different nucleophiles will be discussed at a later stage. The **leaving group** in alkyl halides is halide ion ($X^-$). Relative leaving ability of the halide ion, *i.e.* reactivity of alkyl halides follows the order : RI > RBr > RCl >> RF which can be explained in two ways.

(*a*)     Leaving-group ability of an anion is related to basicity. A strongly basic anion is usually a poorer leaving group than a weakly basic one. Fluoride is the most basic and the poorest leaving group, while iodide is the least basic and the best leaving group.

(*b*)     Iodine has the weakest bond to carbon and thus iodide is the best leaving group ; on the contrary fluorine has the strongest bond to carbon and thus fluoride is the poorest leaving group. Alkyl fluorides are rarely used as substrates in nucleophilic substitution because they are several thousand times less reactive than alkyl chlorides.

In order to ensure that reaction occurs in homogeneous solution, such **solvents** are chosen which dissolve both the alkyl halide (organic compounds) and nucleophiles (generally ionic salts). Two such solvents are ethanol-water mixtures and dimethyl sulphoxide, $(CH_3)_2S = O$ (DMSO).

Kinetic studies (study of rate of reaction with change in concentration) of nucleophilic substitution show that methyl and other primary halides react by second-order kinetics (*i.e.* rate is dependent upon the concentration of two substances, *viz.* alkyl halide and nucleophile) ; while *tert*-alkyl halides react by first-order kinetics (*i.e.* rate depends upon the concentration of only one substance, the alkyl halide). In short,

rate = $k$[RX][OH$^-$]     (For CH$_3$X and 1° alkyl halides)

rate = $k$[RX]     (For 3° alkyl halides)

Secondary alkyl halides show border line behaviour : sometimes sceond-order, sometimes first-order, often a mixture of the two.

The above facts led to the conclusion that nucleophilic aliphatic substitution can proceed by two different mechanisms, named as biomolecular and unimolecular.

### 4.6.3 Bimolecular Mechanism of Nucleophilic Substitution ($S_N2$)

As mentioned earlier, the rate of such reaction is found to be directly proportional to the concentration of both reactants (alkyl halide and nucleophile). Thus we can say that the reaction is first-order with respect to each reactant or second-order overall. The overall second-order kinetic behaviour points out that the rate-determining step of the reaction is *bimolecular.*

The $S_N2$ reactions are believed to be completed in one step. The nucleophile (*e.g.* OH⁻) starts to share its electrons with the substrate carbon from the side opposite* to the bromine atom (*back side attack*), and simultaneously the bromine atom starts removing its shared pair of electrons from the carbon atom **(concerted process).** This leads to the formation of a transition state.

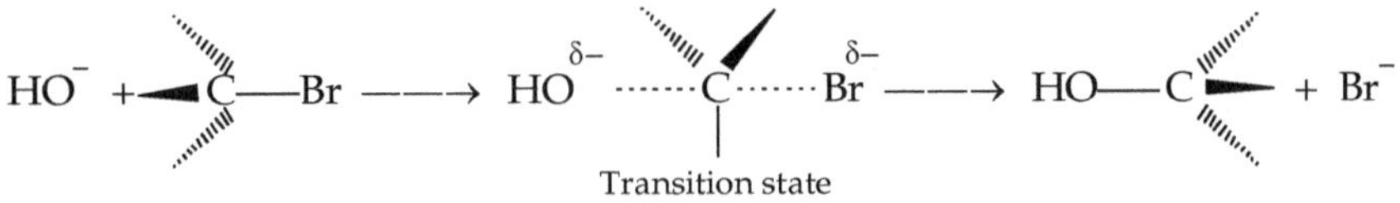

$$HO^- + \overset{}{\underset{}{C}}{-}Br \longrightarrow HO^{\delta-} \cdots\cdots C \cdots Br^{\delta-} \longrightarrow HO{-}C + Br^-$$

Transition state

The $S_N2$ reaction (Note that the nucleophile, OH⁻ attacks the back side of the bromine atom)

In the transition state, carbon atom is partially bonded to the nucleophile (OH⁻) as well as to the leaving group (—Br) ; —OH has a diminished negative charge since it has begun to share its electrons with carbon, while —Br has developed a partial negative charge as it has partly removed a pair of electrons from carbon. The —OH and —Br are located as far apart as possible ; the three substituents and the carbon lie in a single plane, all bond angles being 120°. Thus note the carbon atom in the transition state is pentavalent. The C-substituent bonds are thus arranged like the spokes in a wheel, with the C—OH and the C—Br bonds lying along the axle.

Finally, the C—Br bond is fully cleaved by the energy liberated by the C—OH bond formation, the —OH group takes the position just opposite to that occupied by the —Br. The negative charge on bromine (the leaving group) is stabilised by hydrogen bonding with the solvent.

The $S_N2$ mechanism is believed to describe most substitution of simple primary alkyl halides and to some extent secondary alkyl halides.

**Stereochemistry of $S_N2$ reactions :**

Stereochemistry of $S_N2$ reactions can best be demonstrated by taking alkyl halide having chiral carbon, *e.g.* 2-bromooctane. When (+)-2-bromooctane is allowed to react with NaOH under $S_N2$ conditions, (–)-2-octanol is obtained.

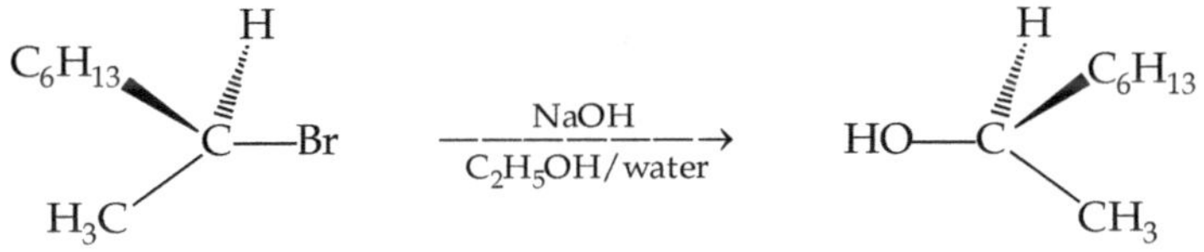

$$C_6H_{13}\overset{H}{\underset{H_3C}{C}}{-}Br \xrightarrow[C_2H_5OH/water]{NaOH} HO{-}\overset{H}{\underset{CH_3}{C}}C_6H_{13}$$

(+)-2-Bromooctane        (–)-2-Octanol

The change in the sign of specific rotation from (+)- to (–)- indicates that the configuration changes during the reaction. Thus it can be concluded that *an $S_N2$ reaction proceeds with inversion of configuration usually referred to as* **Walden inversion.**

Remember that there is no distinct relation between the sign of rotation and R/S specification of different compounds. They may be having different sign of rotation but same specification (R or S), although in the above particular example inversion in configuration (*i.e.* change in specific rotation, happens to be accompanied by a change in specification from S-(+)-2-bromooctane to R-(–)-2-octanol.

It is important to note that during $S_N2$ reaction, configuration of every molecule is inverted *i.e. an $S_N2$ reaction proceeds with complete inversion of configuration.* This can be proved by the fact that a sample of 83% optically pure (+)-2-bromooctane gives 83% optically pure (–)-2-octanol on $S_N2$ reaction.

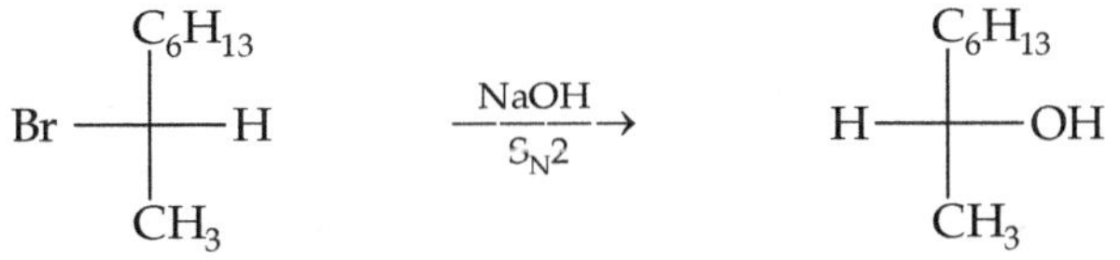

$$Br\overset{C_6H_{13}}{\underset{CH_3}{-\!\!\!|\!\!\!-}}H \xrightarrow[S_N2]{NaOH} H\overset{C_6H_{13}}{\underset{CH_3}{-\!\!\!|\!\!\!-}}OH$$

S-(+)-2-Bromooctane       R-(–)-2-Octanol
$[\alpha] = +32.9°$          $[\alpha] = -8.55°$
(Optical purity 83%)      (Optical purity 83%)

---

*     Attack by OH⁻ on the oppsoite side to that of bromine is because of the fact that both of them are electron rich. It is, therefore, natural that they will remain away as far apart as possible.

## TEST YOUR UNDERSTANDING - 4.3

1.    Determine the specific rotation of (–)-2-octanol obtained by the reaction of (+)-2-bromooctane (of specific rotation = + 24.9°) with aqueous sodium hydroxide. Given [α] for optically pure (+)-2-bromooctane and (–)-2-octanol have specific rotations of + 39.6° and – 10.3° respectively.

**Steric effects in $S_N2$ reactions :** There is a very large difference in reactivity between different types of alkyl halides towards $S_N2$ reactions under the given state of conditions. For example, reactivity of some alkyl bromides with lithium iodide in acetone differs widely.

|  | $CH_3Br$ | $CH_3CH_2Br$ | $(CH_3)_2CHBr$ | $(CH_3)_3CBr$ |
|---|---|---|---|---|
| Relative rate | 221000 | 1350 | 1 | too small to measure |

The above large difference in rate is because of degree of **steric hindrance** offered by increasing number of alkyl groups on the carbon bearing the leaving group, to the nucleophile. This is further evidenced by studying the rate of reaction of different 1° halides with lithium iodide in acetone.

| 1° Alkyl halides : | $CH_3{-}CH_2Br$ | $C_2H_5{-}CH_2Br$ | $(CH_3)_2CH{-}CH_2Br$ | $(CH_3)_3C{-}CH_2Br$ |
|---|---|---|---|---|
| Relative rate : | 1.0 | 0.8 | 0.036 | 0.00002 |

In the above example, we see that although neopentyl bromide, $(CH_3)_3CCH_2Br$, is a primary alkyl halide, it is practically inert to substitution by $S_N2$ mechanism because of steric hindrance. Thus remember that *difference in rate between two $S_N2$ reactions are mainly due to steric factors, and not to polar factors.*

### 4.6.4   Unimolecular Mechanism of Nucleophilic Substitution ($S_N1$)

In the above discussion, it is observed that *tert*-alkyl halides are practically inert to substitution by $S_N2$ mechanism because of steric hindrance. It does not mean that such halides do not undergo nucleophilic substitutions. Actually, it was observed that the hydrolysis of *tert*-alkyl halides occurs by a different mechanism. It follows *first-order* kinetics, that is, the rate depends upon the concentration of only one reactant, the *tert*-alkyl halide which is proved by the fact that the rate does not change either on adding the stronger nucleophile like $OH^-$ ion or increasing the concentration of $OH^-$.

$$(CH_3)_3CBr + H_2O \longrightarrow (CH_3)_3COH + HBr \; ; \; \text{rate} = k[(CH_3)_3CBr]$$

The observations led to the fact that the reaction takes place according to following steps.

**Step 1.**   The carbon-halogen bond breaks heterolytically without any assistance from the nucleophile forming a carbocation.

$$(CH_3)_3C{-}\ddot{B}r\colon \xrightarrow{\text{slow}} (CH_3)_3\overset{+}{C} \; + \; \colon\!\ddot{B}r\colon^-$$

*tert*-Butyl bromide             *tert*-Butyl cation

**Step 2.**   $(CH_3)_3\overset{+}{C} \; + \; \overset{..}{O}H_2 \xrightarrow{\text{fast}} (CH_3)_3C{-}\overset{+}{\underset{..}{O}}\!\!<\!\!{}^{H}_{H}$

**Step 3.**   $(CH_3)_3C{-}\overset{+}{\underset{..}{O}}\!\!<\!\!{}^{H}_{H} \; + \; \colon\!\ddot{O}H_2 \xrightarrow{\text{fast}} (CH_3)_3C{-}OH \; + \; H{-}\overset{+}{\underset{..}{O}}H_2$

*tert*-Butyl oxonium ion     Water         *tert*-Butyl alcohol
(acts as an acid)     (acts as a base)

Step 3 does not occur when the nucleophile is an anion. In this mechanism, since the rate-determining step (slow step which is first) involves only one molecule, it is known as **unimolecular nucleophilic substitution ($S_N1$).**

**Relative reactivity of different alkyl halides towards $S_N1$ mechanism :** Since $S_N1$ reactions involve the formation of carbocation as intermediate in the rate determining step, **more is the stability of carbocation higher will be reactivity of alkyl halides towards $S_N1$ route.** Now we know that stability of carbocations follows the order : $3° > 2° > 1°$, so $S_N1$ reactivity should also follow the same order.

$$3° > 2° > 1° > \text{Methyl } (\mathbf{S_N1 \text{ reactivity}})$$

This is also proved experimentally by carrying out substitution of different alkyl halides by chosing conditions under which $S_N1$ route is very slow as solvolysis in aqueous formic acid (both $H_2O$ and HCOOH are weak nucleophiles)

$$RX + H_2O \xrightarrow{\text{HCOOH}} ROH + HX$$

The relative rate of hydrolysis (which is mainly $S_N1$) of different alkyl halides under these conditions are found as below.

| Alkyl bromide | Class | Relative rate |
|---|---|---|
| $CH_3Br$ | Unsubstituted | 1 |
| $CH_3CH_2Br$ | Primary | 2 |
| $(CH_3)_2CHBr$ | Secondary | 43 |
| $(CH_3)_3CBr$ | Tertiary | 100,000,000 |

This suggests that **steric crowding** that **influences reaction rate in $S_N2$ processes** plays no role in $S_N1$ reactions. On the other hand, **in $S_N1$ reactions, electronic effect,** specifically the stabilization of carbocation intermediate by alkyl substituents **is the decisive factor.**

Additional evidence for the formation of carbocations as intermediates comes from the observations that in certain cases rearranged products are the main products (recall that carbocations undergo rearrangement to the more stable). For example, hydrolysis of 2-bromo-3-methylbutane (a secondary alkyl halide) yields 2-methyl-2-butanol (a tertiary alcohol) as the exclusive product of hydrolysis.

$$CH_3\underset{\underset{Br}{|}}{C}HCHCH_3 \xrightarrow{H_2O} CH_3\underset{\underset{OH}{|}}{C}CH_2CH_3$$

2-Bromo-3-methylbutane → 2-Methyl-2-butanol (93%)

**Mechanism :**

2-Bromo-3-methylbutane $\xrightarrow{\text{slow}}$ 1, 2-Dimethylpropylcation (2°) $\xrightarrow[\text{1, 2-hydride shift (fast)}]{\text{rearranges by}}$

1, 1-Dimethylpropyl cation (3°) $\xrightarrow[\text{fast}]{H_2O}$ $\xrightarrow{\text{fast}}$ 2-Methyl-2-butanol (3° alcohol)

**Stereochemistry of $S_N1$ reactions :** We have observed that $S_N1$ reactions involve the formation of carbocations as intermediates. Further, since carbocations are planar, they can be attacked by the nucleophile in the second (fast) step on either side of the face. Thus if the starting alkyl halide is optically active, the product should be racemic mixture with no optical activity. However, this is rarely observed in practice. Normally, the two enantiomers of the product are not formed in equal amount ; the enantiomer having inverted configuration with respect to the alkyl halide predominates and the second enantiomer of the product is present in lesser amount. Thus the product contains a racemic modification and some amount of the enantiomer having inverted configuration. Hence it can be said that **$S_N1$ reactions proceed with inversion plus partial racemization.** In short, we can say that $S_N1$ reactions proceed both with inversion as well as retention of configuration, number of inverted molecules are always more than the molecules having original configuration. For example, hydrolysis of optically pure (–)-2-bromooctane gives 83% (+)- and 17% (–)-2-octanols, *i.e.* reaction proceeds with 66% net inversion.

$$\text{(–)-2-Bromooctane} \xrightarrow[\text{ethanol}]{H_2O} \text{(+)-2-Octanol (83\%)} + \text{(–)-2-Octanol (17\%)}$$

Net inversion = 66%

Partial but not complete loss of optical activity in $S_N1$ reactions suggests that the carbocation is not completely free of its halide ion counterpart when it is attacked by the nucleophile. Actually ionization of the alkyl halide gives a carbocation halide ion pair. The anion of the leaving group shields one side of the carbocation, and thus the nucleophile attacks the carbocation faster from the side opposite to the leaving group.

Thus more amount of the inverted configuration is formed than that of retained configuration. (The more stable carbocation gives more racemization). Thus note that the products of $S_N1$ reactions are not stereospecific (difference from $S_N2$ products which are stereospecific).

## TEST YOUR UNDERSTANDING - 4.4

1.  (*a*)  Which of the alkyl halide in each of the following pairs will react faster in $S_N1$ reaction ?

    (*i*)   Cyclopentyl iodide or 1-methylcyclopentyl iodide

    (*ii*)  Cyclopentyl bromide or 1-bromo-2, 2-dimethylpropane

    (*iii*) *tert*-Butyl iodide or *tert*-butyl chloride.

    (*b*)  Which of the alkyl halide in each of the following pairs will react faster with sodium iodide in acetone ?

    (*i*)   1-Bromopentane or 3-bromopentane        (*ii*)  1-Chlorohexane or cyclohexyl chloride

    (*iii*) 2-Chloropentane or 2-fluoropentane       (*iv*)  1-Bromodecane or 2-bromopropane

    (*v*)   2-Bromo-2-methylhexane or 2-bromo-5-methylhexane.

2.  In the hydrolysis of 2-bromo-3-methylbutane, the intermediate carbocation rearranges by a hydride shift, but not by a methyl shift, explain.

3.  R-$\alpha$-Phenylethyl chloride, $C_6H_5CHClCH_3$, of specification rotation $-34°$ is treated with dilute aqueous NaOH to give alcohol of $[\alpha]$ $+1.7°$. If the specific rotations of the optically pure (R)-$\alpha$-phenylethyl chloride and (R)-$\alpha$-phenylethyl alcohol are $-109°$ and $-42.3°$ respectively, calculate (*a*) the optical purity of the reactant and product and (*b*) the percentage of inversion and of retention.

4.  Suggest the mechanism whether $S_{N^1}$ or $S_{N^2}$ in the following reactions :

    (*i*)   $CH_3CH_2CH_2X \xrightarrow{\ :Z\ } CH_3CH(Z)CH_3$        (*ii*)  $(CH_3)_2CHCH(X)CH_3 \xrightarrow{\ :Z\ } (CH_3)_2C(Z)CH_2CH_3$

    (*iii*) $(CH_3)_3CCH_2Br \xrightarrow{\ C_2H_5O^-\ } (CH_3)_3CCH_2OC_2H_5$    (*iv*)  $(CH_3)_3CCH_2Br \xrightarrow{\ C_2H_5OH\ } (CH_3)_2\underset{\underset{\displaystyle OC_2H_5}{|}}{C}{-}CH_2CH_3$

5.  Neopentyl halides undergo nucleophilic substitutions very slowly, whatever might be the experimental conditions. Explain.

**$S_N2$ versus $S_N1$ reactions**

| $S_N2$ | $S_N1$ |
|---|---|
| 1. These follow second-order kinetics. | 1. These follow first order kinetics |
| 2. Here the nucleophile attacks on the alkyl halide from back side. | 2. Here the nucleophile attacks on the carbocation which are first formed by heterolysis of the C–X bond. |
| 3. These involve complete stereochemical inversion. | 3. These involve partial racemization. |
| 4. These form unrearranged products. | 4. Rearrange products are formed, where possible. |
| 5. The order of reactivity is $CH_3W > 1° > 2° > 3°$. | 5. Order of reactivity is $3° > 2° > 1° > CH_3W$. |
| 6. These require strong nucleophiles | 6. Weak nucleophiles are OK. |
| 7. Wide variety of solvents are used. | 7. These require good ionising solvent |
| 8. The reaction is stereoselective as well as stereospecific. | 8. The reaction is neither stereoselective nor stereospecific. |

## 4.6.5  Factors Affecting $S_N$ Reactions

However, before going to details of the factors favouring $S_N1$ or $S_N2$ reaction, we must know that the main difference in the two mechanisms lies in the way the nucleophile attacks on substrate. In $S_N2$ mechanism, nucleophile attacks the alkyl halide from back-side of the substrate ; while in $S_N1$, nucleophile attacks on the carbocation, hence here the alkyl halide first undergoes heterolytic cleavage. Thus whichever of these two processes (back-side attack by the nucleophile or heterolysis to form a carbocation) goes faster for a particular alkyl halide determines which mechanism predominates.

$$R-X + :Z \xrightarrow{\text{Solvent}} R-Z + X^-$$

The relative ease of these two processes in turn depends upon nature of substrate (alkyl group as well as leaving group), nature of nucleophile and of course also nature of solvent.

**1.　Nature of alkyl group (R).** The nature of the alkyl group of the substrate exerts a profound effect on the type of mechanism. In alkyl groups, two structural factors are at work.

*(i)　Steric factor.* It largely determines the ease with which a nucleophile can attack the alkyl group from back-side. Larger an alkyl group, more will be difficult for the nucleophile to attack it from back-side.

*(ii)　Accommodation of positive charge.* This factor determines the ease of formation of a carbocation (*i.e.* ease of heterolysis). More is the ability of accommodating positive charge (by delocalization) by a carbocation, more will be the ease of heterolysis.

Thus as we proceed along the simple alkyl series ($CH_3$, 1°, 2° and 3°), the group becomes progressively bulky, steric hindrance increases and hence back side attack becomes more difficult and hence slower, this explains why $S_N2$ mechanism follows the order : $CH_3X < 1° < 2° < 3°$. At the same time, progressive branching in the alkyl group increases ability to accommodate positive charge ; hence heterolysis becomes easier and hence faster. This explains why $S_N1$ mechanism follows the order : $3° > 2° > 1° > CH_3X$.

As mentioned earlier secondary alkyl halides may follow both ($S_N1$ and $S_N2$) or either of the two mechanisms.

Here, we must also consider the reactivity of unsaturated alkyl halides, which are of two types : (*a*) those having unsaturation at α-carbon atom, *viz.* vinyl, alkynyl and aryl halides, and (*b*) those having unsaturation at carbon other than α-, *e.g.* allyl halides.

$$CH_2 = CH—\ddot{\underset{\cdot\cdot}{X}}: \qquad HC \equiv C—\ddot{\underset{\cdot\cdot}{X}}: \qquad \text{[aryl–X]} \qquad CH_2 = CH—CH_2—\ddot{\underset{\cdot\cdot}{X}}:$$

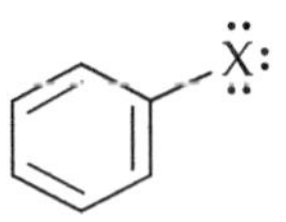

Former are inert towards nucleophilic substitutions because of two factors.

*(i)*　Resonance stabilization of the substrate which results in strengthening of the bond between carbon and halogen.

$$H_2C = CH—\ddot{\underset{\cdot\cdot}{X}}: \quad \longleftrightarrow \quad H_2\overset{\ominus}{C}—CH = \overset{\oplus}{\ddot{X}}:$$

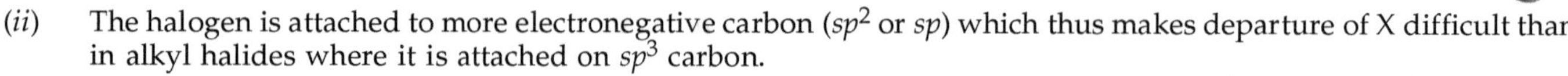

*(ii)* The halogen is attached to more electronegative carbon ($sp^2$ or $sp$) which thus makes departure of X difficult than in alkyl halides where it is attached on $sp^3$ carbon.

On the other hand, allyl halides undergo nucleophilic substitution easily mainly by $S_N1$ mechanism.

$$CH_3CH = CH—CH_2X \longrightarrow [CH_3CH = CH —\overset{+}{C}H_2 \longleftrightarrow CH_3\overset{+}{C}H — CH = CH_2]$$

$$\xrightarrow{OH^-} CH_3CH = CHCH_2OH + CH_3CH(OH)—CH = CH_2$$
$$\text{Normal product } (S_N1) \qquad \text{Rearranged product } (S_N1')$$

**Summary of alkyl, allylic and benzylic halides and $S_N$ reactions :**

*(a)*    *Halides showing mainly $S_N2$ reactions :*

$$CH_3 – X \qquad\qquad R – CH_2 – X \qquad\qquad \underset{\underset{\text{2° alkyl}}{R'}}{R – \overset{|}{\underset{|}{CH}} – X}$$

methyl             1° alkyl             2° alkyl

*(b)*    *Halides showing mainly $S_N^1$ reactions :*

$$R_3C – X \qquad\qquad Ar – \overset{R}{\underset{R'}{\overset{|}{\underset{|}{C}}}} – X \qquad\qquad$$

3° alkyl         3° benzylic         3° allylic

*(c)*    *Halides showing either $S_N^1$ or $S_N^2$ reactions :*

$$Ar – CH_2X \qquad Ar – \underset{R}{\overset{|}{CH}} – X$$

1° benzylic       2° benzylic       1° allylic       2° allylic

2.    **Nature of the leaving group.** The nature of the leaving group has little effect on the type of mechanism. However, it effects the rate of reaction in both $S_N1$ as well as $S_N2$ reactions to same extent. In both cases, leaving group is removed, hence better the leaving group, faster will be the reaction.

Since the leaving group breaks away as a base, it is easier to displace weaker bases as compared to stronger bases. Thus we can say that the less basic the substituent, the more easily it is displaced (by the solvent in $S_N1$ reactions or by an attacking nucleophile in $S_N2$ reactions). This explains why alcohols are resistant to nucleophilic displacement *in non-acidic media* because strongly basic nature of the $OH^-$ group makes it a poor leaving group. However, in presence of acids, the oxygen of the —OH group gets protonated and thus here the leaving group ($H_2O$), being a very weak base displaced easily. Thus alcohols undergo nucleophilic substitutions only in acidic medium. Thus, in general **the weaker the base, the better is the leaving group.** Relative leaving group abilities of the important groups are tabulated below.

**Relative Leaving-Group Abilities**

| Leaving group | Relative rate | Conjugate acid* of leaving group | $K_a$ of conjugate acid |
|---|---|---|---|
| $F^-$ | $10^{-5}$ | HF | $3.5 \times 10^{-4}$ |
| $Cl^-$ | $10^{10}$ | HCl | $10^7$ |
| $Br^-$ | $10^1$ | HBr | $10^9$ |
| $I^-$ | $10^2$ | HI | $10^{10}$ |
| $H_2O$ | $10^1$ | $H_3O^+$ | $55$ |
| $TsO^-$ | $10^5$ | TsOH | $6 \times 10^2$ |
| $CF_3SO_2O^-$ | $10^8$ | $CF_3SO_2OH$ | $10^6$ |

$TsO^-$ is *p*-toluenesulphonate ; their esters are called tosylates ; $CF_3SO_2O^-$ is trifluoromethanesulphonate (esters of the latter are called *triflates*).

---

*    Any species whose conjugate acid has $K_a$ less than 1 cannot be a leaving group in a nucleophilic substitution; *viz.* $OH^-$, $H^-$, $OR^-$, $NH_2^-$, $NR_2^-$.

Since *p*-toluenesulphonates (easily prepared by the reaction of alcohol and *p*-toluenesulphonyl chloride, commonly known as tosyl chloride) are better leaving groups than halides, alkyl halides (chloride, bromide or iodide) can be prepared from alkyl *p*-toluenesulphonates using corresponding NaX as nucleophile.

$$CH_3\underset{\underset{\text{OTs}}{|}}{CH}CH_2CH_3 \;+\; NaBr \;\longrightarrow\; CH_3\underset{\underset{\text{Br}}{|}}{CH}CH_2CH_3 \;+\; NaOTs$$

*sec*-Butyl-*p*-toluene sulphonate    *sec*-Butyl bromide    Sodium *p*-toluenesulphonate

Tosylates undergo nucleophilic substitution ($S_N1$ as well as $S_N2$) in the same way as alkyl halides.

Other good leaving groups are phenoxide ion or 2, 4-dinitrophenoxide ion ; these are weak bases due to dispersal of negative charge on the benzene ring.

*Example 6 :*

**Arrange the following in decreasing order of their leavability.**

$CH_3COO^-, C_6H_5O^-, Cl_3CCOO^-$ **and** $C_6H_5SO_3^-$

*Solution :*

Weaker the base (or stronger the conjugate acid of the base), more will be its leaving capacity. The conjugate acids of the given anions are

$CH_3COOH\ C_6H_5OH$          $Cl_3CCOOH\ C_6H_5SO_3H$

The relative acidic character of the four conjugate acids is

$$C_6H_5SO_3H > Cl_3CCOOH > CH_3COOH > C_6H_5OH$$

Thus the leavability (fugacity) of the four groups is

$$C_6H_5SO_3^- > Cl_3CCOO^- > CH_3COO^- > C_6H_5O^-$$

Alternatively, more the stability of the anion (base), higher is its leavability. Thus

$$C_6H_5-\overset{\overset{O}{\|}}{\underset{\underset{O}{\|}}{S}}-O^- \quad > \quad Cl\!\!\leftarrow\!\!\underset{\underset{Cl}{\downarrow}}{\overset{\overset{Cl}{\uparrow}}{C}}-COO^- \quad > \quad CH_3-\overset{\overset{O}{\|}}{C}-O^- \quad > \quad C_6H_5\overset{-}{O}$$

| Most stable due to three equivalent resonating structures | Stable due to inductive as well as resonance | Two resonating structures are equivalent |
|---|---|---|

# TEST YOUR UNDERSTANDING - 4.5

1.     Give chemical equation showing preparation of octadecyl *p*-toluenesulphonate ; and its reaction with (*a*) potassium acetate and sodium butanethiolate ($CH_3CH_2CH_2CH_2SNa$).

3.     **Nature and concentration of the nucleophile.** Remember that $S_N2$ and $S_N1$ reactions differ in the respect that in the former, nucleophile participates in the rate-determining step, while in $S_N1$ reactions it participates after the rate-determining step. So, nature and concentration of nucleophiles mainly affects $S_N2$ reactions, and it does not play directly any role in $S_N1$ reactions.

In $S_N2$ reactions, a nucleophile transfers its electron pair to carbon of the substrate leading to the formation of transition state. Hence, a stronger nucleophile will react with the substrate faster. Nucleophilic strength or nucleophilicity is a measure of how fast a Lewis base displaces a leaving group from a suitable substrate. By measuring the rate at which various Lewis bases react with methyl iodide in methanol, a list of their nucleophilicity relative to methanol as the standard nucleophile has been compiled.

**Nucleophilicity of some common nucleophiles in water and alcohol**

| Class of nucleophile | Nucleophile | Relative reactivity |
| --- | --- | --- |
| Very good | $R_3P:$, $I^-$, $HS^-$, $RS^-$ | $> 10^5$ |
| Good | $R_2NH$, $HO^-$, $RO^-$, $CN^-$, $N_3^-$ | $10^4$ |
| Fair | $Br^-$, $NH_3$, $Cl^-$, $RCOO^-$ | $10^3$ |
| Weak | $F^-$, $H_2O$, $ROH$ | $1$ |
| Very weak | $RCOOH$ | $10^{-2}$ |

**Trends in nucleophilicity :**

(*i*)     A species with a negative charge is a stronger nucleophile than a similar neutral species. In particular, a base is a stronger nucleophile than its conjugate acid.

$$ {}^-\!\!:\ddot{O}H \; > \; H_2\ddot{O}: \; ; \qquad {}^-\!\!:\ddot{S}H \; > \; H_2\ddot{S}: \; ; \qquad {}^-\!\!:\ddot{N}H_2 \; > \; \ddot{N}H_3 $$

(*ii*)     With increase in electronegativity, nucleophilicity decreases from left to right in the periodic table.

$$ {}^-\!\!:\ddot{O}H \; > \; \ddot{\underset{..}{F}}:^- \; ; \qquad :NH_3 \; > \; H_2\ddot{O}: \; ; \qquad R_3P: \; > \; R_2\ddot{S}: $$

(*iii*)     Nucleophilicity increases down the periodic table, following the increase in size and polarizability.

$$ I^- > Br^- > Cl^- > F^- \; ; \qquad {}^-SeH > {}^-SH > {}^-OH \; ; \qquad R_3P: > R_3N: $$

The rate of $S_N1$ is independent of the nature of the nucleophile (stronger or weaker) because here the nucleophile attacks on the carbocation (a fast step). The net result is that, other things being equal, *a strong nucleophile favours the $S_N2$ reaction, and a weak nucleophile favours the $S_N1$ reaction.*

Thus we can explain that why neopentyl bromide, $Me_3CCH_2Br$ gives unrearranged product ($S_N2$ reaction) with ethoxide ion (a strong nucleophile), but a rearranged product ($S_N1$ mechanism) with $C_2H_5OH$ (a weak nucleophile).

In $S_N2$ reactions, since a nucleophile is involved in the rate determining step, its concentration will directly effect the rate of reaction.

$$ \text{rate} = k[RX][:Z] $$

Hence an increase in the concentration will speed up the reaction and also fraction of the reaction undergoing $S_N2$ reaction. On the other hand, a decrease in $[:Z]$ slows down the $S_N2$ reaction and also the fraction of the reaction undergoing $S_N2$ reaction. The net result is that, other things being equal, *a high concentration of nucleophile favours $S_N2$ reaction, and a low concentration favours the $S_N1$ reaction.*

4.     **Effect of solvent.** Solvents play a dominant and sometimes decisive role in deciding the rate and mechanism of nucleophilic substitution. Change in solvent in a particular reaction may increase or decrease the rate of reaction, even in some cases it may change the mechanism as is evident from following examples.

(*i*)     $$ \underset{(> 91\% \text{ yield})}{C_6H_{13}CN} \; \xleftarrow[< 20 \text{ mts.}]{DMSO} \; CH_3(CH_2)_4CH_2Br + NaCN \; \xrightarrow[> 20 \text{ hrs.}]{aq.\, CH_3OH} \; \underset{(71\% \text{ yield})}{C_6H_{13}CN} $$

It is an example of $S_N2$ reaction.

(*ii*)     $$ CH_3OH \; \xleftarrow[S_N1]{HCOOH/H_2O} \; CH_3Br \; \xrightarrow[S_N2]{H_2O,\, OH^-} \; CH_3OH $$

Although no generalisation can be made, following point should be noted, of course with reservations.

(*a*)     In presence of good ionizing solvents which increases the rate of ionization of the alkyl halide, rate of $S_N2$ reaction decreases while that of $S_N1$ reaction increases.

**Dielectric constants and ionization rates of *t*-butyl chloride in common solvents.**

| Solvent | Dielectric constant | Relative rate of ionization |
|---|---|---|
| Water | 78 | 8000 |
| Methanol | 33 | 1000 |
| Ethanol | 24 | 200 |
| Acetone | 21 | 1 |
| Diethyl ether | 4.3 | 0.001 |
| Hexane | 2.0 | <0.0001 |

(b) Rate of $S_N2$ reactions is fastest in presence of polar aprotic solvents. Aprotic solvents are those polar solvents which do not have —OH group, *viz.* dimethylsulphoxide (DMSO, $Me_2S = O$), N, N-dimethylformamide (DMF, $Me_2NCHO$), acetonitrile ($CH_3CN$) etc.

**Intermolecular versus intramolecular nucleophilic substitution**

A molecule having two functional groups one of which acts as nucleophile and other leaving group can undergo intermolecular or intramolecular nucleophilic substitution. If the two such groups are separated from each other by four or five carbon atoms, intramolecular reaction occurs leading to the formation of five or six membered (*stable*) rings (*intramolecular $S_N$*).

Since three- and four-membered rings are strained (unstable) when the two groups are separated by one, two or three carbon atoms, intermolecular nucleophilic substitution takes place.

## 4.6.6  Nucleophilic Substitution in Acyl Compounds

Acyl compounds (compounds containing acyl group, $R—\overset{\overset{\textstyle O}{\|}}{C}—$ *viz.* carboxylic acids and their derivatives namely acid chlorides, anhydrides, amides and esters) undergo nucleophilic substitution in which —OH, —Cl, —OCOR, —$NH_2$ or —OR' is replaced by some other basic group. Substitution at acyl carbon (unsaturated) takes place much more readily than at alkyl carbon (saturated) atom. High reactivity of acyl carbon towards nucleophilic substitution is due to electronic and steric factors.

(a) Tendency of oxygen to acquire electrons even at the expense of gaining negative charge.

(b) Relatively unhindered transition state is formed ; in acyl substitution a tetrahedral intermediate (a stable situation) is formed from trigonal reactant, while in alkyl substitution a transition state having pentavalent carbon (an unstable situation) is formed from tetrahedral reactant.

The nucleophilic acyl substitution involves two steps.

**First step :**

Transition state
(Becoming tetrahedral)

Intermediate
(Tetrahedral)

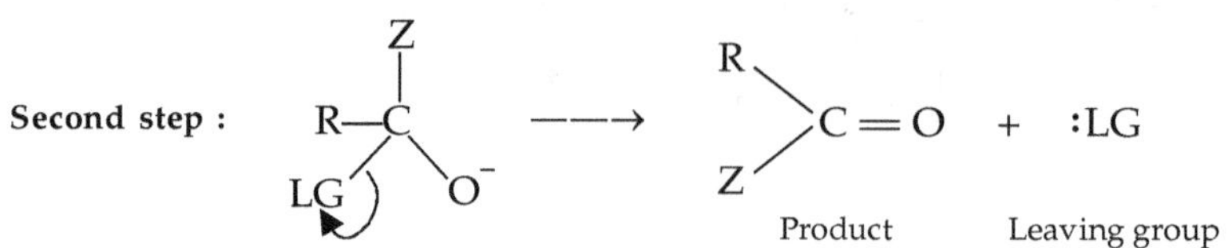

**Second step :** $R{-}C\overset{Z}{\underset{\underset{O^-}{LG}}{|}} \longrightarrow \overset{R}{\underset{Z}{>}}C{=}O \; + \; :LG$

Product       Leaving group

(*i*)    Generally, the overall rate is affected by the rate of both steps, but the first step is more important.

(*ii*)    The first step is favoured by the presence of electron withdrawl group on R which stabilizes the developing negative charge, and it is hindered by the presence of bulky groups which become crowded together in the transition state.

(*iii*)    The second step depends on the basicity of the leaving group (:LG) ; the weaker the base the better the leaving group. For acid chlorides, acid anhydrides, esters and amides, :LG is respectively

$$Cl^- \qquad\qquad {}^-OCOR \qquad\qquad {}^-OR \qquad\qquad {}^-NH_2$$

**Basic character**     Very weak       Moderately weak       Strong bases

Increasing basic character $\longrightarrow$
Decreasing leaving property

Thus acids chlorides undergo nucleophilic substitution most easily, while amides with most difficulty.

Relation between basicity and leaving capacity of the group also explains why aldehydes and ketones undergo nucleophilic addition rather than nucleophilic substitution, although first step is similar to that in acyl nucleophilic substitution.

$$R{-}C\overset{O}{\underset{LG}{\big<}} \xrightarrow{\;:Z\;} R{-}\overset{\overset{O^-}{|}}{\underset{\underset{\boxed{LG}}{|}}{C}}{-}Z \longrightarrow R{-}C\overset{O}{\underset{Z}{\big<}} + :LG \qquad \textbf{(Substitution)}$$

**Acyl compounds**

$$R{-}C\overset{O}{\underset{R'}{\big<}} \xrightarrow{\;:Z\;} R{-}\overset{\overset{O^-}{|}}{\underset{\underset{\boxed{R'}}{|}}{C}}{-}Z \xrightarrow{\;H^+\;} R{-}\overset{\overset{OH}{|}}{\underset{\underset{R'}{|}}{C}}{-}Z \qquad \textbf{(Addition)}$$

**Aldehydes (when R' = H)**
**or ketones**

Note that if aldehydes and ketones, undergo substitution, the leaving group would have been hydride ion (:H⁻) or alkyde ion (: R'⁻) which, as we know, are the strongest bases of all, hence these are most difficult to be removed and instead aldehydes and ketones undergo addition reactions easily.

(*iv*)    Nucleophilic acyl substitution neither involves the formation of carbocations, as in $S_N1$ reactions of alkyl halides nor pentavalent transition state as in $S_N2$ reactions of alkyl halides.

Acyl nucleophilic substitution takes place more easily in presence of acid, because here $H^+$ becomes attached to carbonyl oxygen making the carbonyl grup more electrophilic and thus more susceptible to the nucleophilic attack.

$$\overset{R}{\underset{LG}{>}}C{=}O \xrightarrow{\;H^+\;} \overset{R}{\underset{LG}{>}}C{=}\overset{+}{O}H \longrightarrow R{-}\overset{\overset{Z}{|}}{\underset{\underset{LG}{|}\;\;OH}{C}} \longrightarrow \overset{R}{\underset{Z}{>}}C{=}O + H:LG$$

Undergoes nucleophilic
attack more readily, even
by weak nucleophiles

Thus we can explain why acid derivatives are hydrolysed more readily in presence of acids than in neutral medium; easy hydrolysis of acid derivatives in presence of alkali than in neutral medium is due to strong nucleophile (⁻OH), and discussed in **chapter on acid derivatives.**

### 4.6.7  Electrophilic Substitution Reactions ($S_E$)

These reactions are mainly found in aromatic compounds. For details, consult Ch. 7.

*Example 7 :*

**Observe the following two reactions and answer the questions mentioned below :**

(i) 
$$\underset{\underset{H}{|}}{\overset{\overset{C_3H_7}{|}}{C_2H_5\!-\!\!\!-\!\!\!-OH}} \xrightarrow{K} \underset{\underset{H}{|}}{\overset{\overset{C_3H_7}{|}}{C_2H_5\!-\!\!\!-\!\!\!-OK}} \xrightarrow{CH_3OTs} \text{Product}$$

(ii) 
$$\underset{\underset{H}{|}}{\overset{\overset{C_3H_7}{|}}{C_2H_5\!-\!\!\!-\!\!\!-OH}} \xrightarrow{TsCl} \underset{\underset{H}{|}}{\overset{\overset{C_3H_7}{|}}{C_2H_5\!-\!\!\!-\!\!\!-OTs}} \xrightarrow{CH_3OK} \text{Product}$$

(a)  Pick up the nucleophile in both reactions.

(b)  Write the structure of the product in the two reactions and assign their R, S configurations.

(c)  Is there any relation between the two products, if yes then mention it.

*Solution :*

(a)  The nucleophile in the two reactions are

$$\underset{\underset{H}{|}}{\overset{\overset{C_3H_7}{|}}{C_2H_5\!-\!\!\!-\!\!\!-\overset{-}{O}\overset{+}{K}}} \text{ in (i); and } CH_3O^-K^+ \text{ in (ii).}$$

(b)  In *(i)*, the chiral carbon is in the nucleophile and none of its bonds are cleaved, leading to the same configuration as reactant. However, in *(ii)* the $CH_3O^-$ attacks the chiral carbon of the substrate from back side leading to inversion in configuration.

(c) 

$$\underset{\underset{H}{|}}{\overset{\overset{C_3H_7}{|}}{\underset{3}{C_2H_5}\!-\!\!\!-\!\!\!-\underset{1}{OCH_3}}} \qquad \underset{\underset{H}{|}}{\overset{\overset{C_3H_7}{|}}{\underset{1}{CH_3O}\!-\!\!\!-\!\!\!-\underset{}{C_2H_5}}}$$

Product from *(i)*  —  S     Product from *(ii)*  —  R

The two products are enantiomers.

## TEST YOUR UNDERSTANDING - 4.6

1.  Among the following pairs, pick up the species that undergo nucleophilic substitution more easily

   (i)  $CH_3COCl$ and $CH_3Cl$     (ii)  $CH_3CONH_2$ and $CH_3NH_2$     (iii)  $CH_3COOC_2H_5$ and $CH_3OC_2H_5$

2. For each of the following pairs, pick up the compound (I or II) which undergoes $S_N2$ reaction more easily than the other.

|  | **I** | **II** |
|---|---|---|
| (a) | $CH_3Cl + OH^-$ | $CH_3Br + OH^-$ |
| (b) | $CH_3CH_2Cl + H_2O$ | $CH_3CH_2Cl + OH^-$ |
| (c) | $CH_3CH_2Br + CH_3S^-$ | $CH_3CH_2Br + CH_3O^-$ |

(d)    $CH_3CH = CH\,CH - Br$          $CH_3CH = C\,Br$

                 $|$                            $|$

                 $CH_3$                     $CH_3$

---

## 4.7   Mechanism of Addition Reactions

Like substitution reactions, addition reactions may be initiated by electrophiles, nucleophiles or free radicals. Hence addition reactions may also be of three types, *viz.* electrophilic addition reactions, nucleophilic addition reactions and free radical addition reactions.

$$\text{>C=C<} + E^+ \longrightarrow \text{>C}^+\text{—C<}_E \xrightarrow{Y^-} \overset{Y}{\underset{E}{\text{>C—C<}}} \quad \text{(Electrophilic)}$$

$$\text{>C=C<} + Nu^- \longrightarrow \overset{-}{\text{>C—C<}}_{Nu} \xrightarrow{X^+} \underset{Y}{\text{>C—C<}} \quad \text{(Nucleophilic)}$$

$$\text{>C=C<} + X^\bullet \longrightarrow \underset{X}{\text{>C—C<}} \xrightarrow{X:Y} \overset{Y}{\underset{X}{\text{>C—C<}}} + X^\bullet \quad \text{(Free-radical)}$$

### 4.7.1   Mechanism of Electrophilic Addition

Since a multiple bonded carbon atom can readily supply the comparatively loosely held $\pi$ electrons to the electrophile, *electrophilic additions are characteristic reactions of alkenes and alkynes.* Moreover, $\pi$ electron cloud tends to shield the molecule from attack by nucleophiles. The general mechanism given above for electrophilic addition is applicable for addition of protic acids, *viz.* HCl, HBr, HI, $H_2SO_4$ and $H_3O^+$ (hydration in presence of acid). Let us examplify it by addition of HCl on propene.

**First step :**    $CH_3{-}CH = CH_2 + H{-}Cl \xrightarrow{\text{slow}}$

                $\longrightarrow CH_3{-}\overset{+}{C}H{-}CH_3 + Cl^-$   2° cation (more stable)

                $\times\!\!\longrightarrow CH_3{-}CH_2{-}\overset{+}{C}H_2 + Cl^-$   1° cation (less stable)

**Second step :**    $CH_3{-}\overset{+}{C}H{-}CH_3 + Cl^- \longrightarrow CH_3{-}\overset{\displaystyle Cl}{\overset{|}{C}H}{-}CH_3$

                                      Isopropyl chloride

Order of reactivity among HX is :        HI > HBr > HCl > HF

Such reactions (as that of addition of HX on propene) which can produce two or more isomers, but gives one of them in greater amount than the other, are called **regioselective**, a reaction which is 100 percent regioselective is termed **regiospecific.** For example,

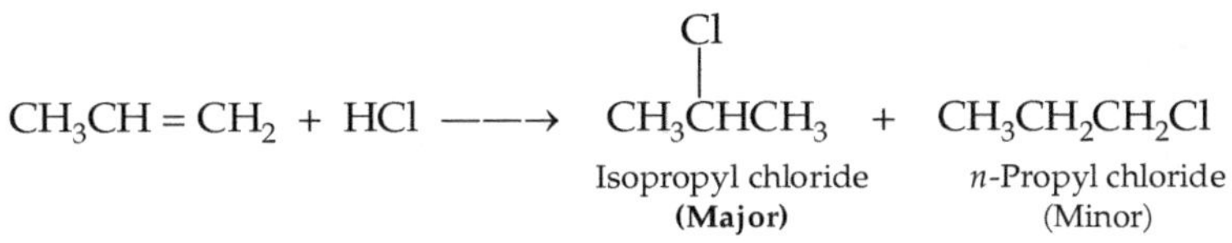

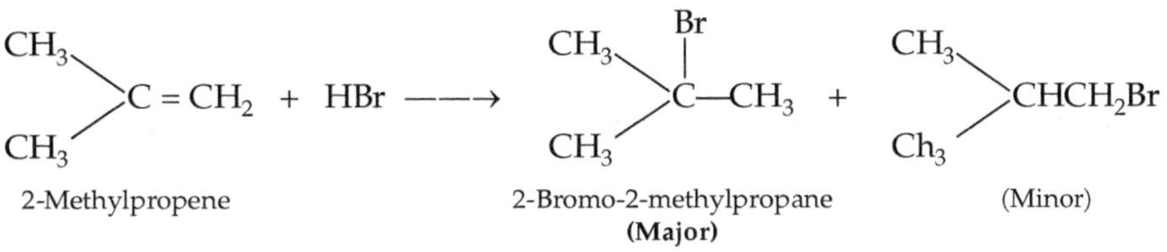

$$CH_3CH=CH_2 + HCl \longrightarrow \underset{\substack{\text{Isopropyl chloride}\\\textbf{(Major)}}}{CH_3\overset{\overset{\displaystyle Cl}{|}}{C}HCH_3} + \underset{\substack{n\text{-Propyl chloride}\\\text{(Minor)}}}{CH_3CH_2CH_2Cl}$$

$$\underset{\text{2-Methylpropene}}{\overset{CH_3}{\underset{CH_3}{>}}C=CH_2} + HBr \longrightarrow \underset{\substack{\text{2-Bromo-2-methylpropane}\\\textbf{(Major)}}}{\overset{CH_3}{\underset{CH_3}{>}}\overset{\overset{\displaystyle Br}{|}}{C}-CH_3} + \underset{\text{(Minor)}}{\overset{CH_3}{\underset{Ch_3}{>}}CHCH_2Br}$$

In such cases, *i.e.* when an unsymmetrical reagent adds on an unsymmetrical alkene, major product is given by **Markownikov's rule** *according to which the negative part of the reagent adds on that carbon atom which has minimum number of hydrogen atom(s).* Alternatively, the compound corresponding to the more stable carbocation is the major product, viz.

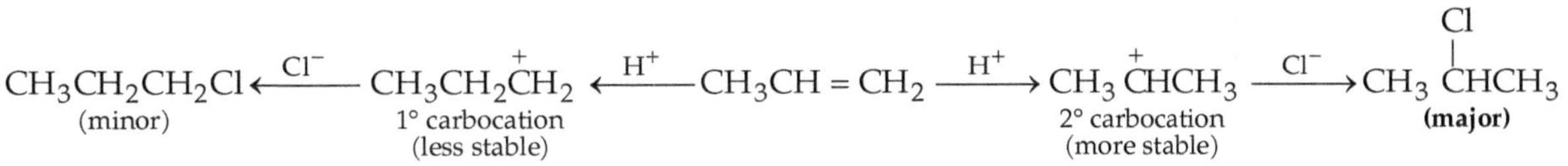

$$\underset{\text{(minor)}}{CH_3CH_2CH_2Cl} \xleftarrow{Cl^-} \underset{\substack{1°\text{ carbocation}\\(\text{less stable})}}{CH_3CH_2\overset{+}{C}H_2} \xleftarrow{H^+} CH_3CH=CH_2 \xrightarrow{H^+} \underset{\substack{2°\text{ carbocation}\\(\text{more stable})}}{CH_3\overset{+}{C}HCH_3} \xrightarrow{Cl^-} \underset{\textbf{(major)}}{CH_3\overset{\overset{\displaystyle Cl}{|}}{C}HCH_3}$$

Since carbocations are formed as intermediate in the above electrophilic addition reactions, such reactions are liable to form rearranged product, where possible, by the 1,2-hydride, 1,2-methyl or 1,2-phenyl shift. Such shifts are possible only when a less stable carbocation is changed to more stable (3° > 2° > 1°). The preference of shifts follow the order

$$\text{1,2-phenyl} > \text{1,2-hydride} > \text{1,2-methyl}$$

For example,

(i)　　$(CH_3)_2CHCH=CH_2 \xrightarrow{H^+} (CH_3)_2C\overset{+}{C}HCH_3 \xrightarrow[\text{shift}]{\text{1,2-hydride}} (CH_3)_2\overset{+}{C}CH_2CH_3$

2° carbocation　　　　　　　3° carbocation (more stable)

↓ $Br^-$　　　　　　　　↓ $Br^-$

$\underset{\text{(minor)}}{(CH_3)_2CH\overset{\overset{\displaystyle Br}{|}}{C}HCH_3}$　　　　$\underset{\text{(major)}}{(CH_3)_2\overset{\overset{\displaystyle Br}{|}}{C}CH_2CH_3}$

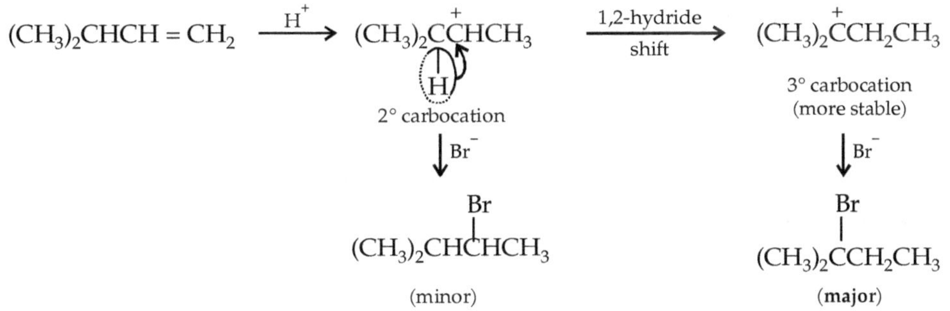

(ii)　　$\underset{\underset{\displaystyle C_6H_5}{|}}{\overset{\overset{\displaystyle CH_3}{|}}{CH_3-C}-CH=CH_2} \xrightarrow{H^+} \underset{C_6H_5}{\overset{\overset{\displaystyle CH_3}{|}}{CH_3-C}-\overset{+}{C}HCH_3} \xrightarrow[\text{shift}]{\text{1,2-phenyl}} \underset{\underset{\displaystyle C_6H_5}{|}}{\overset{\overset{\displaystyle CH_3}{|}}{CH_3-\underset{+}{C}}-CHCH_3}$

2° carbocation　　　　　　　3° carbocation

↓ $Br^-$　　　　　　　　↓ $Br^-$

$\underset{\underset{\displaystyle C_6H_5}{|}}{\underset{\text{(minor)}}{\overset{\overset{\displaystyle CH_3}{|}}{CH_3-C}-CHBrCH_3}}$　　　　$\underset{\underset{\displaystyle Br\ \ C_6H_5}{|\ \ \ |}}{\underset{\text{(major)}}{\overset{\overset{\displaystyle CH_3}{|}}{CH_3-C}-CHCH_3}}$

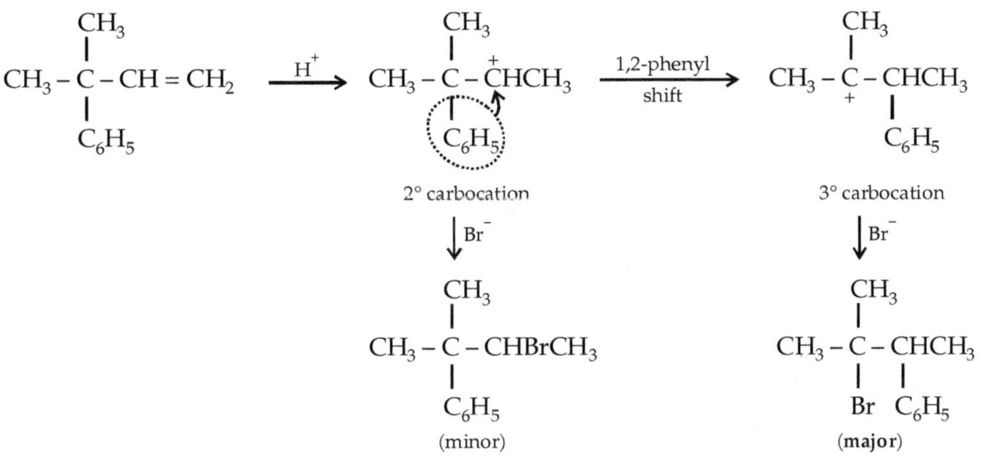

*Example 8 :*
Which compound of each pair is more reactive toward reaction given against each.

(a)    [structure] and [structure] **(addition of HBr)**      (b)    [structure] and [structure] **(addition of HCl)**

(c)    [structure] and [structure] $C_6H_5$ **(addition of HCl)**      (d)    [structure with $CH_3$] and [structure with $C(CH_3)_3$] **(nitration)**

*Solution :*
The first three reactions are examples of electrophilic addition, so higher the stability of the carbocation greater will be its reactivity towards given reagents.

(a)    [structure] $<$ [structure]

    2° carbocation     2° allylic carbocation
                (more stable)

(b)    [structure] $<$ [structure]

    2° carbocation     3° carbocation
                more stable

(c)    [structure] $<$ [structure] $C_6H_5$

    2° carbocation     2° benzyl carbocation
                (more stable)

(d)    Here the two effects (inductive and hyperconjugation) operate in opposite directions. Since hyperconjugation dominate over inductive effect, so nitration (electrophilic substitution) will be governed by hyperconjugation, hence toluene will undergo nitration faster than *ter*-butylbenzene.

$$H-\overset{\overset{\displaystyle H}{|}}{C}-H \qquad CH_3-\overset{\overset{\displaystyle CH_3}{|}}{C}-CH_3$$

    Three hyperconjugative H's      Zero hyperconjugative H

*Example 9 :*
**Give mechanism for the following reactions :**
(i)    $(CH_3)_3\,CCH = CH_2 + HBr$          (ii)   $CH_3CH = CHCH = CHCH_3 + HBr$

*Solution :*

(i)   [mechanism] $CH_3-\overset{CH_3}{\underset{CH_3}{C}}-CH=CH_2 \xrightarrow{H^+} CH_3-\overset{CH_3}{C}-\overset{+}{C}H-CH_3$ (2° carbocation, $CH_3$ shift) $\xrightarrow[\text{shift}]{1,\,2\text{-methyl}} CH_3-\overset{+}{\underset{CH_3}{C}}-CH-CH_3$ (3° carbocation) $\xrightarrow{Br^-} CH_3-\overset{CH_3}{C}-CHCH_3$ (Br, $CH_3$)

2-Bromo-2, 3-dimethylbutane

(ii)   $CH_3CH=CHCH=CHCH_3 \xrightarrow{H^+} \left[ CH_3CH=CH-\overset{+}{C}H-CH_2CH_3 \leftrightarrow CH_3\overset{+}{C}H-CH=CHCH_2CH_3 \right]$

                 2° allylic carbocation               2° allylic carbocation

$\xrightarrow{Br^-} CH_3CH=CH-\overset{\overset{\displaystyle Br}{|}}{C}H-CH_2CH_3 + CH_3\overset{\overset{\displaystyle Br}{|}}{C}H-CH=CHCH_2CH_3$

       4-bromo-2-hexene             2-bromo-3-hexene

**Stereochemistry of Addition of HX on Alkenes**

(i)    When a chiral centre is created due to addition of HX on alkenes, having no chiral carbon, a racemic mixture of the product is formed, because the intermediate is $sp^2$ hybridised carbocation (or $sp^2$ hybridised free radical) either of which is liable to be attacked by the $X^-$ ion (or $X^{\bullet}$) either from above the plane or below the plane.

$$\underset{CH=CH_2}{\overset{CH_2CH_3}{|}} \ +\ HBr \ \longrightarrow\ H\underset{CH_3}{\overset{CH_2CH_3}{\underset{|}{\overset{|}{-\!\!\!-\!\!\!-}}}}Br \ +\ Br\underset{CH_3}{\overset{CH_2CH_3}{\underset{|}{\overset{|}{-\!\!\!-\!\!\!-}}}}H$$

(ii)    In case the alkene has a chirality centre and the addition reaction results in another chiral centre, a pair of diastereomers will be formed.

$$C_2H_5\overset{CH_3}{\underset{CH=CH_2}{-\!\!|\!\!-}}H \xrightarrow{\ HBr\ } C_2H_5\overset{CH_3}{\underset{CH_3}{-\!\!|\!\!-}}\!\!\begin{matrix}H\\Br\end{matrix} \ +\ C_2H_5\overset{CH_3}{\underset{CH_3}{-\!\!|\!\!-}}\!\!\begin{matrix}H\\H\end{matrix}$$

diastereomeric pair

However, the two diastereomers will be formed in unequal amounts because one face of the intermediate carbocation will be more sterically hindered and hence less available for the $Br^-$ ion than the other which is less sterically hindered.

(iii)    For the stereochemistry of the addition reactions on the alkene having no chiral centre but gives two chiral centres, consult **Chemical Properties of Alkenes**.

      **Addition of halogens (*e.g.* Br$_2$) on alkenes** is somewhat different from the above general mechanism of electrophilic addition. Here, again the first step involves the formation of a cation, a cyclic bromonium ion*, but not a carbocation. Note that here also bromine is transferred as positive bromine (electrophile), *i.e.* without a pair of electrons which are left behind on the second bromine atom released as bromide ion. In the second step, the cyclic bromonium ion is attacked by the available nucleophile which may be $Br^-$ or any other species added from outside to form the final product(s).

**First step :**

$$Br\!-\!Br \ +\ \ \rangle C = C\langle \ \longrightarrow\ Br^- \ +\ \rangle\overset{\overset{+}{Br}}{\underset{}{C\!-\!C}}\langle$$

A bromonium ion*

**Second step :**

$$\rangle\overset{\overset{+}{Br}}{C\!-\!C}\langle \ +\ Br^- \ \longrightarrow\ \rangle\overset{Br}{\underset{Br}{C\!-\!C}}\langle$$

*Or*

$$\rangle\overset{\overset{+}{Br}}{C\!-\!C}\langle \ +\ H_2O \ \longrightarrow\ \rangle\overset{\overset{+}{O}H_2}{\underset{Br}{C\!-\!C}}\langle \xrightarrow{\ -H^+\ } \rangle\overset{OH}{\underset{Br}{C\!-\!C}}\langle$$

(if aq. Br$_2$ is used)

---

*    In cyclic bromonium ion, all of its atoms have octet of electrons, while carbon has only six electrons in the carbocation, $BrCH_2-\overset{+}{C}H_2$.

$$BrCH_2-\overset{+}{C}H_2 \xleftarrow{\ Br^+\ } CH_2 = CH_2 \xrightarrow{\ Br^+\ } H_2\overset{\overset{+}{Br}}{C\!-\!C}H_2$$

This is the same reaction which involves the formation of halohydrins (addition of $OH^-$ and $Br^+$ parts of $\overset{-\delta\ \ +\delta}{HOBr}$ used as $(H_2O + Br_2)$.

      Addition of halogens on alkenes follows the order : $F_2 > Cl_2 > Br_2 > I_2$. However, fluorine is so reactive that it not only adds to the double bond but also replaces all the hydrogens with fluorine. On the other hand, iodine adds slowly to alkenes at low temperature and further the di-iodides, being unstable due to large size of iodine present on adjacent carbon atoms, decompose back to give alkene and iodine at room temperature. Inert solvents like $CCl_4$ and $CH_2Cl_2$ are used for halogen addition because these solvents dissolve both halogens as well as alkenes.

### Special features of halogen addition

Addition of two bromine (in case of $Br_2$) or Br and OH (in case of $Br_2 + H_2O$) takes place in *anti*-manner proving the formation of cyclic bromonium ion. Thus addition of bromine on *cis*-2-butene gives only *racemic*-2, 3-dibromobutane, while *trans*-2-butene gives only *meso*-2, 3-dibromobutane. Thus addition of bromine to alkenes is both *stereospecific* as well as *stereoselective*.

cis-2-Butene

I
cis-Bromonium ion

II

III
II and III are enantiomers
(*rac*-2, 3-Dibromobutane)

     Addition of bromine to *cis*-2-butene *via* a cyclic bromonium ion. Opposite-side attacks [(a) and (b)] are equally likely, and give enantiomers in equal amounts.

trans-2-Butene

IV
trans-Bromonium ion

V

VI
V *and* VI *are same*
(*meso*-2, 3-Dibromobutane)

     Addition of bromine to *trans*-2- butene via a cyclic bromonium ion. Opposite-side attacks [(c) and (d)] give the same product.

A reaction in which stereoisomeric starting molecules gives stereoisomeric products is called **stereospecific reaction.** Terms like *syn* addition, *anti* elimination and inversion of configuration describe stereospecific reactions. On the other hand, a reaction in which a single starting material can form two or more stereoisomeric products but one of them predominates is called a **stereoselective reaction.** Terms such as addition to the less hindered side describe stereoselectivity.

---

*Example 10 :*

**Write the major product in each of the following reactions :**

**(a)** 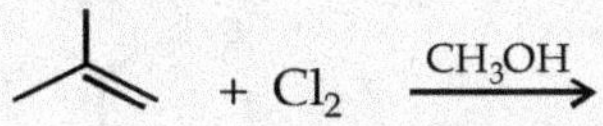 (isobutylene) + $Cl_2$ $\xrightarrow{CH_3OH}$

**(b)** 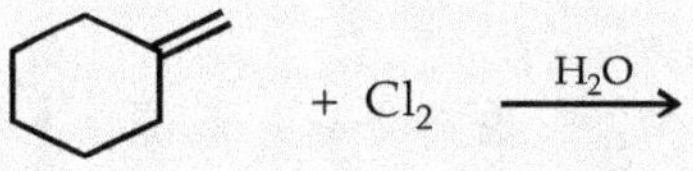 (methylenecyclohexane) + $Cl_2$ $\xrightarrow{H_2O}$

**(c)** 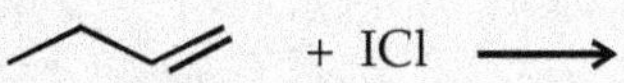 (1-butene) + ICl ⟶

**(d)**  (1-butene) + $Br_2$ $\xrightarrow{H_2O}$

**(e)** 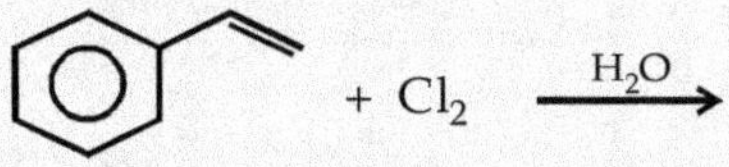 (styrene) + $Cl_2$ $\xrightarrow{H_2O}$

**(f)** 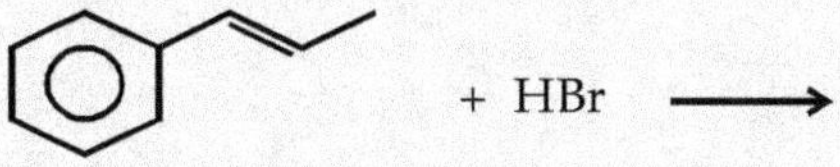 (β-methylstyrene) + HBr ⟶

**(g)** 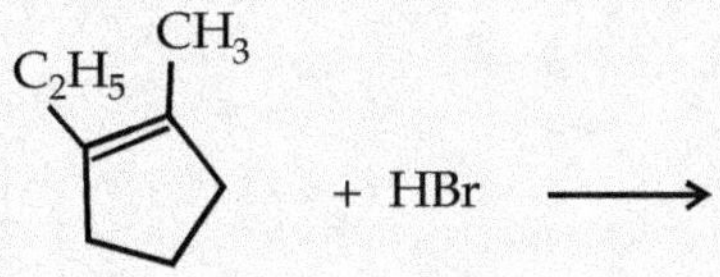 (1-ethyl-2-methylcyclopentene) + HBr ⟶

*Solution :*

**(a)** 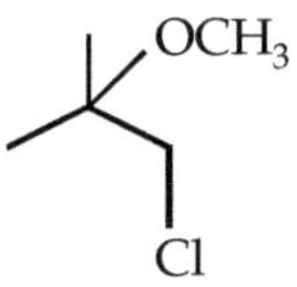 1-chloro-2-methoxy-2-methylpropane

**(b)** 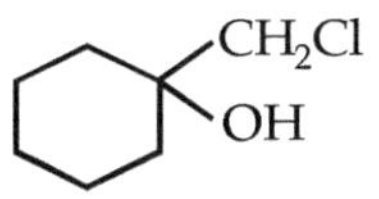 1-(chloromethyl)cyclohexan-1-ol

**(c)** 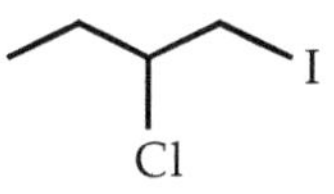 2-chloro-1-iodobutane

**(d)** 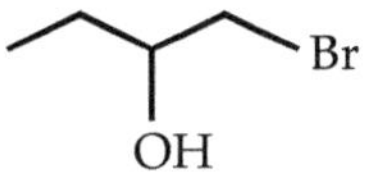 1-bromo-2-butanol

**(e)** 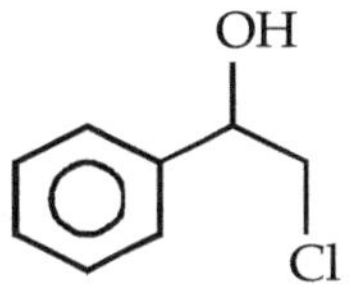 2-chloro-1-phenylethanol

**(f)** 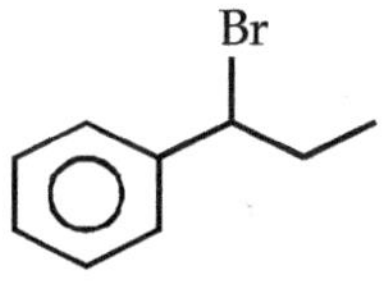 (1-bromopropyl)benzene *(Benzylic carbocation as intermediate)*

**(g)** 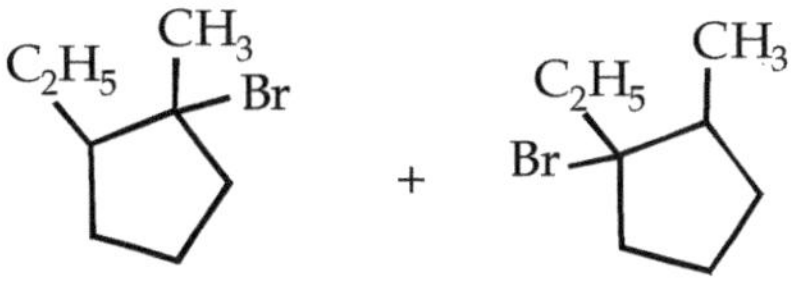 (mixture of cis/trans 1-bromo-2-ethyl-1-methyl... products) +

---

*Example 11 :*

**Give the stereochemistry of the product(s) formed in each of the following reaction :**

**(a)** 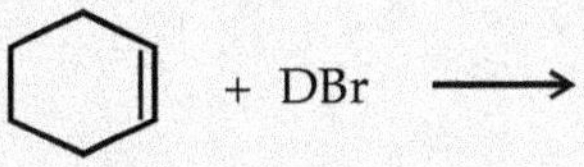 (cyclohexene) + DBr ⟶

**(b)** 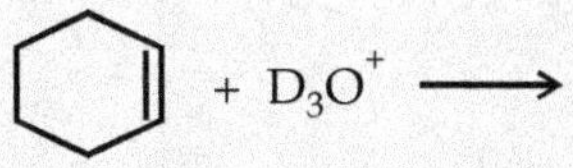 (cyclohexene) + $D_3O^+$ ⟶

**(c)** (cyclopentene) + $Cl_2$ ⟶

**(d)** (1-methylcyclohexene) + HBr ⟶

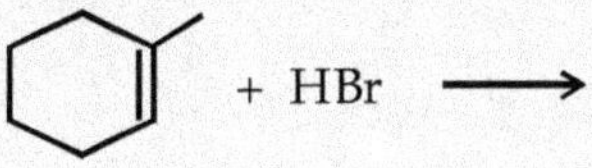

**(e)** 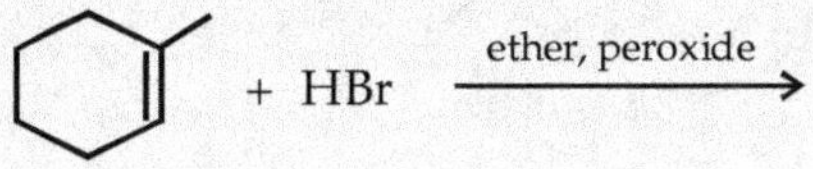 (1-methylcyclohexene) + HBr $\xrightarrow{\text{ether, peroxide}}$

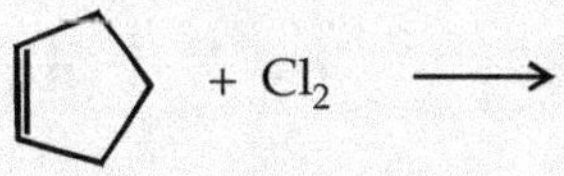

*Solution :*

(a) 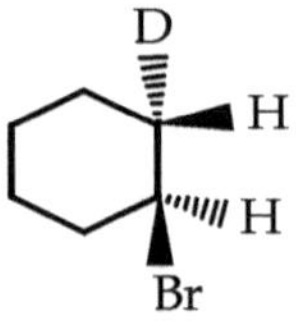  [structure: cyclohexane with D, H, H, Br]  + enantiomer

(b) 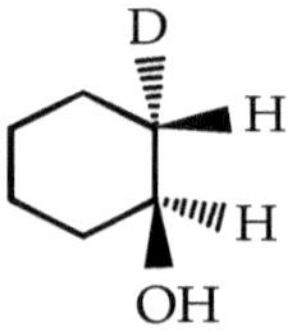  [structure: cyclohexane with D, H, H, OH]  + enantiomer

(c) 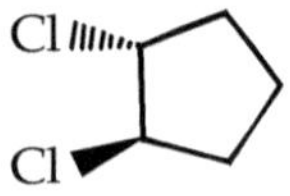  [structure: cyclopentane with Cl, Cl]  + enantiomer

(d) 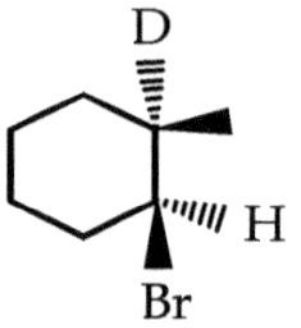  [structure: cyclohexane with D, H, Br]  + enantiomer

(e) 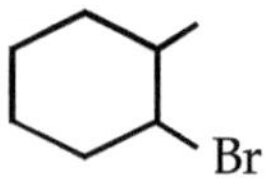  [structure: cyclohexane with CH₃, Br]

---

*Example 12 :*

**Propose mechanism for the following reactions :**

(a) 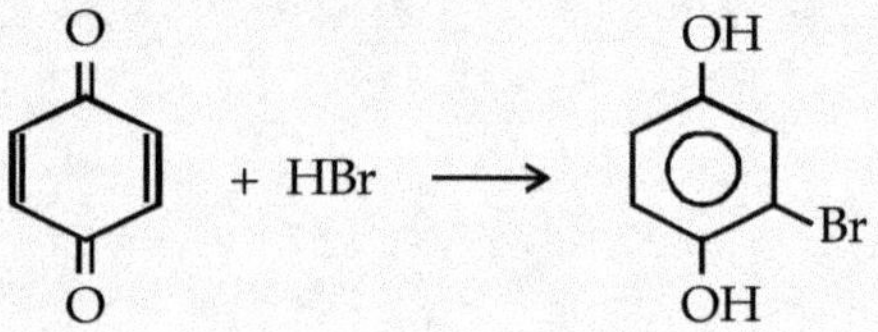  [benzoquinone] + HBr ⟶ [bromohydroquinone]

(b) 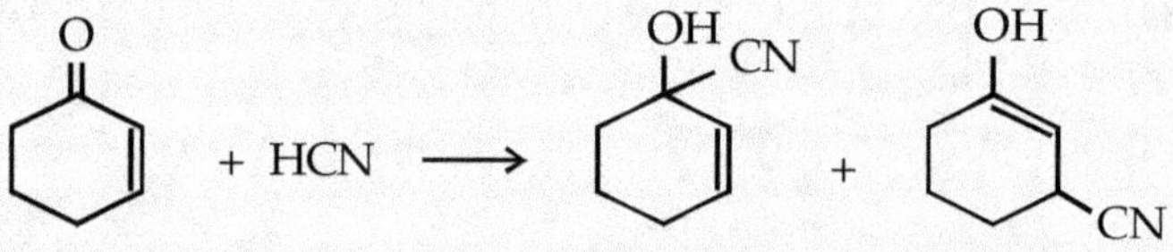  [cyclohexenone] + HCN ⟶ [1,2-addition product OH CN] + [1,4-addition product OH CN]

(c)  $CH_3 - \overset{O}{\underset{\|}{C}} - CH_3$  $\xrightarrow{H_2O^{18}}$  $CH_3 - \overset{O^{18}}{\underset{\|}{C}} - CH_3$

*Solution :*

(a) 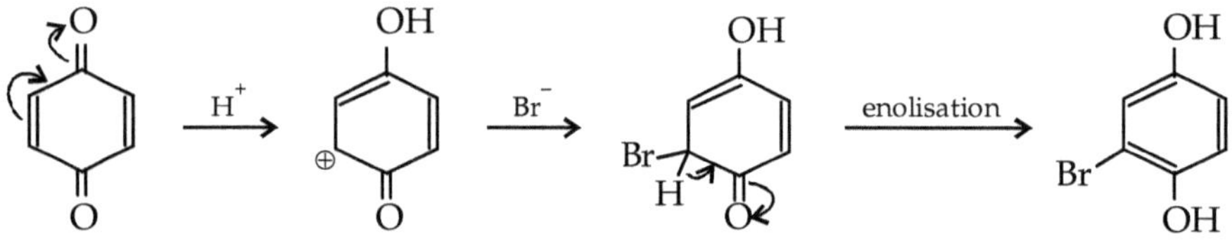  [mechanism: benzoquinone $\xrightarrow{H^+}$ protonated $\xrightarrow{Br^-}$ intermediate $\xrightarrow{\text{enolisation}}$ bromohydroquinone]

(b) 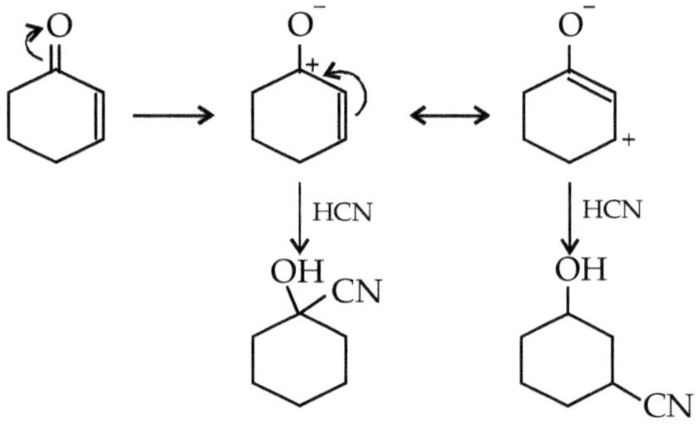  [mechanism: cyclohexenone ⟶ enolate resonance structures]

   1,2-addition (via HCN) → OH, CN product

   1,4-addition (via HCN) → OH, CN product

   1,2-addition          1,4-addition

(c) 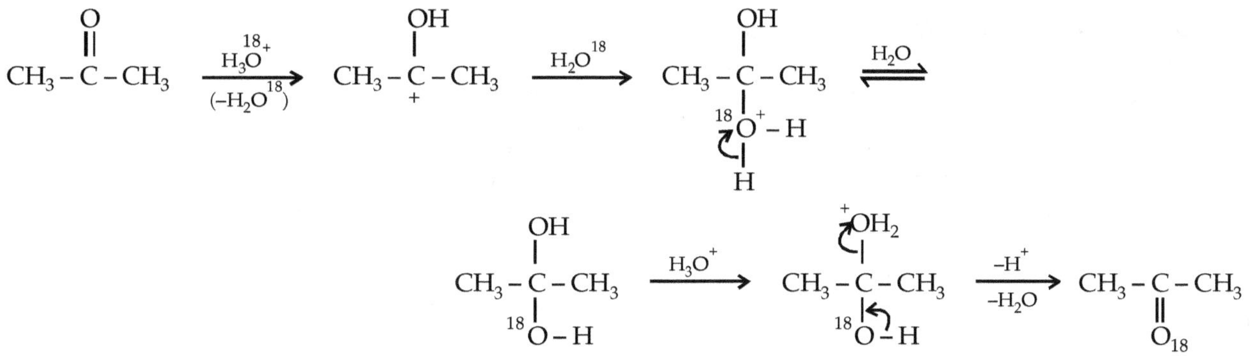 
$$CH_3-\overset{\overset{O}{\|}}{C}-CH_3 \xrightarrow[(-H_2O^{18})]{H_3O^{18+}} CH_3-\overset{\overset{OH}{|}}{\underset{+}{C}}-CH_3 \xrightarrow{H_2O^{18}} CH_3-\overset{\overset{OH}{|}}{\underset{\overset{+}{\underset{|}{{}^{18}O-H}}{|}}{C}}-CH_3 \underset{H}{\rightleftharpoons}$$

$$CH_3-\overset{\overset{OH}{|}}{\underset{\overset{18}{O-H}}{C}}-CH_3 \xrightarrow{H_3O^+} CH_3-\overset{\overset{+OH_2}{|}}{\underset{\overset{18}{O-H}}{C}}-CH_3 \xrightarrow[-H_2O]{-H^+} CH_3-\overset{\overset{}{\|}}{\underset{O_{18}}{C}}-CH_3$$

---

*Example 13 :*

Give the addition product for each of the following reactions with the stereochemistry of the product.

**(a)**   *cis*-3-Heptene + Br$_2$ $\longrightarrow$  

**(b)**   3-Methyl-3-hexene + HBr $\longrightarrow$

**(c)** 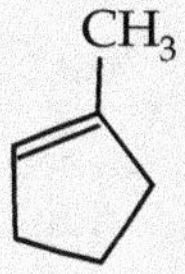   (1-methylcyclopentene) + HBr $\longrightarrow$

*Solution :*

**(a)**   $CH_3CH_2CH = CHCH_2CH_2CH_3 + Br_2 \longrightarrow CH_3CH_2\overset{\overset{Br}{|}}{CH}\overset{*}{\underset{\underset{Br}{|}}{CH}}CH_2CH_2CH_3$

Here although two chiral centres are created, only two isomers (one enantiomeric pair) will be formed because the cyclic bromonium ion is liable to be attacked by the Br$^-$ only from the opposite side, i.e. only *anti* addition (not *syn* addition) is possible.

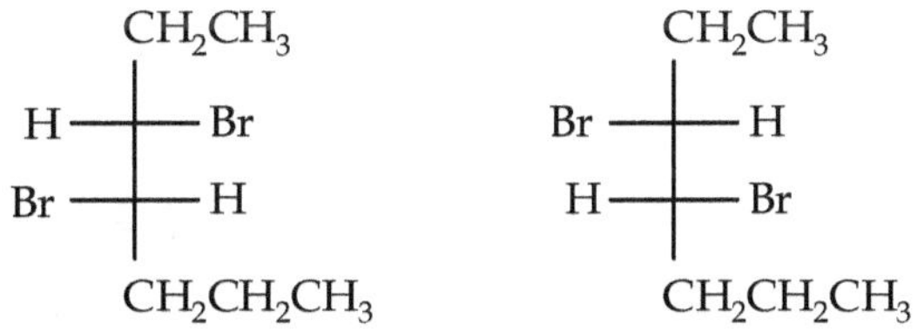

| | CH$_2$CH$_3$ | | | CH$_2$CH$_3$ | |
|---|:---:|---|---|:---:|---|
| H— | \| | —Br | Br— | \| | —H |
| Br— | \| | —H | H— | \| | —Br |
| | CH$_2$CH$_2$CH$_3$ | | | CH$_2$CH$_2$CH$_3$ | |

**(b)** 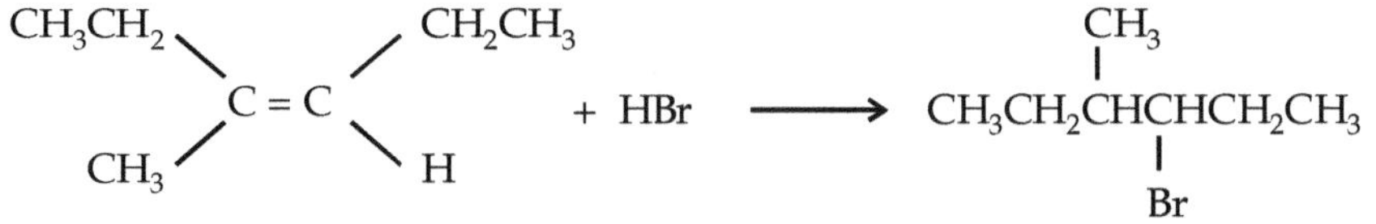   
$$\underset{\underset{CH_3}{\diagup}}{\overset{\overset{CH_3CH_2}{\diagdown}}{}} C = C \underset{\underset{H}{\diagdown}}{\overset{\overset{CH_2CH_3}{\diagup}}{}} + HBr \longrightarrow CH_3CH_2\overset{\overset{CH_3}{|}}{CH}\underset{\underset{Br}{|}}{CH}CH_2CH_3$$

Two chirality centres have been created in the product, the number of stereoisomers formed will be four, which are two enantiomeric pairs.

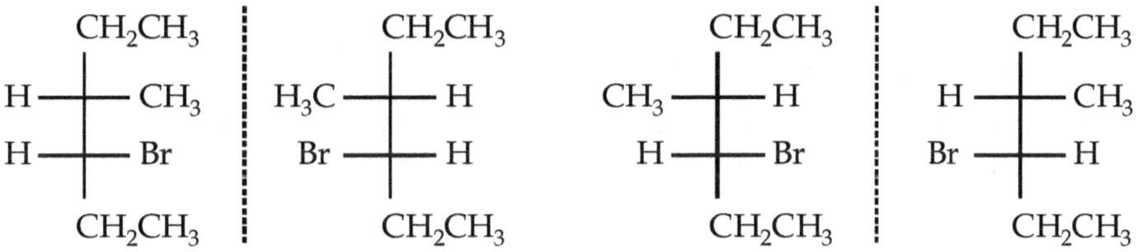

| | CH$_2$CH$_3$ | | | CH$_2$CH$_3$ | | | CH$_2$CH$_3$ | | | CH$_2$CH$_3$ | |
|---|:---:|---|---|:---:|---|---|:---:|---|---|:---:|---|
| H— | \| | —CH$_3$ | H$_3$C— | \| | —H | CH$_3$— | \| | —H | H— | \| | —CH$_3$ |
| H— | \| | —Br | Br— | \| | —H | H— | \| | —Br | Br— | \| | —H |
| | CH$_2$CH$_3$ | | | CH$_2$CH$_3$ | | | CH$_2$CH$_3$ | | | CH$_2$CH$_3$ | |

**(c)**   (1-bromo-1-methylcyclopentane)   (achiral molecule)

### 4.7.2   Mechanism of Nucleophilic Addition

Presence of electron-withdrawing group in an alkene deactivates a carbon-carbon double bond towards electrophilic addition reactions, but at the same time it makes alkene more susceptible to attack by a nucleophile. If the electron-withdrawing group is in conjugation with the carbon-carbon double bond, the intermediate carbanion, formed by the attack of nucleophile stabilizes due to resonance. Hence such alkenes undergo nucleophilic addition reactions. Examples are addition reactions of $\alpha$, $\beta$-unsaturated nitriles, aldehydes, ketones and esters. Addition of ethanol to acrylonitrile in presence of strong base is a typical example. The base converts the weaker nucleophile ($C_2H_5OH$) to a stronger nucleophile ($OC_2H_5^-$).

$$C_2H_5\overset{-}{O} + CH_2 = CH—C \equiv N \longrightarrow \left[ \begin{array}{c} C_2H_5OCH_2—\overset{-}{C}H—C \equiv N \\ \updownarrow \\ C_2H_5OCH_2—CH = C = \overset{-}{N} \end{array} \right]$$

$$C_2H_5OCH_2CH_2C \equiv N \xleftarrow{\;\;C_2H_5OH\;\;}$$

Similarly,   $(CH_3)_2\overset{..}{N}H + CH_2 = CHCN \longrightarrow \qquad (CH_3)_2NCH_2CH_2CN$

Important example is Michael reaction.

However, nucleophilic additions are typical reactions of aldehydes and ketones. The real cause of reactivity of the carbonyl group towards nucleophiles is the tendency of oxygen to acquire electrons and its ability to carry a negative charge. This makes carbonyl carbon electron-deficient and liable to be attacked by a nucleophile. Further, carbonyl group, being flat, is open to relatively unhindered attack from above or below. The reaction takes place in the following two steps.

Reactant (Trigonal) → Transition state (tetrahedral) →

Nucleophilic addition to carbonyl group takes place easily in presence of acids because the latter protonates the carbonyl oxygen which thus causes carbonyl carbon more electron deficient.

note that carbonyl carbon is more electron-deficient

Since alkyl groups are electron-releasing, their presence makes the carbonyl carbon less electron-deficient, and less reactive towards nucleophilic substitution hence nucleophilic substitution on carbonyl group follows the order :

Since the nucleophile attacks only on the carbonyl carbon rather than on oxygen, the addition to carbonyl group is **regioselective**. In case, the carbonyl compound has two different alkyl groups i.e. R $\neq$ R', the product will be a mixture of the two enantiomers.

### 4.7.3   Mechanism of Free Radical Addition

Free radical addition reactions are encountered during addition of HBr (not HCl or HI) on alkenes in presence of peroxides* (recall that in absence of peroxides, additon is electrophilic), hence the reaction is commonly known as **peroxide effect.** The salient features of the mechanism are

(*i*)     peroxides initiate the free-radical reactions.

(*ii*)    hydrogen and bromine add to the double bond homolytically rather than hetero-lytically.

(*iii*)   the intermediate is a free radical rather than a carbocation.

(*iv*)    addition occurs against Markownikov rule.

---

*     Free-radical additon also takes place in presence of light of a wavelength liable to dissociate H—Br into H· and Br·.

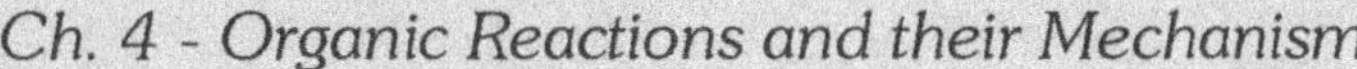

The essential steps of the reaction are as follows.

$$RO-OR \xrightarrow{\phantom{xxx}} 2\overset{\bullet}{O}R$$
$$\text{Peroxide}$$

} **Chain - initiating steps**

$$R\overset{\bullet}{O} + HBr \xrightarrow{\phantom{xxx}} ROH + Br.$$

$$CH_3CH = CH_2 + Br. \xrightarrow{\phantom{xxx}} CH_3 - \overset{\bullet}{C}H - CH_2Br$$
$$\text{2° free radical (more stable)}$$

} **Chain - propagating steps**

$$CH_3 - \overset{\bullet}{C}H - CH_2Br + H-Br \xrightarrow{\phantom{xxx}} CH_3 - CH_2 - CH_2Br + Br.$$

Peroxide effect is neither shown by H—Cl (because bond energy of the H—Cl bond is too high to break on approach of free radicals) nor by H—I because I. radicals are very unstable and hence combine to form $I_2$ molecule.

Polymerisation of ethylene to polyethylene and vinyl monomers to polyvinyl monomers are also free radical addition reactions.

$$nCH_2 = CH_2 \xrightarrow{\text{Catalyst}} -[-CH_2-CH_2-]_n-$$

## TEST YOUR UNDERSTANDING - 4.7

1.   Give structural formula for the carbocation intermediate that leads to the major product in the following reactions :

(*i*)   2-Methyl-1-butene + HCl

(*ii*)   *cis*-2-Butene + HBr

(*iii*)   + HBr

2.   Give mechanism for the additon of HCl on .

3.   Identify compounds A to E in the following reactions :

(*i*)   + HCN $\longrightarrow$ A + B

(*ii*)   $CH_3CH = CH_2 + CCl_4 \xrightarrow{\text{peroxide}} C$

(*iii*)   $CH_3CH = CH_2 + CBrCl_3 \xrightarrow{\text{peroxide}} D$

(*iv*)   $CH_3CH = CH_2 + CHCl_3 \xrightarrow{\text{peroxide}} E$

## 4.8   Mechanism of Elimination Reactions

Elimination reactions involve the loss of atoms(s) or group(s) from a molecule to form an unsaturated species (generally double or triple bonds), thus these reactions may said to be reverse of addition reactions. These reactions may proceed in the following two ways.

1.   **α-Elimination or 1, 1-elimination.** Here the two atoms or groups are eliminated from the same carbon atom leading to the formation of carbenes, *e.g.*

$$CHCl_3 \longrightarrow :CCl_2 + HCl$$

This type of reactions is very rare.

2.   **β-Elimination or 1, 2-elimination.** Here two atoms or groups are removed from two adjacent carbon atoms leading to the formation of a double bond. These are the common elimination reactions and can take place by either of the two mechanisms, namely E2 and E1.

(a)   $H_3C-CH_2Cl + :B \longrightarrow H_2C = CH_2 + H:B + Cl^-$

(b)   $RCH_2CH_2OH \xrightarrow{H^+} RCH = CH_2 + H_2O$

(c)   $RCH_2CH_2\overset{+}{N}R_3OH^- \xrightarrow{\text{heat}} RCH = CH_2 + R_3N + H_2O$   **(Hofmann degradation)**

### 4.8.1 E2 Mechanism

The reaction following this mechanism exhibits second-order kinetics.

$$Rate = k[\text{Alkyl halide}]\ [\text{Base}]$$

Thus doubling the concentration of either the alkyl alhalide or the base doubles the reaction rate, while doubling the concentration of both reactants increases the rate by a factor of 4. Such reactions involve a single step ; base pulls a proton away from carbon and simultaneously a halide leaving group departs from the molecule forming the double bond.

Among different halide leaving groups, reactivity of alkyl halides increases with decreasing strength of the carbon-halogen bond, *i.e.*

$$R\text{---}I \quad > \quad R\text{---}Br \quad > \quad R\text{---}Cl \quad > \quad R\text{---}F$$

Weakest C—halogen bond,

$I^-$ the best leaving group

Strongest C—halogen bond,

$F^-$ the poorest leaving group

Hence iodides are most reactive towards elimination reaction, while fluorides the least which explains why fluorides are not used as starting materials in the preparation of alkenes.

In case, dehydrohalogenation of alkyl halide yields more than one alkene, *the alkene having greater number of alkyl groups to the doubly bonded carbons will be preferred product* (**Saytzeff rule,** which can also be defined as '*in dehydrohalogenation the more stable the alkene, the faster it is formed*'). The more stable alkene is thus known as **Saytzeff product,** while the less stable alkene is known as **Hoffmann product.**

$$CH_3CH_2CHCH_3 \xrightarrow{(CH_3)_3COK} CH_3CH=CHCH_3 + CH_3CH_2CH=CH_2$$

(Saytzeff product)      (Hoffmann product)

Thus the ease of formation and stability of various alkenes is

$$R_2C=CR_2 \quad > \quad R_2C=CHR \quad > \quad R_2C=CH_2,\ RCH=CHR \quad > \quad RCH=CH_2$$

Most E2 reactions give Saytzeff product, however, Hofmann product is preferred under one of the following conditions :

(*i*)     The base used is large, e.g. $Me_3CO^-$.

$$CH_2\text{---}CH-CH_2CH_3 \xrightarrow{Me_3CO^-} CH_2=CHCH_2CH_3$$

Hofmann product

$$CH_3-CH-CHCH_3 \xrightarrow{OH^-} CH_3CH=CHCH_3$$

Saytzeff product

(*ii*)     The alkyl halide is an alkyl fluoride.

(*iii*)     The alkyl halide contains one or more double bonds. Remember that a conjugated alkene is always preferred to non-conjugated alkene.

(*iv*)     Eliminations involving charged substances, e.g. when a quaternary hydroxide is heated strongly (to 125°C or higher), it decomposes to form an alkene and a tertiary amine.

$$CH_3CHCH_2CH_3 \xrightarrow{heat} CH_2=CHCH_2CH_3 + (CH_3)_3N + H_2O$$

1-Butene(95% )

$$N^+(CH_3)_3OH^-$$

This reaction, known as **Hofmann elimination**, is an E2 reaction in which hydroxide ion functions as a base. A novel aspect of the Hofmann elimination is its *regioselectivity*. Elimination in alkyltrimethylammonium hydroxides proceeds in the direction that gives the less substituted alkene (opposite to Saytzeff rule) ; this is known as **Hofmann rule** *or* **Hofmann orientation**.

$$CH_2 = CH-CH_2CH_3 + CH_3CH = CHCH_3$$

Butene-1 (95%)          Butene-2 (5%)

The base ($OH^-$) attacks the most acidic hydrogen ; a primary hydrogen atom is more acidic because its carbon atom bears only one electron-releasing group. Alternatively, it is the less sterically hindered $\beta$ hydrogen that is attacked by the base ($OH^-$ or any other base). Methyl groups are deprotonated in preference to methylene groups which in turn are deprotonated in preference to methines. In case the $4°$ ammonium hydroxide does not have any $\beta$-hydrogen, alkene formation is impossible, rather alcohol is formed by $S_N2$ reaction.

$$HO^- + CH_3-N^+(CH_3)_3 \xrightarrow{\text{heat}} CH_3OH + (CH_3)_3N:$$

As we have observed, E2 mechanism resembles $S_N2$ mechanism, however the two differ in their relative order. Reactivity of RX toward E2 is $3° > 2° > 1°$ (opposite to that of $S_N2$ reactions) which is evident from the following relative rates.

| Alkyl halide | | Product | Relative rate | Relative rate per H |
|---|---|---|---|---|
| (1°) $CH_3CH_2Br$ | $\longrightarrow$ | $CH_2 = CH_2$ | 1.0 | 1.0 |
| (1°) $CH_3CH_2CH_2Br$ | $\longrightarrow$ | $CH_3CH = CH_2$ | 3.3 | 5.0 |
| (2°) $CH_3CHBrCH_3$ | $\longrightarrow$ | $CH_3CH = CH_2$ | 9.4 | 4.7 |
| (3°) $(CH_3)_3CBr$ | $\longrightarrow$ | $(CH_3)_2C = CH_2$ | 120 | 40 |

This relative order, $3° > 2° > 1°$, is due to following two factors.

(*a*)  Increased branching (from 1° alkyl halide to 3° halide) successively provides greater number of $\beta$-hydrogens for attack by base (probability factor).

(*b*)  Increased branching leads to a more highly branched, *i.e.* more stable alkene.

## 4.8.2   Stereochemistry of E2 Reactions

The two groups or atoms are eliminated from *anti* (opposite) positions (*anti elimination*) because *anti* elimination requires the molecule to be in a staggered conformation (a more stable conformer), while *syn* elimination requires eclipsed conformation.

In other words, for *anti* elimination, the two leaving groups must be as far apart as possible. Thus *E*-2-bromobutene forms dimethylacetylene more rapidly than the *Z*-isomer.

$$CH_3-C \equiv C-CH_3$$

*E*-2-Bromobutene          Dimethylacetylene          *Z*-2-Bromobutene

This example indicates that E2 reaction is *stereospecific*, i.e. different stereoisomer of the starting material gives different stereoisomer of the product. This is also reflected from compounds having chiral carbon atoms ; *meso*-isomer gives *cis*-isomer while *d*- or *l*-gives *trans*-isomer on E2 elimination.

Following examples also indicate stereospecificity of E2 reactions.

2-Bromobutane　→ (alc. KOH) → *cis*　　　　　2-Bromobutane　→ (alcoholic KOH) → *trans*

Other interesting example of E2 reaction is dehydrohalogenation of alkyl halides leading to two products.

$$CH_3CH_2\overset{\underset{\displaystyle |}{Br}}{CH}CH_3 \xrightarrow[CH_3CH_2OH]{CH_3CH_2O^-} CH_3CH = CHCH_3 + CH_3CH_2CH = CH_2$$

Butene–2 (**Major**)　　　Butene–1 (Minor)

Further, of the two isomeric butene-2 (*E* and *Z*), *E*-butene-2 (having bulkier groups on opposite sides) is major because it has less steric strain and thus more stable, while *Z*-butene-2 is minor. Thus it can be said that E2 reactions are regioselective (dominance of butene-2 over butene-1) as well as stereoselective (dominance of *E*-butene-2 over *Z*-butene-2).

### 4.8.3　E1 Mechanism

　　E1 reaction proceeds by first-order kinetics. The mechanism is similar to that of $S_N1$ reactions except that here the carbocation loses a proton to form alkene (*cf.* in $S_N1$ reactions, carbocation takes up nucleophile). Since here carbocations are formed as intermediates, the relative order of reactivity of alkyl halides towards E1 should be $3° > 2° > 1°$.

**First step :**

$$CH_3 - \overset{\underset{\displaystyle |}{CH_3}}{\underset{\underset{\displaystyle :Br:}{|}}{C}} - CH_3 \xrightarrow{\text{slow}} \overset{+}{C}(CH_3)_3 \; + \; :\overset{..}{\underset{..}{Br}}:^-$$

**Second step :**

$$CH_3CH_2\overset{..}{O}H + H - H_2C - \overset{+}{C}(CH_3)_2 \xrightarrow{\text{fast}} CH_3CH_2\overset{+}{O}H_2 + H_2C = C(CH_3)_2$$

Base　　　　　　　　　　　　　　Ethyloxonium ion　　Isobutene

### 4.8.4　Characteristics of E1 Reactions

(i)　　Since in the rate-determining step of E1 reaction, the leaving group is removed, and a carbocation is formed as an intermediate, the rate of E1 reaction depends on both of these factors and follows the order.

　　　$3°$ benzylic $\approx 3°$ allylic $> 2°$ benzylic $\approx 2°$ allylic $\approx 3° > 1°$ benzylic $\approx 1°$ allylic $\approx 2° > 1° >$ vinyl

(ii)　　E1 reactions occur in presence of either a weak base or a base in low concentration.

(iii)　　Further, formation of carbocation may result rearranged product, in case when less stable carbocation may change to the more stable by 1, 2-shift. For example,

$$C_6H_5 - \overset{\underset{\displaystyle |}{CH_3}}{\underset{\underset{\displaystyle CH_3Cl}{|}}{C}} - CHC_2H_5 \xrightarrow{CH_3OH} C_6H_5 - \overset{\underset{\displaystyle |}{CH_3}}{\underset{\underset{\displaystyle CH_3}{|}}{C}} - \overset{+}{C}HC_2H_5 \xrightarrow[\text{shift}]{1,\,2\text{-methyl}} C_6H_5 - \overset{\underset{\displaystyle |}{CH_3}}{\overset{+}{C}} - CHC_2H_5 \xrightarrow{-H^+} C_6H_5 - \overset{\underset{\displaystyle |}{CH_3}}{C} = \overset{\underset{\displaystyle |}{CH_3}}{C}C_2H_5$$

2° carbocation

(iv)    In case the removal of proton (second step), can form two products, the major product is formed according to Saytzeff rule. For example,

$$\underset{\underset{Cl}{|}}{\overset{\overset{CH_3}{|}}{CH_3CH_2CCH_3}} \longrightarrow \overset{\overset{CH_3}{|}}{CH_3CH_2\overset{+}{C}-CH_3} \longrightarrow \underset{(\textbf{Major})}{\overset{\overset{CH_3}{|}}{CH_3CH=C-CH_3}} + \underset{(\text{Minor})}{\overset{\overset{CH_3}{|}}{CH_3CH_2C=CH_2}}$$

(v)    **Stereochemistry of E1 reactions :** Since the carbocation is planar, the electrons from the departing hydrogen can move towards the positively charged carbon from either side and thus both *syn-* as well as *anti-*elimination can occur. However, here also *E*-isomer having bulkier groups on the opposite sides will be major product because of its higher stability than the *Z*-isomer.

## 4.8.5  E1cB Mechanism

This is a two step reaction. The first step involves the rapid formation of carbanion by an alkyl halide under the influence of a base. The second step is slow and involves the lose of leaving group (halide ion).

$$\overset{-}{O}C_2H_5 \quad \overset{\overset{\curvearrowright H}{|}}{R\,CHCH_2Br} \underset{fast}{\rightleftharpoons} \quad R\,\overset{-}{C}H\text{-}CH_2 \underset{\overset{|}{Br}}{} \xrightarrow{slow} R\,CH=CH_2 + Br^-$$

carbanion (conjugate base)

Since the rate determining step (slow step) is dependent on the concentration of the conjugate base of the substrate (carbanions) and thus unimolecular, the reaction is known as E1cB **(elimination, unimolecular from conjugate base)**. Reactions proceeding by E1cB pathway are exceedingly rare.

**Acid-catalysed dehydration of alcohols :**

$$RCH_2CH_2-OH \xrightarrow{H^+} RCH_2CH_2-\overset{+}{O}H_2 \xrightarrow[\text{leaving group}]{H_2O \text{ is a better}} RCH_2\overset{+}{C}H_2 \xrightarrow{-H^+} RCH=CH_2$$

However, since 1° carbocations are not quite stable, the above mechanism (E1) is applicable to 2° and 3° alcohols and 1° alcohols follow E2 mechanism, where loss of water and proton take place simultaneously.

## 4.8.6  E2 vs E1

We have already observed that both mechanisms follow the same order (1° < 2° < 3°), although reactivity by both mechanisms increases for different reasons. Reactivity by E2 increases mainly because of greater stability of the more highly branched alkenes being formed ; reactivity by E1 increases because of greater stability of the carbocation being formed in the rate-determining step. Thus it becomes somewhat difficult to know whether an alkyl halide undergoes elimination by E2 or E1. However, this problem can be somewhat solved on the basis of the role by the other reagent, *i.e.,* the base.

We know that E2 is a second-order reaction, *i.e.* here base takes part in the rate determining step; while in E1 base does not take part in rate determining step. Thus the rate of E2 depends upon the nature as well as concentration of the base. On the other hand, the rate of E1 is independent of the nature and concentration of the base. Thus **for a given substrate, the more concentrated the base or the stronger the base the more E2 mechanism is favoured over E1.** Thus *E1 mechanism is encountered only with tertiary or secondary substrates and that too in presence of either a weak base or a base in low concentration.*

*Example 14 :*

**Mention the type of elimination mechanism in each of the following :**

(a) $\underset{CH_3}{\overset{CH_3CH_2}{>}}CHBr$ + $CH_3OH$ $\longrightarrow$

(b) $\underset{CH_3}{\overset{CH_3CH_2}{>}}CHBr$ + $CH_3ONa$ $\xrightarrow{DMSO}$

(c) $Me_3C\,Br + OH^-$ $\xrightarrow{DMF}$

(d) $Me_3C\,Br + H_2O$ $\longrightarrow$

(e) $\underset{Br}{Me_2C\,CH_2CH_3}$ $\xrightarrow{Me_3CO^-}$

(f) $CH_3CH(F)CH_2CH_3$ $\xrightarrow{OH^-}$

(g) (cyclohexane with CH$_3$ and Cl) $\xrightarrow{OC_2H_5^-}$

(h) (cyclohexane with CH$_3$ and Cl) $\xrightarrow{OC_2H_5^-}$

(i) (cyclohexanone with CH$_2$OH) $\xrightarrow{-H_2O}$

*Solution :*

(a) E1 ($CH_3OH$ is a weak base)

(b) E2 ($CH_3O^-$ is a strong base)

(c) E2 ($OH^-$ is a strong base)

(d) E1 ($H_2O$ is a weak base)

(e) $\underset{CH_3}{CH_2 = C - CH_2CH_3}$ (E2, base is strong)

(f) $CH_2 = CHCH_2CH_3$ (E2, halide is fluoride)

(g) (cyclohexene with CH$_3$) (E2, *anti* elimination gives only Hofmann product)

(h) (cyclohexene with CH$_3$) (E2, *anti* elimination gives more preferred Saytzeff product)

(i) (methylenecyclohexanone) + (cyclohexenone) (E1)

*Example 15 :*

**Which of the alkyl halide (I or II) will be more reactive toward E2 reaction?**

          I                                       II

(a) $\underset{Br}{CH_3CH_2CHCH_2CH_3}$　　　　$\underset{Br}{CH_3CH\,CH_2\,CH_3}$

(b) $\underset{Br}{C_6H_5CH_2\,CH\,CH_2\,CH_3}$　　　　$\underset{Br}{C_6H_5CH_2\,CH\,CH_3}$

*Solution :*

(a) II (C bearing Br is less sterically hindered).

(b) I (newly developed double bond is conjugated to benzene ring).

*Example 16 :*

**Predict the product formed in each of the following reaction and give mechanism :**

(a)　$(CH_3)_3C-\underset{\underset{\text{OH}}{|}}{CH}CH_3 \xrightarrow{H^+}$

(b) 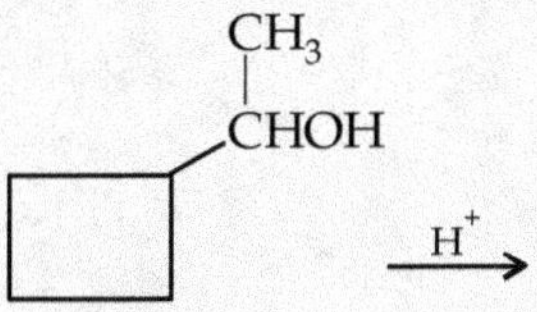　[cyclobutane ring]$-\underset{\underset{}{CHOH}}{\overset{CH_3}{|}}$　$\xrightarrow{H^+}$

(c)　$C_6H_5-CH_2-\underset{\underset{\text{OH}}{|}}{CH}-\overset{\overset{CH_3}{|}}{C}HCH_3 \xrightarrow{Me_3CO^-}$

*Solution :*

(a)　$(CH_3)_3C-\overset{+}{C}HCH_3 \xrightarrow[\text{shift}]{1,2\text{-methyl}} (CH_3)_2\overset{+}{C}-\underset{\underset{CH_3}{|}}{C}HCH_3 \xrightarrow{H^+} (CH_3)_2C=C(CH_3)_2$

　　2° carbocation　　　　　　　　　　3° carbocation

(b)　[mechanism: ring expansion of cyclobutane carbinyl cation]

2° carbocation → (ring expansion) → 2° carbocation ≡ 2° carbocation

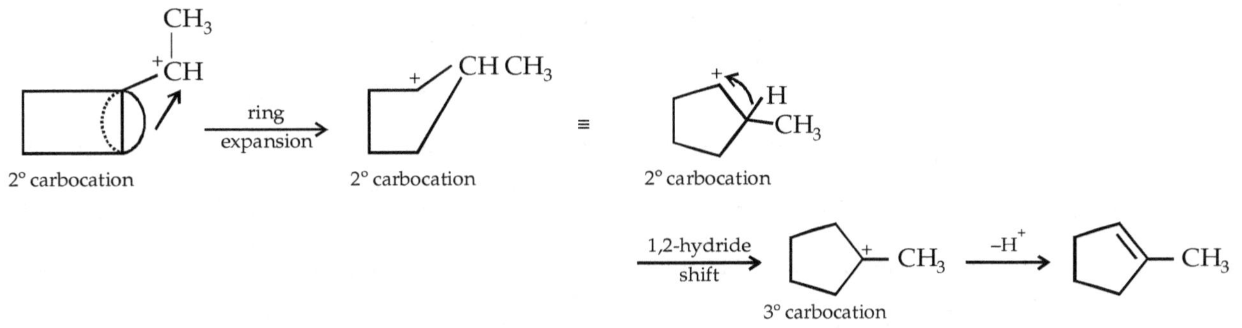

　　$\xrightarrow[\text{shift}]{1,2\text{-hydride}}$ [cyclopentyl cation]$-CH_3 \xrightarrow{-H^+}$ [cyclopentene]$-CH_3$

3° carbocation

(c)　$C_6H_5-\underset{}{CH}-\overset{+}{C}H-\overset{\overset{CH_3}{|}}{C}HCH_3 \longrightarrow C_6H_5\overset{+}{C}HCH_2CH(CH_3)_2 \xrightarrow{-H^+} C_6H_5CH=CHCH(CH_3)_2$

　　2° carbocation　　　　　　　　Benzal carbocation　　　　　　Hofmann product

## 4.8.7　Elimination vs substitution

　　We have observed that the most common substrate for 1, 2-elimination as well as for substitution are **alkyl halides and alkyl sulphonates.** Furthermore, the reagent required for the two reactions (bases and nucleophiles) are similar. Both reagents (bases and nucleophiles) are electron-rich, bases are nucleophilic and nucleophiles are basic. Thus, it is expected that there will nearly always be a competition between substitution and elimination.

　　Let us consider first the $S_N2$ and E2 reactions both of which involve attack of the reagent :Z on the substrate. While acting as a nucleophile, the reagent :Z attacks the substrate on carbon and causes substitution, while acting as a base it attacks the substrate on hydrogen and brings about elimination.

　　Now we know that the relative order of reactivity for the two kinds of reactions is

$$3° > 2° > 1° \qquad \textbf{For E2 reactions}$$
$$1° > 2° > 3° \qquad \textbf{For S}_N\textbf{2 reactions}$$

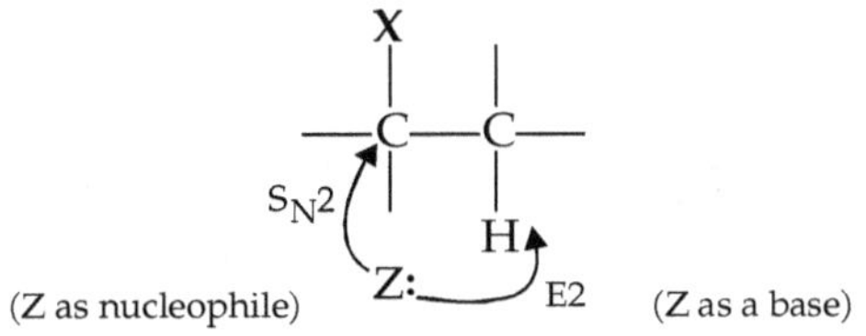

E2 *versus* $S_N2$

(Z as nucleophile)　　　　　　　(Z as a base)

So it can be concluded that primary substrates undergo elimination slowest and substitution fastest, while tertiary substrates undergo elimination fastest and substitution slowest. From the above relative order, it can further be concluded that in bimolecular reactions, the proportion of elimination increases as the structure of the substrate changes from primary to secondary to tertiary.

$$CH_3CH_2Br \xrightarrow{\ ^-OC_2H_5\ } \underset{91\%}{CH_3CH_2OC_2H_5} + \underset{9\%}{CH_2 = CH_2}$$

$$(CH_3)_2CHBr \xrightarrow{\ ^-OC_2H_5\ } \underset{87\%}{CH_3CH = CH_2} + \underset{13\%}{(CH_3)_2CHOC_2H_5}$$

Like the nature of substrate, the nature of the reagent :Z also influences the ratio of the two products.

(a)     A bulky nucleophile or bulky alkyl halide (even primary) will favour E2 reactions, because of steric factor (*cf.* mechanism of $S_N2$ reactions) *e.g.*

$$\underset{1° \text{ Alkylhalide}}{CH_3(CH_2)_{15}CH_2CH_2Br} \xrightarrow[C_2H_5OH]{\ ^-OCMe_3\ } \underset{(87\%)}{CH_3(CH_2)_{15}CH = CH_2} + \underset{(13\%)}{CH_3(CH_2)_{15}CH_2CH_2OC_2H_5}$$

$$(CH_3)_2CHCH_2Br + CH_3O^- \xrightarrow{\ CH_3OH\ } \underset{(60\%)}{(CH_3)_2C = CH_2} + \underset{(40\%)}{(CH_3)_2CHCH_2OCH_3}$$

(b)     Nucleophiles which are also strong bases like $^-OH$ favour elimination while good nucleophiles, which are weak bases (*e.g.* $CN^-$, azide $N_3^-$, $^-SH$ etc.) favour substitution.

2-Chloropropane when treated separately with acetate ion or ethoxide ion undergoes different reactions.

$$\underset{\substack{\text{Isopropyl acetate} \\ (100\%)}}{\overset{\overset{\textstyle OCOCH_3}{|}}{CH_3CHCH_3}} \xleftarrow[\substack{CH_3COOH \\ (S_N2)}]{CH_3COO^-} \underset{\text{2-Chloropropane}}{\overset{\overset{\textstyle Cl}{|}}{CH_3CHCH_3}} \xrightarrow[\substack{C_2H_5OH \\ (E2)}]{C_2H_5O^-} \underset{\substack{\text{Propene} \\ (75\%)}}{CH_3CH = CH_2}$$

This is because $CH_3COO^-$ is a weaker base than $C_2H_5O^-$ (recall that $CH_3COOH$ is a stronger acid than $C_2H_5OH$).

Further, a less polar solvent and high temperature tend to favour elimination, while more polar solvent and a low temperature favour substitution. This explains why hot alc. KOH is used for dehydrohalogenation, while aqueous KOH is used for substitution. So favourable conditions for E2 are bulkiness at either of the two reagents (alkyl halide and nucleophile), strongly basic nucleophiles like $OH^-$ and $OC_2H_5^-$, less polar solvent and relatively high temperature.

(c)     A tertiary alkyl halide is the least reactive toward $S_N2$ reaction but most reactive toward E2 reaction, thus when a *tert*-alkyl halide is treated with a nucleophile under $S_N2$/E2 conditions, only the elimination product is formed.

$$(CH_3)_3CBr + CH_3CH_2O^- \xrightarrow{\ CH_3CH_2OH\ } \underset{\text{Methylpropene}}{(CH_3)_2C = CH_2} + CH_3CH_2OH + Br^-$$

Now let us take $S_N1$ and E1 reactions, both of which involve the formation of carbocation in the rate-determining step. Hence the least stable carbocation (1°) will react immediately with the anion to form substitution product. On the other hand, the 3° cation, having sufficient stability will lose proton to form the more stable (more branched) alkene.

In short, for a particular alkyl halide substitution reactions are favoured by nucleophiles which are weak bases, *viz.* $H_2O$, $C_2H_5OH$, $CN^-$, $N_3^-$, $RS^-$, $HS^-$ etc., and using low temperature (room temperature) ; while elimination reactions are favoured by strong bases like $OH^-$, $^-OC_2H_5$ etc. and using high temperature.

---

*Example 17 :*

**Propose a mechanism for the following reaction :**

*Solution :*

*Example 18 :*

**3,3-Dimethylbutanol-2 loses a molecule of water, when treated with concentrated sulphuric acid to give tetramethylethylene. Suggest a mechanism.** (IIT 1996)

*Solution :*

2° carbocation

3° carbocation
(more stable)

## Summary of $S_N1$, $S_N2$, E1, E2 and E1cB Reactions

| Type of alkyl halide | Poor nucleophile (e.g. $H_2O$, ROH) | Weak basic nucleophile (e.g. $I^-$, $RS^-$) | Strongly basic unhindered nucleophile (e.g. $RO^-$) | Strongly basic hindered nucleophile (e.g. $Me_3CO^-$) |
|---|---|---|---|---|
| Methyl halide | No reaction | $S_N2$ | $S_N2$ | $S_N2$ |
| 1° unhindered RX | No reaction | $S_N2$ | $S_N2$ | E2 |
| 1° hindered RX | No reaction | $S_N2$ | E2 | E2 |
| 2° alkyl halide | $S_N1$, E1(slow) | $S_N2$ | E2 | E2 |
| 3° alkyl halide | E1 or $S_N1$ | $S_N1$, E1 | E2 | E2 |
| $CH_3\overset{O}{\overset{\|}{C}}CH_2\overset{X}{\overset{\|}{CH}}CH_3$ | E1cB | E1cB | E1cB | E1cB |

# TEST YOUR UNDERSTANDING - 4.8

1.  Predict the major product of each of the following reactions :

    (*i*)   Cyclohexyl bromide and potassium ethoxide

    (*ii*)  *sec*-Butyl bromide solvolysis in methanol

    (*iii*) *sec*-Butyl bromide solvolysis in methanol containing 2M sodium ethoxide.

2.  Give various steps involved in the acid-catalysed dehydration of 2, 2-dimethylcyclohexanol to form the major product.

3.  Give various steps involved in the acid-catalysed dehydration of the following alcohols to different alkenes

    (*a*)   1-Methylcyclohexanol                          (*b*)   9-Decanol.

# EXERCISE 4.1  (MCQ - ONE option correct)

**1.** Which of the following is not an electrophile ?
(a)  $Ag^+$
(b)  $H_2C$:
(c)  $SiF_4$
(d)  None

**2.** Consider the following sequence of steps
(i)  A $\longrightarrow$ B
(ii)  B + C $\longrightarrow$ D + E
(iii)  E + A $\longrightarrow$ 2F
Product of the reaction is/are
(a)  B, D, E and F
(b)  D, E and F
(c)  D and F
(d)  F.

**3.** Addition of bromine on ethylene is generally represented as
$$CH_2 = CH_2 + Br_2 \longrightarrow CH_2BrCH_2Br$$
The nucleophilic species present or formed as intermediate in the above reaction are

(a)  $CH_2Br\ \bar{C}H_2$ and $Br^-$
(b)  $CH_2 = CH_2$ and $Br^-$
(c)  only $CH_2 = CH_2$
(d)  only $Br^-$.

**4.** Cyclohexene has three types of hydrogen atoms, marked as 1, 2 and 3. Which hydrogen atom can be removed most easily and which with most difficulty as $H_\bullet$ ?
(a)  1 and 2 respectively
(b)  2 and 3 respectively
(c)  2 and 1 respectively
(d)  All with same ease.

**5.** Insertion of methylene in isobutane, $(CH_3)_2CHCH_3$ can form how many compounds ?
(a)  1
(b)  2
(c)  3
(d)  4

**6.** Extra stability of *tert*-carbocation can be explained due to
(a)  inductive effect
(b)  hyperconjugation
(c)  steric relief
(d)  all the three

**7.** In methyl anion ($:CH_3^-$), carbon is $sp^3$ hybridised. The angle between bonding pairs should be
(a)  109.5°
(b)  < 109.5°
(c)  > 109.5°
(d)  any of the three.

**8.** Which of the following three intermediates have nearly similar geometry ?

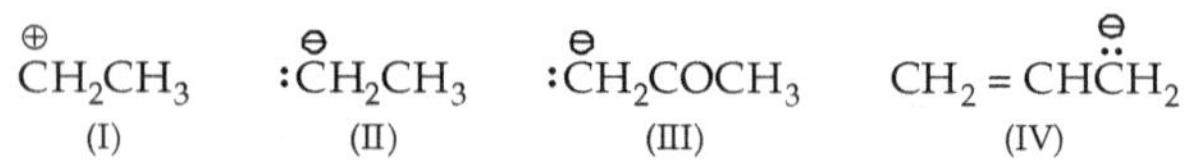

(a)  I and III
(b)  II and IV
(c)  II, III and IV
(d)  I, III and IV.

**9.** Which of the following compound can form carbanion easily ?

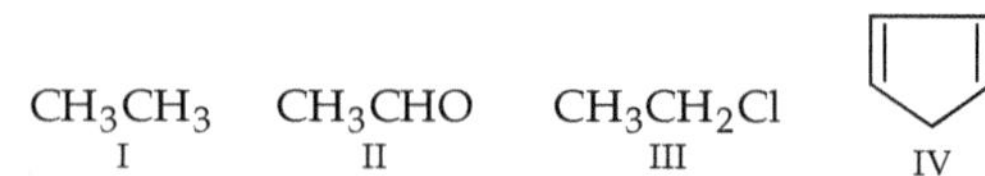

(a)  II only
(b)  II and III
(c)  I, II and III
(d)  II and IV

**10.** $(+)\text{-}C_2H_5CH(CH_3)COC_6H_5 \xrightarrow[\text{(ii) } Br_2]{\text{(i) Base}} C_2H_5CBr(CH_3)COC_6H_5$

Here the product is
(a)  (+) −
(b)  (−)
(c)  (±) −
(d)  Not definite.

**11.** Consider the following species
$H^+$    $OH^-$    $H_3O^+$    $AlCl_3$
I      II      III      IV
Which of the following is/are cationoid ?
(a)  I and III
(b)  I and IV
(c)  II
(d)  I, III and IV.

**12.** Chlorobenzene having chlorine on heavy carbon is treated with sodamide, the product is
(a)  aniline having —$NH_2$ group on heavy C atom
(b)  aniline having —$NH_2$ group on C-12
(c)  both (a) and (b)
(d)  reduction takes place to from benzene.

**13.** The transition state of the rate determining step of a multi-step reaction has
(a)  lowest enthalpy
(b)  highest enthalpy
(c)  medium enthalpy
(d)  unpredictable.

**14.** Enthalpy diagram of a multi-step reaction is drawn below. Can you predict the rate determining step in the reaction ?

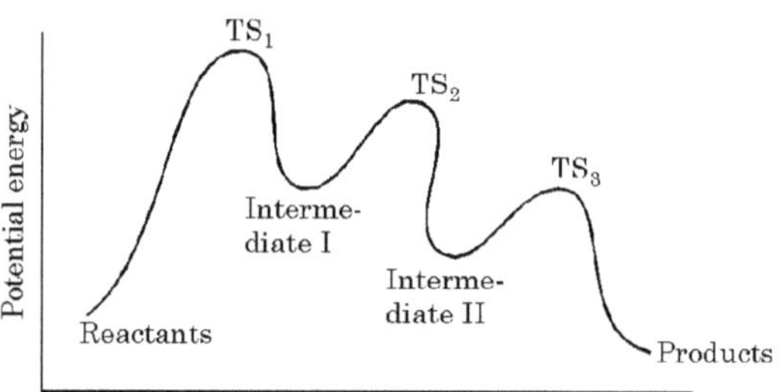


(a)  No
(b)  Yes, first step
(c)  Yes, second step
(d)  Yes, third step.

**15.** The decreasing order of nucleophilicity of $HS^-$, $RCOO^-$, $RCOOH$ and $ROH$ is
(a)  $RCOO^- > HS^- > RCOOH > ROH$
(b)  $HS^- > RCOO^- > RCOOH > ROH$
(c)  $HS^- > RCOO^- > ROH > RCOOH$
(d)  $RCOO^- > HS^- > ROH > RCOOH$.

**16.** During dehydration of *tert*-butanol with an acid, which of the following carbocation is more likely to be formed as an intermediate ?
(a)  $CH_3CH_2CH_2\overset{+}{C}H_2$
(b)  $CH_3CH_2\overset{+}{C}HCH_3$
(c)  Both
(d)  None.

**17.** Polarisation of electrons in acrolein may be written as
(a)  $\overset{\delta-}{CH_2} = CH - \overset{\delta+}{CH} = O$
(b)  $\overset{\delta-}{CH_2} = CH - CH = \overset{\delta+}{O}$
(c)  $\overset{\delta-}{CH_2} = \overset{\delta+}{CH} - CH = O$
(d)  $\overset{\delta+}{CH_2} = CH - CH = \overset{\delta-}{O}$.

**18.** In $CH_3CH_2OH$, the bond that undergoes heterolytic cleavage most readily is
(a)  C—C
(b)  C—O
(c)  C—H
(d)  O—H.

**19.** The bond dissociation energy needed to form the benzyl radical from toluene is ...... the formation of methyl radical from methane.
(a)  equal to
(b)  less than
(c)  greater than
(d)  not certain.

**20.** Which of the following reaction leads to complete racemization?
(a)  Free radical substitution
(b)  $S_N1$
(c)  $S_N2$
(d)  All the three.

21. Which of the following process involves inversion of configuration ?
(*a*) $S_N1$ (*b*) $S_N2$
(*c*) Both (*a*) and (*b*) (*d*) None.

22. An optically active alkyl halide of specific rotation – 34.9° undergoes $S_N1$ reaction, the specific rotation of the product will be
(*a*) + 34.9° (*b*) less than + 34.9°
(*c*) zero (*d*) – 34.9°.

23. The correct order for nucleophilic substitution in the following compounds is

| ROH | RF | $RO^+H_2$ | $ROSO_2CF_3$ | ROTs |
|---|---|---|---|---|
| I | II | III | IV | V |

(*a*) III > I > II > IV > V (*b*) IV > V > III > II > I
(*c*) IV > V > III > I > II (*d*) V > IV > III ≈ I > II.

24. Which of the factor increases the rate of following $S_N1$ reaction;
$RX + OH^- \longrightarrow R{-}OH + X^-$
(*a*) Doubling the concentration of $OH^-$
(*b*) Doubling the concentration of RX
(*c*) Both of the two
(*d*) None of the two.

25. Consider the following reaction
1-Bromobutene-2 + NaOH ⟶
Which of the following statement is true ?
(*a*) It undergoes $S_N2$ reaction
(*b*) It undergoes $S_N1$ reaction and forms one product
(*c*) It undergoes $S_N1$ reaction and forms two products
(*d*) It can undergo $S_N2$ as well as $S_N1$ reaction.

26. The decreasing order of reactivity of the following alkyl bromides towards $S_N2$ displacement is *n*-Propylmethyl bromide (I), *iso*-propylmethylbromide (II), *sec*-butylmethyl bromide (III), *tert*-butylmethyl bromide (IV)
(*a*) I > II > III > IV (*b*) IV > III > II > I
(*c*) III > IV > II > I (*d*) IV > III > I > II.

27. Which of the following does not involve carbocation as intermediate ?
(*a*) $C_6H_6 + Br_2 \xrightarrow{AlBr_3} C_6H_5Br$
(*b*) $CH_2 = CH_2 + Br_2 \longrightarrow BrCH_2 - CH_2Br$
(*c*) $(CH_3)_3COH + HBr \xrightarrow{H^+} (CH_3)_3CBr + H_2O$
(*d*) None of the above.

28. Although aldehydes and ketones also contain a carbonyl group, like acid halides they do not undergo

$R{-}\overset{O}{\overset{\|}{C}}{-}H$ $\quad R{-}\overset{O}{\overset{\|}{C}}{-}R'$ $\quad R{-}\overset{O}{\overset{\|}{C}}{-}Cl$

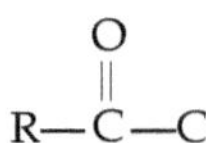

nucleophilic substitution reactions because
(*a*) they do not have electronegative chlorine atom
(*b*) carbon atom of carbonyl group in aldehydes and ketones is less electron deficient
(*c*) hydride ion and methylide ion are strong bases and hence are poor leaving groups
(*d*) none of the above is true.

29. Nucleophilic additions on aldehydes and ketones are catalysed by acids because
(*a*) acids dissolve easily both the reactants
(*b*) acids make carbonyl carbon more electron rich
(*c*) acids make carbonyl carbon more electron deficient
(*d*) acids increase the nucleophilicity of the nucleophiles.

30. During dehydrohalogenation of an alkyl halide, hydrogen of alkyl halide is removed as
(*a*) hydrogen atom (*b*) $H^+$
(*c*) $H^-$ (*d*) free radical.

31. Two reactions of *tert*-butyl chloride are given below to give products indicated against them
$(CH_3)_3CCl + NaF \xrightarrow{H_2O} [A]$
$(CH_3)_3CCl + NaF \xrightarrow{(CH_3)_2SO} [B]$
[A] and [B] are
(*a*) *tert*-Butyl alcohol
(*b*) *iso*-Butene
(*c*) A is *tert*-butyl alcohol, B is *tert*-butyl fluoride
(*d*) A is *tert*-butyl alcohol, B is isobutene.

32. During dehydration of *tert*-butanol, which of the following carbocation is more likely to be formed as an intermediate ?
(*a*) $CH_3CH_2CH_2\overset{+}{C}H_2$ (*b*) $CH_3CH_2\overset{+}{C}HCH_3$
(*c*) Both (*d*) None.

33. A solution of (+)-2-chloro-2-phenylethane in toluene racemises slowly in presence of small amount of $SbCl_5$ due to formation of
(*a*) carbanion (*b*) carbene
(*c*) carbocation (*d*) free radical.

34. Which of the following is least stable ?
(*a*) $C_6H_5\overset{+}{C}H_2$ (*b*) $p\text{-}OCH_3 . C_6H_4 . \overset{+}{C}H_2$
(*c*) $p\text{-}NO_2 . C_6H_4 . \overset{+}{C}H_2$ (*d*) $p\text{-}OH . C_6H_4 . \overset{+}{C}H_2$.

35. Which of the following is fast debrominated ?
(*a*) 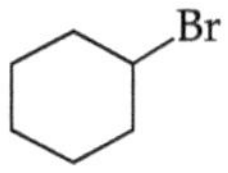 (*b*) 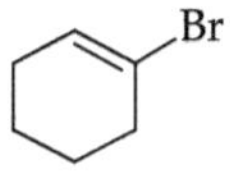
(*c*) 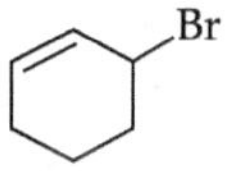 (*d*) 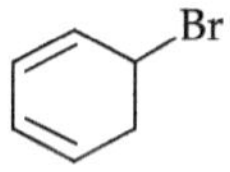

36. Heterolysis of propane gives :
(a) methylium ion and ethyl anion
(b) methyl anion and ethylium ion
(c) either (a) or (b)
(d) methylium and ethylium ions

37. The correct order of decreasing stability of the four carbanions I to IV should be :

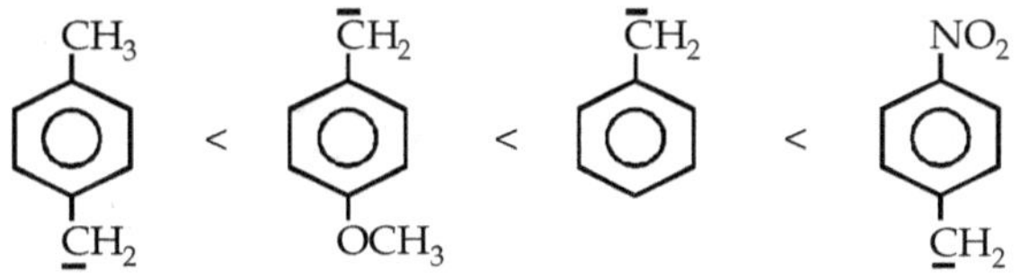

I II III IV

(a) IV > III > II < I (b) IV > III > I > II
(c) I > II > III > IV (d) II > I > IV > III

38. Predict the nature of A and B :
$(CH_3)_3C\ CH_2Br + OC_2H_5^- \longrightarrow A$
$(CH_3)_3C\ CH_2Br + CH_3OH \longrightarrow B$
(a) $(CH_3)_3CCH_2O\ C_2H_5$ and $(CH_3)_3CCH_2O\ CH_3$
(b) $(CH_3)_2C(OC_2H_5)CH_2\ CH_3$ and $(CH_3)_2C\ (OCH_3)CH_2\ CH_3$
(c) $(CH_3)_2\overset{OC_2H_5}{\overset{|}{C}}CH_2CH_3$ and $(CH_3)_3C\ CH_2O\ CH_3$
(d) $(CH_3)_2C = CHCH_3$ and $(CH_3)_2C = CH\ CH_3$

**39.** The structure drawn below has four nucleophilic sites, arrange them in order of decreasing nucloeophilicity.

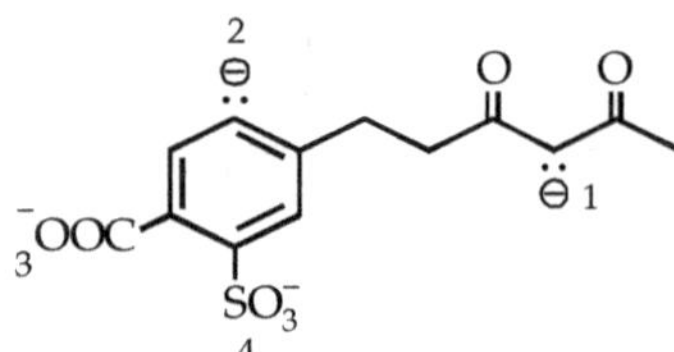

(a)   $3 > 4 > 1 > 2$       (b)   $4 > 3 > 2 > 1$

(c)   $4 > 3 > 1 > 2$       (d)   $3 > 4 > 2 > 1$

**40.** In the following hypothetical structure, which carbon is $sp$ hybridised?

$$\begin{array}{cccc} x_1 & x_2 & x_3 & x_4 \\ - \overset{-}{\underset{|}{C}} - \overset{..}{C} - \overset{.}{C} - \overset{+}{\underset{|}{C}} - \end{array}$$

(a)   $x_2$       (b)   $x_3$

(c)   $x_2$ and $x_3$       (d)   None

**41.** In the above structure, which carbon is $sp^2$ hybridised?

(a)   $x_1$       (b)   $x_2$

(c)   $x_3$       (d)   $x_4$

**42.** The weakest $C - H$ bond is present in

(a)   $CH_4$       (b)   $RCH_3$

(c)   $R_2CH_2$       (d)   $R_3CH$

**43.** Heterolysis of propane gives

(a)   methylium ions and ethyl anion

(b)   methyl anion and ethylium ion

(c)   methylium and ethylium ions

(d)   both (a) and (b)

**44.** Which of the following order is (are) correct regarding stability?

(a)   $\overset{+}{Ph_3C} > \overset{+}{Ph_2CH} > \overset{+}{PhCH_2}$

(b)   $\overset{..}{\overset{-}{Ph_3C}} > \overset{..}{\overset{-}{Ph_2CH}} > \overset{..}{\overset{-}{PhCH_2}}$

(c)   $p-NO_2C_6H_4 - \overset{..}{\overset{-}{CH_2}} > C_6H_5 - \overset{..}{\overset{-}{CH_2}}$

         $> p-CH_3O-C_6H_4 - \overset{..}{\overset{-}{CH_2}}$

(d)   $p-NO_2 - C_6H_4 - \overset{+}{CH_2} > C_6H_5 - \overset{+}{CH_2}$

         $> p\,CH_3O-C_6H_4 - \overset{+}{CH_2}$

**45.** Which of the following species have a trigonal planar shape?

(a)   $: CH_3^-$       (b)   $CH_3^+$

(c)   $BF_4^-$       (d)   $SiH_4$

**46.** A nucleophile must necessarily have

(a)   an overall positive charge

(b)   an overall negative charge

(c)   an unpaired electron

(d)   a lone pair of electrons

**47.** Carbanion is

(a)   an electrophile       (b)   a nucleophile

(c)   a Zwitter ion       (d)   a free radical

**48.** The major product of the following reaction is –

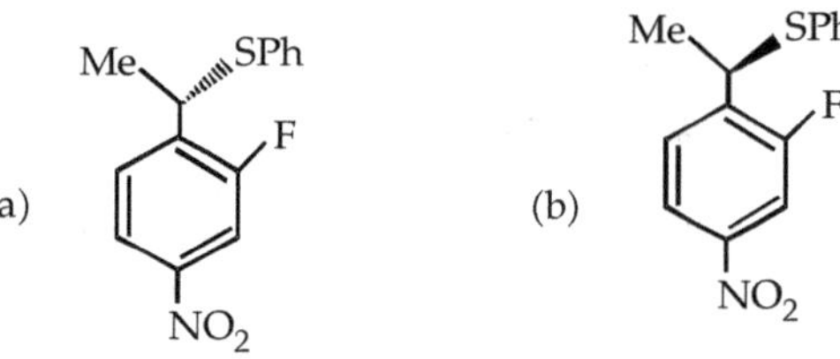

**49.** The correct stability order for the following species is

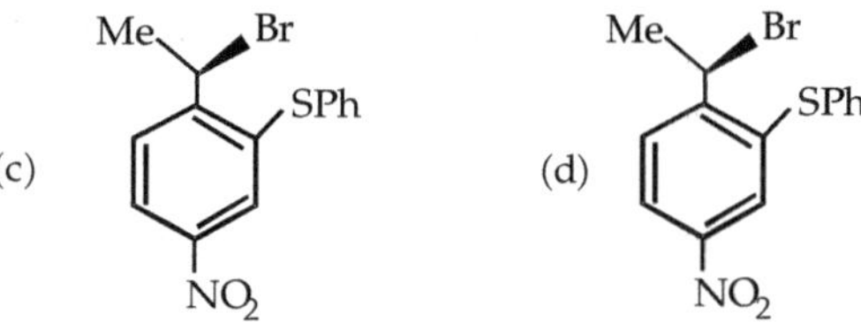

(a)   $(II) > (IV) > (I) > (III)$       (b)   $(I) > (II) > (III) > (IV)$

(c)   $(II) > (I) > (IV) > (III)$       (d)   $(I) > (III) > (II) > (IV)$

---

# EXERCISE 4.2    (MCQ 1 or >1 option correct, Passage based, Matching, A/R)

**DIRECTIONS for Q. 1 to Q. 6 : Multiple choice questions with one or more than one correct option(s).**

**1.** Which of the following statement is true regarding E2 reactions of alkyl halides which follow the following order :

$$3° > 2° > 1° \text{ Alkyl halides}$$

(a)   3° alkyl halides form most stable carbocations

(b)   Increased branching (from 1° alkyl halide to 3° halide) successively provides greater number of hydrogens to be eliminated as $H^+$.

(c)   Increased branching leads to the more stable alkene.

(d)   Increased branching facilitates the formation of transition state.

2.  Which of the following statement is true?
    (a)  $NH_3$ is more basic than $PH_3$ because N lies in a lower period of the periodic table than P.
    (b)  $NH_3$ is more basic because its bond angle is 90° while the bond angle, H – P – H in $PH_3$ is 107°.
    (c)  $NH_3$ and $PH_3$ are equally basic
    (d)  $NH_3$ is less basic than $PH_3$

3.  Pick up the correct statement(s) regarding the hybridisation state of the carbon bearing positive charge.
    (a)  All carbocations are $sp^2$ hybridised
    (b)  Vinyl carbocation is $sp$ hybridised
    (c)  Phenyl carbocation is $sp$ hybridised
    (d)  Carbocations may be $sp^3$, $sp^2$ as well as $sp$

4.  A primary carbanion is
    (a)  more reactive than a secondary carbanion
    (b)  more stable than a secondary carbanion
    (c)  less stable than a secondary carbanion
    (d)  more stable than a tertiary carbanion

5.  Which is/are true statement(s)?
    (a)  Protonation increases electrophilic nature of carbonyl group
    (b)  $CF_3SO_3^-$ is better leaving group than $CH_3SO_3^-$
    (c)  Benzyl carbonium ion is stabilised by resonance
    (d)  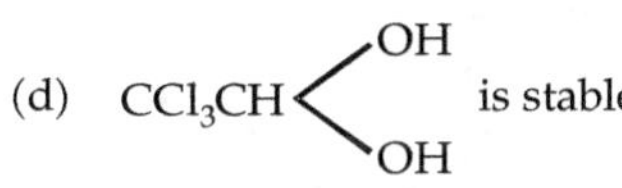 is stable

6.  The relative order of reactivity of $F^-$, $Cl^-$, $Br^-$ and $I^-$ is :
    (a)  $F^- > Cl^- > Br^- > I^-$ in non-polar solvents like DMSO (dimethyl sulphoxide)
    (b)  $F^- < Cl^- < Br^- < I^-$ in polar solvents like $H_2O$, alcohol
    (c)  $F^- < Cl^- < Br^- < I^-$ in DMSO
    (d)  $F^- > Cl^- > Br^- > I^-$ in $H_2O$

**INSTRUCTION for Q. 7 to 15 : Read the passages given below and answer the questions that follow.**

**PASSAGE 1**

7.  The intermediate in the above reaction is
    (a)  carbocation          (b)  carbanion
    (c)  free radical          (d)  none of these

8.  Step 2 involves
    (a)  elimination of $Br^-$
    (b)  rearrangement          (c)  cyclization
    (d)  cyclization as well as rearrangement

9.  Step 3 is
    (a)  reaction with the nucleophile $Br^-$
    (b)  an acid–base reaction
    (c)  Both          (d)  none

**PASSAGE 2**

3° carbocation
with 6-membered ring

10. Step I involves the formation of
    (a)  1° carbocation          (b)  2° carbocation
    (c)  3° carbocation          (d)  a free radical

11. Step 2 involves
    (a)  ring expansion
    (b)  conversion of a less stable carbocation to more stable
    (c)  Both
    (d)  None

12. Step 3 involves
    (a)  the addition of a nucleophile
    (b)  an acid-base reaction
    (c)  both
    (d)  elimination of a proton

**PASSAGE 3**

13. Step 1 involves protonation of oxygen because
    (a)  oxygen is most basic
    (b)  oxygen is most electronegative
    (c)  oxygen can easily accommodate + charge
    (d)  resulting protonated epoxide is highly stable

14. Step 2 is due to
    (a)  Instability of the epoxide ion
    (b)  Formation of more stable 3° carbocation
    (c)  Formation of 2° carbocation
    (d)  None

15. The final product having a $C = C$ is
    (a)  Hofmann product      (b)  Saytzeff product
    (c)  Cope product          (d)  None of these

**Instructions for Q. 16 to 21 : Following questions are Multiple Matching type Questions :**

16.

| Column I | | Column II | |
|---|---|---|---|
| (A) | Carbocations | (a) | E1 |
| (B) | Tetrahedral transition state | (b) | Nucleophilic-addition |
| (C) | Pentavalent transition state | (c) | $S_N2$ |
| (D) | Carbonyl compounds | (d) | $C = C + HX$ |

17.

| Column I | | Column II | |
|---|---|---|---|
| (A) | $(CH_3)_2C = CH_2 + HBr$ | (a) | 1° carbocation |
| (B) | ⬡ $+ CHBr_3 + (CH_3)_3COK$ | (b) | 2° carbocation |
| (C) | cyclohexyl–$CH_2OH$ $+ H^+$ | (c) | 3° carbocation |
| (D) | cyclobutyl–OH | (d) | Carbene |

18.

| Column I | | Column II | |
|---|---|---|---|
| (A) | Carbocation | (a) | Reaction with ethylene |
| (B) | Carbanions | (b) | Reaction with opposite species |
| (C) | Carbenes | (c) | Rearrangement |
| (D) | Free radicals | (d) | Disproportionation |

19.

| Column I | | Column II | |
|---|---|---|---|
| (A) | $S_N1$ | (a) | 3° > 2° (stability of intermediate) |
| (B) | $S_N2$ | (b) | Rearrangement possible |
| (C) | E1 | (c) | A less polar solvent favours |
| (D) | E2 | (d) | Stereospecific |

20.

| Column I (Reaction) | | Column II (Intermediate) | |
|---|---|---|---|
| (A) | Reaction of bromobenzene with sodamide | (a) | Carbocation |
| (B) | Reaction of 1, 3-butadiene with bromine | (b) | A carbanion |
| (C) | Alkaline hydrolysis of chloroform | (c) | Benzyne |
| (D) | Partial reduction of alkynes by Na in liq. $NH_3$ | (d) | Carbene |

21. Match the following :

| Column I | | Column II | |
|---|---|---|---|
| (A) | $C_6H_5CH_2CD_2Br$ on reaction with $C_2H_5O^-$ gives $C_6H_5-CH = CD_2$ | (a) | $E_1$ |
| (B) | $PhCHBrCH_2$ and $PhCHBrCD_3$, both react with the same rate | (b) | $E_2$ |
| (C) | $C_6H_5CH_2CH_2Br$ on treatment with $C_2H_5O^-$ and $C_2H_5OD$ gives $C_6H_5CD=CH_2$ | (c) | $E_1CB$ |
| (D) | $C_6H_5CH_2CH_2Br$ reacts faster than $C_6H_5CD_2CH_2Br$ on reaction with $C_2H_5O^-$ in ethanol | (d) | First order reaction |

**Instructions for Q. 22 to 26 : Following questions are Assertion and Reasoning Type Questions :**

Note : Each question contains STATEMENT-1 (Assertion) and STATEMENT-2 (Reason). Each question has 5 choices (a), (b), (c), (d) and (e) out of which ONLY ONE is correct.

(a) Statement-1 is True, Statement-2 is True; Statement-2 is a correct explanation for Statement-1.

(b) Statement-1 is True, Statement-2 is True; Statement-2 is NOT a correct explanation for Statement-1.

(c) Statement -1 is True, Statement-2 is False.

(d) Statement -1 is False, Statement-2 is True.

(e) Statement -1 is False, Statement-2 is False.

22. **Statement I :** Addition of singlet carbene to alkene is a stereospecific where as addition of triplet carbene is non-stereo specific.

    **Statement II :** Addition of singlet carbene is proceeds in concerted fashion, where as addition of triplet carbene is a two step process.

23. **Statement I :** 2,4,6 trinitro N, N-diemethylaniline is 40,000 times more basic than 2,4,6-trinitroaniline.

    **Statement II :** In the former steric inhibition or resonance causes the availability of $\ell$p on N whereas in the later due to H-bonding of $NH_2$ with $NO_2$ groups make $NH_2$ planar with benzene ring, so easy delocalisation of electron pair of N in benzene ring.

24. **Statement I :** Trichloroacetic acid is stronger than acetic acid.

    **Statement II :** Electron withdrawing substituents decrease the activity.

25. **Statement I :** Styrene on reaction with HBr gives 1-bromo-1-phenylethane.

    **Statement II :** Benzyl radical is more stable than alkyl radical.

26. **Statement I:** Rate of hydrolysis of methyl chloride to methanol is higher in DmF than in water.

    **Statement II :** Hydrolysis of methyl chloride follows second order kinetic.

**Instructions for Q. 27 to 29 : The following questions are True/False Type Questions :**

27. Trimethylmethyl and triphenylmethyl radicals, both being 3° free radical, equally exist in solution.

28. Stability order of carbanions always follows reverse order to that of corresponding carbocations.

29. Among the simple alkyl carbocations, the most stable one is $\overset{+}{C}H_3$ because here the positive charge is dispersed only to small extent.

# EXERCISE 4.3  (Subjective Problems)

**1.** Pick up the stronger nucleophile and stronger base in the following pairs of compounds ?

(*i*)   $NH_2^{\ominus}$ and $NH_3$      (*ii*)   $OH^-$ and $SH^-$

(*iii*)   $H_2O$ and $H_3O^+$      (*iv*)   $CH_3CH_2O^-$ and $CH_3COO^-$

(*v*)   $Br^-$ and $Cl^-$      (*vi*)   $OH^-$ and $F^-$.

**2.** Which of the following behaves as (*a*) a nucleophile, (*b*) an electrophile, (*c*) both or (*d*) neither ?

$Cl^-$, $NO^+$, $H_2O$, $CH_3OH$, $CH_4$, $CH_2O$, $CH_3CN$, $CH_3CH = CH_2$, $AlCl_3$, $BeCl_2$, $Cr^{3+}$, $H_2$ and $SnCl_4$.

**3.** What are ambident nucleophiles ; give two examples.

**4.** Compare the (rate of $S_N2$ reactivity) nucleophilicity of

(*a*)   $H_2O$, $OH^-$, $CH_3O^-$ and $CH_3COO^-$

(*b*)   $NH_3$ and $PH_3$.

**5.** Compare the effectiveness of the following anions as leaving groups

$CH_3COO^-$, $C_6H_5O^-$ and $C_6H_5SO_3^-$, $pK_a$ value of their conjugate acids are 4.5, 10.0 and 2.6 respectively.

**6.** Account for the decreasing stability of the following carbocations :

$$Me_3C^+ \ > \ Me_2\overset{+}{C}H \ > \ Me\overset{+}{C}H_2 \ > \ \overset{+}{C}H_3.$$

**7.** Comment on the role played by the adjacent atom or group on the stability/destability of the following carbocations :

(*a*)   $-\overset{+}{\underset{|}{C}}-CF_3$      (*b*)   $\overset{+}{C}F_3$

(*c*)   $-\overset{+}{\underset{|}{C}}-NH_2$      (*d*)   $-\overset{+}{\underset{|}{C}}-\overset{+}{N}H_3$.

**8.** Give the organic product(s) in the following reactions :

(*i*)   $CH_3CHBrCH_3 + HS^- \xrightarrow[\text{as solvent}]{CH_3OH}$

(*ii*)   $(CH_3)_3CBr + I^- \xrightarrow[\text{as solvent}]{HCOOH}$

(*iii*)   $CH_3CH_2Br + AgCN \longrightarrow$

(*iv*)   $CH_3CH_2Br + S_2O_3^{2-} \longrightarrow$

(*v*)   $CHCl_3 + Me_3COK + CH_2 = CH_2 \longrightarrow$

(*vi*)   (cyclopentane with Cl substituent) $+ \ aq.\ KOH \longrightarrow$ .

**9.** List the following alkyl bromides in order of decreasing (*a*) $S_N2$ reactivity, and (*b*) reaction with alcoholic $AgNO_3$.

$(CH_3)_2C(Br)C_2H_5$,      $CH_3(CH_2)_3CH_2Br$,      $(C_2H_5)_2CHBr$

**10.** Explain the following :

(*i*)   Ethanol does not react with $NaBr$, but reacts in presence of sulphuric acid.

(*ii*)   Although neopentyl chloride, $Me_3CCH_2Cl$ is a primary alkyl halide it does not undergo $S_N2$ reaction.

(*iii*)   *tert*-Butyl chloride undergoes solvolysis slowly than allyl chloride.

(*iv*)   Rate of solvolysis of $(CH_3)_2CHBr$ in presence of 80% water and 20% alcohol is very less than $CH_3CH_2Br$ as well as $(CH_3)_3CBr$.

(*v*)   In aqueous solution, an alkyl halide (RCl) undergoes slow hydrolysis to form alcohol, but the hydrolysis becomes fast on the addition of catalytic amount of potassium iodide.

(*vi*)   On treatment with a strong base, $CH_3CH_2I$ forms ethylene readily than $CD_3CH_2I$.

(*vii*)   Although primary alkyl halides are the least reactive towards $S_N1$ solvolysis, $CH_3CH_2OCH_2Cl$ undergoes $S_N1$ solvolysis easily in ethanol.

**11.** Which of the following reactions is primarily displacement or elimination ?

(*a*)   $CH_3CH_2CH_2Cl + I^- \longrightarrow$

(*b*)   $(CH_3)_3CBr + CN^- \text{ (ethanol)} \longrightarrow$

(*c*)   $CH_3CHBrCH_3 + OH^-(H_2O) \longrightarrow$

(*d*)   $CH_3CHBrCH_3 + OH^- \text{ (ethanol)} \longrightarrow$

(*e*)   $(CH_3)_3CBr + H_2O \longrightarrow$.

**12.** Complete the following reactions and point out the mechanism as $S_N1$, $S_N2$, E1 or E2

(*a*)   $(CH_3)_3CBr + C_2H_5OH \xrightarrow{60°C}$

(*b*)   $CH_3CH = CHCl + NaNH_2 \longrightarrow$

(*c*)   $(CH_3)_3CI + H_2O \longrightarrow$

(*d*)   $(CH_3)_3CI + OH^- \longrightarrow$.

**13.** Arrange the following in increasing order of reactivity towards aqueous HBr

Benzyl alcohol, *p*-chlorobenzyl alcohol, *p*-hydroxybenzyl alcohol, and *p*-nitrobenzyl alcohol

**14.** Arrange different primary isomeric pentyl alcohols in order of increasing reactivity towards aqueous HBr.

**15.** Arrange the following in increasing order of their reactivity towards $S_N1$ reaction

(structures of brominated compounds)

**16.** Among following pairs of alkenes, pick up the alkene which is expected to add HCl readily, assuming that addition is an ionic reaction

(*i*)   (alkene) and (alkene)

(*ii*)   (alkene) and (alkene)

(*iii*)   (alkene) and (alkene with $C_6H_5$ $C_6H_5$)

(*iv*)   (alkene) and (alkene)

**17.** Predict the preferred regiochemistry for the addition of HCl to each of the following :

(*i*)   (cyclohexene)      (*ii*)   (alkene)

(*iii*)   (alkene)      (*iv*)   (alkene)

**18.** Arrange the following in increasing order of reactivity towards the addition of HBr.

Styrene, *p*-methylstyrene, *p*-chlorostyrene, *p*-nitrostyrene.

**19.** Give the mechanism involved in free radical addition of $CBrCl_3$ to 1, 3-butadiene.

**20.** Explain briefly the formation of products giving structures of the intermediates.

(i) (structure) $\xrightarrow{\text{HCl}}$ (structure)

(ii) (structure) $\xrightarrow{\text{HCl}}$ (structure) (only)

(iii) (structure with OCH$_3$, Br) $\xrightarrow[\text{NH}_3]{\text{NaNH}_2}$ (structure with OCH$_3$, NH$_2$)

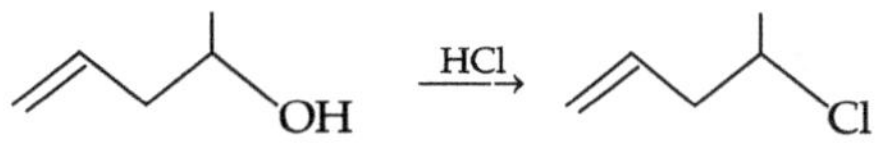

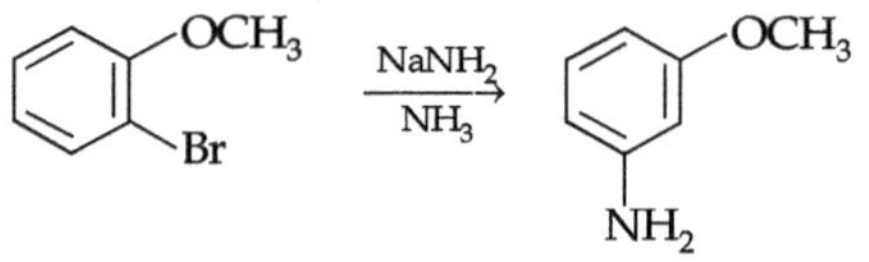

**21.** Arrange the following in decreasing stability order :

(a)

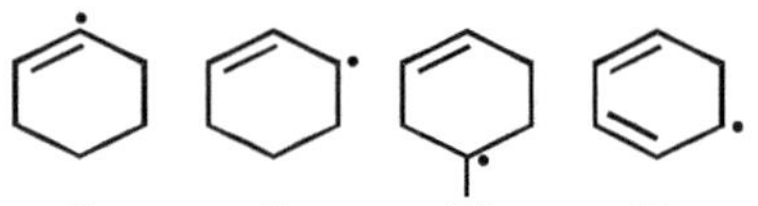

    I     II     III     IV

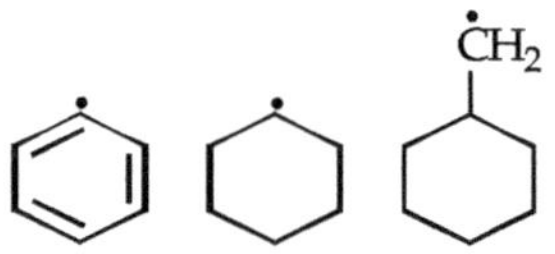

    V     VI     VII

(b)

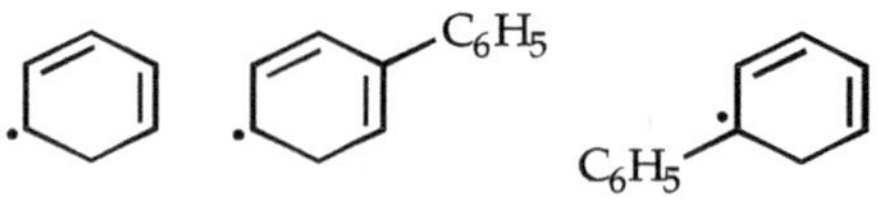

    I     II     III

(c) $: CH_2$, $C_6H_5\ddot{C}H$, $CH_3\ddot{C}H$, $(C_6H_5)_2\ddot{C}$

    I         II        III        IV

(d) Is there any relation betwen the bond energy and stability of a free radical? Cyclohexene has three types of C – H bonds, (marked $a$, $b$ and $c$), which C – H bond is strongest and which one is weakest?

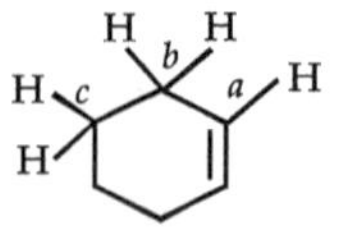

(structure of cyclohexene with H atoms marked a, b, c)

**22.** Complete the following by giving structure of the product :

(a) $CH_3 - N \equiv N \xrightarrow{\text{heat}} N_2 + \ldots\ldots$

(b) $C_6H_5N_3 \xrightarrow{h\nu} N_2 + \ldots\ldots$

(c) $CH_3CON_3 \xrightarrow{h\nu} N_2 + \ldots\ldots$

(d) $HN_3 \xrightarrow{h\nu} N_2 + \ldots\ldots$

(e) $CH_3NCO \xrightarrow{h\nu} CO + \ldots\ldots$

**23.** Write the structure of the missing reactant/product

(a) $CH_3CH_2CH_3 + \ldots\ldots \longrightarrow CH_3CH_2CH_2CH_3 + \ldots\ldots$

(b) $CH_3CH = CHCH_3 + \ldots\ldots \longrightarrow$

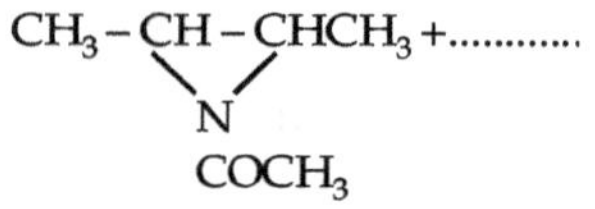

    $CH_3 - CH - CHCH_3 + \ldots\ldots$
           $\underset{\underset{COCH_3}{|}}{N}$

(c)  (structure with MgBr, F) $\xrightarrow{\text{heat}} \ldots\ldots \xrightarrow[\text{liq.}]{\text{NH}_3}$ (structure with NH$_2$)

# SOLUTIONS



**1.** *(a)* **Electrophiles.** $H^+$, $Cl^+$, $Cr^{3+}$, $NO_2^+$ (all have positive charge), $\overset{*}{B}eCl_2$, $\overset{*}{S}nCl_4$ (electron deficient atom, marked by * is present), $SiF_4$ (although every atom has octet, Si can have 10 electrons in its *d*-orbitals).

*(b)* **Nucleophiles.** $Cl^-$ (negative charge), $CH_3CH = CH_2$ (presence of $\pi$ electrons), $H_2\overset{..}{O}:$ (presence of lone pair of electrons)

*(c)* **Both (Ambiphile).** $CH_2 = \overset{..}{O}:$, $CH_3C \equiv N:$ (In these, C is electrophilic ; while O/N is nucleophilic).

*(d)* **None.** $H_2$, $CH_4$ (absence of charge, $\pi$ electrons, lone pair of electrons or $\delta+$ and $\delta-$ charges).

**2.** The part bearing $\delta+$ will act as an electrophile

$$\overset{\delta+}{Cl}-\overset{\delta-}{Cl} \qquad \overset{\delta-}{HO}-\overset{\delta+}{H} \qquad \overset{\delta+}{H}-\overset{\delta-}{Br} \qquad \overset{\delta-}{HO}-\overset{\delta+}{Cl}$$

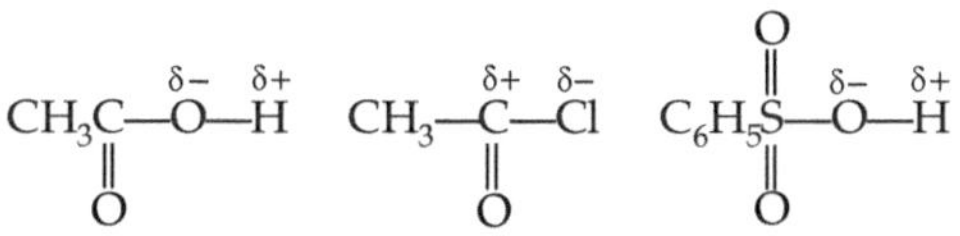

$$CH_3\overset{\delta-}{C}-\overset{\delta+}{O}-H \qquad CH_3-\overset{\delta+}{C}-\overset{\delta-}{Cl} \qquad C_6H_5\overset{\delta-}{S}-\overset{\delta+}{O}-H$$

**3.** Due to high electronegativity of O and Cl in $CH_3COCl$ and Cl in $ICl$, two compounds behave as electrophiles.

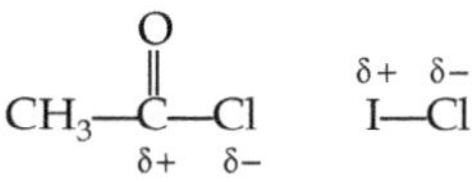

$$CH_3-\overset{O}{\underset{}{C}}-Cl \qquad \overset{\delta+}{I}-\overset{\delta-}{Cl}$$

**4.** *(i)* Addition.

*(ii)* Addition and redox.

*(iii)* Rearrangement ; nothing is eliminated or added ; cycloalkane is converted into alkene.

*(iv)* Elimination (two chlorine atoms are removed from adjacent C atoms ; $\beta$-elimination) and redox (oxidation number of C as well as Zn changes). Organic compound is reduced, while Zn is oxidised.

*(v)* Addition and redox. The two bromine atoms add on two carbon atoms of the ring. Simultaneously note that carbon atoms of the organic compound are oxidised while the bromine atoms are reduced.

*(vi)* Rearrangement ; cyanate (—CNO) functional group is converted into amide group (—$CONH_2$).

*(vii)* Elimination. Note that here both atoms (*i.e.* H as well as Cl) are removed from the same carbon atom, elimination is $\alpha$.

*(viii)* Substitution and redox ; $CH_3CH_2Br$ is reduced.

*(ix)* $\quad$ Addition.

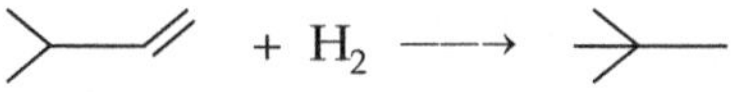

**5.** Try to solve the problem by balancing the charge on the reactant(s) and product(s). Remember that free radicals and carbenes are neutral, the former has one free electron while the latter 2.

*(i)* $(CH_3)_3C^+$ $\qquad$ *(ii)* $:CH_2$

*(iii)* $(CH_3)_3C^+$ $\qquad$ *(iv)* $.CH_3$

*(v)* $:CH_2$ $\qquad$ *(vi)* $CH_2D\overset{+}{C}H_2$

*(vii)* $.CH_3$ $\qquad$ *(viii)* $HC \equiv C:^-$.

**6.** Products are $Me_3COOCCH_3 + AgBr$

**Mechanism**

*(i)* $\underset{\text{Nucleophile}}{\overset{\delta+\ \delta-}{Me_3CBr}} + \underset{\text{Electrophile}}{Ag^+} \xrightarrow{\text{slow}} Me_3C^+ + AgBr$

*(ii)* $\underset{\text{Electrophile}}{Me_3C^+} + \underset{\text{Nucleophile}}{CH_3COO^-} \xrightarrow{\text{fast}} Me_3COOCCH_3$

**7.** *(i)*

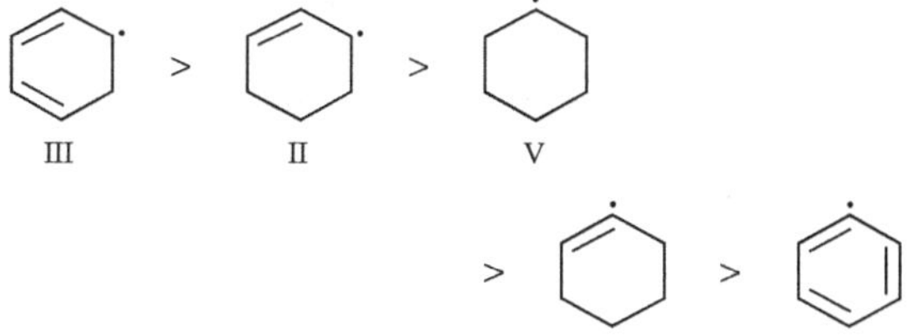

III is most stable because it is an allylic free radical having two conjugated $\pi$ bonds, II is also allylic radical but with one conjugated $\pi$ bond. Relative stability of V, I and IV can better be understood by considering their parent compounds.

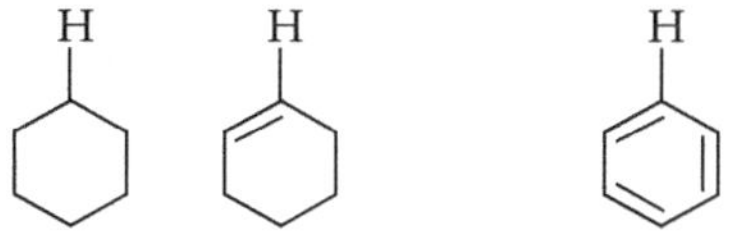

| Parent compound | Va | Ia | IVa |
|---|---|---|---|
| Nature of C—H bond | $sp^3$ (weak) | $sp^2$ (strong) | $sp^2$ (stronger due to resonance) |

Thus it is easiest to remove ·H in Va leading to the most stable free radical and most difficult in IVa leading to the least stable free radical.

*(ii)*

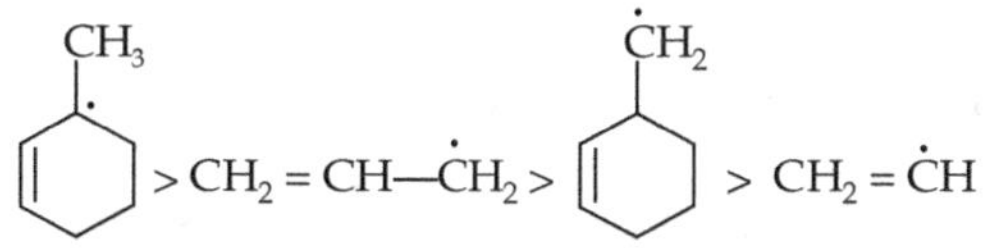

Note that IV and II are both allylic free radicals, their relative stability can be predicted by considering their parent compounds.

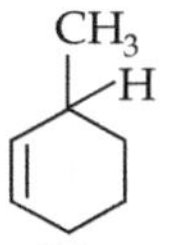

IVa $\qquad$ $CH_2 = CH—CH_3$
IIa (more stable due to hyperconjugations, and thus H· is removed with difficulty)

Stability of III and I can again be considered by taking their parent compounds.

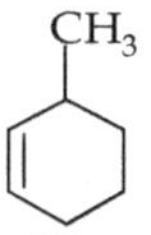

IIIa $\qquad$ $CH_2 = CH_2$
Ia (It is difficult to remove H· from $sp^2$ hybridised C atom)



**1.** *(i)* Negative. Two molecules are changing into one molecule and there is more order (less randomness) in the product, *i.e.* $S_P < S_R$.

*(ii)* Positive. The rigid ring is converted into an acyclic compound which due to free rotation about C—C single bond will have more randomness (less order). Thus here $S_P > S_R$.

*(iii)* Positive. The ions (present in reactants) are solvated by more $H_2O$ molecules than the $CH_3COOH$ (present in product); hence when ions form molecules, several water molecules are set free and hence they will have more randomness, *i.e.* $S_P > S_R$.

**2.** *(i)* Both values increase rate of reaction.

*(ii)* Both values decrease rate of reaction.

*(iii)* Increase in $\Delta H^{\ddagger}$ will tend to decrease the rate while increase in $\Delta S^{\ddagger}$ will tend to increase the rate. Hence the net effect is unpredictable.

*(iv)* The trends will be opposite to those in part *(iii)*; hence here also the net effect will be unpredictable.

**3.** $\Delta H^{\ddagger}$ can be decreased by *(a)* raising $H_R$, *(b)* lowering $H_{TS}$ or *(c)* both of these.

**4.** *(i)* $A + B \longrightarrow C + D$ ; rate $= k[A][B]$.

Here both reactants are involved in the rate expression, so the reaction must be biomolecular. Further, the balanced given reaction involves one molecule of A and one molecule of B, the reaction must have a single (concerted) step.

*(ii)* $r = k[A]$. The rate-determining step is unimolecular and involves only one molecule of A. There can be no prior fast step. Molecule B reacts in the second step, which is fast. A possible two-step mechanism is

$$A \xrightarrow{\text{slow}} C + I \text{ (Intermediate)}$$

$$B + I \xrightarrow{\text{fast}} D$$

*(iii)* $r = k[B]$. On the basis of similar explanation, reaction occurs in the following way :

$$B \xrightarrow{\text{slow}} C + I$$

$$A + I \xrightarrow{\text{fast}} D$$

**5.** The rate expression indicates that one molecule of B and two molecules of A are needed to give the species for the slow step. Since no step is termoloecular, there must be some number of prior fast steps to give at least intermediate needed for the slow step. The second B molecule (given in the reaction equation) must be consumed in a fast step following the slow step to give final products. Two different mechanisms are possible.

*Mechanism I    Mechanism II*

| | |
|---|---|
| $A + B \xrightarrow{\text{fast}} AB$ | $A + A \longrightarrow A_2$ |
| (Intermediate) | (Intermediate) |
| $AB + A \xrightarrow{\text{slow}} ABA$ | $A_2 + B \longrightarrow A_2B$ |
| $ABA + B \xrightarrow{\text{fast}} C + D$ | $A_2B + B \longrightarrow C + D$ |

**6.** The slow unimolecular step should involve decomposition of the intermediate $AB_2$ or $B_2A$. Further all the given number of molecules of the reaction are accounted for in the rate determining step, this should be the final step. Two possible mechanisms can be given.

*Mechanism I    Mechanism II*

| | |
|---|---|
| $B + B \xrightarrow{\text{fast}} B_2$ | $A + B \xrightarrow{\text{fast}} AB$ |
| $B_2 + A \xrightarrow{\text{fast}} B_2A$ | $AB + B \xrightarrow{\text{fast}} AB_2$ |
| $B_2A \xrightarrow{\text{slow}} C + D$ | $AB_2 \xrightarrow{\text{slow}} C + D$ |

---



**1.** According to given statement $+ 39.6°$ is the specific rotation for 100% optically pure (+)-2-bromooctane.

$$\therefore [\alpha] + 24.9° \text{ corresponds to} = \frac{24.9}{39.6} \times 100 = 63\% \text{ optical purity}$$

Since $S_{N}2$ reactions proceed with 100% inversion, the product, (–)-2-octanol, will also be 63% optically pure.

Thus, 100% optically pure (–)-2-octanol has $[\alpha] - 10.3°$.

$$\therefore 63\% \text{ optically pure (–)-2-octanol will have} = \frac{-10.3}{100} \times 63$$
$$= -6.5°$$

$\therefore$ Specific rotation of (–)-2-octanol $= -6.5°$.

$$\text{Br} \overset{\displaystyle C_6H_{13}}{\underset{\displaystyle CH_3}{\rule[0.5ex]{0pt}{2ex}|}} \text{H} \xrightarrow[S_N2]{\text{aq. NaOH}} \text{H} \overset{\displaystyle C_6H_{13}}{\underset{\displaystyle CH_3}{\rule[0.5ex]{0pt}{2ex}|}} \text{OH}$$

(+)-2-Bromooctane        (–)-2-Octanol
$[\alpha] = + 24.9°$      optical purity 63%
optical purity 63%      $\therefore \quad [\alpha] = - 6.5°$

---



**1.** *(a)* $S_N1$ reactions involve formation of carbocation, hence alkyl halide capable of forming carbocation easily $(3° > 2° > 1°)$ will react faster toward $S_N1$.

*(i)* 1-Methylcyclopentyl iodide (3° halide)    will react faster than    Cyclopentyl iodide (2°)

*(ii)* Cyclopentyl bromide (2°)   >   $BrCH_2\overset{\displaystyle CH_3}{\underset{\displaystyle CH_3}{\rule[0.5ex]{0pt}{2ex}|}}CCH_3$   1-Bromo-2, 2-dimethylpropane (1°)

*(iii)* *tert*-Butyl iodide $>$ *tert*-Butyl chloride, C—I bond is weaker than the C—Cl bond.

*(b)* $S_N2$ Reactions involve back-side attack of the nucleophile on the alkyl halide, hence alkyl halide more crowded at the site of substitution will react slowly than the other by $S_N2$ mechanism.

*(i)* $CH_3CH_2CH_2Br$   >   $CH_3\overset{\displaystyle Br}{\underset{\displaystyle}{\rule[0.5ex]{0pt}{2ex}|}}CHCH_3$
1-Bromopropane, 1°     2-Bromopropane, 2°
(less crowded)      (more crowded)

*(ii)* $CH_3(CH_2)_4CH_2Cl$   >   Cyclohexyl chloride (2°, more crowded)
1-Chlorohexane (1°, less crowded)

*(iii)* $CH_3\overset{\displaystyle Cl}{\underset{\displaystyle}{\rule[0.5ex]{0pt}{2ex}|}}CH(CH_2)_2CH_3$   >   $CH_3\overset{\displaystyle F}{\underset{\displaystyle}{\rule[0.5ex]{0pt}{2ex}|}}CH(CH_2)_2CH_3$
2-Chloropentane      2-Fluoropentane

Among halogens, fluorine has the strongest bond to carbon, and fluoride is the poorest leaving group, hence it is least reactive toward $S_N2$ as well as $S_N1$ reactions.

(iv) $\underset{\substack{\text{1-Bromodecane (1°)}\\ \text{(although 1°, it is more}\\ \text{crowded due to bulky}\\ \text{C}_9\text{H}_{19}\text{— group)}}}{CH_3(CH_2)_8CH_2Br}$ $<$ $\underset{\substack{\text{2-Bromopropane (2°)}\\ \text{(although 2°, it is having}\\ \text{smaller —CH}_3\text{ groups)}}}{CH_3\overset{Br}{\underset{}{C}}HCH_3}$

(v) $\underset{\substack{\text{2-Bromo-2-methylethane}\\ \text{(3°, more crowded)}}}{CH_3\overset{Br}{\underset{CH_3}{C}}CH_2CH_2CH_2CH_3}$ $<$ $\underset{\substack{\text{2-Bromo-5-methylhexane}\\ \text{(2°, less crowded)}}}{CH_3\overset{Br}{\underset{}{C}}HCH_2CH_2\overset{CH_3}{\underset{}{C}}HCH_3}$

**2.** A hydride shift produces tertiary, a more stable carbocation ; while a methyl shift produces a secondary carbocation.

$$\underset{\text{2° Carbocation}}{CH_3\overset{CH_3}{\underset{H}{\overset{\oplus}{C}}}-CHCH_3} \xleftarrow[\text{shift}]{\text{methyl}} \underset{\text{1° Carbocation}}{CH_3\overset{CH_3}{\underset{H}{C}}-\overset{+}{C}HCH_3} \xrightarrow[\text{shift}]{\text{hydride}}$$

$$\underset{\text{3° Carbocation}}{CH_3-\overset{CH_3}{\underset{+}{C}}-CH_2CH_3}$$

**3.** (a) According to statement, specific rotations of optically pure (100%) chloride and alcohol are

$$\underset{\text{(R)-(–)-α-Phenylethyl chloride, }[\alpha] = -109°}{H\overset{C_6H_5}{\underset{CH_3}{\rule[-0.5em]{0.02em}{1.5em}}}Cl}$$

$$\underset{\text{(R)-(–)-α-Phenylethyl alcohol, }[\alpha] = -42.3°}{H\overset{C_6H_5}{\underset{CH_3}{\rule[-0.5em]{0.02em}{1.5em}}}OH}$$

However, according to the reaction the actual specific rotations of the reactant and products are – 34° and + 1.7° respectively, different value of specific rotation and opposite sign of $[\alpha]$ of the product indicates that during reaction inversion as well as retention in configuration occurs and the amount of inverted configuration is more than that of retained configuration.

$$H\overset{C_6H_5}{\underset{CH_3}{\rule[-0.5em]{0.02em}{1.5em}}}Cl \xrightarrow{\text{NaOH}} HO\overset{C_6H_5}{\underset{CH_3}{\rule[-0.5em]{0.02em}{1.5em}}}H$$

$[\alpha] = -34°$ *(optical purity = 31%)* $\qquad$ $[\alpha] = +1.7°$ *(optical purity = 4%)*

% of optical purity of the reactant with $[\alpha]$ – 34°

$$= \frac{34}{109} \times 100 = \mathbf{31\%}$$

Similarly, % of optical purity of the product with $[\alpha] + 1.7°$

$$= \frac{1.7}{42.3} \times 100 = \mathbf{4.0\%}$$

(b) Determination of net (after subtracting amount utilised in racemic modification) inverted configuration in the

$$\text{product} = \frac{4}{31} \times 100 = 13\%$$

$\therefore$ % of racemic modification $= 100 - 13 = 87\%$

Hence % of total inverted configuration $= 13 + \dfrac{87}{2}$

$$= \mathbf{56.5\%}$$

and % of retained configuration $= \dfrac{87}{2} = \mathbf{43.5}$

**4.** Remember wherever rearranged products are formed, carbocations must be formed as intermediates which indicate $S_N1$ reaction. Carbocation formation in alkyl halides is favoured by bulky alkyl groups and by weak electrophiles like ROH. $S_N2$ reaction is favoured by alkyl halides having primary alkyl halides and/or by strong nucleophiles like RO⁻.

In (i), (ii) and (iv), rearranged products are formed, thus the mechanism will be $S_N1$. In (iii) usual product is formed, reaction is $S_N2$. However, remember that neopentyl bromide is having Br on primary carbon atom, so its corresponding cation, being primary, is not formed easily. Hence it undergoes $S_N1$ reaction as in (iv) very slowly and in presence of weak nucleophile, in presence of strong nucleophile it undergoes $S_N2$ reaction as in (iii).

**5.** In neopentyl halides, $(CH_3)_3CCH_2X$, $S_N1$ reaction is slow because neopentyl cation is primary $(CH_3)_3C\overset{+}{C}H_2$, and hence its formation is slow. The $S_N2$ reaction is slow because of steric factor, *i.e.* a very large, $(CH_3)_3C$— group, is present on —$CH_2X$.



**1.** $\underset{\text{Octadecyl alcohol}}{CH_3(CH_2)_{16}CH_2-OH} + \underset{\text{$p$-Toluenesulphonyl chloride}}{ClO_2S-\bigcirc-CH_3} \xrightarrow{\text{pyridine}}$

$$\underset{\text{Octadecyl-$p$-toluenesulphonate}}{CH_3(CH_2)_{16}CH_2-\overset{O}{\underset{O}{\overset{\|}{\underset{\|}{S}}}}-\bigcirc-Ch_3} \text{ or } CH_3(CH_2)_{16}CH_2OTs$$

Note that in the preparation of tosylates, C—O bond of alcohol is not cleaved, hence the configuration of the alcohol and tosylate will be same (difference from alkyl halides : R—OH + HCl $\xrightarrow{H^+}$ R—Cl, where configuration of product will not be similar to that of alcohol). Since $p$-toluenesulphonate is a very good leaving group, it will be displaced by nucleophiles very easily.

(a) $\underset{\text{Octadecyl tosylate}}{CH_3(CH_2)_{16}CH_2-OTs} + CH_3COOK \longrightarrow$

$$\underset{\text{Octadecyl acetate}}{CH_3(CH_2)_{16}CH_2-O-\overset{O}{\overset{\|}{C}}CH_3}$$

(b) $CH_3(CH_2)_{16}CH_2-OTs + C_3H_7CH_2SNa \longrightarrow$

$$CH_3(CH_2)_{16}CH_2SCH_2C_3H_7$$



**1.** (i) $CH_3COCl$, (ii) $CH_3CONH_2$, (iii) $CH_3COOC_2H_5$

Oxygen atom of the carbonyl group makes carbon more electrophilic in nature and hence compounds having

$$R-\overset{O}{\overset{\|}{C}}-$$

group are more susceptible to attack by a nucleophilic than the carbon atom of the alkyl group (—$CH_3$).

## TEST YOUR UNDERSTANDING - 4.7

**1.** *(i)*  $H_3C-\overset{CH_3}{\underset{(3°)}{\overset{|}{C}}}-CH_2CH_3$   *(ii)*  $CH_3CH_2\overset{+}{C}HCH_3$

*(iii)* (ethylcyclohexyl cation)

**2.** (alkene) $+ H^+ \longrightarrow$ 2° carbocation $\xrightarrow{\text{rearranges to}}$ 3° carbocation

With $Cl^-$:
2-Chloro-3, 3-dimethylbutane    2-Chloro-2, 3-dimethylbutane

**3.** *(i)* (cyclohexenone) $+ HCN \xrightarrow[\text{addition}]{\text{electrophilic}}$

1, 2-addition (A)  +  1, 4-addition (B)

*(ii)*  $CH_3CH = CH_2 + CCl_4 \xrightarrow{\text{peroxide}} CH_3-\overset{Cl}{\overset{|}{C}HCH_2CCl_3}$  (C)

*(iii)*  $CH_3CH = CH_2 + CBrCl_3 \xrightarrow{\text{peroxide}} CH_3CH(Br)CH_2CCl_3$  (D)

*(iv)*  $CH_3CH = CH_2 + CHCl_3 \xrightarrow{\text{peroxide}} CH_3CH_2CH_2CCl_3$  (E)

## TEST YOUR UNDERSTANDING - 4.8

**1.** *(i)*  (bromocyclohexane) $+ C_2H_5OK \xrightarrow[\text{Strong base}]{\text{elimination}}$ (cyclohexene)

2° Halide

*(ii)*  $CH_3\overset{Br}{\overset{|}{C}HCH_2CH_3} + CH_3OH \xrightarrow[\text{Weak base}]{\text{Substitution}} CH_3\overset{}{\underset{OCH_3}{\overset{|}{C}H}CH_2CH_3}$

2° Halide

*(iii)*  $CH_3\overset{Br}{\overset{|}{C}HCH_2CH_3} + C_2H_5ONa \xrightarrow[\text{Strong base}]{\text{elimination}}$

2° Halide    Strong base

$CH_3CH = CHCH_3$
*cis-* and *trans-* (Major)

**2.**  2, 2-Dimethylcyclo-hexanol $\xrightarrow[(-H_2O)]{H^+}$ 2° Carbocation $\longrightarrow$

3° Carbocation $\xrightarrow{-H^+}$ 1, 2-Dimethyl-cyclohexene

**3.** *(a)* *(i)* (1-methylcyclohexanol) $\xrightarrow{H^+}$ $\xrightarrow{(-H_2O)}$ Carbocation

Carbocation can undergo elimination to form 1-methylcyclohexene and methylenecyclohexane.

*(ii)* $\longrightarrow$ (1-methylcyclohexene) $+ :\overset{+}{O}H_3$  (Major)

*(iii)* $\longrightarrow$ (methylenecyclohexane) $+ :\overset{+}{O}H_3$  (Minor)

*(b)* *(i)* $\xrightarrow{H^+}$ Carbocation $+ H_2O$

*(ii)* $\xrightarrow{H^+}$ $+ :\overset{+}{O}H_3$  (Minor)

*(iii)* $\longrightarrow$ $+ :\overset{+}{O}H_3O$  (Minor)

# EXERCISE 4.1

| 1 | (d) | 6 | (d) | 11 | (d) | 16 | (d) | 21 | (c) | 26 | (a) | 31 | (d) | 36 | (b) | 41 | (b) | 46 | (d) |
|---|-----|---|-----|----|-----|----|-----|----|-----|----|-----|----|-----|----|-----|----|-----|----|-----|
| 2 | (c) | 7 | (b) | 12 | (c) | 17 | (d) | 22 | (b) | 27 | (b) | 32 | (d) | 37 | (b) | 42 | (d) | 47 | (b) |
| 3 | (b) | 8 | (d) | 13 | (b) | 18 | (d) | 23 | (b) | 28 | (c) | 33 | (c) | 38 | (c) | 43 | (b) | 48 | (a) |
| 4 | (c) | 9 | (d) | 14 | (b) | 19 | (c) | 24 | (b) | 29 | (c) | 34 | (c) | 39 | (c) | 44 | (c) | 49 | (d) |
| 5 | (b) | 10 | (c) | 15 | (c) | 20 | (a) | 25 | (c) | 30 | (b) | 35 | (d) | 40 | (b) | 45 | (b) | | |

1. $Ag^+$ has positive charge, hence electron deficient, in $H_2C:$, C has only 6 electrons ; in $SiF_4$, Si can acquire more than 8 electrons by utilizing its $d$-orbitals.

2. In the reaction, A and C are reactants, B and E are intermediates; and D and F are products. This can be observed by addition of the three steps to get the following net reaction
$$2A + C \longrightarrow D + 2F$$

3. The reaction occurs in two steps, in the first step $CH_2 = CH_2$ is nucleophile, while in the second step $Br^-$ is nucleophile

(i) $\overset{\delta+}{H_2C} = \overset{\delta-}{CH_2}$ + $\overset{\delta+}{Br}—\overset{\delta-}{Br}$ $\longrightarrow$ $\overset{+}{C}H_2CH_2Br$ + $Br^-$
Nucleophile₁    Electrophile₂    Electrophile₁    Nucleophile₂

(ii) $\overset{+}{C}H_2CH_2Br$ + $Br^-$ $\longrightarrow$ $CH_2BrCH_2Br$
Electrophile₁    Nucleophile₂

4. Let us study the free radical formed by the removal of three H·'s

Least stable because H· is to be removed from $sp^2$ C    Most stable due to allylic nature    More stable because H· is to be removed from $sp^3$C

5. Isobutane has two types of carbon atoms (1° and 3°) ; hence it will form two products

$CH_3\overset{\overset{CH_3}{|}}{C}HCH_3$ + $:CH_2$ $\longrightarrow$ $CH_3CH_2\overset{\overset{CH_3}{|}}{C}HCH_3$ + $CH_3—\overset{\overset{CH_3}{|}}{\underset{\underset{CH_3}{|}}{C}}—CH_3$
Isobutane     Insertion on 1°C     Insertion on 3°C

6. In the formation of carbocation (as well as free radical) $sp^3$ hybridised carbon atom changes to $sp^2$. This is of special importance in formation of *tert*-carbocation (or free radical) where steric relief is observed. In the parent compound the three bulkyl groups are pushed together due to tetrahedral nature of the carbon atom having bond angle of 109.5° (steric strain) which is greatly relieved in formation of carbocation (or free radical) due to planar structure (120°) of the product, where the three bulky groups are separated from each other by an angle of 120° **(steric relief).**

7. In carbanion, $sp^3$ hybridised carbon atom has three pairs of bonding electrons and one pair of non-bonding electrons. Thus here two types of repulsions are observed : *lp-bp* and *bp-bp* ; since *lp-bp* > *bp-bp* repulsions, angle between two bonding pairs is slightly reduced than the normal tetrahedral value of 109.5°. Thus the geometry of simple carbanions is not exactly tetrahedral, but pyramidal.

8. Carbocations are $sp^2$ hybridised, simple (unconjugated) carbanions are $sp^3$ hybridised but conjugated carbanions are $sp^2$ hybridised because here delocalization of electrons results in the formation of a double bond which requires all involved atoms to lie in the same plane (coplanar), *i.e.* the molecule becomes flat.

$H_2\ddot{C}—\overset{\overset{CH_3}{|}}{C} = O \longleftrightarrow H_2C = \overset{\overset{CH_3}{|}}{C}—\ddot{\ddot{O}}$

$H_2C = CH—\ddot{C}H_2 \longleftrightarrow H_2\ddot{C}—CH = CH_2$ or $\left[ H_2\overset{-\delta}{C}\text{⹀}CH\text{⹀}\overset{-\delta}{C}H_2 \right]$

9. Carbanion from $CH_3CHO$ and cyclopentadiene is stabilised due to resonance and aromatic sextet respectively.

10. Carbanion is formed as an intermediate which being flat can be attacked by $Br_2$ on either face forming racemic mixture.

11. Cationoid (cation-like) are those species which are either cations or behave as cations *i.e.* electron deficient.

13. Rate of a multi-step reaction is determined by the slowest step. Thus transition state of such step will require more energy of activation, and thus the corresponding transition state will have highest enthalpy.

14. In multistep reactions, the step with the highest enthalpy transition state (*i.e.* with highest $\Delta H^{\neq}$ ) is the slowest (rate determining) step.

15. The nucleophilicity of species whose nucleophilic atoms neither lie in the same period nor in the same group of the periodic table should be compared by considering their basic strength or the relative acidic character of their conjugate acids. The decreasing basic character of the species is
$$HS^- > RCOO^- > ROH > RCOOH$$
Conjugate acids   $H_2S$ < $RCOOH$ < $ROH_2^+$ < $RCOOH_2^+$

16. $CH_3—\overset{\overset{CH_3}{|}}{\underset{\underset{CH_3}{|}}{C}}—OH \xrightarrow{\overset{+}{H}} CH_3—\overset{\overset{CH_3}{|}}{\underset{\underset{CH_3}{|}}{\overset{\oplus}{C}}}$
*tert*-Butanol      *tert*-Butyl carbocation

*tert*-Butyl carbocation is formed as an intermediate, which being stable, does not rearrange to the less stable 2° or 1° carbocation.

17. Oxygen, being an electronegative element, can best accommodate negative charge.

18. More the difference between the electronegativies of two concerned atoms, higher will be the chance for dissociation into ions.

19. More the stability of a species greater is the ease of its formation and hence lesser will be the dissociation energy of the bond to be cleaved. Benzyl radical is highly stable due to delocalisation of its odd electron while methyl radical is quite unstable.

20. Free radical substitution leads to complete racemization because the intermediate free radical is coplanar and can be attacked on either of the face equally forming two enantiomers in equal amounts (complete racemization). $S_N2$ reaction involves the formation of transition state in which attack of nucleophile and removal of the leaving group take place simultaneously, hence the nucleophile can attack back-side from that the leaving group. Consequently, compound having inverted configuration is formed (100% inversion of configuration). In $S_{N^1}$ reaction, the nucleophile attacks the ion pair ($R^+X^-$), hence back-side attack of the nucleophile predominates although attack from the side of the leaving group (front-side attack) also takes place. Thus the product will be having both enantiomers, and the enantiomer with the inverted configuration predominates. In short, $S_N1$ reaction leads to partial racemization along with some amount of inverted configuration.

21. Discussed in the above answer.

22. Since $S_N1$ reaction yields racemic modification along with some amount of the enantiomer of inverted configuration ; as far as specific rotation is concerned, the product will be having opposite specific rotation. Further, its value will be less because *optical purity* of the product will be less than that of reactant.

23. The weaker the base, better will be the leaving group. Further, basic character of the groups can be easily judged by acidic character of its conjugate acid (recall that weak bases have stronger conjugate acids). Thus

| Base | $^-OH$ | $F^-$ | $OH_2^-$ | OTs | $^-OSO_2CF_3$ |
|---|---|---|---|---|---|
| Conjugate acid | $H_2O$ | HF | $H_3O^+$ | HOTs | $HOSO_2CF_3$ |

The acidic order of the various conjugate acids is
$$CF_3SO_2OH > TsOH > H_3O^+ > HF > H_2O$$

24. $S_N1$ reactions follow first-order kinetics ; rate = $k[RX]$, hence concentration of the nucleophile does not effect its rate.

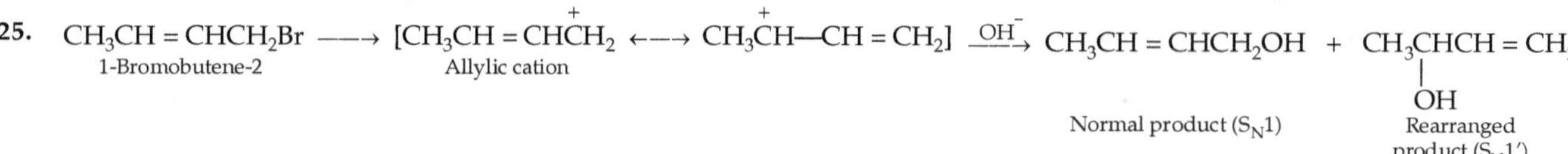

**25.** $CH_3CH = CHCH_2Br \longrightarrow [CH_3CH = \overset{+}{C}HCH_2 \longleftrightarrow CH_3\overset{+}{C}H-CH = CH_2] \xrightarrow{\overline{OH}} CH_3CH = CHCH_2OH + CH_3CHCH = CH_2$

1-Bromobutene-2        Allylic cation        Normal product ($S_N1$)     | OH   Rearranged product ($S_N1'$)

Since allylic cation stabilise easily due to resonance, its formation is easy and hence, the compound undergoes $S_N1$ reaction ; the product formed by rearranged carbocation is known as $S_N1'$ product (unimolecular nucleophilic substitution with rearrangement). It is an example of *allylic rearrangement.*

**26.** All are primary alkyl bromides and undergo $S_N2$ reactions in which nucleophile attacks on the carbon from back side. Thus more the branching on the alkyl group attached to C having Br, lesser will be its reactivity towards $S_N2$ reactions. Thus

$$n\text{-}C_3H_7-CH_2Br \; > \; (CH_3)_2CH-CH_2Br \; > \; \underset{C_2H_5}{\overset{CH_3}{>}}CH-CH_2Br \; > \; (CH_3)_3C-CH_2Br$$

     (I)         (II)         (III)         (IV)

**27.** Addition of halogens to alkenes, involve formation of cyclic halogenonium ion, and not a carbonium ion.

**28.** Stronger a base, poor will be the leaving group.

**29.** In nucleophilic additions on carbonyl groups, nucleophile adds on the electron deficient carbon. Thus any factor which can increase electron deficiency of carbonyl carbon will increase rate of nucleophilic addition on carbonyl compounds. Acids perform this function by protonating carbonyl oxygen which thus becomes more electronegative.

$$\underset{R'}{\overset{R}{>}}C = \ddot{O}: \; + \; H^+ \; \underset{\longleftarrow}{\longrightarrow} \; \underset{R'}{\overset{R}{>}}C = \overset{+}{\underset{..}{O}}H$$

**30.** Reaction takes place in presence of a base (:B) which removes hydrogen as proton.

**31.** $F^-$ is a strong base and causes elimination reaction with *tert*-alkyl halides ; hence the expected product in both should be *isobutene.* However, in presence of $H_2O$, $F^-$ ion is solvated *via* hydrogen bonding and thus can't exert its influence, the weak base $H_2O$ causes substitution reaction. On the other hand, $F^-$ is not solvated in presence of $(CH_3)_2SO$ (DMSO) causing elimination reaction to form isobutene.

**32.** $(CH_3)_3COH \longrightarrow (CH_3)_3\overset{+}{C}.$

**33.** Acid ($SbCl_5$)–catalysed reactions generally involve carbocation as intermediates which here is further confirmed by racemization, since carbocations are flat and can be attacked on either side of the face forming both enantiomers.

**34.** Electron-withdrawing group like $-NO_2$ enhances positive charge on the carbon, thus destabilises the carbonium ion, while electron-pushing group like $-OH$, $-OCH_3$ disperses positive charge, hence stabilises the carbonium ion.

**35.** More the stability of the product, faster is debromination of the parent compound.

## EXERCISE 4.2

| >1 CORRECT OPTION | 1 | (b,c) | 2 | (a, b) | 3 | (b,c) | 4 | (b, d) | 5 | (a, b, c, d) | 6 | (a, b) |
|---|---|---|---|---|---|---|---|---|---|---|---|---|
| PASSAGE 1 | 7 | (d) | 8 | (c) | 9 | (b) | | | | | | |
| PASSAGE 2 | 10 | (b) | 11 | (c) | 12 | (a) | | | | | | |
| PASSAGE 3 | 13 | (b) | 14 | (b) | 15 | (b) | | | | | | |
| MATCHING TYPE QUESTIONS | 16 | (A) - a, d ; (B) - b ; (C) - c, (D) - b | | | | | 19 | (A)-a, b ; (B)-c, d ; (C)-a, b ; (D)-a, d | | | | |
| | 17 | (A)-a, c ; (B)-d ; (C)-a, c ; (D)-b, c | | | | | 20 | (A) – c; (B) – a; (C) – d; (D) – b | | | | |
| | 18 | (A) – b,c; (B) – b; (C) – a; (D) – d | | | | | 21 | (A) – b; (B) – a, d; (C) – c, d; (D) – b | | | | |
| A/R | 22 | (a) | 23 | (a) | 24 | (c) | 25 | (a) | 26 | (a) | | |
| TRUE / FALSE | 27 | False; | 28 | False; | 29 | False; | | | | | | |

## EXERCISE 4.3

**1.**

(*i*)   $NH_2^-$ and $NH_3$. Here nucleophilic site is same (N), hence nucleophilicity and basicity should be of same order. Since the conjugate acid $NH_4^+$ is stronger than $NH_3$, therefore **$NH_3$ should be weaker base and weaker nucleophile than $NH_2^-$.**

(*ii*)   $OH^-$ is a stronger base than $SH^-$ because the O—H bond is stronger than the S—H bond ; while $SH^-$ is a stronger nucleophile than $OH^-$ because S is less electronegative than O.

(*iii*)   $H_2O$ is better nucleophile and stronger base than $H_3O^+$ (Explanation as that of (*i*)).

(*iv*)   On the same line as that of (*i*), $CH_3CH_2O^-$ is a stronger base and better nucleophile than $CH_3COO^-$.

(*v*)   Since the bond dissociation energy of the H—Br is less than that of H—Cl, $Br^-$ will be a weaker base than $Cl^-$. However, electronegativity of Cl is more than Br, $Cl^-$ will be weaker nucleophile than $Br^-$.

(*vi*)   In $OH^-$ and $F^-$, the two nucleophilic atoms belong to same period, hence the basicity and nucleophilicity both decrease with the increase in electronegativity. **Thus $F^-$ should be weaker base and weaker nucleophile than $OH^-$.**

**2.**

(*a*) Nucleophiles (*electron-rich species*) $Cl^-$, $H_2\ddot{O}$, $CH_3\ddot{O}H$, $CH_3CH = CH_2$,

(*b*)   Electrophiles (*electron-deficient species*) : $NO^+$, $AlCl_3$, $BeCl_2$, $Cr^{+3}$, $SnCl_4$

(*c*)   Both : $CH_2 = \ddot{O}$ (electron-rich site O, electron-deficient site C), $CH_3C \equiv \ddot{N}$ (electron-rich site N, electron-deficient site C).

(*d*)   None (*neither nucleophilic nor electrophilic*) : $CH_4$, $H_2$.

3. Species having two different nucleophilic sites are known as **ambident nucleophiles**, *e.g.* $NO_2^-$ and $CN^-$

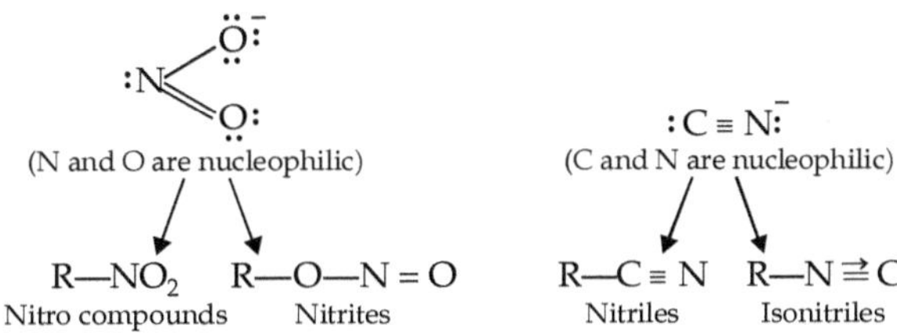

$$R-NO_2 \qquad R-O-N=O \qquad R-C\equiv N \qquad R-N\rightleftharpoons C$$
Nitro compounds      Nitrites          Nitriles          Isonitriles

4. (a) When the nucleophilic site is the same atom (here O), nucleophilicity parallels basicity. Therefore,
$$CH_3O^- > OH^- > CH_3COO^- > H_2O$$
 (b) When the attacking (reacting) atoms are different but in the same periodic family, the one with the largest atomic weight is the most reactive. Therefore, $PH_3 > NH_3$. This order is the reverse of basicity.

5. We know that weaker a base better will be the leaving group. Further we know that weaker a base, stronger will be its conjugate acid and hence lower will be its $pK_a$ value. Thus acid strength of the three conjugate acids is
$$C_6H_5OH \quad < \quad CH_3COOH \quad < \quad C_6H_5SO_3H$$

|  $pK_a$ value | 10.0 | 4.5 | 2.6 |

Hence,
$$C_6H_5SO_3^-, \quad CH_3COO^-, \quad C_6H_5O^-$$

Basic character increases

Leaving property decreases

Thus best leaving group is the weakest base ($C_6H_5SO_3^-$) ; and the poorest leaving group is the strongest base ($C_6H_5O^-$).

6. Greater the dispersal of the positive charge, higher will be the stability of the carbocation. Electron-releasing inductive effect and hyperconjugation is maximum in $(CH_3)_3C^+$ and minimum in $CH_3^+$.
 Further stability of these carbocations can be explained on the basis of steric acceleration. Bulkier the group on the carbon bearing positive charge ($sp^2$ hybridised), more will be steric acceleration (steric relief) in their formation due to conversion of bond angle from 109° present in parent compound ($sp^3$ hybridised) to 120° in carbocation (steric relief). In short,

$$Me_3C-Br \quad > \quad Me_2CH-Br \quad > \quad MeCH_2-Br \quad > \quad CH_3-Br$$
Steric strain and     Maximum                                                          Minimum
hence unstability

$$Me_3C^+ \quad > \quad Me_2\overset{+}{C}H \quad > \quad Me\overset{+}{C}H_2 \quad > \quad \overset{+}{C}H_3$$
Steric relief and     Maximum                                                          Minimum
hence formation

7. (a) Due to strong electron-withdrawing fluorines, a $\delta+$ develops on the atom adjacent to $C^+$. Due to positive charges on adjacent atoms, the species is destabilised.
 (b) Unshared electron pair on fluorine can be shifted to vacant *p*-orbital of $\overset{+}{C}$ (*p-p*-overlap). Hence positive charge is dispersed leading to stability of the carbocation.
 (c) Same explanation as in (*b*).
 (d) Positive charge is present on the two adjacent atoms, leading to destability of the carbocation.

8. Remember a weak base favours substitution, while a strong base favours elimination.
 (i) $HS^-$ is a powerful nucleophile which reacts rapidly with the alkyl halide to form mercaptan

$$CH_3CHBrCH_3 + HS^- \xrightarrow{CH_3OH} CH_3CHSHCH_3$$

 (ii) $I^-$ is a powerful nucleophile but weaker base and reacts by $S_{N1}$ mechanism to form $Me_3CI$, but again iodide is a better leaving group than $Br^-$, it reacts with the nucleophilic solvent $HCOOH$ to form formate

$$(CH_3)_3CBr + I^- \xrightarrow[(-\,Br^-)]{} (CH_3)_3CI \xrightarrow{HCOOH} (CH_3)_3C-O-\overset{\overset{\displaystyle O}{\parallel}}{C}-H$$

 (iii) $AgCN$ is an ambident nucleophile and hence, it will form two products.
$$CH_3CH_2Br + AgCN \longrightarrow CH_3CH_2CN + CH_3CH_2NC$$

 (iv) Since S provides a more powerful nucleophilic site than O, alkyl group will be linked to S.

$$CH_3CH_2Br \;+\; \begin{bmatrix} \overset{\displaystyle O}{\underset{\displaystyle O}{S-S-O}} \end{bmatrix}^{2-} \longrightarrow CH_3CH_2-\overset{\displaystyle O}{\underset{\displaystyle O}{S-S}}-O^-$$

 (v) $$CHCl_3 \xrightarrow{Me_3CO^-} [:CCl_3]^- \xrightarrow{-Cl^-} :CCl_2 \xrightarrow{CH_2=CH_2} H_2C-CH_2$$
an α-elimination

 (vi) No reaction. Although this is a 3° RCl, it does not undergo an $S_{N1}$ reaction because the bridgehead C bonded to Cl is part of a rigid structure and therefore cannot form a planar $R^+$. The bicyclic ring structure does not permit a backside nucleophilic attack on C, ruling out the $S_{N2}$ mechanism.

**9.**   (*a*)   $S_{N^2}$ Reactivity follows the order

$$CH_3(CH_2)_3CH_2Br \underset{1°}{\;>\;} (C_2H_5)_2CHBr \underset{2°}{\;>\;} (CH_3)_2C(Br)C_2H_5 \;\;_{3°}$$

  (*b*)   $Ag^+$ catalyzes $S_{N^1}$ reactivity and thus the order is

$$(CH_3)_2C(Br)C_2H_5 \underset{3°}{\;>\;} (C_2H_5)_2CHBr \underset{2°}{\;>\;} CH_3(CH_2)_3CH_2Br \;\;_{1°}$$

**10.**   (*i*)   $Br^-$ is an extremely weak Bronsted base, hence it can't displace the strong base $OH^-$. However, in presence of acid, $R\overset{+}{O}H_2$ is first formed. Now $Br^-$ displaces $H_2O$ which is a very weak base and a good leaving group.

  (*ii*)   The bulky $(CH_3)_3C$ group sterically hinders backside attack by a nucleophile.

  (*iii*)   Solvolysis goes by an $S_N1$ mechanism. Thus relative rates of different reactants in $S_{N^1}$ reactions depend on the stabilities of the intermediate carbonium ions. $CH_2 = CH_2CH_2Cl$ is more reactive because $CH_2 = CH-\overset{+}{C}H_2$ is more stable than $(CH_3)_3\overset{+}{C}$.

  (*iv*)   $CH_3CH_2Br$ and $(CH_3)_2CHBr$ react by $S_{N^2}$ pathway in which reactivity of the latter halide is very less because of steric hindrance. However, $(CH_3)_3CBr$ reacts by $S_N1$ pathway which involves formation of carbocation, $(CH_3)_3\overset{+}{C}$ formation is very rapid because of steric acceleration as well as inductive effect.

  (*v*)   $$ROH + Cl^- \xleftarrow{\;KI,\, fast\;} RCl + H_2O \xrightarrow{\;slow\;} ROH + Cl^-$$

$I^-$ is a powerful nucleophile which reacts rapidly with RCl to form RI. Further, $I^-$ is also a better leaving group than $Cl^-$, and RI is therefore hydrolysed rapidly to form ROH and regenerate $I^-$, which recycles in the reaction

$$RCl + H_2O \xrightarrow{\;Slow\;} ROH$$

$$\underset{fast}{\xrightarrow{\;I^-\;}} RI \xrightarrow[-I]{H_2O,\, fast}$$

  (*vi*)   This is an E2 reaction which involves the cleavage of C—H (or C—D) bond in the rate determining step. Since C—H bond is broken at a higher rate than the stronger C—D bond, formation of ethylene is easy in $CH_3CH_2I$ than in $CD_3CH_2I$. This ratio of the rate constants, $K_H/K_D$ is called **isotope effect.**

  (*vii*)   Since $S_N1$ reactions involve the formation of carbocations and primary carbocations (from primary alkyl halides) are least stable, 1° RCl are least reactive towards $S_N1$ solvolysis. However, in case of $CH_3CH_2OCH_2Cl$, the carbocation formed has a lone pair of electrons on an atom (O) adjacent to $C^+$, hence delocalisation (by *p-p* overlap) of the positive charge stabilises the carbocation. Therefore, the compound shows $S_N1$ reactivity

$$CH_3CH_2OCH_2Cl \xrightarrow[(-Cl^-)]{} \underset{\substack{\text{Delocalisation of positive}\\\text{charge possible}}}{CH_3CH_2-\overset{\displaystyle\cdot\cdot}{\underset{\displaystyle\cdot\cdot}{O}}\overset{+}{-}CH_2} \xrightarrow{C_2H_5OH} CH_3CH_2-O-CH_2OC_2H_5$$

**11.**   (*a*)   $S_N2$ displacement, $I^-$ is a good nucleophile and a poor base.

  (*b*)   E2 elimination, a 3° halide and a fairly strong base.

  (*c*)   Mainly $S_N2$ displacement.

  (*d*)   Mainly E2. A less polar solvent than $H_2O$ (in *c*) favours E2.

  (*e*)   $S_N1$ displacement ; $H_2O$ is not basic enough to remove a proton to cause elimination.

**12.**   (*a*)   $$(CH_3)_3CBr \longrightarrow (CH_3)_3\overset{+}{C} \xrightarrow{C_2H_5OH} \underset{\text{Major}(S_N1)}{(CH_3)_3COC_2H_5} + \underset{\substack{\text{Very minor (E1) in}\\\text{absence of a strong base}}}{(CH_3)_2C=CH_2}$$

  (*b*)   $$CH_3CH=CHCl \xrightarrow[E2]{NaNH_2} CH_3C\equiv CH$$

Vinyl halides are quite inert toward $S_N2$ reactions.

  (*c*)   $$\underset{(S_N2)}{(CH_3)_3CI + H_2O \longrightarrow (CH_3)_3COH + HI}$$

In presence of a nucleophilic solvent and in absence of a strong base, 3° RX undergoes $S_{N^1}$ solvolysis.

  (*d*)   $$\underset{(E2)}{(CH_3)_3CI + OH^- \longrightarrow (CH_3)_2C=CH_2 + H_2O + I^-}$$

In presence of a strong base ($OH^-$), 3° RX undergoes mainly E2 reaction.

**13.**

This is an example of $S_N1$ reaction because benzyl cation is quite stable. Further, presence of electron-pushing group (*e.g.* —OH) increases stability of the carbocation by dispersing positive charge, while electron-withdrawing groups (—Cl and —NO$_2$) destabilise the carbocation by intensifying the positive charge.

**14.** There are seven isomeric pentyl alcohols, $C_5H_{11}OH$, of which four are primary, two secondary and one tertiary. Primary alcohols follow $S_N2$ pathway and hence isomer having bulky alkyl group will be less reactive. Thus

$$CH_3CH_2CH_2CH_2{-}CH_2OH \; > \; (CH_3)_2CHCH_2{-}CH_2OH \; > \; {\overset{CH_3}{\underset{C_2H_5}{\Large>}}}CH{-}CH_2OH \; > \; (CH_3)_3C{-}CH_2OH$$

**15.** More the stability of the carbocation, higher will be $S_N1$ reactivity of the parent compound.

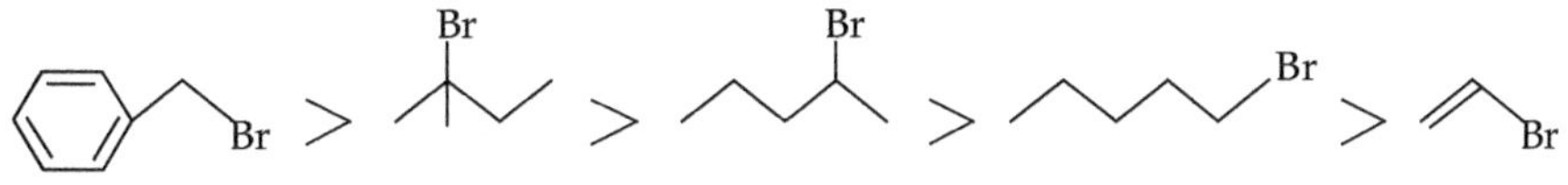

Corresponding cations are

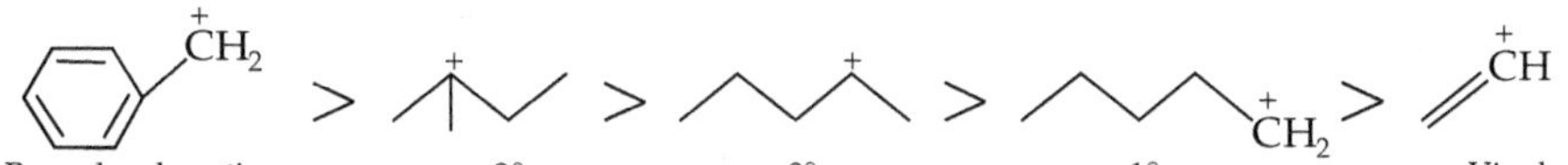

Benzyl carbocation     3°     2°     1°     Vinyl

**16.** Stability of carbocation (Intermediate) determines the reactivity of alkene towards addition of HCl ; more stable the carbocation more will be the reactivity of alkene. Here carbocations of both alkenes are given along with their stability.

*(i)*    $CH_3{-}\overset{\oplus}{C}H_2$   and
   (1° Carbocation)       (2° Carbocation) More stable

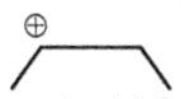

*(ii)*    2° Carbocation    and    3° Carbocation (More stable)

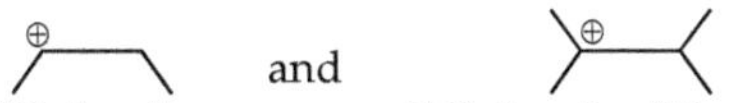

*(iii)*    (2° Carbocation)    and
     2° Carbocation, with conjugation (More stable)

*(iv)*    (2° Carbocation)    and
     2° Carbocation, having conjugated double bond (More stable)

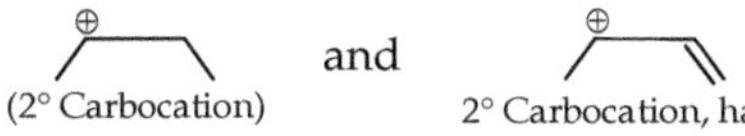

**17.** *(i)*   $\xrightarrow{\;H^+\;}$   $\xrightarrow{\;Cl^-\;}$

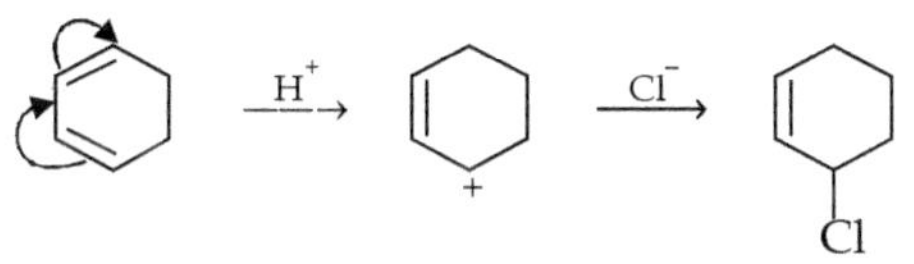

*(ii)*   $\xrightarrow{\;H^+\;}$   3° Carbocation   $\xrightarrow{\;Cl^-\;}$

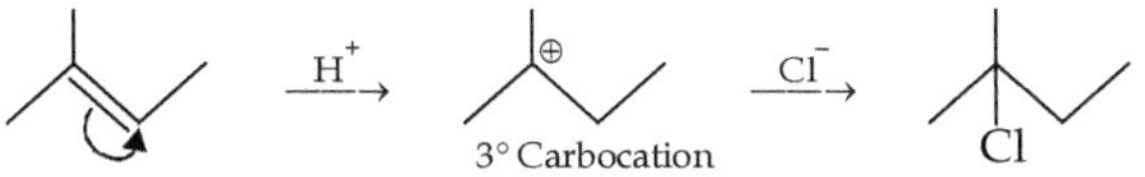

*(iii)*   $\xrightarrow{\;H^+\;}$   3° Carbocation   $\xrightarrow{\;Cl^-\;}$

*(iv)*   $\xrightarrow{\;H^+\;}$   Benzylic carbocation   $\xrightarrow{\;Cl^-\;}$

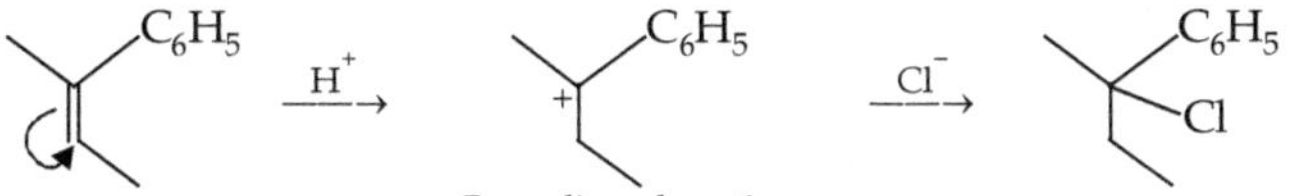

**18.** This is an example of electrophilic addition and involves the formation of carbocation, so more is the stability of the carbocation intermediate higher will be the reactivity of the parent compound. Carbocation stability order, and hence reactivity towards HCl of the parent compound follows the order.

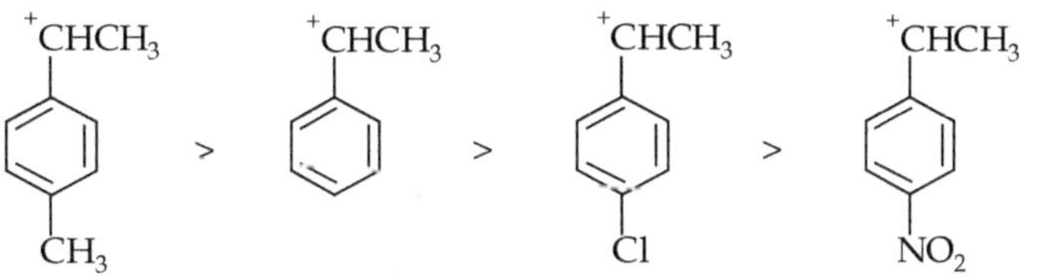

**19.** $CH_2 = CH{-}CH = CH_2 \xrightarrow{\;\cdot CCl_3\;} \left[ Cl_3C{-}CH_2{-}\overset{\cdot}{C}H{-}CH = CH_2 \longleftrightarrow Cl_3C{-}CH_2{-}CH = CH{-}\overset{\cdot}{C}H_2 \right]$

           2° free radical         $\downarrow Br^{\cdot}$

$$Cl_3C{-}CH_2{-}CHBr{-}CH = CH_2 \; + \; Cl_3C{-}CH_2{-}CH = CH{-}CH_2Br$$

       1, 2-addition                 1, 4-addition

**20.** *(i)* Primary alcohols mainly undergo $S_{N^2}$ reactions *via* the formation of a transition state which can form two products.

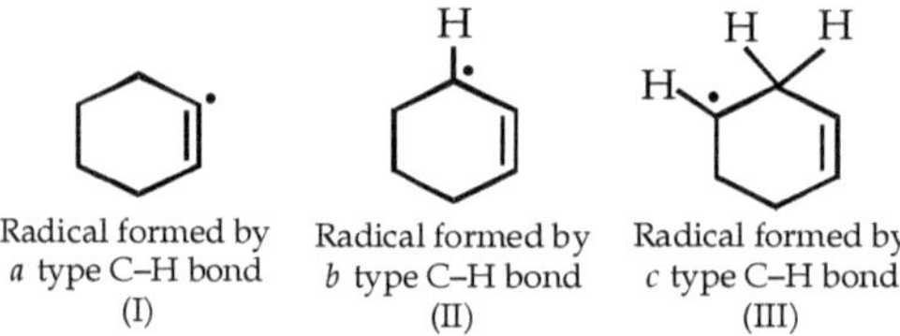

*(ii)* Secondary alcohols undergo $S_N1$ mechanism.

*(iii)*

Benzyne

**21.** (a)
$$\underset{\substack{\text{conjugated} \\ \text{allylic}}}{IV} > \underset{\text{allylic}}{II} > \underset{3°}{III} > \underset{2°}{VI} > \underset{1°}{VII} > \underset{\text{vinylic}}{I} > V$$

(b)
$$\underset{\substack{\text{3° allylic, highly} \\ \text{conjugated}}}{III} > \underset{\substack{\text{2° allylic, highly} \\ \text{conjugated}}}{II} > \underset{\text{2° allylic}}{I}$$

(c) $(C_6H_5)_2 \overset{..}{C} > C_6H_5 \overset{..}{C}H > CH_3 \overset{..}{C}H > : CH_2$

(d) Yes, more is the stability of a free radical, weaker will be the parent bond. Thus write down the structures of the corresponding free radical formed and observe the relative stability of the free radical.

Radical formed by *a* type C–H bond (I)  Radical formed by *b* type C–H bond (II)  Radical formed by *c* type C–H bond (III)

Relative stability of the free radical :
$$\underset{\text{allylic}}{II} > \underset{2°}{III} > \underset{\text{vinylic}}{I}$$

Thus bond energy of the *a*, *b* and *c* C – H bonds :
$$I > III > II$$

**22.** (a) $CH_3^+$  (b) $C_6H_5 \overset{..}{N}:$  (c) $CH_3C\overset{..}{O}N:$  (d) $H\overset{..}{N}:$  (e) $CH_3\overset{..}{N}:$

**23.** (a) $: CH_2, \ CH_3 - \underset{\overset{\displaystyle |}{CH_3}}{CH} - CH_3$

(b) $CH_3C\overset{..}{O}N:$  (c)